CRITICAL INCIDENT MANAGEMENT

CRITICAL INCIDENT MANAGEMENT

Alan B. Sterneckert

AUERBACH PUBLICATIONS

A CRC Press Company
Boca Raton   London   New York   Washington, D.C.

Library of Congress Cataloging-in-Publication Data

Sterneckert, Alan B.
    Critical incident management / Alan B. Sterneckert.
        p. cm.
    Includes index.
    ISBN 0-8493-0010-X (alk. paper)
        1. Organizational effectiveness. 2. Risk management. 3. Management. I. Title.

HD58.9.S7397 2003
658.4—dc21
                                                              2003051841

Visit the CRC Press Web site at www.crcpress.com

© 2004 by CRC Press LLC
Auerbach is an imprint of CRC Press LLC

No claim to original U.S. Government works
International Standard Book Number 0-8493-0010-X
Library of Congress Card Number 2003051841
Printed in the United States of America 1 2 3 4 5 6 7 8 9 0
Printed on acid-free paper

Preface

You are probably reading the preface to see if the rest of the book merits your attention, so I am not going to disappoint you. This book presents those elements most organizations need to plan, prepare, and address critical incidents. Critical incident management requires forward thinking, shifting paradigms, and sometimes ruffling a few feathers. It involves deliberately refining business operations, not spouting business buzzwords while talking around the problem.

Basically, your organization's systems can be defined in terms of its critical assets, meaning those assets required to continue profitably. Pursuing the organization's mission while safeguarding critical assets is the responsibility of every person connected with the enterprise, from the CEO to the parking lot attendant.

The most critical assets in any organization are its people. Valuable employees are challenging to find and difficult to retain but the dividends last longer than the organization itself. They are the company's owners, partners, executives, managers, employees, contractors, interns, and temps.

Data is the business' information, processes, customer lists, employee information, contracts, trade secrets, proprietary information, and intellectual property. In the structure of critical assets, it is ranked second.

Do not let the term *physical facilities* fool you into thinking only of heating and air conditioning. Ranked third, they are a significant part of profitable operations. Physical facilities include office furniture, hardware, workstations, servers, cabling, software, and tangible and intangible items. All factors considered, for these system components to function together successfully requires a complex and well-coordinated dance.

Many organizations spend vast amounts of their resources and capital dealing with outside system attackers; yet, the greatest financial harm originates from attacks inside the company. Although you have read of spectacular and well-publicized attacker events, the most costly, critical incidents originate from inside, e.g., avoidable lawsuits and intellectual property theft.

Critical incident management is a balancing act involving an organization's risk management program, policies and procedures, auditing, critical incident response, legal and law enforcement issues, and privacy. Sometimes you feel like the circus performer who balances the spinning plates while standing on her head. In fact, critical incident management is a lot like playing basketball: the more you sweat before the game, the less you sweat during the game.

You are going to read about matters of planning, preparation, execution, and learning from mistakes. In my experience, most organizations have been reluctant to take preparatory steps toward addressing potential damage caused by harmful events. Due to internal political pressures or poorly conceived programs, organizations spend their resources protecting "junk." It is not a matter of "if"; it is only a matter of "when" harmful events will happen.

This book is written from an Information Technology (IT) perspective, and the reason is simple. We are completely and inexorably dependent on IT for everything in our lives. The concepts detailed here are not academic or theoretical. My intention is to speak plainly and clearly.

This book will mention commercial, shareware, and freeware products. These are not recommendations; they are intended to serve merely as examples. There are new and better products announced daily, so look for products that might be directed toward your specific requirements.

This is a practical book. In my experience, books requiring readers to remember small and seemingly insignificant paragraphs because important sections depend on them later confuse readers and cause them to become disinterested. I know I do. I have a redundant style of writing. I tell you what I am going to tell you, I tell you, and then I tell you what it was I told you (say that three times, quickly). This is not my invention; it was borrowed from some very good instructors I have had over the years.

Experience Note When I was in the United States Air Force and subsequently at the Federal Bureau of Investigation, many times I sat in meetings where the person delivering the presentation seemed to be drowning in minutiae. After a moment, the ranking person would generally interrupt the speaker with a command to "get to the point."

So that is the style in which I wrote this book; getting to the point and not wading through seas of trivia.

Please note the book contains many bulleted lists, and exhibits in the form of tables and figures, constituting items to be incorporated into reports and other documents. The text intentionally emulates presentations in which the speaker knows the audience is knowledgeable of relevant topics and is providing meaningful instruction.

Do not get confused when I constantly refer to employees. The term references anyone who has any type of regular access to an organization. Whether they are contractors, vendors, consultants, part-timers, interns, temporary employees, or unpaid family members (including your brother-in-law), they all fall under my broad category of employees.

My view of enterprise includes any type of business structure, profit, not-for-profit, nonprofitable, barely profitable, and government agencies. The size and nature of your organization are not important for most of the chapters because the concepts are intended to be adaptable.

Notice the paragraphs labeled Experience Notes. These are small but interesting paragraphs to lighten your reading.

I make reference to senior managers. They are the "C" levels of executives: CTO, CFO, CIO, CISO, CSO, Chief Legal Officers, Chief Network Administrators, Chief Auditors, and Senior Managers. This book is directed primarily to you.

I avoid giving specific names, dates, and places. It is not my intention to harm or embarrass people for something they may have done or said.

We live in a litigious world. Stockholders, employees, competitors, managers, executives, and government agencies are successfully suing organizations today.

Litigation poses a serious risk, and wise managers are taking affirmative steps to close or at least minimize their exposures. One of the most viable defenses will be your ability to show due diligence in safeguarding your critical assets. This book provides steps you can implement to legally defend your actions.

Experience Note I once had a professor that said, "anyone with $25 for a filing fee and a typewriter can file a lawsuit." He was right.

I am going to make references to events taking place in the courts. Court decisions can negatively affect your organization and often can be avoided by demonstrating some professionalism and common sense. If you and your staff do not have legal knowledge, seek experts. You will be glad you did. Legal decisions can be anticipated and effectively addressed, but you have to consider them as manageable and not as merely unavoidable.

Overall, the philosophy of this book is one where "an ounce of prevention is worth a pound of cure." I do not like professional surprises. I would rather deal with backed-up data than try to recover it from a devastated hard drive. I believe organizations must have proactive programs consisting of tested plans, developed and executed by trustworthy people, instead of chaotic alternatives. I am going to address these steps in each of the six chapters.

The book begins with the need for establishing a risk management program, including elements of critical asset identification, threats, vulnerabilities, information classification, disaster recovery, and restoration. It may seem like a daunting task, and it is, but it is like eating an elephant — it is done one bite at a time. Take special note of the risk management section on dealing with the press; most organizations fail when they deal with press inquiries during crises.

The second chapter deals with policies and procedures. Recently, there has been a surge of literature published about these subjects. Much of it has merit and will go a long way to improve your business' performance. More than one organization has been saved from the fires of ruin because of having well-developed policies and procedures. When reading about policies and procedures, do not get mired in definitions. Take the steps to get them drafted, vetted, approved, and implemented. Get the auditors to see to their adherence.

Auditing is the third chapter. Auditors must look at policies, procedures, standards, processes, and the way organizations safeguard their critical assets. Saving your hard-earned assets is the name of the audit game.

The fourth chapter deals with critical incident response. Identifying a critical incident, handling its investigation, reporting, and evidence collection will be covered. There are two overarching concepts in this chapter: do not perform evidence collections and examinations for which you do not have the expertise, and do not do anything that is going to alter the evidence. Here, I discuss the development of critical incident teams, including their structure, development, function, funding, and reporting requirements.

Chapter 5 deals with the matter of law enforcement, what it can do, and how to deal with it. Computer-related crimes including economic espionage, theft of intellectual property, and trade secrets are described here.

Completing the book is a chapter on privacy. Like it or not, it is the wave of the future. Depending on the activity, people are entitled to different levels of privacy; with that in mind, I am going to provide some insight into the reasonable expectations in this area.

A little about me. Many years ago I spent some time dealing with secure electronic communications as part of my U.S. Air Force experience. At that time, communication networks were considered sophisticated, and they actually were if judged by the standards of their early years. I joined the Federal Bureau of Investigation, and for the next 24 years enjoyed many experiences while assigned to Dallas, New York City, San Juan, Puerto Rico, and Salt Lake City. Regardless of some opinions, I found the support employees, Special Agents of the FBI, and police officers in the trenches of law enforcement dedicated to preserving our freedoms. God bless them.

Thanks to my family and particularly to my wife, Tina, for her infinite love and support.

I would also like to thank Rich O'Hanley and his staff for their professional abilities and attitudes.

I am certain there are mistakes in this book. Please excuse me; I have taken every effort to ensure accuracy. If you find something you want to discuss, feel free to email me at absterneckert@yahoo.com.

The Author

Alan B. Sterneckert is the owner and general manager of Risk Management Associates. A retired Special Agent, Federal Bureau of Investigation, Mr. Sterneckert is a professional specializing in critical incident and risk management, IT systems security, and systems auditing.

During his 24-year tenure with the FBI, Mr. Sterneckert was responsible for many significant investigations into multi-national white collar crime and narcotics trafficking organizations. He was stationed in Dallas, New York, San Juan, and Salt Lake City.

Before entering the FBI, he was a member of the U.S. Air Force, where he specialized in communications and information security.

He graduated from Weber State University (B.A.) and Long Island University (M.S.). He holds the following professional certifications: Certified Information Systems Auditor (CISA), Certified Information Security Manager (CISM), Certified Information Systems Security Professional (CISSP), and Certified Fraud Examiner (CFE).

When not consulting or writing, he can be found fishing for Arctic grayling and cutthroat trout.

Contents

1 Risk Management.. 1
  Ancient History: My, How Time Passes when You're Having Fun..................... 1
    Recent Events.. 1
    Game Plan.. 2
    Maginot Line 3
    Senior Management Responsibilities 3
  Critical Incidents: Damaging Critical Assets.. 3
    Critical Asset Priority 3
  Risk Definitions: No Dictionaries, Please.. 5
  Yes, Sir. I'm Motivated! Fear, Uncertainty, and Doubt................................. 7
  PDD 63 (President's Decision Directive) 8
  The Law Is the Law 8
  CIA: Not the Central Intelligence Agency.. 9
  Down to Risk-Business 10
  GOOOAAALLL! 10
  Plan to Plan 11
    Assessment and Critical Incident Program Requirements 11
    Plan 12
    A Word about Charting.. 12
    Acquire and Implement 13
    Monitor and Revise... 13
  Risk Assessments 14
  A Little Organization, Please 14
  Best Practices in Risk Assessments 16
    Executive Sponsorship 16
    Scope 16
    Information Resources.. 16
    Team Management Dynamics... 17
  The Facts and Only the Facts 18
  Ask Good Questions of Good People and You Will Get Good Answers........ 20
  And Now a Word about Asset Criticality.. 20
  Mathematics Can Be Simple, even for the Mathematically Challenged 21
    Single Loss Expectancy and Annualized Loss Expectancy 21

Are You Threatening Me? 22
Protection Strategies 26
    Personnel 26
    Data 28
    Data Classification 28
    Need-to-Know 28
    Backups 29
    Physical Facilities 30
    Redundant Physical Facilities 30
    Facilities Outsourcing 30
    Get Organized 31
Disaster Recovery Plans: Murphy's Law 32
    Basic Employee Training 33
Who's in Charge Here, Anyway? 35
    Emergency Management Team 35
        Transportation Sub-Team 35
        Emergency Operations Sub-Team 35
        Communications Sub-Team 36
        Data Recovery Sub-Team 36
        Facilities Sub-Team 36
        Administrative Support and Supplies Sub-Team 36
    Press Relations 36
        Key Press Items 37
    Original Documentation 37
    Test the Plan 37
Risk Assessment Reports 38
    Simple Risk Management Advice 38
    Just when You Thought You Were Done 39
Suggestions 39

2 Policies and Procedures 41
Policies, Procedures, Standards, and Politics 41
Et Tu, Policy 42
Trust Models: Trust Me, I'm a Good Person 44
The Policy of Policy Development 44
    Team Leadership 45
    Policy Team Members 45
    Common Policy Components 45
    Executive Approvals 46
    Policy Exemptions 46
    Changes 46
    Violations 46
    Do the Policy Right the First Time 48
    Vetting Policies 48
Policy Writing Techniques 48
    Plain Language 48
    Spelling and Grammar 49
    Gender Words 49
    Eternal View 49
    Application 49
    Responsibility for Compliance 50

Policy Distributions 50
Enhancements to Written Policies... 50
    Audio/Video Productions.. 50
    Classroom Training Sessions... 51
E-Mail Policy: Avoiding Hidden Risks.. 51
Information Tsunami... 51
To Keep or Not to Keep, that Is the Question.. 53
    Document Retention... 53
What's in that Cute Little E-Mail Mailbox? 54
Employees Must Think before Clicking the Send Button: Is There
an Undelete Button?... 54
    Confidentiality 55
    Negotiations.. 55
    Bad News 55
    Plain, Professional Language 55
    Attachments 56
    Spam 56
    Message Priority 56
    Forwarded E-Mail... 56
    Salutations and Signatures 56
    Spelling and Grammar 56
    Encrypted Communications 57
    E-Mail for Managers... 57
    Out-of-Band Communications 57
Employee Privacy Expectations and Legal Rights 57
    ECPA 58
    Privacy Arguments 59
    Privacy Acknowledgments 59
    Reasons to Monitor and Audit Employee Behavior 59
    Employees Working at Home... 59
    Part-Time and Full-Time Employees... 60
    Harassment, Discrimination, and Defamation 60
    Employee Copyright Concerns.. 61
    Employees and Trade Secrets.. 62
    Employee Labor Organization 63
    Spamming, Spoofing, and the Organization 63
    Attorney–Client Communications Using E-Mail.. 64
    Passwords 65
    Something that the Person Is 66
    Something a Person Knows.. 66
    Something a Person Has... 66
    Shoulder Surfing 67
    Security through Obscurity 67
    Employee Software Installation 68
    Copyright Violation.. 68
    Use of Banners 68
Connecting to the Internet: Policies and Procedures of Survivability............... 69
Systems Development Lifecycle (SDLC)... 71
    SDLC Benefits... 72
    SDLC Supports the Use of an Integrated Product Team 72
    Management Controls... 73

Documentation...73
System Accreditation and Certification 74
Physical and Environmental Safety..76
Network Management Policies...77
Forensics Policy: Looking for Evidence 78
Wireless Network Security..82
Service Set Identifier (SSID)..83
Virtual Privacy Network (VPN)..84
Secure Sockets Layer (SSL)..84
Wireless Policies 84
Network Vulnerability Assessment Policies: Why Am I Hearing about
My Network Leaking Sensitive Information on the News? 85
Plan to Conduct Vulnerability Assessments....................................86
Identify Exposures 86
Resolving Exposures 87
Vendor Policies and Procedures 87
Outsource Potentials..88
Consultant Procedures...88
Outsource Vendor Selection Procedures 89
Evaluating Proposals..89
Policies and Procedures Involving Outsourcing: What Is Yours and
What Is Mine?...89
Employee Privacy Policy 91
Internet Firewall Policy..91
Authentication 92
Firewall Types...92
Application Firewalls 93
Hardware Firewall Architectures 93
Firewall Administration...94
Firewall Administrators...94
Remote Firewall Administration...95
Intrusion Detection Policies...95
Network and Host IDSs 96
Host-Based IDS...96
Web Server Security Policies and Procedures....................................97
Web Server Policies and Procedures 97
Information Systems Support Policies 98
Data Entry 99
Technical Support...99
Securing Systems 100
The Auditors Are Coming. The Auditors Are Coming.....................103
Systems Development and Programming Policies..........................104
Data Controls 104
Disaster Recovery and Business Continuity 104
Workstation Audit Policies 105
Information Technology Human Resources Management Policies:
Yes, Virginia, IT Employees Really Are Different............................105
Getting the Best Candidates for the Position.................................105
Job Interviews...106
Performance Reviews 107
Employee Termination 107

Employee Departures on Good Terms...108
Employee Training 108
 Mentor Assignment 108
Conclusion 109

3 Auditing 111
Auditing for the Masses..111
 Auditor Responsibilities...111
 Internal Controls 112
 General Controls 112
 Specific Controls 112
 Separation of Duties and Least Privilege......................................112
 Authority and Responsibility...113
 Documentation..113
 Performance Checks and Accountability 113
Auditors: Who Are They? 113
 Managers Are Not from Venus, Auditors Are Not from Mars 113
 Auditor Attributes..114
  Personal...114
  Leadership...114
  Functional Abilities...115
 Code of Ethics and Conduct 115
 Free and Independent..115
 Organizational Impairments...116
 External Impairments 116
 Personal Impairments 116
Controls..117
 Considering the Universe in the Set of Subsystems......................118
Subsystem Interaction and Reliability...118
 Risks Affecting Auditors..119
 Generally Accepted Government Auditing Standards (GAGAS) 120
 Audit Procedures 120
Evidence Collection: Evidence Is not just Evidence 121
 Interviews 121
 Interview Preparation 122
 Doing Your Homework...122
 Interview Steps..123
 Interviewing for Evidence of Controls...123
 Interview Analysis..124
 Questionnaires 125
 Flowcharts 126
 Types of Flowcharts 126
 Taking Care of the Stakeholders..128
Audit Management Planning 129
 Audit Risk...130
 Planning the Audit...130
 Audit Programs 132
 Standard Audit Programs 133
 Developing Your Audit Program...135
 Useful Internet Web Sites..136
 Common Attacks...136

Flawed Systems...136
Auditing Common Systems Vulnerabilities....................................137
    Buffer Overflows..137
    CGI Scripting...138
    Remote Procedure Calls 139
Audit Work Papers..143
Audit Report..143
Audit Conferences: More (but Important) Meetings You Need
to Attend...145
Opening Conferences...145
Other Conferences..145
Exit Conferences...146
Summary of Audit Steps 146
Audit Program for a Small IT Department..147
Vulnerability Self-Assessments...150
Vulnerability Self-Assessment...151
    Hardware 151
    Physical Security...151
    Emergency Power Management...152
    Environmental Conditions 152
    Configuration Management 152
    Network Protocols...152
    Disaster Recovery and Business Resumption 153
    Software 153
    Media..153
    Employee Security Awareness Training 154
Specialized Auditing Matters 154
Auditing Databases...154
Database Definitions...154
Access Controls...156
Discretionary Access Controls 156
Mandatory Access Controls...156
Software Controls and Update Protocols..157
Database Concurrency Controls in a Distributed Environment......157
Audit Trail Controls 158
Object Reuse 158
Database Existence Controls..158
Domain Servers...159
Protecting against DNS Cache Corruption.......................................162
Auditing UNIX...163
UNIX Shadow Password File..166
Format of the /etc/passwd File..167
Format of the Shadow File...168
Auditing Windows NT...168
Network Vulnerability Assessments: The Practical Examination of
Your System...171
Rules of Engagement..173
Social Engineering 174
IP Address Confirmation 176
Assessment Safety 176
Discovering the Character of the Audit Target 177

Tools 177
What Parts of the System Are Alive? 180
Identifying Operating Systems... 183
Domain Name Server, DNS, and Zone Transfers 184
Automated Vulnerability Tools 185
Doing Your Homework.. 187
Web Application Vulnerability Assessments..................................... 191
HTML Examination 192
Testing for Indexed Directories.. 192
Web Server Examination 193
Accidental Error Messages 194
More Unexpected User Input.. 195
Overflow Vulnerabilities... 195
Hidden Form Elements 195
Get vs. Post Commands in CGI Forms 196
Web Page Referrer Fields.. 198
Unicode Input Attack 198
Cookie Pal... 198
Achilles 199
Automated Web Tools.. 199
    Whisker 200
    SiteScan 200
    Brutus... 200
Quality Control Issues... 201
Reporting Vulnerability Assessment Results 201
Audit Findings... 202
Audit Issues... 202
Auditing Remote System Administration 202
Firewall Auditing: First We Build an Impregnable Barrier, then We
Punch Holes in It.. 204
    Barbarians at the Wall 204
    Firewall Rulebase... 205
    Look at Logging... 206
Auditing Wireless Networks: Who Is Listening to My Network Traffic? 206
    Basic Wi-Fi Architecture... 207
    802.11b Information Packet Types... 208
    Wi-Fi Network Detection 208
    802.11b Headers 208
    WEP 209
    Cloaking SSIDs.. 209
    Wi-Fi Audit Program Features 209
    Wireless Denial-of-Service Attacks 211
    Auditor Considerations for Wireless Networks 211
Auditing Security Measures Preventing Automated Attacks 212
    Root Tools to Gain Access 212
    Who Uses Attacking Tools?... 213
        Due Diligence.. 214
Auditing E-Commerce Web Sites 214
    Credit Card Authentication... 215
    Settlement 216
    Chargeback Issues 216

Audit Program Items 216
Implementing Fraud Screening to Identify High-Risk Transactions 217
Signs of Possible Online Credit Card Fraud 218
Auditing Workstations.. 219
First Steps 220
Organizing and Searching File Systems.. 221
    Wilbur... 221
    Little Images 221
Unformatting and Undeleting.. 222
Windows Registry Investigations... 222
E-Mail Sent by Employees 224
Looking in all the Right Places 225
Telling the Tale with Cookies 226
Auditing Windows NT and XP.. 227
Keystroke Monitors... 227

4   Critical Incident Response and CIRT Development......................... 229
Critical Incident Management.. 229
    Critical Incident Response.................................... 230
    Firefighter Response Model 231
    Critical Incident Response Strategy 231
    Critical Incident Planning.................................... 232
    Command Post Operations....................................... 233
Critical Incident Detection: How to Know What Is Serious and
What Is Not 235
    Critical Incident Symptoms 236
    Response Strategy... 236
    IP Addressing in Brief.. 237
    IP Addresses.. 238
    Reviewing DNS 239
    Resources... 240
    Locating the Origin of Denial-of-Service Attacks............. 240
    UNIX Logging 240
    Windows Logging... 241
    Application Logging... 241
    Hardening Servers... 242
    Backup Frequently... 242
    User Security Training 243
    System Security Architecture.................................. 243
    Time Stamps... 244
    System Monitoring Structure 244
    Business Issues 245
    Legal Issues 245
    Political Issues.. 245
    Critical Incident Response Tools 246
    Critical Incident Response Personnel.......................... 247
    Mission Statement 247
    Responding to the Scene 248
    Critical Incident Checklist 249
    System Map 250
    Investigation at the Crime Scene.............................. 250

Interviews 250
Interviewing Users 251
Interviewing System Administrators 251
Interviewing Managers 252
Determining a Response Strategy 252
Restoring Service Operations 253
An Attack Is Underway 253
Where Is the Attacker? 253
Law Enforcement Relations 254
Suspicious Activity Reports 256
Law Enforcement Liaison 256
Types of Attacks 257
Administrator Facilitated Attacks 258
Senior Manager's Approval 259
Other Relative Issues 259
Business Considerations before Legal Actions 260
Collecting Evidence 260
What Is Evidence? 260
Evidence Prioritization 261
Examining Computer Evidence 262
Policies and Procedures 263
Common Mistakes when Handling Evidence 263
Chain of Custody Schedule 264
Evidence Tags 265
Activity Log 265
Witness Reports 265
Recorded Statements 266
Hostile Interview Environments 267
Performing Forensic Duplication: When a Clone Really Is a Clone 267
Steps to Follow when Collecting Evidence 268
Different Approaches to Media Duplication 269
Removing the Target Hard Drive 270
Attaching a Hard Drive 271
A Word about BIOS 271
Power-On Self Test 272
BIOS Passwords 272
Hard Disk Construction 274
Relative Addressing 275
Windows DOS-Based File Allocation Table 276
Undeleting in Windows-Based Operating Systems 277
Information Hiding in the Windows FAT 278
Windows NT File System 278
UNIX File System 279
Forensically Sound Duplication Tools 281
Forensic Media Duplication Tools 281
Producing Hash Values 281
Boot Disk 282
Boot Disk Creation 283
Disabling DRVSPACE.BIN 283
Physical Write Blockers 284
Using Safeback in Forensic Duplications 284

UNIX dd Commands 285
EnCase 285
Forensic Investigation: Not Exactly a Needle in a Haystack 285
Physical Level Search 286
File Slack and Free Space.. 287
DOS-Based Operating Systems File Deletions 287
Reading E-Mail Headers.. 288
E-Mail Processing.. 288
E-Mail with Firewall Headers 290
Relaying 291
Common E-Mail Headers 292
Network Resources.. 292
Networking Review 292
Responding to Windows NT Incidents 293
Tools in the Tool Bag 293
Storing the Data... 293
To Turn Off or not to Turn Off.. 294
System Users 294
Open Ports and Listening Services 295
Processes Running on the Target Computer... 295
Collecting Volatile Live-Time Evidence.. 296
Examining the Evidence: Taking a Look when You Have Time 296
Evidence on Windows Operating Systems... 296
Logical File Review in Windows... 297
Going Native 298
Changing User Passwords... 298
Cracking User Passwords.. 299
Looking at the Windows Registry 299
Autocomplete Entries in the Registry... 299
Good Places for Evidence 300
Recycle Bin... 300
Partitions.. 302
Partition Status 302
Password-Protected and Encrypted Files.. 303
Print Spooler Files 303
Windows NT Logging.. 304
Offline Log Reviews 305
Looking for Specific Words... 306
Looking at Relevant Files.. 306
Chronology of Events... 307
Legal Cautions.. 307
UNIX-Based Investigations 307
UNIX File System Analysis... 307
Undeleting UNIX... 308
Data Hiding Techniques 309
Coroner's Toolkit 309
Hiding Files.. 310
Steganography... 311
Strong Encrypted Protections... 312
File Recovery Alternatives for UNIX/Linux 312
Understanding File Permissions.. 312

File Stamps 312
Baseline Comparison for SUID/SGID Files 314
System Configuration... 314
User and Password Accounts 314
Log Files 314
Types of Malicious Code Attacks: Even Kevlar Will not Stop all Attacks 315
Viruses 315
Trojan Horses and Logic Bombs.. 316
Things to Do after a Malicious Code Attack................................. 317
Digital Bloodhounds... 317
IP Addresses 318
Resolving IP Addresses 318
Trace Route 319
Dynamic Host Control Protocol Tracing....................................... 320
Investigating the Identity of the Attacker...................................... 321
Domain Registration Payments.. 322
Nicks and Monikers... 322
Anonymous Re-mailers... 323
Forming a Critical Incident Response Team...................................... 324
CIRT... 325
Using Outside Consultants... 325
Using In-House Talent 326
Ad Hoc CIRTs 327
CIRT Requirements and Roles... 327
Added CIRT Responsibilities.. 328
CIRT Funding... 328
Who Does the CIRT Support? 329
CIRT Communications.. 329
Developing Critical Incident Cost Analyses 330
CIRT Composition: What Kind of Skills and Talent Do I Need
for a CIRT?.. 331
Legal Unit 332
Public Relations.. 332
Human Resources Unit... 332
IT Investigative, Analysis, and Forensic Experts........................... 332
IT Security Officers.. 333
Systems Administrators... 333
Telecommunications Specialists.. 333
Database Managers... 333
Engineers/Software Developers.. 333
System Owners 333
CIRT Management Skills 334
Technical Skills... 334
Team Skills 334
Communication Skills 334
People Skills... 335
Incident Reporting 335
What Should I Do if I Have Been Hit? 336
Response Steps for Legal Actions 336
CIRT Success Metrics... 338
CIRT Development Life Cycle 339

5 Legal Matters **341**
   Legal Functions: More than Speeding Tickets 341
   Investigators' Goals 342
   Common Types of Unlawful Acts 343
   Copyrights, Trademarks, Service Marks, Patents, and Trade Secrets
   Comprising Intellectual Property.. 343
       Works that Can Be Copyrighted.. 344
       Copyright Protection.. 345
       Duration of Copyright Protection.. 345
       Copyright Infringement 345
       Criminal Actions in Copyright Cases 345
       Criminal Copyright Forfeiture 346
       Works that Cannot Be Copyrighted... 346
       Trademarks and Service Marks Protection 346
       Criminal Prosecution for Trafficking in Counterfeit Goods
       or Services 346
       Protected Works... 346
       Trademark and Service Mark Protection 347
       Trademark and Service Mark Ownership................................. 347
       Public Notification 348
       Internet Domain Names and Registered Marks 348
       Cybersquatters.. 349
       Cybersquatter-Victim Protection.. 349
       Patent Protections 351
       Qualifications for Design Patents... 351
       Qualifications for Utility Patents.. 351
       "Firstest with the Mostest" 351
       Filing for Patent Protection... 352
       Patent Ownership 352
       Patent Terms 352
       Patent Validity 352
       Trade Secrets.. 352
       Protected Trade Secrets.. 352
       Criminal Forfeiture... 353
       Obtaining Trade Secrets Protection... 354
   Fraud in the Workplace.. 354
       Employee Fraud Controls 355
       Management Functions in Fraud Control 355
       Accountability... 355
       Records 356
   Evidence, Its Collection, Preservation, Analysis, and Introduction
   at Trial.. 356
   The Cost of Computer Crime... 357
   Criminal Law... 358
       Allegations 359
       The Investigation 359
       Witnesses 359
       Grand Juries 360
       Subpoenas and Summons... 361
       Search Warrants.. 362
       Court Orders 364

Testimony 365
Expert Testimony 365
Defense Arguments Relative to Expert Witnesses 366
Computer Evidence 366
Means of Collecting Electronic Evidence under Federal Statutes 367
Federal Legal Requirements for Electronic Surveillance 367
Evidence 370
Criminal Procedure 370
Criminal Discovery 371
Electronic Discovery 372
E-Mail as Evidence 372
Criminal Plea Bargains 373
Trials 373
Sentencing 374
Appeals 374
Civil Suits 374
Plaintiff's Burden of Proof 375
Civil Processes 375
Civil Discovery 376
E-Mail Discovery 376
More on Civil Discovery 377
Federal Laws Applicable to Computer-Related Crimes 378

6   Privacy **381**
Privacy Expectations 381
Information Ownership 382
Information Vulnerability in the Organization 382
Threats to Information Privacy 383
Privacy Protection 383
Information Assets Inventory 384
Technology Relevant to Privacy Protection 384
Policies and Procedures 385
Auditing Privacy Practices 385
Web Site Privacy 386
Safeguarding, Processing, and Storing Privacy Data 386
Nonconsent Information Use 388
Employee Privacy Training 388
Privacy Training Best Practices 389
Handling Privacy in Supply Chains 389
Employee Privacy: Is Monitoring the Same as Spying? 391
Legalities in Employee Monitoring 391
Oral Communications 392
Wire Communications 392
Trap and Trace and Pen Register Installations 393
Video and Still Camera Monitoring 393
Monitoring E-Mail and the Employee Workstation Conduct 394
Employee Legal Defense 395
Employee Monitoring Best Practices 396
Employee Polygraphs 397
Industry-Specific Privacy Issues 397
Access to Financial Records Is Denied to Government Agencies 397

Gramm–Leach–Bliley Act 398
Health Insurance Portability and Accountability Act 398
Fair Credit Reporting Act 399
Family Education Privacy Rights 400
Cable TV Privacy Act 401
Wrongful Disclosure of Videotape Rental or Sale Records
(18 U.S. Code 2710) 401
Children's Online Privacy Protection Act (COPPA) 402
Federal Privacy Act 405
Safe Harbor Issues in the United States 405

Appendix A 409
Port Numbers (Updated 2/9/2003) 409
Well-Known Port Numbers 409
Port Assignments 409
References 449

Appendix B
Site Security Handbook RFC 2196 451
Status 451
Abstract 451
Table of Contents 451
Introduction 452
Purpose of this Work 453
Audience 453
Definitions 453
Related Work 454
Basic Approach 454
Risk Assessment 454
General Discussion 454
Identifying the Assets 455
Identifying the Threats 455
Security Policies 456
What Is a Security Policy, and Why Have One? 456
Definition of a Security Policy 456
Purposes of a Security Policy 457
Who Should Be Involved when Forming Policy? 457
What Makes a Good Security Policy? 457
Keeping the Policy Flexible 459
Architecture 459
Objectives 459
Completely Defined Security Plans 459
Separation of Services 460
Deny All/Allow All 460
Identify Real Needs for Services 461
Network and Service Configuration 461
Protecting the Infrastructure 461
Protecting the Network 462
Protecting the Services 463
Protecting the Protection 465

Firewalls.. 466
Security Services and Procedures 468
  Authentication 468
    One-Time Passwords 469
    Kerberos... 469
    Choosing and Protecting Secret Tokens and PINs 469
    Password Assurance... 470
  Confidentiality 471
  Integrity.. 471
  Authorization.. 472
  Access 472
    Physical Access.. 472
    Walk-Up Network Connections.. 473
    Other Network Technologies... 473
    Modems.. 473
  Auditing 475
    What to Collect 475
    Collection Process 476
    Collection Load 476
    Handling and Preserving Audit Data 477
    Legal Considerations 477
  Securing Backups 477
Security Incident Handling.. 478
  Preparing and Planning for Incident Handling..................................... 479
  Notification and Points of Contact.. 481
    Local Managers and Personnel 481
    Law Enforcement and Investigative Agencies 482
    Computer Security Incident Handling Teams.................................. 484
    Affected and Involved Sites 484
    Internal Communications... 485
    Public Relations: Press Releases 485
  Identifying an Incident... 486
    Is It Real? 486
    Types and Scope of Incidents 487
    Assessing the Damage and Extent 487
  Handling an Incident.. 488
    Types of Notification and Exchange of Information 488
    Protecting Evidence and Activity Logs... 490
    Containment.. 490
    Eradication 491
    Recovery 491
    Follow-Up 492
  Aftermath of an Incident.. 492
  Responsibilities.. 493
    Not Crossing the Line... 493
    Good Internet Citizenship 493
    Administrative Response to Incidents 493
Ongoing Activities 493
Tools and Locations 494
Mailing Lists and Other Resources 495
  Mailing Lists... 495

        CERT™ Advisory 495
        VIRUS-L List 495
        Internet Firewalls.. 495
        USENET Newsgroups... 496
        World Wide Web Pages... 496
    References 496

Appendix C **503**
    Tools.. 503
    Vulnerability Lists 504
    Bulletins and Listservs.. 504

Index 505

Chapter 1

Risk Management

Ancient History: My, How Time Passes when You're Having Fun

There was a time when computers occupied entire buildings with their support units staffed by hundreds of workers. Instead of model numbers, these computers were given names like the Bombe, Colossus, and Eniac. In those primitive times, it was sufficient to have a risk management process with the objective of protecting an organization's assets after a natural disaster struck. Protective measures usually consisted merely of having extra business supplies stockpiled in a supply closet. Having malicious employees on staff was unthinkable. Formalized program assessments, testing, and revising were not part of those early processes; they were afterthoughts assigned as a lesser part of official responsibilities. It seems risk management processes were guided by the attitude of "hope for the best, and pray for the rest."

Recent Events

A few days after the September 11, 2001, attack on the World Trade Center, computer systems around the world felt the destructive and economically significant attack of the NIMDA computer virus. It propagated across the world with remarkable speed and attempted several different ways to infect computer systems until it achieved entry and began destroying files. NIMDA went from nonexistence to worldwide in less than a week. In the United States alone, it attacked 86,000 computers and caused significant problems in seemingly well-protected industries. It forced businesses and individuals offline and required some organizations to entirely rebuild their systems.

While the actual damage of NIMDA is unknown, industry sources estimate that the overall financial impact of system attacks resulting from malicious code reached $13 billion in 2001 alone. At Carnegie-Mellon University, the CERT (Computer Emergency Response Team) reported approximately 3700 computer attacks in 1998; in 2002, CERT reported more than 110,000 attacks.

In the span of less than 20 years, the world shifted control of essential business processes in manufacturing, utilities, finance, and communications to networked information systems. All sectors of the world economy are being affected: energy production, transportation, public health, emergency services, defense industrial-base, shipping, agriculture, food, and education. This shift resulted in lowering the cost of doing business and significantly raised productivity.

Attacks concentrating on information systems occur frequently and have serious consequences, causing loss of revenue, loss of life, and disruption of critical services. Effectively countering these attacks requires a concerted effort on the part of public and private organizations.

The following trends are emerging:

- Computer systems are increasing in sophistication and becoming more integrated in our lives.
- Computer-system-related incidents are increasing in number, sophistication, severity, and cost.
- Critical incidents occur every day.
- Risk management programs will significantly reduce risks and result in continuing profitable operations.
- It is a mistake to assume that current levels of system damage caused by inside and outside attackers are indicators of the future. It is anticipated that significantly worse events will occur.
- It is the responsibility of each organization to secure its systems.

Organizations must be aware that the process of securing and protecting systems must be continuous as new vulnerabilities are created or discovered almost daily. CERT has noted that not only are cyber incidents and the number of attacks occurring at an increasing rate, but the number of vulnerabilities that an attacker can exploit is also increasing. Organizations faced with problems that allow unauthorized entry or damage to a computer system more than doubled in recent years.

In 2000, there were 1090 separate system vulnerabilities, with 2437 reported in 2001. In a recent survey conducted by the Computer Security Institute (CSI), 90 percent of the respondents used antivirus software, yet more than 85 percent had experienced damage attributed to a virus. In this same survey, 89 percent of the survey respondents had installed network firewalls and 60 percent had installed intrusion detection systems, but 90 percent reported network security breaches and 40 percent had their systems accessed from outside the network. This CSI survey indicates that good security practices include not just installing security devices, but that policies and procedures must be observed in business operations as well.

Game Plan

As part of the critical incident management process, there is a need to develop a risk management program beginning with planning models, critical asset identification, risk assessment, disaster recovery, protective measures, and reporting. Building on this process, it will be integrated into the areas of policy formulation, auditing, critical incident response, critical incident team development, law enforcement relations, and privacy. Approaching this process is going to require some forward thinking about conventional risk management models while being introduced to some new topics.

Too often organizations form asset protection strategies focused on perceived rather than actual weaknesses. They protect those things they perceive as important. At times critical assets are those that are "pet" projects of the boss or they appear important to the risk team, but when examined they are actually not as critical as they seem.

Organizations often spend significant resources protecting "junk." They fail to compare negative-event impact with the need for continuing profitable operations.

Here is an example worth remembering: after the terrible destruction of September 11, 2001, the New York Stock Exchange was operational within five days. Many ask how the NYSE was able to recover and restore services in such a short time. The answer is simple. The NYSE had an effective and efficient plan, and the plan was executed.

In the successful implementation of a critical incident management program, assets, threats and their frequency, and vulnerabilities are considered along with their degree of impact. Simply stated, risk management is the process of proactively addressing risks before they occur, when they occur, and the process of resuming profitable operations after they occur. It is important to consider all relevant risks when planning for safeguards and disaster recovery.

Maginot Line

Early in the 20th century, France spent millions of francs constructing the Maginot Line defenses, anticipating an invasion similar to previous land invasions. At that time, these defensive fortifications were considered impregnable. During the 1940 German Army invasion, blitzing soldiers bypassed the Maginot Line, traveling through Holland and Belgium, thereby rendering these expensive fortifications useless.

Senior Management Responsibilities

As a senior manager, it is your task to know your organization, assets, threats and their frequency, vulnerabilities, and safeguards. Managers usually think of risks originating outside the company's walls. They tend to think of critical incidents as pesky attackers attempting to enter their networks or malicious persons targeting their businesses with denial-of-service (DoS) attacks. As damaging as these threats may be, they are small when compared with the internal threats that are more financially damaging. Too often businesses trust employees because they are co-workers, friends, and family members who would not damage their employer. Think again.

Critical Incidents: Damaging Critical Assets

Critical incidents are adverse events negatively affecting the ability to continue profitable operations. Critical incidents are defined in terms of risk, where risk is the probability of harmful events happening. Critical assets are those assets absolutely required for the organization to continue profitably, and profitability is the achievement of the organization's goals.

Critical Asset Priority

Critical assets are essentially divided into three supporting pillars listed in rank order:

1. Human resources
2. Data
3. Physical facilities

Addressing risks is very similar to knowing your adversary: know the risks, accept the risks, mitigate the risks, transfer the risks, and avoid the risks. It is important to know which events can have a detrimental effect on your organization's assets. Harmful events are best understood when they are quantified in the form of a schedule showing the relationships between assets, threats and their frequency, vulnerabilities, and cost-effective safeguards.

By accepting risks, you are not denying their probability or their impact; rather, you have decided to take measures to protect your assets. By addressing risks, you are committed to implementing cost-effective, asset-protecting safeguards. The most desirable asset safeguard is one that avoids risk altogether, so the asset never suffers diminishment. A subset of risk avoidance is one where the negative impact of the harmful event is postponed, hopefully forever.

The process of transferring risks can also be addressed by implementing safeguards protecting specific assets. An example of a "transferring risk" safeguard is the out-sourcing of employee payroll and benefits processing. By passing this responsibility to someone else, accompanied by specific contractual performance requirements, the risk is passed from the original enterprise to the processor. In the event of a critical incident, the asset, risks, and attendant expense are transferred elsewhere.

Mitigating risks is the process by which their probability of happening is reduced. The subset of mitigating risks is reducing their harmful effects on assets. This mitigation process can be highly complex, involving sophisticated strategies, or it can be as simple as instituting a company-wide policy.

In considering risks, the value of a proactive program is not necessarily determined by its complexity and expense. Never underestimate the value of a simple, well-written policy. An example of a simple policy is employee Internet use. Employees, as a condition of their employment, agree that Internet use is permitted only as part of their official duties. Policies, read and acknowledged by each employee, prohibit personal Internet use.

Experience note: An example of a critical incident that can seriously damage business operations is a senior employee, Bob, who gets a little bored after lunch and begins to surf the Internet from his workstation. He is aware of the business-only policy, but chooses to ignore it. Because most of the office is an open bullpen, privacy in his workplace does not exist. After checking his Internet e-mail, he does some online shopping, and because none of his co-workers are looking, he takes a peek at some soft pornography Web sites. He begins to lose track of time and surfs to some sites that are more offensive. While Bob is clicking through some pop-ups, Doris, the office manager, enters his work area. Seeing the Web sites Bob is viewing, Doris remarks that they are very offensive. She reports her experience to her supervisor and visits the local EEO office. This is the third time she has seen Bob browsing pornography at his workstation, and she has reported the matter to her company's management each time. But this is her last straw; she has had enough. Bob has been warned about his pornography browsing but because his technical skills are not easily replaced, his activities have not resulted in adverse personnel action. After exhausting her administrative remedies without resolution, Doris files a civil suit, naming her employer and Bob as defendants. Because the court filings are public, there is significant news coverage and the organization's good image is irreparably tarnished. A large monetary settlement is made and Bob is fired.

One information manager stated, "There is a generally accepted statistic that places risk at an acceptable level: 1 percent. This is a risk. That's all the motivation I need; expect the best, but plan for the worst."

Risk Definitions: No Dictionaries, Please

In the business world, everyone has different ideas relative to the meaning of terms, so here is a small glossary that will make sure we are on the same page of music.

annualized loss expectancy (ALE): The expected loss, expressed in money units, for a given asset as a result of a given threat.

annualized rate of occurrence (ARO): Calculated frequency of a threat expressed in fractions of a whole.

asset: Something of value, divided into one of three pillars: personnel, data, and physical facilities. Assets include tangible (hardware) and intangible (intellectual property) items.

asset value: The total replacement value of an asset.

attack: An attempt, successful or not, to gain access to a computer system by bypassing security controls.

attacker: People using technical or social means to gain access to facilities, employees, or systems.

authorization: Access privileges granted to a user, process, or program.

backup: Exact copies of files and programs to facilitate recovery.

banner: A notice appearing as users gain access to facilities or systems advising they may be monitored.

BIOS: Basic input/output system.

BOT: Short-speak for robot; a script or program that runs automatically.

critical assets: Assets needed to assure continuing profitability of operations.

cost/benefit: Is the cost of the safeguard worth more than the value of the asset? Essentially defined as the "biggest bang for the buck."

DMZ: Demilitarized zone; used in establishing a buffer zone between the organization's interior network, usually protected by a firewall, and the exterior open-ended network, such as the Internet.

exposure value: The amount of anticipated asset loss attributable to a given threat. Usually expressed in a percent value.

ECPA: Electronic Communications Privacy Act, Title 18, United States Code, Sections 2701–2711.

fault tolerance: Assets required assuring profitability. What does the organization really need to continue profitably?

FUD: Fear, uncertainty, doubt.

granularity: Size of the units under consideration.

hacker: Person using technical or social means to gain access to facilities, employees, or systems; an attacker.

hash: Mathematical procedure easily computed, but the calculation of its reverse is infeasible. A one-way hash function produces a mathematical product of a file resulting in a fingerprint of that file.

host: Any device on a network; same as node.

malware: Software capable of performing unauthorized functions on a computer system.

pornography: An obscene item recognized by most children, yet not clearly defined by some of our great legal minds.

qualitative: Process expressed in the experience of the evaluators.

quantitative: Process measured in numeric terms.

risk: The probability of something harmful happening to assets.

risk analysis: The process of identifying assets, threats, and vulnerabilities and contrasting with safeguards. There are two means of risk analysis: quantitative and qualitative.

risk analysis report: A narrative and tables reflecting critical assets, threats, vulnerabilities, cost/benefit analyses, and recovery program.

root: Person logged on has complete system privileges, same as administrator; possesses the system's crown jewels.

safeguards: Protective measures, the purpose of which is to ensure assets are available to meet business profitability requirements.

single loss expectancy (SLE): This expression is the value (V) of the asset multiplied by the exposure factor expressed as a percent (E): $E \times V = SLE$.

spam: Unsolicited, unwanted e-mail.

system: Combination of many elements, human resources, data, physical facilities, the objective of which is to achieve profitability.

trap door: Hidden mechanism circumventing access and security controls; same as back door.

Trojan horse: A piece of software that mimics a valid function but whose purpose is to cause damage.

threats: Event causing potential harm to an asset.

vulnerability: A weakness that can be exploited by a threat.

Following is a list of commonly used abbreviations:

AES Advanced Encryption Standard

ASCII American Standard Code for Information Interchange

BIOS basic input/output system

CA certification (or certificate) authority

CCIPS Computer Crime and Intellectual Property Section (Criminal Division, U.S. Department of Justice)

CPU central processing unit

CTC Computer and Telecommunications Communicator (U.S. Attorney's Office)

DES Data Encryption Standard

DNS Domain Name System (or Service)

DoJ Department of Justice

ESN electronic serial number

FBI Federal Bureau of Investigation

FRR false rejection rate

FTP file transfer protocol

Gb gigabyte

hex hexadecimal

HTML Hypertext Markup Language

HTTP Hypertext Transfer Protocol

IDEA International Data Encryption Algorithm

IM instant messenger

IP Internet Protocol

IRC Internet relay chat (or channel)

ISDN Integrated Services Digital Network

ISO International Standards Organization

ISP Internet service provider

kbps kilobits per second

KBps kilobytes per second

LAN local area network

mbps megabits per second

MBps megabytes per second

MIME Multipurpose Internet Mail Extensions

MoA/MoU memorandum of agreement/memorandum of understanding

NNTP Network News Transfer Protocol

PBX private branch exchange

PCMCIA Personal Computer Memory Card International Association

PDA personal digital assistant

PGP Pretty Good Privacy

PIN personal identification number

Ping Packet Internet Groper

PKI public key infrastructure

RA registration authority

RFC request for comments

ROM read-only memory

RSA encryption Rivest-Shamir-Adleman encryption

TCP Transmission Control Protocol

TCP/IP Transmission Control Protocol/Internet Protocol

TLD top-level domain

TTL time-to-live

URI Universal Resource Identifier

URL Uniform Resource Locator

WAN wide area network

WWW World Wide Web

Yes, Sir. I'm Motivated! Fear, Uncertainty, and Doubt

In a perfect world, organizations would voluntarily take every possible step to protect critical assets, but that is not the case in the business world. The motivation for initiating a risk management process is probably based on the FUD factor. Regrettably, fear, uncertainty, and doubt motivate many businesses to engage asset protection programs. Fear of criminal or civil actions, doubts about continuing market share, and uncertainty of public perceptions resulting from adverse publicity, all count toward motivating businesses to initiate and develop a risk management program. Because some businesses were either negligent or delayed in protecting assets, legislative bodies have passed laws and regulations requiring asset protection.

In the United States, Congress passed specific regulations and laws governing security and privacy aspects of government agencies, civilian agencies, and private organizations in the fields of healthcare, finance, and even videotape rentals. U.S. government civilian agencies must comply with the Government Information Security Reform Act; GISRA mandates that information systems must undergo a security assessment that is submitted each year to the OMB (Office of Management and Budget) or it is possible the agency may not receive its funding. Private industries are legislated and regulated to protect data they collect in the pursuit of their business processes.

PDD 63 (President's Decision Directive)

There are several key areas where laws, regulations, and directives have been enacted requiring industries to preserve their assets for the protection of their investors, benefactors, or place in the National Critical Infrastructure. In May 1998, the President of the United States through PDD 63 required that specific measures were taken to protect the National Critical Infrastructure:

> The President's policy ... [s]ets a goal of a reliable, interconnected, and secure information system infrastructure by the year 2003, and significantly increase[s] security to government systems by the year 2000, by ... [i]mmediately establishing a national center to warn of and respond to attacks. Ensuring the capability to protect critical infrastructures from intentional acts by 2003, PDD 63 addresses the cyber and physical infrastructure vulnerabilities of the Federal government by requiring each department and agency to work to reduce its exposure to new threats. It requires the Federal government to serve as a model to the rest of the country for how infrastructure protection is to be attained. It seeks the voluntary participation of private industry to meet common goals for protecting our critical systems through public–private partnerships. It protects privacy rights and seeks to utilize market forces. It is meant to strengthen and protect the nation's economic power, not to stifle it. Seeks full participation and input from the Congress.

The Law Is the Law

Congress has taken an active role in passing laws and regulations governing the means that business will employ to preserve and protect their assets. In light of these laws, it is important to know exactly who is going to be held legally accountable: senior managers. Of course by law, custom, and practice, they are the persons responsible for protecting business assets from damage and destruction. And when inquiries are made, senior managers are held responsible for the successful operation of their organization.

Laws and regulations have been enacted affecting the protection of company assets and it is senior management's responsibility to know them. You cannot hide behind

Exhibit 1   Laws Affecting Industries

Regulation	Organization	Information
Foreign Corrupt Practices Act (1997)	Industrywide	Accountability for record keeping
IRS Procedure 86-19	Industrywide	Requirements for computer-related tax records
Accreditation Manual for Hospitals (1994)	Healthcare	Guidelines for information management
Gramm–Leach–Bliley Act (15 USC 6801)	Financial institutions	Protection of personal financial information
Office of Foreign Asset Control (OFAC)	Financial and money service institutions	Prohibition of doing financial business with specified persons, nations, and businesses
Health Insurance Portability and Accountability Act of 1996 (HIPAA; 45 CFR 164)	All industries associated with healthcare services	Protection of personal healthcare records

ignorance because it is your responsibility to know how they affect your organization. Exhibit 1 is a small sample of the laws currently affecting the way businesses must protect their assets.

Exhibit 1 represents only a very small portion of the laws and regulations requiring organizations to preserve their data assets. It is not enough that a company has exercised sound business practices; it has to comply with the law or it can be found noncompliant and face the legal consequences. Penalties for failing to comply with laws and regulations can vary greatly. In the case of failing to preserve the confidentiality of personal financial records, the injured party can sue the offending financial institution. In other cases, it is a criminal act to disclose financial or healthcare information for profit without the data owner's informed consent.

As a logical legal extension, senior managers responsible for instituting and maintaining data protection likely will be held personally liable through civil and criminal actions. Legal mandates must be integrated into your critical incident management process. Compliance with current legislation is an area to be carefully discussed with your legal counsel and auditing departments. In today's litigious society, you can bet that failure to comply will result in offended parties seeking their pound of legal flesh.

CIA: Not the Central Intelligence Agency

Historically, risk managers divide information asset protection measures into three broad categories: confidentiality, integrity, and availability. The categories are relatively simple to remember as CIA; not to be confused with the well-known intelligence agency. Think of CIA applying to the three critical asset pillars of human resources, data, and physical facilities. Confidentiality considers sensitive assets that must be secure and protected from unauthorized eyes. Integrity references the whole quality of the asset, meaning it is free from degradation and preserved in the form intended by its owners. Availability is the quality all assets need. They should be accessible by authorized persons when they are required.

Down to Risk-Business

Remember, risks are simply defined as the probability of harmful events. Looking at it another way, risk is a wager, like playing Blackjack. You have to calculate the odds, knowing when to raise your bet or when to fold.

Risk management programs ask these questions:

- What are the odds that a critical incident will happen?
- What is the worst that can happen?
- What are the odds that partial or total asset destruction will happen?
- How will that event affect my ability to continue profitably?

Of course, there is a corollary that should be weighing on every senior manager's mind: "will my business survive these harmful events?"

A general theme repeated throughout this chapter is that "an ounce of prevention is worth a pound of cure." Addressing risks proactively is often a business requirement, not an elective, as laws and regulations mandate safeguards. It is more economical to identify and address risks before they happen than to deal with postincident chaos and ensuing financial losses. Regardless of the strength of an organization's risk management plan, there are going to be points of vulnerability. However, it is wise to expect that despite the best preventive efforts, disasters happen. In managing risks, there are no perfect solutions. Accept this idea and plan accordingly.

If risk management were tight enough to address every vulnerability, it would be so tight employees could not do their jobs. There is such a thing as "acceptable" risk, although balance is defined by functional protection.

Experience Note Systems administrators tell of the ultimate firewall being an off-switch. While this may be true, if a system were switched off, it would be impervious to attacks, but no one could use it.

Risks are not distributed evenly throughout the enterprise; risks must be considered in the light of their specific impact on each critical asset. Assets must be prioritized relative to their criticality in continuing profitable operations after a harmful event. An example of this is the server where engineers test Web page designs. Exploiting vulnerabilities on this server has a lower critical asset impact than unauthorized entry to the file server holding the company's client list. For this reason, the safeguards protecting the test server are significantly less than those surrounding the client list.

Professional due diligence involves assuring adequate controls and processes are in place to protect an organization's systems. The responsibility for due diligence starts at the top of an organization, with the senior managers, and filters downward. These same managers are responsible for seeing that their employees understand what is expected of them in protecting the organization's assets and that employee performance is directed to that end. Developing these processes can seem daunting but "eating an elephant is a process begun one bite at a time." As with all endeavors, we need to devise a plan.

GOOOAAALLL!

The basis of planning is deciding and defining deliverables. In this case, the deliverables are:

- Avoidance of the critical incident
- Transferring critical incident
- Postponing the incident or mitigating the incident's effects

Critical incident analysis consists of two parts: information collection and analysis. Data collected should be a comprehensive snapshot of critical business processes, including the infrastructure supporting mechanisms. Practice good program design. Before embarking on any plan, be certain to review the business' strategic plan. Of course, there are many different names for this business plan. It could be something as simple as the business plan the bank required before granting the business its last loan; or it could be the grand strategic plan presented at the last stockholders' meeting. Regardless, it is strongly recommended that careful review is made concerning the details of this plan before initiating any type of risk management program. Consider the alternative: if you take the time to develop a plan and program that are not congruous with business operations, who is going to support it? In addition to a lack of support, imagine the embarrassment of presenting a risk management plan and someone discovers that it is at odds with the company's goals.

The most important step to be taken at this time is project ownership and leadership. You need to have a project owner. Who better to accept the task than the program's originator? Step up and accept the responsibility. You are also going to need an executive sponsor for the risk program. This person needs to be passionate about the project's value, a real fanatic. If mere lip service is your sponsor's attitude, you need to find another sponsor because you are increasing your odds of failure.

With the project's orientation matching the organization's goals, an enthusiastic executive sponsor, and you in the driver's seat, you are ready to begin to put your plan together. This means you have selected your deliverables, and will begin to select your team to devise the plan and develop the program.

Experience Note Function is more important than form.

Plan to Plan

> Learn to plan or plan to fail.
>
> **— Unknown**

Assessment and Critical Incident Program Requirements

Take the time to scope the program. In short, this step means take the time to decide how large a view this project requires. Commit this scope to paper; too narrow a view and the project will not address enough critical issues, too wide of a view and the material will be too diluted. With restated emphasis, this is the point to make certain the project has passionate executive-level sponsorship, a dedicated owner, and assurance that its goals are aligned with current business plans. Many projects fail because they do not have a solid foundation. In broad terms, the risk management program will take steps to identify and prioritize critical assets, determine threats and their frequency, identify vulnerabilities, identify safeguards and their effectiveness, and execute postcritical incident processes to resume business operations.

Plan

Start the team formulation process by including people from relevant business units that will be impacted by the project, and whose actions will facilitate the project's efforts. Team members should feel like they have a stake in the project team possessing knowledge and creativity. Look for employees who have track records of successful team participation. Based on the size of your organization, there could be many units that will be affected. It is strongly recommended that you include input and participation from at least the following areas:

- Executive committee member
- Legal
- Human Resources
- Information and physical security
- Senior systems administrators
- Auditing managers
- Finance/Budget

Assemble the team, develop the team's goals and motivate them. The more passionate the team members are, the more likely the project will succeed.

Formulate an outline for your plan using the collective abilities of your team. Ask for their comments and input. Disseminating clear, brief, direct, and concise ideas should be considered part of your team's "best practices." In all cases, be certain to document all your steps. You can direct e-mail and memo copies to a specially designated computer folder. Copies of paper memos, correspondence, work papers, notes, and meeting minutes should be archived. Documenting your efforts will save your proverbial bacon with auditors and the legal department.

Meetings are not forums for the same persons to propound their ideas constantly. If you do not need a meeting, do not schedule one. Taking notes during telephone calls and e-mailing them to participating employees for their review and adoption is a good idea. After they have been reviewed, amended, and adopted, direct them to a project file for retention. If there is a conference call or meeting, make certain there are designated start and end times, and an agenda with objectives. Do not allow meetings to fall into the abyss of uselessness.

Minutes of the meeting may seem like an unnecessary step, but remember you might be explaining the process to a group of stockholders from a witness chair in the future. Keeping accurate records of the team's efforts will demonstrate professional diligence and measure your leadership and dedication to this project.

A Word about Charting

This is a good time to invest in drafting a few charts documenting steps, assignments, and progress. There are many volumes available detailing the manner to complete impressive charts.

Experience Note   The preferred method is KISS ... "Keep It Simple Simon." Frankly, the simpler the chart, the easier it is to follow.

Depending on the complexity of the task, Gantt charts are functional for the majority of projects. However, if you require many simultaneous steps, Critical Path Method charts accompanied by a detailed legend with completion deadlines might be a better alternative. Examples of these charting methods are found in Exhibit 2

Exhibit 2   Example of Simple Gantt Chart

No.	Task Name	Duration (days)	Start	Finish	Communications	Complete (%)
1	Select Team Members	0	2/8/03	2/8/03	Personal discussion	0
2	Meet w/Team	1	2/8/03	2/8/03	Schedule meeting	0
3	Proposed Plan	4	2/18/03	2/21/03	E-mail	0
4	Deliver Draft Plan	0	2/22/03	2/22/03	E-mail	0
5	Plan Approval	1	2/26/03	2/26/03	Conference call	0
6	Decide Acquisition and Implementation Needs	2	3/12/03	3/13/03	E-mail	0
7	Decide Timetable for Implementation	0.5	3/13/03	3/13/03	E-mail	0
8	Resource Acquisition	10	3/13/03	3/23/03	Designated team members	0
9	Implementation	30	3/24/03	4/24/03	Designated team members	0
10	Monitoring and Testing	90	4/24/03	7/24/03	Designated team members	0
11	Revising Program	5	7/25/03	7/30/03	Entire team	0

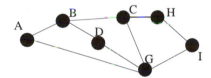

Exhibit 3   Example of Simple Critical Path Method Chart

and Exhibit 3. Remember these are only examples; create and modify your charts to fit your team's needs and goals.

In the Critical Path Method (CPM) chart, dots represent steps that must be taken. Letters identify actions, positions, persons, and completion deadlines. Using the CPM chart, you can address essentially the same type of information contained in the Gantt chart through careful explanation in the chart's legend. As an example, dot A is the team selection and notification, while dot B is the risk questionnaire development. Charts are merely tools and are not as important as the planning, accomplishment, implementation, and documentation of the risk program.

Acquire and Implement

After completing your plan of action, acquire the human resources and materials needed to implement the risk program and put it into place.

Monitor and Revise

Once the program is in place, prudent managers will step back, monitor its utility, and test its function. Any failings, real or perceived, should be addressed and the program should be revised to implement these changes. Remember, rather than address changes in a willy-nilly fashion, implement change controls in your planning process. Change controls follow the same process as planning. Assess the requirements of the proposed changes, determine their effects, obtain comments from affected persons and positions, pass these changes through the planning participants, and then implement them on a pilot basis, measuring their effect. If they are successful, implement them fully. Depending on your perspective, it is better to proceed cautiously than fix preventable blunders.

Risk Assessments

Risk assessment is a business issue, not a technical one. This is the second step in bringing your critical incident plan to fruition. Risk assessment is the process by which the organization's management understands the impacts associated with potential threats and calculates maximum downtime before the organization ceases to be profitable. Risk assessment requires widespread interaction with relevant business units and sometimes places team leaders in the middle of having to soothe tempers and calm bruised egos. Like planning, there are many different approaches to successful risk assessment. Some are very complicated and require an incredible degree of abstract understanding, while others are simple and effective.

Experience Note Occam's razor: "All things being equal, the simplest solution is usually the best."

Risk assessment comes to a conclusion when an organization's executives make formal decisions relative to their fault tolerance. Fault tolerance is the level of functionality required by an organization to continue profitably.

A Little Organization, Please

It is preferable to assemble a small team to collect and evaluate information used to create the risk analysis. The size of the business will dictate the size of your team. It is important not to have a risk analysis team of excessive size. Large teams seem to be more difficult to manage and they are generally less functional than smaller ones.

Experience Note An elephant is a horse designed by a large committee.

The risk team's responsibilities are:

1. Gather and organize necessary data
2. Perform critical asset, threat, risk, and cost/benefit analyses
3. Formulate protection strategies
4. Report results

Gathering and organizing information might consist of documenting the results of e-mail and personal interviews where persons within the organization are interviewed, as well as collecting already existing documentation. This does not mean contacting employees in management positions only, it means talking to employees having operations knowledge. The most time-consuming interviewing method is the personal interview. There are circumstances that dictate a boardroom-to-boiler-room scale of questioning, which depends on the size and structure of the organization as well as the experience of the risk team. Personal interviews allow clarification and free exchange of ideas; however, if the team is faced with a large-scale organization, it is strongly suggested that you use a combination of sending questionnaires via e-mail first, then review them and conduct personal interviews of more-critical positions.

Respondents usually provide valuable information in the way of their opinions about critical assets and perceived threats. Take the necessary time to review each returned questionnaire. Frequently overlooked is the organization's internal documentation. If the organization has had a recent security audit or other type of operational assessment, ask to see the final report. A related and useful document is the organization's last audit report. Search for the organization's response to the audit. It will likely contain the findings of the audit and the corrective actions taken.

Ask for data flowcharts, organization charts, and lines of authority, human resource directories, equipment inventories, policy and procedure manuals, and software inventories. All these documents will help identify critical assets.

Experience Note Remember these documents are very sensitive and deal with the very core of an organization, so approach the subject diplomatically. Provide appropriate security to these documents. They should be reviewed on a need-to-know basis.

Performing a threat analysis is a multi-faceted task. The first step is the identification of critical assets required to continue profitable operations over a given period of time after the critical incident happens. Critical asset prioritization is an essential part of the threat analysis process. Threats must be considered, as they impact specific assets. Threats must be considered in light of their frequency and whether they will affect critical assets in part or as a whole.

Keep threat assessments within reason. It is unreasonable to consider the chance of hurricanes impacting the Rocky Mountains or snowfalls in Brazil. Frequently, risk assessments measure the impact of threats such as fires, floods, hackers, and viruses, and ignore the employee who is sending off-color jokes through the organization's network. The risk team must consider the probability of malicious or unethical employee behavior negatively affecting assets.

Likely the most-valuable source of employee behavior policy information may be found in the employees' handbook or the organization's Human Resources Department. If the business has weak or nonexistent employee behavior policies, this should be brought to the attention of the executive sponsor. Immediate action is required to address this matter.

Formulating protection strategies starts with evaluating asset safeguards already in place, the effectiveness and cost of those safeguards as they relate to protected assets, and future safeguard needs. An important idea supporting protection strategies uses the "what-if" idea. This process takes place in imaginary scenarios:

- What if an employee e-mailed an offensive joke from his workstation to other employees in the company?
- What if an intruder compromised a mental health patient's records?
- What if an employee steals the organization's trade secrets or intellectual property?

This method has the effect of adding safeguards to the protection strategy testing to determine the difference each safeguard makes in relation to its cost and effectiveness. A good question to be posed by the risk team: What is the level of fault tolerance in each of these "what-if" scenarios? In considering "what-if" scenarios, the risk analysis team must have a good knowledge of the business organization, its processes, and excellent communications skills. During the process of completing the project, if the team discovers it does not have sufficient knowledge of a subject, then the team must decide to augment their knowledge and seek outside resources.

Reporting results is the most important task performed by the team.

Experience Note   "If it is not written, it does not exist."

So it is with the report that will be developed by the team, at a minimum it must be in a logically organized written form. Oral presentations can be made to augment the report, but for legal and audit purposes, a formal written document must be created. Reports should be written as stand-alone documents, meaning readers having little knowledge of the organization's function can understand the report and gain a reasonable grasp of the process, analysis, and recommendations. The language of these reports should be plain, digestible, and jargon-free.

Experience Note A government worker was asked to explain a document with this language: "The PIC was TDY to NCA to correct anomalies in the ALCCS."

Nothing glares in a reader's face more than having to constantly refer to glossaries or to look up hundreds of technological abbreviations.

Best Practices in Risk Assessments

Executive Sponsorship

Remember, this was mentioned a few pages ago. It is important. Executive-level managers must have a stake in this project. The project's sponsor must be enthusiastically supportive. This person will run interference for the team seeing their recommendations are implemented. Absent this degree of support, the team's efforts become merely an exercise. Senior employees and managers should be targeted to participate as team members as they are likely to be the repositories of much of the organization's institutional knowledge.

Scope

Risk analysis should include operational areas, but be mindful that a project of overly broad scope will likely fail. On the other hand, if the scope is too narrow, it will not be sufficiently detailed to be useful.

Experience Note Correct scope is like a good shoe, it has got to fit correctly or it is not useful.

Information Resources

Collect current organizational charts that include some idea of not only the job title, but also the job performed at that position. Obtain a copy of the organization's strategic or business plan. It is just a drill unless the project's results can support the business' objectives. Charts documenting the company information flow, asset inventory, organizational charts, process and transaction flows, and reporting structure should be in the possession of the team before the interrogatory/questionnaire process begins.

Select risk team members very carefully. Members should come from different business divisions, and their knowledge should be sufficient to address most general business topics and process areas. It is more important to assemble the team based on identifying the right people rather than who is available. The team's basic design is what provides the platform upon which the members do their work. Taking the time, thought, and energy to make that platform as sturdy as it can be is a good investment whether people will be working around the same conference table or scattered around the globe.

Team Management Dynamics

There are several approaches to team building and management. One view supports the idea that team members should not be stationary and should be rotated frequently. This is similar to the airlines model where crew members are usually working together only for the duration of the flight. On the next flight, a whole new flight team is assembled.

There is a belief that team members become complacent when they work together frequently and there is little chance of cross-checking one another for work quality. However, a 1994 National Transportation Safety Board study revealed that 73 percent of all incidents occurred on a new crew's first day of flying together and almost 44 percent took place on a crew's very first flight. What is the lesson in this study? One interpretation is that teams are most vulnerable to problems when they are starting, before they have had a chance to learn how to work together.

There are many reasons why stable teams perform better. Members develop familiarity with one another and with their collective tasks; consequently, they do not waste time getting settled in and getting oriented. Teams composed of professionals build a shared pool of knowledge that is more comprehensive than that of any single team member. Collectively, they learn which member is skilled in a particular area and they learn how to deal with members who are less skilled without disrupting the team's overall progress. Before a group can be developed into a successful team, there needs to be a team unit with shared responsibilities for clearly defined, worthwhile work. Leadership of the team can be successful if they perform well in these areas:

- Define and compel the team's direction
- Executive support enabling and empowering the team to do its job
- The leader should have expert coaching skills

Leaders should be mindful of using rhetorical inventions to motivate their team members; they do not work in the long run. If the fishing boat captain tells the line-baiters they are fishing for tuna, it may motivate them for a while. But there comes a time, when they are baiting hooks and they never get to land the fish, they are just baiting hooks for others. They realize their work is trivial and unrewarding.

Team support structures must be simple, avoiding the belief that self-managing teams can work everything out on their own. Avoid the "bigger is better" team structure idea. Generally, a large team will hamper its ability to create something useful. So why do companies organize such large teams in the workplace? Emotional issues are usually to blame. Large teams distribute individual accountability and it is more politically acceptable; giving all relevant parties a voice, they will accept the final product.

Expert coaching skills can promote team effectiveness by helping members learn to work and manage themselves. Teams need leadership exercising authority to direct efforts toward goals, not mandating minute details. Sports coaches demonstrate different leadership styles during the course of the game. At the beginning of a game, the coach takes a more-motivational approach showing that the team has worked hard and has a chance to win the game if the members play together and at their best. During halftime, the coach moves more toward a consultative approach where the game plays are reviewed, successes and failures are analyzed, and strategy is revised based on how things are going. After the game, the team reviews the game, the coach emphasizes critical interventions, helping the team learn from experience and build their skills for future games. Good coaching helps a team develop a task-oriented performance strategy; bad coaching identifies a team's problems and tells members how to fix them.

Experience Note Teams sometimes have one member with a particularly strong personality who was able to sway decisions to her point of view. Regrettably, she had an agenda protecting favored programs that were not essential for business continuity resulting in a skewed risk assessment.

Good coaching can usually help a well-designed team succeed, but no amount of good coaching can make a poorly designed team successful. Well-created and developed teams are likely to have less need of coaching sessions as they encounter fewer problems outside their own capabilities. Those teams become skilled at coaching themselves and enter a spiral of increasing capabilities and effectiveness.

Experience Note In the absence of leadership, most teams will drink sand.

The Facts and Only the Facts

Using questionnaires is one of the most effective and efficient means to collect information from a wide variety of persons. The ideal situation is one in which the interviewer conducts the interview in person, thereby answering qualifying questions from the interviewee. Work from an organizational chart, workflow chart, and the knowledge of the risk team members are the best methods to determine the appropriate persons to be interviewed.

In the case of critical employees, team members will want to conduct those interviews personally. Personal interviews should be brief and to the point, lasting no more than 30 minutes. Interviewers should take quick notes and complete their documentation after the interview has been completed. Interviews should logically begin with a brief review of the control standard outlining the official policy. Validating that the interview subject is in compliance with those policies can be attempted here, but compliance should really be left to the auditors as it may adversely affect the interview's results. Notes taken during the interview are merely reminders of the content of the interview and are not intended to be a verbatim transcript. Keep a copy of the notes, along with all the completed questionnaires as part of the team's work papers. These documents may be important if the enterprise is targeted for an audit or legal action. Having relevant documentation is the mark of professional due diligence and can prove that a required task was completed.

There are automated questionnaires and programs that facilitate the risk analysis process. They are commercially available and can be used in place of the customized questionnaires (see Exhibit 4 for a sample).

A well-written questionnaire will generally provide the structure needed by the team to document the needed information. At first, it is important that the questionnaire is the same for all recipients, as this will greatly help in evaluating and comparing

Exhibit 4   Sample Questionnaire

Background
- Date
- Name and title of person completing questionnaire
- Contact information
- Brief description of business function of unit focusing on time-critical processes linked to functions and interrelationships

Operational Impact
- Estimation of impact resulting from business interruption. This category may be divided into sections of time, i.e., 24 hours, 2 days, 5 days, 1 week, etc. (loss of customer service capabilities, loss of internal customer/management services, etc.)
- Loss of confidence (affecting customers, partners, shareholders, regulatory agencies, employees, general public)

Financial Impact
- Estimations of revenues lost due to business interruption. This section should also be divided into sections of time, i.e., 24 hours, 2 days, 5 days, 1 week, etc. These estimates should include revenue losses, lost trade, interest paid on borrowed funds, penalties for late payments to vendors, contractual fines or penalties, canceled orders owed to late delivery, etc.
- Expenses attributable to extraordinary circumstances. These estimates should include temporary employees, emergency purchases, rental or lease equipment, wages to idle staff, temporary relocation of office and employees, etc.

Critical Assets
- List those personnel assets required to maintain profitability for 24 hours, 2 days, 5 days, 1 week, etc. These assets should be listed by position and should include a brief summary of job responsibilities
- List those data assets required to maintain profitability for 24 hours, 2 days, 5 days, 1 week, etc.
- List those physical facilities required to maintain profitability for 24 hours, 2 days, 5 days, 1 week, etc. These assets should include HVAC, equipment, supplies, workstations, software, etc.

Threat Identification
- List those items and their frequency that pose a personnel threat to your business operation such as strike, illness, bombing, criminal action, civil action, extortion, embezzlement, pornography, etc.
- List those items and their frequency that pose a threat to your data such as unauthorized intrusion, data destruction, virus, denial-of-service, theft of intellectual property, data corruption, etc.
- List those items and their frequency that pose a physical or natural threat to your business operation, including physical threats such as flooding, fire, earthquake, loss of electrical power, vandalism, terrorism, etc.

Vulnerabilities (Weaknesses)
- In order of priority, list those specific vulnerabilities that could affect your business unit. These items may be listed as physical security, IT security, training, weak financial controls, weak separation duties, etc.
- In a brief narrative, what has been your experience with those vulnerabilities?

Safeguards
- List safeguards that are already in place that will protect critical assets
- List the initial and continuing costs of those safeguards
- In a brief narrative, what safeguards should be implemented to protect critical assets?

Other
- Are there any other persons you would suggest asking these or similar questions?

the responses. Team members should formulate their questions based on the organization's documentation and their knowledge and experience. Questions should address those items that will progress toward identifying critical assets, threats and their frequency, vulnerabilities, and safeguards. Be sure to track the completed questionnaire responses, as that will assure the various business divisions and units are adequately represented in the survey.

Ask Good Questions of Good People and You Will Get Good Answers

Here are some best practices in the formulation of questions for the questionnaire:

- *Ask intelligent questions of knowledgeable people.* The team should elicit quality results from a pool of knowledgeable people. Do not waste their time. If the question is superfluous or specious, remove it.
- *Include a catch-all section in the questionnaire.* If you have asked the wrong person, ask to be directed to the correct one. No one is perfect.
- *Provide information so the interviewees know their response is important and valuable.* Explain to the recipient the assessment process, how their information contributes to the project of risk management, and how this process affects the overall business. Accomplish this step with a cover e-mail or as a preamble to the personal interview.

The information collection process is not a test. Consequently, there is no right or wrong answer. When conducting interviews, remember this process is not adversarial; sometimes a thick skin is desirable if the person being interviewed has something on their mind. When someone is responding, ask that responses reflect their personal knowledge first and then address any speculation. A bit of reflective listening may go a long way in successfully completing this process.

Experience Note   "Not everything that can be counted counts, and not everything that counts can be counted" (Albert Einstein).

And Now a Word about Asset Criticality

Contemporary with risk assessments, asset prioritization comes into play. Considering fault tolerance, it is the organization's ability to continue profitable operations when confronted with emergencies. Fault tolerance basically defines the minimum level at which organizations can profitably exist. Asset criticality can usually be determined by asking questions such as:

- How would you handle an operation interruption of the following durations? 1 hour? 8 hours? 24 hours? 48 hours? 72 hours?
- Which assets are you required to have in these time periods to maintain profitable operations?

Ranking assets according to their criticality is generally expressed in the context of continuing profitable business operations. Here is a proposed structure to rank assets according to their criticality:

- *High*. These assets are absolutely essential for business operations. There is no redundancy for these assets and fault tolerance is low. Business operational tolerance to interruption is extremely low with the cost of interruption being very high. For the organization to continue profitable operations, it would need to arrange to have these specific assets or duplicate assets immediately available. The availability time for these assets would be measured in minutes, not hours.
- *Medium*. These assets are somewhat replaceable by duplicate means or can be performed manually for a very limited time. Absence of these assets is tolerable for a short time. There is a somewhat higher tolerance for interruption.
- *Low*. These assets may be substituted with some difficulty, but are somewhat tolerant to interruption for a longer period of time than the more-critical assets. However, these assets require reinstatement when the organization is restored after a critical incident.
- *Routine*. These assets may be interrupted for an extended period of time with little or no cost to profitable operations. Assets of this nature are very fault tolerant. After the organization is restored to complete operation, these assets become a consideration.

Mathematics Can Be Simple, even for the Mathematically Challenged

Threat analysis is where we will compare the nature of threats, their frequency of occurrence, with the value of the asset. The risk team should consider the response information in the completed questionnaires, their own experience, and the expertise of those outside the risk team. Do not be proud, it is acceptable for the team to consult with others who have more experience in certain business operations.

There are two assessment concepts, one of quantitative analysis and the other of qualitative analysis. The distinction is fairly simple; quantitative is a process where numeric values are assigned to elements of risk analysis. In this fashion, those who are inclined to measure differences and similarities in numeric form are very comfortable. In the qualitative model, asset values, threat frequency, and safeguard efficiency are indicated by values reflecting the experience of the risk team. Values are based on subjective expressions stated in relative terms, with the credibility resting with the team. Qualitative reports usually require much less explanation, and therefore depend more on the strength of the team's writing ability.

Executives, auditors, and stockholders are more likely to understand risk assessment reports in the quantitative model. They appreciate the risk report's granularity with the advantage of being more difficult for distorted findings. One of the more important features to consider is that risk reports will be reviewed by outside people who do not have the view, knowledge, or experience of the risk team.

Experience Note In the face of disasters, litigation is always a question. Consequently, one of the first documents sought is the most-current risk analysis report.

Single Loss Expectancy and Annualized Loss Expectancy

The National Institute of Standards and Technology lays the foundation for the standards used to calculate single loss expectancy (SLE) and annualized loss expectancy (ALE).

This is a good time to deliver the mathematical formula for arriving at the single loss exposure: take the replacement value of an asset and multiply it by the exposure value to arrive at the SLE. For example, we value a file server at $50,000 excluding data, and we know that it is located in the basement of an office building. According to the local county recorder's office, the office building's basement is located 15 feet beneath the flood plain. Consequently, the company has been paying for flood insurance since the date it moved into this location. A review of news articles and information from the local weather bureau showed the area surrounding the office building has been severely flooded as a result of hurricanes four times in the past 20 years. Because the basement is located beneath the flood plain, it is reasonable to assume the equipment located there would be a total loss if flooded. So, the asset exposure factor would be expressed as 100 percent, and the chance of flooding is one in five.

Doing the calculation, we find that replacement value of our server, minus data, is $50,000 and the exposure factor is 100 percent. The expressed SLE is $50,000.

Now calculate the ALE by multiplying the SLE ($50,000) by the annualized rate of occurrence (ARO). This is expressed as 1/5. Remember, a flood occurred once every five years. This is expressed as SLE × ARO = ALE. Turning the crank on the numbers reveals an ARO of $10,000. The purpose of this drill is realized when we complete the risk analysis report; we're going to schedule the SLE and ARO for critical assets.

Are You Threatening Me?

There are many classification and analysis practices in identifying and classifying threats. Threats may be classified in many ways. Start the risk assessment by thinking outside the organization and consider the origin threats as having either human or natural causes.

Experience Note An accurate analogy is business structure compared to an onion. If you remove the onion's layers one at a time; you will go deeper and deeper until you reach its core.

So it is with your enterprise; identify and examine the risks on the periphery and work your way inward, eventually reaching the center. When you are trying to classify threats and their probability of happening, you will need percentages to determine such things as frequency, and the degree to which they affect assets. Following is a list of a few common threats and some resources that can be contacted to collect relevant information. When contacting these resources, it is suggested that you collect information relative to the threats' frequency, location, and degree of severity measured in a relevant time period for your locale.

- *Earthquake:* Geology departments at local universities and the U.S. Geological Survey.
- *Fire:* National Fire Protection Association.
- *Flood, tornado, hurricane, wind storm, snow, ice storm:* National Oceanic and Atmospheric Administration and the National Weather Bureau.
- *Criminal and hacker threats:* Talking with the local chapter of the National Infrastructure Protection Center (NIPC), sponsored by the nearest field office of the FBI, you should be able to gain an idea of the latest criminal and

system-attacker threats. Most FBI offices have a designated Special Agent as the NIPC coordinator whose job it is to see to the success of the local NIPC chapter. This is the most likely person to contact. More information can be obtained through the FBI Web site (http://www.fbi.gov).

Human threats, both internal and external to the organization, are the most unpredictable and potentially the most destructive. Human threats are more mobile, devious, and plentiful than natural threats. Imagine that one of your trusted system engineers becomes dispirited one day and resigns. If the engineer were malicious, can your imagination stretch far enough to conceive of the damage that could be done with knowledge of your operation? Another scenario of the "what-if" model is born.

The following categories are not intended to provide a comprehensive list of human-based attacks, but merely to serve as a reference. New attacks on technology emerge daily, as do their solutions. Here are a few examples of human-based threats:

- *Unauthorized intrusions.* These malicious acts may originate outside or inside the organization. They are characterized by gaining access to one or more systems. Often attackers install programs allowing reentry to the system. Usually the intruder has concealed his/her true identity and may be masquerading as a legitimate user by modifying data, perusing or stealing sensitive information, etc.

- *Unauthorized program execution.* This is not necessarily the same as the unauthorized intruder. Perpetrators compromise a host or a network service such as Domain Name System (DNS). Once compromised, intruders install and run scanning tools to locate other vulnerable systems while removing traces of their presence in the compromised system. From these compromised systems, intruders can launch intrusion attacks on remote systems, with tracing efforts stopping at the compromised systems. From a frequency perspective, it is likely that most outside network scans are launched from compromised systems with the intention of disguising the attacker's identity.

- *Denial-of-service attacks and distributed denial-of-service attacks.* These are attacks originating at sources inside and outside an organization with the purpose of destroying the organization's ability to conduct business. Examples of these threats are network flood attacks resulting in systems crashes.

- *Privilege escalation.* Privilege escalation means raising access privileges without authorization. Attackers, inside and outside, may not be able to gain privileges immediately when they enter a computer system; usually they attempt to escalate privileges by exploiting vulnerabilities either in applications or in the operating system. It is a common practice for intruders to exploit programming weaknesses in the Common Gateway Interface (CGI). CGI programs are commonly used to provide user interaction with Web pages. By manipulating the input information, it is possible in some CGI programming to gain root access to Web servers. With this privilege level, the attacker is free to deface the Web page, gain access to the host network, redirect shipments, and steal credit card or other sensitive information.

- *Worm and virus attacks.* Viruses are programs that are typically executed through opening e-mail attachments, sharing infected disks, or opening documents containing macros. Worms, on the other hand, are similar to viruses in that they are self-replicating, but they have the object of filling the victim-computer's hard drive.

■ *Back doors or remote control programs.* These are methods employed by attackers to gain repeated access and control of their victim's systems. Often an e-mail attachment is sent to the intended target having the payload of a remote control program. It may be disguised as something very desirable to the victim.

Experience Note   Investigators have seen remote control programs disguised as anti-virus program updates or photographs of famous personalities. Once installed, the program gives the attacker complete control over the victim's computer allowing the attacker to peruse files, install software, or send e-mail in the victim's name.

■ *Malicious programming.* This is programming that has been installed with a date or event trigger. An example is the discontented programmer who had unauthorized access to the computer's payroll code. He modified the code so that if his name and Social Security number were not part of the payroll run, then the computer would delete the current payroll information. After several months, the employee was eventually dismissed for performance issues. When the payroll was run, the computer did not see his name and Social Security number, so it deleted the payroll data. This resulted in the business having to recover the payroll data from backup media, but it was still an unnecessary delay and expense.

There are also many legal threats that can have a very negative impact on a business' operation. If successful, these risks can be more devastating to the organization than the technological threats. Following are a few examples:

■ *Discrimination and a hostile work environment.* E-mail is used everywhere in business operations. However, e-mail can also be misused, posing a very serious threat. Employees and persons outside the organization might recount offensive jokes or spread offensive stories and pornographic material. E-mail misuse can and will lead to a hostile work environment if viewed by someone that finds the e-mail offensive. Discrimination is defined as the prejudiced or prejudicial outlook, action, or treatment of an individual on the basis of age, gender, race, religion, national origin, or sexual orientation.
■ *Defamation.* Defamation is defined as oral or written false statements that wrongfully harm a person's reputation. Oral defamation is referenced as slander and written as libel. It should be noted that defamation laws differ from state to state. If an employee posts false information to a newsgroup or circulates e-mail causing harm to an individual or organization from the employee's workstation, both the organization and the employee may be held legally liable for the action.
■ *Harassment.* This is unwanted behavior targeting a specific person or group of persons. Consider that an employee is the victim of unwanted, sexually harassing messages posted to the company's bulletin board.
■ *Privacy violations.* This act discloses information intended to be private by its owner. Safeguarding confidential information is currently an object of legislation, making its unauthorized disclosure a serious unlawful act.

Experience Note   Consider that a famous celebrity visited a hospital for treatment. During the celebrity's stay, hundreds of hospital staff accessed and reviewed her records without authorization or need. This is another court case that will be monetarily decided.

There are threats and vulnerabilities that can occur within an organization, regardless of management's intentions. Consider an Internet hosting facility with hundreds of servers in its communications center. The building is the size of a large warehouse and, having been recently constructed, has the latest and greatest innovations. The fire extinguishing equipment consists primarily of large tanks of inert argon gas. Its purpose is to flood a fire with the inert gas, displacing the oxygen and extinguishing the fire, thereby preserving equipment and data. This is a fine idea for preserving equipment and data; however, no one considered that there are people working in the communications center who will suffocate before they can reach an exit, due to the large size of the facility. This concept was subsequently analyzed in the "what-if" scenario. The extinguishing system was replaced with another that did not threaten the communications center employees.

Think of malicious employees who have an intimate knowledge of your business operation and are predisposed to do damage. No one is in a better position to commit acts of sabotage, if they are inclined.

Experience Note During the Industrial Revolution, European workers were afraid of losing their jobs to mechanization. In the affected countries, wooden shoes called *sabot* were worn. Workers were able to stop the machinery by throwing their shoes into the works; hence the word *sabotage*.

The threat posed by employees and former employees surpasses the other threats.

- *Vulnerabilities*. Vulnerabilities are weaknesses in the organization that allow a threat to possibly trigger a loss. Vulnerabilities apply to specific threats and assets. Surveying employees who use and manage the organization's systems is a critical part of identifying vulnerabilities. Mapping assets, threats, vulnerabilities, and remedies is the risk team's task. Scheduling them together allows the analysis of their interrelationships. In mapping critical assets, threats and their frequency, vulnerabilities, safeguards and cost/benefits, examine carefully the safeguards area.

- *Insurance*. Insurance is not a consideration at the time of risk analysis. Insurance generally is a means to obtain money after the damage has already happened. While this is an excellent idea, money in the pocket will not immediately restore lost personnel, lost data, or lost facilities in time to continue critical functions. Acquiring critical assets takes time, and regardless of the amount of money, the longer an organization is without profitable operations, the less likely it is to remain in business. Consequently, insurance is an excellent item to have as part of your risk management practices in the long term, but the focus here is the idea of risk assessment and immediate business restoration procedures.

- *Safeguards*. Safeguards are expensive measures; consequently cost/benefit analysis is imperative. They cost money and deplete resources, but if designed and implemented correctly, they can save your critical assets. Do not spend more to protect an asset than its value to the organization. For example, an organization has a Web page used to provide advertising of its services, but almost all of its sales are derived from a well-developed reseller network. Realistically, the Web page contributes little to overall profits. However, in his responses to the risk team's questionnaire, the company's CIO thinks the Web page is very informative and critical to the organization. The Web server has been identified by the CIO as so critical to business operations that it rests behind its own firewall. Costs of the firewall and its related maintenance exceed the Web page's value. When the risk team performs their assessment, they nix the Web page as being superfluous. Of course, there is a requisite soothing session between the risk team leader and the CIO.

■ *CIA*. There are several overriding factors in scheduling these interrelationships; CIA (confidentiality, integrity, and availability) are the relevant qualifiers along with fault tolerance in deciding asset priority. Exhibit 5 provides a proposed risk schedule where relationships between assets, threats, vulnerabilities, and safeguards are illustrated. Of course, this exhibit is intended as a representative model and should be customized to organizational needs. Frequently, teams are challenged by difficult decisions when a potentially lost asset severely affects operations in the long run, but in the short run its loss does not affect much. The risk team should make decisions of this nature supported by its executive sponsor. The goal is the resumption of profitable operations as soon as possible after a critical incident. Once this level of operation is achieved, longer-term considerations can be addressed.

Protection Strategies

Many times, risk assessment teams produce a report that prioritizes the organization's assets, threats, vulnerabilities, and safeguard effectiveness, but they do not complete the next logical step and produce a critical asset protection strategy. Executives and managers will want to know the steps they should take to protect critical assets. It is strongly suggested that protection strategies should be drafted addressing the three asset pillars: personnel, data, and physical facilities.

Personnel

Too often, the overlooked area of critical asset protection strategy is human resources: the employees needed to restore profitable operations after a critical incident. What if a critical employee is impacted by an incident? Could this event create a single point of failure? In order to raise our level of human resource fault tolerance, there is a need to have redundant critical employee resources. Protection strategies could include cross-training employees to fill positions deemed important avoiding single points of failure.

Another viable alternative is the emergency contractor. For example, a qualified engineer is hired to assist on an important system's project that always seems to elude completion. Such a project could be the requisite documentation of a wide area network, WAN. With the completion of this project, the company may want to continue with the engineering contractor for several days each month to clean up other necessary projects. The services could cover periods of regular employee vacation or other absences such as family leave. This contract employee would guarantee that a qualified, well-versed engineer could complete projects, fill in during scheduled employee absences, and handle emergencies.

Another consideration is the use of outsourcing. If a business outsources certain critical functions, then continuing these services, postcritical incident, is merely integrating them into the business recovery and restoration program. The risk team would be well advised to consider protection strategies composed of a series of controls addressing each category of critical assets in broad terms rather than being limited to specific critical assets.

Exhibit 5 Risk Assessment Schedule

Business Unit	Asset	Asset Replacement Value (SLE/ARO)	Rank (High, Med., Low Routine)	Threat and Frequency (1 to 10)	Vulnerabilities	Safeguard	Safeguard Annual Costs	Info.
Human Resources	Payroll applications	SLE = $$$ ARO = percent	High	Unauthorized system access Attempted frequency = 10	Access	Firewall	$$$	None
	Payroll data	SLE = $$$ ARO = percent	High	Unauthorized system access Attempted frequency = 10	Access	Firewall and partitioned subnets	$$$	None
Sales	Client list	Irreplaceable	High	Corrupt data Frequency = 7	Data input and access	Employee access requests	$$	None
Warehouse	Inventory listings	SLE = $$$ ARO = percent	High	Unable to track	Correct input	Field checking	$$	None

Exhibit 6   Information Classification Schedule

Criticality	Classification	Fault Tolerance
Most critical and sensitive	Top-secret information; unauthorized disclosure would cause grievous organizational damage (e.g., cryptographic technology)	Less than 24 hours
Seriously critical and sensitive	Secret information; unauthorized disclosure would cause serious organizational damage (e.g., private party healthcare information)	25 to 48 hours
Critical and sensitive	Confidential information; unauthorized disclosure would cause significant organizational damage (e.g., pricing of raw materials for manufacturing facilities)	2 to 5 days
Sensitive	Restricted-for-internal-use-only information; unauthorized disclosure would cause some organizational damage (e.g., employee's nonpublic wage structure)	5 to 10 days
Public	Unauthorized disclosure would cause no damage	10 days or more

Data

Protection strategies relating to data must consider data classification and backup. Data by itself is critical only as it supports critical business functions or it satisfies legal or financial business requirements. It is noteworthy that data includes files stored electronically or on paper. This means data must be identified relative to its nature as well as its storage. Data classification will identify the criticality and sensitivity of data for business restoration processes as well as provide levels of security.

Data Classification

The U.S. government uses an information classification schedule similar to the one shown in Exhibit 6. Of course, if terms like "top secret" are by nature too military for your company, feel free to change them to terms such as "absolutely essential."

Accompanying data classification is access control. There are many different types of theories in this area, some with complex relational matrices and mathematical progressions. Keeping with the KISS idea, the overriding concept should be that only authorized personnel should have to access human resources, data, and physical facilities, with their access restricted to those items needed to perform their authorized tasks. There are many different schemes for access control but the overarching concept is "need-to-know."

Need-to-Know

The bottom line is that if someone does not have a legitimate need-to-know, they are denied access. Deny all access unless specifically authorized. When considering access controls, the more critical the data, the more restricted access must be. This is an axiom.

Access controls must extend to personnel, data, and the organization's physical facilities.

It makes good business sense to restrict access to sensitive personnel. For example, organizations are not going to have meetings where outside guests are allowed to ask technical questions of research engineers who are developing sensitive voice encryption devices. It is for this reason that access to critical personnel must be limited while they are in their official capacities. Outsiders do not have a need to know.

Experience Note As a condition of their employment, U.S. government employees with access to sensitive information must report contacts with foreign individuals and the content of communications. In some cases, these employees must submit to polygraphs about their foreign contacts.

The higher the criticality of data, the more restricted the access should be. It must be emphasized that persons having access to sensitive data never share that access with anyone for any reason.

Access sharing is not an employee's choice to make, regardless of position. Granting access can only be performed by either the owner or by a formally designated person. How many times have employees given out their passwords, allowing access to data or facilities because they were just being nice, only to have data or facilities compromised?

Experience Note This is an example of "loose lips sinking ships." Government contractors are usually very sensitive about their wage structures as they compete for contracts based on performance and costs. During the annual company picnic, the husband of one of the contractor's employees overheard a conversation where most of the company's wage structure was discussed. Some weeks later, over drinks, he repeated what he had overheard to a few friends. As the drinks poured, his conversation was overheard by the chief financial officer of a competing contractor who was seated at a table nearby. The contractor's next bid submission was aced by the competitor because the government salary structure was known and the contractor was bankrupt within a few months of losing the renewal bid.

Backups

Data backup practices are as varied as organizations. These practices must be based on established and audited company policies identifying critical data and managing that data's integrity. Work and information flow of the business will dictate in large part the type and frequency of backup practices.

In the case of individual workstations, data backup continues to be one of the greatest vulnerabilities. It is a matter of practicality because so much data is created and stored at the workstation with few backup copies made. If employees take the protective step of creating backups, they usually store them next to their workstation or somewhere in their office. By doing this, any harm that befalls the workspace will affect the workstation and the backed-up data. A viable organizational policy is one that requires employees to back up workstation data on two disks: one is picked up and transported for offsite storage at regular intervals, and the other rests with the owner, stored at the secure location of the owner's choosing.

Security of the company's data is important. There are data storage companies that use unmarked vehicles to transport data to secure facilities. It is important that these data storage facilities are sufficiently secure and separated from the original site so they do not fall victim to widespread threats. Another concern is how much advance notice will be required to locate and deliver the data to a designated site.

In recent times, offsite storage area networks have gained popularity, allowing organizations to back up their data via very large-capacity transmission lines to sites that store the data many miles from the clients. These facilities may be owned by the organization or contracted as outsourced companies. Data backup can take place many times during a 24-hour period, and that data can be subsequently downloaded to any site designated by the organization. It is also a common practice for these data transmissions to be encrypted so they are secure in transit, authentication, and storage.

Something to consider are laws governing the encryption of certain types of transmitted and stored data, so consult with your legal counsel before implementing any policies and procedures. Backed-up data is a required business practice; you cannot recover and restore what you do not have, and the longer you are without data, the greater are the odds your business will not survive. Remember, backing up data includes electronic and paper-based documents.

Physical Facilities

Protection strategies concerning physical facilities encompass such items as physical safety of personnel, data and systems, HVAC (heating, ventilation, air conditioning), uninterruptible electrical power, conditioned electrical power (restricting electrical power to 120 volts), secure restrooms, and adequate lighting. There are laws and regulations governing conditions under which your employees may safely and reasonably work. For example, according to recent legislation, it is a requirement for employees handling heavy loads to be provided with back supports and safety equipment.

Another area of concern is the physically challenged employee or client. It is a legal requirement that reasonable accommodations must be made for these folks to function in the workspace.

Redundant Physical Facilities

As with other critical assets, redundancy of physical facilities can go a long way to business resumption in the face of disasters. As far as the extent of these facilities, here are some observations and recommendations. In a perfect world, optimum conditions would be having exactly duplicated facilities. Balance in this arena can be achieved in several ways.

Consider the expense of duplicating your facilities. Now consider entering a partnership with someone that has similar facilities and sharing the expense with them.

Experience Note One of the better plans recently observed was when partners not in competition had duplicated facilities they used to lessen the workload on their primary facilities. When an emergency occurs, the capacity of the extra facilities is sufficient to carry on critical functions. This action takes care of the problem of ramping up duplicate hardware and software as these are in daily use already.

Because the partners were not located near one another, the possibility of the same natural disaster striking both of them simultaneously was very small. It occurred that these facilities were actually engaged during an actual disaster. They worked very well, despite the fact that one of the partners had suffered almost a complete loss of primary facilities. Critical business functions were restored within a few hours.

Facilities Outsourcing

Another viable alternative is facilities outsourcing. Vendors offer mobile facilities equipped with office equipment, hardware, and software tailored to the needs of their clients. Delays are minimal in arriving at the designated site, setting up, and having the client's employees arrive for operation.

Other alternatives involve hot, warm, and cold facilities. Organizations may wish to have their own facilities; how well these facilities are equipped determines their readiness. Hot sites are facilities where complete facilities including office equipment, communications, hardware, software, and other critical items are ready for use. Installing current data and transporting employees are the only tasks remaining before these facilities can be activated. Essentially, these are turnkey operations. Their greatest advantage is that they require very little preparation before they are ready to go online. The cost is going to be high and must be weighed against the benefits. Organizations with low fault tolerance will want to look at such alternatives.

Warm sites are less equipped than hot sites. They contain a minimum of facilities and require substantially more preparation than hot sites. As a general case, they require the installation of some equipment and software. It is not unusual for their preparation to require anywhere from one to two days before they are made operational. The advantage is that they are not as expensive as other alternatives.

Cold sites are building shells with heating, air conditioning, and flooring; telephone lines may not be connected. Facilities of this type require substantial preparation before they can be made functional, taking two to five days. Cold sites have the advantage of costing less than other alternatives, but should be considered only for organizations that are very fault tolerant.

Experience Note We have gone so long with so little, we can now do everything with nothing.

Get Organized

After the risk management plan has been developed, implementation should begin by addressing the critical assets in each relevant business unit. Exhibit 7 is a sample schedule.

Exhibit 7   Asset Protection Schedule

Business Unit Critical Asset	Protection Control	Description
Human resources/ payroll applications	Backup policy Firewall maintenance	Develop policies/procedures limiting outside and inside access and to update firewall software and access control list Use mandatory access control lists instead of discretionary access control
Human resources/ payroll data	Policy/software	Develop procedures and obtain software for backing up data; obtain and implement intrusion detection software
Sales	Policy/practices Modify sales application	Operational controls allowing input fields to accept only correct data input from sales Only business unit management may approve sales database access
Warehouse	Policy/practices Modify inventory application	Operational controls allowing only correct data input; only business unit management may approve inventory access

Disaster Recovery Plans: Murphy's Law

Murphy's Law states "if anything can go wrong, it will at the worst possible time." Disaster recovery is not a proactive topic. It is the time when safeguards, either whole or in part, have broken down and the organization is now engaged in survival and business restoration activities.

Disaster recovery planning is a complex and labor-intensive process. It requires the redirection of valuable technical staff, processing resources, and, of course, funding. You can minimize the impact of such a project on scarce resources by considering the development and implementation of disaster recovery and business resumption as part of the organization's routine business planning activities. Approaches to this topic should be straightforward and uncomplicated. Remember KISS.

Recovery procedures are designed to prioritize the organization's resources to minimize disruptions, minimize financial losses, and ensure timely resumption of profitable operations.

Because there are no two organizations structured alike, plans should be developed in consideration of priority-ranked critical assets in the worst possible scenarios.

Experience Note Plan for the worst, but expect the best.

In all likelihood, organizations will experience a mixture of disaster consequences. Outages affecting manufacturing or sales cost millions of dollars, while outages affecting archived data files may be relatively small. The following questions should be asked of relevant business units in assessing the consequences of disasters and the need for recovery:

1. At what time does the unavailability of a specific critical asset impact profitable operations?
2. Do specific assets generate revenue? If so, how much does it generate in 1 hour? 1 day? 2 days? 1 week? 1 month?
3. What are the intangible losses (public confidence) that would occur in the event of a critical asset not being available for 1 hour? 1 day? 1 week? 1 month?
4. How quickly can this critical asset be recovered in the event of an outage?
5. How long did it take to recover this critical asset in the last disaster recovery test or in the last actual disaster?
6. Do key employees understand how 1 hour of a critical asset's unavailability impacts profitability?
7. Will employees need to be sent home because they cannot continue to work without a critical asset for 1 hour? 24 hours? 2 days? 1 week?
8. Are you required by law, regulation, or stakeholders to make disaster recovery data available for audit? What are the liabilities of ignoring these requirements?

Sensible contingency plans should have the following core elements:

1. Management resumption plans
2. Emergency operation plans
3. Emergency communications plans

Management resumption plans include aspects that assume a few positions may be filled by a variety of employees. Who would act in the CEO's place during a crisis if the CEO is unavailable? Several possibilities should be designated and trained so operations may continue as smoothly as possible. The most important aspect of this challenge is that a qualified candidate or set of candidates is trained to fill the position in an emergency. Again, having a set of qualified substitutes assures operational redundancy and fewer single points of failure.

Emergency operation plans include those processes needed to continue profitable operations. It is imperative these operations begin as soon after the critical incident as possible. Specific teams composed of trained employees addressing critical needs should be developed, trained, and tested. This is a continuous process as operations are dynamic processes with constant changes in personnel, facilities, and data. It is important to have required assets designated in their priority ranking so the most critical assets are recovered first with less critical assets following.

Emergency communications can take many forms, depending on the size and needs of the organization. One of the most vital elements of an emergency communications plan is the ability to contact employees and see to their safety. There must be a mechanism developed and in place, where all employees might be contacted and a determination made as to their safety. After that step has been taken, decisions such as how employees can be transported to an emergency relocation site can be made. Remember, human resources are the most important critical assets.

Every business function contains critical tasks that absolutely must be performed and secondary tasks that are important after the critical tasks have been completed. Of course, critical functions require critical assets. The longer the organization continues in its disaster recovery mode, secondary tasks will usually be forced to critical ranking.

Written in the form of an operations manual, or procedures guide, organizations should have their critical tasks documented along with information and business process flowcharts. This recovery guide will provide immediate help to employees involved in both day-to-day operations and of exceptional use during recovery operations. In the face of a disaster, lacking an operations manual with policies and procedures promotes arbitrary and baseless decisions based upon an employee's recollection or interpretation of a policy that was understood, but not committed to a written document.

Informal or unwritten functional responsibilities will cause confusion, ineffective task prioritization, and misunderstandings. Job descriptions must be formalized as poorly defined or nonexistent positions make performance accountability impossible. During a disaster is not the time to discover you do not know who is responsible for backing up the enterprise e-mail servers.

Position descriptions must be developed, maintained, and regularly reviewed relevant to job description, levels of authority, and reporting requirements. Manuals describing position policies and procedures will be introduced in legal proceedings. Count on it.

They must be drafted with this end in mind. The content and tone of all policy documents should reflect the organization's professionalism, as they will for the basis of business operations during the period of the emergency.

Training employees relative to their duties and responsibilities before an actual disaster is critical to the recovery plan's success. Standardized employee training results in a teamwork effort and identifies how employees will perform during an actual disaster. Employees should be knowledgeable about their roles in an emergency and their specific responsibilities in disaster response and recovery. Practical training reduces development errors, improves procedures, and reduces miscommunications. The point behind practical training is the development of the employees' comfort, confidence, and performance.

Basic Employee Training

Employee recovery program training consists of these basic components:

- *Orientation.* All new employees, regardless of position, should receive orientation training regarding the organization's philosophy, mission, reporting structure, chain of command, goals, and priorities.
- *Transfer or promotion.* All employees, as they are transferred or promoted to a new position, should be thoroughly trained in their new emergency duties, policies, internal control mechanisms, and related responsibilities.
- *Disaster recovery and business resumption procedures.* This training should include the organization's stance, reporting requirements, individual duties and responsibilities, and performance expectations in the event of an emergency. Cross-train employees so they may reasonably perform job duties of other employees. Care must be exercised in this area, as internal controls require a separation of duties and least privilege. Employees should possess only as much privilege as they need to perform their assigned tasks, and jobs must be separated from each other. If individual employees have too much privilege or there is insufficient separation of duties, fraud and abuse are the likely outcome. Regardless, if an employee is a manager in Human Resources, there is no reason why this employee cannot be cross-trained as a sales manager and take this role in the event of an emergency.
- *Knowledge of facility's emergency shut-off procedures.* All employees must have knowledge of the appropriate shut-off devices for electricity, gas, and water. They should know how and when to extinguish these utilities. Employees must know the location of fire extinguishing equipment, first-aid kits, survival equipment, and emergency supplies. Employees must know when and how to notify emergency personnel such as police, fire department, or emergency medical personnel.
- *Evacuation and emergency staging areas.* All employees should know and be able to perform their assigned responsibilities for evacuating building structures, location of staging areas, and performance expectations.
- *Procedures for alerting personnel of an emergency.* All employees should be trained relative to what actually constitutes an emergency, when they should notify inside and outside emergency personnel, and their responsibilities for all stages of the recovery effort.
- *Emergency processes.* These are procedures established for identifying and reacting to disasters. It is important that designated and trained employees are in a position to identify the nature and extent of the disaster and react according to the organization's emergency/disaster plan.
- *Employee notification process.* These procedures call for notifying relevant and designated employees in the event of a disaster. A notification list must include home addresses and telephone numbers, cellular telephone numbers, pager numbers, and mobile device e-mail addresses.
- *Emergency operations center.* This section of the contingency plan should also include the processes for setting up an emergency operations center (EOC). EOCs may be as simple as a preselected location where telephone communications are available, or something more elaborate as a specially designed EOC where very sophisticated communications equipment includes telephone, LAN, wireless wide-area computer network terminals, Internet, radio equipment, etc.
- *Emergency recovery processes.* These procedures and instructions are relevant to the assessment of asset damage following a disaster. In this process, there is a specified means for determining whether a disaster exists, the extent of

asset damage or destruction, and a mechanism for invoking the disaster recovery plan.

- *Business recovery processes.* These are the procedures that assure the most-critical assets are recovered and implemented first. Through this part of the plan, critical profitable operations are restored first and other assets are restored in priority order, according to a specified timeline in compliance with the business disaster recovery plan. This is the section that prioritizes the restoration of assets according to the risk assessment.
- *Relocation procedures.* Instructions for relocating the emergency operations are found here. Relocation sites may consist of a cold site, a warm site, or a hot site. Cold sites are locations where organizations may relocate with a minimum of equipment and services. Frequently, these sites require significant effort and delay before they can be activated, usually three to five days. Warm sites usually contain equipment and facilities requiring less effort, and are operational within 48 to 72 hours. Hot sites are equipped with redundant systems and applications for minimum profitable operations to continue within 24 hours of the disaster. In essence, hot sites are fully equipped and are just waiting for backed-up data to be installed. Frequently, organizations form partnerships with similar entities to establish and equip mutual hot sites. The significant disadvantage of this venture is an event where both partners require the site at the same time.
- *Salvage operations.* These are instructions for salvaging undamaged or partially damaged assets. Often these assets consist of components of facilities, computer and paper records, etc. This is the section that details the filing of insurance claims and the possibility of reoccupying the original business site.

Who's in Charge Here, Anyway?

Emergency Management Team

The emergency management team is structured according to the organization's needs and culture, having overall responsibility to coordinate the activities of all the other recovery teams. This team's roles and responsibilities should be defined in the disaster recovery plan. This is a team that must function with the idea that upper-level managers are not going to be available during a disaster. In fact, they assign functions to specific members of subordinate teams. Following is a proposed structure of recovery-function teams following generic business functions.

Transportation Sub-Team

This team is responsible for coordinating the transportation of critical personnel to the emergency recovery site. Their duties may include informing employees of their new work locations, scheduling transportation, and arranging food and lodging.

Emergency Operations Sub-Team

This team should consist of shift operators and at least one supervisor who will activate a systems recovery site and manage operations there during the disaster recovery and business resumption stages. These are the employees who arrive first on the scene, activate all the facilities and activate other sub-teams.

Communications Sub-Team

This team travels to the recovery site and establishes a user/system network. They will be responsible for restoring critical communications assets such as telephone service, ISP services, value-added network services, LAN services, and last-mile connections.

Data Recovery Sub-Team

The data recovery sub-team may have the responsibility of retrieving critical data assets from storage. Members visit the data storage facilities and collect the data necessary to resume operations, or they coordinate with the software and communications sub-teams downloading pertinent data to the recovery site.

Facilities Sub-Team

These team members are going to install, test, and make critical systems operational. They set up the offsite facilities with everything the critical employees need to conduct critical business functions. After installations are completed, they will act as the help desk, and monitor performance, addressing problems as they arise.

Administrative Support and Supplies Sub-Team

These team members assume the responsibility of seeing that all the administrative support required by the critical assets is delivered to the site on a timely basis. Items such as payroll, benefits, insurance, leave accounting, official and unofficial emergencies, office supplies, morale boosters, and equipment replacements are their responsibilities.

Experience Note A quote I heard attributed to General Norman Schwartzkopf, "When in command; command!"

Press Relations

More than one organization has committed serious mistakes while attempting to deal with members of the press. The most effective tool in dealing with the press is timely information. Businesses have been credited with taking appropriate action during critical times, by the way they dealt with the press. Here are a few general observations:

- Have a plan and a structure to handle press inquiries.
- Do not lie or misrepresent the facts. Credibility is everything.
- Never insult or derogate anyone, for any reason.
- Sarcasm or press-critical remarks are best never expressed.
- If you do not have something to say, do not ramble.
- All microphones and cameras, manned or not, are live.
- All reporters record conversations.
- You are never "off the record."
- Never say anything that has more than one definition or interpretation.
- Never act cute or funny.
- Sincerity counts. If you cannot be sincere, find someone who can.

- Speak plainly, and on about a 12th-grade level. Avoid all jargon and technical speech.
- If you do not know, do not speculate. If you are asked for an estimate, estimate very carefully.
- If you promise anything, do it! Press people have long memories.
- Make opening remarks and distribute written copies of these remarks to the press before speaking.
- Depending on the situation, it is strongly suggested that you designate a knowledgeable and experienced employee as the spokesperson.

Key Press Items

Following are press-related leadership items that must be in place before a crisis situation:

- *Business plan.* This information provides the media person with the "big picture" information. This plan describes (in plain language not business-speak) the organization's values, goals, and business strategies.
- *Public relations policy and procedures.* Statement mandating press relations, company press policies, and actions.
- *Designated spokesperson.* This person is part of the emergency response plan. Arrange for the spokesperson to have experience addressing the press corps before an emergency. Consider filling this position with someone from the local area who is knowledgeable about language, culture, and local customs.
- *Media contact log.* Keep a journal of every journalist and story. Know who contacted the organization, when, topics, their contact information, what you promised, any delegated items, and when you are due to get back to them. If you do not provide accurate and timely information, it will be likely the press will quote someone less qualified as their source.

Original Documentation

Recovering business operations after a critical incident often requires the use of original documents and critical records not stored as backed-up electronic data. Business recovery plans should include steps for the consolidation and storage of original and critical documents in a secure location. Storing critical documents away from the business will preserve them in the event of total physical destruction of the organization. Critical documents include contracts, service agreements, corporate papers, insurance policies, and personnel and financial records.

Test the Plan

Contingency plans are dynamic documents designed to adapt to business changes as they occur, including changes in personnel, data, and physical facilities. A mock critical incident test should be staged at least once annually, with only a minimum number of employees advised of the date and the test scenario. The point of this exercise is to test the plan, training, people, and equipment. Have a test reflecting likely emergency scenarios.

Experience Note While participating in a critical incident exercise with thousands in attendance, the emergency teams faced a mock bombing scenario. Emergency response teams arrived at the scene and began attending to the "injured." Emergency responders did not think to scan the area for hazardous materials as they transported the injured to local hospitals. When they arrived at the hospitals, the proctors overseeing the exercise informed everyone that the bomb site was surrounded by a very hazardous substance that was carried into the emergency rooms by the injured and the attending paramedics. Each emergency room was then quarantined as a result of the spreading contamination, closing down every hospital in the metropolitan area. This test showed the immediate need to alter conventional emergency response procedures by more in-depth "what-if" scenarios.

Using possible critical incidents will determine if the plan works or not. Do not announce when the test is going to take place, nor should you broadcast possible scenarios. It should be a surprise, just like an actual emergency. If too many employees are aware of the exercise, the test results will not reflect behavior during actual emergencies. After the exercise, schedule a time for debriefing and postmortem critique. Gather all appropriate employees together and scrutinize responsibilities, behaviors, and results in an organized and constructive way. Remember to document the plan, the exercise, and the critique. The auditors and other examiners will ask to see these documents.

Risk Assessment Reports

Risk assessment reports should be drafted in common business language. It is not unusual for several levels of employees to review narratives, accompanying charts, and the work papers. Other report reviewers may include internal and external auditors, bank examiners, legislatures, stockholders, lawyers, law enforcement agents, prosecutors, judges, and possibly juries.

The risk team is drafting a report that many people will review and, depending on their experience, training, and background, might draw conclusions differing significantly from those intended. Use explanatory narratives if necessary for each abbreviation and acronym to avoid misunderstandings.

In Exhibit 8 is a proposed format for the risk assessment team's report. Of course, this example is a model that can be modified to suit your particular circumstances.

Simple Risk Management Advice

In many circumstances, risk management exists in business units isolated from one another. Here are some considerations when developing a risk management program:

- In terms of a calendar month, if you are right 95 percent of the time, you are wrong one day per month. So, no matter how confident senior managers might be, rely on the experience of the risk team.
- No senior manager knows it all. Do not fall into the trench of "if I didn't think of it, it isn't any good."
- Do not ignore historical data to predict future events; however, you should include possible catastrophic events in your risk management models.
- Most often a simple spreadsheet will do. Do not fall into the quagmire of overly complex models.
- Integrate all business units and avoid isolating critical business functions.

Exhibit 8   Risk Assessment Report

To: (Intended audience at the "C" level)

From: (Risk Assessment Team)

Subject: Risk Assessment for XYZ Corporation

> **Introduction:** Predication of the project, participants, and methodology

> **Scope:** Detail the scope and purpose of the risk assessment project

> **Summary:** Include a brief synopsis of the project with particular emphasis on asset criticality and protection strategies

> **Details:** Narrative describing the risk assessment in detail emphasizing critical assets, threats and their frequency, vulnerabilities, and safeguards with their accompanying effectiveness and cost/benefit

> **Disaster Recovery Steps:** Describe in substantial detail the necessary steps to disaster recovery and business resumption. A logical organization would be to address recovery steps in terms of business units, critical assets, and their timeline for restoration

> **Recommendations:** List recommendations, their estimated costs, and a reasonable time for implementation

> **Observations:** This is the location of any candid or confidential information

> **Attachments:** Inventory of attached work papers

Just when You Thought You Were Done

After the report is done, and it has been presented and adopted by anxious executive committee members, the teams enjoy a celebratory lunch and you think you are done. No, you are not.

Organizations are not static entities; they have to change to meet daily challenges. As organizations change, so must their critical incident management program. Risk management planning is not a two-month project, and it is definitely not a project that once completed can be filed and forgotten. Depending on the size and structure of the organization; changing legal and regulatory requirements; FUD factors (fear, uncertainty, and doubt), the organization needs to determine when to conduct risk management assessments.

Suggestions

All organizations must have a critical incident management program consisting of risk management, disaster recovery and business resumption, policies and procedures, compliance auditing, critical incident response programs, Critical Incident Response Teams, legal and law enforcement relationships, and privacy management.

Qualified team members selected from senior staff of the organization's business units can perform risk management. Enthusiastic executive-level managers should be the sponsors of risk management teams. Their primary task is the collection of information relative to critical assets (those assets required for profitable operations), threats and their frequency, vulnerabilities, and safeguard effectiveness.

Risk management efforts should be documented in the form of reports, notes, and work papers, with these items being archived. Risk assessment teams are responsible for information collection and analysis, reporting their findings, and making recovery recommendations. They should write the report, keeping in mind that it will have a wide audience outside the organization. Test all aspects of the emergency response plan, including teams, sites, programs, equipment, procedures, and employees. After the exercise, have a positive critique session to revise and improve performance. Then implement plan changes under the change control policy. Archive all reports, notes, and minutes for future reference.

Chapter 2

Policies and Procedures

Policies, Procedures, Standards, and Politics

Modern organizations have developed into a complex waltz of human resources, data, equipment, facilities, processes, policies, and procedures. For most of us, our daily activities are not scripted and rely on policies and procedures to create an efficient and productive environment. Developing and implementing fixed policies often seems like a futile exercise, yet unless there is a formal architecture, employees end up spinning their wheels.

In the same sense that countries require laws governing the conduct of their citizens, organizations require policies to govern the conduct of their critical assets. Policy development and enforcement is neither an academic drill nor an exercise just to placate auditors. It is an essential component of sound business operations. If appropriate conduct were decided on a voluntary basis, it would be observed about as often as those who make a complete stop at stop signs without a police officer present. True, it does happen, but not often.

Policies are the methods by which business processes are documented and disseminated. Not all policies are going to apply to all business units. Consequently, policies may have general coverage areas, or coverage that is directed to specific business units and even specific functions. They provide employees with limits, alternatives, and governance. Formal policies allow senior managers to conduct their business without constant intervention, enabling employees to work within defined frameworks. They reduce the range of individual decisions and encourage managers to deal with items that are only outside that framework.

Policies assure equitable access to secure resources for authorized users. They make certain that safe, consistent, correct procedures are being employed to conduct the organization's work. Many policies are not optional; rather, they are mandated by legal and regulatory requirements while others are based on fear, uncertainty, and doubt (FUD).

Ask any system administrator how many times he or she has repeated the company's policy mandating that employees not open e-mail attachments. Before long, the system administrator has to deal with an employee who has done exactly the opposite.

There is another purpose for developing written policies and procedures to help guide the practice and performance of professionals who are faced with a combination of mundane tasks and crisis-related activities requiring an immediate decision. Professionals such as lawyers, accountants, auditors, scientists, physicians, and others are dependent on policies to assure their efforts are directed toward specific accepted practices. The logic behind policies for professionals assures that the work is done the same way, regardless of who is doing it, as the accepted manner of completing the task is consistent from professional to professional.

Under most circumstances, senior employees are expected to be promoted, leaving vacancies behind them. The generally accepted idea is that the employee accepting the position will be able to "hit the ground, running," because there will be written policies and procedures left by the employee vacating the position. Written policies and procedures refined by the incumbent ensure that the employee filling this position will be able to work effectively and efficiently at this job with a minimum of delay. These policies bridge the gap between two employees doing the same job at different times, locations, or even business divisions.

When followed, these policies guarantee the consistency of the work performed previously or in different locations. They form a core of institutional communication between the experienced, knowledgeable person who developed or enhanced the work plan, and the new person assuming the position. Policies address ways to handle routine situations, and can form a directory of operating procedures to be used in unique circumstances. As a learning tool, policy documents form a basis for describing new procedures or explaining the application of special circumstances to others.

Written policies and procedures form essential components of the organization's management system because they detail management instructions that are often the result of high-level discussions or legislated requirements. Statements of policy, especially as they relate to critical incident management, are the manifestation of executive direction in the organization's environment. As practical instruments of managers, written procedures bind the organization's philosophy to the actual work-related task.

Et Tu, Policy

Policies constitute an established course of action directed toward accepted business goals and objectives. Procedures are methods by which policies performed. Standards are definitions of quality generally accepted by industry. An example of standards is the Institute of Electronic and Electrical Engineers standard 802.11. This is a measure for standard information technology telecommunications and information exchange between information networks.

Each procedure has an action, decision or repeated step. In other circumstances, the word procedure can also take a variety of usages such as, Standard Operating Procedure (SOP), Department Operating Procedure (DOP), or Quality Operating Procedure (QOS). Regardless of the terminology used, policies are written to carry out the details of the business process. In some business cultures, there may not be a significant distinction between policy and procedure. In other cultures, there may be a great difference between policy and procedures.

In times passed, there were many businesses that did not think they needed well-developed policies and procedures. However, in today's legislated world, there is hardly an organization that is not specifically addressed by laws and regulations. For example, in the area of healthcare, data collected must undergo a high level of access restriction because failure to do so could result in criminal or civil penalties. The content of privacy statutes, directed to healthcare providers, is detailed in very specific language.

Organizations must ensure that the content of policies and procedures does not violate rules, regulations, and laws under which they must operate, and good business sense. The rationale for establishing policies that are disseminated throughout an organization is twofold:

1. They establish clear and consistent processes. Organizations must show widespread uniformity in applying laws and regulations.
2. To allow employees, who are not legally minded, to have confidence that they are performing their duties in conformity with the law. For example, a township finance office has the responsibility of accounting for sales tax revenues collected from local businesses. Local ordinances require such taxes to be paid to the township government one quarter after collection. Recently, the township council decided they would offer certain qualifying business rebates on their collected sales taxes as an incentive to remain in the township, as there had been some difficult economic times. The township had a policy that described the process for creating, amending, and depreciating policies. Accordingly, the finance office drafted, vetted, and implemented a series of policy changes. Policy changes were proposed by the finance office and vetted through their legal counsel, the audit unit, and the township executive committee. After all parties approved the policies, they were adopted and installed. Corresponding changes in check processing software were made for tax rebate checks having two signatures: (1) the signature of one of the five township executives and (2) the signature of the comptroller. This policy observed changes made to the law and the internal controls of least privilege and separation of duties. Under the policy, no one person or office could authorize the release of revenue rebate checks.

There are many other reasons for documenting policies:

- *Performance standards*. Written policies enable managers and their subordinates to define and understand their requirements, boundaries, and responsibilities. Policies create performance baselines to which subsequent changes can be referred, enabling orderly process changes to be made.
- *Performance metrics*. Policies enable managers to determine whether a subordinate's action was simply poor judgment or an infringement of the rules. If specific rules did not exist, then employees could not be held accountable for their actions. Having a written baseline of performance expectations, those in authority can decide if disciplinary action or reward is warranted.
- *Management metrics*. Policies provide substantial freedom to employees in the performance of their duties, allowing them to make decisions within previously defined boundaries. Well-defined policies allow employees to do their jobs without micro-managers meddling in their work. In this same vein, policies enable managers to manage by exception rather than by controlling every action and decision of their subordinates. Before an action begins, employees know the rules and are more likely to produce the right result the first time.
- *Quality models*. The International Standards Organization developed a series of worldwide quality standards known as ISO 9000. This is a set of documents addressing quality systems applicable to most settings. They specify requirements and recommendations for the design and assessment of management

systems, ensuring that goods and services reach specified requirements. ISO 9000 standards apply to most processes and require that policies and procedures are documented, understood, and executed.

The Capability Maturity Model® (CMM) process developed by the Scientific Engineering Institute located at the Carnegie Mellon University is a framework that describes key components of effective systems and software development. The CMM is very powerful as it provides the necessary detail to understand the requirements of each maturity level, allowing organizations to examine and compare their practices. In this fashion, gap analyses are completed and improvements are prioritized addressing specific needs. The CMM has five maturity levels, with each level requiring specific policies and procedures before advancing to the next level.

Both ISO 9000 and the CMM are important industry standards representing desirable and pursued quality standards. They are important to organizations in terms of process improvement, but they also are considered an excellent source for policy content.

Experience Note Quality is remembered long after the price is forgotten.

Trust Models: Trust Me, I'm a Good Person

There are three trust models described here:

1. *Trust everyone all of the time.* It is the easiest trust policy model to follow, but not practical and definitely not sensible. Some businesses stopped following this model after they discovered their trusted employees had looted the company's bank accounts.
2. *Trust no one at any time.* This is the most restrictive policy and also one that is not practical. Some organizations attempt to function on this model, but do not function very well.
3. *Trust some people some of the time.* This model emphasizes caution in providing access to critical assets on an as-needed basis and only in sufficient amounts permitting employees to do their jobs. Controls are instituted ensuring trust is not violated. Usually the most-favored model is one that requires a bare minimum of privilege and as trust is gradually built, privilege escalates.

The Policy of Policy Development

Good policies address potential threats. If there were an absence of threats, there would be little reason for policies. Organizations need comprehensive policies. A good example is the United States needing policies that address national defense. The state of Colorado does not need a national defense policy, as there are no security threats posed by other states, nor is Colorado in a position to execute treaties with other nations. Nevertheless, Colorado is a significant member of the United States and thereby provides resources to the national defense posture of the whole United States. Unified policies provide a framework for identifying threats and vulnerabilities and a basis for effective safeguards.

Policies are about strategy. You cannot decide countermeasures for information leakage if you do not have policies mandating enforceable countermeasures. For example, you cannot expect 20 software engineers, each of whom is in charge of a small degree of program security, to behave coherently unless there is a unified policy with the same goals in mind. Of course, employees have a policy in mind when they define and implement safeguards, but written policies direct them to a mutual goal.

Every organization needs policies addressing its many functions. Policies should detail who is responsible for policy implementation, enforcement, audit, and review. Policies must contain a very brief explanation as to the reason they exist. Seemingly arbitrary policies delivered from on high with little or no explanation are likely to be ignored completely. Clear, concise, coherent, and consistent policies are more likely to be adopted and followed by the workforce.

Most well-developed policies share many of the same elements. Some are drafted so these elements are specifically identified while others are subtle, requiring a thorough reading and a bit of head scratching.

Experience Note Employees, regardless of their position in the organization, prefer the explicit policy style. They want it right between the eyes, reading and understanding the policy, not guessing at its implied meanings.

Some employees will resist policies, regardless of their intent. They view policies as impediments to their ability, restricting their freedom. Sometimes they feel the organization does not trust them and intends to overly govern their behavior. Employees fear that policies will be difficult to incorporate into their business activities or difficult to follow. Managers tend to worry that restrictions placed by policies will adversely impact the organization's morale and profitability. Obviously, the most desirable deliverable goal in policy drafting is the win-win-win scenario. Managers win, employees win, and the organization wins. This strategy requires skill, daring, and terrific delivery.

Team Leadership

Successful policy development teams must have a fanatical executive sponsor. This senior manager needs to be a "true believer." The policy development team needs to have a leader with excellent business knowledge, analysis, management, and communications skills.

Team leaders are able to guide and direct the team's efforts by:

- Asking questions that stimulate ideas and fruitful discussions.
- Using reflective listening skills.
- Directing but not overly managing the team's discussions.
- Developing and fostering an informal and relaxed atmosphere.
- Celebrating the achievement of milestones and objectives.

Policy Team Members

Carefully select the policy development team members. The team development model presented in Chapter 1 is also applicable here. Team members should be selected from relevant business units. There is a decided advantage if members have the ability to write in plain, simple language.

Common Policy Components

All policies must be given an effective date. Effective dates cannot be before the release date of the policy, but prior events can be included as part of the policy statement.

Every policy should be subject to a review or expiration date. This date assures that the policy will be reviewed periodically to determine if it is still needed. In this way, old policies may be updated, obsolete policies can be abandoned, and new requirements can be incorporated into existing policies.

Affected business units or positions should be listed as the policy audience. If the policy is companywide, then it should clearly state this fact; however, if it is applicable to just a few people, then those positions should be specifically detailed. Avoid the tendency to make policies just to impress someone such as a new operations officer or company president. Make policies that matter.

Experience Note "If it's not broken, don't fix it." Do not adjust or amend policies unless absolutely necessary.

Executive Approvals

Policies should specify which executives approved them. They should be named along with their official title in the policy document. Here are two points on executive approvals:

1. Do not name an artificially high officer who has little relevance to the policy as the authorizing person. This may result in the policy being challenged without a knowledgeable defense.
2. The authorizing officer should be of sufficient authority so that higher-ranking executives could not overrule if the policy were challenged.

Policy Exemptions

Just as important as the body of the policy is the process outlining how exemptions can be requested. If exemptions are not possible, then the policy should state why. It is not important to state the conditions under which exemptions may be granted; just the process for requesting them. It is likely that if you are overly explicit in defining the exemptions, you will receive a deluge of similarly worded exemption requests.

Changes

Policies cannot remain unchanged forever. Successful policies have explicit procedures for generating succeeding policies. In some cases, policy changes are merely a technical review while others will require a full narrative justification, including a process for combining old procedures with newer ones.

Violations

All policies must contain an explanation of consequences when employees violate them. Disciplinary actions can vary from the least level, where a violator's supervisor must acknowledge that the policy has not been followed, to severe disciplinary action resulting in the employee's dismissal and prosecution. The level of discipline must be commensurate with the importance of the policy. For example, a new employee violates a policy that requires e-mail to be used only for job-related purposes. It is

Exhibit 1 Policy Format

Paragraph Number	Heading	Information
Address block	Date: To: Position title From: Policy authors Subject: Policy name	Standard memo address block
1.0	Purpose	Predication and purpose of policy, including the authority for this policy and effective date
2.0	Revision history	Previous policy history; set date for future review, revision, and by whom
3.0	Affected personnel	Specify business units and positions to which this policy applies; state who is responsible for policy compliance
4.0	Policy name	State the policy in clear and precise terms
5.0	Exemptions	State exemption application processes
6.0	Disciplinary actions for noncompliance	State what will happen in the case of noncompliance in very clear and precise terms

sufficient for his supervisor to issue an information reminder about the use of e-mail. However, if a senior employee were to send an e-mail containing obscene language or racial insults, this would likely result in counseling the employee, and depending on the circumstances, suspension without pay or even dismissal. Exhibit 1 is a common format for policy headings.

The policy purpose section explains the objectives of the policy. When drafting purpose statements, consider using a consistent opening paragraph containing one or two sentences. Avoid rambling or flowery sentences; the language should be sufficiently comprehensive and concise in meaning. Do not use abbreviations, which abbreviations cause confusion and provide a basis for misunderstanding.

The revision history shows previous revisions to the policy and provides a historical view of the document, showing the policy as it was instituted and how it was revised since that time. In the case of ISO 9000 or the Capability Maturity Model, policy and revision histories are requirements. This section is a good place to set dates for a future review, noting who should perform this review and why.

The affected personnel section identifies the employees to whom the policy applies. It states the users of the policy and should identify the affected persons by business unit positions rather than specific persons by name, e.g., "All server systems engineers" rather than specific employees such as "John Doe."

The next heading, the policy's body, is the most important. In this section, the general attitude of the company, its goals, mission, and vision are reflected. This is the section that should include any clarifying narratives or definitions. All readers should have a common vocabulary if they are going to clearly understand the policy. Avoid stating the policy in part, then referring the reader to another section for the rest of the policy. Regardless of the length, state the policy completely. The whole purpose of writing an easy-to-read policy is to assist the reader to understand and remember the information on the first reading.

Exemption processes should be the next section. State the process by which exemptions may be obtained. Be certain to detail the written format that exemption applications need to follow and specify the position to which they should be submitted for consideration.

Disciplinary actions should be plainly stated in the policy for noncompliance. Accountability, responsibility, and employee empowerment are current management tools that are available in explaining the policy.

Do the Policy Right the First Time

Avoid drafting, vetting, and approving a policy only to discover shortly thereafter that it does not address the problem. Get it right the first time. Policy teams lose credibility and senior management support if they complete the process and need to undo or revise the policy a few days later.

Vetting Policies

We live in a litigious world. Laws, contracts, union agreements, regulations, and international treaties affect the workplace. Policies must pass through an established vetting process where they can be reviewed for consistency and compliance. The complexity of this process depends on the policy, the size of the organization, and the policy's affected universe. At a minimum, these are the parties that should review the policy, making any corrections before it is adopted: affected business units, Human Resources, union representatives, Legal, Audit, Finance, and Executive Committee. Failure to adequately vet a policy might adversely affect the company and preclude it from doing business.

Policy Writing Techniques

Writing policies is a lot like creative writing. Very few folks have the skills right away, but with some experience and practice nearly everyone can write policies and become proficient at drafting a document that is easy to understand and carries substantial weight in the organization. Here are some general best practices in drafting policy documents.

Plain Language

Generally, policies are written to specific employees in particular business units. For example, information technology policies are replete with language and abbreviations that are so cryptic that other employees have little appreciation or understanding of the policy's purpose or direction. Policy language should aim to be as clear as possible and every sentence should say exactly what it is intended to say. For example, a drafted policy may say an employee is entitled to two weeks of vacation annually. What does this policy mean? Does the employee accrue vacation time during the year? What is the term of that year? Is it a calendar year or other term of year? Can the employee take vacation in less than a two-week period? Is the term "2 weeks" a 15-day period or is it 10 work days?

Policies should be drafted in the simplest words possible that still convey the meaning to the reader. Avoid colloquial terms, unexplained foreign language terms, technical terms, and slang. For example, what is the meaning of the term "rip-off." Today's usage would include definitions such as defraud, theft, or embezzle. However, to those of previous generations it refers to an action similar to removing wallpaper.

A major problem with technical writers is that they often aim at correctness and choose the biggest and most specific words. Remember, words serve little useful purpose if they are not understood. Policies should not be written like college textbooks requiring exhaustive study. Employees do not have the time or interest to engage in deep study. On the other hand, do not draft policies using terminology that makes them seem simplistic and condescending.

Spelling and Grammar

Avoid careless spelling and grammar mistakes. Word processors and spreadsheet applications have spell checkers and grammar checkers for a reason: the credibility of your policy documents depend on them.

Gender Words

In recent years, writers have been trying to avoid using "he" because it implies masculinity and possible bias. Sometimes we see a trend of using the terminology of "he/she" or "he or she." This phraseology gets tiresome very quickly in written form and is very awkward in conversation. It is acceptable to use a combination of "he and she" in writing or in conversation, depending on the location of the intended audience. It is important to remember to geography of the audience; for example, in some Middle Eastern nations it is appropriate to use the male gender and masculine words, while other nations prefer nongender words such as "team members" or "performance analysts." Policy documents must avoid offending employees if they are going to be considered credible. When drafting policies, it is a matter of credibility to be sensitive to the intended audience.

Eternal View

Policies should be in a written tone as though they have always existed and will continue to exist. Unless specific references are critical to the policy's application, avoid references to specific products, current computer architecture, or technologies. Also, policies should always refer to positions in the organization rather than to specific persons. Whenever possible, policies should not reference an employee's name, address, telephone number, floor, or mail station unless absolutely necessary. Rather, policies should reference positions such as the Human Resources Manager, located at a given location, telephone number, mail stop, and so on. If named business functions are referenced in the policy, they should be carefully identified, leaving no uncertainty in the mind of the reader. Be certain to do your homework when referring to a position; with recent restructuring and business unit consolidations happening on a daily basis, it is important that the correct position and office is named.

Application

"I did not think it applied to me." This is a common explanation given to auditors when an employee avoids policy compliance. The most-effective way to remove this excuse is to specifically state who must comply with the instructions of the policy. Such application statements are probably best stated in the context of which employees are responsible for adherence rather than stating those employees who are not required to comply. For example: "This policy applies to all employees who have remote network access." This is a much better policy statement than "This policy does not apply to those without remote network access."

Responsibility for Compliance

Well-written policies will explicitly identify the group or individual responsible for enforcing policy compliance. This statement can include those responsible for monitoring compliance, auditing adherence, and those who are responsible for uniform application of the policy across the organization.

Policy Distributions

Drafting is not the only step to developing complete and effective policy documents. Policies must be disseminated to the target audience in the most-effective and efficient means possible.

Experience Note While conducting an operational assessment, the auditor asked to see the organization's manual of policies and procedures. She was presented with a six-volume set of operational and administrative policies and procedures comprising near 3000 pages. These binder pages were a hodgepodge of legal terminology, operational guides, and executive mandates. Later the auditor was presented with additional policy volumes relevant to procurement requirements, a funding guide, and an operations policy binder. There was no central index, nor were there searchable electronic versions available. These volumes were kept at several locations and access was very limited to two of the volumes. The auditor asked to whom these policies applied? The senior manager replied, "all employees."

To be truly effective and efficient, policies must be distributed to the intended audience to convey the message. It is not reasonable to expect all policies to apply to all employees at all times. Applicable policies should be distributed to the intended audience in a timely and effective fashion. After distributing the policies, it is important in some cases for employee acknowledgments to be executed and returned to the Human Resources unit for accountability purposes. This would be the case with policies such as the use of e-mail.

Consider the use of online policy manuals. Using this online method, a smaller number of policies with application to specific business departments or functional units can be developed, disseminated, and easily modified. They are easier to disseminate and are more easily updated and distributed than the larger companywide paper versions.

Enhancements to Written Policies

Other media can augment policies, making them more appealing and useful to intended readers. Reading policies is not very interesting to most employees. These supplements generally consist of some kind of electronic media for them to be effective.

Audio/Video Productions

Many organizations have started to use media convenient for the telecommuter. Video productions can be easily downloaded to the computer of an offsite employee, who can then review it at leisure and send an acknowledgment to the office. Once stored on the employee's computer, these productions can provide future reference for the employee.

Classroom Training Sessions

Most organizations offer formal classroom training sessions to present policies to employees and to obtain feedback from them. Classrooms provide the opportunity to learn from other attendees relative to policy methods and wording. The classroom setting provides an opportunity for attendees to meet with the instructor as well as other employees, and to exchange viewpoints. Instruction of this type may be restricted to the individual employee or include groups sharing policies.

Each organization has a culture that functions best in some environments but not in others. Before arbitrarily spending time and money offering supplements to written policies, weigh each media option and select carefully.

E-Mail Policy: Avoiding Hidden Risks

In today's business environment, organizations must be aware of potential liabilities by developing and implementing comprehensive management programs that address e-mail creation, content, retention, privacy, and deletion. E-mail has replaced the telephone call as the preferred means of business communication. Through e-mail threads, employees record their thoughts and read the thoughts of others. Wrongful statements, disparaging remarks, and off-color jokes can be read at future dates. The result is written ammunition that can make or break organizations should a lawsuit or criminal action follow.

Experience Note   In recent litigation about diet pills, some of the most embarrassing evidence against the manufacturer came from internal e-mail exchanges among its own employees. One insensitive message reported an employee expressing her dismay at the thought of spending the balance of her career paying "fat people who are a little afraid of some silly lung problem." The remark was a reflection of the employee's attitude to a rare but fatal condition some diet-pill users developed. Of course, the judge and jury in awarding damages carefully considered these e-mail messages.

In the past, if an investigator was trying to discover what employees were saying or thinking at a given time, the best evidence would generally come from notepads, calendars, diaries, desk pad scrawl, and other informal documents. However, with the use of the computer workstation and the prevalence of e-mail in the workplace, experts can have access to a virtual library of written documents located on hard drives, file servers, and backup media. E-mail records provide important insight about how decisions were made and the timeframe in which they were made. The fact that organizations lack viable e-mail policies means that senior managers do not give it the priority it deserves. It is a mission-critical tool present in daily business and personal life. If not managed properly, e-mail can pose serious risks.

Information Tsunami

E-mail is at the crux of what many consider the information tsunami. E-mail is not just a messaging protocol; it constitutes a document-generating storage and commu-

Exhibit 2   Sample Acceptable E-Mail Use Policy Language

Employees, contractors, and associated persons of the XYZ Corporation may not use the e-mail
   system, network, or Internet/intranet/extranet for any reason other than official purposes. This
   includes e-mail sent and received by the XYZ Corporation. Employees do not have a reasonable
   expectation to privacy in sending or receiving e-mail. E-mail is considered property of the XYZ
   Corporation and is not confidential and may be monitored and read by personnel of the XYZ
   Corporation at any time.

---

nication system vital to business processes. The question arises about e-mail and its
management, with little attention paid to the actual extent of the risk potential. Often
the knowledge contained in e-mails relates to other electronic documents. It makes
good business sense for e-mail to be retained within the organization's overall
electronic document management program. This strategy ensures that all information
relating to a particular topic can be located in a single system. E-mail and attachments
must be considered and managed as business knowledge in the same fashion as
paper-based documents.

Many companies interact with their customers electronically. Managing inquiries,
confirmation, orders, financial information, and purchasing patterns are all part of a
process called Customer Resource Management. CRM can provide tremendous value
to an organization; having all customer interactions (including e-mail conversations
between staff members and clients) in one location can bring customer service benefits
and address potential legal liability issues by documenting exchanges. In legal proceedings, e-mail leading to a contract agreement may be as important in determining
the spirit of the contract as the actual contract itself. If fraudulent conduct is alleged,
and the e-mail records of that conduct are missing or deleted, the resulting judgment
the organization will experience can be severe.

E-mail is not a transitory communications medium similar to a telephone call;
rather it is a repository of information and accumulated knowledge. As e-mail has
permeated our personal and business lives, becoming a vital productivity-enhancing
medium, it has eclipsed verbal communications. It stands as a documentary record
of deliberations and proceedings. E-mail must be considered critical business records
to be preserved and accessed on demand for internal and external requirements. The
ability to sift through waste and capture e-mail of importance requires good policies
coupled with compliance procedures.

To reduce risks, organizations must carefully devise acceptable e-mail use policies.
Settle for nothing less than professional commentary coursing through the organization's e-mail system. Good e-mail is businesslike, with an absence of obscene, vulgar,
insensitive, defamatory, or offensive language. Good e-mail is well written and free
from ambiguity and grammatical problems. Employees must understand and acknowledge that all e-mail content and e-mail attachments sent and received by the organization are the property of the organization. Exhibit 2 is a sample of acceptable e-mail
use policy language. This policy statement leaves nothing to the imagination. Employees should have no trouble understanding that e-mail sent and received from the XYZ
Corporation is the company's property, it is for official purposes only, is not confidential, and may be read at any time. Language of this type clearly states that the e-
mail system is FOUO, For Official Use Only. This policy clearly eliminates personal
use and anything other than use related to the business of XYZ Corporation. The
policy is sufficiently broad, and avoids becoming mired in superfluous definitions and
over-qualification. Using language of this nature eliminates off-color jokes, pornography, rumor mongering, and disparagement as acceptable.

To Keep or Not to Keep, that Is the Question

Business-related records, including e-mail, must be managed throughout their lifecycles according to logical and reasonable policies. Often, laws and regulations mandate the structure of these policies and procedures. There are no significant differences between paper- and electronic-based documents in that they may not arbitrarily be preserved or destroyed. They tell the story of the organization and how it conducts its business, including information that lawyers might have the right to review and introduce at court. There are circumstances where deletion of e-mail may be perfectly legitimate or it may be impossible to do, depending on circumstances. In e-mail deletion, there is no way to be absolutely certain that all copies have been destroyed, because an e-mail can be forwarded to many different accounts, stored in backup media, relocated to other e-mail accounts outside the organization, or made an attachment to another e-mail. The organization is clearly responsible for the maintenance and organization of e-mail records. Failure to implement safeguards and legal compliance invites censure from legal and regulatory bodies and may result in enormous search costs if retrieval is legally demanded.

Organizations functioning in highly regulated areas such as healthcare, securities, commercial aviation, government, and utilities are at risk. Due in part to specific laws and regulations, these firms typically meet their industry's requirements for document retention and destruction. Accordingly, businesses are regulated in what they must do relative to information indexing, auditing, information retrieval, etc. Regulations direct relevant industries to develop and enforce policies mandating the retention of all e-mail for future compliance auditing purposes.

Depending on the legal and regulatory requirements, there is no good reason to retain e-mail indefinitely. One of the most important elements of successful policy development is the existence of an electronic document creation, use, transmission, retention, and destruction policy. The present is a good time to implement one. Currently, many prominent organizations do not have a policy detailing how employees must categorize paper- and electronic-based documents, storage, and destruction schedule.

Document Retention

Backing up all e-mail and electronic documents is tantamount to recording all telephone calls. If there is no good reason to do so, there are many compelling reasons not to do so. If an organization is the subject of a civil suit or criminal investigations initiated, every e-mail message that is stored will be subject to production and subsequent review. In essence, this means every flippant remark, every sarcastic message, every mistakenly routed e-mail will be subject to legal scrutiny and subsequent judgment.

Organizations should ask themselves if they are using e-mail to document decisions. If so, are those messages intermingled with less formal, potentially risky e-mail that could sway legal decisions? Are there policies about e-mail destruction? What is the duration of e-mail storage? What is the method of destruction? Is the destruction method thorough? Is it possible that destroyed records might be forensically restored?

How many startling revelations were made as a result of e-mail being introduced in antitrust proceedings as a result of a software developer's employees retaining their e-mail? Organizations seeing these legal difficulties have become more cautious about retaining e-mail. If you want to reduce potential risks, but are uncomfortable about deleting your e-mail messages, shoot for a compromise. Many organizations have policies to destroy e-mail backup media after 30 days. One month of retention enables the employer to retrieve data in the event of a system crash, but only a small number of stored documents are in the system awaiting exposure to legal demands for their production.

Depending on the personnel and systems architecture, an organization may back up e-mail on a daily, weekly, or monthly basis. It is wise to err on the side of caution; the longer you retain electronic documents, the greater the risk surrounding it. So, given the risks in retaining e-mail, why do so many companies insist on backing up all their electronic correspondence? Simple; senior managers want to maintain formal records of all business discussions and decisions. Sometimes they are lazy or insecure about business processes. Others are naïve about the risks associated with retaining electronic messages.

It is a matter of education. Managers in charge of backing up data are not aware of the legal exposures attached to these backed-up files and think they are merely doing their jobs. They have been careful to ensure that regardless of the type of system or computer crash, data is not lost and users can return to their online business with a minimum of delay. Consequently, systems administrators are directed to err on the side of caution and retain electronic communications far longer than necessary.

What's in that Cute Little E-Mail Mailbox?

The problem with e-mail storage and retention is basically this: you do not know what your employees are keeping in their e-mail mailboxes. If you are auditing workstations and you review the results, you may be shocked or amazed at what is found. Talk to your employees, explaining the risks surrounding the retention of e-mail and the reason for the destruction policy. Policies should direct employees not to retain old e-mail messages. Policies should consider that some employees may want to store e-mail on their workstation hard drives or on floppy disks, and this practice should be discouraged. Make it very clear that saving messages to hard drives and floppies violates retention policies. If e-mail is going to be saved, it must be saved in project folders or other pertinent files. In this way, e-mail is accessible and retrievable. Emphasize the risks associated with the retention of e-mail outside of policy mandates. Employees should understand that workstations are audited and one of the areas of compliance is the storage of e-mail on hard drives and other media. Through training, employees should be instructed how to delete e-mail, and should receive an explanation of how the delete folder works. Many employees will not understand that e-mail messages may sit in the delete folder unless the user manually takes steps to empty it.

Consider installing and configuring software that automatically empties employees' e-mail folders at designated intervals. Assign limited e-mail space on your mail server for individual accounts. Reducing the size of e-mail accounts will encourage employees who retain e-mail to delete it, as they will simply run out of room. Exhibit 3 is a sample policy for e-mail retention.

Employees Must Think before Clicking the Send Button: Is There an Undelete Button?

Just because e-mail is one of the quickest ways to communicate with others does not necessarily mean it is the most appropriate way to do business at all times. When

Exhibit 3   Sample E-Mail Retention Policy

All e-mail more than 30 days old will be automatically purged from server mailboxes, mail queues, and backup media. Individual e-mail accounts will be limited to 2 MB in size. Users are explicitly prohibited from saving e-mail to hard drives or other media for a period of more than 30 days. If specific backup is required, it should be saved to specific program or project files. Employees do not have a reasonable right to privacy, and workstations will be periodically audited for policy compliance.

you are training employees in the use of e-mail, there are some other important factors to consider.

Confidentiality

E-mail is not private. Messages that are sensitive or private must never be sent through e-mail. Employees should understand there are many persons who have legitimate access to their e-mail, not the least of which are senior managers, systems administrators, auditors, and sometimes investigators. Additionally, there are attackers who are illegitimately engaged in accessing e-mail accounts.

Experience Note   Remember, if it is not there, it cannot be found.

Negotiations

These exchanges are best conducted either face-to-face or through telephone conversations. Regardless of whether they are related to an employee's salary, contract negotiations, or the price of cabbage, dialogues of this nature are best held until the parties can discuss them verbally.

Bad News

Train all employees never to use e-mail to deliver bad news or to discuss performance-related or emotionally charged issues. Senior managers must thoroughly understand this principle. Without the benefit of facial expressions, vocal intonations, and body language, hurt feelings can result.

Experience Note   During the last economic downturn, a senior engineering manager received his dismissal notice through an e-mail where several employees were listed in the address block. He learned of their lay-off before they did. This same manager and other senior managers had also received their last performance review through an e-mail. He remarked the company did not leave him with warm and fuzzy feelings when he left.

Plain, Professional Language

Obscenity, vulgarity, profanity, defamation, off-color remarks, and just plain nasty talk have no place at work or in e-mail. Electronic communications are not private and can be read by a variety of persons today and in the future. Plain, courteous, professional language is the language of business. Risks associated with this type of activity are extremely damaging to the organization and to the individual employee.

Experience Note A good measuring stick of correct language is as if your mother, boss, the press, or your best friend were looking over your shoulder. Do not fall into the trap of treating e-mail messages too casually. If you would not say it in a crowded room filled with friends, do not say it in an e-mail.

Attachments

Organizations must be cautious about sending and receiving e-mail attachments. Instruct employees to copy and paste items into the body of the e-mail. If it is not possible, the sender should ask the recipient if the item can be sent as an attachment. Employees should be cautious about opening attachments and they should be mindful that this is primary way that viruses are distributed. If the e-mail users are technically minded, train them so they recognize that attachments with extensions of .exe, .vbs, and .src should never be opened. Systems administrators should consider using software that denies executable attachments from being delivered to the organization's interior networks.

Spam

Instruct employees never to reply to unsolicited or unwanted e-mail, affectionately known as spam. Replies usually have the effect of confirming active e-mail accounts for spammers who may sell or trade viable e-mail accounts to other spammers, thereby compounding the problem. Irate replies usually go to empty e-mail accounts as spammers often use one-time e-mail addresses.

Message Priority

Do not indicate that your e-mail is urgent if it is not. Do not oversell e-mail messages. Reserve urgent notifications for those e-mails that are truly important.

Forwarded E-Mail

Instruct employees they must not forward e-mail, attachments, and the latest newsletters willy-nilly. They may find them interesting, but most recipients will not. Be respectful of your intended e-mail recipient's time. They may not be very excited about receiving the latest and greatest magazine articles about salad dressing.

Experience Note Do not click the Forward button, just because you can. Ask the e-mail originator for consent to having the message forwarded.

Salutations and Signatures

Incorporating salutations and signatures into the text of an e-mail threat will establish the employee's role and position. An additional benefit is derived from using salutations and signatures: they provide beginnings and endings to messages attributable to specific individuals.

Spelling and Grammar

Instruct employees to use proper language construction, spelling, and grammar that distinguish professional conduct. Use spell-checking and grammar-checking software before sending e-mail. Avoid word and sentence constructions that have double meanings. Do not editorialize or rant in e-mail messages. Red herrings cost time and money. Employees should be frequently reminded that it is possible their messages will be introduced in a court of law.

Encrypted Communications

There are many ramifications of encrypted e-mail communications. Employees can exchange e-mail, assured of its integrity and confidentially. While this is certainly an advantage, it is easy to e-mail proprietary information to outside parties, using crypto-technology. E-mail encryption programs can be easily purchased and in some cases are free. If organizations are going to monitor e-mail communications, they are not going to be able to read encrypted messages. More than one employee has used the company's encrypted e-mail to send sensitive information to waiting competitors without fear of being caught.

Experience Note Weigh e-mail encryption use very carefully in policy construction.

E-Mail for Managers

Managers should remind employees that e-mail and the attendant systems are the property of the organization and are being monitored. Each time a manager reminds employees of this fact, it should be documented so it can be retrieved and formally acknowledged by employees. Human Resources units should have signed acknowledgments from all employees.

Experience Note Under current laws, if employees are allowed to develop a reasonable expectation of privacy, organizations lose the ability to monitor and audit the activities of their employees.

All employees are subject to the organization's policies. No one is outside this policy unless specifically and formally exempted. Exemptions must be justified and individually approved. Being a senior manager is not sufficient justification for an exemption. Managers and auditors must enforce the organization's e-mail policy consistently and equitably. Do not allow special rights to some employees that are not enjoyed by all employees.

Out-of-Band Communications

If communications are very sensitive, employees and managers particularly must know about out-of-band (OOB) communications. OOB communications are outside the regular communications channels. They may include conversations through cellular telephone calls outside the workplace, e-mail communications between computers outside the workplace, encrypted communications, etc. OOB communications alternatives should be available to employees with a reason to use them.

Examples of e-mail privacy policies are given in Exhibit 4 through Exhibit 7.

Employee Privacy Expectations and Legal Rights

In years passed, electronic communications were not issues. However, today's employers are being named in lawsuits with claims of harassment, copyright violation, invasion

Exhibit 4   Expectation of Privacy

Computers, computer systems, and computer accounts are provided to assist users in the performance of their jobs. Computers, computer systems, communications systems, and related media equipment are the property of the XYZ Corporation and may be subject to monitoring, recording, or audit at any time. Users do not have an expectation of privacy in anything they speak, communicate, create, send, store, or receive on these systems.

Exhibit 5   Waiver of Privacy Rights

Users expressly waive any right of privacy in anything they create, store, send, or receive on the Internet or any other computer network. All users consent to allowing personnel of the XYZ Corporation or its assignees to access, audit, and review any and all materials users create, store, send, or receive on the computer or through the Internet or any other computer network.

Exhibit 6   No User Privacy in Communications

The XYZ Corporation reserves the right to monitor any and all aspects of its computer system, including but not limited to monitoring workstation usage, computer network usage, monitoring sites visited by users on the Internet, monitoring chat rooms, newsgroups, messaging services, reviewing materials downloaded or uploaded by users, as well as e-mail sent and received by users.

Exhibit 7   Automated User Monitoring

Users understand that the XYZ Corporation may use automated means to monitor material created, stored, sent, or received on its computer network.

of privacy, discrimination, and defamation. Often, these matters are related to inappropriate e-mail, Internet, and software use by employees. Laws, regulations, and court cases are deciding the means by which companies may govern the conduct of their employees. Organizations can take protective measures in the development and implementation of comprehensive written policies addressing employee expectations.

In most organizations, employees believe their e-mail and Internet activities are private and businesses do not have a legal right to monitor their electronic communications.

ECPA

Under the provisions of the Electronic Communications Privacy Act (ECPA), an employer-provided computer system is the property of the employer, and as such the employer has the right to monitor all e-mail traffic and Internet browsing on its system. In spite of the ECPA language favoring the employer's right to monitor electronic communications on company systems, there has been a significant rise in lawsuits where employers are being sued for allegedly invading the privacy of their employees. Many of these cases are based on an employee's reasonable expectation of privacy. If an employee might convince a court to rule against the employer's right to monitor the employee's activities because the employee has a reasonable expectation of privacy, then the employee will prevail.

Privacy Arguments

It is possible that employees could successfully argue that because the employer had not monitored e-mail in the past, there was an expectation the employer would never do so. Consequently, by inaction the employer granted a *de facto* expectation of e-mail privacy to the employee. If organizations reviewed employee conduct only under selective circumstances, offended employees could logically argue their cases did not fit those circumstances.

Privacy Acknowledgments

Most organizations have solutions at hand to avoid legal actions of this nature. Use written policies to deliver explicit notice to employees that they do not have any expectation of privacy. A wise business practice would deliver such notices as part of new or transferring employee orientation with signed acknowledgments from the employee. Employers should advise their employees that they do not have an expectation of privacy and accept their written acknowledgment to that effect at least annually. These documents should be archived for future retrieval.

Reasons to Monitor and Audit Employee Behavior

An organization demonstrates respect for its employees and concern for its future by explaining that only authorized persons will be allowed to review the staff's electronic activities. Educate employees that the purpose behind monitoring their activities is not spying, rather it is managing the organization's risks. Review risks facing the business and the benefits employees enjoy, mostly in the area of profit, if the company reduces their risks.

Employee activities may be subject to monitoring, including but not limited to telephone conversations, office areas, and common areas such as gyms or lunchrooms, hallways, equipment rooms, etc. Employees have levels of privacy in areas such as restroom stalls, private restrooms, and clothes changing areas.

Before drafting policies addressing employee privacy, consult with competent legal counsel specializing in employee privacy matters before implementing relevant policies. There are many laws, regulations, and court cases affecting these matters. Do not depend on outdated information; seek the most-current legal interpretations before adopting a privacy policy (Exhibit 8 and Exhibit 9).

Employees Working at Home

Employees should understand that they do not relinquish their right to privacy in their personal dealings. They have an expectation of privacy, provided their activities

Exhibit 8   Privacy Statement

The XYZ Corporation provides office facilities, supplies, and equipment to each employee for business use only. XYZ Corporation may monitor and access any and all office facilities at any time without notice to users. No one has an expectation to privacy or confidentiality in their use of office facilities. Office facilities include but are not limited to desks, cabinets, computer workstations, networks, correspondence, e-mail, Internet usage, work rooms, lunchrooms, restrooms, gymnasium, hallways, telephone usage, voice mail usage, locker rooms, and parking areas.

Exhibit 9   Electronic Privacy Statement

All information created, accessed, downloaded, uploaded, and stored using XYZ Corporation
applications and systems is the property of XYZ Corporation. Users do not have any right to
privacy relative to any activity conducted using XYZ Corporation's computers, computer systems,
software, or equipment. XYZ Corporation may review, read, access, audit, or monitor any and all
activities on XYZ Corporation's system or on any other system access by use of XYZ Corporation.

do not have anything to do with the organization. It is the organization's responsibility
to educate them so they understand that any time they access assets of the organization,
it is possible these connections may be monitored and audited. Telecommuters must
understand that policies that apply to the office also apply to them in the field. Do
not frighten your telecommuters, but they should know that if they are accessing the
company's computer equipment through their personal equipment, this equipment
falls under the same rules as if it were in the company's space.

The risks are the same, whether the employee is located outside office or not.
Consequently, it is a wise idea to provide telecommuters with company-owned equipment and policies governing its use rather than expect telecommuters to use their own
equipment. If employees are sharing their personal data with that of the company, it
could prove to be very embarrassing and expensive in the event of a lawsuit.

Part-Time and Full-Time Employees

Organizations should not distinguish between full-time and part-time employees in
mandating that business equipment may only be used for business purposes.

Experience Note Several years ago, a government official was asked to surrender his
government-owned laptop computer. This equipment was designated for
official use and was assigned to him for his use exclusively. Auditing the
laptop discovered images that were objectionable on the hard drive. An official
investigation followed. The official explained his son had made use of the
computer on several occasions and the images were results of that use.
Because the images and the son's use of the equipment were violations of
policy, sanctions were sought.

Managers should remind their employees about official use of computers, supplies,
and equipment. These items are not to be used for personal use under any circumstances, as the risks to the organization are too high. All employees should understand
that computers used in official activities are subject to unannounced audits. Auditors
will be reviewing the equipment and its use for policy compliance. Employees should
understand that in the event of legal action, computer forensic experts will access
hard drives and other storage media. It is likely that these experts will take steps to
restore deleted or otherwise destroyed files. Whatever activity an employee might
have engaged in would be open to review.

Experience Note If there are no violations of official use policies, there will be no
objectionable materials found.

Harassment, Discrimination, and Defamation

The most efficient way to control risks is to set policies and control content. Establishing
policies addressing the rules of conduct and language will emphasize the point that
employees are expected to abide by policies in their official conduct.

Exhibit 10   Language Use in Communications

XYZ Corporation employees are prohibited from engaging in any activities that would be interpreted as racial or ethnic slurs, religious slurs, harassment, intimidation, stalking, threatening others, or engaging in any illegal or unethical activity including but not limited to pornography, menacing, terrorism, espionage, theft, and trafficking in illicit drugs or paraphernalia.

Professional conduct means no racially oriented content, no sexually oriented content, no harassment, no menacing, no ethnic slurs, no religious slurs, no sexual preference slurs, no profanity, and no obscenities.

As with most organizations, Human Resources management units have policies addressing matters of equal employment opportunity and the establishment of a work environment free of hostilities. Policies of this nature generally use language such as:

> It is the policy of the XYZ Corporation to provide equality of opportunity for all employees or employment candidates regardless of race, color, religion, gender, national origin, age, physical or mental disabilities, or sexual orientation. It is the policy of the XYZ Corporation to promote full realization of equal opportunity through employment and to maintain a workplace free of discriminatory policies and practices.

Policies of this nature apply equally to recruiting, hiring, training, promotions, employee development, separations, and awards.

All employees must be allowed to work in an environment free from unsolicited and unwelcome verbal and physical sexual advances. Sexual harassment, in any form, undermines the integrity of the employment relationship. Policies of this character have the purpose of removing from the working environment all activities of a sexual nature which create an intimidating, hostile, or offensive work environment or impede the ability of a person to perform a job. Managers, supervisors, and executives are accountable for enforcing standards of office behavior and are expected to take immediate action addressing sexual harassment (Exhibit 10).

Employee Copyright Concerns

Laws and regulations concerning copyrights extend to items such as text, images, music, video, audio, software, and presentations found everywhere on the Internet. All are protected under U.S. copyright laws. Just as employees are often in the dark about privacy, so are they usually ill informed about copyright infringement matters.

Experience Note While looking for images to jazz up his presentation, an employee downloaded several pieces of clipart from a presentation he saw on the Internet. He included artwork that was copyrighted, exposing his organization to allegations of infringement.

Another case is the department head who, because of some recent budgetary restrictions, installs a popular office suite on several workstations from a single licensed copy, also exposing the organization to infringement allegations.

Organizations can protect themselves from this type of unlawful behavior through employee education and compliance auditing. Companies are responsible for the wrongdoings of their employees. Should an employee violate copyright laws, orga-

Exhibit 11   Copyright Sample

The XYZ Corporation does not allow the unauthorized use of copyrighted materials in any fashion. Materials that are marked as copyrighted or not should be considered as copyrighted and may not be used unless explicit permission is obtained authorizing their use.

Exhibit 12   Software Copyright Sample

The XYZ Corporation does not allow the installation of software that has not been authorized by correct licensing. In this same spirit, XYZ Corporation does not allow copies of software found on its computer equipment to be made for personal use. Users may not import, duplicate, copy, store, or distribute copyrighted materials without authorization. Doing so may violate licensing agreements and/or copyright laws.

nizations and their offending employees could be held criminally and civilly liable for these actions (Exhibit 11 and Exhibit 12).

Employees and Trade Secrets

The theft of proprietary information is likely one of the greatest threats to a nation's business competitiveness. Numerous subjects have been generally recognized as constituting trade secrets: computer programs, chemical formulae, plans, blueprints for products, manufacturing methods, certain databases, technical plans and data, and patent applications pending approval. There are several qualifiers for determining if information is a trade secret:

- What measures have been taken to protect the information's secrecy?
- Is the information generally known by other businesses?
- What is the value of the information to the information's owner and its competitors?

In 1996, Congress passed a law, the Economic Espionage Act of 1996 (Title 18 United States Code Sections 1831–1839), imposing criminal liabilities on anyone who intentionally steals a trade secret. In the language of this act, trade secrets focus on information in the following forms:

> ...all forms and types of financial, business, scientific, technical, economic, or engineering information, including plans, patters, compilations, program devices, formulas, designs, prototypes, methods, techniques, processes, procedures, programs or codes, whether tangible or intangible, and whether or how stored, compiled, or memorialized physically, electronically, graphically, photographically, or in writing...

(18 USC 1839)

E-mail makes it easy for persons with authorized or unauthorized access to company plans, market strategies, client lists, manufacturing processes, materials pricing, and other critical information to transmit it to people who have no business reading it. It only takes a moment for information to be transmitted to competitors by disgruntled employees looking for revenge or a few extra dollars.

Exhibit 13   Proprietary and Sensitive Information Sample

XYZ Corporation does not allow sending proprietary or sensitive or confidential information to any unauthorized party. The authorized transmission of such information requires proper approval and may only be done through approved means.

Exhibit 14   Employee Responsibility Statement

I, _____, acknowledge that I have read a copy of the XYZ Corporation policies and procedures regarding computer and computer systems use. I acknowledge that I do not have any expectation of privacy using XYZ Corporation equipment, nor do I have any expectation of privacy on the XYZ Corporation premises. I understand that the XYZ Corporation may access, read, and monitor my activities while engaged in my assigned duties. I further understand my work area, workstation, files, correspondence, Internet activities, and work product may be audited for compliance with policies, procedures, regulations, and the law at any time and without announcement. I further understand I may be subject to disciplinary action for violating these policies and procedures. If I have committed violations of law, then my actions will be reported to the authorities. I have read these policies and procedures and I understand them.

Signed _____ Dated _____

This is a policy point to emphasize with the organization's next training session. Company secrets and proprietary information should not be shared with unauthorized readers for any reason. Fortify the position by installing equipment and software to monitor employees' activities and advise them their activities are monitored (Exhibit 13 and Exhibit 14).

Employee Labor Organization

E-mail or company-sponsored electronic bulletin boards provide easy and economical means for employees to organize themselves. Senior managers need to be aware of this fact and write their polices to address labor organization activities. Under current provisions of the National Labor Relations Act (NLRA), 29 USC 158 (a)(1), when employees use the property of the employer to self-organize, it must be weighed against the employer's property rights. It is an unfair labor practice for an employer "to interfere with, restrain, or coerce employees in the exercise of rights guaranteed" under Section 7.

Employers may not prohibit all labor-organizing activities by employees; however, employers may restrict the times and locations in which its equipment and facilities are used for organizing. Employees do not have a statutory right to use their employer's equipment for any reason, personal or labor-organization purposes. Employers have the legal right to mandate that their equipment and premises are to be used solely for official and business purposes. However, when an employer permits employees to use company resources for nonwork-related activities, such as personal messaging or homework, then Section 7 of the NLRA has been interpreted to require the employer not to discriminate against labor-organizing uses (*Roadway Express v. NLRB*, 831 F.2d 1285, 1290; 1987.)

Spamming, Spoofing, and the Organization

Many people feel that unsolicited e-mail, known as spam, is a demonic presence, and lawmakers have led crusades in an effort to eliminate it. There are legal liabilities assumed by those who engage in spamming practices.

Exhibit 15   Sending Unsolicited E-Mail or Spam

Users may not send unsolicited e-mail to persons with whom they have no prior relationship. Users may not send e-mail with "spoofed" information. Users must never alter the From line or any other attribute of origin in e-mail, newsgroups, bulletin boards, or any other means of communication. Users may not use any means to disguise or conceal their identities while performing their duties at the XYZ Corporation.
Administrators must configure all e-mail hardware and software denying e-mail relays from outside the XYZ Corporation systems.

Businesses sending spam may suffer the wrath of Internet citizens. Many spammers use spoofed (fake) e-mail addresses to avoid the flood of unhappy spam recipients.

Experience Note Recently, a large ISP filed a successful lawsuit against a company in the spam business, and compelled the company to stop sending spoofed e-mail return addresses. Currently, there are no federal laws requiring spammers to use their true e-mail addresses in correspondence, but this may change soon as Congress and several states are considering legislation.

In the California Business and Professional Code, section 17538, businesses offering goods or services for sale through the Internet or other electronic communication means must reveal their identity and address. Violations are punishable by up to six months confinement and/or fines of up to $1000.

Spammers frequently search for poorly configured SMTP servers that allow relay e-mail from outside their organization's network. In other words, spammers can point their e-mail traffic to be transmitted to a poorly configured SMTP server and it will transmit their spam to be sent to thousands of addresses. Does this mean that if a company had a poorly configured SMTP service, it could be held liable for allowing a spammer to use it to send spam? This is a matter for the courts to decide (Exhibit 15).

Attorney–Client Communications Using E-Mail

Saving time and money, businesses are using e-mail to communicate with their attorneys. Communications of this sort might contain remarks regarding strategy in anticipated litigation, settlement offer amounts, details of negotiations, tax planning, employee information, and other highly sensitive information. For the most part, communications between attorneys and their clients are protected against review by third parties.

The crux of the attorney–client relationship is confidentiality. Confidentiality ensures that clients may speak freely with their attorneys revealing the complete facts of their cases without fear of having these facts revealed. Confidentiality between attorney and client is based on two doctrines:

1. The fact that every attorney is under ethical obligation to maintain client communications as secret. Purposeful or accidental revelation of attorney–client communications would likely result in disbarment and a costly lawsuit.
2. Attorney–client communications are shielded from being discovered in litigation, and prevent attorneys from having to provide testimony about those communications. In short, this privilege permits a client to refuse to reveal the communication and prevents others from discovering it from the client's attorney.

...and Procedures

All a...
appe...
represen...
of the indiv...
protected by a...
responsible for o...
in error. Be advised...
copying of this e-mail, ...
error, please contact (Attor...
incurred in notifying this atto...

...rney–Client E-Mail Footer Sample

...mmunications in the XYZ Corporation will use the following footer
...ntial e-mail: This e-mail and any attached files are confidential and
...nt communications. These documents are intended solely for the use
...to which they are addressed. This communication contains material
...t privilege. If you ar not the intended recipient or the person
...e e-mail to the inteded recipient, you have received this e-mail
... dissemination, isclosure, forwarding, printing, storage, or
...ments, is strict prohibited. If you received this e-mail in
...Address, and lephone Number) immediately. Any costs
...ffice will be rsonably reimbursed.

Exhibit 17   Attorney–Client E-Mail

Attorney–client e-mail within the XYZ Corporation, either house counsel or any attorney representing the XYZ Corporation, should include this no cation at the beginning of the communication: "ATTORNEY–CLIENT PRIVILEGED COMMUNCATION. DO NOT READ, COPY, STORE, OR FORWARD WITHOUT PERMISSION."

Many questions surface in addressing electronic communications between attorneys and clients: Is the privilege lost if the computer system suffers system errors and the communication is compromised? Are unencrypted messages sent over a public network, such as the Internet, considered confidential? Is it necessary for attorney–client communications to be encrypted? There are many bar associations and courts that have not thoroughly decided the matter as of yet. However, if reasonable precautions are taken to secure the confidentiality of the communication, this is at least a good starting place. If a communication is revealed by mistake and the client or his attorney is not negligent in revealing the message, the privilege will likely be upheld. But, if there is an indication that a public network is used to transmit attorney–client communications and if those communications could be easily be misaddressed, is it unreasonable not to use encryption to protect the integrity and authentication of the messages? In other words, if the use of encryption is a reasonable precaution protecting the confidentiality of the privileged communication, is it an indication the client did not intend to keep the communication confidential? Only the courts and legislatures can answer these questions.

Communications between attorneys and clients are protected as confidential. Organizations should take reasonable precautions to assure that messages are correctly addressed and are not forwarded to unintended third parties. It is very important that attorney–client messages are clearly identified as confidential. Organizations may consider using a form of encryption in the exchange of attorney–client e-mail (Exhibit 16 and Exhibit 17).

Passwords

Passwords are one of the methods by which access is authorized and authentication is performed. It is the same whether an employee is gaining physical access to an office space, file, or the company's computer network. Security is assured by allowing only authorized persons to access critical assets. Password usage following to verify identity, and probably not the most secure means in.d something a

Experience Note There is an old adage that identities are only an authorized means: something a person is, something a personirements for access person has. Using any two of these will raise the.son. person is allowed access. Having all three ite almost guarantees that the requestor is the

Something that the Person Is

Something about the person would clude bint, signature, or retinal pattern, then techniques measuring a person's physical attributes such as a voice int, finystem that is authenticating the person transmitting the collected inforation to requesting access.

Something a Person Knows

Passwords or pass-phrases are items qualifying as something a person knows. They are the most commonly used method of controlling access. Strong passwords are a combination of letters, numbers, and special characters, preferably comprised of at least eight or more digits, and should only be known to the accessor. Pass-phrases are simple phrases where key characters are extracted and entered as passwords. For example: % The famous British Secret Agent was James Bond, 007 %, the password is translated as %TfBSAwJB007%.

Something a Person Has

Several techniques can be used in the authentication method of something possessed by an individual. One technique is a magnetically encoded card such as a smart card or bank cash machine card. Smart cards are credit-card-shaped devices embedded with a programmable electronic device. According to current literature, smart cards are extremely difficult to counterfeit and virtually impossible to spoof.

When someone attempts to gain access to a bank cash machine, they insert a card with a magnetic strip containing account and identity information along with their personal identification number. This accomplishes two of the three security methods.

Another example is a device held by the requestor where a password provides access to the device initially. A one-time password is generated by the handheld device and manually entered into another access device by the holder. This password is valid for only one entry attempt. This is another method where two of the three methods are employed to verify the person's identity.

If the password access method alone is used, it is possible for a third party to steal or guess the password, compromising entry. Any activities of this person are going to be attributable to the password possessor. To prevent possible theft of passwords, employees should never write them down.

Experience Note In conducting an unannounced operational assessment, the auditor discovered that more than 80 percent of the workstations audited had valid passwords written on small pieces of paper and attached to the bottom of their keyboards or mouse pads.

Shoulder Surfing

Employees should be aware of "shoulder surfers" where someone, an employee or company visitor, is watching over their shoulder while the individual is entering their password for access.

Access software should be configured requiring passwords and other access devices to be changed at least every 60 days or less. Regardless of the access, it is imperative that passwords and other configurable access methods are changed on a regular basis for workstations, computer networks, office space, server rooms, washrooms, etc. Additionally, all employees must understand the policy that under no circumstances, regardless of the requesting person's position, may they share their passwords or access devices.

Experience Note In an operational assessment, cold telephone calls were made from outside telephone numbers to company employees. In three of ten individuals, system access passwords were disclosed to the callers and one of the three offered the use of his smart card to the caller.

Security through Obscurity

There is an argument that is frequently made for security-through-obscurity. This is roughly translated into persons not having a need to know are not given information about the organization's security measures. As an example, employees should not disclose the means by which office space access is gained nor should they discuss the method by which workstation access is made. In this fashion, intruders are kept in the dark during their attempts to gain unauthorized access. The idea rests in that if intruders do not know, they have to attempt to gain access through multiple means. A frustrated intruder may go somewhere more attractive (Exhibit 18 and Exhibit 19).

Exhibit 18   Employee Responsibility for Entry Methods

Employees of the XYZ Corporation are responsible for safeguarding their passwords and other access-gaining methods. These methods must never be disclosed to anyone unless specifically authorized by the Chief Security Officer. Under no circumstances are passwords to be disclosed for any reason to anyone. Employees are individually accountable for transactions made using their access methods. Users may not disguise their identities while gaining access to any XYZ Corporation property, file, information, or device. Users have individual responsibility to report the actual or suspected theft or compromising access methods to their supervisor or CSO immediately.

Exhibit 19   Password Maintenance

XYZ Corporation employees have the responsibility to select obscure passwords having at least eight characters selected from alphabetic, numeric, and special characters. At least two of the password's digits must be capitalized and at least two must be special characters such as #$%&*. These password standards apply to all entry devices, physical and network. Systems administrators and security officers must configure appropriate software to ensure passwords comply with these security standards, and are changed at least every 60 calendar days. Administrators are responsible to configure software allowing three attempts before the user is locked out for period of at least 15 minutes.

Employee Software Installation

Employees who open e-mail attachments or download files from the Internet may cause severe damage to an organization's computer system, allowing unauthorized intruders to gain entry and possibly cause catastrophic data loss.

Employees who introduce media from outside sources into the organization's workstations could seriously jeopardize the organization's security and possibly create a critical incident. Viruses, Trojan horses, and other destructive software cost businesses millions of dollars each year and have spawned a major industry of computer-protection software companies. These examples of malware (malicious software) come from downloaded software and media introduced by employees from outside sources, and opening e-mail attachments. Recent advertising pronouncements claim that more than 200 viruses are released on the Internet each month. Additionally, downloaded software may contain applications that allow unauthorized individuals to take control of company hosts and workstations with devious persons accessing sensitive information such as credit card numbers.

Copyright Violation

Permitting employees to install personal software begs the question if there is correct licensing for this software. If an employee installs a copy of personal software on his company laptop and has the same copy installed at home for his family's use, and there is only a one copy license, the business may be in a position of legal liability.

Experience Note While conducting a workstation audit, the auditor discovered an installed copy of very expensive three-dimensional imaging software. The employee explained that her son had copied the software from his employer. She had used the software to create attractive images for her last presentation made to the company's senior managers. Interestingly, not one senior technical manager asked how the images were created for the presentation. This situation could place the employee in serious legal problems, and could legally jeopardize her employer for allowing this to happen.

Introducing software or media from anything other than officially sanctioned sources allows the introduction of potentially harmful programs and from questionable sources and can raise serious problems with software licensing. In short, allowing employees to install software greatly increases the organization's risks (Exhibit 20).

Use of Banners

Log-in banners and entry notices should be incorporated as part of any business' official use policies. Banners remind users that they are using a system intended for business purposes only, and that accessing the system constitutes their consent to monitoring. Entry notices announce to employees and others that their activities are subject to monitoring and there is no expectation of privacy upon entering an organization's property. Because users see banners and notices each time they log in or enter the workplace, there are some doubts as to their effectiveness because users accustomed to seeing them ignore them. It is likely that an unauthorized intruder will enter the system or premises bypassing banners and notices altogether. Regardless, implementing log-in banner and entry notice policies, that specifically state that system use and company property are for official purposes only and use of the system or entry to the company property means that the user consents to monitoring, goes a

Exhibit 20   Employee-Installed Software and Storage Media Use

Employees of the XYZ Corporation may install software from approved sources only, specifically the Workstation and Network Maintenance Unit. A list of approved software and sources is available from them. Downloading or installing software from any other source is strictly prohibited.

Employees are permitted to use storage media, floppies, zip disks, CD-R, CD-RW, DVD-R, and the like, purchased by the XYZ Corporation only. Before using any media, employees are requested to scan it with the latest antivirus application. No user is permitted to introduce media from any other source into any XYZ Corporation workstation, computer, or network.

Exhibit 21   Entry Notice Banner

All persons accessing XYZ Corporation systems or property consent to having their activities monitored while on the premises. There is no expectation of privacy while on property owned by the XYZ Corporation. All activities conducted here by visitors and employees must be official in nature.

Exhibit 22   Log-In Banner Policy

All users of XYZ Corporation computing equipment, communications, and networks are advised their entry constitutes consent to monitor their activities. This system is for official use only.

long way to strengthen the organization's argument that a given user exceeded his or her authorization by accessing the workspace or using the system for unauthorized purposes (Exhibit 21 and Exhibit 22).

Connecting to the Internet: Policies and Procedures of Survivability

Computer networks such as the Internet that do not have central administrative controls or unified security policies should be called open-ended networks. Because of their open-ended nature, there is no realistic way to determine just how many nodes are attached to the network. Regardless of the best efforts of information security officers, no degree of hardening will assure that a computer system that is connected to an open-ended system can be made invulnerable to attacks. However, if systems were designed with the goal of delivering profitable services while maintaining properties such as confidentiality, integrity, and availability, they would go a long way to contributing to an organization's survivability in the face of disasters.

Today's large-scale networks are highly distributed in an effort to improve efficiency and effectiveness by permitting high levels of integration. These levels of integration, while providing great strength of communication between networks, also carry elevated risks associated with unauthorized intrusion and compromise. These risks can be somewhat mitigated by implementing survivability in an organization's systems. Survivability incorporates risk management, fault tolerance, performance testing, and auditing.

Survivability is easily defined as the capability of a system attached to an open-ended network to continue to deliver profitable services in the presence of accidents, attacks, or systems failures.

The terms *accidents, attacks,* and *failures* are meant to include all potentially damaging events. Attacks include intrusions, viruses, worms, Trojan horses, and denial-of-service attacks. Any system with an overly restrictive structure because of attack threats may significantly reduce its functionality while directing excessive resources to protect and monitor its assets.

Failures and accidents are risks caused by deficiencies in the system itself, or in an external item on which the system depends. Failures may be attributable to design errors, human errors, hardware failures, coding errors, or corrupted data.

Accidents are usually described as random events such as naturally occurring disasters such as floods, blizzards, earthquakes, etc.

For a system to achieve high levels of survivability, it must react to and recover from damaging events while continuing to deliver efficient and effective services. In fact, reaction and recovery must be at acceptable levels whether or not the cause of the damaging event is ascertained. Levels of survivability are central to the notion that the system is sufficiently redundant that even if significant portions of the system were damaged or destroyed, the system would continue to meet demands.

For example, a survivable financial system maintains confidentiality, integrity, and availability of critical information when nodes or communication systems are not functioning as a result of harmful events. This financial system is survivable owing to its robust design. It recovers and delivers critical services in a timely manner in the face of disaster. The hallmark of a survivable system is the identification of critical services, the essential components that support them within the system and the ability to deliver these services in spite of harmful events. These are some of the key elements of survivable systems connected to open-ended networks:

- *Resistance to attacks.* Strategies include strong user authentication and verification, configuration management, change controls, upgrade and patching policies, audit policies, antivirus policies, e-mail policies; partitioned sub-networks; firewalls; proxy services; network address translation services; redundant data backup copies and critical services; and well-developed risk-management programs.
- *Recognition of system attacks.* Strategies include detecting intrusion attacks and understanding the current state of the system such that evaluating the extent of damage can be accomplished effectively.
- *Creation of event and transactions logs.* These logs must document the external and internal activities taking place on the network. Having details contained in these logs can go a long way to saving your system administration and legal bacon. Many experienced administrators strongly suggest that logs are maintained on Write Once, Read Many (WORM) media. This logging media will prevent a malicious person from deleting his or her harmful activities once done.

Experience Note A senior employee attempted to access sensitive personnel performance review records. She installed tools that permitted her to delete the activity logs, only to discover when she was dismissed that the systems administrators had installed WORM logging media a few weeks before.

- *Recognition of intrusion attack patterns.* Strategies include virus scans, systems vulnerability scans, internal integrity checking, logging, audits, system monitoring, and network monitoring.

- *Recovery of full or critical services* is based on critical asset prioritization, recovery, and business resumption.
- *Development and implementation of strategies for restoring the following:* compromised data, critical functionality, limiting extent of damage, maintenance or resumption of critical services, and the eventual restoration of services as time and resources allow.
- *Restoration of critical data and applications.* Use of alternative services, use of redundant components with same or similar interface, operational procedures to restore system configuration state, containment and isolation of damage, and practiced ability to operate critical services with reduced resources.

Risk management planning requires that risk management decisions and financial balances must be made by senior managers with guidance and recommendations of technical experts in application and data domains, security, and software engineering. System survivability depends at least as much on risk management development and implementation as it does on the technical abilities of the organization's employees. Experts in security and technical issues have the role of providing senior managers with the information necessary to make informed risk management decisions.

In the design of new systems or refitting older systems, survivability imposes structures on all phases of system and software development processes. At the requirement and specification levels, critical assets must be identified. Requirements for damage resistance, recognition, recovery, and resumption should be specifically addressed. System architectures should address survivability equally with other performance properties as capacity, reliability, and maintainability. In the selection of commercial off-the-shelf software, solutions should be chosen with survivability as one of the highest priorities.

Software solution design and implementation should include techniques for containment and isolation, replication, restoration, and migration of critical assets. Survivability solutions must be integrated into both new and existing systems, avoiding systems failure due to attack, accident, or natural disasters.

Systems Development Lifecycle (SDLC)

The SDLC is a mechanism assuring that systems meet established requirements and further the organization's business strategic goals. It provides a structured approach to managing projects, beginning with the justification for initiating development or maintenance efforts and concluding with system disposal.

Most organizations spend millions of dollars annually in the acquisition, design, development, implementation, and maintenance of information systems. The need for secure and reliable system solutions is easily recognized by the dependence on computer systems needed to provide products and administer daily activities.

SDLC methodology establishes policies, procedures, and guidelines managing project development, planning, requirements analysis, design, development, integration and test, implementation, and operations, maintenance, and disposition of information systems. The SDLC is not the do-all, be-all, end-all methodology. There are many permutations of it, but those concepts will not be addressed in this section. However, SDLC is one development method that has a proven track record and should be integrated with already-existing organization policies and procedures.

SDLC Benefits

- Reduced risk of project failure
- Consideration of user requirements throughout the system's lifetime
- Early identification of technical, performance, and management issues
- Description and disclosure of all costs guiding business decisions
- Realistic user expectations of what the system will deliver
- Identification of systems and processes that are no longer cost effective
- Measurements of project progress to enable necessary corrections
- Supports effective resource and budget planning and accountability
- Identifies current and future business requirements

SDLC Supports the Use of an Integrated Product Team

The SDLC project team can provide for the project's success. It should be an interdisciplinary group composed of a senior management project sponsor, a project manager, and team members responsible for planning, implementation, and delivery. Team members should comprise senior employees representing business units such as user groups, human resources, program/functional management, quality assurance, security, legal, telecommunications, data administration, database administration, logistics, financial, systems engineering, test and evaluation, contracts management, audit, physical facilities, and configuration management. Working together in a proactive, open-communication, team-oriented environment can build a successful project by providing decision makers with the necessary experience and information to make the right decisions at the right time.

The SDLC has nine phases or steps that will be briefly described:

1. *SDLC System Concept Development Phase.* This project concept initiates the development lifecycle. It begins when a business need, based on operational requirements, is identified. Once the operational requirement is expressed, the approaches for meeting it are reviewed for necessity, feasibility, reasonableness, and appropriateness. The need may involve development of a new product or the modification of an existing system. Senior managers are usually the responsible officials for approvals and funding before the planning phase can begin.
2. *Planning Phase.* A program plan is developed documenting the approach to be used, including the formulation of methods, tools, resources, schedules, user input, funding, audit, and risk management.
3. *Requirements Analysis Phase.* User requirements are formally defined along with the requirements of system performance, data, risk management, and maintenance. All requirements are detailed to such a level that it is sufficient for designers to proceed.
4. *Design Phase.* The external characteristics of the system are designed during this phase. Operating environments are established, major sub-systems with their required inputs and outputs are defined. At this time, processes are allocated to resources. User input is documented, reviewed, and modified, and final approval is made. Internal characteristics of the system are described, specified, and designed. Required logic specifications are prepared for software modules.
5. *Development Phase.* Detailed specifications produced during the design phase are translated into hardware, software, and communications links. Software is integrated, tested, modified if necessary, and retested.

6. *Integration and Test Phase.* System integration, risk management, and user acceptance are conducted during this phase. Users, audit, and quality assurance units validate the functional requirements, as defined in the functional requirements documentation. It is important that these functional requirements are satisfied by the developed system.

7. *Implementation Phase.* The systems are installed and made operational initially in a test environment. After successful testing, the system is made operational in a production environment. This phase continues until the system is operating in production in conformity with user requirements and design parameters. Its security is certified. In this phase, it is accepted or rejected by users.

8. *Operations and Maintenance Phase.* By now the system is operating and is monitored for continued performance, satisfying user requirements. If needed, system modifications proceed through a requirements and necessity phase; they are scheduled, designed, tested, and implemented. If more than relatively simple modifications or changes are identified, the system will reenter the planning phase.

9. *Disposition Phase.* Disposition activities ensure the orderly review, modification, and termination of the system. Emphasis is granted to the preservation of data processed by the system in order for data to be migrated to another system or stored in compliance with records management policies, laws, or regulations for future accessing and processing.

Management Controls

The SDLC requires the following comprehensive management controls:

- Structured approach to systems development, operation, and disposal
- A senior management sponsor, preferably someone with a cheerleader's enthusiasm
- Project management limited to a single, accountable project manager
- Comprehensive project planning required for each system project
- Projects proceed when sufficient resource availability is assured
- Organized and accessible documentation of all steps, decisions, deliberations, agreements, requirements, plans, proposals, schedules, risk management, security measures, quality controls, funding, auditing, and meetings

Documentation

The SDLC specifies that documentation shall be generated during each phase. The principal categories of documentation are divided into two types:

1. Process documentation details actions taken for developing, implementing, testing, and maintaining the system. Process documentation includes but is not necessarily limited to plans, notes, meeting minutes, deliberations, funding, schedules, charts, funding expenditures, auditing documents, quality control decisions, reports, and time and attendance reports.

2. Product documentation includes matters that detail the system itself, what it is, how it is operated, how it is maintained, and future disposal. Examples include but are not limited to technical manuals, user manuals, operations

manuals, maintenance manuals, systems requirements documentation, and design documentation.

It should be noted that some documentation will remain relatively static throughout the system lifecycle and some will be continuously changed. Some documents are revised documenting the results of analyses performed during operations. Each document should be collected, stored securely, and protected for future reference. It is important that regulatory and legal issues are addressed before any documentation is destroyed. Undocumented or inadequate documentation of decisions and events can cause significant confusion or wasted efforts and can intensify the effect of team member turnover. Activities should not be considered complete, nor decisions made, until there is sufficient documentation of the activity or decision. In the case of some very large projects, there cannot be advancement to the next SDLC phase without the required audits, management reviews, and appropriate approvals.

System Accreditation and Certification

The accreditation process in the SDLC ensures that the system will operate within an acceptable threshold of risk, and complies with the system security policies and any legal and regulatory requirements. At the completion of each lifecycle phase, the accreditation manager (usually the senior manager responsible for accepting the system) reviews the certification results in the design documentation to determine if the system design should proceed to the next lifecycle phase or if the design should be altered to reduce risks. The decision to halt or progress will depend on the acceptability of identified risks and compliance of the system's design to the applicable policies.

System accreditation is the process forcing managers and technical staff to find the best risk management processes, given the system's technical structure, operational constraints, and business requirements. By completing the system accreditation process, the senior managers accept the risks associated with the system.

The role of certification in the SDLC is similar to the role of system quality assurance in that the certification process validates, verifies, and tests the system's features. Certification evaluates the system to determine whether the system operates according to the requirements and does not deliver new functionality introducing new risks. Certification includes total system performance and security policy compliance in security validation, security verification, security testing and evaluation, and system risk assessments. In addition to determining the system's compliance to security and policy requirements, the certification process must ensure the system complies with technical and regulatory requirements. It is important that applicable policies and safeguards are identified as early as possible in the SDLC.

Security officers, auditors, quality control employees, and management responsible for accreditation have security responsibilities. Security officials are closer to the day-to-day operation of the system and direct, perform, and monitor security tasks. The general system manager will have responsibility for the organization supported by the system. Accreditation is not a decision that should be made by the security office, rather it is the duty of the business manager to accept the system along with its associated risks. Formalization of the system accreditation process reduces the potential that systems will be placed into a production environment without appropriate management review.

Management acceptance of the system must be based on an assessment of management, operational, and technical controls. Because the security plan establishes the system protection requirements and documents the security controls in the system, it should form the basis for the system's accreditation. System accreditation is usually supported by a technical or security evaluation (or both), risk assessment, contingency plan, audit, and acknowledged policies of acceptable user behavior.

Reaccreditation should occur after any significant system change and at least every two to three years. If there is a high degree of risk, it should be performed more often. Following are the minimum security controls that must be in place prior to accrediting a system to begin processing. These principles should be made part of policies regarding systems development.

- The level of controls should be consistent with the level of data or system sensitivity
- Technical and security evaluation complete
- Risk assessment conducted
- Policies of acceptable behavior established and acknowledged by users
- Disaster recovery and business resumption plans developed and tested
- System survivability and security plan developed, updated, and reviewed
- System meets all applicable laws, regulations, policies, and operations standards
- Safeguards operating as intended
- Auditing processes developed and implemented

Experience Note While conducting an operational assessment, the auditor asked the senior operations manager for documentation detailing the business' billing process. The company had been in business for several years and had a small staff of software engineers. It was their business practice to send billing to their clients on the first day of each month. The operations manager stated that the engineers took care of monitoring the billing process. It was not really necessary to have any documentation of the process as most of the engineering staff was competent and the did not see any reason to be concerned. The auditor interviewed the engineers and found that only one engineer had a thorough understanding of the billing software and process. Other engineers were able to generally recite the process, but were not intimately knowledgeable of it. The interviewer discovered the billing system had not been developed through any organized process; rather, it had been developed on an *ad hoc* basis over the years. No certification or accreditation processes had ever been done. Asking a few more questions revealed there were no documents about the billing software or processes. The auditor discovered one engineer had enough privilege to stop the billing application and create, delete, and modify accounts while the billing cycle was running (Exhibit 23).

Exhibit 23 System Development Policy

All information systems developed or acquired by the XYZ Corporation will be done with the goal of maximizing survivability and will be subject to the Systems Development Lifecycle (SDLC). At all times, appropriate documentation will be developed and archived. As an integral part of systems development, all systems will undergo an accreditation and certification process before being accepted and placed into production environments.

Physical and Environmental Safety

Physical and environmental safety controls are developed and implemented to protect the physical facility housing employees, data, and equipment. An organization's physical and environmental policies should address at least the following topic areas:

- *Access Controls.* Physical access controls restrict the entry and exit of personnel, equipment, and media from an area. The granularity of access controls should be commensurate with the value of the items located in that area. For example, there should be very limited access to servers and cabling. Anyone exiting an office area carrying equipment or media must provide appropriate approvals. Physical access controls should address not only the area containing system hardware but also locations of cabling used to connect elements of the system, supporting services such as electric power, backup media, and any other elements required for the system's operation. It is important to assess the effectiveness of physical access controls in each area, during normal business hours, and at other times, particularly when an area may be unoccupied or occupied by maintenance employees.

- *Fire Safety Factors.* Fires are a significant threat because of the potential for complete destruction of both hardware and data, the risk to human life, and the pervasiveness of the damage. Smoke, toxic gases, and heat from a fire can destroy lives and critical data and damage systems throughout an entire building or business campus. Consequently, in addition to the annual local fire marshal inspection, it is important to evaluate the fire safety of buildings. It is a solid business practice to have fire safety as part of the company's audit program.

- *Utilities Failures.* Systems and the people who operate them have an expectation of a well-regulated operating environment. Consequently, failures of electric power, heating, and air-conditioning systems; water; sewage; and other utilities usually cause service interruptions damaging hardware and data, making working conditions unbearable. Organizations should take every precaution to ensure that utilities function properly, and in the event of failures, the organization must make certain there are redundant systems available to continue profitable operations. Risk planning will consider the degree of redundant utility systems and how long they should be available.

- *Building Collapse.* Organizations should be aware that a building might be subjected to loads greater than it was designed to support. This results from earthquakes, snowfalls, or explosions that displace or weaken structural members, or a fire that destroys structural supports.

- *Plumbing Leaks.* Water leaks do not occur frequently, but when they happen they can be very disruptive. An organization should know the location of water pipes that might leak or burst, endangering employees and equipment. Businesses should take appropriate steps to reduce risks by relocating pipes and fire extinguishing equipment and clearly identify shut-off valves.

- *Workplace Safety.* Employees must be safe in the workplace. Laws, regulations, and policies demand it. Auditors and managers should frequently assess workplace safety by walking around and looking for cables crossing walk areas, unsafe equipment placement, lack of safety equipment in areas such as loading docks, overloaded electrical connectors, unsafe elevators, etc. (Exhibit 24).

Appropriate and adequate controls will vary depending on the individual system requirements. The following list shows the types of controls for a system in a computer

Exhibit 24   Workplace Safety Policy

The XYZ Corporation will take every reasonable step to ensure workplace safety for employees, data, and equipment. Such measures will be in compliance with laws, regulations, building codes, and sound safety practices.

room. It is not intended to be all-inclusive or to imply that all systems should have all the controls listed.

- Card keys for building and work area entrances
- Twenty-four hour guards at all entrances and exits
- Cipher lock on computer room door
- Dedicated heating/ventilation/air conditioning system
- Humidifier, if appropriate
- Emergency lighting
- Fire extinguishers rated for electrical fires
- B/C-rated fire extinguishers
- Smoke, water, and heat detectors
- Emergency power-off switches
- Surge suppressors
- Emergency replacement equipment
- Zoned dry-pipe sprinkler system
- Uninterruptible power supplies for critical equipment
- Power strips and power suppressors for peripherals and computers
- Separate controlled access to server and cabling rooms
- Protection for water-sensitive equipment in the event of fire

Network Management Policies

Network management policies include resource accountability, reporting errors and malfunctions, and preventative maintenance. There are some repetitions of policy elements here, but it is recommended that this section is reviewed. Network protection policies address the continuing need for risk analysis, security awareness and training, security administration, and facilities security. Following are some measures that address network management policies:

- Initiate and maintain a formal inventory of network components such as hardware, applications, and attendant components including serial numbers, physical location, version numbers, and dates of acquisition, implementation or installation.
- All company network users must be formally authorized to use the network. All users must request access in writing, accompanied by the approval of their supervisor or manager. All access requests, approvals, and denials are retained and archived.
- Regularly review network configuration ensuring that all attached components are authorized and configured correctly. Any attempt by employees to alter network configurations by installing unauthorized software or hardware must be reported immediately. Verify network interface equipment and configurations after a unit has been serviced or an audit has been performed. Verify the identity of network interface card user at time of unit maintenance. Deny

access to anyone having no authorized network interface card, and report violations.

- Depending on the type of work, maintain logs of all network transactions including but not limited to identity of user, log-in time, files accessed, transactions performed, and log-off time.
- All media where logs, when feasible, are recorded on WORM media.
- Through manual or automated means, all logs are reviewed and filed daily as permanent records.
- All security and risk-related events are to be reported immediately and receive immediate senior management attention.
- All corrective actions are documented and reported in a timely fashion.
- Develop and maintain a schedule of preventative maintenance activities for applications, and equipment. Any hardware and software not conforming to policy, procedures, or standards will be addressed appropriately, with reports made to senior managers. Ensure there is documentation relative to the time and type of maintenance performed on all network components.
- Remove any and all data from storage media, e.g., floppy disks, hard drives, tapes, and CDs, before equipment is delivered to maintenance or disposal personnel.
- Periodic risk assessments and audits are the responsibility of the network owner and the audit unit. Documentary evidence of these processes is to be made and maintained.
- Risk analyses will be performed during the network's SDLC design stage and at any time changes are made to the network design or components. These analyses should measure, among others, the network's vulnerability to:
  - Improper disclosure of information
  - Fraud, theft, and abuse
  - Inadvertent harmful errors
  - Financial losses to the organization
  - Harm to individuals' privacy rights
  - Loss of intellectual property
  - Loss of continuing profitable operations
- Employees responsible for the company's network security and administration must have the necessary experience and should receive sufficient formal training to be able to perform their duties.
- All network users are required to attend training sessions and sign an agreement regarding their security responsibilities, privacy, proper use of network facilities, and the safeguarding of data.
- Employees have the responsibility to challenge strangers and other individuals who do not possess appropriate identification badges. At no time is an employee to allow someone access to any area by holding open a door equipped with an access control device.
- All user activities and their accounts are subject to unannounced audits.

Forensics Policy: Looking for Evidence

Experience Note Imagine Alice, a senior manager, rarely takes vacations, voluntarily works many hours in excess of her scheduled duty-day, and recently acquired a condominium at a prestigious European resort. Alice's accounts payable unit has been previously audited with few findings.

For economic reasons, Alice's company is reorganized with the audit unit under different leadership. During the next audit, the auditors are encouraged to look outside routine programs. One of the auditors takes the time to thoroughly reconcile the accounts payable with business addresses, discovering several disparate companies with the same Post Office box. Closer examination reveals more than nine paid accounts with the same physical address and the same mailing address.

The company's security office conducts a preliminary investigation; Alice is suspended and sent home. The company has a policy precluding any personal expectation of privacy regarding her workstation, office space, or its contents.

A security officer contacts the contracted computer forensics investigator, Bob, with whom he has established a business relationship. The company has a policy that this professional will be notified under these circumstances. Additionally, the company's legal department notified the police department. Because Bob is a retired police computer forensics officer, he will conduct the initial investigation and report his findings to the police department.

After arriving, Bob asks if the company has the authority to enter Alice's office. Conferring with the human relations management and legal units, it is determined the company has a policy where its employees waive privacy rights as part of their employment and there is a document acknowledged by Alice to this effect. It is also the company's policy that its equipment may be used only for official purposes and nothing of a personal nature is permitted.

As part of any investigative process, the forensic investigator initiates an activity log where he documents his investigative steps. This document contains a schedule where the time he was notified is noted, as well as the time he arrived at Alice's office, the organization's employees with whom they spoke, and the results of those conversations. His experience and training have taught him that his words and actions are subject to scrutiny should he testify later.

As with all evidence, a chain-of-custody schedule is initiated by the forensics officer, where he documents the location, time, date, item name, and identifying number, the seizing person's identity, and the person to whom the evidence is released.

Upon entering Alice's work area, Bob notices that the door is locked. Without entering the office, the officer begins taking photographs at the office doorway. He takes special care to photograph the location of papers left on the desk, walls, and Post-It notes near her computer. He carefully photographs the back of Alice's computer and makes notes regarding the cabling. He notes Alice's bookcase containing many books about computer programming, computer architecture, and networking.

Returning from his van, the investigator retrieves a forensics workstation he purchased as part of his professional forensic examiner's certification process. He removes Alice's workstation hard drive while logging each step. Using specialized software already installed on his workstation, he makes exact bit-by-bit duplicates of the workstation hard drive. In anticipation of making these copies, he had prepared three new compatible hard drives by subjecting them to a cleansing process, completely removing the possibility of any data being present on them before he uses them as evidence.

With the duplication process underway, the detective goes about the process of seizing relevant documentation and other media, including CDs, floppy disks, and a box of accounting software. This is not the accounting software authorized for use on Alice's machine. After the box's contents are quickly inspected, a series of floppy disks are found near the box marked "Oro." One of the floppy disks is labeled "Particulares."

All of the items seized are marked with an identification tag and are inventoried. A copy of this inventory will be provided to the security officer upon completion and will be treated as evidence. Plainly marked on the inventory is name of the item, its tag number, location where it was found, and the name of the officers who found it.

For several hours the process continues. The investigator suggests to the security officer that he should contact his superiors and determine if there is someone who can retrieve Alice's network activity logs over the past six months. He also asks to be present so he can later testify as to how they were accessed and that he witnessed the process. Interviewing Alice's co-workers reveals that Alice announced the receipt of a large inheritance, and stated that she would not need to work in the future.

The investigator contacts the police department and delivers all the evidence along with his logs and notes. The police perform an analysis of the materials. They discover the accounting software was used by Alice and is secured by a password. The police examiners have specialized commercial software to "crack" the password, finding the "Oro" floppy disks contain a list of real estate properties along with their purchase price and location. The disk marked "Particulares" is a list of personal identification numbers for bank accounts and passwords for Internet e-mail accounts. The matter is presented to the district attorney's office, which authorizes prosecution. Simultaneous to her indictment, the company's legal unit, acting in conjunction with the prosecutor's office, files a lawsuit naming Alice as the defendant.

There are many compelling reasons for employing computer forensics, but before business managers make the decision to do so, they need to understand what it is and when to use it. Risk management is the leading reason for deploying computer forensics. Any business that does not have a policy and procedure to stop malicious behavior may count on being victimized with little recourse against the perpetrator. Computer forensics is the investigative practice of collecting, examining, and analyzing evidence retrieved from computers and computer-related equipment. At times it would seem that computer forensics analysis is akin to magic in that trained, experienced professionals can find relevant evidence through sophisticated collection and restoration techniques. More than one competent analyst has been called "a miracle worker."

Collecting and analyzing computer evidence is useful for confirming or dispelling concerns about whether an unlawful act has been committed. Further, this type of work has been able to document workstation, applications, and network vulnerabilities after a critical incident.

Organizations today must have policies regarding when computer forensics examiners should be called in. Usually information-related threats involve a computer of some kind or a communication's network because they are the means by which companies conduct their business and information processes. Businesses employ computer forensics when there is a serious risk resulting from compromised intellectual property, a threat of lawsuits stemming from employee conduct, or potential damage to their reputation or brand. There are many organizations that regularly use forensic means to audit employee workstations with the idea that employees who know and recognize they are being monitored are less likely to stray from policies and procedures. When a random selection of employees' computers is made monthly, and forensic examinations are conducted, the appropriate steps are taken if unauthorized use, pornography, or abuse is discovered.

Any experienced computer forensics examiner starts and completes assignments with his or her testimony in mind. This means the examiner must always collect, analyze, and preserve evidence according to the rules of evidence. A good standard for this professional is the Federal Rules of Evidence. Basically, the examiner has three important tasks: finding, preparing, and preserving evidence.

Another aspect of forensic computer examination is the testimony of the forensics professional. This person must never attempt to perform an examination for which he or she is not trained. There are times when untrained or inexperienced persons are tempted to conduct examinations, which can corrupt or damage potential evidence. Just because a person has a detailed knowledge of computers and networks does not mean the person is qualified to conduct forensics examinations. Following is a list of what to look for when selecting forensics computer examiners:

- Prior experience in computer forensics examinations
- Specialized training
- Specialized experience in collecting, analyzing, and preserving evidence
- Experience as an expert witness
- Possession of pertinent professional certifications
- Personal and professional integrity; examiners must withstand thorough scrutiny on technical and personal levels
- A laboratory equipped with tools for evidence recovery

Another matter of significance: organizations should understand that reporting unlawful activities is required under many state statutes and is required under U.S. law. According to Title 18, USC 4, "whoever, having knowledge of the actual commission of a felony cognizable by a court of the United States, conceals and does not as soon as possible make known the same to some judge or other person in civil or military authority under the United States, shall be fined under this title or imprisoned not more than three years or both" (Exhibit 25).

Exhibit 25   Forensics Examination Policy

The XYZ Corporation may employ forensics computer examination and analysis during the course of its business processes. Upon the discovery of any unlawful act, the XYZ Corporation will report allegations to the appropriate authorities. The XYZ Corporation may pursue legal recourse in the form of administrative, civil, and criminal processes against persons or entities sponsoring or committing unlawful acts. All unlawful acts will be reported to the authorities in a timely manner.

Wireless Network Security

Wireless technologies cover a wide range of capabilities geared toward different needs and uses. Wireless local area networks (WLANs) permit users to move a laptop or personal digital assistant (PDA) from place to place within their work area without the need for cables, with the advantage of not losing network connections. There are networks utilizing Bluetooth protocols that permit data transmission between network components. Bluetooth technology can eliminate cables formerly required for printers and other peripheral devices.

Alas, there is a downside; risks are inherent in any wireless technology. Some risks are the same or similar to those of conventional wired networks, while others are exacerbated by the nature of wireless connectivity. The most notable difference between the wired and wireless networks is the communications medium and the risks associated with that medium. Communications transmitted through the airwaves are openly available to being intercepted. Attackers have the ability to locate and communicate with wireless networks with much-less effort than invading wired ones.

Losing confidentiality, integrity, and availability are risks associated with wired networks, and they are easily achieved in wireless networks. Malicious users may gain access to company systems and information and compromise critical asset confidentiality, integrity, and availability. Following are some examples of risks associated with wireless networks:

- All vulnerabilities existing in wired networks also apply to wireless technologies.
- It is possible that unauthorized intrusions may gain access to an organization's wireless network, bypassing firewall safeguards.
- Sensitive information not encrypted before transmission is subject to being intercepted and disclosed by third parties.
- Malicious entities may steal the identity of legitimate users and use them.
- Malware including viruses, Trojan horses, and back door programs permit damage and continuing unauthorized network access, reducing availability and potentially disrupting business operations.

Organizations should not deploy wireless technologies unless they thoroughly understand and manage the accompanying risks. In light of current wireless communications protocols, most commercial products provide inadequate protection and present significant unacceptable risks to business operations. Senior managers must proactively address these risks, protecting their critical assets before wireless network deployment. Often due to apathy or a lack of understanding or education, many organizations poorly administer their wireless networks, relying on "default" installation settings, failing to control access to their access points, failing to implement factory-provided security configurations, and not developing a security policy suitable to the wireless environment. Such wireless safeguards include firewalls between wired and wireless systems, packet screens where unneeded services and ports are blocked, and implementing strong encryption such as Virtual Privacy Network (VPN), or file encryption technologies before data is transmitted.

Organizations must understand the technical and security ramifications of wireless technologies. While wireless connectivity seems like the best solution to connection-without-cables, it is an immature technology coupled with relatively poor security, potential for lax administration, and limited user awareness. In wireless environments, data is transmitted through the air without any control over the geographical limits of these broadcasts. Organizations are unable to exercise typical physical and logical controls that are employed in wired networks. In short, data transmitted over a wireless network can be captured and transactions begun by unauthorized third parties. Because of radio wave attenuation, building construction, and the capabilities of high-gain antennas, the distance for controlling wireless technologies preventing eavesdropping can be extremely difficult to control.

Following are some suggested best practices to help address wireless network risk issues:

- Organizations must formulate and enforce compliance of applicable policies addressing the use of IEEE wireless standards of 802.11 (a, b, g, and others), Bluetooth, and other wireless technologies. These policies must be implemented before the deployment of wireless connectivity.
- Configuration management and strict change controls must be adopted ensuring that equipment has the latest software patches, including security features addressing vulnerabilities.
- Organizations will adopt configuration standards for all wireless network hardware and software, ensuring consistency of operation. These configurations will reflect steps to proactively address risks. It is noteworthy that many wireless technologies have weak user authentication. Wireless systems using Wired Equivalent Privacy (WEP) have been demonstrated as being subject to unauthorized transmission capture and intrusion, leaving this encryption method of somewhat questionable value.

However, regardless of whether WEP's protection is considered strong, medium, or weak, it is certainly better than open transmissions without encryption. If a wireless system uses 64-bit encryption, by all means use it; and if your wireless system supports 128-bit encryption, better still. In most systems, WEP is disabled at the default installation, so you must manually enable it before thinking your system is protected.

If your system allows the option of setting authentication to Shared Key, it is a wise idea to enable this feature. Change WEP keys on a regular basis, even as often as daily or weekly to help avoid data capture and network intrusions.

Service Set Identifier (SSID)

SSID is essentially the wireless network's identification. SSID helps to secure the network by ensuring the proper clients can access the system's access point. In the wireless platform, the access point is essentially a small transceiver operating on the designated frequency. For example, in an 802.11b system, the AP operates on the 2.4-GHz band with a few hundred feet of range, and in certain circumstances this can be extended to more than 500 feet. The AP is the location where the Internet and the internal network are connected, with the access point then broadcasting to any receiver capable of processing its traffic. This broadcast is received by wireless transceivers known as clients. Because the transmissions travel in all directions, they may possibly be received by intended and unintended recipients.

If WEP is disabled and the SSID is broadcast, it may be captured by anyone. Attackers may begin by compromising the network's access password. In order for clients to gain system access, they must have the SSID and the system password. If passwords are transmitted in the clear, they might be intercepted by any suitable client.

Wireless systems manufacturers usually install default SSIDs. Intruders are well aware of these default SSIDs, consequently changing the default SSID makes your network more difficult to access by someone who is not authorized.

Disabling any options for broadcasting the SSIDs is a good idea. This ensures the client SSID matches the access point SSID before any access is permitted. There is a secondary benefit of concealing the SSIDs — it hides the existence of your wireless network to the world.

Virtual Privacy Network (VPN)

Use of VPN technology between networks and clients assures strong user authentication and message privacy. VPNs are basically closed networks implemented through open-ended networks, including wireless. They allow for secure, authenticated transmissions to take place between designated points. If unauthorized persons intercept VPN-protected traffic, it is encrypted so there is little that can be done with it. Without the correct VPN technology, keys and passwords can be read. Such technology is very cost effective and secure, allowing confidentiality and message integrity over wireless networks.

Secure Sockets Layer (SSL)

Another technology worth considering in a wireless environment is the deployment of SSL technology. Simply stated, SSL provides a secure connection between a workstation's Web browser and a specific Web server. Data transmitted between the server and client is encrypted using technology called public key encryption, ensuring only the intended recipient can decrypt and read the information. In order to secure SSL, each Web site has its own unique digital certificate that defines the public and private encryption keys used during secure communications. If you leave the secure site and browse to another, the original SSL connection is closed. If you return to the SSL secured site or another SSL secured site, a new secure connection is made using a different set of encryption keys. By *de facto* standard, SSL is the most popular Web-based message security protocol with practically all online purchases and monetary transactions using it.

SSL effectively permits secure transmissions to take place between intended points and stifles intruder attempts to read them. SSL coupled with WEP provides an effective means to pass information over a wireless network with little fear of some unauthorized person reading your traffic.

Wireless Policies

Following are some examples of wireless network policy considerations:

- Organizations will actively sponsor administrator and user security awareness training to raise consciousness about the risks associated with wireless technologies.
- Organizations must have policies specifically addressing employees who are permitted to install wireless equipment and software.
- Organizations must have policies that describe the type of information that can be transmitted over a wireless network.

- Organizations must have policies requiring the reporting of the loss of wireless devices, fixed and mobile.
- Organizations must have policies requiring the reporting of security incidents.
- Organizations must have policies requiring network user IP addresses to be assigned dynamically via DHCP (Dynamic Host Control Protocol).
- Organizations must have policies regarding use of wireless VPN technology.
- Organizations must have policies regarding the use of SSL technology on Web sites.
- Organizations must have configuration policies regarding wireless equipment.
- Organizations must have policies regarding the implementation of WEP.
- Organizations must have policies requiring firewalls to be installed, configured properly, and maintained on all wireless network equipment.
- Organizations must have policies prohibiting the use of equipment or software that would extend the useable range of wireless network equipment.
- Organizations must have policies requiring all wireless equipment to be audited for legal, regulatory, and policy compliance.

Network Vulnerability Assessment Policies: Why Am I Hearing about My Network Leaking Sensitive Information on the News?

Every organization contains risks, ranging from finance to procurement. Given the risks in doing business through the Internet, it is surprising how many businesses are not finding more ways to enable safeguards and protect their critical assets.

Experience Note If you search the IRC (Internet Relay Chat) chat rooms for credit card hackers, you are going to find a large number of chat rooms complete with automated applications known as "bots" to verify credit card numbers and related information. Entering these chat rooms reveals literally dozens of participants attempting to verify credit cards, addresses, names, addresses, and banks. Searching the World Wide Web will reveal many Web sites also dedicated to verifying credit card information. Where is the wellspring of this credit information? In large part, it comes from poorly secured Web sites and networks where intruders have gained access downloading credit card numbers and relevant information for the purpose of committing fraud or selling the data to someone else so they can commit fraud.

Frequently, there is one technique that is overlooked by organizations when developing systems: the vulnerability assessment policy. This is the process of attempting to exploit system vulnerabilities to gain unauthorized access to sensitive information. Vulnerability assessments are attacks originating from a friendly system assessment team targeting a computer system to discover ways of breaching the system's security controls, penetrating the protection afforded to sensitive information, obtaining unauthorized services, or damaging the system by denying services to legitimate users. These policies form a base of testing discovering features, functions, and system capabilities that may be unspecified and unknown to its developers and users. Vulnerability assessments attempt to discover system capabilities that are flaws in the design, implementation, operation, documentation, change controls, and maintenance.

A vulnerability assessment is as thorough as the talent, training, skills, and diligence of the employees performing it. It can place reasonable limits on the knowledge and experience required for the intruder to gain unauthorized access. That knowledge applied to safeguards and protective measures can restrict intruder access below this limit, and give some degree of assurance that the system is operating securely.

Performing the vulnerability assessment utilizing the organization's own resources has certain advantages in the area of in-house knowledge building, employee control, reliability, and trustworthiness. It may lead to discovering risks before attackers do and assist in highlighting the enterprise's security position. There is a lot of preparation that must be performed in the construction of an effective vulnerability assessment. Policies and procedures must be drafted, approved, and installed; relevant employees must be trained; and there must be stringent compliance auditing, a well-developed change management process, and postmortem critique conducted of the assessment where flaws and improvements are addressed.

As with any job, policies and practices must address the means by which vulnerability assessments are conducted. Before the actual vulnerability assessment, there must be a strong foundation of policies and procedures. It is important to ensure that the underlying policies relevant to the organization's network security are in place, facilitating the process. These documents will be the principles underwriting the actions taken when planning and executing the assessment. The organization's vulnerability assessment policy should address the following active components.

Plan to Conduct Vulnerability Assessments

The planning step will include gathering relevant information, defining the assessment activities, defining roles and responsibilities, and making relevant employees aware of the need to make changes based on the findings of the assessment.

A comprehensive vulnerability test plan will improve the odds of achieving system penetration. Penetration planning establishes the ground rules, limits, and scope of the process. The plan identifies the object being assessed and determines when the test is complete. Some planning steps may include interviewing system administrators, reviewing appropriate hardware and software documentation, and reviewing appropriate policies and procedures relative to targeted systems.

Create and develop a good penetration team. Desirable characteristics for the team members include experienced vulnerability testers, employees knowledgeable of the target system, creative people with unusual ideas, SDLC development methods, access control structures, and programming abilities in several languages. Successful team members are characterized by being patient, detail-oriented, having good people and communications skills. One key requirement is of highly ethical, mature professionals who can protect proprietary, sensitive data and flaws in the target system.

Encourage the assessment team to use a variety of mechanisms to achieve unauthorized access, involving exploiting hardware, software, and human resources vulnerabilities. With senior management's consent, more than one vulnerability assessment team has asked for and received root passwords from an employee.

Identify Exposures

This phase may include a variety of tasks. It may include but not be limited to reviewing the resulting data from the assessment phase, actually deploying mechanisms to discover system vulnerabilities and linking findings to the management process so that individual accountability for assessment findings is established and risk issues can be resolved. Of course, this step must be conducted with a great deal of cooperation from senior managers and employees responsible for the system's development, monitoring, and maintenance.

Vulnerability assessments should be framed in the organization's policy as a method to reduce risks and raise profitability. If there are risks associated with negligence on the part of individual employees, senior managers should weigh the assessment's findings in light of employee accountability.

Resolving Exposures

This phase resolves the risks identified in the previous phase. Before any substantive steps can be taken to address assessment findings, an investigation must be done to determine if the risk is in fact relevant to continued business operation. If risks are identified that do not have bearing or insignificant bearing on business operations, then it is possible they may be excused as irrelevant.

Performing a vulnerability assessment can provide a point-in-time representation of the organization's risk position. In fact, this mechanism is insufficient. There must be a method incorporated into the organization's policies and procedures ensuring that the vulnerability assessment process is conducted on a frequent or continuous basis. Only in this manner can policy minimize network risk. Vulnerability assessments are best employed to discover broad capabilities of the target system and flaws contrary to security policies, rather than resulting in a gaming situation between the target system's administrators and the assessment team trying to penetrate a protected asset.

An organization's vulnerability assessment policy must require that all known flaws are repaired. As part of their postmortem critique, the system assessors may suggest the implementation of corrections or safeguards. After the system has been repaired, policy should require that the system is reevaluated to confirm the fixes and to ensure no other flaws were introduced by the repairs or implemented safeguards. An organization's reevaluation process is a complete repetition of the vulnerability assessment process.

By completing policies requiring continuous vulnerability assessments, you facilitate the identification of potential risks before attackers do. Early detection allows the opportunity to address assessment findings before attackers can exploit the vulnerabilities resulting in damage to the company's critical assets.

Experience Note A side benefit of vulnerability assessment policies: you want to hear about findings while you can address them and before they become banner headlines.

Policies requiring continuous vulnerability assessments can deliver a picture of how secure sensitive information is, and go a long way in preventing having to read about critical assets being stolen or compromised in the news.

Vendor Policies and Procedures

The size of business operations and the uneven demand for services influence the type and amount of outsource services required. Within the business, available funds are balanced with needs, and often they are not in agreement. Service vendors outside the organization come in a variety of flavors including consultants, technical service and hardware vendors, and contract human resources. Good business sense, based on ethics and morals, is the best policy in dealing with outside vendors.

Several units within the organization come into play when selecting outside services. The organization's purchasing unit should provide information about vendors, their reliability, financial status, reputation in the business community, and whether they will be in business a year from now. This is information that should be at hand before negotiating a contract.

The legal unit must review any vendor contracts before they are signed and large amounts of capital committed. One of the more-important tasks the legal unit performs is the review of the contract's performance language where there are penalties assessed in the event the vendor fails to complete its responsibilities.

The legal units must ensure there is contract language detailing that promised services or products meet the organization's expectations. This language needs to dovetail with SDLC provisions if services or products must be certified and accredited before the contract is fulfilled. If the project involves classified materials, the legal unit is responsible for requiring and verifying that contractors have security clearances.

The organization's audit unit should be included in the contract review to see that important provisions are detailed that will require its involvement. Such details involve auditing of ongoing contract compliance by the vendor. Auditors should be involved if the vendor provides services within the provisions of the SDLC. The contract should allow the review of development procedures and the quality of the services or product.

Outsource Potentials

Following are possible areas for outsourcing efforts:

- Operations that are difficult to staff and manage
- Providing special skills not available within the organization
- Reducing internal operation costs by not having to develop skills that will be used infrequently
- Delivering system improvements or benefits more quickly than can be performed internally

Consultant Procedures

Outsourcing consultant services can be a valuable asset if the proper relationship is developed. Consultants can just as easily be acquired or employed for all the wrong reasons. Following are several wrong reasons for contracting a consultant:

- *Not having clear goals and performance expectations.* Having very clearly defined goals and performance expectations will permit maximum benefit to be derived from consultants.
- *If there is bad news for projects in trouble, let the consultant deliver it.* Wrong idea. If a project is in trouble, the future of the organization's credibility may be at stake. Handle any internal project problems within the organization. Do not outsource them.
- *Contracting a "hired gun" from out of town to impress the locals.* For some unknown reason, the distance the expert traveled, the cost of the expert, and the perception of the expert's skill set frequently impresses employees. Senior managers have an ability to be impressed with experts who have many titles

behind their names. It is not unusual that a consultant came up with a solution that was the same as one developed by your own employees.

■ *Weak senior management.* Project managers lacking decisive skills will often attempt to employ consultants to make decisions for them. Consultants are contracted at the staff level of an organization. They should not be substituted for poor managers.

Outsource Vendor Selection Procedures

Choosing vendors for services, software and support, and hardware requires evaluation procedures. When a business decides it requires a vendor to submit proposals, a request for proposal letter is sent to all possible vendor candidates.

In the case of hardware, this request approach details the proposed time period, professional and financial references, hardware and hardware configuration, architecture, and requests a price quote. With software and support, a request defines the target system and asks the vendor to provide a support performance objective for a specific configuration. System operation performance requirements include systems design, configuration and architecture, types and number of users, production volume, maintenance and operation objectives, and price. Outsource service proposals should include at least the following items:

■ Professional and financial references
■ Objective of delivered services
■ Security requirements
■ Services delivery schedule
■ Documentation
■ Pricing

In all request for proposals, there should be a deadline by which proposals must be received by the organization to be considered viable.

Evaluating Proposals

All received vendor proposals should be analyzed in detail. There should be common elements addressing the specific proposal requirements. Organize an *ad hoc* committee to evaluate the submitted proposals and discuss them. Be mindful that there may be laws and regulations governing the request for proposals and their submission. Most notable are organizations requiring legal adherence of those doing business with federal, state, and local governments. Some governments have requirements where selection preference is granted to vendors doing business within municipal boundaries. In some cases, these restrictions are codified as regulations or laws, and in other cases they merely follow custom or tradition. Failing to observe such restrictions can result in protracted grievance proceedings and litigation.

Policies and Procedures Involving Outsourcing: What Is Yours and What Is Mine?

An organization's policies and procedures must govern the interaction between the organization and outside contractors.

Experience Note It is not unusual for a consultant or integrator to hold an organization hostage, demanding rewards or some form of exorbitant compensation before delivering the goods.

Instead of structuring a relationship based on the value of service they are contracted to provide, they base it on the necessity of doing business, as they are the only people who have the source code. In other cases, they have not delivered sufficient documentation for the organization's employees to maintain the system, thereby requiring their continued services. It is essentially a monopoly of one. Because the organization does not have the source code to their custom system, it has lost control of one of its critical assets. Regrettably, this condition is usually brought to the company's attention after it has already happened. The situation grows more desperate as the company is reluctant to notify its lawyers, fearing that the contracted developers might sabotage the source code by modifying it to render it useless at some time. When structuring systems development projects performed by outside contractors, these are a few policy suggestions to reduce risks:

- *Get the source code.* Be certain to investigate the work history of the contractor, and by all means contact all professional references to ascertain if there were any past problems. The organization must ensure it receives the source code, and there are contractual arrangements with strict requirements to this effect. No excuses are acceptable. The source code must be installed according to the organization's certification and accreditation policies.
- *Licensing and documentation.* Purchase the appropriate licenses for the source code. Businesses want to replicate the development environment exactly, having the ability to keep the code up to date during the maintenance development phase. Make certain the contractor is drafting the required documentation of effort. This documentation should be subject to inspection and audit by the organization's representatives before the product is delivered. If the organization has the resources, any agreements must permit a representative of the organization to conduct an ongoing review of the code. This inspection must also include documentation.
- *Confirmation.* Confirm that you are going to receive what you contracted. Force a rebuild of the programs if you are not satisfied. If you have to pay for it, consider it the cost of doing business.
- *Secondary plan.* Have in the wings a backup developer or other reliable resource familiar with the code base and system design. What if the contractor becomes disabled and is unable to complete the project?
- *Ownership and delivery.* The organization's policy should require that the contract stipulates who is going to own what. Who owns the software? Does the organization own the software or merely a license to use it? Does the organization own the software to such an extent it may do what it wants with it? Write the contract carefully, and by all means have an attorney familiar with these issues review it before signing.

The best outcome is one of complete control where the organization has its asset with the system working as intended in the event of a problem with the developer. What does the organization have to do in the event the developer fails? Much will depend on the contract's language, your lawyer, and the developer. If you have to go to litigation in order to enforce the contract, you may not have possession of your

Exhibit 26   Protecting Employee Personal Information Policy

The XYZ Corporation will exercise every reasonable safeguard in the collection, storage, use, and dissemination of employee information. XYZ Corporation employees have a reasonable right to view their personal information, may make truthful corrections to this information, and must consent before dissemination is made of their information outside the XYZ Corporation.

application, and litigation takes time. By the end of legal wrangling, it is possible everyone loses.

Employee Privacy Policy

Personal privacy is a cherished value closely linked to concepts of personal freedom and well being. At the same time, personal privacy parallels fundamental principles of the First Amendment to the Constitution, the most important hallmark of personal freedom, the protection of free flow of information in society.

Most organizations require personal information about their employees to carry out business goals and objectives. It is imperative that collected information is safeguarded from intentional or accidental disclosure. Increasingly, automation of personal records permits this information to be used and analyzed in ways that would reduce employee privacy without adequate safeguards.

Organizations must have policies requiring compliance with legal, regulatory, and moral safeguards relative to employee information. These policies should assure that information technologies sustain and do not erode personal information protections in the organization's use, collection, and disclosure of personal information.

It is important that organizations constantly evaluate legislative and regulatory requirements involving the collection, use, and disclosure of personal information (Exhibit 26).

Internet Firewall Policy

Because the Internet is not trustworthy, an organization's system connected to the Internet is vulnerable to abuse and attack. Enabling a firewall between the organization's local area network and the Internet can go a long way to control access between trusted parties and less-trusted ones. A firewall is not a single component; rather it is a strategy for protecting an organization's Internet-reachable assets. Firewalls serve as gatekeepers between the untrustworthy Internet and the more-trusted organization networks.

The primary function of a firewall is to centralize system access controls. If remote users, authorized or not, can access the internal networks without traversing the firewalls, their effectiveness is diminished. If a traveling employee has the ability to connect to his office workstation, circumventing the organization's firewall architecture, then an attacker can do the same. Firewalls have the ability to allow network services to be passed or blocked; consequently, system administrators must consult with firewall administrators relative to which services are necessary for business operations. All unnecessary services must be disabled, denied, or blocked.

Firewalls provide several layers and types of protection:

- Firewalls can block unwanted traffic, essentially partitioning the inside network from the outside network.
- They can direct incoming traffic to more trustworthy internal systems.
- They can conceal vulnerable systems that cannot be secure from the Internet.
- They can provide audit trails logging traffic to and from the organization's private networks and the Internet.
- Firewalls can conceal information such as system addresses, network devices, and user identification from the Internet.

Authentication

Firewalls located at the perimeter of the organization's network, interfacing between the Internet and the internal networks, do not provide user authentication. Host-based firewalls usually provide these types of user authentication:

- *User names and passwords.* User names and unique passwords are compared against authorized user lists and verified by correct passwords. This is one of the least secure methods.
- *One-time passwords.* One-time passwords using software or hardware tokens produce a new password for each user session. Old passwords cannot be reused if they were stolen, intercepted, or borrowed. This method is one where the user must know something and must possess something before gaining access.
- *Digital certificates.* Digital certificates use a certificate generated using public key encryption from a trusted third party. This access method is one where the user must know something and have something.

Firewall Types

Packet-filtering firewalls are gateways located at network routers that have packet-screening abilities based on policy rules granting or denying access based on several factors:

- *Information packet source address.* It is capable of denying system access from specific source addresses; for example, it is possible to deny outside entry of any information packet having a source address of a competing company.
- *Information packet destination address.* It is capable of denying access to any internal workstation or host based on its IP address; for example, all traffic can be blocked attempting to connect to the client list file server.
- *Service port.* Firewalls are capable of blocking or allowing access to specific services; for example, connection attempts to workstation TCP Port 139 are denied.

Packet-filtering firewalls offer minimum security but very low cost. They can be an appropriate choice for a low-risk network environment. However, there are some drawbacks:

- They do not protect against IP or DNS address spoofing.
- Attackers will have direct access to any host on the internal network once access has been granted by the firewall.

- Strong user authentication is not a feature supported with many packet-screening firewalls.
- They do not generally provide complete or useful logging features.

Application Firewalls

Application firewalls use server programs, called proxies, running on the firewall. These proxies arbitrate transactions between interior and exterior networks. They accept requests, examine them, and forward legitimate requests to internal hosts that provide appropriate service. Application firewalls generally support functions as user authentication and logging features. Application firewalls require that a proxy is configured for each applicable service such as FTP, HTTP, etc.

Application-level firewalls generally offer the solution of network address translation (NAT). This feature may be configured so that outbound traffic appears as if the traffic had originated from the firewall itself. In this fashion, all IP addresses of the hosts behind the firewall are protected from discovery in that once they depart the firewall outbound, they all have the same IP address.

- Application firewalls supporting proxies for different services prevent direct access to internal network services, protecting the business against insecure or poorly configured internal servers.
- Application firewalls generally offer strong user authentication.
- Application firewalls generally provide detailed logging of user activities.

Hardware Firewall Architectures

Firewalls can be configured in many different hardware architectures providing various levels of security with different installation and operation costs. Organizations should match their risks to the type of firewall architecture selected. The following briefly describes firewall architectures.

- *Multiple-homed host.* This is a firewall that has more than one network interface card, NIC. Each NIC is logically and physically connected to separate network segments. A dual-homed host, one with two NICs is the most common example of a multi-homed host. One NIC is connected to the external or untrusted network, like the Internet, and the other NIC is connected to the internal or trusted network. In this configuration, the key point is not to allow computer traffic to be passed from the untrusted network directly to the trusted network. The firewall acts as an intermediary (Exhibit 27).
- *Screened hosts.* Screened firewall architecture uses a host called a bastion host. It usually has two network interface cards, but may have several NICs, making

Exhibit 27   Multiple or Dual-Homed Firewall Policy

In the configuration of multiple or dual-homed firewalls, routing by the firewall will be disabled, meaning that information packets from untrusted networks such as the Internet shall not be directly routed to the internal or trusted networks. All unnecessary network services will be disabled on XYZ Corporation hosts with firewalls configured appropriately denying ingress and egress traffic.

Exhibit 28   Screened Sub-Network Policy

In the XYZ Corporation, a screened sub-network shall be deployed by partitioning a perimeter network in order to separate the internal network from a more-external network. This measure assures that if there is a successful attack on the bastion host, the attacker is restricted to the more-exterior or perimeter network by the screening router that is connecting the internal and external networks.

Exhibit 29   Firewall Administration Policy

It is the policy of the XYZ Corporation to have two firewall administrators for each work shift. The Chief Technology Officer or designee shall designate them. These employees shall be responsible for the installation, correct configuration, and maintenance of the firewalls. The primary administrator shall be empowered to make approved changes to the firewall and the secondary administrator shall only do so in the absence of the primary administrator, avoiding duplicate or contradictory firewall access.

it a multiple-homed device. All outside hosts connect to this device rather than allowing direct connection between inside and outside hosts. To achieve this character, a filtering router is configured in such a fashion as to remove all unnecessary services, thereby earning its name as a hardened host. If superfluous services and features are removed or disabled, they cannot be exploited to gain unauthorized access. In the bastion host, a filtering router is installed and configured so that all connection traffic from between the internal and external networks must pass through the bastion host. No direct internal-network-to-external-network connections are allowed.

Bastion hosts can be deployed to partition sub-networks from other interior networks; for example, an interior network handling company e-mail is partitioned by a bastion host from another interior network where employee records are kept. This architecture is known as a screened sub-network, and adds an extra layer of security by creating a separate but connected internal network or sub-network (Exhibit 28).

Firewall Administration

Firewalls consisting of hardware, software, or appliances have to be the ongoing job of a responsible and senior employee. After all, this employee literally has the "keys to the kingdom." It is a wise business practice to have two firewall administrators, assuring continuity and institutional knowledge in the event of an absence (Exhibit 29).

Firewall Administrators

For each duty-day, it is recommended that two experienced employees are available to address firewall issues. In this manner, the firewall administrator function is constantly covered. It is compulsory that these employees have a thorough understanding of network architectures, TCP/IP protocols, and security policies (Exhibit 30).

Exhibit 30   Firewall Administrator Policy

In the XYZ Corporation, employees tasked with firewall administration must have significant hands-on experience with networking concepts, protocols, architectures, designs, configurations, and implementation so that firewalls are installed, configured. and maintained correctly. Firewall administrators will be responsible for securing computer traffic between secured network elements and less-secure network elements. It is expected that firewall administrators will complete periodic training on networks and firewalls in use.

Exhibit 31   Firewall Administration Policy

In the XYZ Corporation, firewall administrators will be on duty at all times. All firewall administration must be performed from the local terminal attached to the firewall host. Access to the firewall host is not permitted via remote access. Physical and logical access to the firewall host or the local terminal is strictly limited to the primary and secondary firewall administrators.

Exhibit 32   Firewall Backup Policy

In the XYZ Corporation, firewall software, configuration data, access control data, database files, etc., must be backed up daily, permitting efficient firewall systems recovery in the event of outage. Backup files will be stored securely on Write Once, Read Many media. At all times, backup files are to be secured with access granted appropriately.

Remote Firewall Administration

Firewalls are usually the first line and sometimes the last line of defense against attackers. By design, firewalls are supposed to be difficult to attack directly, causing attackers to attack the accounts on the firewall itself. Additionally, there should be no user accounts on the firewall host other than those of the administrators. User names and passwords must be strongly protected. One of the most common protections is strong physical security surrounding the firewall host and permitting firewall administration from one attached terminal. Only the primary and secondary firewall administrators should have physical access to the firewall host. Depending on the sensitivity of the data stored on the protected network, it is strongly recommended that firewall administrators are not allowed to remotely access firewalls. Depending on the business' operations, it may be prudent to have a firewall administrator on duty constantly. What degree of profit losses will be incurred if users are unable to access information assets because of firewall problems? Although having a firewall administrator on duty full-time, in the long run it provides increased integrity and availability for firewalls and the systems they protect (Exhibit 31 and Exhibit 32).

Intrusion Detection Policies

You are a senior manager with the responsibility of overseeing the company's network administration and security. Your platforms range from servers, firewalls, routers, and related equipment. Your employees are above average in their technical skills and do their best to develop and maintain a secure operating environment. Yet, you find yourself dealing with the skills of an aggressive and persistent attacker. Many senior managers put their trust in firewalls and rely on their administrators to lock down network services and workstations. Other managers have enough wisdom and knowledge to marry effective policies and procedures with technology-based security solutions.

For most businesses, a combination of network administrator skills, policy and procedure, and technology solutions are the approaches best addressing system vulnerabilities.

The IDS dream is a set of distributed systems that identify and sound alarms when systems are being attacked in real-time. Regrettably, it is easier to dream the dream than implement the system. Current IDS products are extremely valuable security tools but generally they do not deliver as much as advertised.

Network and Host IDSs

The host-based vs. network-based intrusion-detection strategy debate has been raging for some time. Currently, the consensus is moving toward a unified approach combining the two technologies.

Network-based products are built on the concept of a real-time wiretap. A sensor examines every information packet traveling through the system. These sensors apply a set of rules or attack "signatures" to the captured packets, attempting to identify hostile traffic. Basically, network IDS sensors are network sniffers with built-in, rule-based comparison engines. If a malicious packet is detected, then the network IDS sounds the alarm.

But the network IDS approach has its problems. It does not scale very well in that it has difficulty keeping up at network speeds of 100 Mbps. With gigabit network speeds arriving in business networks, these network IDS systems do not keep up with the traffic. Additionally, network IDS systems are based on attack signatures that will always be a step behind the latest vulnerability exploits. IDS product vendors have not caught up with all the known attacks, and there are new attacks announced every few days.

Nevertheless, network IDS enjoys some advantages. The greatest feature is stealth. Network IDS can be deployed in an unobtrusive manner, with little or no effect on existing systems. Once deployed, network IDS sensors will listen for attacks, regardless of the destination.

Host-Based IDS

Host-based IDS primarily function within the system audit and event logs. In place of identifying attack-profile packets, they aim to identify known patterns of local and remote users doing things they should not be doing. One type of host IDS product produces a one-way hash of critical files located on a host. These files include user accounts, configuration, and audit operations. If anything changes in these accounts, e.g., an intruder establishes an account on the root level, then the host IDS would notify the system administrator. The host IDS cannot identify what, but it can tell the administrator that something important has changed. Host IDSs have their problems in portability. They run only on specific operation systems platforms so it is possible your favorite operation system is not on the list.

IDSs in general are incredibly useful but the hope of turning them loose on your systems and giving them control is not feasible. IDS technology is not very mature but it is getting better. It is strongly recommended that IDS technology is given serious implementation consideration. But it should be considered being used in conjunction with other critical asset preservation measures and not replace any of them.

Web Server Security Policies and Procedures

Most businesses, governments, and organizations have external Web sites describing their purpose and structure, and often provide the opportunity for public interaction. E-commerce on the Internet is not something that only large businesses can afford to do. It can be a profitable operation for every "Mom and Pop" enterprise as well. For security reasons, Internet Web servers are usually positioned inside the packet-screening firewall that faces the Internet and inside the firewalls that protect precious interior networks. Such architecture has a good security track record if implemented correctly, and is called the demilitarized zone (DMZ).

Organizations may also choose to develop and deploy intranet Web sites for employee use. In these cases, the Web servers are located inside the interior network, as these systems are not intended for outside eyes. Regardless of the organization's size and whether it has Internet or intranet Web sites, considerable amounts of money and resources are spent in the development of a suitable Web site that is informative yet practical. In a very real sense, the company's Web site reflects the organization's branding, image, and business reputation.

The development, maintenance, management, and administration of the company's Internet Web site is usually assigned to a team of experts within the enterprise or outsourced. It is possible a director of online marketing development is responsible for identifying and implementing new online business development opportunities while the company's Webmaster takes charge of the site's technical excellence, content development, management, and security. On the part of the Webmaster, there is a development team responsible for site design, coding, graphics, and business features such as shopping carts.

Internal company Web sites are generally used for posting information relevant to employees. Birthdays, presentations, corporate calendars, directories, organizational charts, and project information are often posted. Project management information posted to an internal network can provide a central reference point for the project team and senior managers with project oversight. Internal Web sites do not have the same visibility as Internet Web sites, but they have the same need to be managed through specific policies and procedures.

Web Server Policies and Procedures

- It is highly recommended that the Chief Information Officer formally approve the content and operation of any Web server to be connected to any organization system.
- Any and all Web site content and features must be approved and installed by the organization's Webmaster.
- Under no circumstances will sensitive information be made available on any company Web site internally or externally accessible.
- All enterprise Web sites must be reviewed, vetted, and approved in the same fashion as officially released reports or other outside correspondence.
- At all times, copyrights will be protected and observed.
- There should be no reason for control of the Web server other than from the Web server's console. Logging on to the Web server from any device other than this console is not permitted, and the server's software should be configured accordingly.

- Systems administrators, firewall administrators, and Webmasters are to report any and all attempts to gain unauthorized access to the Web server located on either the Internet or internal intranet.
- Incoming packet traffic will be scanned and connections to unapproved Web sites will be immediately reported to senior managers.
- Systems maintenance will include the installation of operating systems and applications patches.
- Senior administrators and Webmasters are responsible for change management. Any and all changes must be justified, documented, and submitted to a thorough quality control process before installation.
- Senior administrators and Webmasters are responsible for monitoring system performance, taking appropriate security measures, and ensuring Web sites reflect the highest quality standards.
- Implementation of common gateway interchange (CGI) scripts will be strictly monitored and controlled.
- In order to avoid buffer overflows, systems developers must keep buffer sizes defined when accepting data. In order to avoid CGI vulnerabilities, regular testing will be performed and appropriate security measures taken.
- All user input to any Web site, internal and external, will be filtered for appropriate content.
- In the case of third party applications interacting with programs that contain buffers that do not check for incoming data correctness, it is important that these applications are monitored and patched appropriately.

Information Systems Support Policies

Workstations, servers, and mainframes require many of the same support policies. Work areas must be clean and air conditioned. On a daily basis, housekeeping resources must enter all work areas except the data library, server, and mainframe rooms for cleaning. There must be policies eliminating the presence of food, beverages, and smoking in the vicinity of computer equipment and media. This may be a harsh idea but more than one laptop/desktop has met its end by a spilled café grande.

Data libraries where real-time and backed up data are stored are perhaps the most critical areas of the workplace. Generally, data libraries store magnetic tapes, optical disks, magnetic disks, application media, and paper-based documents. Often, there are data libraries required for ready access on the office site, while remote data libraries store materials in the event of disaster.

There should be policies governing the conduct of data libraries and the duties of the data librarian. The primary duty, of course, is to support the business' computer operations. Following is a list of data librarian duties for policy consideration:

- Upon receipt of new media, the librarian compares quantity received with the original order and billing information. If incorrect, the librarian notifies the operations manager.
- Inspects all media for physical damage. If any media is damaged, the librarian notifies the operations manager.
- Logs all new media and assigned identification numbers.
- Acknowledges all receipts and deliveries with the operations manager.
- At no time is the librarian to have access to applications or information systems of any kind, preserving separation of duties and least privilege.

Data Entry

Many senior managers have forgotten that data entry is still a vital part of business operations. There is a need to convert raw, bulk data such as credit card applications into a familiar format for use by information systems. Many companies utilize both centralized and decentralized data entry systems. In fact, it is becoming very popular to package and ship forms to foreign countries with relatively low labor costs for data entry. In most cases, the equipment of choice is the online monitor and keyboard; there are others consisting of bar code readers, optical or magnetic character readers, and voice recognition. Policies and procedures for online data entry are as follows:

- All employees and terminals are identified by proper codes to ensure that only authorized equipment and employees enter data.
- When the data is displayed on the monitor correctly, the operator keys in the proper code to transmit the data to the computer.
- All data is checked by the computer system, ensuring that the correct data is being entered. For example, if a field is no more than seven numerical characters in a specific range, the computer will not allow the operator to enter incorrect characters.
- All data entered are logged by terminal number and the data entry employee.
- At no time are the data entry employees to have access to computing hardware outside what is necessary for them to enter data.
- At no time are the data entry employees to have access to applications other than what is necessary for them to enter data. These last two steps help preserve separation of duties and least privilege.

Technical Support

The primary purpose of the technical support units is to provide technical services to computing equipment and software users. There are basically four sections for which they have responsibilities:

1. *Communications.* The communications support unit is responsible for hardware, software, wiring, cabling, maintenance, and lease services for the operation of all business communications. Included here are the local area networks (LANs), wireless networks, and wide area networks (WANs). They also are responsible for telephone communications, including cellular and wireless, and their respective billing.
2. *Database administration.* The database manager is responsible for a number of administrators who are responsible for maintaining and controlling the processing related to the company's databases. Their related duties include:
   - Selection and maintenance of database software
   - Control database access and employees who can create information, read specific information, change information, add information, and delete information
   - Maintain file and database backups
   - Provide consultations to relevant database users
   - Provide disaster-planning procedures and test them
   - Report immediately any security breaches or data corruption
   - Maintain directory services
   The latter duty, depending on the organization's size, can constitute a sizeable part of the database administrator's duties. A directory is a collection of

information for a given application. It may hold all the information relating to each application such as user access and logons. They are responsible for the directory's integrity and security. It is important to maintain a division between database support unit employees and production applications so separation of duties and least privilege are observed.

3. *Software support.* These are the program engineers responsible for supporting the operating systems, applications, and in-house developed and purchased software applications. Some of their responsibilities include but are not limited to:

    – Make approved changes to the operating system software when directed by senior managers in writing.
    – Document all changes to any production software.
    – Report immediately any security issues in any production software.
    – Report immediately any physical security breaches.
    – Inform computer operators of programming changes in written form.
    – Test new software before introducing to a production environment.
    – At no time should any programmer have access to live data in any form. Further, at no time should any single employee, programmer or otherwise, have the ability to change the operating system code or any of the production applications. These restrictions will help maintain an atmosphere of least privilege and separation of duties.

4. *Workstation/server help desk.* These are the employees responsible for affecting the majority of the organization's computer users. They generally address issues such as:

    – Workstation and server configurations. They establish standard operation procedures, ensuring that all workstation and server configurations are the same from machine to machine and platform to platform. With standard configurations observed, they can readily identify security or abuse issues and handle them.
    – Provide service to employees having difficulty with their equipment and software.
    – Service and maintain peripheral equipment.
    – Make recommendations of equipment and software.
    – Monitor performance and provide feedback to senior managers.
    – Train users to maximize equipment and software use.
    – Maintain inventory of hardware and software.
    – Maintain hardware and software licensing.
    – Provide and maintain list of approved software applications.
    – Test and approve software and equipment for security and place into production.
    – Approve installation of specified software applications.
    – Report any security violations involving users.

As with other employees, there must be a separation of duties in that these employees must never have the ability to access live production data, operating system code, or application programming.

Securing Systems

In protecting individual workstations, including mobile computing devices such as laptops, notepads, and personal digital assistants, there is an old saying that the best defense is a good offense.

Having proactive procedures will help ensure security and privacy, and minimize the risks associated with computer operations. Workstation security can be assured by having standard hardware and software configurations, maintenance, and disposal policies and procedures. The following steps are general while course deviations should be addressed on an individual basis:

- *Install the most-recent operation systems and application security patches.* Regrettably, some popular operating systems and applications have notorious security and operating flaws, making them easy prey for intrusions and the installation of malicious software (malware). To make sure your systems are protected, download and install updates as they are made available. It is the responsibility of the users and maintenance staff to ensure these updates are installed and documented. Documentation should reflect the individual device, identified by unique name or serial number, the type of update installed, date of installation, and by whom.

- *Do not allow the installation of unauthorized software.* Have a procedure where there is a list of authorized software that can be installed. Use software from recognized companies and install all update patches. Do not allow the installation of shareware or freeware programs. No one knows what these programs contain in the way of allowing damage to occur to your system. Besides, recognized companies generally have some kind of quality controls, and there is a performance expectation of a packaged product. In the event there is a problem, there is a viable party from whom to seek civil recourse for damages.

- *Do not allow any unauthorized configurations.* As an example, if file or printer shares are disabled, employees must not be allowed to enable them.

- *Do not allow employees to install any hardware.* Only authorized employees are allowed to install authorized hardware. For example, no employee is permitted to install modems in their workstations. This action creates a monumental security risk to the network.

- *Keep all configurations the same.* Regardless if there are network services, the organization should follow a standard configuration procedure for those applications. This facilitates auditing and security testing. Develop and maintain a standard installation and configuration procedure for all authorized software.

- *Keep your workstation off-limits.* Workstations should be physically secured when not in use. If the workstation is located in an office, the door should be locked when the workstation is not in use. If the workstation is used for very sensitive work, having a removable hard drive that is secured at the end of the workday is a good idea. Laptops may be secured by having software that encrypts the hard drive. In this fashion, if the hard drive was removed from the laptop and installed in another computer, it still would not be easily accessible.

- *Other workstation security measures include using a BIOS password.* The basic input/output system (BIOS) is a special piece of software incorporated in most computers. BIOS controls the startup of the computer and has the ability to be configured for a password before the computer may be started. In the event someone forgets their password, there are ways to circumvent the process but they usually require some time and specialized knowledge. BIOS passwords are similar to locks in that most locks will thwart a casual thief, but they will not stop a professional.

- *Create a password-protected screensaver activated after a few minutes of inactivity.* This feature is usually incorporated as part of the workstation's operating system. When activated, the screensaver continues to block anyone from seeing behind it. A password is required for deactivating the screensaver. If a malicious user attempts to restart the computer, depending on the operating system, it may require a password to restart the computer; if this is not the case, when a BIOS password is installed, it will prevent any system restart.

■ *Install operating systems that create individual password-protected user profiles.* Many operating systems, such as Windows NT or XP and Linux allow individual password-protected user accounts to be created. In this fashion, the system boots and as it launches the operating system, it requires a password before the user may access the operating system, applications, and data.

■ *Install biometric devices, which is equivalent to installing a deadbolt on a door.* Biometric devices restrict access to systems based on the unique physiological characteristics recognized by the device. Examples of effective biometric devices are fingerprints, iris and retina scans, and voice.

■ *Disconnect from open-ended networks such as the Internet when you are not actively using them.* As long as you have an active connection to an insecure open-ended network, malicious persons have a channel to access your workstation. These can be minimized by disconnecting from the open-ended network. This means disconnecting your dial-up modem, DSL (Digital Subscriber Line) connection, or ISDN (Integrated Services Digital Network) terminal emulator when you finish each session. If attackers cannot reach the system, they cannot do anything malicious.

Experience Note A computer security professional lecturing at one of the national computer system security conferences had a few minutes of free time and wanted to access the wireless network to download his e-mail. After completing the process, he remained connected to the wireless network for some time while his laptop was inactive. He was still connected when he saw e-mail being read on his computer. He realized he had not accessed the wireless network of the conference; rather, he had connected to a Trojan horse network disguised to look like the official network. The attackers had captured his e-mail account password and were in a position to read and send e-mail through his account.

■ *Install personal workstation firewalls to protect your workstation while it is connected to the network, whether the network is closed or open ended.* Many employees think their computers are protected by the network firewalls, and indeed they are. Having a personal firewall installed is another layer of protection against attackers. Individual workstation firewalls are usually inexpensive.

■ *Disable cookies for privacy.* If cookies, small bits of code sent from Web sites to your browser and stored on your hard drive for identification and tracking purposes frighten you, then disable them. Most browsers have security features allowing you to be prompted for accepting cookies and you have the choice of accepting them or not. Regardless, it is prudent to delete cookies on a regular basis. Within most browsers there are methods to delete cookies. It is important to note that cookies are not generally malicious in themselves, but they are read by some Web sites and used to track the Internet browsing habits of the workstation's users.

■ *Avoid spyware.* There are small applications that are somewhat malicious in that they track your Internet browsing habits and are considered more intrusive than just ordinary cookies. Some spyware lodges itself in the operating system's registry and lettered drives. Scanners are readily available that search the workstation's drives and remove the offenders. Users should scan for spyware at least weekly.

- *Protect the user's identity.* Applications offer to save your login name and password so you do not have to enter them each time you visit the site. By activating his feature, you are allowing the login name and password to be stored in the workstation's hard drive and anyone with access to your hard drive can capture these bits of information.

- *Some word processors incorporate the user's registration information in the content of the document.* Of course, this information will not be displayed by the word processor, but can be viewed when displayed in a simple text editor. Be mindful of this feature when you enter application registration information.

- *Install and update your antivirus software.* This is a matter of good business sense. Antivirus software must be installed on all workstations, must be activated upon the system's startup, and must be updated regularly. Most antivirus programs look for viruses and other types of malware. Fortunately, most antivirus developers sell update subscriptions and their applications can be configured to retrieve updates automatically. With the amount of malware circulating on open-ended networks, it makes sense to activate the antivirus shielding while using the Internet and scan for malware at least weekly.

- *Disable file and printer sharing features in the workstation's operating system.* This is a favorite vulnerability permitting attackers to gain unauthorized access. If you must allow this type of sharing, be sure to enable the password feature with a very strong password. Regardless, it is strongly recommended that unless there is a very compelling reason, disable file and printer sharing on all workstations.

- *Collect all sensitive trash daily for burning or shredding.* There has been more than one active password collected from unburned trash.

- *When it is time to dispose of computer-related equipment and media in the form of floppy disks, hard drives, CDs, CD-Rs, and the like, it is important to have very specific procedures.* All computers should have their hard drives removed before disposal. All media, including hard drives, should be burned in the incinerator. Commercial burning at very high temperatures is the only reliable way to be assured of media destruction.

Experience Note Several years ago, a government agency sold its antiquated equipment at auction. To the agency's horror, the recipients quickly discovered they could unerase and unformat the hard drives and related media, recovering the agency's data. Untold embarrassment ensued.

The Auditors Are Coming. The Auditors Are Coming.

Audit policies and procedures are needed to ensure that employees are meeting management objectives, legal and regulatory requirements, and addressing risks. Auditing is covered in the next chapter, so it is only going to be lightly addressed here. Management audits assure that resources are being properly utilized and monitored:

- Develop and implement policies addressing human resources management, data, and facilities.

- Ensure that projects are completed on schedule and within budget.
- Ensure that projects have been completed utilizing quality models such as the SDLC.
- Develop and maintain business priorities and long-term strategies.
- Assure that controls are in place for risk detection, prevention, and correction.

Systems Development and Programming Policies

These audits are more technical than management audits and require more knowledge and detail. Frequently, organizations do not have policies governing operations, so employees are left to their own devices, making decisions they are not qualified to make. Systems development involves activities ranging from purchasing commercial off-the-shelf software systems, to developing in-house systems, to purchasing turnkey systems. All systems development must be considered in the light of confidentiality, integrity, and availability.

Organizations must have written policies and auditing programs for:

- Systems design and development through quality models
- Systems selection and procurement criteria
- Systems application development
- Program testing
- Systems implementation
- Systems monitoring
- Systems disposal
- Systems change controls
- Systems documentation
- Systems quality assurance

Data Controls

Data control policies have the objectives of addressing confidentiality, integrity, and availability of data. These features are audited in the following areas:

- Input controls to any operation must be addressed by policies and procedures. Because input varies considerably, so will policies.
- Output controls address electronic and printed media.
- Database management controls must be established by policies with compliance assured by audit activities.
- Database information backup and storage policies.

Disaster Recovery and Business Continuity

Disaster recovery audit policies also address business continuity. Audit policies must require that auditors obtain evidence that these are in place and combined with regular unannounced testing. Audits of this nature address the existence of the following policies:

- Establishment of a Risk Management team
- Critical asset identification and prioritization
- Threat: impact analysis

- Existence of critical asset safeguards
- Disaster recovery plan
- Establishment of Disaster Recovery team
- Designated employees to address public and press inquiries
- Business continuity plan
- Plan testing

Workstation Audit Policies

These audits address the use of workstations and all company-owned equipment and facilities, including:

- Access restrictions to workstations
- Inventory of software and hardware reconciled with licensing and purchase documents
- Evidence of policy and individual compliance for the procurement and installation of software and hardware
- Evidence of individual compliance with policy regarding official use
- Evidence of individual compliance with policy regarding network and workstation security
- Policy and individual compliance with regular data backup
- Evidence of policy and individual compliance with workstation housekeeping

Information Technology Human Resources Management Policies: Yes, Virginia, IT Employees Really Are Different

Policies governing IT human resources differ from those used in other business units because they require some stringency. Polices and procedures to hire the best-possible candidates will decrease human resource risk factors and raise the possibilities of "getting the biggest bang for the buck." IT employees are very different than others in the business world. They have very specialized skills, training, certifications, and experience that are very portable. Consequently, many IT employees feel more loyalty to their profession than to the company, requiring policies and procedures to accommodate these differences if the business unit is to function at the level that is normal for the profession and if the turnover rate is to be minimized.

Getting the Best Candidates for the Position

There are successful procedures for obtaining the best IT candidates when combined with the more-traditional methods:

- Pay a meaningful bounty to current employees for recruiting and hiring qualified people.
- The Human Resources management office should have a standardized procedure for screening employment candidates so only qualified candidates are considered. Often the creation of forms requiring basic information as to the candidate's education, training, professional experience, professional certifications, and professional recommendations provide an effective mechanism of measuring the candidates for jobs. Accepting résumés is a traditional first step in developing a qualified candidate pool but some candidates have an ability

to mischaracterize their abilities, so it is recommended the standard job form is sent to candidates who appear most qualified.

Experience Note While conducting an audit of a Human Resources management unit, a stack of resumes was reviewed as part of the audit program. The auditor was shown job requirements for a systems analyst and a submitted resume where a candidate purported to have 15 years of IT management experience. The Human Resources manager sent a standardized experience form for completion to the candidate, requesting a detailed explanation of his management experience. After completion, the form reflected the candidate had been a data entry supervisor where he was responsible for several data entry specialists and had never worked with the actual network or anything that would qualify that person in systems analysis or development.

- Consult with the person leaving a position that can describe the job better than anyone else. In the event of a new position, locate persons who are in the same or similar position for their input.
- After the most qualified candidates are found, confirm their work experience at their previous employer. This is a frequently ignored area. Take the time to speak with their former supervisor and ask job performance questions. Determine if this person is eligible for rehire.
- If there is a bonding or other similar requirement, obtain a waiver from the candidates and obtain a credit report.
- Do not forget to verify their professional references. It is recommended that each qualified candidate provide at least three. It is recommended the references should be thoroughly interviewed about the qualifications of the candidate.
- In the case of very-sensitive positions, require a complete background investigation to be performed by a competent and experienced firm. These background investigations should be required every few years of employees in sensitive positions. They are worth the time and expense.
- Avoid nepotism. The controls needed for IT business operations are stringent at best; hiring relatives may cause unnecessary problems. Individuals related to each other tend not to abide by the same rules as nonrelatives. Often they tend to cover up more errors and have higher rates of orchestrated thefts and embezzlements.

Job Interviews

Candidate interviews are a necessary part of the selection procedure. They usually begin after the candidates have passed preliminary screening processes.

Structured interviews are generally characterized by a list of questions suitable for interviewers with little training to ask. The questions can be divided among the interviewers or repeated using different versions looking for response consistency. This approach is very restricted and narrow.

Semistructured interviews are usually characterized by only a few major questions prepared by the interviewers in advance. Conducting this interview requires a higher degree of technical skill and preparation but allows for more flexibility than the structured interview approach. At this time, the interviewers are more able to probe the areas that seem to merit more detail from the candidate.

The unstructured interview is best conducted by senior managers and very experienced interviewers. Topical areas are covered during the interview, but the interviewer retains the freedom to adapt to the individual candidate. The reliability of this interviewing method may be questioned at some time but if it is conducted carefully and thoughtfully, it does provide the interviewer with substantial information about each person.

As soon as the candidate interview is concluded, each participating interviewer should document his objective analysis of the candidate in writing. These notes and analyses should be archived and maintained in the event of future litigation. The interviewers should make an informed recommendation to the hiring manager. If the decision is close, the hiring manager may wish to speak with the interviewers or even have a second interview with the candidates.

Performance Reviews

Most companies have employee performance review procedures in place. IT systems professionals may require specialized procedures as their performance is a function of ability as well as professional skill and personal effort. Following are several procedures that should be considered when addressing individual performance matters:

- There should be formalized criteria against which an employee's performance is measured. This criteria is not merely a job description; rather, this document sets out the performance expectation of the employee in that job. It is important that the performance criteria match the level of professional expectation for each position level. For example, if an employee is an entry-level programmer, the performance measurement criteria should be geared toward that of an entry-level programmer.
- Consider job performance measurement criteria that have unacceptable levels, acceptable levels, and truly exceptional levels of performance.
- Job performance criteria should escalate with the employee's escalating abilities.
- There should be monetary and other award incentives for employees who perform well.
- Employees should read and acknowledge their job performance criteria.
- Consider a formalized career path for employees. Can they increase their responsibilities and pay according to formalized methods?
- Performance evaluations should be face-to-face at least annually. Senior managers need to speak with their employees and let them know how they are doing. Managers should seriously consider having semiannual performance reviews so the employee is not shocked at his annual performance review. If someone is doing very well, he should be acknowledged.
- Spot awards recognize employees in a particular task. These tokens are generally something a senior manager has available to hand to an employee, recognizing his good work on the spot.

Experience Note Emperor Napoleon recognized that his soldiers would literally march through the greatest battles if recognized with bits of metal and ribbon.

Employee Termination

To protect the organization, senior managers should use special termination procedures, as departing employees have many opportunities to vent animosity with destructive results. These are a few examples of special procedures when dealing with employee terminations:

- Employee is notified away from the work area.
- Employee's systems passwords are removed before the notice is delivered.
- Employee immediately returns company identification and any company property including tokens, smart cards, laptops, etc.
- Employee is accompanied as he packs his belongings and is escorted from the building. In some cases, the organization may want to pack the employee's personal items and send them to his residence. At no time is the employee left unaccompanied after termination notice is delivered. If transportation is required, it should be provided.
- The internal auditing unit is notified and all employee activities in the network and workstation are audited for a period of 90 days. It is a frequent occurrence that employees with a feeling they are going to be terminated will do damage in that time period.

Employee Departures on Good Terms

Employees departing on good terms, for a variety of reasons, should have an exit interview by someone other than their direct manager. This interview has the purpose of learning exactly why the employee is leaving. Data collected from departing employees may indicate undesirable situations or conditions exist and need correction.

In all cases, as soon as the employee gives notice of departure it is prudent to notify the auditors. After the person leaves the organization, his network and workstation activities should be audited for a period of at least 90 days. This action will attempt to discover if the employee is leaving with intellectual property belonging to the organization, and determine if there are any retaliatory events waiting to happen in his absence.

Employee Training

Employee training procedures begin with the orientation of new employees and continue to help them meet the changing skills required by their jobs. IT employees are generally required to have specialized skills that quickly become obsolete, and for this reason they move on to other jobs that may provide the opportunity to acquire new skills. The scope of training is vast and covers an employee as he reports for his first day at work and continues throughout his professional career.

Records of employee training are begun during the initial orientation, and document education, skills, and experience before the employee enters the company. Documentation of all education and training should be kept and archived after the employee's departure from the organization. With this as a basis, future education and training benefiting the employee should be assessed and used, if necessary, to justify the individual's training program from in-house or outside resources.

Mentor Assignment

Sometimes a "personal touch" is a prudent step in employee development. An employee is assigned to a mentor to develop professional skills. The mentor should be positive, personable, someone who can make the employee comfortable about asking questions, and someone very knowledgeable in his area of expertise.

Conclusion

The details of this chapter should make it very clear that policies, procedures, and standards play a critical role in determining legal and regulatory requirements, employee conduct, and system survivability. They must be carefully crafted to reflect the organization's strategic thinking. It is crucial that policies, procedures, and standards be formalized in all organizations regardless of their size and nationality. Not all policies and procedures apply to all employees, but it is imperative they be accessible and searchable by appropriate employees. Having them will save the organization's bacon when the need arises.

Chapter 3

Auditing

Auditing for the Masses

In summary terms, risk management identifies, prioritizes, and safeguards critical assets, while policies, procedures, and standards address employee conduct. Auditing is the process of assessing whether employees and business operations are in compliance with the organization's policies and procedures as well as applicable laws and regulations. Auditing is the investigation and measurement of employee behavior and business operations based on collected evidence. Counted together, risk management, policies and procedures, and auditing form the first three integrated steps in proactively addressing critical incident management.

Auditing is the compliance extension of your risk management program where operations, policies, and procedures are examined to determine whether operations are lawful, effective, efficient, and profitable. Auditing will determine that the organization's critical assets are accounted for, prioritized with adequate safeguards, and whether recovery and restoration procedures are implemented and tested. Fundamentally, auditing is also a comparison and analytical process comprised of collecting and evaluating evidence regarding management assertions and the actual state of the organization's operations. In fact, the most-critical part of auditing is the degree of separation between an organization's assertions and established system-addressed risk criteria. Any differences between assertions and the actual-state falls into a category called the "gap."

Experience Note Easy-to-digest definitions remove the mystery from the auditing process and permit stakeholders to understand it.

Information technology auditing is a carefully planned and executed business process involving the collection and evaluation of evidence to ascertain if a computer system safeguards critical assets and facilitates organizational goals being achieved.

Auditor Responsibilities

In the sense of their function, auditors must not have any direct responsibility or authority over any of the activities that they examine or could examine in the future.

Operational assessments and employee performance appraisals do not, in any way, relieve employees of their professional responsibilities. Auditors must be authorized to have full and unrestricted access to relevant equipment and information including computer files, documents, records, property and employees. They must have a high degree of freedom in all audit-applicable business areas with the exception of specific restrictions imposed by law.

Internal Controls

Managing critical assets, their safeguards, controlling potential frauds and improving effectiveness and efficiency can best be achieved if senior managers establish a structure of internal controls. There really is not a great deal of universal details in this area as all organizations are different in their mission and function. Let's define internal controls here in the context of formal systems that prevent, detect, and correct policy violations, unlawful and abusive events. These are the three most important levels of general controls: prevention, detection, and correction.

General Controls

General controls are those internal controls having wide application to most areas of business operations. For the most part, they include but are not limited to specific system applications:

- Planning and organization controls
- Physical and logical access controls
- Human resources
- Risk management
- Communications controls
- System development controls

Specific Controls

In broad terms these are controls with application to specific applications:

- Access controls
- Data input controls (these include all system data inputs)
- Processing controls
- Output controls

The overarching governing structure for specific and general controls is that of CIA, confidentiality, integrity, and availability. In current auditing views, there are many components where internal controls apply for example, separation of duties and least privilege, clear lines of authority and responsibility, adequate documentation, access control, management supervision, individual accountability, performance checks, and audit trails to name a few.

Separation of Duties and Least Privilege

Separation of duties basically means that separate employees should be responsible for initiating transactions, processing transactions, recording those transactions, and maintaining custody of critical assets. Least privilege means that employees have the knowledge and authority to perform their jobs and nothing more. For example, in a small organization an accounts payable clerk has the responsibility of preparing billing payments. She reviews the billing for its correctness and prepares wire transfer documents. By observing the concepts of separation of duties and least privilege, she does not have the authority or the ability to release funds. So, she prepares a voucher with the attached billing documentation and submits these materials to the finance vice-president who authorizes the transfer of funds. In the event the payment amounts are over $10,000, the organization's policies and procedures mandate that two vice-presidents approve the electronic wire transfer. Once the payment is approved, the transaction information flows to another employee that is responsible for posting the transaction to the organization's financial records.

Authority and Responsibility

Clear and well-defined lines of authority and responsibility are essential in controlling systems. In today's business environment, the distinctions between authority and responsibility may not be clear. It is frequently difficult as many resources are shared among many users. For example, database use is common among many users in a business organization. When several authorized users have simultaneous access and, through some unknown means, the data becomes corrupted, it is not always easy to fix responsibility.

Documentation

Documents and records are essential in providing an audit trail of activities within any system. Electronic and paper-based documents are used to support the initiation, execution, payment, and recording of transactions. Documentation is intended to provide an accurate record of events and acts. Documents should provide a tangible record in which events can be reconstructed from their content. In a well-designed system, audit trails document the actions and events occurring during business operations as well as those documents required to administratively run the business.

Experience Note "If it's not written, it doesn't exist."

Performance Checks and Accountability

Checks of performance and accountability are done by auditors because employees are likely to forget policies and procedures, make genuine mistakes, become careless and negligent, or intentionally fail to follow procedures. Individual employee accountability is tied to performance and competence as well as continuing responsibility.

Auditors: Who Are They?

Managers Are Not from Venus, Auditors Are Not from Mars

This is a difficult question that could literally be debated for many years without resolution. Who makes the best auditors and where are they found? One of the first general standards for all auditors, is they must collectively possess adequate professional ability to complete their required tasks. This does not mean they know all things about all things in the organization. What it does mean is that auditors must have the skills and knowledge about the area they going to audit. They should have a thorough knowledge of the target's business environment relative to the nature of the audit being performed. Auditor qualifications apply to the audit team collectively and not necessarily to each individual auditor. Acceptable skills could include, but not be limited to such areas as, accounting, statistics, law, engineering, computer science, business administration, public administration, economics, social sciences, and mathematics.

Auditing is a field that requires significant ongoing education in professional disciplines. Auditors generally plan to complete at least 40 hours annually of continuing relevant education and training in order to remain current in their discipline. Continuing professional training should include topics such as, audit methodology, assessment of internal controls, principles of management, computer information systems management, statistical sampling methodology, evaluation design, and data analysis.

Auditor Attributes

Following are some important characteristics to consider when selecting candidates as auditors:

Personal

The auditor determines when decisions can be made and exercises authority sparingly. She shares appropriate information with the correct people in a timely fashion. She exercises correct judgment and maintains a professional demeanor at all times. She understands the limits of her knowledge and knows when to call others seeking their expertise. In other words, she does not think she knows all things.

She builds trust by demonstrating honest and direct behavior yet is acutely aware of sensitive issues. Auditors do not compromise their ethics, nor will they tolerate a compromise of ethics by others. This may seem a bit rigid, but considering that auditors must prize their credibility highly, it is not unreasonable. It is important to note that auditors in essence are not ever off-duty. They are aware that their off-duty conduct affects their on-duty credibility. Auditors are professionals that understand that if they engage in activities that call their personal judgment into question, their professional judgment may be called into question on the assessments they make on the job.

They consistently develop comprehensive plans to accomplish their goals and take the initiative to meet or exceed deadlines in anticipation of timelines. They are adept at multitasking and handle multiple tasks simultaneously prioritizing work by focusing on significant problems.

Leadership

Auditors take an active role in preparation of presentations delivering oral and written presentations that are grammatically correct, logical, clear, concise, and relevant. They incorporate business and personal experiences in the communication of ideas to others. An auditor is thoroughly knowledgeable in emerging and current trends applicable to her tasking as well as her profession. She possesses excellent negotiation and persuasion skills and is adept at exercising various types of negotiation styles. She presents her point of view yet is sensitive and adept at leading herself and others to win/win conclusions. She discusses matters in a factual, professional fashion yet delivers her point of view in a passionate and persuasive manner. She effectively and efficiently recognizes and manages potential conflicts.

Functional Abilities

She knows her profession and is experienced and well trained in her craft. Auditors routinely provide advice to senior managers on the assertions that need to be provided regarding systems' confidentiality, availability, and integrity. She leads the audit team in drafting the audit management plan, program, and final report and determines the requirements of any postmortem actions. She effectively and efficiently collects evidence regarding assertions and conformity criteria. When appropriate, she will direct the evidence collection efforts of others.

Code of Ethics and Conduct

Auditors must subscribe to a formalized, universal code of ethics. For example, a code of ethics for holders of the Certified Information Systems Auditor (CISA) certification has been established by the Information Systems Audit and Control Association (ISACA).*

Codes of ethics are usually required by professional organizations and typically address the following areas of auditor conduct:

- Establishment and compliance with information systems controls, standards, and procedures
- Trustworthy service and reporting to stakeholders throughout the audit process
- Avoidance of participating in improper acts personally and professionally
- Confidentiality of observed and collected audit evidence
- Auditor independence
- Professional competence through participation in continuing professional development
- Due diligence when conducting audits and documentation of sufficient evidence supporting conclusions and recommendations
- Communication of audit results to appropriate stakeholders
- Education of stakeholders in the audit process to enhance understanding of systems and the audit process

Free and Independent

External auditing is often called independent auditing as qualified individuals outside the organization being audited do the audit. External auditors represent the interests of third-party stakeholders such as creditors, government agencies, and stockholders.

Internal auditors operate as independent appraisers established within an organization examining and evaluating activities as a service to the organization itself. Internal auditors perform a wide variety of tasks including assessing compliance with legal obligations, assessing operational efficiency, detecting and pursuing fraud and system vulnerabilities. External auditors are distinguished from internal auditors in that they represent outside constituents, while internal auditors represent the interests of the

---

* ISACA's code of ethics may be found at www.isaca.org.

organization. Their efforts are not necessarily exclusive, internal auditors often cooperate and assist external auditors in performing audits achieving efficiency and reducing audit fees. External auditors depend on the independence and competence of internal auditors in relying on their work. Independent internal auditors add value to business processes. Internal auditors often collect evidence throughout the fiscal period that can be used at year end to conduct more-efficient, less-costly external audits.

In auditing and all related matters, auditors must be free from personal and external impairments to their independence. Auditors must be organizationally independent and should maintain an independent attitude and appearance.

Experience Note Auditors must be mindful of engagements where they anticipate an offer of employment or other career-altering event while they are completing an audit. More than one auditor has been offered employment or promotion before their audit engagement was completed.

Auditors must consider not only if they are independent with their attitudes and beliefs, but also whether there is anything about their situation that might lead others to question their independence. All situations must be considered, as it is essential that auditors consider themselves to be impartial and that knowledgeable third parties consider them to be independent.

For auditors, there are essentially three very general types of impairments to independence: organizational, personal, and external. If any of these impairments affect their ability to do their work and report their findings impartially, the auditors must decline the engagement.

Organizational Impairments

Internal auditors may be affected by their job-placement within the structure of the business entity where they are employed. Auditors must be sufficiently removed from managerial, political, and organizational pressures ensuring that they can conduct their audits independently and report their findings, opinions, recommendations, and conclusions objectively. In the case of external auditors, they may be presumed to be independent of the audited entity if there are no personal, external, or organizational impairments.

External Impairments

There may be factors external to the auditor interfering with an auditor's ability to form objective and independent opinions, recommendations, and conclusions. There may be interference or undo influence that improperly limits or modifies the scope or methodology of an audit.

Personal Impairments

Regrettably, there are circumstances in which auditors may not be impartial or perceived by knowledgeable third parties as being impartial. It is important for an auditing unit to have policies and procedures in place to determine if auditors have any personal impairment affecting their ability to conduct audits. Although the responsibility rests on the shoulders of the individual auditors, audit managers and executives need to be alert for impairments affecting the judgment and performance of their audit staff. Auditors must be responsible for notifying the appropriate official about any personal impairment. Personal impairments include, but are not limited to the following:

- Official, professional, financial, or personal relationships that might cause the auditor to limit the methodology, extent of the audit inquiry, limit disclosure, or minimize or slant the audit findings in any way.

Experience Note An auditor was engaged to perform an audit and, after arriving to conduct his work, discovered the target of the audit was his brother's former commanding officer. This was the same person who had delivered a career-devastating performance appraisal to his brother. The auditor asked to be removed from the audit for personal impairment reasons.

- Preconceived ideas toward the audit or the organization on which the audit is going to be performed; any feelings that the auditor has that could taint audit results require that the auditor is removed from the audit engagement
- Previous responsibility for decision making or management authority that would affect current operations of the entity to be audited is considered biasing
- Personal biases (including business, political, religious, or social convictions) resulting from employment or loyalty to a particular group or organization
- Direct or indirect financial interest in the audited entity

Controls

Auditors are charged with evaluating the reliability and operational effectiveness of controls. Controls are broadly categorized as systems that prevent, detect, or correct policy violations, unlawful or abusive events.

The overarching purpose of controls is to reduce risks occurring in the organization adversely affecting critical assets. Preventive controls may be exemplified as instructions contained in a data input field where the user will not be allowed to incorrectly input data. Preventive controls reduce the probability of harmful events occurring in the first place. Detective controls are systems where errors in the system are identified. For example, a data input program identifies erroneous data entered into the system and notifies administrators.

Corrective controls are typified by a program using special instructions to correct data that has been altered during transmission between the data entry point and the storage facility. Auditors have the responsibility of ascertaining if controls are in place and functioning adequately. Their task extends to seeing that at least one control addresses each prohibited event in the context of it possibly occurring.

There are harmful events not addressed by controls, as they are not cost-effective. This is where the judgment of the auditor comes into play. If the cost of the control exceeds the value of the critical asset, it is not cost-effective to implement the control. It is not the auditor's responsibility to make this decision. The matter is reported and left to the determination of the senior managers. If the auditor has performed her task with professional due diligence and reported her findings adequately, the audit findings resolution rests with senior management. Auditors are within their authority to make operational recommendations but if these recommendations are not followed, the responsibility is shifted to senior management.

Even if a prohibited action or event is addressed by a control, auditors must determine if the control is functioning effectively and efficiently. Frankly, it is not

Exhibit 1   Management Functions

Senior management	Senior managers ensure the information system is well managed; responsible for overall profitability
Information systems managers	Have responsibility for planning, implementing, and control of all information technology systems; advises senior management in appropriate matters
Systems development managers	Responsible for information systems design, implementation, and maintenance
Data administration management	Responsible for planning, addressing, and related issues of the organization's data
Operations management	Responsible for planning and operation of day-to-day operation of the information technology systems

sufficient to merely identify a control; it must be verified that this control is functioning properly. This functional verification process is known as "testing." If an auditor does not make accurate and timely decisions, it is possible the risks to the organization will become unmanageable.

Considering the Universe in the Set of Subsystems

Auditors usually take the first step to understanding a complex system by dividing it into its subsystems. Subsystems are the basic components of the greater-system that perform a function needed by the business in achieving its goals. This process is commonly known as factoring. Basically, subsystems are defined by the function they perform. Auditors look first for the system functions that have been performed, and then factor those functions as they relate to the different subsystems. For example, an insurance company has as one of its primary functions the processing of claims. A subsystem of the claims processing system is the data entry from claims filed by policyholders and received by the company by mail. The fashion in which the auditor chooses to factor systems may vary according to the auditor and the system. However, auditors frequently factor systems in two basic forms, managerial functions and application functions. Exhibit 1 is an example of managerial functions performed in a system.

The second factor considered by auditors is application functions needed to ensure reliable data processing. Information technology systems can be considered from a business-process point of view. These steps are going to vary widely depending on the industry, location, and whether public or private sectors. Typically, organizations will have some form of the following application-related business processes such as sales, account collections, payroll and human resources management, acquisitions, accounts payable, inventory, warehousing, and financial accounting. In the organization, application systems are factored into subsystems related to the business process. Exhibit 2 is a table reflecting application subsystems.

Subsystem Interaction and Reliability

Auditors usually begin their analysis with the lowest level of subsystem activity attempting to identify all the different types of events that occur in these subsystems. Through this effort, the auditor begins to build a vision of what happens in the organization's business processes. Auditors must be mindful of two levels of prohibited

Exhibit 2   Application Functions

Outside boundary	Components that interface between the user and the information technology system
Data input	Components that capture, process, and enter commands and data into the information technology system
Processing	Components that form the architecture for decision making, ordering, classification, and organization of data
Database	Components that define, add, modify, and delete data
Communications	Components that transmit data between inside and outside information technology systems
Output	Components that collect and present data to users

events, prohibited events that are presently occurring and prohibited events that might occur in the future. In this vein, it is important for the auditor to focus her attention on the major process functions and how each subsystem supports the process's mission. One of the most important aspects of identifying permissible events in management subsystems is the determination of how a particular function should be performed within the subsystem. After the auditor performs research in the management subsystem, it should be clear how the management subsystems vary between circumstances in each relevant business unit.

A valid basis for identifying events in applications subsystems, attention must be placed on the transactions that occur as data is input to the subsystem. Events in an application subsystem cause changes in the application's state when the data is received in the form of input. More events take place as the application processes the transaction. Permitted events occur if the transaction and processing are authorized, complete, accurate, and not redundant. If anything otherwise occurs, a prohibited event occurred.

Risks Affecting Auditors

Information technology auditors must be concerned with four essential goals:

- Safeguarding critical assets
- Data integrity
- System effectiveness
- System efficiency

All auditors must consider that errors or irregularities will cause financial losses to the organization. Auditors collect evidence to achieve their goals, but there are inherent risks in these efforts. There is a risk that auditors may fail to detect actual or potential misstatements or process errors through the course of the audit. Experienced auditors approach and design their audit programs in such a fashion as they can fully articulate and document their efforts to minimize audit risks. If they fail to adequately address audit risk, audit results will not be valid and will not represent the true state of the system.

Assessing the levels of control risk associated within an audit segment, auditors consider the reliability of, and implementation of management and application controls. It is important to remember that management controls are fundamental controls in that they govern all application systems. In this hierarchical view, the absence of some or all management controls is a serious matter and reason for immediate action on the part of senior managers.

Once auditors have evaluated a management control and it is discovered that it spans the business unit's operation, it should function in relevant subsystem applications. For example, if an auditor reviews an adequate sample and discovers that an organization enforces high documentation standards of software development, it is likely these standards are enforced throughout the software development unit. Therefore, it is unlikely the auditor will review all documentation in all software development projects. Rather, she will select a representative amount ensuring that adequate documentation standards are observed thereby addressing any audit risk.

Experienced auditors estimate the level of detection risk they might achieve within a given set of audit procedures. They develop a good understanding of the probability these procedures have in detecting material loss or misstatements. It is very important that auditors choose audit procedures that provide the organization with an acceptable level of detection risk. In light of deadlines and limited resources, addressing audit risks must be focused on areas where they can deliver the highest payoffs.

Frequently, auditors cannot collect evidence to the extent they would prefer because they must spread their abilities among so many demands. They must be careful in the terms of where they apply their audit practice and how they interpret the evidence they collect. Throughout the audit, they must continuously make decisions based on their experience and training. It is their knowledge of audit methodology, material evidence collection and acceptable risks that guides them in making decisions as to what should be reported, to whom, and when.

Generally Accepted Government Auditing Standards (GAGAS)

According to GAGAS 4.21, auditors should obtain a sufficient understanding of internal control to plan the audit and determine the nature, timing, and extent of tests to be performed. According to GAGAS 4.21.1, auditors must consider the following when conducting an audit:

- The extent to which computer processing is used in each significant accounting application
- The complexity of the entity's computer operations
- The organizational structure of the computer processing activities
- The kinds and competence of available evidential matter in electronic and paper formats to achieve audit objectives

Audit Procedures

Auditors generally use five types of procedures in collecting evidence for their audits:

1. *Procedures in obtaining an understanding of system controls.* Auditors will make inquiries, inspections, and observations to obtain an understanding of the controls that exist, the design of the controls, and whether the controls have been implemented. Inquiries, inspections, and observations can be used in obtaining an understanding of the controls affecting the company's asset safeguards. It is important to remember the three critical asset pillars: human resources, data, and physical facilities.
2. *Tests of controls.* Auditors will make inquiries, inspections, observations, and reperformance of control procedures to determine whether controls are oper-

ating effectively and efficiently. These tests deal with whether controls have been designed and whether they are effectively operating. For example, the auditors will determine if the operations manager reviews system response times and what substantive steps she has taken to address unacceptable system response times.

3. *Transactions tests.* These tests are designed by the auditors to detect errors or irregularities in system transactions that affect the organization. For example, an auditor would verify that accounts payable transactions are correctly posted in the business' financial journals and ledgers. Auditors must evaluate the limits of transaction effectiveness and efficiency. For example, auditors sample system response times for individual transactions attempting to determine if they are within acceptable limits.

4. *Analytical review.* Tests of an analytical nature look at relationships between data items in identifying areas. For example, an auditor examines two years of inventory levels to determine if there are substantive levels of fluctuation requiring further investigation. Auditors may employ similar procedures in evaluating the effectiveness and efficiency of an organization's operation: These are comparisons between two related procedures concerning effectiveness and efficiency. For example, auditors will design a model where the amount of document processing by the system is evaluated and compared with the previous two years.

5. *Tests of system results.* These are tests of management's assertions regarding effectiveness and efficiency. For example, senior IT management may assert that system response time over the past two years is three seconds. Auditors will design a sampling technique where a survey of system users is made to determine the validity of this assertion for the applicable period.

Evidence Collection: Evidence Is not just Evidence

There are three techniques used by auditors in collecting evidence that allows them to understand an organization and its application systems:

- Make a judgment about the levels of inherent risk associated with an organization's management and its application systems.
- Obtain an understanding of an organization's controls sufficient to make a judgment about the types and levels of controls in the applications system.
- Design and perform tests of the existence and reliability of controls on which the organization can depend.

Auditors commonly use the evidence collecting techniques of interviews, questionnaires, and flowcharts to complete their audits.

Interviews

Auditors use interviews to obtain qualitative and quantitative information during their evidence collection efforts. Their objectives are to elicit candid, complete and honest answers from the interviewees. At this point, it is important to differentiate between interviews and interrogations. The reason behind an interrogation is to elicit information about some wrongdoing. Inherently, it is an intrusive method of obtaining information using accusatory language and demeanor. Interviewing is a technique eliciting information from someone who has more information than the interviewer who is requesting a response from a fellow professional. It is a kinder, gentler approach to eliciting information than an interrogation.

Auditors must conduct effective interviews, but first, they must understand the interviewee's motivation for answering the auditor's questions. Usually, the respondent's motivation to reply to questions asked during the interview is a function of how they perceive the interview to be a means of reaching their goals or something the respondent wants. For example, if a respondent sees the audit as a process in assisting them in attaining their performance goals, they will likely answer questions frankly and directly. However, if the interviewee views the auditor's interview as a process hindering their work, it is possible their answers will be evasive, incomplete, and even antagonistic. Wise auditors ask themselves, "What's in the interview for the respondent?"

Interview Preparation

Auditors may control the amount of interview stress by limiting the number of difficult questions asked. In this fashion, more stressful interviews should be shorter. Experienced auditors take sufficient steps to alleviate any respondent fears before the interview begins. Interviewers should be aware of the interviewee's desire to pursue topics that interest them if they perceive the auditor to be a responsible person. The auditor's task is one of establishing a professional rapport as quickly and effectively as possible. This is another one of those good judgment areas for auditors. Adept auditors clearly communicate the purpose and intent of the interview at the outset to show empathy, professional and responsible demeanor, and promote mutual trust and respect.

Experience Note Taking a moment to talk to the interviewee about something other than work is a technique that works well.

Doing Your Homework

Before beginning an interview, auditors should be mindful that the information they require is not available from anywhere else. Frankly, if interviewees perceive the interview is a waste of their time, they may become disinterested and less than forthright. Doing their homework involves auditors identifying those employees who can provide them with the best information on a particular topic. Organizational charts are usually the first source.

Another good source of information is the organization's line-of-authority documentation and brief job descriptions. Through senior managers, auditors may obtain an idea as to the division of business units and corresponding employee responsibilities. Additionally, senior managers may wish to make introductions between their employees and the auditors. Senior managers can be very helpful in locating facilities for performing interviews where the atmosphere is not disruptive and scheduling mutually convenient times.

Interview content must be thoroughly prepared before beginning the interview. Nothing will leave a respondent colder than an auditor who has no idea about what they want to do during the interview. Auditors should make a list of goals they wish to achieve during the interview. Some auditors go so far as having a script of questions they want to ask divided by specific topic area.

Auditors may use open or closed questions in their interviews. Closed questions merely require a yes or no answer. Open questions usually begin with the words:

how, why, when, who, or what. Open questions may be asked at the beginning of topic areas followed by closed questions where more clarification is needed. For example, "What are the types of controls you have over the entry of data from credit card applications?" This question might be followed by "Do you have manual or automated data input quality inspections?"

Interview Steps

At the outset of the interview, the auditor should state the purpose of the interview and confirm with the respondent that the interview corresponds to the arrangements made earlier. No one likes to be surprised in showing up for an interview just to find it is not the interview they were expecting. Here are a few steps to facilitate productive interviews:

- Take a moment to state the purpose of the interview. Auditors may wish deliver the goals of the interview at the beginning.
- Take another moment to briefly establish a personal rapport.
- Do not digress during the interview, stay on track.
- Mirror the voice, tonality, volume of speech, eye contact and rate of the respondent
- Ask if the auditor can take notes. Ask if they want copies of the auditor's interview notes.
- Be a good listener; wait for the respondent to reply.
- Allow the respondent time to think.
- Answer any questions from the interviewee.
- Keep it professional, avoid familiarity.
- Review responses for accuracy.
- Typical questions should cover at least the following basic topic areas:
    - What is the nature of your business? Briefly describe your business unit's operations.
    - How many employees are there? What are their duties? Where are their workstations and their respective locations?
    - What was the date of the last hardware/software inventory? Where is the location of the inventory documentation?
    - What was the date of the last risk analysis? Is there a risk management program? Where is the documentation? When was the last test of your disaster recovery/business resumption plan?
    - Provide documentation for these business processes:
        - ☐ Policies, procedures, standards
        - ☐ Human resources, data and facilities safeguards
        - ☐ Last audit documentation
        - ☐ Legal and regulatory issues
        - ☐ Human resources issues
        - ☐ Employee training and continuing education
        - ☐ Security awareness program
        - ☐ Business unit or organizational issues

Interviewing for Evidence of Controls

Interviews can be very useful in obtaining evidence of the existence of controls and the procedures. By way of widely accepted measures, there are already formulated audit programs to address internal controls and their implementation. Examples of these programs are ISO 17799, available at www.iso.ch and COBIT™ (Control Objectives for Information and related Technology) and ISACA, available at www.isaca.org. These programs attempt to provide generally accepted internal control guidance for auditors and are worth reviewing before beginning an IT audit engagement.

The object of the auditor's employee interview is to determine the present condition of the system and compare this condition with the audit program criteria. In the pursuit of interviews, the auditor should ask employees for evidence of the controls in the form of questions:

- May I see it?
- Please show me how you _____.
- May I observe you working?
- How do you perform the process of _____?
- Is it possible for you to delete transaction logs?
- Please show me if you can do this _____ operation.

An experienced auditor will interview several employees having similar jobs in order to compare results and decide whether policies and procedures are being practiced or not.

Interview Analysis

As soon as possible after the interview, the auditor should prepare a written report of the interview from the notes taken. Be certain to separate fact from inference and speculation.

Facts are those things that the interviewee has heard, seen, or in which she has materially participated. They know the facts because they were there. Inference is a logical extension of the interviewee's mind — for example, if a cat and a mouse were placed in a box and the top closed and placed where it is under constant observation. A few minutes later the box is opened; the mouse is discovered to be gone. It is inferred that the cat ate the mouse even though no one actually observed it. Speculation is merely that the interviewee is guessing about something. For example, if there is a sudden increase in system processing time and the interviewee indicates the reason is attributable to increased input error rates, but cannot offer any observation or other substantive proof, then the response is speculative.

Do not discount the value of speculation. Wise auditors give speculation due consideration depending on the credibility, experience, and training of the interviewee. Many experienced auditors include speculation at the end of their interview report accompanied by proper qualifications.

Interview notes and written reports should be retained as permanent parts of the auditors' work papers. Senior managers should not be surprised when knowledgeable attorneys or investigators request audit interview notes and reports as legal processes. They are looking for evidence that the audit work papers can reconstruct audit events.

Experience Note In some cases, the destruction or failure to retain auditor work papers is a violation of law and regulation, depending on the industry. In other cases, destroying work papers after being notified of a pending investigation or legal action is running the risk of contempt of court.

Questionnaires

Auditors may use written questionnaires as effective means to collect evidence. Responses obtained to questions asked on questionnaires indicate the presence or absence of controls or the incorrect application of controls. They can elicit users' comments about the effectiveness and efficiency of a system or subsystems. There are basically three major aspects of their design:

1. Design of questions
2. Design of responses
3. Design of layout and structure

The primary focus on questionnaire design is the crafting of questions to ensure the respondents understand the facts required. It is not unreasonable that some questions are redundant ensuring the respondents understand which facts are being requested. Questions need to be self-explanatory. If the question asks about input field limits, then it is expected the anticipated respondent already knows what input field limits are and when they apply. Here are a few questionnaire best practices:

- Make certain the questions are specific. Rather than ask if input fields are controlled, ask which applications examine input field correctness.
- Use simple, plain language.
- Avoid technical jargon.
- Avoid abbreviations; use specific language instead.
- Avoid ambiguous language.
- Avoid leading questions. Leading questions suggest answers that respondents should reply. For example, "Do employees use the human resources system interface?" A much better question is phrased as, "How is human resources information obtained online, and by whom?"
- Avoid hypothetical questions. Stick to the facts. Do not ask questions based on assumptions. For example, "How often would you use the human resources system in a month's time?" This presupposes that the respondent knows about the human resources system and uses it monthly.
- Avoid questions that require extensive and accurate recall. "How many times did you use the human resources system during the past two months?" This is a question that cannot be easily answered. Instead, ask the respondent if he/she keeps a record of their use of a particular system.
- If the questionnaire has a scale of responses, make certain they are applicable to the topic. If the questionnaire asks the location of fire extinguishers in the warehouse, then ask if fire extinguishers are present, how many are present, and their locations. Make certain the questionnaire is directed to the right employees. Asking the finance unit questions about the location of fire extinguishers in the warehouse is not going to produce relevant answers.

The layout and structure of a questionnaire affect its accuracy. If the questionnaire is mailed, its layout and structure will likely affect the response rate. Its objective is to be well-received with clear, simple, logical, and appealing construction. The length of a questionnaire also affects the success of completion. If questions and questionnaires are too long, respondents lose interest and provide answers that may not accurately reflect their observations. Care must be taken to craft the flow of questions through the questionnaire. At the beginning, general questions should be asked placing little stress on the respondent with more difficult questions placed toward the middle or end of the topic areas.

Flowcharts

Control flowcharts illustrate that controls exist in a system and where these they are located in the system. There are basically three purposes of flowcharts for auditing purposes:

1. *Comprehensive.* The construction of this type of flowchart highlights areas where auditors do not have a thorough understanding of either the system or the controls located in the system.
2. *Evaluation.* Auditors use control flowcharts to recognize patterns that show control strengths or weaknesses.
3. *Communication.* Auditors may use control flowcharts to communicate their understanding of the target system and its related controls to other parties.

Experience Note Auditors ask respondents for their flowcharts before creating their own. It is likely most business units already have control flowcharts.

Types of Flowcharts

There are many different types of flowcharts that can be crafted. There are flowcharts for analysts, designers, engineers, managers, or programmers detailing individual understanding.

Document flowcharts have the purpose of showing existing controls over document-flow through the components of a system. These flowcharts are typified by their vertical structure. The chart is read from left to right and documents the flow of documents through the various business units. An example of document flowchart is shown in Exhibit 3.

The second popular type of flowchart is the data flowchart. This diagram has the purpose of showing the controls governing data flows in the system. Data flowcharts are used primarily to show the channels that data is transmitted through the system rather than how controls flow. It is important to note that data flowcharts are not particularly useful in gaining an understanding of controls placed in the physical or resource level of a system. In other words, data flowcharts do not illustrate controls in prevention of detection of errors (Exhibit 4).

System flowcharts are the third type of illustration showing the controls located at the physical or resource level. System flowcharts show the flow of data to and through the major components of a system such as, data entry, programs, storage media, processors, and communication networks. These types of flowcharts demonstrate how the controls are placed to ensure the correct functioning of the named components (Exhibit 5).

The fourth type of flowchart, the program flowchart, shows the controls placed internally to a program within the system. For example, illustrating the process modules within a program aids the auditor in gaining an understanding of the means by which data integrity is preserved during processing (Exhibit 6).

Experience Note Unless there is some very pressing reason to create flowcharts, they are very time consuming and frequently are not understood or appreciated by the intended audience. Think twice about spending the time before doing them.

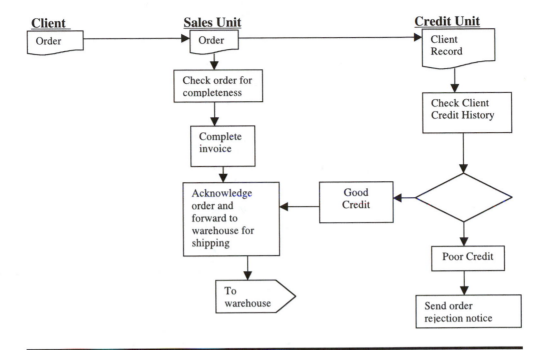

Exhibit 3   Document Flowchart

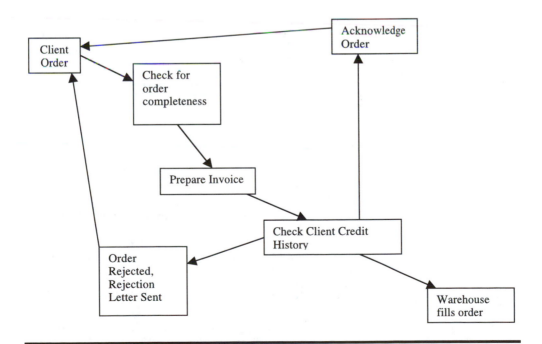

Exhibit 4   Data Flowchart

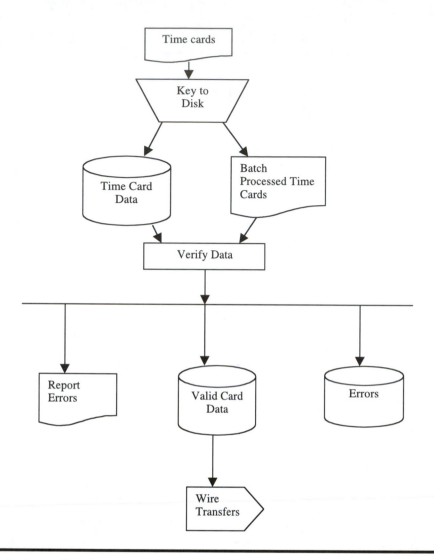

Exhibit 5   System Flowchart

Taking Care of the Stakeholders

Although this practice is not really part of the collection of evidence, it is relevant. In any audit process, no one likes surprises. Experienced auditors will initiate and foster dialogues with stakeholders during the audit. It is unwise for auditors to play "Gotcha" with audit results, besides most folks lose their sense of humor resulting from this behavior.

Experience Note A "stakeholder" is someone who has a professional interest in the audit and its outcome.

Here are a few best practices in the care and feeding of stakeholders:

■ Keep audit stakeholders briefed during the audit process. Keep them briefed of any serious negative trends or indications of fraud or abuse. Ensure that verbal briefings reflect exactly the same terminology that is going to be found

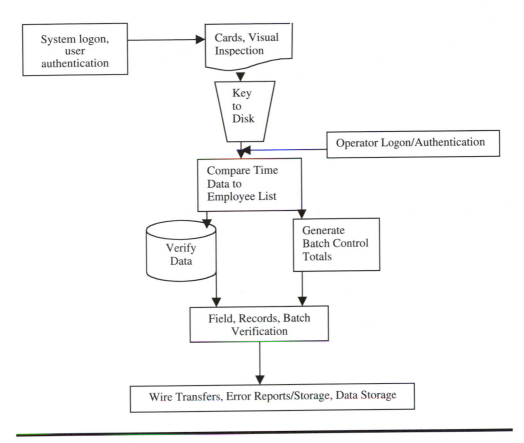

Exhibit 6   Program Flowchart

in the audit report. Discrepancies of this nature cast serious doubts on auditor credibility.

- Keep the audit manager briefed regularly throughout the audit process.
- Reports should not be overly brief nor should they be overly verbose. They should be concise and supported by brief and relevant narratives.
- Auditors should feel they have the independence to stray from the audit program, but a logical explanation is necessary if they spend significant time outside the formal program.

Audit Management Planning

Audit management planning is the initial step for an audit. This process defines the understanding of the objectives to be accomplished by the audit, assigning the appropriate number of trained employees, obtaining the background information, understanding the legal obligations, performing analytical review procedures, and identifying the areas of risk in the audit. Here are the major steps of an IT audit:

- Preliminary audit work
- Obtain understanding of control structure
- Assess control risks
- Controls testing
- Form audit opinion and issue report

Audit Risk

Auditors must make judgments on the acceptable levels of audit risk. It is important to remember that the levels of risk will vary across the different segments of the audit, as there are systems that are more susceptible to errors, ineffectiveness, inefficiencies, and fraud.

Experience Note   As unpopular as it is to say, there is a school of thought that equates audit "irregularities" with fraud. Fraud is when a person lies to obtain money or something of value and obtains it.

An example of different types of risks associated with different segments of the audit, systems involving handling of cash are very susceptible to theft, where data processing systems are usually susceptible to inefficient resource allocation. In planning to manage audits, the most difficult judgment is the level of acceptable risk relevant to each audit segment. It is for this reason that auditors should be knowledgeable and experienced persons. Auditors must understand the control environment and the associated risks by examining management and application controls already in place. For example, when auditors review system development activities, they are seeking to understand the controls that are associated with these tasks.

They attempt to understand the business processes, including components such as human expertise, information technology, communications, management controls and application controls so they can assess related vulnerabilities and attendant risks. By understanding processes, components, behavior, and intended results, auditors can provide appropriate safeguard recommendations, if any apply.

Planning the Audit

In order to conduct an audit properly, a comprehensive audit management plan must be crafted.

Experience Note   If you do not plan, you are planning to fail.

The audit management plan should be action oriented, by listing the primary objectives to be performed. It should be tailored to the specific targeted business unit or division.

In drafting the audit management plan, a thorough review must be made of the organization's policies, with particular attention paid to risk management activities.

Experience Note   There is some confusing terminology that should be clarified here. The purpose of integrated critical incident management is the continuation of profitable operations before business-harmful events happen. It is a wise business decision to take a proactive approach to critical incident management so risk management policies and procedures are designed and implemented. In essence, risk management is a series of steps where critical assets, including human resources, data, and facilities required to maintain profitability are identified and prioritized. Critical asset threats and their frequency, vulnerabilities, and existing safeguards are identified. In the event of a critical incident, meaning an incident affecting critical assets and profitability occurs, the organization has disaster recovery procedures in place to recover critical assets. As soon as critical assets are recovered, the process of planned business resumption takes place. In this phase, basically the business is returned to normal operating stature.

In the crafting, development, and implementation of policies, procedures, and standards, the organization is providing a process governing the activities of its employees consistent with the particular organization's goals and objectives. In many cases there are laws, regulations, and requirements affecting how the organization must conduct all or part of their business processes. Risk management is an integral part of the policy and procedure implementation. Auditing is basically an impartial review and investigation into the application of the organization's policies, procedures, and standards.

In crafting the audit management plan, the organization's strategic plan and objectives should be reviewed. This is essentially the basic guiding documentation for the organization. Depending on the business' units that are being audited, their applicable policies, procedures, and standards should be carefully reviewed. Job descriptions, organizational charts, lines of reporting, lines of authority, and chains of command should be made part of the information cache used to form the basis of the audit management plan.

In some business environments, audit management planning requires the auditors to conduct a preliminary survey through questionnaires to establish the appropriate scope addressing relevant business risks, develop the audit management plan, and direct auditor activities within the audit program. Often senior audit managers prepare questionnaires, also known as interrogatories, and send them to appropriate senior managers of the audit target. When completed, these questionnaires will provide the auditors with comprehensive visibility into the processes of the business unit.

These questionnaires may help auditors identify critical areas on which they need to focus their attention rather than taking a scattered, "shotgun" approach. As part of this preliminary questionnaire survey, auditors should review systems and processes to identify key controls already in place.

General questions that should be asked in preparing audit management plan questionnaires include but not limited to:

- What are the critical issues regarding this business unit's operation?
- What are the critical assets of this business unit?
- What are the critical management functions?
- What are the critical applications?
- Does this business unit process sensitive data?
- What are the risks to the business unit?
- What substantive steps have been taken to address these risks?
- What processes are least tested in the unit's business unit's daily operations? For example, if the business unit suffers from frequent power-outages and uses emergency power sources, including uninterruptible power sources and emergency generators, to restore operations, then power recovery requirements are likely to be well-formulated and tested. However, in the case of a complete disaster recovery plan, it may not be tested, and in fact, may not exist at all. The audit management plan should be the governing document for the "biggest bang for the buck."

Another valuable source in the development of an audit management plan is the review of previously performed audit reports. Many times these documents will identify potential weaknesses that should have been corrected or addressed earlier. The audit management plan is merely that, an activity plan. It should address those areas to be evaluated, and not too much more. Audit programs are different from audit plans in that they are comprehensive documents delving into the audit's "nuts and bolts."

Exhibit 7   Audit Management Plan for Firewall Administration Unit

Audit Step

Planning
1   Discuss nature and scope of audit with key senior personnel
2   Discuss audit requirements with senior managers
3   Assemble required audit staff and build team
4   Draft comprehensive audit program
5   Draft initial budget

Reporting
1   Hold opening meeting with appropriate personnel at initiation of audit
2   Use standard audit reports format including compilation of audit findings and
      recommendations
3   Hold closing meeting with key managers to review draft of final audit report
4   Identify key senior managers in the event of reporting irregularities before audit conclusion

Preliminary Audit Steps
1   Identify key employee contacts for audit
2   Obtain appropriate organization and business unit documentation including
      A   Strategic business plans
      B   Relevant policies, procedures, and standards for firewall administration unit
      C   Relevant documentation to gain an understanding of the operations of the firewall
            administration unit

Audit Procedures
1   Understand unit's business practices and compare with organization's policies, practices,
      and standards
2   Understand and document business process flows
3   Interview pertinent employees in firewall administration unit to gain an understanding of
      their functions, risks, and other relevant issues

Testing
1   Testing will be performed to increase auditor's understanding of the firewall administration
      unit's function and activities
2   Testing will increase the auditor's understanding of managerial and application controls
3   Auditor will test if relevant controls are operating correctly and consistently
4   Auditor will test metrics to manage firewall administration
5   Auditor will test the correct design, development, and implementation of firewall
      administration

Experience Note   Audit management plans are considered part of the auditor's work
         papers and must be retained. Their absence is considered a lack of professional
         due diligence or even evidence destruction.

   Exhibit 7 is a brief example of an audit management plan.

Audit Programs

Audit programs are guides specifically directing auditors' activities.

Experience Note Although there are procedures for auditing, none are so restrictive that auditors cannot review areas outside the audit program with sufficient logical justification. Auditors have found fraud by going outside their audit program, looking in the company parking lot and asking why the accounts payable clerk is driving an expensive luxury car.

The audit program is a comprehensive, detailed document addressing the relevant audit areas, and in some cases, the methodology of the audit. It is an action-oriented document, with much more detail than the audit plan. An audit program has the following purposes:

- Provides detailed communications to the intended recipients and audit team members of the audit objectives
- Facilitates direction, scope, and control over the audit process; directs team members having specialized skills and knowledge to specific areas
- Delivers a record of the audit process
- Directs the collection of evidence in specific areas
- Suggests the sampling methodology to be used in specific audit areas
- Documents the professional due diligence of the audit process, including planning, fieldwork, and supervision
- Becomes included in the auditors' work papers and is thereby maintained for future review
- In some cases, it documents specific audit assignments

Standard Audit Programs

There are several standard security assessment or audit programs. There are certain advantages for auditors to use one of the standard audit programs:

- They usually have a history of successful engagements and results.
- They frequently have been adopted by industries as governing instruments.
- They may save a significant amount of auditor resources by suggesting business operations to be tested.

One of the most comprehensive standard information technology programs is the COBIT™ program. The Information Systems Audit and Control Association (ISACA, www.isaca.org) developed this program. It is a generally applicable and accepted standard for information and information technology control. COBIT is fully adaptable and applicable for enterprise-level and smaller organization information technology areas. It starts from a control framework, it is management oriented, and it is based on critical review of tasks and activities regarding business operations.

COBIT deals with three levels:

1. *Domain.* This is a natural grouping of processes, often matching an organizational domain of responsibility.
2. *Processes.* This is a series of jointed activities with natural breaks.
3. *Activities.* Actions needed to achieve a measurable result. Activities have a life cycle where tasks are discreet.

Control objectives domains are divided into four areas:

1. Planning and organization
2. Acquisition and implementation
3. Delivery and support
4. Monitoring

One of the more-popular security guidance standards is BS 7799, a British Standard Institute program publication. It was submitted to the International Standards Organization who published it as the *Code of Practice for Information Security Management* and was subsequently published by ISO under the number 17799 in 2000.*
The stated purpose of 17799:2000 is to

> give recommendations for information security management for use by those who are responsible for initiating, implementing or maintaining security in their organization. It is intended to provide a common basis for developing organizational security standards and effective security management practice and to provide confidence in inter-organizational dealings.

ISO 17799 is a general organizational management and best practices guide intended to deliver secure system operations. It is not applicable to all organizations and does not attempt to address all required internal controls. It generally covers the following areas:

- Policies
- Security architecture
- Information controls
- Human resources
- Physical security matters
- Access control
- Business continuity procedures

The United States government through the National Institute for Standards and Technology (NIST, www.nist.gov) has several high-quality guidance publications relevant to security practices in information technology systems:

- Generally Accepted Principles and Practices for Security Information Technology Systems
- Security Issues in the Database Language SQL
- Computer Security
- Guidelines for Automatic Data Processing Physical Security and Risk Management
- Guide for Developing Security Plans for Information Technology Systems
- Engineering Principles for Information Technology Security

These U.S. government documents are general and high-level documents adaptable to most organizational structures and functions. They can provide auditors with a variety of domains that should be considered when developing audit plans and programs.

---

* Available at www.iso.ch.

Developing Your Audit Program

Developing proprietary audit programs is one of the challenges facing audit managers. There are several sources that should influence the program that will be designed by the audit manager and her team. Logically, the first place to begin is with the organization's risk management program. Attention should be paid to the structure and details encompassed in this document. Audit managers crafting their audit plan should see if the organization's critical assets have been identified, prioritized, and classified relative to their sensitivity and their criticality. They should also look to see if the organization has detailed relevant threats, their likelihood of occurrence, and systems vulnerabilities with accompanying safeguards.

Experience Note When critical asset safeguards are considered, it is important to place them in the context of cost/benefit. Do not protect junk!

It is very likely that pursuant to the risk management program, critical assets were divided into relevant pillars such as human resources, data, and physical facilities. The structure of the risk program may easily serve as one of the supporting documents of the audit program.

Audit managers and their teams are going to thoroughly review the organization's policies, procedures, and standards ascertaining if they address potential risks facing the business. From their review, the audit team will design their audit program. The program will have divided the organization's policies, procedures, and standards according to their relevance to the audit. It will also have determined the applicability of any laws and regulations and test to ascertain if they are being observed by the organization.

The organization's policies and procedures should be broken into the basic elements, and from there the audit program is drafted. For example, the organization has a policy governing the method that packet screen firewalls are going to be deployed on the network's perimeter and this policy states that there is an access control list for permissible computer traffic. The auditors should review this policy to determine the specific elements of permissible traffic. They should query the systems administrators to determine the appropriate protocols, e.g., FTP, POP3, DNS, etc. Audit managers will design their audit program to include sampling and testing those policies and relevant documentation. Included in the audit program will be all facets of firewall operation, development under the SDLC, and effectiveness. Connected to the firewall audit is a review of all aspects surrounding the management, selection, training, and deployment of firewall administrators.

Designing the audit program from the organization's operations, policies, procedures, and standards is the most effective means of completing a meaningful audit; however, it is probably the most time consuming. This means of crafting an audit program can be tedious and challenging but the resulting program, if skillfully done, will likely result in an on-target and highly effective audit report.

It is prudent for auditors to review and know the target's business operations, hardware, operating systems and applications so they may determine if updating and change management controls have been implemented in a timely and correct fashion.

Gaps, meaning areas of risk not addressed by existing policies and procedures, or policies and procedures that go unnoticed by employees, must be reported as findings in the audit report. For this reason it is imperative that the audit team be composed of broadly experienced individuals that will recognize and credibly articulate their findings.

Useful Internet Web Sites

Fruitful areas for drafting audit programs may be found at these Web sites:

> www.cert.org
> www.sans.org
> www.cve.mitre.org
> http://icat.nist.gov
> http://www.securityfocus.com

These sites present the most-common system vulnerabilities and exploits (CVEs). Their purpose is the orientation of system managers and auditors in determining if their systems contain common security flaws and provide means addressing them. There are comprehensive lists, published by the above institutions, detailing commonly occurring system vulnerabilities. Some are named the "Ten Most Critical Vulnerabilities" or the "Twenty Most Critical Vulnerabilities." Regardless, they list the most commonly found vulnerabilities based primarily on surveyed systems administrators, security officers, or auditors. Many businesses use their lists to prioritize their efforts so the most commonly occurring risks are addressed first. They provide a basis of commonly exploitable system flaws allowing auditors to direct their efforts in these areas first with the prevailing logic being that these vulnerabilities comprise the majority of successful system attacks.

Common Attacks

Most attackers are opportunists who take advantage of the easiest and most convenient attack route. Commonly, attackers attempt to gain access through the best-known system flaws with readily available tools from the Internet. Because they count on organizations failing to address their system risks, attackers identify flawed systems and attack them using commonly known exploits. It is for these reasons that auditors may wish to pay particular attention to these vulnerability lists as the first place to concentrate their efforts.

Flawed Systems

There are many reasons for flawed systems. Auditors should be aware that some operating systems and applications were not initially designed as production software. Such was the case with UNIX. Over the past twenty years, it has been pinched, tweaked, and patched until we have the platform we have today. After all this development, you would naturally think UNIX and its accompanying applications are perfect. No, they're not.

Other programs are rushed to market with such speed; there was insufficient time to look at software vulnerabilities that programmers were not able to address. Another important fact is that approximately two million hosts are added to the Internet each month. Many of them do not have system administrators, auditors, and other support staffing, ensuring system security. For the most part, many administrators have become victims of the directive of "keep the system up, regardless of what it takes."

Because many businesses are understaffed and currently shorthanded, they get around to crafting and enforcing policies, risk management, and audits when they have the time. The responsible persons were too busy doing other things to pay attention to default configuration vulnerabilities.

Auditing Common Systems Vulnerabilities

Buffer Overflows

During 1996, a series of articles about buffer overflows and the havoc they can create was published, changing application security forever. One such article authored by Aleph One, "Smashing the Stack for Fun and Profit," detailed the profound effects of buffer overflows on poor programming practices.*

In essence, buffer overflows occur when an attacker or other malicious user stuffs more data into a buffer than is allocated. For the technically inclined, this type of overflow input is generally associated with C programming language functions similar to *strcpy ()*, *strcat ()*, and *sprintf ()*. These are merely examples as there are many other types of exploitable functions. Buffer overflows cause a segmentation violation to occur. This type of input can be exploited to gain access to the target system. Buffer overflows are not limited to remote attacks, they can also occur from within the local network.

In this example, the UNIX-based application, *Sendmail,* will be used. Suppose there is a fixed-length buffer of 255 bytes. This buffer defines the amount of data that can be stored as input to the VRFY command. In this example, the *Sendmail* application will be running at Root. What is the result if an attacker connects to the *Sendmail* application and sends a block of data consisting of 10,000 "V"s to the VRFY command rather than the expected user name? The system will crash, essentially causing a denial-of-service attack, as the VRFY buffer is overrun because it is only designed to expect an input of not more than 255 bytes of user input. If the attacker inputs a specific code that overflows the buffer and executes the command */bin/sh,* the attacker could reach root access.

When the attack is executed by the system, a special assembly code known as *egg* is sent to the VRFY command as part of the string used to overflow the buffer. On being overrun, the attacker can set the return address of the offending function allowing the alteration of the program flow. Instead of the function returning to its proper memory location, the attacker executes the code that was sent included as part of the buffer overflow data that will run with root privileges.

It is important to note that buffer overflow codes are specific to systems' architecture and operating systems. For example, a buffer overflow targeting a BSD UNIX, based on an Intel processor will not be effective on a Solaris operating system running on a SPARC processor. From this brief explanation, auditors can see that buffer overflows are extremely dangerous and are the bane of most system administrators. For the most part, attackers must be fairly talented to create a workable *egg*; however, most system-dependent *eggs* have been discovered and programmed, and are available from attacker Web sites on the Internet.**

Many common system vulnerability lists have a description of the exploit, the systems on which it is effective, and the CVE (Common Vulnerability and Exposure) number.***

---

* This article is available at www.2600.net/phrack/p49-14.html.

** Another reference paper detailing the effects of buffer overflow attacks written by "Dildog," titled "The Tao of Windows," can be found at www.cultdeadcow.com.

***CVE numbers can be referenced for explanation at www.cve.mitre.org.

In the Domain Name Server, DNS, known as BIND, Berkley Internet Domain, there are security vulnerabilities in older versions prior to 8.2.2 with patch 5. Good reason for auditors to look at the application update and change policy of the organization, right? Older and unpatched BIND versions can be corrupted by attackers that allow them to redirect Internet traffic to sites not of the owner's choosing. Poorly configured BIND can allow attackers to download all the names, operating systems, and IP addresses of the organization's internal network. With this knowledge, attackers can search for specific tools targeting machines in your network to gain unauthorized access to your systems.

CGI Scripting

Common Gateway Interface (CGI) is the means by which Web page developers collect and display your input to a Web-based form. CGI scripts are frequently written in PERL (Practical Extraction and Report Language) and uploaded to the CGI-BIN directory located on the Web server. In some cases, developers and vendors have distributed these scripts with vulnerabilities already in them.

CGI scripts can be written in almost any standard input programming language, but PERL is the most common. It is important to note that for each executed CGI script there is a new process started that will be terminated when the CGI has finished. Usually data is sent to the server to be executed or manipulated, and is returned to the user in the form of HTML or images.

By way of review, CGI processing generally follows this way: The user accesses a Web page that requests user-input. After making the input, the user clicks the Send button and sends the data to the Web server for processing. The server forwards the data to the CGI application, sometimes called the CGI script, as these are small programs, where the user-input is processed. After processing the data, it is returned to the server and the server returns the data to the user. It can be seen the potential for vulnerabilities exist with the user-input data. CGI is used to perform functions that normal Web pages cannot. For example, CGIs manage databases of user accounts, calculations, form-input data processing, etc. There are easily available CGI scripts available as part of Web servers, downloaded from CGI Web sites, or developers may write their own.

Before placing a Web server into a production environment, developers should make certain the CGI code has been thoroughly reviewed by quality control managers and auditors for programming errors. It is imperative that CGI scripts are tested thoroughly and retested before being allowed into a production environment. It is equally important that CGI scripts have delimited input in that only expected input and input length are permitted, denying all other types of input.

Attackers have discovered they can corrupt these scripts and cause them to do things they were not intended to do. For example, it is possible for attackers to access collected credit card numbers by corrupting the CGI scripts. It is also possible for attackers to gain root access to the Web server and deface your E-commerce site. If you do not have any production need for CGI scripts, remove them from your system.

In keeping with policy and procedures, auditors should note that all unnecessary services should be disabled or removed thereby reducing the number of vulnerabilities. Also, ensure the Web server software is updated and documented regularly. This will go a long way to minimizing unauthorized intrusions.

Remote Procedure Calls

RPC allows a computer to launch and run a program on another computer. Many client-server architectures depend on this functionality. Those systems that are most frequently affected by RPC vulnerabilities are those based on the UNIX platform, such as Linux, Solaris, AIX, HP-UX, and IRIX. It is important to remember from an auditing perspective that RPC vulnerabilities can be exploited by buffer overflows resulting in the attacker being granted root privileges. The best means to deal with RPC vulnerabilities is to update the operating system's security patches. And, if RPC functionality is not necessary for system functionality, disable or remove it.

Default installations of operating systems and applications frequently use installation scripts to facilitate the installation of the software. In many cases, most of the program's functions are enabled with the least amount of interaction from the installer. Installation scripts usually install more features than the majority of users need. Although this installation action is convenient for users, it deposits potentially dangerous vulnerabilities. They become more serious, as administrators and managers do not actively update software components. For example, it is common for some operating systems and applications to install default passwords for many of their features. If these features or default passwords are not disabled or removed, they provide an easily accessible entry-point for the attacker. In addition, many users do not realize the default features that have been installed. Left unattended, these services provide ready access to attackers both inside and outside the organization. Likewise, it is important that all software is updated on a regular basis, allowing for patches and newer versions to address current vulnerabilities. Change control, management, and documentation is not just a drill. It is a matter of system survivability.

Experience Note The fewer open ports and services available on a system, the fewer the opportunities for system vulnerabilities.

Software installers must have standard installation procedures mandating the removal or disabling of unnecessary features and updating software. It is important these installation procedures are written and disseminated to all employees authorized to install software and hardware. Auditors must review the software installation process, making certain all unnecessary features, passwords, and services are removed or disabled, and that all software is regularly updated and those updates are appropriately documented.

Weak, default, or missing passwords is another common systems failing. Most of today's systems are configured to use passwords as the first, and many times, the only line of access restriction. User identification is relatively easy to acquire, and regrettably many business have unauthorized dial-up access that bypass firewall protections.

A more glaring problem is the account that does not have any password protection. As a matter of business sense, all weak passwords, accounts without passwords, and default passwords must be removed from the system or disabled. System attackers usually look for applications and accounts with easy password access. They have downloaded utilities that attack password accounts and are successful more often than not when poor password policies and procedures exist. Auditors should carefully review the company's password and software installation policies and procedures. Testing passwords is easily accomplished by using commercial software solutions available from vendors such as www.accessdata.com.

It is not a matter of *if* a critical incident will happen; it is only a matter of *when*. Count on it, it will happen, and it will happen at the worst possible moment. It is

Murphy's Law! Recovery from critical incidents requires accurate, reliable, easily accessible backups and tested methods of restoring data. It is a common mistake for organizations to make frequent backups of their data, but never take the time to verify that the backed-up data is viable or that their recovery and business restoration procedures will actually work under the worst possible conditions.

One of the secondary faults of backed-up data is that of physical security and accessibility. More than one security administrator has lost sleep after discovering an attacker has entered the company's system and destroyed sensitive information. Because the backed-up data was stored on a server within the system, the attacker destroyed those files also.

Auditors must ascertain if a system is vulnerable in the face of critical incidents using the simple work paper shown in Exhibit 8.

Exhibit 8   Backup and Data Recovery Audit Program

Backup and Data Recovery

Objectives of this audit segment are to ascertain adequacy of policies, practices, and standards in management and application controls relevant to the backup and recovery activities of the XYZ Corporation's Information Technology Unit, for the period xx/xx/xx to xx/xx/xx.
Overarching principles in these audit objectives are confidentiality, integrity, and availability of critical information resources.

1   Obtain and review organization chart and related job descriptions and responsibilities for Information Technology Unit
2   Verify critical functions and if these job functions follow principles of least privilege and separation of duties
3   Obtain and review documents containing relevant policies, procedures, and standards
4   Test appropriate documents to determine if the backup and recovery policies, procedures, and standards are in compliance with current legal and regulatory requirements
5   Observe and document where critical backup files are stored
6   Determine and document if the backup media has sufficient shelf life to store data
7   Determine and document security measures for backup media
8   Verify and document if backup media are stored in low-fire-hazard containers
9   Verify and document the availability of backup media to XYZ Corporation
10 Test and document accuracy of backup media by performing exercise requiring backed-up data
11 Verify and document test time requirements in obtaining and restoring data in backup media
12 Test document procedures requiring information to be backed up
13 Determine and document if procedures for identifying critical data and their retention periods are appropriate
14 Verify and document qualifications of employee responsible for administration of backed-up data
15 Determine and document if there are single points of failure in the XYZ Corporation's information backup and restoration system
16 Obtain and test samples for accuracy of original information with the backed-up information
17 Observe and document employee activities relative to information backup and restoration
18 Identify and document senior manager responsible for employee compliance with backup and recovery procedures
19 Identify and document ownership of backup media
20 Identify and observe methods by which backup and restoration takes place

The more open ports you have listening with services on your system, the greater number of attackers that will try to connect and break into your system. If a system feature or service is not absolutely essential, disable or remove it. The IT world would be much safer if this policy were practiced.

Auditors can scan 65,535 TCP and UDP system ports by using a port scanner utility. The most popular and configurable scanner is Nmap.* There are other port scanners that work as well, but it is probably the most powerful port-scanning tool currently available. Instructions on downloading, installing, configuration, and help files are available at the Web sites. Running Nmap does essentially three things:

1. It will ping a number of hosts to determine if they are alive.
2. It will portscan hosts to determine which services are listening.
3. It will attempt to identify the host's operating system.

Running a scanning utility will show the auditor the specific system ports and services that are open on the target system. Once done, the auditor compares the list with the allowed services in the organization's policies and procedures. Any discrepancies should be immediately investigated and reported.

On UNIX systems, most services are controlled by *inetd* and the corresponding system configuration file, *inetd.conf*. *Inetd.conf* lists the services listening on any given port, and this configuration tool can be used to close unneeded ports. If a service in the *inetd.conf* has been removed, restarting the system stops the port from being opened. There are other services started in */etc/rc* or */etc/rc.local*. Consult your system's documentation about disabling these scripts as UNIX features vary between versions. In the case of Windows NT products, consult with the Window NT system's documentation about disabling or removing services on open ports.

Incomplete or missing logging is a frequent system fault. When systems are attacked, your saving grace is the existence and completeness of logs. Without logs, you will have no idea what happened in your compromised system and, worse yet, no one will know when the system became corrupted, so no one will know how far in the past data and applications will need to be restored. It is possible that the attacker still has access to the system. Logging must be done on all critical systems. It is highly recommended that logs are written to Write Once Read Many, WORM, media such as CD-Rs. Logs should be sent to remote systems making their compromise that much harder. Logs should be saved and backed up in the same fashion as other valuable data. Auditors should review logs in determining if unacceptable behavior has taken place. For example, if an employee has the responsibility for accounts payable, why would this employee be logged as viewing a sensitive project under development? Another auditing test may consist of comparing logs stored as backups and logs present on the system. If there are discrepancies, an attacker may have altered the logs after they were backed up to conceal her activities.

Improper or nonexistent filtering of incoming and outgoing address packets is a common mistake made by firewall administrators. There is a popular denial-of-service attack where the attacker sends literally millions of packets containing spoofed IP addresses of the target system to the target system. Receiving the spoofed packets, the target system crashes. However, if routers and other network devices are configured to filter incoming (ingress) and outgoing (egress) traffic, a high level of protection is afforded. Here is an example of some egress and ingress filtering rules:

---

* Nmap is available for UNIX at www.insecure.org/nmap, and for Windows NT at www.eeye.com/html/Research/Tools/nmapnt.html.

- All ingress packets must not have a source address of any of the organization's internal network.
- All ingress packets must have the destination address of the organization's internal network.
- All egress packets must have a source address of the organization's internal network.
- All egress and ingress packets must not have a source or destination address of an address of the internal network and must not have an address in RFC 1918;* these include addresses: 10.x.x.x/8, 172.16.x.x/12, or 192.168.x.x/16, and the loopback network address, 127.0.0.0/8.
- All IP addresses with the IP options field set should be blocked.
- All reserved, dynamically assigned addresses (DHCP, Dynamic Host Control Protocol) and multicast addresses must be blocked including:
  - 0.0.0.0/8
  - 169.254.0.0/16
  - 192.0.2.0/24
  - 224.0.0.0/4
  - 240.0.0.0/4

In Windows systems, there is a protocol known as the Server Message Block that enables file sharing over networks. Although many employees have the best of intentions, they knowingly or ignorantly change the configuration of Windows, allowing coworkers to access and write to their files. By doing so, they also make these files available to attackers. Additionally, the default installation of some operating systems allows file and printer sharing.

Experience Note Exploiting file and printer shares is probably the most common attack.

This is a simple checklist to address unprotected sharing:

- Ensure that workstation file and printer sharing are disabled. Remember that they will likely be enabled from a default installation.
- If file sharing is determined to be absolutely essential, ensure that specific files are accessed with strong passwords.
- In the case of Windows NT platforms, use file permissions to ensure that only enumerated users have access privileges.
- Block ingress connections, at the firewall, to the NetBios session service on port 139 and port 445.

This list of common system vulnerabilities is not intended to be a comprehensive list, but it should provide some degree of guidance. There are security lists available on the Internet and should be considered dynamic documents, as they frequently change as systems and vulnerabilities change. Many system vulnerabilities are application or operating system specific and many are not. Auditors must keep abreast of current vulnerabilities as they apply to critical assets, ensuring they are incorporated in the organization's risk management program, policies, and procedures, and audit programs.

---

* Referred For Comment document number 1918 may be located at www.ieee.org.

Experience Note Auditors are generally the last line of proactive defense against onslaught of risks. If they do not discover the problem, it will likely go undiscovered until the critical incident brings the organization to its knees.

Exhibit 9 is a brief example of an audit program for a small organization's IT unit.

Audit Work Papers

Audit working papers are essential tools of auditors. They support the auditor's opinion. They should be inclusive, comprehensive, and serve to:

- Support the record that the audit was performed in conformity with auditing fieldwork standards
- Aid the auditor in conducting, assigning, and coordinating the audit
- Provide evidence of supervision and review
- Assist in planning and executing the next audit
- Provide a means by which audit steps may be reconstructed at a later date
- Provide evidence of professional due diligence

Experience Note The last item has been one of the most important work paper purposes. It is strongly recommended that each work document contains a heading detailing the business unit, purpose of the work paper, and the date; a place for the preparer to initial and date, thereby adopting the content of the work paper; a place for the audit reviewer or manager to initial and date, thereby adopting the content of the work paper and all audit work papers must be collected into binders, organized by content, indexed, and archived.

It is important to note that audit management plans, program, interview notes, sampling methodology, related notes, and the final report are considered work papers.

Audit Report

Audit reports are the expected results of an audit. This is the document everyone wants to see. It contains the "guts" of the audit by describing the audit's objectives, methodology, predication, findings, and recommendations and surprisingly, may offer words of praise. In the final report, auditors should meet expectations but not drown their intended audiences with excessive narratives, jargon, and techno-speak. Reports should get to the point early and not dawdle excessively in narratives. If the audit report is lengthy, and most are, include an executive summary section. If during the audit, criminal or potentially damaging activities are discovered, they should be brought to the attention of senior managers immediately on their discovery. Wise auditors will document their conversations and make them a part of the final audit report. It is the responsibility of the person discovering criminal activity to report it to authorities.

Experience Note If anyone has questions concerning their obligation to report federal criminal matters, he would be wise to review 18 U.S. Code 4. If anyone does not have access to the latest paper-based version of the federal criminal statutes, they can be located at: www.findlaw.com. It is not considered a bar to individual prosecution to say you reported criminal acts to your senior managers.

Exhibit 9 is an outline of an audit report.

Exhibit 9   Audit Report for XYZ Corporation Backup and Recovery Unit

Table of Contents
This table of contents should include major sections, with references to the tabbed work papers
   located in a separate binder.

Executive Summary
Restate conclusions for each audit objective listed in the audit program summarizing significant
   findings and recommendations.

Background
Provide background information about the purpose/mission of the audited area. Include reason
   for audit such as suspected irregularities or routine audit interval. Indicate in this section
   whether this is a follow-up on a previous audit.

Audit Objectives
List audit objectives in an organized fashion.

Scope and Methodology
Identify audited activities, time period audited, and nature and extent of audit tests performed.
   This is the section to explain any sampling methodologies used in controls testing.

Audit Results
This section should be restricted to documented factual and supported statements. Statements
   of opinion, assumption, and conclusion, such as "disclosure of health care information is a
   violation of employee privacy," are more effective than "internal data controls were weak."
Auditors can make recommendations that are preceded by a narrative of the finding, followed
   by the corresponding manager's response to the recommendation. In other words, the results
   of the audit report are presented to the managers for their input before the final report is drafted.
   If the manager's response is excessively long, then a summary of the response should be included
   in the report and the complete response tabbed and placed as part of the appendices.

Conclusion
The auditor's opinion or conclusion based on the objectives of the audit should be stated.

Prior Audit Results	Prior Recommendations	Prior Management Responses	Current Year Follow-Up

Senior Audit Manager   Senior Operations Manager

Appendices with Corresponding Tabs

A. The Nature, Timing, and Extent of Audit Tests

B. Follow-Up on Last Audit's Recommendations
The following table summarizes the last audit results, recommendations, management
   responses, and the results of our current audit results.

C. Standards for the Professional Practice of Internal Auditing
Standards for the Professional Practice of Internal Auditing require that we plan and perform
   audits with the objective of obtaining reasonable assurance about whether internal controls
   are effective; whether internal controls provide reasonable assurance that XYZ Corporation is
   complying with applicable laws and regulations; and whether internal controls provide
   reasonable assurance that management understands the extent to which XYZ Corporation's
   operational objectives are being achieved effectively and efficiently. This audit includes
   examinations on a test basis, control environment, risk assessment, management control
   activities, application controls, and monitoring and development activities. We believe our
   audit provides a reasonable basis for this report.

Audit Conferences: More (but Important) Meetings You Need to Attend

Opening Conferences

Opening conferences occur at the initiation of the audit and should communicate the scope of the audit, the audit's objectives, introduce the audit staff, agendas, schedules, and relevant handouts. In part it is an opportunity to explain in professional terms the purpose and expected results of the audit to the employees who are going to be going to be participating in the audit. The entrance conference should be conducted with the following in attendance: Directors, or department heads responsible for the area being audited, managers and their subordinates who work in the specific audit target and any appropriate senior employees.

A typical entrance conference will have an agenda similar to the following:

- Welcome
- Introduce auditors and related audit participants
- Review audit objectives
- Review audit steps
- Review time schedule
- Identify relevant points of contact for each step
- Describe the audit process from the auditor's and target's perspective
- Set up first contact appointments
- Conclusion

Other Conferences

During the course of the audit, there will likely be reasons for other conferences. For example, if an auditor finds there is something of a fraudulent nature, this should be brought to the attention of senior managers immediately. This meeting will take place behind closed doors. It is recommended that conferences between the entrance and exit conference take place away from the eyes of employees. If held before employees' view, they tend to foster unwarranted speculation, and damaging rumors can be fomented. Conferences of this type should be scheduled away from the work area being audited. In the case of reporting potential criminal activities, it is strongly recommended that the persons participating in this conference communicate through out-of-band means. Cellular telephones and communications methods, not using the organization's communication networks, are the best out-of-band communications. Involve the appropriate levels of staff including senior managers, legal unit, security unit, and risk managers in all conferences.

One point of professional due diligence is the discussion of the audit findings somewhere toward the end of the audit with the senior managers of the unit being audited. This gives them a chance to see any "hot grounders" headed their way. Responding to the auditor's findings is an effective way of determining if the auditors "hit their marks" with their work. Most senior managers realize their strengths and weaknesses before the audit takes place. Often the audit results merely provide them with the motivation to take corrective action.

An end of audit conference provides a formal means for a meeting of the minds and makes a matter of record of the audit's performance in the eyes of the responding managers. If there are serious differences between the auditor's findings and the manager's responses, it may be the auditors did not have a sufficient grasp of their material or they were not diligent in their efforts. In a worst-case scenario, it could mean the senior managers were out of touch with their business processes. In the former case, it is the responsibility of the audit managers to see that audit team members receive training to bring their skills up to par or find ways to motivate them to diligently perform their tasks.

Meetings whose purpose it is to preliminarily discuss their findings, allow senior managers an informal opportunity to discuss the audit findings and recommendations. This is a useful technique in addressing significant findings and permits the meeting's participants to determine if a follow-up audit is going to be needed.

Experience Note. In the case of significant, relevant findings or irregularities, it is strongly recommended that a follow-up audit is performed.

Usually, follow-up audits are very narrow in their scope focusing entirely on those significant findings of the previous audit. Follow-up audits are much abbreviated, do not have opening or closing conferences and are staffed only with enough auditors to review the findings for compliance.

Experience Note. Remember, conference agendas, schedules, and notes are all part of the audit record and considered work papers. These documents should be archived because you never know who is going to request them.

Exit Conferences

The auditors have completed their work, the report is done, and it is time to bring the audit to a close. Often, auditors deliver a performance survey to the managers of the target business unit. Such surveys have the purpose of collecting information about the performance of the auditors and the audit in general. Audit managers commonly use these surveys in completing the auditors' performance appraisals.

The agenda below is typical of a closing conference:

- Welcome
- Review audit objectives
- Review audit steps
- Briefly review controls adequacy
- Briefly review controls recommendations
- Present draft report
- Field any questions from the attendees
- Conclusion

Summary of Audit Steps

By way of summary, here are some steps to successfully completing audits:

- Preparation
  - Predication for audit, routinely scheduled or based on an allegation
  - Form audit team from qualified employees
  - Prepare audit management plan
  - Prepare and deliver preliminary questionnaires
  - Prepare audit program
  - Prepare audit budget

- Field work
  - Entrance conference
  - Audit field work
  - Audit status conference
  - Prepare draft of report including senior management responses
  - Exit conference
- Conclusion
  - Prepare final audit report
  - Complete audit performance survey
  - Schedule follow-up audit, if necessary

Audit Program for a Small IT Department

Exhibit 10 is an example of an audit program covering general controls for a small business' IT department. It will provide an example on which to build for future audits.

Exhibit 10   General Controls Review for IT Department

Information Technology General Controls Review Audit Program for XYZ Corporation

General Controls	Where applicable, review previous audit report findings and recommendations relevant to data processing activities. Ascertain if appropriate corrective actions have been completed. Describe and document any and all corrective actions relevant to previous audit's findings and recommendations.
	Where applicable, review the findings and recommendations of regulatory agency reports applicable to the XYZ Corporation's information technology business processes. Describe and document the computer platforms used by the XYZ Corporation and the applications installed on each relevant platform. Information pertinent to computer platforms includes: ■ Equipment model ■ Manufacturer's name ■ Quantity Information for installed software applications should include: ■ Name of the application ■ Vendor name/internally developed ■ Current version number
	Document that adequate hardware and software inventory has been completed in the last year. Ascertain, by sampling, if there is a correct number of licenses corresponding to the installed applications.
IT Organization	Obtain current organization chart and accompanying job descriptions for the Information Technology Unit. Ascertain that key functions (i.e., systems programming, application programming, computer operations) within the IT unit are appropriately segregated. Describe if there is an implemented doctrine of least privilege in the IT unit.
	Through interviews with IT personnel, evaluate proper segregation of critical processing functions.
	Document and describe the function of the IT steering committee or an equivalent committee within the XYZ Corporation.
Data Processing Center Access	Evaluate the location of the data processing center and its position in the building in which it is lodged. By sampling and interview, determine that there are no combustible materials are stored on the floors surrounding the data processing center. Describe the fire suppression system and ascertain its adequacy in light of critical asset priorities.

Exhibit 10   General Controls Review for IT Department (Continued)

Data Processing Center Access	Tour the data processing center. Describe and document measures that have been taken to restrict physical access to this center and the surrounding facilities including cabling closets, electrical facilities, and telecommunications closets.

Identify all entrances to the data processing center and ensure that each adequately restricts access. Ascertain if these doors are adequately alarmed for intruders and unauthorized exits.

Describe and document all measures requiring data processing center visitors are screened for identification and purpose and that they are required to sign-in and are accompanied at all times while visiting the XYZ Corporation office space.

Describe and document surveillance methods including but not limited to, security guards and electronic card keys are used to restrict data processing center access.

Describe and document all computer environmental controls that have been installed and are active:

- Fire suppression/control equipment.
- Uninterruptible power supplies attached to individual critical equipment
- Emergency power system, e.g., generators
- Temperature and humidity control equipment with appropriate redundancy relevant to employees and equipment
- Emergency power switches
- Smoke and water detectors
- Emergency lighting for the data processing center and exits

Describe the steps taken to test and maintain the above equipment.

Describe and document the location of system consoles used to operate the system; determine if all are located within the data processing center and are secure from all be specific access.

Data and Information Security	Determine existence of data and information security policy. Ascertain if this policy is communicated and acknowledged by appropriate employees.

Obtain a copy of information security policy are review for adequacy of coverage. Consider whether this policy includes all types of data including electronic and paper-based. Consider whether the policy addresses ownership, confidentiality, integrity, and availability of information.

Determine how system resources (i.e., batch, online transactions, datasets, and sensitive utilities) are protected on all computing platforms including mainframe, minicomputer, and microcomputer. Identify all installed applications that provide their own security mechanisms. Ensure the following capabilities have been implemented:

- Unique and nonsequential user identifications are assigned to all users
- Unattended terminals are automatically logged off after five minutes of inactivity
- Applications are configured requiring users to change passwords every 60 days or less
- In cases of sensitive areas, biometrics or tokens are required to sign in along with passwords

Document and describe policies and procedures requesting and removing access to systems. Document and evaluate policies and procedures established to remove users from the system when an employee departs the XYZ Corporation. Document policies and procedures auditing the activities of departing employees covering a period of 90 days before their actual departure. Document and describe to whom the results of these audits are provided.

Exhibit 10   General Controls Review for IT Department (Continued)

Select a sample of at least five users defined to the system's security configuration and ensure that system access has been properly authorized and documented.

Select five datasets and document steps that ensure appropriate access has been implemented.

Observe the establishment of at least three new user accounts and document procedures.

Identify those users that have been granted privileges on the security features. Document and describe the procedures for monitoring the activity of the privileged users. Verify existence and regular review of user activity and transaction logs.

Systems Development and Application Maintenance

Obtain an understanding of the systems development and change management processes.

Document and describe the methodology the XYZ Corporation implemented for the development of new systems, including hardware and software. Document the adequacy of the methodology for procuring commercial off-the-shelf software systems.

Document and describe the adequacy of the Systems Development Life Cycle and consider the following elements:

- User participation in all phases including feasibility, planning, development, implementation, monitoring and disposal
- System testing
- Certification and accreditation
- Proper review and approval by appropriate officers at the completion of key stages in the SDLC

Select and sample five systems in the development life cycle process. Review documentation to determine compliance with the SDLC methodology.

Document and describe the application change management process. Review procedures to ascertain the status of the following functions:

- Documenting the program change request, including feasibility, necessity, and implementation approvals
- User approval of the system change request
- System changes implemented into the production environment by employees not responsible for making the changes, thereby observing adequate separation of duties and least privilege

Select and sample five recently completed program changes and review change management documentation for compliance to the organization application program change policies and procedures.

Document and describe the adequacy/existence of a test environment for the development, testing changes and systems prior to their implementation into the production environment.

Document and describe the organization's emergency program change management procedures.

Select and sample five emergency program management changes to determine compliance to the organization's established policies and procedures.

Document and describe the organization's policies and procedures for making rate changes (i.e., tax rates) to appropriate applications.

Document and describe the programming standards implemented by the XYZ Corporation. Consideration should be directed to standards featuring naming conventions and use of structured code.

Document and describe what, if any, security steps have been implemented regarding the security of source code and other sensitive/proprietary files.

Exhibit 10   General Controls Review for IT Department (Continued)

System Operations	Describe the process implemented for scheduling production batch processes. Ascertain if users authorized all changes prior to installation to the production environment. Select and sample ten schedule changes and review for established procedure compliance.
	Document and describe means by which schedule of production environment is controlled. Ascertain adequacy of these controls.
	Document and describe means by which production output is distributed to users and steps taken to ensure sensitive materials are adequately safeguarded and controlled.
Backup/Recovery	Review system backup, recovery, and business recovery policies and procedures.
	Document and describe processes implemented to ensure that system backup is performed adequately to permit timely restoration of services.
	Document and describe through observation the frequency of the backups and determine that all files and programs are being backed up properly.
	Document online transaction backups that provide recovery for updated databases.
	Document and describe policies and procedures ensuring that backup copies of system, programs, and data files are stored in adequate offsite storage facilities.
	■ Determine if there are any regulatory or legal requirements applicable to this information storage and ensure compliance.
	■ Determine adequacy of backup copy inventory.
Contingency Planning/ Disaster Recovery	Observe that the written business resumption plan has been developed, implemented, and tested at least annually. Through examinations, ascertain if the plan is current and includes all key business components.
	Describe the scope of the business resumption plan tests performed and obtain the results of the last test. Included in these test results should be the results of the posttest critique.
	Document, describe, and evaluate the hot-site contract, if applicable, to ensure hot site adequately addresses all critical assets. Determine if contractor is completing contract requirements and in substantial compliance.

Vulnerability Self-Assessments

Audits are generally very time consuming and require a great degree of planning and coordination before they can be successfully completed. Comprehensive audits consist of thorough review controls detailed in policies, procedures, standards, and vulnerability testing. These steps are expensive and for this reason audits are generally performed annually at best. Many organizations need to design more expedient methods by which they can assess their risks, enter the self-assessment. Self-assessments can be used as checklists helping senior managers address vulnerability elements during systems design phases and after the system goes into production, before they become findings in the next audit.

In the perfect world, application vulnerability assessments actually begin in the planning stages of the Systems Development Life Cycle. When the system design phase begins, vulnerabilities should be identified and addressed before the system goes through the acquisition and implementation phases.

Vulnerability Self-Assessment

It is important in vulnerability self-assessments that all steps document policies and procedures addressing risk-elements. It is also important that if system vulnerabilities are identified during the course of the self-assessment, they should be made part of the company's risk management and audit processes.

The following discussion is a checklist that can be used in system vulnerability self-assessment.

Hardware

- Describe the system infrastructure. Is there a diagram illustrating the topology? Is there an organizational chart reflecting job description and hardware responsibilities?
- Document and describe the data outlets for servers, workstations, printers, modems, video cameras, CSU/DSU (network interface equipment), switches, hubs, load balancing, routers, firewalls, gateways, VPN appliances, etc.
- Document and describe the cabling between the major hardware components.
- Describe the location, organization, and person responsible for the relevant hardware documentation.
- When was the date of the last hardware inventory? Was all hardware accountable? Were there any instances of unauthorized hardware installed?
- Is all hardware authorized?
- Is there a policy addressing official use of personal equipment?
- Document and describe all pertinent hardware components that have software installed with default configurations. Why?
- Document and describe access control lists, ACLs, for the firewall configurations including interior and exterior firewalls.
- Document and describe perimeter router filtering policies, rules, and enforcement.
- Document and describe the standard software installation policies and procedures for each hardware platform.
- Document workstation access measures such as: BIOS passwords, Screensaver Passwords, Tokens, Biometrics, and Smart Card requirements.

Physical Security

- Document and describe the location of fire suppression equipment.
- Document any and all equipment that is not physically secure. Why?
- Describe server and workstation boot processes. Do these equipment configurations have floppy drives (A) disabled for booting processes?
- Are there BIOS, Basic Input/Output Information System, passwords? Do workstations have screensaver passwords? Are hard drives of mobile computing devices encrypted? Does mobile equipment have antitheft devices?
- Are hard drives and removable media, containing sensitive information, secured in approved receptacles during idle periods?
- Describe safeguards protecting equipment/media from theft.
- Describe the location and safeguards of all publicly accessible equipment, including mobile units, e.g., laptops, PDAs, cellular telephones, PBX (Telephone Branch Exchange) equipment.

Emergency Power Management

- Are there sufficient resources in the form of auxiliary power generators, uninterruptible power supplies, and electrical power conditioners for all user needs?
- Is there individual hardware protection for power surges and voltage spikes?

Environmental Conditions

- Are specific environmental needs met for employees, data, and equipment?
- Are heating, air conditioning, and ventilation equipment in conformity with building and safety codes?
- Is the employee work environment safe?

Configuration Management

- Describe hardware and software configuration management. Who is responsible for configuration approval?
- Are the protected interior systems connected to systems, through modems, terminal equipment, or PBX equipment having weak security procedures?
- Are IP or IPX addresses accountable? When was the last inventory?
- Are telephone numbers accountable? When was the last inventory?
- Is information, within the organization, classified relative to its sensitivity? Does information have an owner?
- What is the means by which access is granted to information resources?

Network Protocols

- Have all nonessential network services been disabled or removed on all relevant equipment?
- Can any system be accessed by telephone, and if so, why?
- Can any system be accessed wirelessly, and if so, why?
- What security precautions have been implemented in wireless environments? Is there adequate supporting documentation?
- Are wireless security precautions adequate for the traffic?
- Are cabling cabinets/closets secured? Who has access, and why?
- Are rooms containing networking equipment secured with restricted access? Who has access, and why?
- Document all network equipment with remote configuration. Why?
- Is network equipment accessible from consoles other than those located immediately next to the equipment? Why?
- Have Web services been placed in a DMZ?
- Are interior networks protected by firewalls?
- Are sensitive interior networks partitioned by firewalls?
- In the case of sensitive information, what is the justification of having open-ended networks connected?
- Has intrusion detection technology been installed at the network and host levels?
- Is there a procedure to respond to IDS alarms?

Disaster Recovery and Business Resumption

- Have critical assets been identified and prioritized?
- Has there been a risk management program implemented? Has this risk plan been thoroughly tested in the past 12 months?
- Do employees know of shut-off procedures for water, electricity, and gas?
- Is there a business resumption program? Has it been tested in the past 12 months?
- Is there a critical incident management program?
- Is there a Critical Incident Response Team?
- Is there a business resumption plan? Has it been tested in the past 12 months?
- Are there application and network transaction logs? With what frequency are they reviewed?

Software

- Is there a list of authorized software to be installed on systems? Document authorized software lists.
- Is there a policy regarding employees authorized to install software?
- When was the last software inventory? Did this inventory include version numbers?
- Is there a policy that addresses personally owned software?
- Is there a standard configuration procedure for all authorized software installations?
- What are the procedures for remote access to network/applications/workstations?
- Are nonessential ports and services disabled?
- Has antivirus software been installed and updated? How often is it run?
- Have all applications and operating systems been updated with appropriate security patches?
- Are software licenses audited regularly? When?
- Are applications/operating systems protected by access control procedures?
- Who are the employees having access to data? Why?
- Who are the employees having access to production systems? Why?
- Who is capable of accessing production code/applications/operating systems?
- Do engineers/programmers/help desk employees have access to data? Why?
- Are there system maintenance accounts? Who has access?
- What justification is needed for user accounts?
- Are departing employees' accounts audited before exiting? Are former employees' accounts disabled appropriately?

Media

- Are media containing sensitive information appropriately secured during use and in idle periods?
- Is there a policy regarding the use of personally owned media?
- Is there a policy regarding scanning all media antivirus software?
- Are media regularly backed up with copies secured offsite?
- Is there a test of the integrity of backed-up media?

- Is backed-up media tested for systems recovery? How long do recovery steps take?
- Is printer output protected?
- Is media, containing sensitive information, appropriately labeled?
- Is there a procedure for media destruction and disposal?
- Are there efforts requiring passwords to be changed regularly, minimum length, and containing special characters and capital letters? Are passwords required for application and operating system access? Are biometrics used to grant system access? Are Tokens/Smart Cards required for system access?
- Are there documents showing that user authentication mechanisms are installed to limit system, building, and workspace access?
- Are procedures requiring employee background investigations in place? Have the professional and personal references of all employees been verified? Have the professional qualifications of all employees been verified?
- Is there appropriate separation of duties and least privilege?

Employee Security Awareness Training

- Have employees been trained relative to risks and their management?
- Is security awareness training mandatory for all employees? Are there documented attendance records?

Specialized Auditing Matters

Auditing Databases

Today's database subsystems are applications providing functions related to defining, creating, deleting, modifying, and reading data in an information system. By way of review, the principal components of a database subsystem are the database management system, DBMS, used to manage data; the application programs performing operations on the data, central processor in which operations are performed and the storage media maintaining copies of the database. The database subsystem is also called a knowledge base reflecting the power of the data maintained in the database.

As in all auditing practices, the overarching controls design stem from CIA, confidentiality, integrity, and availability.

Auditing database subsystems is an examination of the controls governing the database, beginning with policies and procedures where access to the database is controlled preventing unauthorized access. Auditors must examine the implementation of the various types of integrity controls. There are many good texts about database design and implementation. Before an auditor attempts to engage a review of database operations, it is strongly suggested she have sufficient training and experience. As in all audit practices, auditors should not audit areas where they do not possess expertise.

Database Definitions

Before the discussion travels too much farther, here are some definitions that may be needed by an auditor engaged in database subsystem examination:

Accountability is achieved with two types of access restricting mechanisms, user identification and user authentication controls. Compliance with these controls is achieved through auditing. Major auditing concerns for databases are directed to information security events including logins, granting and revoking access privileges to relations, user activity logs, etc.

Experience Note Several years ago a government worker, having broad access to databases containing extremely sensitive information, decided to illicitly sell his knowledge and services. He was aware that his database activities were logged, but he was equally aware those logs were infrequently reviewed. The database was configured in such a fashion that anyone with access to the database was capable of viewing and copying information outside the their assigned duties. Over a period of years, he accessed information for which he did not have a need to know and sold it. The employee was discovered through exterior means and subsequently prosecuted for his criminal activities.

These are a few definitions that should help the auditor in database assessments:

- *Aggregation:* The result of combining distinct units of data when handling information. Aggregation of data at one level may result in the total amount of data being designated at a higher privilege level.
- *Data manipulation:* Populate and modify the contents of a database by adding, modifying, deleting, and creating rows and columns.
- *Discretionary Access Control:* DAC is a method by which access to objects is restricted to authorized users or groups of users. Access is discretionary in that access privileges may be passed to users either directly or indirectly by the object's owner.
- *Inference:* Derivation of new information from known information. An inference problem refers to derived information that may be classified at a level for which the user does not have privileges and a need to know. The inference problem is that of users deducing unauthorized information from information they have legitimately acquired. The problem of database inference has significant consequences. For example, physicians specialize in the treatment of specific diseases. It is possible for healthcare provider staffs to infer a patient's ailment by identifying the attending doctor. This type of information could be easily gleaned by viewing the patient information accompanied by the doctor's name. Drugs are also generally associated with a particular disease consequently; it is possible for staff members to infer a patient's ailment by identifying prescriptions.

Experience Note Auditors should be mindful of the possibility of users gaining unauthorized information through inference resulting from poor database design or access controls.

- *Mandatory Access Control:* MAC is a procedure of established access controls relating to resources assigned a classification level and users are assigned clearance levels. For example, users are not allowed to read a resource classified at a certain level, unless their clearance level is equal or greater than the resource's classification.
- *Referential integrity:* A database has referential integrity if all foreign keys reference existing primary keys.
- *Schema definition:* Used to define the structure of the database, integrity constraints, and access privileges.
- *Schema manipulation:* Modify the database structure, integrity constraints, and privileges associated with the tables and views within the database.

■ *Transaction management:* The ability to define and manage database transactions.

Access Controls

Access controls in the database subsystem have the function of denying unauthorized access and data manipulation. In the case of discretionary access control, DAC, users can specify who can access data they own and what action they have with respect to that data. Conversely, mandatory access control, MAC, requires an administrator to assign security attributes, such as object classifications and employee clearances. These classifications are fixed and cannot be changed by database users.

Discretionary Access Controls

With discretionary access controls, a typical user may be authorized to perform the following functions within the database:

■ Create a schema.
■ Create, modify, or delete views associated with a schema.
■ Create, modify, or delete relations associated with the schema.
■ Create, modify, or delete tuples in relations associated with the database schema.
■ Retrieve data from tuples in relations associated with the schema.

These are privileges granted to users who are designated as the owners of a particular schema along with its related views. There is an important type of privilege, that of a user granting their privileges, or a portion of them, to another user. Privilege propagation is the case of a user granting privileges to another user, who in turn grants privileges to another user.

In the propagation of privileges, it is important for an auditor to determine the allowable degree of privilege propagation. It is equally important for an auditor to examine the degree of privilege revocation. For example, if it is discovered a user has abused her privileges, what affirmative steps were taken to revoke her access privileges?

Mandatory Access Controls

In MAC, database user access to a resource is governed by a strict security policy. Database resources in the way of data-objects/attributes and record/relations are assigned classification levels. It is also a common practice to assign a classification level to each record/relation equal to the highest classification level assigned to a data/item/attribute in the record/relation. When differing levels of classification are present in the database, users are not allowed to view all the data present in the database. They may view only those items they care cleared to see.

Managing access control rules are often done through the operating system and the database management system. For example, the operating system permits only authorized users to access the database subsystem, while the database management system restricts access and the degree of user data manipulation. Auditors must be aware this is somewhat of a redundant security procedure, but one that safeguards database contents.

When a database is distributed, it is even more difficult to ensure that database access and integrity are maintained and that complete and consistent access rules are enforced throughout the enterprise. It does not matter if the database is replicated at multiple sites, or if a different database is distributed to different sites from a central location, auditors should collect evidence that multiple access control mechanisms are implemented and are universal in supporting replication.

In any processing subsystem, the issue of data integrity is one of the primary audit concerns. In database management systems, the application software directly accesses and updates the database, however, the database management system depends on the application software to pass across the correct sequence of commands and update parameters taking appropriate actions when certain types of exceptions arise.

Software Controls and Update Protocols

Application software update protocols ensure that changes to the database reflect changes to entities and associations in data the database is supposed to reflect.

- *Ensure all records are processed correctly.* If a master file is in sequential order, correct end of file protocols must be followed in an update program to make certain records are not lost from either a transaction or master file. Designing and implementing correct end of file protocols can be complex if multiple sequential transaction files and multiple sequential files are concurrently processed. Auditors should collect evidence that these protocols have been designed where they can detect, prevent, and correct end of file errors.
- *Sequence check transaction and master files.* During batch update processes, the transaction file is often sorted prior to the update of the database master file or the database tables. There are times when the master file or tables, intended to be updated, might be sorted in a particular order. It may seem duplicitous for the update program to check the sequence of the transaction as it processes each record. Regardless, there are situations that occur resulting in records on the transaction or master file that are out of sequence.
- *Single-record multiple-transaction processing order.* Database programs frequently receive multiple transactions targeting a single master record, also known as a tuple. The order in which transactions are processed against the master record is important. Different types of transactions must be given transaction codes resulting in them being sorted in correct order before being processed against the master record.
- *Suspense accounts.* Suspense accounts are essentially a file for monetary transaction where a master record could not be located at the time the update was attempted. Monetary transactions, for which a master record cannot be located, must be charged to a suspense account. If they are lost because someone fails to correct their mismatch, someone may receive a product rebate payment to which they were not entitled. Auditors must be mindful that suspense accounts, relating to data mismatches, must exist and any suspense accounts with more than a zero balance show there are processing errors needing correction.

Database Concurrency Controls in a Distributed Environment

Databases stored at multiple sites are deemed to be in a distributed environment. In one configuration, a replicated database copy is stored at all sites, and in another configuration, pieces of a database can be stored in different partitions with each partition stored at one site. Data concurrency and deadlocking problems are usually addressed by a two-step process. First step, before a transaction can read data, it must establish a read-lock on the data item. In like fashion, before a transaction can write to a data item, it must establish a write-lock on the data item. Second step, different transactions are not allowed to establish conflicting locks simultaneously. Essentially, this two-step rule means that two transactions can own read-locks on the same data item, but a read-lock and a write-lock or two write-locks are not permitted at the same time. Until a transaction releases the lock, it cannot establish additional locks. Releasing a lock provides another transaction — the opportunity to obtain control over the data item. For this reason, a transaction must commit its database changes before releasing its locks to avoid inconsistent results.

Database concurrency and deadlock problems can become serious threats to distributed database integrity unless the database management system has appropriate control levels. With replicated and distributed databases, the system must ensure that all accessible database versions are kept in a consistent state. There are some replicated database procedures that require that all data items are locked before update operations proceed. Auditors must determine the locking and updating protocols that ensure data integrity is established and maintained in a distributed environment. Further, it is important that auditors ascertain the procedures by which database administrators handle data error and conflict reports.

Audit Trail Controls

Audit trails or logs are electronic records reflecting the chronology of events occurring in the database or the database definition. Most systems require a complete set of events to be recorded such as, creation, deletions, modifications, and specific records accessed. If audit trails do not exist, it is be impossible to determine how the database arrived at its current state, who retrieved a record or who executed a specific transaction.

There are several important characteristics of audit trails. All transactions must have a unique time stamp confirming that a transaction was directed to the database definition or the database itself. Time stamps identify the unique time that the transaction caused a series of events to take place so a documented history is created. It is important to note that audit trails must record not only the time and the transaction, but also the user account from which the transaction occurred. Auditors must be mindful of the length of time that audit trails must be retained. In many cases, laws and regulations applicable to the specific industry or type of data strictly mandate how long an audit trail will be retained.

Object Reuse

It is important for auditors to address issues concerning object reuse in the database management system and operating system. Operating systems are responsible for deallocating system resources, such as files used to store tables. In order to maintain confidentiality and integrity, data stored in these resources and objects must be zeroed or replaced with random information before being reassigned.

Database Existence Controls

Existence controls in the database subsystem must be able to restore the database in the event of loss or corruption. All backup procedures involving the maintenance of a previous version of the database and corresponding audit trails. Recovery procedures generally take two forms. The first is the current state of the database must be restored if the entire database or a portion of the database is lost or corrupted. This activity involves a "roll-forward operation" where a prior correct version of the database is restored along with the log of transactions or changes that have occurred to the database since its last backup copy was made.

The "roll-back operation" is where the current invalid state and the updates are rolled back undoing the updates that caused the database to be corrupted. The log of database changes is used to restore the database to the prior valid state. Auditors must carefully examine the possibility of fraudulent behavior in rolling back database operations, making changes to the database; allowing the database to process the data, then rolling back the database to its prior state, without error report generation and audit trail recording.

Experience Note Database administrators had the ability to roll-forward and roll-backward the database during monthly accounts payable processing cycles without generating error reports. Further, these same administrators had the ability to edit the audit trails so there were no records made of their activities. During a monthly billing process, administrators stopped the billing database, inserted several fabricated accounts to be paid, and allowed the process to pay these accounts. Once the process had paid the bogus accounts, they rolled back the operation to the time before they inserted the bogus accounts, and allowed the operation to continue. They merely inserted the accounts, the accounts were paid, and they restored the database to its original state. The system's audit trails were edited in such a fashion, so it appeared nothing had happened in the transaction log. The system was not configured to generate error reports accounting for roll-forward and roll-backward events. After a routine audit discovered the administrator's excessive privileges, an analyst discovered the embezzlement. The offending employees were subsequently indicted and convicted.

Domain Servers

Domain name servers (DNSs) literally translate names suitable for understanding by most people into network addresses. For example, www.myexample.com is sent to a DNS and translated to the numeric address of 192.165.23.22. Of course, the latter address is one that is routable and understood by computer networks. Essentially, DNS is a database of network addresses visited by network users. If the local DNS is not able to resolve the URL, Uniform Resource Locator, it will query the next highest domain server and eventually resolve the alphabetical URL to the familiar numeric network address before being routed.

Because DNS servers are frequently exposed to open-ended networks, such as the Internet, they are subject to a wide variety of attacks. For example:

- Attacks targeting the name server software allowing an intruder to compromise the server and take control of the DNS host
- Denial-of-service attacks directed to a single DNS server affecting an entire network by preventing users from translating host names into IP addresses
- Spoofing attacks trying to induce a DNS server to cache false resource records leading users to unintended sites
- Information leakage from zone transfers exposing internal network information that could be used to plan and execute future attacks
- A DNS server could be an unwitting participant in attacks on other sites

As any software application, DNS software evolves with each version release. Essentially, all older DNS versions have widely known vulnerabilities that attackers will exploit. In most cases, vulnerabilities that appear in one version are patched in subsequent releases. Running the latest version of DNS software does not guarantee security; however, it will minimize the likelihood of exploitation.

Auditors should be mindful there are steps that can be taken to secure a DNS server that only as to deliver DNS to a single audience and it can be optimized for that particular function. It is useful to use separate DNS servers configured to play specific roles. It is a useful procedure to have different security policies applied to servers respective to their function. For example, having an external DNS server used only as an external name server is a sound business procedure. This DNS server should provide resolution for zones for which it has authoritative information. In other words, it provides DNS services for Internet or open-ended networks and your internal network's users.

Exterior DNS servers should not contain any information about your internal network addressing or topology. It should be located in the Demilitarized Zone, DMZ, meaning it is behind a packet screen firewall facing the open-ended network and in front of the application firewall that protect the sensitive interior network. Architectures of this nature look like a sandwich with the DMZ located between the slices. DMZs are the areas where Web servers, outside e-mail services, and name servers reside.

Having an internal DNS server is commonly used to provide name resolution services to internal network clients. This DNS server is configured to provide query answers from trusted internal hosts and not from the Internet. It is located behind the packet screen, the DMZ, the application firewall as a member of the internal network. Adopting these security procedures will result in the external DNS server configured to provide little resolution service other than answering queries for which it is authoritative. Internal DNS servers can be protected by restricting the server to respond only to known and trusted hosts. In this fashion, if the resolving server was compromised or its cache corrupted, the outside DNS server's authoritative zone information would not be affected, thereby limiting the potential for damage. In this same vein, if the internal DNS server were also configured to be authoritative for internal zones only, a compromise of the external DNS server would not affect the normal name service operation of the internal network.

As a matter of network security and protection, organizations operate their DNS servers on dedicated hosts. Hosts that run the DNS services do not provide other services; consequently, there is no need for them to respond to non-DNS traffic. In such a dedicated DNS host configuration, it reduces the possibility of the DNS server being compromised by a weakness in any other piece of software located on the same host as the DNS. As a further sound security procedure, administrators disable or remove any unnecessary software or hardware features from the DNS host. The logic supporting this procedure is if unnecessary software and hardware are not present, attackers cannot exploit them.

For DNS servers providing external name resolution, everything but traffic from the Internet to port 53 UDP and port 53 TCP on the DNS server can be safely filtered and denied entry. Similarly, internal network DNS servers can be filtered allowing only internal clients access to ports 53 UDP and TCP on the name server and allowing the internal DNS server to make outbound queries to other internal DNS servers.

Exhibit 11 reflects a packet-filtering table for a typical DNS packet filter.

Experience Note Auditors should be mindful of packet screening policy tables similar to the one above. Auditors should request to see the policy tables for all

Exhibit 11 Packet Filtering Security Table

Function	Description	Source IP	Source Port	Destination IP	Destination Port
Public name service	Inbound queries	Any	53/udp, 53/tcp, >1023/udp, >1023/tcp	Nameserver	53/udp, 53/tcp
Public name service	Query replies	Nameserver	53/udp, 53/tcp	Any	53/udp, 53/tcp, any 53/udp, 53/tcp, >1023/udp, >1023/tcp
Internal name server	Queries from clients	Internal Network	>1023/udp, >1023/tcp	Nameserver	53/udp, 53/tcp
Internal name server	Replies to clients	Nameserver	53/udp, 53/tcp	Internal network	>1023/udp, >1023/tcp
Internal name server	Outbound recursive queries	Nameserver	>1023/udp, >1023/tcp	Any	53/udp, 53/tcp
Internal name server	Replies to recursive queries	Any	53/udp, 53/tcp	Nameserver	>1023/udp, >1023/tcp

network traffic permitted to pass to through the packet screen as part of their due diligence. It is a matter of some gravity if such screening policy tables are flawed or absent. It is not unreasonable for auditors to test these packet screen policies and their implementation by placing a packet generator, such as Nmap outside the network and a packet detection device using Windump or TCPdump on the inside of the packet screen.

TCPdump is a network information capture program developed at Lawrence Berkeley National Laboratory. It is a UNIX-based program consisting of an executable with a network capture driver program. The purpose of this utility is the interception, capture, and display of information packets passing through the network. If TCPdump were installed on computer connected to the target network, it will capture all passing information packets. The Windows version of TCPdump is called Windump.*

Attackers will typically attempt to exploit packet-screening flaws.

Zone transfers are used to transfer DNS information from one DNS server to another. Restricting zone transfers is a significant step in security DNS services. Implementing restrictive zone transfers has the secondary benefit of preventing others from taxing your system's resources as it prevents intruders from gaining a list of the contents of DNS zones. Zone transfers are the delivery of the cached information held in the DNS service. Attackers obtaining zone transfers from your internal DNS server will allow them to see the IP addresses as well as the architecture of your internal network. Denying attackers this type of information raises your internal network's security. An attacker who is able to complete a zone transfer can use that information to identify new targets on your internal network such as routers, mail servers, other DNS servers, file servers, databases, and anything else in your DNS records.

A common administrator mistake is to restrict zone transfers from the primary master DNS server only, while neglecting to restrict transfers from slave servers. Because it is possible to obtain a zone transfer from a slave server, it is important that auditors ensure that all authoritative DNS servers have restrictions placed on zone transfers.

In BIND 8 or 9, use the allow-transfer substatement:

```
options {
  allow-transfer {192.168.4.154;};
};
```

or specific to a zone:

```
type master;
zone "my example.com" {
  file "db.myexample.com";
  allow-transfer {192.168.4.154;};
};
```

Protecting against DNS Cache Corruption

DNS servers can operate in one of two ways when responding to queries:

---

* Both TCPdump and Windump are freely available at www.tcpdump.org and windump.polito.it.

scalability, enhanced fault tolerance, and ⬚⬚ds-based interoperability. Windows NT Advanced Server was promoted as an a⬚ds-based interoperability server for Novell NetWare, Banyan VINES, and Microsoft networks providing ⬚n server for Novell NetWare, Banyan accounting, and database servers such as ⬚m for business solutions as financial, as Microsoft Mail. ⬚⬚ver, SNA Server, and e-mail servers

Windows NT Server 4.0, Terminal Server ⬚ consisted of three components:

- The Windows NT Server multi-user c⬚ which made it possible to host multiple, simultaneous client sessions.
- The Remote Desktop Protocol, allowing co⬚nication with a server that has Terminal Server enabled over the network.
- The "super-thin" Windows-based client softwa⬚ which displayed the familiar 32-bit Windows user interface on a range of des⬚ hardware. The Windows 2000 Server family offers features as centralized ⬚licy-based management, faster deployment options and Active Directory.

Here are a few areas that auditors may wish to review when completing their Windows NT server audits:

- Ensure that appropriate levels of auditing are enabled by selecting the NT event viewer under policy, file systems.
- Auditors should select the File manager and ensure that the server is using the NTFS as its file scheme. FAT or file allocation table is not secure.
- Auditors should review the security log file size. There should be sufficient file space for one week's activities because the log is overwritten when it is full. View the log file size through the event log settings.
- Auditors should review the documented frequency of reviewed log events.
- Auditors should ensure the Web server is in the DMZ and is not a member of a domain or Domain Controller.
- Auditors should ensure that only essential services are installed and operating. All nonessential services should be disabled or removed.
- Auditors should access the *add/remove programs* of the NT server and determine if any of the following programs have been installed according to the organization's policies and procedures:
  - ☐ Certificate Server
  - ☐ FrontPage 98 Server Extensions
  - Internet Connection Service for RAS
  - The following subcomponents under Internet Information Server (IIS):
    - ☐ File Transfer Protocol (FTP) Server
    - ☐ Internet NNTP Service
    - ☐ Internet Service Manager (HTML)
    - ☐ SMTP Service
    - ☐ World Wide Web Sample Site
    - ☐ Microsoft Index Server
    - ☐ Microsoft Message Queue
    - ☐ Microsoft Script Debugger
    - ☐ Microsoft Site Server Express 2.0
  - The following subcomponent under Transaction Server:
    - ☐ Transaction Server Development
    - ☐ Visual InterDev RAD Remote Deployment Support
    - ☐ Windows Scripting Host
- Auditors should attempt to access the security log from a nonprivileged account noting any deficiencies.

- Auditors should use the *~~ve programs~~* to determine which updates are applied and reconc~~arity/current.asp~~ ~~ag~~inst the Microsoft Security Bulletins at: www.microsoft.com/tech~~r~~services should only be started manually and
- Auditors should note tha~~t~~he server starts. should not be running ~~b~~uilt-in accounts (Administrator etc.):
- Auditors should verify~~es~~ (length of passwords, expiration period, etc.)
  - Review password ~~s~~hips and the privileges of these groups.
  - Review group me~~t~~he audit logs for successful access to the NT registry.
- Auditors should rev~~i~~~~a~~nd confirm that these logs are reviewed, at least daily, Auditors should ve~~r~~ by administra~~t~~ors.
- Auditors should ~~r~~ew permissions and determine their appropriateness for users and ~~u~~ser ~~gro~~ups.
- Auditors shoul~~d~~ ~~d~~etermine if a backup of the NT Registry is performed at least bi-week~~ly~~ with a ~~b~~aseline Registry copy retained.
- Auditors should ~~v~~erify all trust relationships between NT Domains.
- Auditors should ~~d~~etermine if workstations are operating on Windows environments other tha~~n~~ NT, there should be Screensaver and BIOS passwords. The use of Screen~~s~~a~~v~~er and BIOS passwords are permitted, and encouraged, in NT environmen~~t~~.
- Auditors shoul~~d~~ review all remote NT access for adequate controls.
- Auditors shoul~~d~~ verify Access Control Lists for the following files and functions:

Directory or File	Suggested Privileges
C:\	Administrators: Change Users: Read
C:\WINNT\	Administrators: Change Users: Read
WINNT\config\	Administrators: Change Users: Read
\WINNT\inf\	Administrators: Change Users: Read
\WINNT\profiles\	Administrators: Change
\WINNT\system\	Administrators: Change Users: Read
\WINNT\System32\	Administrators: Change
AUTOEXEC.NT	Administrators: Change
CONFIG.NT	Administrators: Change
C:\...*.EXE, *.BAT, *.COM, *.CMD, *.DLL	Administrators: Change

- Auditors should review interfaces and security for connections to other LANS.
- Auditors should review the administrator account and ensure it had been named something that will not attract the attention of attackers. Wise administrators routinely establish "decoy" administrator accounts having few privileges. As a matter of course, administrators should review logs for this decoy account looking for attacker activity. Legitimate administrator accounts must have a password consisting of at least ten digits and require special characters, numbers, and capital letters. This password must be changed monthly.
- Auditors must ensure that all default accounts, such as *Guest*, have been disabled or removed.

- Auditors must ensure that all unnecessary features have been disabled or removed. For example, IP routing in NT permits packets from one interface to be routed to another interface, if IP routing is not disabled.
- Auditors must ensure that the target system has been configured to unbind WINS Client from TCP/IP. If WINS is bound to TCP/IP attackers may access machine information using tools and direct NetBios specific exploits at the target. Auditors may use the *bindings* tab of the Network Manager to test for unbinding NetBIOS and all other unnecessary protocols.
- Auditors must ensure that strong encryption has been applied to the Security Account Manager (SAM). This is the database where passwords are stored. It is important for auditors to remember that because the SAM data is encrypted, it does not preclude someone from downloading the SAM file and using a password cracker program to obtain the passwords.
- Auditors should review local TCP/IP configured filtering. Microsoft IIS server supports filtering and rules for IP addresses. IIS should have ports 80 and 443 open with all other ports denied.
- Auditors should review auditing of user and system activities. It is important to note that the default installation of NT does not enable auditing. Ensure appropriate levels of auditing are enabled.
- Auditors should ensure that the default NT installation of samples and unused ODBC drivers are removed.
- Auditors should ensure that NT null user sessions are disabled. NT uses null user sessions to remotely download user names and share names. Auditors should determine whether the following Registry key is set to a value of 1: HKEY_LOCAL_MACHINE\System\CurrentControlSet\Control\LSA\RestrictAnonymous.
- Auditors should ensure that NT file system, NTFS, cannot auto-generate 8.3 names for backward compatibility with 16-bit applications. Auditors should verify that the following key value is set to 1: HKEY_LOCAL_MACHINE\SYSTEM\CurrentControlSet\Control\FileSystem\.

This is merely a representative sample of the potential areas to be audited in the Windows NT environment. A very good reference guide for security and auditing Windows NT systems is available through www.trustedsystems.com/index.htm.

Network Vulnerability Assessments: The Practical Examination of Your System

Network vulnerability assessment is a hands-on approach in ascertaining your system's obvious vulnerabilities and their locations. There are many risks that are associated with these types of audits that go largely ignored by senior managers.

Experience Note An auditor was examining the business' network software development process for compliance to the company's policy and procedures. She discovered the programmers and engineers were not observing any of the policy requirements and were basically approaching their development phases in a haphazard fashion. She detailed her findings in a preliminary report to senior managers who told her that they had evolved past the SDLC and other quality methods. Instead, they were writing their code, installing it, and using the network vulnerability assessment as a quality control to determine any weaknesses existing in their software. Her audit report findings were lengthy and specific.

In conducting network and other types of practical vulnerability assessments, it is paramount that auditors adopt a holistic view of auditing. Auditing is the process by which prohibited, abusive, and irregular activities are found and reported. If a concerted auditing effort is adopted, the entire system consisting of the three pillars of human resources, data and physical facilities will be measured as part of risk management and operational efficiency.

Vulnerability assessments only measure those vulnerabilities that are within the scope of the rules of engagement, the knowledge of the auditors, and those system vulnerabilities that are present at the time of the assessment. It should be made clear that network vulnerability assessments must be considered as part of the whole audit picture. They are not a substitute for poor systems design and management.

Network vulnerability assessments are the part of the audit program whose purpose is the practical identification of system vulnerabilities. If vulnerabilities are found, and they will be found, they will be reported as findings, accompanied by recommendations in the audit report. It is a fair statement that you cannot repair system weaknesses, unless you locate them first. If during a comprehensive audit, senior managers fail to locate and repair system vulnerabilities, it is a safe bet that attackers inside and outside the organization will find and exploit them. The general goals and objectives of system vulnerability assessments are as follows:

- Measure levels of system risks.
- Ascertain practical compliance with organization's policies and procedures. (This usually involves a high-degree of employee and senior manager embarrassment.)
- System vulnerability assessments comprise an important part of the comprehensive auditing effort and clearly demonstrate professional due diligence.

Audit team members should be carefully selected for their experience, people skills, communications skills, good judgment, system knowledge, and knowledge of software and intrusion and attacker tactics. It is recommended they have a good knowledge of programming in languages such as C, C++, Java, and PERL. Programming skills and network knowledge enable auditors to review open source tools, fix or modify them, and write their own programs, if necessary. It is worth remembering that running automated tools without an understanding of the underlying protocols and issues is dangerous and generally will not provide sufficient insight when documenting findings in the audit report. Skills such as persuasive sales are a valuable commodity if the audit team is going to engage in social engineering. Often the question is asked if this is "white-hat," "black-hat," or "gray-hat" system attacking.

Experience Note   Personally, the author thinks the "hat" business is a bit of nonsense. Some organizations are caught up in the idea of hiring individuals of questionable character, but who have a great deal of skill. Many are convicted felons. Think of this example, "Would you hire a professional thief to make a security survey of your business?" Prudent business managers should engage professionals of known abilities with impeccable references, not soon-to-be indicted attackers.

Questions arise whether organizations should outsource system vulnerability assessments or develop the skills internally. Correct answers are not easily decided as there are advantages and disadvantages to both sides. There is some degree of risk in outsourcing vulnerability assessments unless a significant amount of research is done.

Experience Note There are many outside "system security consultants" that are reformed attackers. Some have even spent time in prison for their criminal behavior, while others have been defendants in lawsuits centered in their unlawful behavior.

So before contracting outside vulnerability auditors, it is prudent to discuss their backgrounds, experience, bonding, the length of time they have been in business, and references. Demand they provide a long list of satisfied clients and a few that were not so satisfied. Contracts should be carefully crafted enumerating liabilities and responsibilities.

It is strongly recommended that several lawyers, having experience with services of this nature, review the details of the contract before being finalized.

It is the practice of most consultants to spend an inordinate amount of time keeping skills current to explore and exploit system weaknesses. For some, their skills' improvement and bragging rights are something that borders on obsession. On their own time, they explore system weaknesses to the exclusion of other pursuits. Many consultants can tell you about successfully gaining root access to systems that were considered impregnable by its owners. Regardless, if the decision is made to use contractors, your sensitive assets are subject to capture by the outsiders. You are giving them the key to the business' crown jewels.

Experience Note It is quite likely that today's system audit consultant will not be employed by the firm for more than a short time. She knows your system's vulnerabilities when she decides to exploit them.

If the organization decides to develop inside talents, there are many suitable training courses available that can provide the skills necessary to perform a respectable system vulnerability assessment. Training of this nature is valuable and can be used as part of an employee development program. It is important to note that systems auditing skills are a serious commitment in that they require constant upgrading and expansion as new technologies emerge and new weaknesses are announced.

Rules of Engagement

Rules of engagement govern the level and extent of vulnerability assessment efforts. Develop a written agreement between the audit manager and appropriate levels of senior management, as the vulnerability assessment process is extremely invasive. In this statement the questions of who, what, when, where, and how should be thoroughly, but briefly addressed. For example, the purpose of this vulnerability assessment will be to test the effectiveness of procedures ensuring that attackers cannot obtain unauthorized access to the organization's critical assets of human resources, data, and physical resources.

Assessment procedures define the methods and means by which the various evaluation events will take place. These procedures can be expressed in the following areas:

- *Assessment standing.* Determine and define when the assessment will begin, the scope of the assessment, and when the assessment will end.
- *Vantage point.* What will be the vantage point of the assessment? Should the auditors consider themselves as outside the organization, or inside the orga-

nization? Obviously, the vantage point will affect the assessment objectives and the time involved. In the insider vantage point, the auditors are provided as much pertinent information as possible. For example, auditors will have the source code for CGI scripts, network topology and architecture, IP addresses, etc. With this degree of information, the auditors may test the system more thoroughly looking for subtle flaws that might otherwise escape notice. Besides, this approach saves time and resources.

On the other hand, outsider testing provides little, if any, relevant system information to the auditors in the anticipation their stance is that of an outside attacker. This approach requires a great deal of time and effort to complete an accurate and meaningful assessment. Proponents of this type of assessment claim it provides a realistic approach to system evaluation in light of the fact outside attackers will not have insider information. The fact of the matter is with the large number of attacks attempting to gain access, or extinguish services, this approach requires a significant time investment, and it is likely that new vulnerabilities will be discovered before they can be tested against the system.

There are two more vulnerability modes, passive and aggressive. Passive testing means the auditor can take only a distant view, essentially a "looking glass" approach. This is a safe way of testing, but it is not going to provide the type of detail that should be narrated in the "findings" section of an audit report. The auditor discovers a system's vulnerability and reports findings without further exploration and system exploitation. Aggressive testing takes the approach of exploiting all discovered vulnerabilities and exploring just how far the auditor can penetrate the system before coming to an end.

How far should the auditor pursue an exploit? The answer should be explicitly detailed in the rules of engagement. However, it is recommended that the auditor pursue a vulnerability to the extent possible without doing damage to the system. Only in this fashion can the risk potential be measured and reported. It is further recommended that in a system vulnerability assessment, the procedure should be to locate a weakness, exploit it, and leverage that weakness to gain wider access to the target system.

Social Engineering

Social engineering is the tactic of having contact with the organization or persons associated with the organization and through ruse, pretext, or misdirection, attempt to gain information that would facilitate an unauthorized intrusion. It is possibly the least most popular means of auditing a system and must be thoroughly addressed as a tenet in the rules of engagement for the vulnerability assessment. Social engineering tests employees and their training.

Experience Note When organizations suffer a successful social engineering attack, it makes banner headlines. Employee training and compliance auditing will help in avoiding these disasters.

Auditors and senior managers must be mindful that attackers are employing these tactics, so using them in a measured fashion has great benefits in probing vulnerabilities. In essence, social engineering involves getting employees to voluntarily surrender information that can be used to gain an advantage that would not be available without it. It can be as easy as a telephone conversation, going through someone's wastepaper basket, or using an unprotected workstation.

The primary tool of the social engineer is the telephone. Typically, a talented auditor can obtain more critical information and cause greater damage by working making a few telephone calls than the best network attacker. Among the most common approaches are:

- Posing as a member of the target organization's technical support staff
- Playing the role of a disgruntled customer/user seeking a password change
- Calling the technical support staff and enlisting their aid in getting a workstation connected to their network
- Going through the waste paper baskets located in open office areas after work hours and before it is collected
- Using unattended workstations or servers
- Going through the trash collected by the maintenance staff
- Going through the organization's dumpster (consider this a major undertaking and avoid unless deemed necessary)
- Making copies of notes and other materials left out on desks after hours

Experience Note One of the most interesting, inventive, and legendary social engineering activities was the new maintenance employee who was seen posting small signs around an office area. These signs announced a new telephone number for the company's technical support unit. When one of the senior managers asked the employee who it was that requested he post the signs she responded that she was new and did not know the person who asked The manager did not follow it up any further. After about a week, the company's technical support staff sent an e-mail to their manager asking what happened to all their calls. They had not received a trouble call in several days. It was discovered that when calls were made to the "new" telephone number for the technical support unit, a recorded message stated that all agents were busy; and requested the caller to verify his identity with network logon name and password. It was discovered that the callers' network accounts had been accessed and sensitive information taken through terminals located inside the company during off-duty hours. Additionally, the organization had not verified the identity and background of the maintenance person.

If the rules of engagement permit, auditor's can use social engineering for gaining access to the company's systems. For example, an auditor, not previously introduced to the target organization arrives early at the organization and loiters near the entrance. When an employee passes security and enters the office space, the auditor, acting as a new employee, offers the excuse they are new and have forgotten their identification badge, and follows the employee inside. Or an auditor telephones the network administrator and misrepresents himself as a member of the management staff and asks the administrator for her e-mail account password to be reset. The administrator provides a one-time use password without verifying the caller's identity and the auditor accesses the manager's e-mail account. Should such tactics be allowed? If the audit is going to test the risk management training provided to the employees, the answer is yes. Regardless, the use of social engineering tests must be addressed in the rules of engagement. If auditors do not test the system's vulnerabilities, attackers will. Again, it is not a matter of *if* an attacker attempts this type of intrusion; it is only a matter of *when*.

Senior managers and auditors must arrive at a level of understanding of whether the employees are going to be advised of the system testing or not. If employees are aware of system testing, they will likely be on guard and on their best behavior. However, if the rules of engagement allow the auditors to fully explore and exploit if the system crashes due to an attack, the administrators can take appropriate action without panic. But, not advising employees has advantages, in that auditors will observe the true performance of how employees react to system attacks and how recovery efforts are brought to pass. Obviously, telling or not telling employees of the system assessment is a matter for careful consideration by senior managers with the matter fully documented in the rules of engagement. Safeguards are typically deployed in the event of electing not to notify employees to avoid having embarrassing calls made to law enforcement.

The last area of preparation includes the area of permission. Appropriate levels of permission must be obtained before conducting this type of system vulnerability assessment. This is an area of good judgment. Auditors must do a thorough job, but they cannot damage any critical assets in any fashion including employee morale. On the other hand, the more realistic these tests are, the more useful will be their results. Use good judgment in crafting the rules of engagement and obtaining the appropriate levels of permission.

IP Address Confirmation

In this step, business functions must be mapped to physical system and information about how the systems operate must be recorded. It is a wise audit step to obtain a list of the organization's IP addresses, to whom they are assigned, and where they are assigned, including the type of device. DNS name resolution can be used, but if something happens to the name server, or if the IP address resolution is incorrect, the actions taken by the auditors could be slowed or result in the wrong systems being audited.

Ownership of the IP addresses should verified and confirmed before beginning the assessment. A very simple, but effective tool for IP resolution having a host of other features is available from: www.samspade.org. This tool is very intuitive, easily configurable, and will automatically select the correct Internet registration authority reflecting IP address ownership. Confirming IP addresses is good audit practice and serves to verify whether the organization has accurately completed their asset inventory.

Assessment Safety

Although auditors will have the best intentions, it is a wise practice to have a safety protocol for those moments when adverse things happen. When auditors download freeware/shareware or purchase their tools, it is a wise procedure to scan these utilities for malware being present. It only takes a moment to update the antivirus software and scan the product for worms, viruses, and Trojans.

During the audit is not the time to experiment with a new tool. An audit tool should be carefully exercised to ensure the auditor has a thorough knowledge of its use before using it in an audit. Additionally, assessment tools should be updated, as new versions become available. Newer versions will likely address newly announced weaknesses that may be missed by older pieces of software.

Auditors should have emergency contact information for appropriate management levels for each of the sections they are evaluating. These contacts must be 24/7. It is the experience of most system auditors that if anything can go wrong, it will at the least opportune moment.

Experience Note Murphy's Law will be in full effect during every audit step; plan on it.

Auditors should document all their actions and information captured during the assessment. Notes should be recorded to a central file for each member of the audit team. Some auditors go so far as to enable keystroke logging on their workstations to record all their actions. Record all IP addresses and netmasks targeted by your scanner tools. It is important to note when your system's IP address changes at any time during the assessment. This will help you keep directed and on track when performing the assessment. Additionally, it will simplify configuring the scanning tools. Using the IP addresses from the organization's inventory will shorten the time scanning tools are run. In this fashion, auditors only have to cover the territory once. Auditors should document the start and stop times of their tools. These documents will comprise a section in the auditor's work papers and will be referenced in the audit report.

Discovering the Character of the Audit Target

As a general first step, auditors will research public source information about the audit target. One of the most logical steps is to look up the domain registration information of the audit target. There are many manual Web sites providing Internet domain registration. These are just a few:

- www.arin.net
- www.networksolutions.com
- www.allwhois.com

Domain registration queries will provide information similar to the sample shown in Exhibit 12.

Tools

This is a good place to discuss tools such as SamSpade, and the audit features they offer. Most of these tools offer similar features and prove to be invaluable during a vulnerability assessment. SamSpade provides a GUI (graphical user interface) that expedites its configuration. It runs on Windows 9X, ME, NT, and XP. As part of its functionality, it performs queries such as whois, ping, DNS Dig (Advanced DNS request and zone transfer), traceroute, finger, SMTP mail relay checking, and Web site crawling. Using SamSpade and similar tools are intuitive and self-explanatory so it would be a waste of time to fully describe their features and configuration. However, before using this tool, and others, auditors are cautioned to become familiar with their capabilities and risks. Additionally, all the tools listed below include very well written *help* files as part of their product (Exhibit 13).

Similar tools are easily found on the Internet, caution is urged in making certain with whom you are doing business, make certain the tools come from reputable vendors and locations. Examples of similar tools may be located at www.ipswitch.com (WS_Ping ProPack) and www.nwpsw.com (NetScan Tools).

Attentive auditors review the domain registration and notice the technical contact is not located at the same address and telephone exchange as the target enterprise. Several conclusions may be drawn from this information.

The Web host is a contractor or the company that has its hosting facilities located outside its headquarters.

The response also gives some insight into the e-mail naming conventions for the target. This information could be useful if an attacker wanted to find e-mail addresses she could target.

Exhibit 12   Domain Registration Queries

Registrant

Interexample Online LLC (INTEREXAMPLE-DOM)

100 Broadway

New York, NY 10007

    Netname: INTEREXAMPLE-BLK-0

    Netblock: 197.123.123.0 – 197.000.254.0

    Domain Name: INTEREXAMPLEONLINE.COM

Technical Contact

    Bob Robertson

    P.O. Box 1234

    New York, NY 10007

    Telephone: 212–555–0000

    E-mail: Brobertson@webhosting.com

Administrative Contract

    Alice Wincelowitz

    Interexample Online LLC

    100 Broadway

    New York, NY 10007

    Telephone: 212–999–0000

    E-mail: AliWincelowitz@Interexampleonline.com

Billing Contact

    Alice Wincelowitz

    Interexample Online LLC

    100 Broadway

    New York, NY 10007

    Telephone: 212–999–0000

    E-mail: AliWincelowitz@Interexampleonline.com

NS1.INTEREXAMPLEONLINE.COM 197.123.123.1

NS2.INTEREXAMPLEONLINE.COM 197.123.123.2

Record last updated on 10-May-2003

Database last updated 1-June-2001

In discovering more of the audit target, the auditor will look to the Internet for more information. Using such resources as www.google.com or www.hotbot.com will locate information about the target, its employees, and publicly available information. Google may also be used to query newsgroups for postings made by employees using the organization's domain name. This technique can be useful if employees are posting information about their company's vulnerabilities while using the organization's e-mail system.

Frequently, attackers publish the company's network vulnerabilities in newsgroups or chat rooms. Experienced auditors will query newsgroups and participate in chat rooms to determine if relevant system vulnerabilities are available.

Auditors often search public information areas such as the Securities Exchange Commission database known as EDGAR (www.sec.gov) for information about the target's filings. Two of the most informative filings are the 10K and 10Q. The form

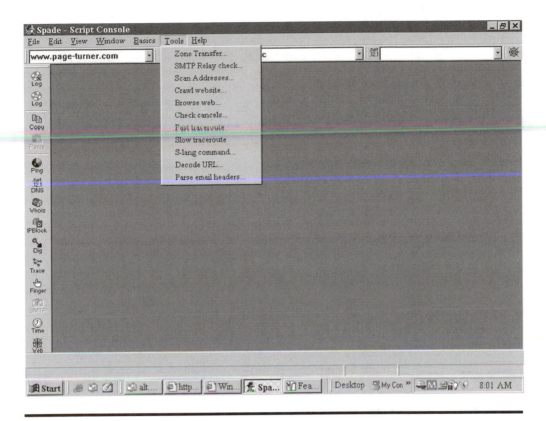

Exhibit 13   SamSpade

10Q provides visibility into the company's activities in the last quarter, while the 10K is an annual filing describing the company's previous year. Reviewing these documents can provide information about recent mergers and acquisitions. It is possible the entities recently blended to form today's organization may allow the auditor to discover already documented vulnerabilities and permit unauthorized entries.

Additionally, SEC filings and posted annual company reports provide a wealth of information for the attacker. It is not unusual for attackers to collect personal information about owners and senior managers, including private e-mail addresses, residences, financial holdings, automobile ownership, marital status, social security numbers, credit histories, etc.

In the case of smaller organizations, auditors may purchase subscriptions to services that provide detailed information about individuals on a query-fee basis. If the rules of engagement allow this type of review, the type of information available about the target's senior management is almost limitless. These agencies collect information from magazine subscriptions, real estate transactions, driver's permits, professional organizations, clubs, and innocuous areas such as dog and cat licensing. Companies using this type of information collection are legitimate and are easily locatable on the Internet. Not all companies use legal means of information collection; so be wary and deal only with reputable agencies.

Auditors must be fully aware that collecting private information is sensitive, but if the auditor can find the information, so can those who intend harm. It should be within the rules of engagement to discover available information. Auditors must make appropriate recommendations as to the information disclosed by employees that could result in jeopardizing their safety. If a regulatory agency or law does not require disclosure of information, do not do it. Making it a matter of audit programs will ensure its compliance with policy and procedures.

Auditors should carefully document their public information discoveries in a detailed schedule as part of their final report. Making a printout and including it as part of the work papers is an accepted practice. This information will become very useful as the vulnerability assessment continues.

If the rules of engagement permit the auditor to travel where attackers venture, it would be wise to enter the world of chat. Downloading a shareware chat client from, www.mirc.com will provide the means to speak with others about their knowledge of the audit target's vulnerabilities. Using this vehicle requires a fair degree of skill and is not going to be valuable unless the auditor has used this communication medium previously. However in the hands of a skillful professional, chatters frequently know an organization's critical asset vulnerabilities and exploits.

Experience Note At a credit card clearinghouse, an auditor discovered several chat rooms and Web pages providing free scripts targeting the clearinghouse's Web site as well as open chats about the audit target's credit card network vulnerabilities. These scripts were designed to verify credit card information using the clearinghouse's computing facilities. When the auditor queried the persons chatting and the persons supporting the Web pages, it was discovered they were located virtually everywhere: Brazil, Russia, Philippines, Malaysia, and the United States. Auditors should not underestimate the value of chat rooms in determining an organization's vulnerabilities.

What Parts of the System Are Alive?

One of the most basic steps in a network vulnerability assessment is the port scan on a range of IP addresses and network blocks in order to ascertain which systems are alive and functioning. There are many tools available to perform this function:

- For UNIX, go to http://packetstorm.securify.com/Exploit_code_archive/fping.tar.gz for the fping tool.
- Nmap, which is probably one of the most useful vulnerability tools for UNIX platforms, is found at www.insecure.org/nmap.
- A Windows version of Nmap may be found at www.eeye.com/html.research/tools/nmapNT.html. Instructions for tool use are located at the corresponding Web sites.
- Another ping scanner known as SuperScan can be found at www.foundstone.com/rdlabs/proddesc/superscan.html, Exhibit 14.

Ping scanning will provide an inventory of active targets. While Nmap and other tools will provide many types of port scanning results, it is suggested that the results of ping scans be used to determine which devices should be port scanned.

Ping scans usually produce results similar to the following example:

```
[localhost] $ fping -f discov.txt
194.168.2.154 is alive
194.168.2.168 is alive
194.168.3.2 is alive
194,168,3,104 is alive
194.168.3.209 is alive
```

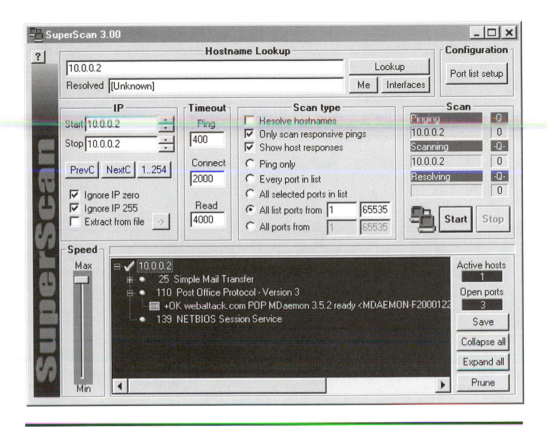

Exhibit 14   SuperScan

With the ping scan completed, auditors may compare the results with the organization's policy and procedure documentation. If the inventory and the ping discovery do not match exactly, there are several possibilities:

- There is a rogue piece of equipment located on the system waiting to be exploited.
- There are IP addresses showing as assigned to a particular piece of equipment.
- It is possible the IP address-related equipment is disabled, misplaced, or stolen.

If a security-conscious system's employee has disabled the ICMP (Internet Control Management Protocol) ping function, there are some additional tools and techniques that may be necessary for system discovery.

Typical TCP (Transmission Control Protocol) ports and UDP (User Datagram Protocol) ports are numbered from 0 to 65534. Ports that have services listening on them are known as sockets. Services that are installed and active can lead to systems vulnerabilities and exploits. Depending on the rules of engagement and the thoroughness of the audit, a port scan of all TCP and UDP ports could take several hours for each hardware device to be examined. However, if there is sufficient time, a thorough end-to-end review of ports is recommended as part of any thorough vulnerability assessment.

Using Nmap can provide many options relative to the fashion in which the port scan is conducted. Some of these options include:

Exhibit 15   Sample Output of Nmap

Port	State	Protocol	Service
TCP Scan			
21	open	tcp	ftp
22	open	tcp	ssh
23	open	tcp	telnet
79	open	tcp	finger
111	open	tcp	sunrpc
UDP Scan			
53	open	udp	domain
111	open	udp	sunrpc
123	udp	ntp	
137	open	udp	netbios-ns
138	open	udp	netbios-dgm
177	open	udp	xdmcp
1024	open	udp	unknown

- Ping sweep
- SYN Stealth
- FIN Stealth
- UDP Port Scan
- Fast Scan
- Host name
- ICMP Ping
- Range of Ports
- Use Decoys
- Get indentd Info

For a sample of Nmap output and results, see Exhibit 15 and Exhibit 16.

Look at the scanner output and guess which port an attacker would choose to exploit. Consider it the vulnerability of choice. If the attacker cannot find a host with open ports, it is a simple matter to find another host on your target network, run a port scan, locate the active services, and exploit them. If there are unnecessary services listening on ports, it is a simple matter for the attacker to research possible methods to gain entry and make her move.

In addition to the scanners listed above, the auditor has available the *netstat* command as part of UNIX and Windows NT platforms. Getting help with *netstat* is as simple as obtaining a command line from DOS or UNIX and inputting *netstat?*; entering this command results in the display of netstat's switches and functions.

Exhibit 17 is an example of netstat's output.

Using the *netstat* command is an expedient means to determine the listening services on a single workstation or server. This practice assumes a reasonable sample is being taken by the auditors. Using this method is recommended when conducting individual workstation or server audits. The *netstat* output should be printed using the *printscreen* option located on the keyboard and saved as part of the audit work papers.

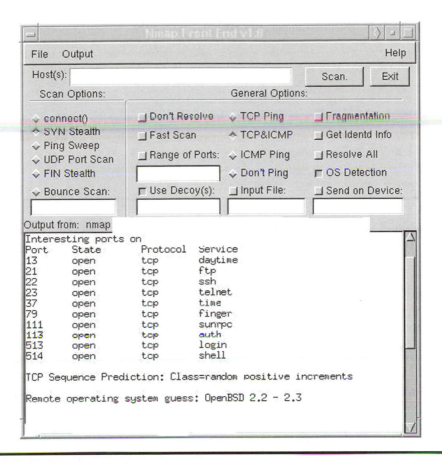

Exhibit 16   Sample of Nmap Results

Exhibit 17   C:\ netstat -na

Proto	Local Address	Foreign Address	State
Active connections			
TCP	0.0.0.0:80	0.0.0.0:0	LISTENING
TCP	0.0.0.0:139	0.0.0.0:0	LISTENING
TCP	0.0.0.0:445	0.0.0.0:0	LISTENING

Identifying Operating Systems

Nmap can also be used to identify an operating system by examining its response to nonstandard TCP/IP packets. Nmap has this capability as a feature, by simply adding –O option. The output is similar to the example in Exhibit 18.

For a good reference for TCP stack fingerprinting, go to www.insecure.org/nmap/nmap-fingerprinting-article.html. Stack fingerprinting is not foolproof, but it is a valuable method to confirm that a specific operating system is present on a specific IP address. Stack fingerprinting results should be included in the comparison between the actual inventory results and those created through the vulnerability assessment. Any disparities should be resolved before being listed as a finding in the audit report.

Exhibit 18   Localhost #nmap –O –sS

Starting nmap V. 2.2 by Fyodor <fyodor@dhp.com,www.insecure.org/nmap/)
Host (192.166.201.0) seems to be a subnet broadcast address (returned 1extra
pings). Interesting ports on Interexample.com (192.166.201.0):

Port	State	Protocol	Service
22	open	tcp	ssh
111	open	tcp	sunrpc
1025	open	tcp	unknown

TCP sequence prediction: Class = random positive increments
Remote operating system guess: Linux 2.1.2–2.1.22

Such resolution actions will disclose the accuracy of the inventory and discover any prohibited activities.

Domain Name Server, DNS, and Zone Transfers

A frequent misconfiguration found in many DNS servers is allowing untrusted users to perform a DNS zone transfer. Zone transfers permit a secondary master DNS server to update its zone database from the primary master DNS server. This provides for redundancy when running DNS, if the primary name server becomes unavailable. It is similar to having expected redundancy. Normally, a DNS zone transfer needs only to be performed by secondary master DNS servers; however, many DNS servers are poorly configured allowing a copy of the primary master DNS server database to be transferred to anyone who requests it.

This is not necessarily a bad practice and if an organization were to keep their interior and open-ended DNS servers partitioned; it will not generally be a problem. The matter gains strength when an organization has only one DNS server for both the exterior open-ended networks and the sensitive interior networks. In this case, internal hostnames and corresponding IP addresses are revealed through the DNS zone transfer to an attacker. Providing internal IP addresses to an untrusted user is analogous to providing a complete architectural map of your interior network.

Experience Note   Allowing zone transfers from the interior system's DNS to any exterior DNS is poor business procedure and should be addressed appropriately.

An easy way to perform a zone transfer is to use the *nslookup* client already provided as part of the UNIX or Windows NT installation. An example of using the *nslookup* is shown in Exhibit 19.

Exhibit 19   [bash] $ nslookup

default server: dns2.interexampleonline.com
address: 197.123.123.2
>> server 197.123.123.2
Default server: [197.123.123.2]
Address: 197.123.123.2
>> set type = any
>> ls –d interexampleonline.com..tmp/zone_out

Exhibit 20

acct20	1D	IN	A	194.178.22..0
	1D	IN	HINFO	"IBM" "WinWKGRPS"
	1D	IN	TXT	"Location : Server Room"
ce	1D	IN	CNAME	gandolfo
au	1D	IN	A	194.178.22.1

This script allows *nslookup* to run in interactive mode. It should produce the default name server it is using. Under general circumstances, it should be the organization's DNS server, or the DNS server provided by the host. Setting the record type to *any* allows the zone transfer of any DNS records available. Exhibit 20 is an example of the zone transfer output.

There are automated zone transfer features with the SamSpade tool that will speed the assessment process. There are several important records displayed as part of the zone transfer: internal IP addresses, names of hosts, locations, and other information useful for the attacker. Auditors should include DNS zone transfers as part of their audit program. Restricting zone transfers will definitely increase the time necessary for attackers to probe your network for IP addresses and host names.

Auditors should recommend that exterior and interior DNS servers be partitioned between a DMZ and firewalls. This architecture provides that the outside network connects to a packet screening firewall, the DMZ contains the outside DNS server to handle exterior addressing. The inside network connects to the DMZ and is protected by a firewall consisting of an application firewall (proxy). Interior name servers should never be used for exterior network name resolution and should be located on the inside of the proxy service. Interior DNS servers should be configured so they deliver and accept zone transfers from the interior network only, never from outside the DMZ. HINFO records can be used for identifying the system's operating systems. HINFO should be disabled on exterior DNS services.

Automated Vulnerability Tools

General-purpose vulnerability scanners will perform a wide variety of security tests against network resources. Some scanners combine host and network tests via local agents installed on the target. It is important to note that some tests performed by automated scanners will compromise the audit target in order to verify the vulnerability or to collect more information. It is essential to address these issues in the rules of engagement, and it is prudent to alert appropriate levels of management before executing these audits as they tend to send administrators into the stratosphere.

Once configured with a range of primary targets such as IP addresses or system names, automated scanners provide the following results:

- Locate targets from the IP range.
- Inventory services present on each target.
- In some cases, automated tools infer new targets from gathered data.
- Automated tools will launch individual tests for identified services. An example of this individual test is the tool's ability to relay e-mail through a mail server.

Experience Note Automated vulnerability tools have one significant advantage: if auditors do not use them in conducting vulnerability assessments, attackers will.

From a practical view, the results of an automated vulnerability scanner should be considered a minimum vulnerability baseline. During the execution of the scan, if there are many high-risk findings, then the network has serious issues, and senior management must be notified immediately. However, it is a fair statement that if the automated tool finds few, if any, high-risk issues, there may be many undiscovered potential exploits. They are not anywhere near perfect. For this reason, vulnerability assessments are only a part of the audit program.

There are some serious limitations of automated tools:

- The results are merely a snapshot of the system at the time of the scan.
- The tool only evaluates the system according to the tool's configuration.
- The tool is only as good as its attack signature database. If the database is not updated continuously, the results of the scan will likely be poor. Because new vulnerabilities are announced frequently, the tool's database must be modified to reflect these new issues.
- The tool does not evaluate compliance with specific policies, procedures, and standards.
- The tool will only consider known vulnerabilities with Common Vulnerabilities and Exploits (CVEs) revealed almost weekly, automated tools provide only relative measurements.
- False positives are common in the results of vulnerability scans. In other words, tools report too many false alarms. The test may have been flawed or the auditor used an excessively ambitious test numbering. In other words, the same vulnerability is reported with different names. It is only a tool and requires intelligent operation.
- False negatives are also common and may be worse than the false positives.

There are two types of automated vulnerability scanners, network-based and host-based. Network-based scanners attempt to gain visibility into vulnerabilities from the outside. This type of scanner is generally launched from a remote system, outside the organization, without authorized user access. For example, network-based scanners examine a system for such exploits as open ports, application security exploits, and buffer overflows.

The host-based scanners usually require a software agent or client to be installed on the host. The client then reports back to the managing station vulnerabilities it finds. Host-based scanners look for features as weak file access permissions, poor passwords, logging faults, and so on.

Exhibit 21 lists some of the more-popular vulnerability scanners. The listed products are intended only to provide a small sample of available tools. These products are listed for reference and feature comparison only; none of the comments should be considered recommendations.

These are dynamic pieces of software. Their features, capabilities, and sometimes existence change frequently, so do your research and comparison. Make certain your choice of automated tool fills your needs.

Of course, there are freeware vulnerability scanners that are also worth mentioning.

- SARA was introduced in 1999 and has received Internet support. Visiting the Web site (www.arc.com/sara) reveals some vulnerability updates.
- SAINT was introduced in 1998 and also has received Internet support. The Web site (www.wwdsi.com/saint) has software, documentation, and updates.

Exhibit 21   Vulnerability Scanners

Target Host Platform	Network-Based	Host-Based
Windows NT	CyberCop, ISS Internet Scanner, NetRecon, Nessus	ISS System Scanner, Bindview
UNIX (HP-UX, Solaris, AIX)	CyberCop, ISS Internet Scanner, Nessus, NetRecon	Bindview, Enterprise Security Manager
AS/400	CyberCop, ISS Internet Scanner, Nessus, NetRecon	Enterprise Security Manager
Netware	NetRecon, Nessus	Bindview, Enterprise Security Manager

- Nessus was introduced in 1998 and has received widespread Internet support. The Web site (www.nessus.org) has hundreds of updates, currently more than 1200 modules. This is a very powerful tool, primarily UNIX-based, but there is some Windows NT capability. Nessus is a free, open-source code, general-purpose vulnerability scanner. It is freely available to legitimate users as well as the attacker community. Nessus consists of a client/server architecture with modular plug-ins for individual tests. Nessus is typical of most sophisticated vulnerability scanners in that it is updated frequently, flexible in its configuration, and comprehensive in its vulnerability report functions.

From the auditor's perspective, the value of the tool's report is important; however, it frequently contains so much information that, unless boiled down to a useable document, it overwhelms the audit report. Before including the scanner's report as it is generated in the work papers is prudent, as it demonstrates the depth of the assessment. Only after testing the scanner's report results, eliminating false positives and negatives, should they be included in the body of the audit report (Exhibit 22 through Exhibit 26).

Nessus is open to development and freely available. It can be modified to fill specific requirements and is constantly being updated with more modules. As you can see from the list of vulnerability families (Exhibit 26), Nessus is a thorough and comprehensive scanning tool.

Experience Note It is important to notify senior managers before administering an automated vulnerability tool.

Their function mimics attacker-profiles, triggers intrusion detection equipment and causes a substantial exercise of firewall resources. If not properly configured correctly, automated scanners running at full-throttle can absorb all network resources acting like a denial or service attack. These are matters to be addressed in the rules of engagement.

Doing Your Homework

Auditors should carefully research vulnerabilities found after executing an automated scan. It is possible there are vulnerabilities that require immediate attention and it is quite possible there are repeated vulnerabilities. Auditors must be careful before hitting the panic button; it is possible the vulnerability may be a false positive. Verify the existence of all reported vulnerabilities before including them as findings.

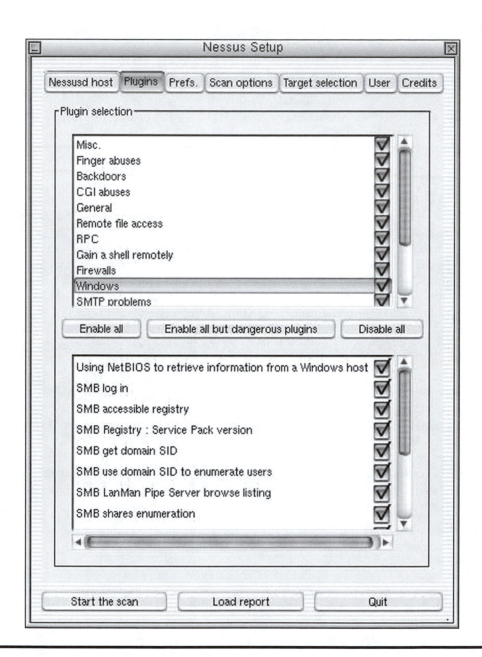

Exhibit 22   Nessus Plugins

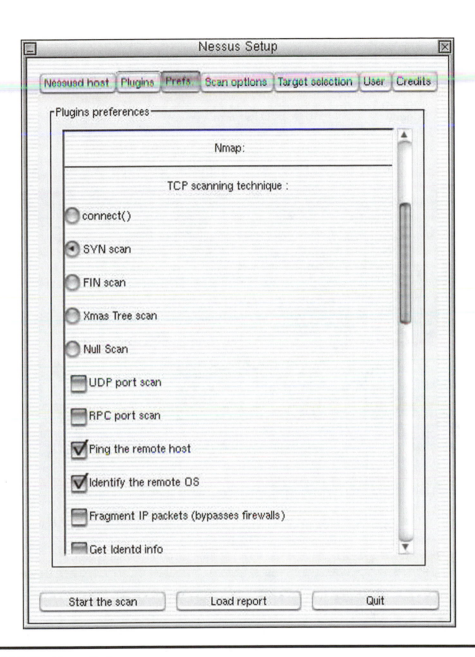

Exhibit 23   Nessus Preferences

Exhibit 24   Nessus Plugin Families[a]

Backdoors	CGI abuses	CISCO
Denial of service	Finger abuses	Firewalls
FTP	Gain a shell remotely	Gain root remotely
General	Miscellaneous	Netware
NIS	Port scanners	Remote file access
RPC	Settings	SMTP problems
SNMP	Untested	Useless services
Windows	Windows : User management	

[a] There are currently 1093 vulnerability-testing plug-ins in the database.

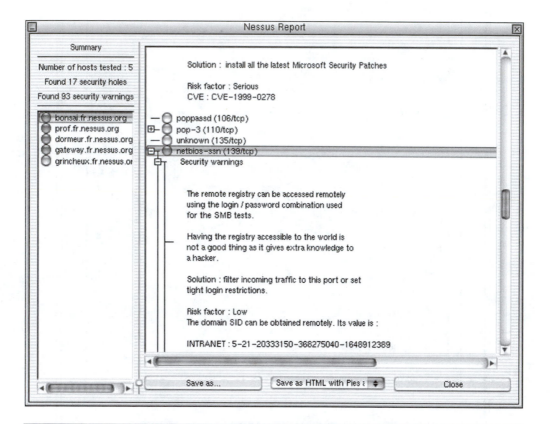

Exhibit 25   Nessus Report Sample

There are a few essential places to research this type of information:

- Automated scanner vendor Web sites
- Antivirus software vendor Web sites
- Specialty Web sites such as www.securityfocus.com/vdb, www.cert.org, and www.cve.mitre.org

Another useful Web site for vulnerability information is the ICAT Metabase. This database is a searchable index of system vulnerabilities. ICAT links users to a variety

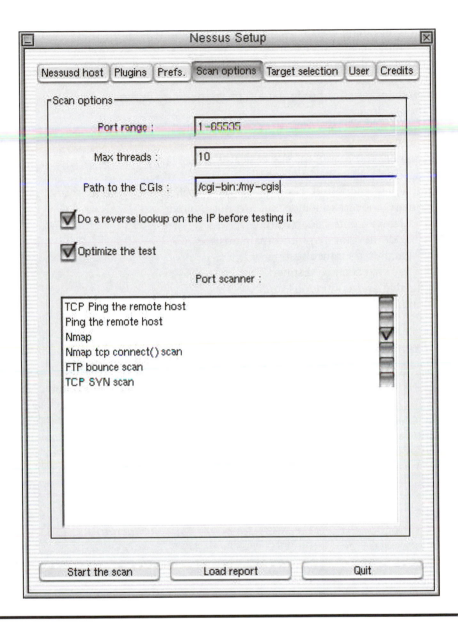

Exhibit 26   Nessus Scan Options

of publicly available vulnerability databases and software Web sites. It is a searchable index of resources and can be found at: http://icat.nist.gov/icat.cfm.

Web Application Vulnerability Assessments

One of the most attractive business frontiers is E-commerce. For the first time in history, a business can have its doors open to the entire world where users can make purchases with nothing more than their credit cards in hand. Businesses are drawn to E-commerce to disseminate company information, sell products and services, provide customer service, and gain a competitive advantage. Most organizations with a presence on the World Wide Web have installed preventive and detection controls in the form of installing DMZs, firewalls, and intrusion detection equipment, and hiring competent employees. Senior managers are surprised at what an attacker can do with a Web-browser and a little creativity.

Auditors must be aware there are logical steps in reducing risks, but the majority of vulnerabilities are found in faulty programming, misconfiguration, and absent systems monitoring.

Auditors must be aware that risks are controlled by:

- Knowing the organization's critical assets
- Knowing threats and vulnerabilities
- Implementation and compliance with policies, procedures, and standards; primary concerns include but are not limited to:
  - Change control management
  - Code development and maintenance
  - Quality assurance testing
  - User acceptance testing
- Effective and continuous audits
- Continuing risk management

HTML Examination

As a logical first step, auditors should carefully examine the HTML, HyperText Markup Language, composition of the organization's Web site. Attackers examine the Web page coding as one of their first steps to gaining as much knowledge as possible about their targets. Basically, auditors should download all the pages comprising the organization's Web site and examine the HTML coding. Often there are valuable programmer comments, passwords, telephone numbers, names, contractor's information, and business addresses, commonly placed within the HTML. For example:

```
<HTML>
<HEAD>
<TITLE> Welcome to the XYZ Corporation HomePage </TITLE>
<BODY> BGCOLOR = "#0000FF" TEXT = #FFFFF">
</Body>
</HTML>
<! — Any problems call Alice Doe at ABC Web Design, Waterfront,
San Diego, CA, XXX-555-1234 or e-mail me at alicedoe@ABCWebDe-
sign.com — >
```

An examination of this Web page HTML reveals the XYZ Corporation is using an outsource Web design firm, and the page designer has listed her name and contact information. This information could be very useful to an attacker who was interested in doing a bit of social engineering with Alice Doe or her employer.

Testing for Indexed Directories

Auditors should obtain a list of the indexed Web page directories. The manual process is a slow one, where the browser is used to request specific directories. For this reason, it is more expeditious for the auditor to obtain a list of indexed directories from the Web page administrator. However, if a true outside view is sought, the auditor can deploy her browser in this fashion (http://www.xyzcorporation.com/images).

If the browser returns the images directory, it is important for the auditor to examine each and every file related to the Web site. More than once, auditors have discovered files that were not innocent files.

Experience Note While conducting an audit of a client's Web site, the auditor began to survey the files accessible from the URL address line of the browser, using the format of www.xzycorporation.com/files. After downloading the files, it was discovered that one of them contained personally identifiable employee information.

Web Server Examination

Auditors may frequently access a company's Web site and determine the presence of specific Web servers. In UNIX and Windows environments, auditors may use the telnet client. By requesting a bogus file, the server file returns an error message and often the Web server will be correctly named. With this knowledge, an attacker merely researches the Internet for known vulnerabilities and executes them. For example:

```
# telnet www.xyzcorporation.com 80
Trying 275.xxx.xxx.xxx
Connected to
XYZCorporation.
Escape character is ^
GET/no-such-page.html HTTP/1.0 (At this time the auditor presses
the Enter key twice)
HTTP/1.0 error 404 Not Found
Server: IIS-1.0 (This is the Internet Information Server version
1.0)
Content-Type: text/html
Content-Length: 295
```

Another useful tool for auditors is found at the Web site www.netcraft.com. This tool is useful whether Web sites are SSL, Secure Sockets Layer, enabled. By completing a few entries, the netcraft tool will display information about the particular Web site of interest including the Web server and operating system.

Experience Note It is possible that savvy administrators have changed the banners in their server responses, so it is beneficial to verify the information before listing it as a possible finding.

Although this is not considered a high-risk vulnerability, but there are many advantages in concealing system information from attackers. Attackers using techniques to identify the Web server and its version will browse the Internet in an effort to obtain vulnerability information that can be used to exploit the server. So, if they do not have accurate information, they must resort to another means to identify the Web server. It is not a perfect remedy. Efforts to conceal information will often discourage the casual attacker but probably will not dissuade the more-motivated ones.

In a Window's environment, the HTTP server field may be edited via a hex editor in the W3SVC.DLL file and in a UNIX environment, the TCP/IP stack may be changed following the instructions at http://ippersonality.sourcefourge.net. It is suggested that the Web server response should be changed to reflect something nonsensical such as *Vital O/S 2003*.

There are many advantages in the practice of security through obscurity. Auditors have a variety of tools available when mirroring a Web site. The advantage of mirroring a Web site is that auditors can view it at their leisure and conduct an in-depth review of the HTML as well as its construction. There are Web site mirroring tools at www.webstripper.net, www.esalesbiz.com/extra, and www.softbytelabs.com.

Web site mirroring software will generally follow all links on a Web site and copy discovered files to the auditor's hard drive. In configuring them, rules can be set limiting the software to specific domains or preventing downloading certain file types.

Experience Note WGET is a UNIX tool to mirror Web sites and may be found at http://wget.sunsite.dk.

Once a Web site has been downloaded, the auditor can open the pages in a simple text editor application, such as Notepad or Vi, and review the HTML content. Auditors should review coding for e-mail addresses, names, addresses, passwords, and other information useful to an attacker.

Accidental Error Messages

It is not unusual for Web servers to mishandle unanticipated user input. They fail to adequately address incorrect input and frequently provide verbose error messages that can provide valuable information to an attacker. For example, if a user incorrectly entered her user name information, the system might respond with an error message such as *We were unable to find an account for this user name, click here to enroll*. If the user inputs an incorrect password, the system might respond with an error message such as *You have entered an incorrect password, you can reset it by clicking here*.

Attackers can use overly informative error messages to either launch a denial-of-service attack or attempt to engage a brute-force attack against the password entry. A more appropriate error message is one similar to: *There has been a user error; please provide the correct input*. Auditors must be mindful that authorized user logons should never be the same as the user names used by the organization's e-mail naming conventions. From an attacker's point of view, the e-mail user naming convention being the same as the user name logon is having half the problem solved for a successful attack.

Some Web sites permit an unlimited number of failed sign-on attempts without being locked out. The vulnerability in this flawed practice is that user accounts can be compromised via brute-force attacks targeting the Web site's password entry.

Brute-force attacks are either manually or automatically performed where alphabetical and numerical combinations are tried as data entries to gain entry. From a preventive control stance, the sign-in policy should be that the user is locked out for a specified time after three failed sign-on attempts.

Experience Note Remember, even this policy is not without a threat potential in that an attacker can target the sign-on with incorrect data entry and lock out a legitimate user when she attempts entry. Having a viable and acceptable user reactivation policy is an important aspect of this preventive control.

There is a useful password-guessing tool to be found at www.tlsecurity.net/windows/cracker/webcracker.htm. This tool will automatically brute-force passwords in HTTP basic authentication and form-based authentication. Auditors should attempt to gain entry through brute-force methods as a means of testing entry security.

Another method that may have some success in defeating brute-force entry tools is to avoid direct linking to the sign-on function. For example, Web pages found behind the sign-on function should have a referrer field where the originating Web page of the user is checked against the allowed Web page URL, uniform resource locator.

Another method defeating some attacks is the error message, *"inactivity timeout."* This action causes the user's session to be terminated after a predefined period of inactivity. Auditors may test and verify this procedure by opening a Web page session in a sensitive area such as an E-commerce site where financial or personal information is collected. The server should terminate the session after predetermined period of user inactivity. This step prevents someone from hijacking the user's session.

More Unexpected User Input

There are a variety of ways that user input can be different from what was anticipated by the Web page developers. The size of the input can be too large, or too small. The input's content can be inappropriate in that alternate characters or executable scripts may be used causing the server to execute the input. Developers should incorporate user input screening in their programming routines. These are the types of input that should be filtered:

- Metacharacters are special characters that represent something other than what they are themselves. For example, the ; (semicolon) is a command separator and the ? (question mark) is a match for a single character.
- HTML delimiter characters such as "<" and ">".
- Path redirection such as "/../" or ".." indicate the user is attempting to access the directory structure outside the Web server's Web page. These are known as regular expressions and must be screened before being processed by the server.

Experience Note User input must always be screened with all improper input denied.

Overflow Vulnerabilities

Improperly validated user input to the Content-Type header can cause a buffer overflow condition. As a result of nonvalidated user input, excessive data copied onto the data stack can overwrite critical parts of the stack frame such as the calling function's return address, potentially permitting remote code execution with root privileges on the Web server. It is important for auditors to determine if user input is checked for correctness and any input other than the expected input merely returns an error message.

Additionally, it is important that not only user-supplied input is screened and verified, but everything coming from the user's browser to the Web server should be filtered. Users can put executable code within the URL address and without proper filtering, it is possible that user input may be executed by the server.

Hidden Form Elements

HTML supports a form element called "hidden." These variables along with their included values are sent to the user by the Web server and in return get embedded into the HTML response to the user. These hidden elements were never intended to be seen by the user nor were they supposed to be changed or manipulated.

Users can alter these HTML elements changing their values causing unexpected input results. It is relatively a simple process for the auditor to download the Web page, change the HTML in a simple text editor, save it and then replace the Web page in the browser and have the page submitted to the Web server. For example:

```
<Form Action = " http://www.xyzcorporation.com/cgi-
bin/search.cgi"
Method = "Post">
<TD><Input type = "text" name = "query" size = "30" MAXLENGTH
= "40"
<Value = ""></TD>
<TD align = center><input type = "submit" value = "search"></TD>
<Input type = "Hidden" name = "user name" Value = search"></form>
```

Users may change the last value statement to [*value* = *"/etc/password"*]. It is possible if the user input were not filtered, it could result in the password file being passed from the server to the user's browser. There is a practical rule of thumb, when filtering user input, it is best to define permitted characters and deny everything else as opposed to attempting to predict everything that is not permitted and removing those elements. Basically, the rule is this one, if it is not specifically allowed, it is denied. For example, if a form is requesting a person's telephone area code, nothing more than three numeric digits are acceptable and all other entries are denied resulting in error messages.

Attackers can easily use search engines such as www.Google.com to find potentially vulnerable fields in Web pages. For example, if an attacker were looking for vulner-abilities on the XYZ Corporation Web page, she enters the following in *Google: "type = hidden"* and *"name = price" site: xyzcorporationonline.com.* Using search engines with entries similar to this entry will reveal all pages within the domain, *xyzcorporationonline.com* that contain strings of *"type = hidden"* and *"name = price."* These hidden fields are used to pass price information to the Web server. If the user-input information is not screened for correctness, the price paid may be significantly less than the actual price. For example, a Web page that states the purchase information for a particular product. Frequently, the page is downloaded to the user's browser and a request of the user is made to indicate the number of the product the user wishes to purchase. The user downloads the HTML and changes the price of the product from $500 to $5 using a text editor, saves the modified page and submits the page to the server for processing. The order is processed as there is no more field checking in the shopping cart software. With the order shipped, the vendor is shorted $495. It is important that auditors consider that this type of financial attack is possible by testing the shopping software and making certain that all user-inputs are checker for correctness.

Get vs. Post Commands in CGI Forms

Auditors should carefully examine the method used by Web developers to collect and send user-supplied data. In world of HTML and where CGI, common gateway interface scripts are used, there are two methods of transmitting data. In HTML, the default method for form requests is *Get* so if the developer did not specify the attribute from the *Form* tag, the system will assume the developer meant *Get.* The *Get* method is the easiest request method. It requests a document from the Web server. When the browser uses the *Get* method to request a document from the Web server, the request looks like this example:

```
GET HTTP1.0/index.html
```

When a form is submitted using the *Get* method, the URL-encoded data is tacked onto the end of the URL that's requested, with a question mark inserted between them as a separator. So, if the auditor were to submit the data in a form using the *Get* method, it could look something like:

```
GET HTTP/1.0/CGI-BIN/SAMPLE.CGI?USER NAME = ALICE+DOE
```

The Web server is programmed to send everything after the question mark to the CGI script *sample.cgi* file for processing. A problem with the *Get* method is that it does not provide any privacy to the user. Using the *Get* method has some possible user-related problems:

- It exposes user parameter values in the user's Web browser history file.
- It exposes user parameter values in the Web server's audit logs.
- It exposes user parameter values in the server's proxy logs.
- It exposes user parameter values at other Web sites via the HTTP referrer field.

It is possible that using the *Get* method may cause URLs to contain sensitive information such as account numbers, passwords, user names and addresses. Browser security exploits may permit malicious Web sites to steal the user's browser history file. If an attacker should gain physical access to the user's workstation, it is possible for her to steal the browser's history file and all the user-sensitive information it contains.

From the auditor's point of view, the preferable HTML method for forms is the *Post* method. The *Post* method sends the form data back to the Web server after the headers are sent. Using the *Post* method adds the attribute as:

```
METHOD = "POST"
```

to the *Form* tag used to create the HTML form. For example:

```
user name = Alice+Doe
```

The *Post* command tells the server to expect more data after the reset of the header is sent. A blank line is included between the header and the posted data to let the server know when the browser is finished with its header and is starting to send the actual form data. There is a difference between the *Get* and the *Post* methods in the way the form data is communicated from the Web server to the CGI program. In the *Get* method, data is stored in an environment variable, where it can be accessed by the CGI program. In the *Post* method, the data is submitted to the Web server and from there directly to the input of the CGI script.

So what is the best method for form handling in CGI? For nonsensitive routine matters, *Get* is an acceptable form handling method. There are many examples of search engines on the Internet that use *Get* as the form handler. For form data where there should be some expected or required degree of security, the *Post* method of form handling is the preferred method. Auditors reviewing HTML downloaded from the audit targets Web pages should be looking for these distinctions.

Web Page Referrer Fields

Current versions of HTML support the HTTP referrer header field. When a browser follows a link, the referrer field can contain the URL of the page the user came from. The referrer field can also be present when a form is submitted to the Web server for processing. Web Servers can check the referrer field when receiving a completed form and reject it if it did not come from the permitted URL. If this filtering action is performed, attacks from anywhere other than the specified URL should fail. Auditors should be mindful of referrer fields in the case of sensitive information being provided as form-input.

Unicode Input Attack

Unicode is one the Internet community's attempts at forming a single set of characters across all languages. Web servers such as Microsoft's Internet Information Server, IIS, supports the Unicode character set. Accepting and processing Unicode potentially leads to vulnerability exploits in the IIS Web server's reading and executing the Unicode script supplied by the attacker.

This attack is common and usually one of the first launched by attackers when an IIS Web service is found. There are easily available scripts that can be downloaded from the Internet that do not require the attacker to have any knowledge of their function before using them. The Unicode bug in IIS is basically one where a prohibited Unicode encoding of the *"/"* allowed users to craft URLs that could jump outside the Web document directory and call the command shell command, *cmd.exe* inside the Windows file system. The exploit is successful because IIS performs only one security check after the first script decode and as a result performs the request, as there is not a subsequent security check performed after the second decode pass. This vulnerability is run in the URL like this:

```
http://www.xyzcorporation.com/scripts/…%255c…%255cwinnt/
system32/cmd.exe?/c+dir+c:\
```

The URL causes the IIS Web server to interpret the Unicode characters as back slashes, bypassing the normal Web server filtering for such events, and moves two directory levels above the location of the/scripts/directory, and targets the/winnt'system32/cmd.exe.

Following are some examples of double decode variations:

```
%255c
%%35c
%%35%63
%25%35%63
```

These are not the only combinations. Many more are possible. For these reasons, user-input validation becomes very important. Auditors should also examine the system and change controls Web servers receiving the latest update patches as Microsoft currently delivers an IIS patch addressing these vulnerabilities.

Cookie Pal

Cookies are small fields of text data created in a file that a browser stores and uses to maintain its state and to retrieve information from the Web server. However, if an

E-commerce site is using cookies, Web servers can be fooled into delivering more information than they should. For reference, there are basically two types of cookies, session and persistent.

Session cookies remain only in the system's memory and are temporary fields of data held in the workstation until the client's browser is closed. Supposedly they are valid for the time the user is using specific Web site services. Session cookies are generally valid for finite periods of time. Unlike session cookies, persistent cookies are held on the workstation's hard disk and are read by the browser when requested to do so. For example, in Microsoft's Internet Explorer, persistent cookies are held in the C:\Documents and Settings\Administrator\Cookies directory.

The Cookie Pal application is a shareware program available at: www.kburra.net/. Cookie Pal permits control of both the session cookie and the persistent cookie before being lodged in memory or recorded on the hard drive. Basically, Cookie Pal intercepts the request in the Web server's response and displays it in a dialogue box.

Remember, cookies frequently hold user information as stored user names, passwords, preferences, mailing addresses, and online identification. It is important to note that often cookies contain a significant amount of information valuable to an attacker. Attackers do not usually have access to cookies unless they can gain access to a user's workstation. Cookie Pal allows an auditor to intercept a cookie and examine its contents. This is an extremely useful technique when auditing the cookies being placed by the organization's Web site.

A possible attacker ploy is to modify the cookie containing the number of times the Web page had been visited by a user. It may be possible to change the cookie reflecting the number of user visits with some exorbitant number of visits possibly causing a server buffer overflow to occur if the user-input is not checked for correctness.

Achilles

Achilles can be one of the more useful tools for actively auditing Web applications. It is a Windows-based utility and is capable of acting like a Web proxy, where information is captured before being sent back to the Web server. It is a free tool and available at: http://www.digizen-security.com/projects.html.

Achilles allows the user to intercept Web page information, modify it, and send it forward to the server. This ability to modify information on the fly is a tremendous ability permitting an attacker to efficiently attempt code-injection or value changes before the information goes on.

Achilles' configuration is fairly straightforward. Click on the "Intercept Server Data (text)" checkbox in Achilles, and then make a request of the Web server. The client's request will get intercepted, as well as the server's reply. The server's reply can reveal the cookies being set, management attempts on the part of the server, and any fields that may be modified later by the user before being sent onto the Web server.

Automated Web Tools

Automated Web site vulnerability tools look for vulnerabilities in CGI scripts and other exploitable areas. Network vulnerability tools sometimes have utilities testing Web site weaknesses. They may simulate attacks in the fashion of Nessus having modules that test areas such as password strength and CGI vulnerabilities.

Whisker

Whisker is a PERL language-based CGI scanner and it is one of the most comprehensive CGI vulnerability tools. It scans a target Web site and compares it against a database of known vulnerabilities. Applicable vulnerability database files are updated from the Whisker Web site. It is configurable and has a default database of script files that is fairly comprehensive. It is available from: http://sourceforge.net/projects/whisker/.

Basically, it is a universal tool and can be used in a UNIX or a Windows environment if PERL is downloaded on the scanning computer. To use Whisker, execute it from the command line and provide a target IP address or host name of the target Web server. It is a bit difficult for someone not comfortable programming in PERL; however, it is considered as one of the best CGI vulnerability scanners available. Using Whisker is run from the command line like this:

```
C:\nt\whisker\v1.4>whisker.pl -h 127.X.X.6
whisker/v1.4/rain forest puppy/www.wiretrip.net -
 = - = - = - = - =
 = Host: 127.X.X.6
 = Server: Apache/1.3.0 (Linux 6.2)
200 OK: HEAD/cgi-bin/creditcards
200 OK: HEAD/clearinghouse/
```

In this case, Whisker identified the Web server as Apache version 1.3.0 running on Linux version 6.2. Whisker identified two important links that could provide temptations for an attacker interested in obtaining credit card information or information about the clearinghouse.

SiteScan

SiteScan is a fairly useful tool for finding Web site vulnerabilities.* It is a Windows-based tool and is easy to install, configure, and launch. There is a bit of a downside in that this tool is dated. However, many of the exploits identified by this tool are relevant for auditing purposes as Web site administrators frequently fail to keep their systems updated with the latest patches.

Brutus

This is essentially another password brute-force testing tool.** It is a fairly simple tool to use and delivers an easy way to test authentication mechanisms via brute-force attacks. Brutus is Windows-based and is a tool that is not restricted to HTTP. Brutus can attack FTP, telnet, POP3, and SMB password accounts. Because Web servers were intended to handle large numbers of requests, it is one of the easier areas on which to force an intrusion and gain access.

Experience Note Automated vulnerability tools are effective and for the most part efficient. However, they should not be used as the sole means of assessing systems. Automated tools are limited to the vulnerabilities listed in their database or the potential passwords located in their dictionaries. They cannot examine policies, procedures,

---

* Available at www.hackers.com/html/archive.5.html.
** This tool is a download from www.hoobie.net/brutus.

and standards. They are merely tools, among all the tools, available to the auditor and should not be allowed to replace experience and good judgment.

Quality Control Issues

There are quality matters about which auditors should be concerned. Assessments of Web-enabled applications are important and generally require a significant amount of work. Evaluating Web applications is much easier while in the testing phase before they enter the production environment. Web application assessments should be completed after the Quality Assurance Unit has done their job, and before actual User Acceptance Testing, UAT, is commenced especially if real customers are going to be used. It is possible that real customers have malicious intent or they accidentally discover a security flaw during the UAT. Auditors should remember the following:

- Test sign-on processes
- Test sign-off processes
- Test modified user-supplied input
- All user input must be filtered at the Web server for proper size and content type before being accepted and acted on by the CGI scripts
- All CGI Output in the form of HTML and HTTP must be scrubbed of comments, error messages, sensitive information, and hidden tags that identify the Web server's version and any third-party products
- All CGI defaults must be removed or secured before going into a production environment
- Test error messages for degree of information
- Test logical sequences
- Test HTML in Web page content assuring that it does not contain any sensitive information
- Web application assessments are dependent on the knowledge and expertise of real people; using a manual and automated approach generally assures accuracy

Reporting Vulnerability Assessment Results

It is recommended that automated vulnerability assessment results occupy a separate section of the audit report. Of course, before any automated tool results are made part of the audit report, auditors must verify the findings of their tools. It is not professionally diligent to take the tool's results and include them in the audit report without further corroboration.

Audit team members must verify reported vulnerabilities. With this being said, once verified vulnerability findings should be ranked relative to their risk and potential for exploitation. Rankings should generally fall in three categories, low, medium, and high. In the realm of exposure, vulnerabilities may be labeled to detail the area required for leveraging the vulnerability usually defined as "remote" or "local." Remote vulnerability permits an attacker to exploit the system's weaknesses from across the network without having prior access to the target system. A local vulnerability requires the attacker to have some type of system access before being able to exploit vulnerabilities. Before completing the report, auditors must answer the question, "how popular is the vulnerability I have found, and if exploited what is its greatest impact?" Many vulnerabilities and corrective actions may be found at these Web sites:

- www.sans.org/top20htm
- www.cert.org
- www.cve.mitre.org
- www.securityfocus.com

If the auditor's findings are among the more common vulnerabilities listed at these Web sites, the chances are very good that your vulnerabilities are currently being attacked and have already been exploited or they will be shortly. Auditors should make their findings known to senior managers as soon as possible and recommend which controls should be implemented. Vulnerabilities that are found will likely be listed among the CVEs at www.cve.mitre.org along with their corresponding corrective action. If corrective steps are taken, auditors should verify the corrections making certain they are noted in the final report.

Audit findings detected during the automated vulnerability assessment should be evaluated in the light of their business impact. In other words, they should be gauged according to their potential to adversely affect the organization's critical assets.

- *High:* These findings are the most significant and pose an immediate danger to the security of the company's critical assets. These findings must be addressed before the audit report is drafted. Do not wait. Report these findings to senior managers immediately.
- *Medium:* These audit findings should be addressed according to a specific timeline.
- *Low:* These are low priority findings and should be noted and implemented on a scheduled later date. They do not pose a risk at the present time.

Audit Findings

Audit findings generally have several elements. These elements include a title, risk rating, description, potential risk impact, affected systems, recommendations for corrective action, and references for further details (Exhibit 27).

Audit Issues

Audit reports should contain possible system issues. Issues are narratives of industry best practices regarding particular risk factors. They should be included in the auditor's report to augment a specific finding or to enhance the overall understanding of a particular topic. For example, an issue may detail best practices for configuring ingress traffic on your exterior router. Issues do not generally have risk ratings and should be presented in professional tones.

Auditing Remote System Administration

Generally, administrating a network consists of updating user accounts, examining logs, establishing and maintaining standard configurations, and installing and updating software. Administrators perform these tasks from either the location of the workstation or server or from a remote location. For the administration team who has several hundred servers and several thousand workstations, handling these tasks remotely is the most effective and efficient way of doing business.

Exhibit 27 Automated Vulnerability Sample Finding Report

Finding	*DNS Cache Corruption Potential*
Description	Versions 4.5, and below, of the DNS application known as BIND are vulnerable to attack where individuals cache incorrect name server information on the DNS server. This action allows the attacker to "spoof" the DNS name server and redirect Web access to another Web page. Further, this vulnerability permits the attacker to bypass name-based authentication mechanisms.
Potential business risk	Because the XYZ Corporation uses E-commerce extensively, comprising approximately 89 percent of its current business revenue, this vulnerability permits users to illicitly access the interior File Transfer Protocol, FTP, server, xxx.xxx.xxx.xxx from the Internet. This is a high-priority audit finding and was verbally brought to the attention of Ms. Senior Audit Manager, on 12 December 2002 at approximately 1600 hrs.

Name	*Affected System* IP Address	*Information*
NS1.exampleonline.com	xxx.xxx.xxx.xxx	DNS Server
Recommendation	On 12 December 2002, at approximately 1700 hrs, the BIND DNS server was updated to version 9 with all attendant security patches. This implementation was made as a "clean" installation and was implemented across the XYZ Corporation and its subsidiaries. This recommendation was forwarded to its business partners who were urged to update their systems.	
References	CERT Advisory CA-97.22 BIND	

Here are a few considerations that should be part of the auditor's program in systems with remote configuration capability:

- Ensure that the system accepts administration commands from only an authenticated administrator. Client systems must use strong authentication and traffic encryption mechanisms. Under no circumstances should the administrator send her password in clear text to the system on which she is going to work. The only logical exception for transmitting the user password in clear text is the use of one-time passwords transmitted from the administrator and accepted by the target system.
- Auditors must ensure that the system permits administration to take place from the authenticated host only. It is important that the system receiving the administrator's attention authenticates her identity through means distinct from IP addresses or DNS names, as attackers can easily spoof (falsify) such information. In the case of UNIX, using an authentication tool such as secure shell, SSH, is recommended. In other cases, establishing a VPN, Virtual Privacy Network, where the identity of the administrator is assured and the computer traffic is encrypted through a tunnel, is also highly recommended.
- Auditors must ensure that all administration tasks are operating at the minimum privilege necessary. Administrator tasks should only be performed at minimum privilege levels and not higher. It is a wise consideration to review the separation of duties among administrators so privilege levels are restricted to just a few employees. Of course, the size of the operation will generally dictate

the number of privileged individuals. This procedure eliminates risks in having a single point of failure with one administrator.

- Auditors must ensure that administrator information cannot be intercepted, modified, or read by attackers. Mechanisms such as encrypted traffic or VPNs will go a long way ensuring that traffic travels between the administrator's system and the system being serviced in a private and unaltered fashion. If the administrators' communication packets can be read by unauthorized persons, not only does this pose a serious risk to the target system, but this information could be used to attack other systems.
- Auditors should determine if administrators have created checksums of critical system files before placing the system in a production environment. This will permit administrators to know if important files have been altered, deleted, or created by attackers hoping to corrupt the target system.

Firewall Auditing: First We Build an Impregnable Barrier, then We Punch Holes in It

If administrators were to name the hardware/software device that is the most critical for system security, they would most likely name the firewall. Of course, firewall architects will swear their equipment and software will stop all illicit intruding traffic and possibly rampaging elephants.

Barbarians at the Wall

In the firewall assessment process, it has to be determined exactly what it is the organization is expecting of its firewalls and that the firewalls are performing at that level of expectation. Assessing the firewall is done with a copy of the organization's policies in hand before verifying the firewall's rulebase. Basically, auditing a firewall consists of two steps. The first step consists of testing the firewall itself and ensuring it is secure. The second step is testing the firewall's rulebase ensuring that only authorized traffic is permitted to pass through it. After all, the firewall's purpose is to deny entry to all traffic, except traffic that is specifically enumerated as being permitted to pass in the rulebase.

These are steps that should be included in the firewall audit program:

- Demonstrate that the firewall is physically secure having very restrictive access. No one should have access without a very specific reason to the machine where the firewall is located. In other words, is the firewall secure from everyone except those having a need-to-know?
- Is remote access permitted to the firewall? Is there a very serious need for remote administration? If not, is the firewall accessible from terminals outside its physical location, and why? Is the firewall accessible only from the physically attacked console?
- Is the operating system used to support the firewall fully armored? Have all unnecessary hardware and software features not needed to support the firewall's operation been removed? Does the firewall reside on a machine used for other functions other than the firewall? It is strongly recommended that all firewalls, regardless of their type and configuration, reside on dedicated machines, devoid of other applications.

There are many checklists available for locking down operating systems. The platform supporting the firewall should be a barebones installation with only the features and ports required to support the firewall opened and enabled.

Experience Note An auditor was engaged in a firewall audit and asked to review the system supporting the network firewall. The administrator admitted the auditor to the secure firewall room and showed her to the computer supporting a proxy service. The auditor noticed a pair of speakers attached to the computer and asked why these were present. The administrator stated she used the computer to listen to music while working in the room. After a closer inspection, the auditor noted the installation of a sound card, supporting sound software, MP-3 software, a media player, and a CD-RW in addition to the already installed CD-ROM. Her audit report reflected her findings.

Auditors may want to scan the firewall ports from internal and external views looking for UDP and TCP open ports. On most correctly configured firewalls, auditors should find few open ports, and auditors should not be able to "ping" the firewall and receive a response.

Experience Note Auditors should employ a number of scans, other than the Ping, in their firewall assessment.

Auditors should be aware that many firewalls have open ports as a matter of default installations. For example, in some firewall installations, ports 256 and 258 are open for administration of the firewall by default. All ICMP ports should be closed thereby thwarting an attacker's ability to map the internal system. If administrative ports are required, then a formal policy should reflect which specific ports are to be open and that only specific IP addresses are allowed to connect to them. Obviously, the idea behind the firewall's configuration is to deny all connections except those specifically allowed.

Firewall Rulebase

The goal behind examining the rulebase is to ensure that the firewall is enforcing what is expected of it, any exceptions should be considered a performance gap and finding. Examining the actual firewall policy can be done by assessing the processes allowed to pass denying all others. This can be accomplished by placing a laptop, with a scanning program such as Nmap installed, on the outside of the firewall and attempt to scan a system located on the inside of the firewall. Placing a workstation on the inside of the firewall with and TCPdump, or Windump, installed will allow the auditor to examine all passing traffic and determine if the written firewall policy is reflected in the passing traffic.

Because firewalls may be used to partition segments of a network, it is prudent to scan network segments. For example, if a firewall is connected to the outside open-ended network such as the Internet, a scanning computer should be connected to this outside connection. The scanner should scan the firewall looking for the protected DMZ network segment and test the permitted traffic rulebase. From this point, other network segments can be scanned from the scanning machine's perspective. It is a wise step for an auditor to validate the DMZ rulebase and attempt to penetrate the internal network. This basically determines the probability of an attacker compromising the DMZ, containing such services as DNS and Web services, and gaining access to the protected internal network. It is important for auditors to note that if they have

Exhibit 28　Firewall Policy Sample

Direction	Source Address	Destination Address	Protocol	Source Port	Destination Port	Notes
In	External	Internal	TCP	>1023	80	Request external client to internal server
Out	Internal	External	TCP	80	>1023	Response internal server to external client
Out	Internal	External	TCP	>1023	80	Request internal client to external server
In	External	Internal	TCP	80	>1023	Response external server to internal client

the organization's policy in one hand and their scan results are different, then they have an item requiring quick resolution. If the auditor discovers open doors in firewalls, this is cause for immediate and positive action before attackers can launch against these potential exploits.

Before merely listing the open ports and unnecessary services, auditors should assess the degree of risk they pose to the organization. By doing this, the auditor extends her view beyond the firewall and begins to gain visibility into the internal network.

Experience Note　Ranking vulnerabilities according to their risk is part of professional due diligence and good procedure. It is the auditor's goal to identify the existence of system vulnerabilities. The system should not be limited to the firewall's function; rather it should extend beyond.

Exhibit 28 is a sample of a typical firewall policy for Web service on port 80.

For each of the firewall's permitted protocols, the firewall should have a policy statement similar to the one above where allowed traffic is scheduled with all others being denied passage. There should not be any services for which there are not rules. Exceptions are considered deviations and should be identified as audit report findings.

Look at Logging

After assessing the permeability of the firewalls, take a serious look at firewall logs:

- Did the firewall detect all the earlier scans and were expected alerts made to the appropriate employees?
- What was the extent of the firewall's logging?
- If the firewall did not log all the scans, why did not it?
- How extensive is the logging? Is the logging capability remotely accessible?
- Is the media holding the logs erasable?
- Are firewall logs stored within the interior protected network?
- Has the machine holding the logs been fortified against attacks?

Auditing Wireless Networks: Who Is Listening to My Network Traffic?

In today's business environment, the installation of wireless networks has taken a center-stage position. Wireless permits an organization to use networked devices in locations where Cat 5 cable is not available.

The Institute of Electrical and Electronics Engineers (IEEE, www.ieee.org) has taken a lead position in the creation and development of wireless networking protocols. In 1990, IEEE established the 802.11 working group. One of their goals was the creation of a wireless local area network (WLAN) standard. The standard specified an operating frequency in the 2.4 GHz band that had been specified for industrial, scientific, and medical use. Seven years later, in 1997, the IEEE adopted the first WLAN standard with data rates of 1 Mbps and 2 Mbps. In 1999, the working group approved two extensions to the 802.11 protocol. The first, 802.11a, operates in the Unlicensed National Information Infrastructure band of 5 GHz with a transfer rate of 54 Mbps. This standard protocol only allowed clients within 40 to 50 feet, due to power restrictions enforced by the Federal Communications Commission (FCC). The second adopted standard is one of the more popular WLAN protocols, 802.11b. This protocol operates on the 2.4 GHz band with operating distances sometimes exceeding 1000 feet and has speeds near 11 Mbps. It is the 802.11b standard known popularly as "Wi-Fi," Wireless Fidelity.

Basic Wi-Fi Architecture

One basic workstation to other compatible client is known as the independent basic service. It provides peer-to-peer communication links between two or more wireless devices with the use of an Access Point, AP, device. In other words, the devices connected via the wireless links are known as "cells" and generally do not have any outside connections other than their connections to each other. This connection structure is known as "Ad hoc." For example, three laptops are connected via their 802.11b wireless network interface cards. In this fashion, they may transact their business through this rudimentary peer-to-peer wireless network.

Experience Note Peer-to-peer wireless networking is the default setting for most wireless network cards.

The most common WLAN infrastructure is known as the "basic service set" where an access point (AP) and at least one wireless client are required. The AP is a device that acts as a router connecting networks, and the wireless client acts in a similar fashion to a Network Interface Card for the client device. APs are relatively small hardware devices that require very little technical knowledge and time to install. In most cases, APs can be purchased for less than $200. Wireless clients are easily installed in desktops and laptops and frequently cost less than $100. In most WLAN architectures, the AP is the connection point between the LAN and the Internet or other open-ended network, while the wireless clients are installed in workstations and mobile systems.

Connections between the AP and its clients are initiated with the proper Service Set Identifier, SSID. Basically, the SSID is the name the owner gives the WLAN network. It is supposed to provide a logical separation between the AP and its clients. In theory, clients must have been configured with the same SSID as the AP in order to connect. It is important to remember that APs act in very similar fashion to routers, and the wireless clients act in similar fashion to NIC cards.

Experience Note It is possible for wireless clients to be placed in a promiscuous mode by placing the word "any" or leaving the configuration blank in the client's SSID configuration. In essence, this configuration will sniff the air for WLANs and possibly connect if the network does not have any other security features. Some APs are configured to broadcast their SSIDs to any receiving wireless clients. In this fashion, the wireless client connects to the sending AP without being required to know the SSID beforehand.

Most WLANs have the ability to be configured for Wired Equivalence Protection, WEP. This is an encryption method between the AP and clients. Due to flaws in WEP, it is possible for attackers to record a significant amount of the encrypted traffic between AP and clients, deduce the encryption, and decipher the traffic. This attack requires a significant amount of recorded traffic and specialized software. Regardless, successfully attacking a wireless network, featuring WEP, can be done by tenacious persons. It is simply a matter of patience and skill.

Experience Note Any traffic that is encrypted is better than clear text traffic. If a wireless network is passing traffic of a sensitive nature, the traffic should be passed over a Virtual Privacy Network, VPN, ensuring privacy and authentication. Many manufacturers are offering APs supporting VPN technology at inexpensive prices.

802.11b Information Packet Types

Beacon packets are typically transmitted continually by APs. These packets contain the SSID, maximum transfer rate, and MAC address of the AP. Generally, APs send from six to ten beacon packets every second. Probe packets are sent by clients to APs while attempting to join a network. Probe packets request the SSID of the network it wishes to join. If an AP permits the client to associate with the target network, the AP responds with a response containing the SSID. Data packets are simply TCP/IP encapsulations of the data being exchanged between the client and the AP. Ad hoc packets are similar to beacon packets, except they are exchanged client card to client card instead of through an AP.

Wi-Fi Network Detection

Active detection is the condition where the client transmits probe packet requests and listens for responses to them. This is the process followed by Netstumbler (www.net-stumbler.com). Active detection requires the wireless client to be located within the radio frequency range of the AP to exchange traffic with the target network.

Passive detection is the process where the client merely listens to all detectable traffic in the air and extracts pertinent information from the intercepted packets. The client needs to be within the useable range of the AP to detect the packets. Passive detection cannot locate an AP that is not broadcasting. The wireless sniffer application, Airsnort, available at airsnort.shmoo.com, uses this listening detection method. If an attacker uses the passive detection method, it is virtually impossible to detect an attacker monitoring the target network.

802.11b Headers

Wireless network headers contain the most basic packet information: the MAC of the transmitting source, destination, SSID, WEP information, supported transfer rates, the channel, and the direction of the communication. It is important for auditors to note that WEP only encrypts the data packets. Packets in the link-layer such as beaconing, probes, etc., are not encrypted. They are exchanged in clear text.

WEP

WEP effectiveness is determined by its key-length, the number of flawed systems generating packet traffic, and the traffic levels on the network. If there are no systems generating data traffic, then attackers are not going to have the opportunity to capture weak keys. WEP has the flaw of being a shared secret key encryption method. Once the system's key is compromised, all systems must be updated with a new WEP key. The new key must be of a greater length or the newly generated and shared key will have the same weaknesses as the compromised key. Compromised keys may result from attackers, former employees, or lost systems.

Cloaking SSIDs

Currently, there are many manufacturers that have the feature of blanking the SSID from the beacon packets. Unless the client knows the correct SSID, it cannot associate with the AP and join the network. However, this protection is possibly transparent as a client joining the network, the AP sends its SSID to the client in the clear. This becomes important in that every time a client exchanges traffic with an AP, the SSID is broadcast in clear text. Legitimate users actually facilitate the AP sending the SSID. Attackers can force an AP to disclose its SSID by attacking it with jamming transmissions and as the clients attempt to rejoin the network, there is an exchange of the SSID in cleartext. Jamming consists of any strong 2.4 GHz transmitter.

Some manufacturers attempt to protect APs by disabling their beaconing ability. This is not a panacea either, such as cloaking the SSID is disclosed as users join the network. Auditors should remember that APs not transmitting the SSID and having their beaconing disabled are merely steps toward system security. Like WEP, they are not the only steps.

Wi-Fi Audit Program Features

Signal strength is one of the features of WLANs that permits attackers to gain a foothold in your system. Walls, doors, glass, and other types of building construction will not provide sufficient containment of the wireless signal. The AP placed inside a typical office can transmit a signal anywhere up to 1000+ feet. In many settings, a signal broadcast in any direction will place it in a neighboring office, road, or parking lot. Vertical signal reception must also be considered in that offices located above and beneath should be factors when selecting a location for the AP. Attackers have been known to engage in a practice known as "war driving," in which they spend their time driving from location to location equipped with a laptop, wireless client, and specialized software in search of unsecured Wi-Fi networks. Some attackers have gone as far as integrating their war-driving network interceptions with GPS and have created maps where wireless networks and their corresponding SSIDs are listed. Several Internet Web sites are dedicated to showing the location and SSIDs of unsecured networks. Of particular interest to attackers are those unprotected wireless networks located in business conference rooms. Software designed to locate unprotected wireless networks is available from www.netstumbler.com.

Many wireless network administrators feel that configuring their networks to recognize specific Network Interface Cards in the form of their individual MAC, Media Access Control, addresses is a measure that goes a long way to securing their networks from unauthorized intruders. MACs are individually significant digital addresses assigned to NICs. MACs identify the specific component and theoretically belong only to that component and none other in the world.

So, if an administrator configures her system to accept only specific MACs, then all others should not be permitted access. In this fashion, MAC filtering provides a significant degree of wireless network security. It is important to remember that there are software utilities that allow attackers to spoof their MAC addresses, however considering the large number of possible digital MAC combinations, there are a hundred million combinations, and the probability of guessing a MAC address is practically impossible. So if an intruder successfully spoofed an authorized MAC address, the intruder has had access to an authorized piece of equipment or has successfully intercepted an authorized MAC that was broadcast in the clear without being encrypted such as a VPN. Having an accurate inventory of equipment and accompanying identifying numbers, such as the MAC, can provide some avenue as to how the MAC was compromised.

Features associated with Wired Equivalent Privacy (WEP) have given wireless administrators and senior managers a false sense of security. In short, it is possible to break WEP contingent on the tenacity, and luck, of the attacker. Even when WEP is properly deployed on a wireless network, it is possible to break the encryption and gain access to the AP. It is important to know that WEP encryption keys are static and configured manually.

WEP protocol requires the same secret key to be shared by all wireless clients within the cell. The flaws are highlighted in the manner that WEP uses Initialization Vectors, IV, in establishing the encrypted link between the AP and the authorized clients. If a determined attacker intercepts a sufficient amount of wireless traffic, he can penetrate the wireless network's WEP and gain access using available software.*

Beyond the idea of restricted MACs and WEP deployment, the only viable solution of private and authorized system traffic is the deployment of a Virtual Privacy Network, VPN. This is not without its issues, but it is a means of allowing only authorized clients to use the system's facilities and provides an encrypted tunnel between clients and other system components. The following factors determine whether it is worth the trouble to deploy a VPN system:

- What is the sensitivity of the traffic this system is going to be seeing?
- What is the importance of privacy?
- Is it important for my wireless network to eliminate unauthorized users?
- Is my wireless network connected to other sensitive system components? What are the risks if an attacker gained access, through the wireless network, to other network elements?

Experience Note Recently, an auditor saw a financial processing sub-network that was separated from the organization's other internal network by a firewall. None of the workstations in the financial unit was allowed Internet access as an added precaution due to the perceived sensitivity of the unit's work. Many employees complained they were being treated poorly, so their organization established a wireless network with separate Internet workstations on each employee's desk allowing them to use the Internet for official purposes. This wireless network was not connected to any internal network and only serviced the employee's Internet needs.

---

* Such software is available at http://sourceforge.net/projects/airsnort/, http://airsnort.shmoo.com/, or http://www.dachb0den.com/projects/bsd-airtools.html.

Wireless Denial-of-Service Attacks

Wi-Fi networks can become victims to denial-of-service attacks in the same fashion as wired networks. They have some of their own issues distinct from conventionally wired systems.

- Users with malicious intent can configure a wireless client to transmit thousands of connection requests to an AP eventually leading to a complete shutdown of the AP. This makes a strong auditor argument for system logging and having the MACs assigned to specific machines with accurate inventories.
- Extraneous radio frequency (RF) generation can result in Wi-Fi jamming from sources such as an arc-welder. Having an AP that cannot receive the transmissions of its assigned clients due to powerful RF jamming from a nearby construction project or body and fender repair shop will not receive intended traffic.
- In wireless systems, it is possible to reach a saturation of RF devices. This is true in 802.11b, 802.11a, 802.11g, and Bluetooth systems. In essence, there are more users than the system can handle.

Auditor Considerations for Wireless Networks

Wireless networks have a different set of system security countermeasures than hard-wire systems do. These are some audit program features that may be worth incorporating:

- APs should have the correct antenna configuration.
- If the system has the ability to attenuate the signal strength, has the broadcast signal strength been reduced sufficiently to cover the intended area and no more?
- Turn off the SSID broadcasting at the AP. If this is not possible, consider using another vendor if restricting unauthorized users is a primary consideration.
- What SSID naming convention was used? SSIDs should not disclose any useful information about the wireless system, for example: Finanzoffice, HRMail, or BWINET.
- What is the level of security dependence on the client's MAC as an access authenticator? Wireless systems must not solely depend on MAC layer filters as their only security measure. This is one of those steps that should be part of the whole system authentication process. Remember that MACs can be spoofed.
- Does the target system have an Intrusion Detection System, IDS, configured to alert administrators in the event an excessive amount of ARP, Address Resolution Protocol, replies are detected on the system? Remember that ARP associates MAC with IP addresses.
- Is the system configured with software tools that will provide notification when IP to MAC bindings change. One such tool is called Arpwatch and is available at www.nrg.ee.lbl.gov.
- Has a VPN solution been effectively implemented between the target system and the clients? Use a third party VPN solution to connect the clients to a single AP with each use being routed to the appropriate VPN endpoint in the organization's network.
- Are there multiple APs to access different segments of the system, each with a unique SSID?

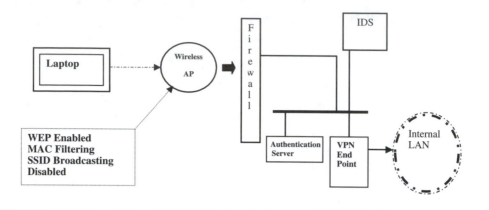

Exhibit 29   Typical Wireless System

- Does the organization's current policy prohibit the installation of APs and other hardware/software without prior written approval of the information security officer?
- Are all APs logically located outside the organization's perimeter firewall?
- Are all unused internal switch ports disabled?
- Is there a systemwide mechanism to monitor any new MAC addresses on the organization's internal system? How effective is this monitoring?

Exhibit 29 is an example of a wireless system with the laptop representing a variety of wireless client devices. It is important to note that the AP is located outside the firewall and computer traffic is required to be authenticated and pass through the VPN endpoint before entering the internal network.

Auditing Security Measures Preventing Automated Attacks

Root Tools to Gain Access

Attackers are those who are attempting to gain unauthorized access to your business and personal systems. It does not surprise anyone that attackers do not have programming or profound knowledge of communications systems in order to gain "root" or "administrative" access to a system or application.

Tools of the attacker's trade, inside or outside your organization include programs that will give them what they want, administrator or root access to the target. Attackers currently have the ability to launch automated tools to scan ports looking for sockets.

Experience Note Sockets are programs listening at Transmission Control Protocol, TCP, or User Datagram Protocol, UDP, ports waiting to connect to incoming traffic.

The act of gaining administrator or root access is commonly called "rooting" or "busting root" on a system. Attackers use tools scanning networks and even standalone machines for exploitable applications and other vulnerabilities. Once a system is successfully compromised, virtually any type of malicious code can be installed. Sensitive data including proprietary information may be captured and stolen, or Web pages can be vandalized, or services may be installed allowing attackers to launch denial-of-service attacks, DoS, targeting other systems. When the information packets are traced, they show a return to your compromised system.

Experience Note   Many legal experts do not understand that the return address on information packets, commonly known as Internet Protocol, IP, does not necessarily reflect the IP packet's true origin.

Computer networks that have been compromised by attackers often have the logged evidence of their origins erased making the determination of who and where the attacker is virtually impossible. Often lawyers and law enforcement officers ask for the IP address of someone sending an obscene e-mail only to find the IP address is incorrect and not traceable.

Who Uses Attacking Tools?

Automated network and vulnerability scanning tools may be used for legitimate auditing reasons as well as illegitimate purposes. This is not the case with attacker root tools. In the Internet community, attackers having little if any true technical skill and even less regard for the resources of others are known as "script kiddies."

Usually, script kiddies have little, if any, idea who or why an exploit works; nevertheless, they are successful because they have the leisure time and resources to scan thousands of systems without any consideration of the damage or resources they waste. Script kiddies locate root tools and other vulnerability tools on the Internet, download, install, configure, click, and attack.

A few years ago, attackers needed a port scanning tool, similar to Nmap, to explore and map large ranges of networks. Once done, the attacker would then review the data her tool had collected. She looked for specific open ports, vulnerable versions of operating systems, or exploitable services. From this, she would construct a list of potential targets. After deciding the easiest way to gain entry, the attacker would enter the system, install malicious code on the compromised systems, erase the log files that documented her activities, and repeat the process on the compromised systems to launch attacks on other systems to disguise her identity.

With the arrival of automated root tools, an attacker does not need to manually scan systems for open ports or operating system information. The actual technical knowledge required earlier is no longer required. Attackers, using automated root tools, merely point them to a range of IP addresses and launch the tool. Every network device within the specified address range will be tested for potential vulnerabilities. All collected data will be organized by the root tool and will launch attacks against exploitable machines. If the tool is successful, the root tool will delete log entries attempting to remove traces of its intrusive activities.

The ramifications of this type of point-and-click attacking are frightening for system professionals and users. Today, a relative novice can attack literally hundreds of systems in a matter of a few hours. If only one in two hundred machines is vulnerable, the attacker can have visibility into dozens of vulnerable machines by one night's work. Entire networks may be caught if they are not properly updated with the latest security patches or if they have been improperly configured. Root tools can be configured to attack the systems surrounding the target. As an example, if a packet screen is improperly configured, a compromised interior network server can be used by the attacker to attack machines on the interior network.

What is the defense against automated attacker tools? It boils down to protection based in system's best practices:

- Workstations and servers must install updated antivirus software because root tools may spread via e-mail and Web scripts. Today's antivirus software will detect and stop root tools.
- Disabling services. Remove or disable unnecessary services from all system devices is an important step in defending against root tools. Many root tools spread from compromised services. Consequently, this step will go a long way to effectively thwarting their effects.
- Firewalls. Packet screens filtering ingress and egress traffic will be effective. Partition sensitive interior systems using firewalls. This measure can be used to prevent and contain the proliferation of root tools.
- Intrusion detection systems can act like alarms by alerting employees of malicious activities.
- Update your systems. Successful root tools depend on the frequency of security holes in a system or its connected systems. Systems must be updated with the latest patches to thwart these automated tools.

Experience Note Do not allow secure systems to be connected to a system having lower levels of security than your own. If you do, they will be used as launching pads against your system.

Due Diligence

If one of your systems becomes compromised, follow your policies and procedures in taking it offline. If you allow it to remain active, the root tool is going to spread to other systems.

Following good system policies and procedures can thwart automated root tools. It is imperative that these steps receive the attention of the auditors and self-assessment, so systems can function correctly. It is not magic, just good business procedure.

Auditing E-Commerce Web Sites

Using the Internet for E-commerce is not an obscure concept; it is a matter of good business sense. However, if retail organizations ignore the malicious abilities of attackers, they are selling themselves short. There are dozens of Web sites, and an equal number of news groups and chat rooms, dedicated to verifying stolen credit card information so they can use it to commit fraud or sell it to someone else who would commit fraud in the future.

There are a number of entities involved in online credit card transactions:

- *Credit card holder.* The person or organization to which a credit card has been issued.
- *Issuing financial institution.* The financial institution that issues the credit card to the credit card holder, also known as the "issuer."
- *Acquiring financial institution.* This institution contracts with merchants to accept and process their credit card transactions. It is possible for acquirers to contract with third-party processors to provide these services. Acquiring financial institutions are also known as "merchant banks" and the organizations' accounts are known as "merchant accounts."

- *Payment gateway.* This is a service allowing an E-commerce merchant to connect to the acquirer or its merchant processor to complete a credit card transaction in real-time.
- *Service provider.* Includes any third-party support entity, e.g., shopping carts, Web servers, payment processors, fulfillment houses, etc. This term is also used to describe a payment gateway alliance.

Of course, online credit card transactions not only include the entities above, but they also include three essential processing actions:

1. *Authorization.* This action takes place at the time a credit card transaction occurs. It is the process by which an issuer approves, or declines, a credit card transaction.
2. *Authentication.* This process involves the verification of the cardholder and the credit card. At the time of authorization, the E-commerce merchant should use fraud prevention controls and tools to validate the credit cardholder's identity and the credit card being used to make a purchase.
3. *Settlement.* When a product has been purchased by a cardholder, the E-commerce merchant can initiate the settlement of a transaction through an acquirer and initiate the transfer of funds from the issuer to the merchant account.

This is an example of a real-time processing for an online credit card transaction. It is not as complicated as many people think. Processing events may vary slightly depending on the acquirer relationship, business requirements, and systems used, but they generally follow the credit card authorization process:

- The cardholder orders items from an E-commerce merchant by entering the credit card number, identifying information, and any shipping information.
- The information transmission is transmitted through the Internet to the merchant server. The payment gateway receives the information from the merchant server; the information is formatted, and transmitted to the acquirer.
- The acquirer electronically sends the authorization to the issuer, who approves or declines the transaction.

Credit Card Authentication

It is the responsibility of the E-commerce merchant to apply tools and controls in verifying the cardholder's identity and validity of the transaction and avoid fraud. These are a few generally accepted tools and controls in avoiding fraud:

- *Address Verification Service (AVS).* This service allows the E-commerce merchant to check a cardholder's billing address with the issuer. AVS provides online merchants with a key indicator verifying whether the transaction is valid or not.
- *Credit Card Verification Value 2 (CVV2).* This is a three digit number printed on the signature panel of the credit card helping to validate that a customer has a genuine card in her possession and that the credit card account is valid. CVV2 numbers are present on most major credit cards.
- *Advanced fraud screens.* These fraud-detection services examine the transactions generated by online E-commerce sites. These services calculate in real-time the level of risk associated with each transaction and provide the merchant

with risk scores. These scores permit merchants to identify potentially fraud-ulent orders and behavior patterns.

Settlement

This process is the operation by which money flows from the issuer to the acquirer. Once the goods or services have been delivered, the E-commerce merchant captures and batches the related transactions for settlement. The batch is electronically submitted to the various acquirers for processing.

The acquirer electronically submits the transaction to issuer for payment. The issuer transmits the payment to the acquirer who credits the E-commerce merchant's account.

Chargeback Issues

With literally millions of credit card transactions, it is inevitable that there will be chargebacks. Chargebacks are transactions that are returned to the acquirer, to the issuer, then to the merchant. There are many reasons for chargebacks:

- Customer disputed transactions
- Fraud
- Authorization issues
- Inaccurate or incomplete transaction information
- Transaction processing errors

The majority of chargebacks are initiated when the cardholder reviews her bank statement and notifies the issuer that there is a problem with a transaction. When this happens, the issuer usually requests an explanation of the problem from the cardholder. If the issuer determines there is a basis for a chargeback, then the matter is referred to the acquirer who debits the merchant's account. It is generally the responsibility of the merchant to resolve the chargeback.

Audit Program Items

E-commerce merchants must take all possible steps to reduce and treat risk. Auditors can play a significant role in this arena and should include audit program items that tip the scales in the E-commerce merchant's favor.

- Record all key elements of fraudulent transactions, names, addresses, shipping addresses, e-mail, credit card numbers, and items purchased. Auditors should verify the existence and currency of a database containing this information.
- Document that all fraud database items are used for comparison before any transactions are processed by the merchant.
- Establish internal transaction controls to identify high-risk transactions prior to authorization. These controls should include:
  - Setting review limits based on the number and dollar amount of transactions approved within a specified number of days. Adjust these limits to fit prior cardholder purchasing patterns.
  - Setting review limits based on a single transaction amount.
  - Ensuring that velocity limits, frequency by which the credit card number and associated information, are checked across multiple characteristics, includ-

ing shipping address, telephone number, and e-mail address. The term "velocity" in this context is degree of frequency that a credit card is used at an E-commerce Web site. It can also mean the number, within a given time period, that credit cards are submitted from a single IP address. Is there a mechanism prescribed by policy that requires contact with customers who exceed these control limits in an effort to determine whether the cardholder's activity is authorized and legitimate?

- In the Web server interface, does it require the cardholder to input the card type, e.g., MasterCard, American Express, etc.? Does it also require the customer to input the card number and CVV2? Does the merchant's Web site verify that the card type and numerical sequence identifying the card type coincide?
- Does the merchant's Web site require the cardholder to enter the card's expiration date and is there a mechanism to verify that the credit card number, name imprinted on it, and the expiration date coincide?
- Does the merchant's Web site require a customer to enter a legitimate e-mail address?
- Does the merchant's Web site require a customer to enter a legitimate CVV2 number and are these numbers verified with the credit card's other pertinent information?
- Has the merchant implemented AVS verification?

Implementing Fraud Screening to Identify High-Risk Transactions

In the E-commerce world, the greatest risk is that of fraud committed by customers. There are a variety of tools and techniques that will help identify and deal with online fraud.

- Implement fraud screening tools to identify high-risk credit card transactions. This can include online transactions:
  - Matching credit card data stored in the organization's internal negative files.
  - Exceed velocity limits and internal controls.
  - Identify the persons, potential credit card attackers, who are submitting Authorize-Only transactions that are never captured or settled.
  - Identify the persons, potential credit card attackers, who are submitting transactions of low amounts, less than $5, to a Web site in an attempt to merely verify the credit card number and cardholder's information.
  - Notification of an AVS mismatch.
- Develop and implement an effective manual transaction review procedure to investigate high-risk credit card transactions. The purpose of this activity is to significantly reduce online fraud as a percentage of revenue, thereby minimizing the impact on legitimate sales.
- Treat anonymous e-mail addresses as high-risk. It is important to note that many online merchants have discovered that anonymous e-mail addresses have a substantially higher fraud rate than e-mail accounts with well-known Internet Service Providers. Organizations should take more steps requiring these types of e-mail addresses to pass additional verification requirements before permitting them to transact online credit card business.
- Identify and screen high-risk shipping addresses. Fraud can be reduced by comparing the client's shipping address to high-risk shipping in third-party databases and in the organization's own negative files. Of particular note is the shipping address located in a different mail-code than the billing address's

mail-code. Particular attention should be paid to mail drops, prisons (of particular note in a prison address is the inclusion of the inmate number), hospitals, and addresses of known fraudulent activity.

■ Organizations should develop and implement policies and procedures addressing shipping addresses different from the billing address.

■ Organizations should treat addresses outside the merchant's country as being high-risk. Transactions involving cards issued outside the merchant's country of origin and having foreign shipping and billing addresses should be regarded as high-risk. Organizations must be careful the AVS will not likely be useful in such cases. Organizations should require higher transaction scrutiny and customer verification for international online transactions. Controls should be enforced regarding transaction velocity thresholds for these transactions. Internal policies and procedures must address cases where there is not third-party AVS available, where billing and shipping addresses differ, and the client uses an anonymous e-mail address.

■ Organizations must assess risks based on the purchase of merchandise that is easily remarketed, for example electronic products or jewelry.

■ Organizations should have a policy regarding contacting the credit card issuer to confirm cardholder's information prior to shipping goods related to a high-risk transaction.

Signs of Possible Online Credit Card Fraud

These are some of the possible indicators that attackers are attempting to commit fraud at the E-commerce Web site. Organizations need to be mindful of these signs and take appropriate steps to avoid becoming a victim of fraud. Auditors should include these signs as being addressed by the organization's policies and procedures in their audit programs.

■ *Multiple credit cards being used from a single IP address.* Multiple (more than two) cards are a good indication a fraud scheme is afoot.

■ *Orders consisting of several of the same item.* Having multiples of the same item increases the fraudster's chances of success.

■ *Orders composed of "big-ticket" items with rushed shipping.* These are usually items identified as having maximum resale value with little regard for shipping costs increasing the profit potential for the criminal.

■ *Orders shipped to a single receiving address but purchased on multiple cards.* These transactions could also be characteristic of account numbers generated by special software or stolen.

■ *Multiple transactions on one card or similar cards with a single billing address or a single card with multiple shipping addresses.* This activity represents an organized fraudulent activity rather than one individual at work.

If an online transaction is approved by the credit card issuer, the organization should consider sending a confirming e-mail to the customer before completing and sending the order. If the transaction is declined, the organization should have policies and procedures that specify the means by which the organization handles such transaction declinations.

Auditors should review the method by which the company handles declined transactions. Consideration should be given to having customer service employees review online transaction authorizations declined by issuers and obtain corrected information or an alternate payment that allows the organization to safely proceed. These employees must be mindful of transactions containing incorrect card expiration dates, incorrect billing addresses, incorrect name spelling, incorrect mailing addresses, or incorrect CVV2 information. Incorrect information should be retained as part of the organization's negative information database that is used for comparison with future transaction attempts.

Attackers can gain access to a business' online Web site through shopping carts or payment gateway processor systems. Attackers are also very adept at finding security holes in weak or default passwords. With an attacker invading an E-commerce site, it is possible for the attacker to emulate the merchant and begin processing debits and credits without the merchant's knowledge. It is a fraudulent practice for attackers to offset the deposit credits with debits, thereby attempting to avoid detection by deposit-volume monitoring by the true merchant's bank.

Here is a short checklist for merchants to monitor online authorizations and transactions:

- On a daily basis, organizations must review their transaction logs for Authorize-only transactions and small amount transactions (less than $5). An unusually high number will likely indicate attackers testing the merchant's system.
- On a daily basis, organizations must review their transactions for an unusually high amount or volume of credits. This could indicate fraud.
- On a daily basis, organizations must review their transactions for identical transaction amounts.
- On a daily basis, organizations must review their transactions for multiple transactions from a single IP address.
- Organizations must thoroughly review their online transactions before they are settled. This affords the opportunity to void potentially fraudulent or erroneous transactions before they are submitted for settlement.
- All pertinent passwords must be at least ten characters in length, with a combination of special characters, numbers, and capital letters. These passwords must be changed at least every 30 days or less.
- All credit card numbers and related cardholder information must be stored on a secure server inside a guarded interior system and away from the DMZ where the Web site is located.

Auditing Workstations

Auditing workstations is one of the most invasive things an auditor can do to an employee. It must be approached with thoughtful consideration and professional demeanor. Auditors must respect the privacy of employees who are not violating policies and procedures. Exercising good judgment by ensuring the auditors have mature attitudes generally goes a long way in workstation audits.

The unannounced workstation audit is an activity that must be predicated on legal and sound policies and procedures. If an organization is going to undertake the workstation assessment process, employees must understand and acknowledge that they do not have a reasonable expectation to privacy for any of their activities conducted on the company's systems.

Audit teams must ensure that they have full concurrence and cooperation of senior managers before engaging in these types of audit practices. Prudent audit team managers will make certain that the organization's legal department is regularly consulted to determine if there have been any recent legislative changes affecting employee privacy before beginning workstation audits. Workstation auditing should not be restricted to stationary desktop systems, but should include all mobile devices including laptop, handheld, wireless, and cellular devices used on the job.

Since Microsoft created its first operating system for Intel processors, there has been an increasing market share for their products. As a result of this rapid and ever-increasing expansion, most offices use Microsoft products and mobile environments. Consequently, this section will concentrate on auditing workstations with Windows operating system environments.

First Steps

Begin at the beginning. Workstation audits must include employee work areas.

- Are there policies and procedures requiring the proper treatment of paper trash? How often does the employee dispose of her trash?
- Where does the employee print her jobs? Is there waste paper present at the printer?
- Does the organization have policies and procedures regarding the shredding or burning of trash?

Auditors should take a careful look at the areas surrounding the workstation. Are passwords written and hidden beneath mouse pads or keyboards? What sensitive materials are left unattended on desk areas?

With a physical review of the work area completed, the first step that should be taken by workstation auditors is the process of "unhiding" files. By clicking the *My Computer* icon, and selecting *View* and then *Folder Options*, the auditor may select the tab for *View*. Within this pane will be a selection for showing all files. Auditors should select this option to reveal any files the users may have hidden.

Experience Note An auditor was referred an e-mail for review to determine its compliance with company policy regarding official use. Once received, the auditor opened the e-mail and its obscene attachment in the form of a Microsoft Word document. She started her analysis. She opened the e-mail text in a simple hex editor allowing her to view the hexadecimal coding of the document. She easily located the MAC (Media Access Code) address of the sender. Checking with the inventory control specialist, she located the workstation of the alleged sender. She opened the Word document attachment in a text editor, Notepad, and began looking for the GUID (Globally Unique Identifier). This information is an essential component of Microsoft Word's architecture and is useful in determining the origin of the attachment. After comparing the MAC of the workstation and the GUID, the auditor determined they were the same person, and identified that the attachment had been composed in a copy of Word personally registered to that particular employee. It was composed outside the organization's office space, as all software products are registered in the company's name and not the name of any employee. She began the workstation audit, and located the MAC in the browser cookie file. It was found in a cookie marked, "microsoft.txt." It was the same as the workstation's ethernet card. This went a long way to showing the MAC had not been spoofed. After reviewing obscene attachment text as a final step, the auditor provided a written report to the human resources unit for their action.

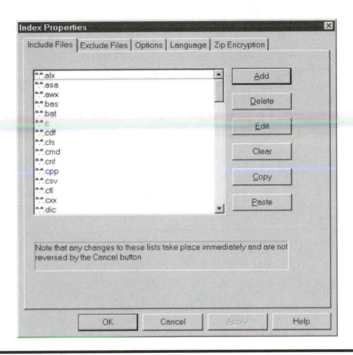

Exhibit 30   Wilbur Configuration

Organizing and Searching File Systems

It is important for auditors to be able to organize, search, and display files lodged on media contained within the target workstation or server.

Wilbur

There is a simple, free application known as Wilbur that easily accomplishes the task of organizing a disks files available at www.redtree.com. It is a freeware Windows-based utility that creates an index of the target media, hard drives, floppies, or CD-Rs. Wilbur will search every file on the target media by the type of file, for example, spreadsheet, word processing, images, html, zipped files, etc. This is very useful if the auditor is looking for images with the extension of jpeg or gif. Having an index of image files will provide the auditor with additional insight into the user's Internet browsing practices. This is particularly useful if the auditor is looking for browsing outside the organizations stated policies. This application can also look into the content of files for specific words displaying the file and the text. Wilbur permits descriptions to contain wild card searches and logical expressions facilitating the auditor's efforts to find the specific files. Searches can be constrained by combinations of, file names, contents, folder names, file size, attributes, and file modification dates (Exhibit 30 and Exhibit 31).

Little Images

In most cases, reviewing hundreds of images is tedious and somewhat tiresome for auditors. In many cases, large organizations have frequent complaints dealing with employees who engage in unauthorized pornographic Web site browsing. In other

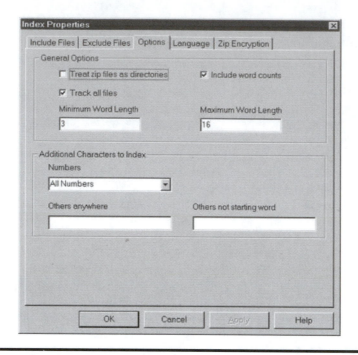

Exhibit 31   Wilbur Options

cases, employees may be engaged in stealing intellectual property or other sensitive information. Using a simple application known as ThumbsPlus, auditors can create a catalog of image files. ThumbsPlus is available at www.cerious.com. Auditors using this program can select the workstation's drive unit, or directory and the program creates an image catalog displaying all image files. Conscientious auditors can quickly scan the images produced in small aspect and determine if any are offensive.

Unformatting and Undeleting

Many users believe that once the file has been deleted, it is gone forever and cannot be restored to a useable state. Further, users may also believe that once a drive has been reformatted, the information previously contained there is gone. Information may be recovered from deleted files and reformatted disks by using simple utilities. Norton Utilities, currently owned and distributed by Symantec (www.symantec.com), provides applications that will unerase deleted files and unformat media that have been formatted. Norton's is not the only software suite that has these utilities. Auditors can easily locate other suitable programs on the Internet.

It is not practical for auditors to restore all deleted files within the hard drive's multi-gigabyte structure; nevertheless, if auditors identify suspicious files, they have the option of restoring them and possibly recovering their contents. Using unerase and unformat programs are fairly easy and are usually well documented in the help file or literature accompanying the program.

Windows Registry Investigations

The Windows Registry is a database containing information about every program installed on the workstation. Wise auditors will not go idly poking around in the workstation's registry without some degree of expertise, as this is one sure way to make the machine completely unusable if you do not know what you are doing. In essence, the registry contains information about the workstation's users and their configuration preferences.

The Windows operating system registry consists of at least two files: System.dat and User.dat. If the workstation has been configured for multiple users, each user will have their own copies of these files in the Windows\Profiles\user name file. Auditors can boot the workstation into DOS and type *scanreg/restore* from the DOS prompt launching the DOS version of the registry checker. This will provide a list of existing registry backups and their effective dates. Highlighting the one selected to deliver the restoration and follow the prompts after that.

The best way to view the registry is with the editor provided by Microsoft and already found in Windows. If the auditor is reviewing Windows 9X or ME, it is a matter of going to the *Run* selection from *Start,* and entering *regedit*. In the case of NT, *regedit32* is entered. It is a good idea to create a backup of the registry in the event something goes wrong. While in the Registry menu, select Export Registry file. This will prompt for a file name. Saving this file will provide a copy of the Registry.

Operating within the Registry Editor is similar to exploring files in the Windows Explorer. Registry entries are arranged like file system trees. Located on the left side of the are folders indicated by icons. These are called "keys." Keys contain other keys or values and values may be of three types: binary, string, or DWORD (double word 32 bit). If there is a plus (+) sign next to a folder, clicking on it opens other folders and drops down the list of subkeys.

There can be a host of information stored in the Registry; for example, locate the HKEY_CURRENT_USER key, and expand it to find the Software key; expand it, locate the Current Version key, and finally select the DocFindSpecMRU. In the right window pane, you can see the contents of this folder. Reviewing the contents of this file will provide the search history of the workstation. This can also be confirmed by reviewing the search terms contained in the file search utility found in the *start, find,* and *folders* utility. Basically, looking at this Registry entry shows where the workstation users have used the *Find* function and what their search parameters were. Reviewing the search function will reveal if the user has forgotten where she concealed files in the operating system's file system. For example, Alice is engaged in periodically siphoning money from accounts payable and later makes credit entries that offset these debits. She has concealed a small spreadsheet where she tracks the stolen amounts being careful not to take too much too frequently. This spreadsheet is hidden within her workstation's file system. After a three-week vacation, she returns to work and has forgotten where she has hidden the spreadsheet. She clicks on the *Find* function and begins searching for her spreadsheet. By performing this search, her search parameters are logged in the Registry and can be retrieved by others.

The Explorer/RunMRU is another registry key worth reviewing as it contains infor-mation about user activities. This window will display the most recent commands launched from the *Run* function that is accessible from the *Start* button. The *Run* history will show those commands entered by the users. This information is also available from the *Run* function and clicking on the little box to the right of the entry box. This information is useful in determining if users were running unauthorized software or if they were mapping the interior network using utilities found in the Windows operating system such as *Ping, Netstat, Tracert,* and *Nbtstat*. These networking routines are used by Windows to perform its networking function, and if used manually, will provide a very good map of the architecture and naming conventions used in the organization's system. *Ping* is used to verify connections to hosts; *Netstat* displays protocol statistics and current TCP/IP connections to the workstation; *Tracert* determines the route taken to a network destination; and *Nbtstat* displays protocol statistics and current TCP/IP connections using NetBIOS over TCP/IP. Auditors should be mindful there are very few reasons that employees, outside of those having direct system responsibilities, should be routinely using these commands. It is important to note that these network commands may be run from the DOS prompt function within Windows and these commands will not be recorded in the Registry. Employees interested in the organization's system architecture would likely use these commands to discover details in order to facilitate an attack. Auditors should be mindful that an employee using these commands might just be curious about the system. If there are tools present on the workstation or stored elsewhere in the system, they should be located before making any recommendations.

Another Registry area worth the time for an auditor to investigate is one that records the URLs entered by the user during Web browsing sessions. Remember that this will only be useful if Microsoft's Internet Explorer is operating as the default Web browser. The keys pertinent to this folder are located in the Microsoft Registry under the key named *TypedURLs*. It also reveals the user's Web browser Startpage. In this folder is a list of all the URLs the user typed into the Internet Explorer's Address field. As an auditing tool, this resource is very useful as it provides a partial record of the Web sites visited by the workstation user. The importance of this investigation is it reveals that the user intentionally typed the URL into the address blank calling the Web page to view.

The HKEY_LOCAL_MACHINE key records information about the individual workstation and the network. The *Network/Logon* key contains the last user name used to log onto the network and is a good place to look if the auditor is attempting to correlate the workstation's user with workstation activity.

E-Mail Sent by Employees

E-mail is a reasonable place for a workstation audit. It is often the source insight into the employee's daily activities. It is likely that the organization has a policy relating to employees using only the internal system's e-mail services. In this fashion, e-mail content may be examined for inappropriate use and the possibility that users may be using e-mail to transmit sensitive or intellectual property outside the company.

At times, a suspicious e-mail is the first indication that an employee is outside of organizational policies and might be guilty of other things. Auditors may think of e-mail as the database of the employee and their contacts while on duty. Individual messages are often stored in the folders that were installed as a matter of application default or in the folders the employee created. Auditors should investigate the default folder structure within the e-mail client. Looking at the *Sent, Outbox, Drafts, Inbox,* and *Deleted* folders may provide some insight into the employee's e-mail activities.

Auditors should note that just because a workstation has an e-mail client, such as "Eudora" or "Outlook" installed, does not necessarily mean all the e-mail activity of the user is recorded. Web-based e-mail has distinct advantages for employees. By not using the e-mail server of the organization's network, the employee can bypass any backup and recording of e-mail being sent. Employees may transmit and receive e-mail without any concern their traffic is going to be examined later from inside the company.

Web-based e-mail allows users to send, receive, and store e-mail from multiple computers and from a wide variety of locations. Because the e-mail is stored on a server with Internet access, the user is free to conduct her e-mail business from any computer having Internet access.

Interested workstation auditors may wish to access the browser's *History* file and look for the dates and times the user accessed their Web-based e-mail service. Viewing the *History* file will provide the URL and date the Web site was visited by the user. Auditors may also wish to look into the browser's *Favorites* or *Bookmarks* file where the user may have bookmarked those Web sites she wishes to visit again. Having bookmarked a Web site is a fair indication the user intended to visit it again. Frequently, users will not delete the *History* file, and auditors will discover that the user has at least visited an Internet e-mail site.

Auditors may wish to visit the *Cookies* file easily located by the Windows *Find* function. Often, *Cookies* are deposited on the user's workstation by Internet e-mail sites to facilitate user recognition and logon. By examining this file, auditors may see if the user has visited Internet e-mail or other sites.

This is another more subtle purpose for Internet e-mail use: the users wishing to visit Web sites and avoid being detected by the interior gateway filter. By visiting an Internet e-mail site and sending URLs for prohibited Web sites to herself, an employee may circumvent content filters located on the interior network. She merely visits the Internet e-mail site, sends herself URLs for Web sites that are going to be filtered by the company's system, and clicks on them through the Internet e-mail site.

Looking in all the Right Places

Auditors performing workstation audits should be mindful of areas that generally retain information providing useful insight into the workstation user's day. Before attempting to perform an audit on the target workstation, auditors should visit the business' Help Desk Unit and inquire about recent requests for assistance made by the users of the workstation they are going to audit. Employees requesting efficient file transfer applications such as FTP, file transfer protocol, should have their workstations carefully screened. Unless an employee is engaged in system or Web page development, there is not a legitimate reason to have FTP software.

Experience Note Auditors suspecting an employee was using unauthorized software performed an audit on her workstation after normal work hours. They did not discover any unauthorized applications on her workstation. However, using the *Find* feature of Windows, auditors found an interesting file called ""."//.old." The file's extension was not conventional, so the auditors opened the file and looking at the *Properties* of the file determined that the extension of the file should have been *exe*. Changing the extension of the file to *exe* opened an FTP client containing an IP address located on the Internet and password. Perusing the transfer log revealed the employee had been transferring proprietary information outside the company including soon-to-be-released products, suppliers, price lists, and client lists. The employee was subsequently prosecuted and convicted. Additionally, she and her partners were sued for damages with monies recovered by her former employer.

Experience Note Reviewing the Internet activity logs is another logical place to start the workstation audit. Auditors should coordinate their efforts with appropriate levels of system administrators in obtaining and sorting the employee's Internet activity logs. Auditors should be looking for Web sites that are contrary to organization policy and Web sites that "just don't look right."

Reviewing the contents of the Windows *Recycle* folder will give the auditor an idea of the discarded items no longer wanted by the user. Looking in this folder will often disclose discarded items from Web pages and any other discarded items. Reviewing the *Recycle* folder may possibly disclose if the user had attempted to install unauthorized software. Auditors should be mindful that reviewing the *Add/Remove Software* function located in the *Control Panel/Systems* folder generally reveals if the user has installed unauthorized software. If the user is not careful, there can be hardware device conflicts that have not been resolved that can reveal any attempts to install hardware. Reviewing the *Device Manager* will generally disclose if the user has installed or attempted to install unauthorized hardware.

Auditors should be mindful that most browsers have a *History* file containing the Internet browsing history of the user. This file may be located by the *Find* function of Windows and may be accessed by clicking on one of the entries. Generally, the entries are cataloged by the week they were accessed. For example, there will be headings such as "54 Weeks Ago," indicating that these were the Internet Web sites visited 54 weeks ago from the time of the current date. Because the listed Web sites are identified only by their URLs, it is a wise auditor who takes a representative sample for examination.

Directories that can provide the auditor with valuable information are *Temp* and *Temp Internet*. These directories hold items that are meant to be discarded in the future. For example in the case of *Temp* downloaded applications or applications needing a temporary file for installation are going to be found here. Frequently, users frequently ignore this file when they delete the program not realizing a copy was deposited on their hard drive. In the case of the *Temp Internet* file, this file acts as a depository for a variety of Internet-related items, including downloaded images, Web pages, and cookies. Searching through these items can provide information about the user's Internet browsing habits. Depending on the browser, sometimes there are *Cache* files that serve essentially the same purpose as *Temp* or *Temp Internet*. Browser *Cache* files may be accessed and reviewed for the same purposes as any other "temp" file.

Most Windows systems keep many of the images relative to visited Web pages. These images can be easily displayed by using an application such as *ThumbsPlus* or they can be found using their extensions. Auditors may input gif or jpeg in the *Find* function of Windows and the lower pane will display the image files.

Telling the Tale with Cookies

Cookies are text files useful in holding the user's name, password, and other information pertinent to a specific Web site. Sometimes cookies contain custom settings for a given Web site and other data the Web site uses in tracking the user's visit.

From an auditing perspective, cookies may hold information relative to Web sites, as they contain information for the browser's preferred configuration of the site. For example, they may contain preferences for Web site viewing without music or with a particular background color. Cookies do not indicate whether the user intentionally went to the Web site or not. They merely indicate that the viewer was at the Web site for the cookie to be deposited at the browser's cookie file.

Because cookies are text files, they can easily be viewed in a text editor such as Windows Notepad. When viewed in the Windows pane, they will appear similar to the following example: aliceandbob@adlinks[1].txt or alice@yahoo[2].txt. When viewed in the text editor, they will appear similar to the following example: *Uid0oxd823903.0x17d7rr0ads.adlinks.com/0o02375044590230*0*. Looking at the text will reveal the visited Web site: *adlinks.com*.

There are no formal requirements for cookies, so it is sometimes difficult to obtain consistently useful information from them other than to see the Web site's URL.

It may be sufficient for auditors to know the URLs visited by the user and correlate this information with the properties of the images contained on the user's workstation. If auditors will right-click on the cookie, they will view the properties of the cookie including the date it was created and the day it was last modified. Because it is being viewed by the auditor, the date it was last accessed will be the date it was viewed by the auditor.

Auditing Windows NT and XP

An integral part of these Windows operating systems is the feature of activity logging or auditing. As a matter of policy and procedure, organizations are advised that operating systems having the ability to enable auditing are strongly recommended. When enabled and correctly configured, auditing causes entries to be made to an event log. Event logs are divided into sections: System Messages, Application Messages, Security Logs, and Iexplore.

The event viewer function is used at "administrator" privilege level to view logs. The time that the event log is retained depends on the configuration settings, telling the workstation when to overwrite the oldest entries. The success auditors have in viewing logs depends on the implementation of policies and procedures relating to proper operating system configurations.

It is important for auditors to have a fair sample of user-activity on which they may draw their assessment sample. If too small, the sample will not reflect the user's activity and if too large, the sample contains too much information to be useful. Default configuration settings will generally overwrite logs in a few days or a week at most. Often the purpose supporting logs is that of debugging systems, not monitoring user-activity. Auditors should be mindful that if suspicious user activity has triggered an audit, it might be advised to have the security manager activate and configure the target workstation's logging feature to capture a larger number of events with greater granularity before actually performing the audit.

Keystroke Monitors

Auditors must be mindful there are hardware and software solutions that provide for the capture of every keystroke made on a given keyboard by the user. It is possible to configure them to either retain all the keystroke information on the workstation's hard drive or send the information via e-mail to the intended recipient. Other versions take snapshots of the target's monitor. Such keystroke software applications are available from www.spectorsoft.com.

Auditors should know these programs are not one hundred percent accurate, but provide a significant degree of insight about what the user is doing on her workstation. Keystroke monitors are generally invisible to the user, but if a user is very computer-savvy he can be discovered with a degree of effort. These users provide an important tool to auditors who are actively looking for illicit or unlawful activity. Because there are legal issues when using keystroke monitors, consult with legal counsel before installing them.

Chapter 4

Critical Incident Response and CIRT Development

Critical Incident Management

In modern organizations, the combination of easily available data, poorly administered safeguards, and malicious individuals make systems vulnerable and attractive to attacks. Almost daily, we hear of businesses being robbed of critical information assets or suffering outages through virus infections or denial-of-service attacks. Computer networks are still relatively new, having their birth only 30 years ago. It sometimes seems hard to put in perspective, but the vaunted Information Highway was just getting its feet of the ground in the early 1980s. And, as information became an extremely valuable commodity, the exploitation of vulnerabilities seemed to keep pace with the growth of network systems.

Illustrating this point is one of the most famous misdeeds, the 1988 "Morris Worm" incident resulted in a significantly large percentage of the network systems with Internet connections being corrupted and removed from service. This was the catalyst that caused Internet users to have postmortem meetings where they decided that preventative, detective, and corrective steps had to be made active parts of their business practice.

For the past seven years, the Computer Crime and Security survey has been conducted jointly by the Computer Security Institute (www.gocsi.com) and the Federal Bureau of Investigation's San Francisco, California, office. The purpose of this survey is to raise levels of computer system awareness while measuring the magnitude and frequency of computer crimes. The 2002 survey results are based on 503 responses from computer security professionals practicing in U.S. business and government agencies. Responses to this survey confirm that computer systems threats continue to spiral upwardly with corresponding financial losses following.

Here are a few highlights from the most recent survey:

- 90 percent of the survey respondents detected computer security breaches in the last twelve months.

- 80 percent acknowledged financial losses attributable to the computer security breaches.
- Of the 503 respondents, 44 percent estimated their financial losses at more than $455 million.
- The most serious financial losses occurred through the theft of proprietary information with 26 respondents reporting more than $170 million and 25 respondents reporting more than $115 mission in financial fraud.
- Of the respondents, 74 percent reported their Internet connection as the more-frequent point of attack than their internal system.
- In 1996, only 16 percent acknowledged reporting intrusions to law enforcement, but in 2002, 34 percent reported their intrusions to law enforcement authorities.
- 40 percent detected systems' penetration from outside the organization.
- 78 percent detected employee abuse of Internet access privileges or inappropriate use of e-mail.
- 38 percent suffered unauthorized access or misuse of their Web sites in the last 12 months, while 21 percent reported they did not know if there had been unauthorized access or misuse.

Patrice Rapalus, CSI Director, remarked that the Computer Crime and Security Survey has served as a reality check for industry and government:

> Over its 7 year life span, the survey has told a compelling story. It has underscored some of the verities of the information security profession; for example, that technology alone cannot thwart cyber attacks and that there is a need for greater cooperation between the private sector and the government. It has also challenged some of the profession's 'conventional wisdom;' for example, that the 'threat from inside the organization is far greater than the threat from outside the organization and that most hack attacks are perpetrated by juveniles on joy rides in cyberspace. Over the 7 year life span of the survey, a sense of the facts on the ground has emerged. There is much more illegal and unauthorized activity in cyberspace than corporations will admit to their clients, stockholders, and business partners or report to law enforcement. Incidents are widespread, costly, and commonplace. Since September 11, 2001, there seems to be a greater appreciation for how much information security means not only to each individual enterprise but also to the economy itself and to society as a whole. Hopefully, this greater appreciation will translate into increased staffing levels, more investment in training, and enhanced organizational clout for those responsible for information security.

Experience Note The most frequent system attacks originate outside the business organization, but the most successful attacks are those committed by insiders.

Critical Incident Response

The best response to critical incidents is characterized by the "ounce of prevention is worth a pound of cure" philosophy. It is much more financially prudent to implement a sound risk management program characterized by written policies, procedures, and standards, with compliance ensured by comprehensive and unannounced audits, than it is to deal with financially devastating events after they happen.

But there are times when "bad things happen to good people" and a response must be made to a critical incident occurring despite your best efforts. It is virtually impossible to predict when someone is going to attack your system and steal your critical information except to say it is not a matter of *if* as much as it is a matter of *when*.

Firefighter Response Model

Responding to a critical incident is similar to responding to a fire. Fire departments work tirelessly to educate us about the best means to prevent fires. Safety training starts with simple programs when we are young by talking about fire-related hazards at home and school. Television and radio public service announcements tell us of the safety measures we can take to safeguard our lives at home. We see fire-safety slogans telling us "only you can prevent forest fires" and similar signs as we enter campgrounds and picnic areas. Sometimes we are visited by Fire Marshals inspecting our facilities, making certain there are marked exits and equipment to extinguish fires and save lives.

When the worst happens, a company of firefighters responds to an emergency:

- Respond to emergency contact numbers
- Trained to handle wide-ranging emergency situations
- Organized in the deployment of their tactics and equipment
- Frequently cross-trained as Emergency Medical Technicians
- Confirm that an emergency exists and the nature of it
- Take all appropriate steps to control the emergency
- Take all appropriate steps to prevent the fire from destroying priority order:
  - Lives
  - Surrounding property
  - Property where the fire is presently burning
- Take every possible step to collect and preserve evidence of criminal behavior but not at the risk of life and property
- Testify at judicial proceedings about their actions and findings
- Conduct reviews and critique improving their performance

Critical Incident Response Strategy

No one would argue that responding to critical system incidents is a complex area that is not as easy as taking a pill and waking up feeling better in the morning. Critical Incident response methodology closely follows that of the firefighters:

- Precritical incident preparation. Designated and specially trained response personnel, contact methods, equipment, and tool availability and response posture.
- Detection of critical incidents.
- Initial response evaluation. This is a preliminary step in which an initial investigation is performed and an evaluation is made quickly to determine which type of response is appropriate.
- Response. This is the step where necessary resources are deployed responding to the critical incident. The response goals are very similar to those of the firefighters: contain the damage, prevent it from further spreading, dedicate efforts in a priority manner, and pursue resumption of normal operations.
- Response posture strategy. This step is where the preliminary facts are ascertained and a "best response" plan is proposed. At this time, the proposed plan

is passed to senior managers for their review and approval. It is imperative that this step be accomplished within the framework of response demands and priorities. Time is of the essence, dawdling is not acceptable here. Depending on the nature of the emergency, there will be times that an immediate hammer-to-nail response is made and there will be times when the matter may be handled the next business day.

Experience Note Be careful of "crying wolf" too frequently; if every case is declared an emergency, there are no emergencies.

- Law enforcement notification. Having previously established a relationship with law enforcement authorities, responders know whether they should collect the evidence first, or secure the crime scene and wait for officers to respond.
- Legal determination. Responders must include their legal counsel in the decision process surrounding response strategy. On receiving the responder's observations and recommendations, legal counsel should be prepared to render an opinion whether the responders should collect evidence for future legal proceedings, notify law officers so they can collect relevant evidence or take immediate steps to correct damage and restore operations possibly destroying evidence. It is possible that in destroying evidence that responders are violating laws or regulations by not preserving evidence and not coordinating their efforts with law enforcement authorities. For this reason, senior managers and legal counsel must be part of the decision process.
- Evidence collection. This step collects key evidence with interviews, photographs, sketches, and physical evidence.
- Forensic duplications. This step provides bit-by-bit, forensically sound, duplications of critical media.
- Recovery. Responders take appropriate steps to isolate, contain, recover from the incident, and resume business operations.
- Reporting. Take appropriate steps to draft accurate and timely reports to stakeholders and law enforcement authorities, where applicable.
- Postmortem. This is the after-action critique and report of the actions taken during the critical incident response.

Critical Incident Planning

If you do not plan, you're planning to fail.

Writing and implementing a critical incident plan ensures that emergencies are addressed carefully, thoroughly, and in conformity with risk management programs. As part of the response plan, draft checklists where common incidents are addressed minimizing the required time for response actions. For example, having a response checklist addressing a workstation virus will be significantly different from an employee who is discovered stealing intellectual property and e-mailing it to a competitor.

Here are some recommended elements for a critical incident response plan:

- Obtain and follow the organization's risk management plans. If your organization does not have one, today is an excellent time to start one. This plan should provide details relative to the priority of critical assets, their restoration, and the steps to be taken for resuming profitable operations.

- The critical incident response plan should outline the means of detecting emergencies, collecting preliminary information, assessing the gravity of the system attack, systems affected, spread of damage, steps necessary to stop damage, and protect personnel, data, and facilities. The recommended plan structure is simple, direct, and understandable.
- The critical incident response plan should provide a means to easily contact all relevant employees and outside resources.
- The critical incident response plan should provide specific instructions about policies, procedures, and legal requirements.
- The critical incident response plan should provide templates for any documents required during the emergency. For example, the plan should include a template for logging responder's actions and significant events during the response.

Many critical incident response plans fail because they do not include a response-owner and a senior management correspondent as part of the process. A response-owner is the employee responsible in most cases for the response the emergency receives including relevant actions from start to completion. The senior manager correspondent is the employee who will deliver information to stakeholders.

Command Post Operations

This is a sensitive topic relative to the initiation, staffing, and operation of a command post. Do not think that CPs are intended only for military or government operations because all agencies, while addressing emergency situations, should consider this response strategy. Basically, a CP is a temporary business unit assembled to address one of more crises and will remain in operation until all emergencies are stable and settled. CPs work very closely with regular business operations but have the executive "horsepower" to function independently in decision making, assigning resources, taking action, and following up.

CPs are staffed with specialists assigned particular tasks with dedicated resources at their disposal. In their most common configuration, CPs are housed in segregated facilities located within the business' headquarters. If this is not possible, plans should include relocating the CP to a secondary and equipped facility. They should be equipped with dedicated facilities such as office space, electrical generation, high-speed satellite-linked Internet connections, telephones having multiple direct lines separate from other business units, satellite-linked television for news reception, and a LAN connecting CP workstations to the business LAN and the Internet.

CP reporting structure is funnel-shaped. Information flows from telephone calls, radio, news broadcasts, and e-mail to those designated for information processing. Telephone callers may be employees, specialized response teams, members of the press, stakeholders, or the general public. Carefully trained employees are tasked to interview outside callers and collect information. They are trained relative to the information they may disclose because any comments will be attributed to the organization.

Individuals collecting information for the CP should complete a simple contact report form synopsizing the information from their call, news broadcast, or e-mail. This form may be paper-based or electronic with one copy being passed to the function-point (the single point where all collected information flows), another copy is passed to the data input unit, and the last copy is retained and archived as "work papers." If it is significant, she immediately briefs the function-point and follows the briefing with the written contact report form.

The function-point unit is the person or unit that screens incoming information and makes a determination of where the information should be routed, its priority and processing action. The function-point is a critical position requiring decisions to be based on sound business sense. The data input unit is responsible for routing the information to the unit or employee assigned to the task by the function-point. Another unit must be responsible for collecting the work papers and organizing them for future review and retrieval.

Within the CP are several critical business unit representatives. Depending on the nature of the emergency, these are suggested units that should have representatives in the CP:

- Legal
- Human Resources
- Public/Media Relations
- Senior Management
- Operations Staff
- Maintenance Staff
- Supply/Logistics Staff
- Communications Staff
- Data Input Staff
- Function-Point staff

At least in the initial stages, it will probably be required that the CP is open and staffed for 24 hours.

Experience Note CP staff will have stages of burnout. Replace all staff members at the end of their 8-hour shifts. At the end of shifts, there should be a briefing by the outgoing shift of the events so the oncoming shift knows what has happened during the past eight hours.

There is a good reason to maintain an events log — so the oncoming employees can review it for reference purposes. Activity logs and other work papers could be made part of legal actions, so care in this area is advised. Employees should be trained that documenting facts is acceptable, while documenting opinions or editorializing are not.

Experience Note While working in a CP, an employee made a note that was later maintained as a work paper about an event that was only hypothetical and not actual. However, when legal action was sought, the plaintiff introduced the note was as if the event actually happened. Despite the defendant's protestations and objections, the note was accepted as evidence causing significant damage to the defendant's case.

Once the emergency begins to abate, staff, duty-hours, and activities can be reduced. It is a common practice having CP unit leaders meet every half-hour during the first few hours of CP operations. At this time, they should bring important events to briefings along with any concerns. Meetings should last not more than a few minutes and are driven by the nature and treatment of the emergency.

CP employees should understand that press inquiries can have grave consequences for the organization. They should be trained to handle press calls in an appropriate manner. For example, in the face of a disaster, the CP receives a telephone inquiry from a noted news organization; the employee handling the call accepts the information and documents the inquiry by completing the contact report form. Once completed, the form is passed to the function-point where it is screened again and passed to the public relations unit at the CP for handling. One copy of the intake report is passed to the data-input unit that is creating a chronology database of events, and while making an assignment to the public relations unit with a request, they respond when the assignment is completed. In this fashion, assignments can be tracked whether they have been completed or not. Frequently, the input unit will list all uncompleted assignments and pass them to the function-point that will screen them again deciding if they need to be completed in light of the most recent events. Once the public relations unit receives the assignment from the function-point, they contact the news organization and provide appropriate information.

Critical Incident Detection: How to Know What Is Serious and What Is Not

The first step in dealing with critical incidents rests with becoming aware that an adverse event has happened. The detection of critical events happens through a variety of avenues:

- Suspected critical incidents may be detected by a review of firewall logs.
- Suspected critical incidents may be detected as suspicious user activity.
- Suspected critical incidents may be detected by intrusion detection systems.
- Suspected critical incidents may be detected by systems administrators.
- Suspected critical incidents may be detected by systems auditors.
- Suspected critical incidents may be reported from contacts outside the organization.
- Suspicious events reported by users.
- Suspicious events reported by help desk operators.

In the course of detecting critical incidents, it is important to have the function point, where these activities can reported. Employees should be regularly familiarized with the procedure directing them to the location where they report suspicious activities. Function-points can be employees or a business unit where potential incidents may be reported 24/7. It is their responsibility to accept the report, elicit as much relevant information as possible, record the details, triage the event, and decide to activate the response plan or not. Using an incident reporting checklist ensures all the pertinent information is recorded so an appropriate determination might be made. When eliciting information, get the facts first, then the complainant's speculation and "good-guesses."

Here are some of the key areas for an incident report checklist:

- Current time and date
- Person accepting information
- Person reporting information
- Nature of the critical incident
- When, how, why, where, and who of the critical incident
- Systems involved (software, hardware, employees, etc.)
- Key contact information for reporting employee, including reporting chain
- Describe any need for out-of-band communications

■ Describe estimated priority of critical incident
■ Recommendations from the reporting party

If you do not know that an incident has taken place, it is difficult if not summarily impossible to determine if your systems have been compromised. The function-point should get as many of the facts as are available at that time. If information is not collected in a timely fashion, it cannot be determined which sensitive data, systems, or networks have been attacked and the extent of damage that has been done to your operation's confidentiality, integrity, and availability. Detecting critical incidents in a timely fashion is imperative. If you can compare the current systems state with the last time you knew the system was uncorrupted; responders should know what is needed to restore operations.

Critical Incident Symptoms

There are some suspicious activities that might escape the notice of Intrusion Detection Systems, firewalls, and less-than-vigilant systems monitoring. Their discovery sometimes depends on attentive administrators, help desk employees, auditors, and log-entry analyses. Here are a few examples:

■ Unusual login accounts. These include failed login attempts — attempts to enter dormant or default accounts. In this category is included the new or unusual account not created by administrators. Often this rogue account is a mysterious root account or a privileged user account.
■ Unusual account activity during irregular work hours. It seems that attackers often attempt to gain access during hours when administrators are assumed to be least likely to notice their activities. Attackers assume the system may be unattended or poorly staffed at these times.
■ Unfamiliar files or applications. Usually these types of programs are "backdoor" programs facilitating the unauthorized access of an attacker. They often take the form of something innocuous such as */etc/inetd.d/* or ".." (this is read as space-dot-dot).
■ Unauthorized changes or escalation of file and directory privileges.
■ Use of commands not normally related to an employee's job. This is an event that is often revealed when reviewing log entries. Log entries reveal that a user (not an administrator) is executing commands such as extracting downloaded programs using the *tar* command and subsequently compiling code.
■ Presence of unauthorized utilities. Finding password cracking utilities and other tools used by attackers in the system indicate a potential problem.
■ Erasures or gaps in log entries. This is another one of those activities that quickly indicates there is trouble afoot. If there are gaps or erasures in logs, it is likely someone has attempted to cover his tracks.

Response Strategy

The objective of creating a response strategy is to determine the most appropriate method responding to the critical incident. Of course, before heading off into the sunrise with technical guns blazing, there are at least three immediate considerations that must be made:

1. Technical factors
2. Business factors
3. Legal requirements

In formulating your response strategy, much depends on the character of the emergency. You do not want to treat arterial bleeding with a gauze and tape when you should be calling a surgeon. Here are some dependent factors that will significantly impact your decision process:

- Are the affected systems impacting profitable operations?
- If information was stolen, what was its level of sensitivity or classification?
- Which business functions are being impacted and at what level?
- Has the incident been contained or is it continuing?
- What is the origin of the emergency? Is it internal or external to the organization?
- Is the critical incident public knowledge?
- What are the legal reporting requirements? Does the law require this matter to be reported immediately to authorities? Who are those authorities? Should this matter be handled as a human resources matter? Should this matter be handled as a civil suit?
- What, if any, steps should be immediately taken to discover the identity of an outside-agency attacker?
- What is the fault tolerance level of the affected systems?
- As of this moment with the incident contained, what are the financial losses?

Critical incidents will vary greatly from being infected with the latest virus to the loss of extremely sensitive information. Depending on the size of the affected company, the theft of sensitive information as credit card information could result in financial ruin. Even in a larger business, a successful class-action suit resulting from negligently failing to safeguard personally identifiable information can result in significant monetary losses and incalculable damage to business reputation.

Information collected during the initial emergency assessment phase will significantly impact the manner in which a response strategy is formulated. Contained within the response strategy are estimates of your organization's ability to respond to the critical incident, public perceptions, legal and regulatory requirements, as well as an impact assessment on critical assets.

Experience Note Remember "haste makes waste." Responders should act deliberately but not dawdle.

Actions taken in response to critical incidents must be made with some degree of alacrity, but attempting to address matters without a firm set of facts is not likely to be productive.

IP Addressing in Brief

By way of review, Internet Protocol, IP, addresses are those numbers assigned to network devices that serve as their identification. It is a decimal notation that divides a 32-bit address into four 8-bit fields. An IP address consists of the following components: Network ID and Host ID. For example, in the IP address 204.9.205.21, the network ID is 204.9.205 and the host ID is 21.

For practical purposes, Internet IP addresses are divided by classes A, B, and C. Network classes are only applicable in Internet environments as closed networks may assign addresses in any form their naming convention policies allow.

- Class A networks begin at address 1.xxx.xxx.xxx through 126.xxx.xxx.xxx
- Class B networks begin at address 128.xxx.xxx.xxx through 191.xxx.xxx.xxx
- Class C networks begin at address 192.xxx.xxx.xxx though 223.255.255.xxx
- Class D networks begin at address 224.0.0.0 through 239.225.225.225
- Class E networks begin at address 240.0.0.0 through 247.225.225.225

Class D networks are reserved for multicasting and Class E networks are reserved as experimental.

There are other reserved IP addresses for example. IP address 225.2.100.1 is a multicast address to be received by a group of hosts on the network. Multicasting is the transmission of information to specific hosts.

Broadcasting is the transmission of information to be received by all hosts on a network. For example, the IP addresses 255.255.255.255, 192.9.205.255, 180.10.255.255, and 10.255.255.255 are broadcast IP addresses.

A unicast IP address uniquely identifies a specific host on a network. The datagram with a unicast IP address is received and processed by one single host. For example, the IP address 204.10.95.214 is a unicast IP address.

IP Addresses

Exhibit 1 should help put things in perspective. Class is for the most part an outdated concept but still used to explain and understand the basic structure of the Internet. The Internet authorities have ceased allocating IP addresses according to class, and all routing through the Internet has implemented Classless Inter-Domain Routing (CIDR). Currently, the preferred means for expressing the size of a network is to use the number of bits in the subnet mask.

Exhibit 1   IP Address Blocks

IP Address	Description
127.xxx.xxx.xxx	Local loopback address. The value of the last 3 bytes is ignored. The datagram with this IP address is never transmitted over the network.
0.0.0.0	Local host
xxx.0.0.0 xxx.xxx.0.0 xxx.xxx.xxx.0	Local host IP address. The x represents the network ID bits.
0.xxx.xxx. 0.0.xxx.xxx 0.0.0.xxx	IP address of a host in the local network. The x represents the host ID bits.
255.255.255.255	Limited broadcast address. Datagram with this address will be received and processed by all the hosts in the local network. This datagram is not forwarded to other networks by routers.
xxx.255.255.255 xxx.xxx.255.255 xxx.xxx.xxx.255	Directed broadcast address. The datagram with this IP address is received by all the hosts in the specified network. The x represents the network ID bits.

Exhibit 2   CIDR Addressing Blocks

CIDR Block Prefix	Equivalent Class C (#)	# of Host Addresses
/27	1/8th	32
/26	1/4th	64
/25	1/2	128
/24	1	256
/23	2	512
/22	4	1,024
/21	8	2,048
/20	16	4,096
/19	32	8,192
/18	64	16,384
/17	128	32,768
/16	256	65,536
/15	512	131,072
/14	1,024	262,144
/13	2,048	524,288

CIDR divides IP addresses into host and network portions. Instead of being limited to network identifiers of 8, 16, or 24 bits, CIDR uses prefixes from 13 to 27 bits. In this fashion, blocks of address can be assigned to networks as small as 32 hosts or those with over 500,000 hosts. This allows for address assignments tailored to an organization's specific needs. CIDR addresses include the standard 32-bit IP address and information on how many bits are used for the network prefix. For example, in the CIDR address of 102.13.0.48/8, the "8" indicates the first eight bits are used to identify the unique network leaving the remaining bits to identify the specific host (Exhibit 2).

Reviewing DNS

Domain name services are structured in a hierarchy with the highest level being the last component of the DNS address. DNS names can be up to 255 characters long and are not case-sensitive. They must start with a letter and may only consist of letters, digits, and hyphens. DNS was originally introduced in the United States and the final component of an address was intended to indicate the type of organization hosting the domain. Some of the three letter final labels such as .edu, .gov, .mil, and .biz are in common usage today. When resolved, these DNS names will indicate the IP address of the host. The purpose of DNS is to register meaningful names with numeric IP addresses, while the process of reducing a DNS name to its IP registration is called "resolution."

In some cases, there are two letter codes indicating the country of origin as part of the domain name as defined in ISO 3166, available at www.din.de/gremien/nas/nabd/iso3166ma/codlstp1/en_listp1.html.

If a DNS name cannot be resolved locally, the DNS server will communicate with other DNS servers reaching higher-level servers attempting to resolve the name. If it is unsuccessful, it will attempt to contact the ultimate authority or root server for the domain, e.g., .gov, .org, etc. This process is called the recursive resolution of addresses.

Resources

Binary mathematics, IP address architecture, CIDR, DNS, TCP/IP, and network sub-netting are topics that could fill volumes and are outside the scope of this book, but here are a few resources that will provide valuable information in these areas:

- A review of IP networks and subnetting is available at www.learntcpip.com
- A review of DNS, domain name service, is available at www.ietf.org/rfc/rfc1034. txt?number=1034
- A review of CIDR is available at www.ietf.org/rfc/rfc1517.txt?number=1517
- A review of IP address formatting is available at www.ietf.org/rfc/rfc1166. txt?number=1166
- A review of TCP/IP protocols is available at www.ietf.org/rfc/rfc1180.txt?number=1180

Locating the Origin of Denial-of-Service Attacks

Denial-of-service attacks, DoS, are extremely difficult to trace to a source IP address. For argument sake, DoS attacks include Distributed denial-of-service, DDoS attacks with the distinction being the DoS emanates from a single IP address where the DDoS attack emanates from multiple, even hundreds of IP addresses. Typically, DoS attacks originate from spoofed or compromised accounts making it virtually impossible to trace them to a single source machine.

Investigators have the option of contacting the system administrators of compromised systems and hope they have adequate logging to take the next step backward in the direction of the perpetrator, but eventually it seems there is a system in the tracing chain that does not have enough information to complete the trace. The path toward the attacker will end there.

Experience Note Because law enforcement authorities generally have very limited abilities outside their jurisdiction, it may be very helpful for the affected system administrators to contact the system administrators of the previous systems in the chain. Often law enforcement authorities may accept information collected pursuant to the business activities of administrators but may not direct administrators to contact their counterparts, as this would possibly taint the evidence as the officers could only collect the information through a warrant or international treaties.

UNIX Logging

UNIX is a platform that offers much in the way of logging features. Here, as in many systems, it is wise to alter the default-logging configuration.

Experience Note Of all the preparatory steps that responders can take before a critical incident, adequate logging is probably the most useful. Logging permits the reconstruction of events and is one of those "save your bacon" policies.

The principle file for logging is UNIX *syslog*. This file stores logging information in one, or more, configurable locations. Logging is configurable through the *syslogd* file located at */etc/syslog.conf*. Within this file, there are two significant configurations, *action* and *selector*. *Action* controls the location that the logging message is stored, while the *selector* controls the message's priority and facility. Essentially, this means the selector field controls where the logging message is generated, and the severity of the message.

Logging all security-related events is accomplished in this example:

var/log/syslog

Because attackers will attempt to delete or alter system logging, it is strongly recommended that all messages are logged and stored, remotely avoiding the possibility that an attacker could gain root privileges to the same system where the messages are generated and stored. Configuring systems to log their messages to a remote logging server is accomplished by this example:

```
auth.* @xxx.xxx.xxx.xxx
```

Of course, the *xxx.xxx.xxx.xxx* is the IP address of the remote logging server.

UNIX is capable of logging the commands that each user executes. This log file is found, depending on the variety of UNIX used, in the */var/adm*; */var/log*; or */var/adm* files. Enabling this level of logging is one that will significantly help emergency responders in their efforts to reconstruct the damaging events on the system.

Experience Note There is a major consideration for UNIX process tracking in that it will generate large logging files as essentially every action taken by a user is generating an entry. There must be a compromise reached where meaningful logging is created in the event of an emergency, yet there must be some controls placed on the amount of logging as it will soon consume all available storage.

Windows Logging

Enabling Windows NT server logging, in Microsoft's terms, is called "auditing," and must be manually done by the administrator as it is not done by default at installation. It is accomplished by following this path: *Start | Programs | Administrative Tools | User Manager | Audit Policy*. The following events are the minimum level of logging:

- User logon and logoff
- Security policy changes
- Shutdown and restart

Windows allows the auditing of file and directory permission changes. In order to accomplish this task, merely right-click on the target file or directory and choose Properties from the displayed menu. In this dialog box, choose the Security selection tab and choose Auditing. From this Directory Auditing dialogue box, you can choose the auditing of events surrounding the selected file or directory such as the success or failure of attempts to change privileges.

Remote logging in Windows is accomplished with third-party software: Kiwi Syslog Daemon, available at www.kiwisyslog.com/products.htm.

Application Logging

There are many applications that allow logging of significant events. Each has its own configuration requirements. However, these are several minimum steps that should be considered when implementing application logging:

- Log messages to a directory or file secured so that only authorized employees can access it.
- If possible, log messages to a secure, remote server.
- Record logs on WORM, Write Once Read Many, media.
- Log as much information as will be necessary to reconstruct system events.
- Ensure that all logging includes the relevant IP addresses of inside and outside the organization.

In the case of Microsoft's Internet Information Server (IIS), there are several layers of meaningful auditing. By accessing the Management Console, administrators may view and change the auditing capabilities. At the time of installation, IIS has logging enabled by default but by viewing the Extended Logging Properties dialogue box, you can see the type of logging available: *Date, Time, Client IP Address, User Name, Server IP, Cookie, Server Port,* and *Bytes Sent,* to name a few.

Hardening Servers

In a perfect world, all system components would be impregnable and all applications would not need to be protected from attackers by hiding them behind firewalls. Regrettably, most of us do not live in that world, so a system must be fortified against attacks. By taking a few preincident precautions, you can save yourself a lot of time and resources when the emergency occurs.

Here are a few proactive suggestions:

- Ensure all versions of operating systems, applications, and hardware are the most current available.
- Ensure that all software updates have been installed for all operating systems and applications. Changes must be approved and documented.
- Ensure that all services, not absolutely essential for the server's function are disabled or removed.
- Ensure that all unnecessary hardware is removed or disabled.
- Ensure there is a standard installation procedure for all hardware and software.
- Never accept default software configurations for production environments. Always review configurations and thoroughly test systems before placing them in production.

Experience Note Attackers are depending on default configurations for their success. Many attacks can be thwarted by correctly configuring software.

- Backup regularly and include critical data, applications, and configurations.
- Ensure all changes are documented, recorded, and approved before implementation.

Backup Frequently

Procedures must demand that regular and frequent backups take place. Backing up data and system configurations will help you discover attacker-related changes and expedite restoration. Backups are only as good as the originals. Test backup copies by attempting to restore operations by using backed-up copies. Many businesses have copies and when critical incidents occur, they discover their backups are insufficient.

If the only available backup copies were made after the system was compromised, they are not going to be much help. However, if good backups were made before the incident, they will be invaluable in determining the changes made to the system by the attacker.

User Security Training

Users, whether employees or not, are the most significant threat to system security. Even the most seasoned systems managers are surprised which system flaws can be exploited either intentionally or by accident. It is for this reason that user education is essential in maintaining system security. Users should know what types of emergency actions are acceptable and those that are not. Employees must be trained to know the basic steps regarding critical incident response.

Bare-essential employee training for critical incidents should include the following:

- In normal business operations, they must recognize those events that are indicative of emergencies.
- In the event of a critical incident, they must know and follow applicable policies and procedures.
- They must know that nothing is more important than lives. Data and physical facilities can be replaced.
- Ensure employees do not take any corrective or restorative steps unless advised by senior managers and CIRT members.
- Ensure employees do not take any investigative steps, unless directed by the CIRT.

System Security Architecture

Arguably, there are numerous steps that can be taken ensuring the security of a system. The most secure system denies all access and privilege but is absurd and unworkable. So a compromise is needed, and one that is basically transparent to the users.

Experience Note The best system security is transparent to the users.

Network administrators are those who are charged with the responsibility of the system topology, architecture, and secure operation of the network. Administrators are tasked with the day-to-day enforcement of the organization's policies, practices, and standards. Emergency responders are usually dependent on administrators recognizing potential emergencies, standardized configurations, and documentation for their effectiveness. For example, administrators are responsible for the creation and enforcement of policy for packet screens. If they do not have standardized configurations and documentation of access control lists; responders effectiveness will be severely hampered addressing a firewall breach.

Generally, network security is dependent on the following:

- Firewalls consisting of packet screens, inspections, and proxies
- Intrusion detection
- User authentication
- User privileges
- Activity log reviews
- System monitoring

- System audits
- Encryption

Time Stamps

Administrators should make certain that all logs and indeed, all applicable functions are timestamped recording the same time and synchronized for all machines across the network. Using the Network Time Protocol is an efficient way of achieving system-wide temporal parity. Having the same time synchronized with all devices will greatly aid a responder when she is attempting to reconstruct events from log files.

System Monitoring Structure

This seems to be a recurring theme, many businesses have no idea what they have and where it is located. Although having a current hardware and software installation standard particular to each item seems to be obvious. Each time a piece of hardware or software is installed, the authorized person should have a standard installation procedure checklist created specifically for that item governing installation and configuration. From a responder's perspective, fewer things are more frustrating than learning that servers, having the same hardware, software, and function, are configured differently.

Here are some items to have ready when the responder makes contact:

- Ensure all relevant documentation is current and available.
  - Software manuals corresponding to the installed versions
  - Hardware manuals
  - Documentation for software configuration procedures
  - Cabling diagrams
  - Schematics and relevant diagrams
  - Organizational chart, job descriptions, and reporting authority
- Ensure all relevant logs are securely stored and part of the backup procedures.
- Have a current inventory of the locations of hardware and software. The inventory should include items such as:
  - Manufacturer
  - Date of acquisition
  - Serial numbers
  - How the hardware is being used
  - Peripheral equipment attached
  - Names and versions of installed software accompanied by authenticity codes
  - Owner
  - Users
  - Physical location
  - Configuration of hardware
  - Configuration of software
  - Updates installed
- Network topology map. Having a current and accurate topology map is extremely helpful during a critical incident. Under the best of circumstances, the topology map includes relative details as connected hosts, relevant applications, switches, hubs, routers, firewalls, NICs, terminal equipment, location

of network storage devices, location and types of cabling or wireless linkage, and open-ended network connections. In order to give responders an accurate picture of the system, this map should also include the physical location and connectivity (including IP addresses and device names) of each device. Many employees will object to performing and updating this document, but it is absolutely necessary in preparing for emergency responses.

Business Issues

In business priorities, often we consider business decisions before any others. For example, when an employee is discovered stealing proprietary information and transmitting it to competitors, the organization goes into self-preservation mode minimizing its risks and preserving its critical assets. Seldom is the offender criminally prosecuted or civilly sued. As a matter of routine course, the offending employee is suspended pending the outcome of an investigation, and, if it is discovered the employee was violating policies, she is dismissed without any future legal action.

The damage an offending employee has done usually spans tangible and the intangible critical assets. Tangible losses are sustained in that valuable information was stolen and passed to competitors. In the avenue of intangible damage, she caused incalculable harm to the business reputation of the company. It is possible the financial losses suffered by the loss of credibility will exceed those from the stolen property.

This is a quandary — should managers legally pursue an offender and risk public scrutiny by airing their seemingly dirty laundry or should they dispose of the matter privately and risk becoming a target for attackers knowing they will not receive serious punishment? Organizations should consider if they fail to legally pursue attackers and criminals with full vigor, they accept current circumstances and fail to deter future attackers. In many cases, the decision is simple to make as laws mandate that suspicious or criminal activities must be reported to law enforcement authorities.

Legal Issues

Adverse legal actions can drive an otherwise well-run business into oblivion. Responders should consult with legal counsel whenever administrative, criminal, or civil proceedings might be the result of employee behavior or an outside originating attack. Considering laws and business positions, it is possible that legal counsel will advise against a particular course of action and suggest alternatives.

Political Issues

Shades of company politics can substantially color the fashion in which an organization handles its crises. Suppose for a moment that it is the atmosphere within an organization to accept all employees at their word, trusting them, it is likely they are provided substantial freedom in their work. In this atmosphere, identifying and handling critical incidents caused by employees would be a matter of little significance. In such environments, few company resources, if any, would be dedicated to addressing critical incidents. However, if the organization has a more realistic culture where it vigorously safeguards critical assets, it will allocate the necessary resources to monitor compliance with its policies and procedures.

Experience Note Performing an audit on the organization's Chief Legal Officer's workstation, the auditor discovered pornography. After a careful review, it was determined some of this material was in violation of federal laws as well the company's policies. The auditor advised her supervisor and jointly they briefed the Chief Executive Officer presenting examples of the images. It was well known that the CEO and CLO were close friends. Subsequently, the CLO was dismissed and criminally prosecuted.

Critical Incident Response Tools

Assembling a response toolkit composed of carefully selected and constantly updated hardware and software is an important aspect of critical incident response preparation. Preferred platforms include robust hardware with a full complement of software suitable to address the onsite requirements of the organization's systems.

Suggested hardware tools:

- External hard drives of large capacity
- Network interface cards compatible with LANs in the organization
- CD-RW drive
- Wireless NICs for 802.11a,b and g.
- Floppy drive
- SCSI card and controller
- SCSI hard drive with large capacity
- Surge suppressor power strips
- SCSI cables and terminators
- Several lengths of CAT 5 cables
- Several lengths of telephone cables with RJ-11 connectors
- Ribbon cables with more than three plug connectors
- Coaxial cable and connectors
- CD-Rs (at least 200 or more)
- Labels sufficient for all CD-Rs
- Laptop to EIDE adapter connector for connecting laptop hard drives to the forensic desktop
- Zip and Jazz drives
- Camera and film or removable memory card
- Portable printer and paper
- Sketch pad
- Labeling markers
- Toolkit containing tools to tag and mark hardware fasteners
- Bags into which evidence may be tagged and stored
- Labels and tags for marking evidence

Suggested software tools:

- Disk-write blocking utilities
- Boot disks for DOS and UNIX
- Unerase utilities for DOS, NT, and UNIX
- Unformat utilities
- Bootable CDs for DOS and UNIX
- Disk Editor
- Internet browser
- E-mail clients such as Eudora, Pegasus, or Outlook

- Resident operating systems on the forensic computer, including Windows 98, DOS 6.22, Windows NT, XP, Linux, or UNIX (Some investigators use DOS 6.22 or 7.0 to examine files.)
- Safeback, EnCase, Ghost, or other forensic software used to create bit-by-bit exact images of the target's media
- Word processor and label maker for evidence inventory and tags
- Spreadsheet or database applications for evidence inventories
- Drivers for the hardware in the forensic computer
- Viewers like Quickview Plus or other software allowing the viewing of a wide variety of files
- ThumbsPlus Image finder and publisher
- File organizer like 'Wilbur' (Wilbur is available at redtree.com) suitable to organize the files present on the target media

Critical Incident Response Personnel

The time to formulate a critical incident response team is not the morning after an incident occurs. That's a matter of too little too late. Responding to emergencies requires specially trained and experienced employees.

Experience Note One of the most serious transgressions committed by inexperienced responders is attempting techniques outside their area of training and expertise. During a crisis is not the time to experiment or try new techniques. They attempt to perform processes and analyses in which they have little training or experience during a crisis. Such behavior destroys evidence or causes recovered evidence to be useless in legal actions.

Here are desirable characteristics of response-team members:

- Attention to detail
- Knowledgeable in several programming languages, e.g., C, Perl, Assembly, HTML, XML, PHP, COBOL, Java, and JavaScript
- Thorough knowledge of the organization's systems
- Not rushing important tasks
- Attention to detail
- People skills
- Knowing their limitations
- Well-developed communication skills
- Not easily intimidated

Mission Statement

The mission statement of the responders should include at least the following elements:

- Respond to all critical incidents through an organized and deliberate process
- Investigations will be complete and free from bias and prejudice
- Through well-established policies, procedures will seek to immediately assess the scope of damage and take appropriate steps
- Control and contain the emergency
- Thoughtfully collect and document all evidence with consideration given to future legal actions

- Protect employee privacy rights in accordance with laws, regulations, and policy
- Establish liaison with federal and local law enforcement authorities reporting all incidents when appropriate
- Be available for testimony at legal proceedings
- Advise stakeholders of critical incidents and provide them with sound recommendations when requested
- Generate reports accurately reflecting facts, circumstances, events, actions, and recommendations
- Conduct postmortem critique with the goal of improved efficiency and effectiveness

Responding to the Scene

As a baseline, responders will be involved in a six-step methodology when addressing critical incidents:

- Make all necessary preparations for emergencies. Such preparations include personal training and skills updating, network preparations, and equipment/software preparations.
- Detect critical incidents. This includes but is not limited to collecting relevant information from system administrators, Web administrators, security administrators, auditors, human resources administrators, legal unit, firewall administrators, and intrusion detection equipment.
- Investigate incidents effectively and efficiently.
- Create a response strategy and present it to the appropriate senior managers before proceeding with the incident response.
- Respond to the emergency.
- Critique and postmortem. Responders, clients, and stakeholders should conduct a candid and productive analysis of the response with the objective being to improve service.

When those responding to the critical incident are advised of the emergency, there are generally two questions in their minds:

1. What happened?
2. Which is the best action to take?

As with most investigations, conducted by the law enforcement or corporate security officers, the initial stage is essentially obtaining information about the critical incident and making an assessment. Every situation is unique to itself. When collecting information about the incident, you ask what happened from those who are already there and determine if any have direct knowledge.

The first bit of information is usually the notification that something adverse has happened. Investigators should query employees present during the incident about their knowledge. On the completion of these initial interviews, this level of knowledge is usually sufficient to formulate a response strategy and make recommendations. At this particular time, it is important for investigators to ensure that actions and recommendations are measured with the exigencies of the scene.

Critical Incident Checklist

Once investigators learn of a critical incident, they begin by asking questions. Depending on their level of experience and the frequency of such events, they may not ask the right kind of questions or enough questions. At the onset, they should ask questions sufficient to determine the basic facts. Questions will likely involve the location of the affected systems, administrative and management contacts, extent of damage, and if the emergency has been contained or is spreading. They may not receive an answer to every question and in the heat of the event, they might not remember to ask the right questions. Having an emergency response checklist will go a long way to avoiding asking duplicate questions or forgetting to ask questions that should have been asked.

- Identity, location, and title of person calling
- Time and date of call
- Brief description of critical incident:
  - When did it occur?
  - Where did it occur?
  - How was it detected?
  - Who detected it?
  - What is happening at this moment?
- What systems are affected?
  - What is the impact to users now?
- Systems questions:
  - Hardware involved?
  - Software involved?
  - Type of network at the affected systems?
  - Physical location of affected systems?
  - How are the users affected?
  - Is the damage contained?
  - How was the damage contained?
  - What recovery steps have been taken?
- Who is the senior manager for this location? Contact information?
- Who is aware of this problem currently?
- Has the problem been discovered by the public?
- Attacker questions:
  - Is the attack inside or outside the organization?
  - What is the classification and extent of the stolen information?
  - What is the IP address? Has it been resolved to a domain?
  - Has there been any contact with the administrator of that domain?
  - Is the attack a denial of service?
  - What is the level of damage?
  - What steps have been taken to minimize the effects?
- User questions:
  - Have logs been examined and what do they show?
  - Is there remote access to the affected machine?
  - Have there been any changes to firewalls or access control lists?
  - Are there any auditing activities planned or taking place now?
- Contacts:
  - Who can be contacted for more information?
  - Who are the administrators and managers of the affected systems?

System Map

As part of responder preparation, it is strongly suggested that a map showing the topology, architecture, and locations is created and maintained. The location of the affected system may allow a responder to draw certain conclusions about the emergency. For example, if the affected systems are located in a secure area and do not have any connections to open-ended networks, it is obvious an employee is responsible. However, if the affected system is connected to open-ended networks like the Internet, Frame Relay, or X.25, investigators must broaden the universe of likely sources.

From the responder's perspective, there are basically three details that a topology and architecture map will provide, broadcast domains, open-ended network connectivity, and network-attached devices. Broadcast domains are those areas of shared traffic. They show trust-relationships and will generally show that an affected system will likely affect the systems within the broadcast domain. Connectivity with open-ended networks includes any point that is connected to a network that extends outside the protected network.

Reviewing system maps, responders gain an idea of the location of devices such as PBXs, routers, firewalls, intrusion devices, hubs, switches, workstations, and servers. Some documents might be of sufficient detail to display the physical location and MACs of relevant devices. Accompanying systems maps are policies and procedures regarding such items as the filtering rules, access control lists, authentication means, and other applicable policies and configuration procedures.

Experience Note Investigators must review all applicable policies and procedures in the creation of their response strategy. One of the questions senior managers will likely ask, when briefed about a critical incident, is the existence of policies and procedures relative to the response strategy.

Investigation at the Crime Scene

After completing an initial assessment, investigators should have a basic understanding of the situation. However, more information is generally needed before being able to decide the next steps. It is necessary to conduct a few interviews and engage in a few hands-on activities before making the first report to senior managers.

Interviews

Interviews are essentially guided conversations. Correctly done, they are extremely useful in gleaning information about the incident. Obviously, any information will have a significant affect on the way a plan of action is formulated and pursued.

Experience Note There is a word of caution when conducting interviews — remember that it is possible the person who is being interviewed is the cause of the problem. Document all interviews carefully and thoroughly.

When interviewing employees, a great deal of caution should be used. It is very unwise to use language that would appear to be accusatory. Interviewers must be aware of employees' legal rights, for example, if an employee is threatened with her job in order to obtain a confession of a criminal act. Such action will likely render the statement useless for future criminal prosecution, as statements of this nature must be voluntary and not coerced.

Interviewing Users

Users can provide a great deal of relevant information depending on the circumstances. Often users report unusual happenings to the help unit first. Experienced help unit employees should not dismiss strange happenings quickly. There are times that erratic system indications are a result of attacks.

Experience Note The help unit received repeated calls over a period of several days from one of the company's senior employees regarding e-mail that was marked as open, yet the employee insisted she had not opened it. At lunch, the help unit employee was having lunch with her supervisor and described the mysteriously opened e-mail. The supervisor explained she had some experience with "monitoring" software and visited the complaining employee. After a short interview, the help unit supervisor discovered the employee's anti-virus program had been disabled. Enabling the anti-virus program and launching it, she discovered a copy of "Back Orifice" had been installed on the workstation. She recognized that Back Orifice was a program that would allow a user to remotely access and operate a workstation. Without delay, the supervisor asked the nature of the mysteriously opened e-mail and found that many dealt with sensitive financial matters. The critical incident response team was immediately notified. They discovered that Back Orifice had been secretly installed on the workstation and through a bit of research, they discovered the employee that had opened and read the e-mail.

Users, help unit employees, auditors, security officers, and senior managers should be encouraged and trained to notice and report events that identify critical incidents. After a user reports her system problems, it is incumbent on the responder to complete the process. A complete interview will answer "who, why, what, where, when, and how" of the alleged incident.

Experience Note When is it appropriate to report an incident? This is a difficult question to answer and much depends on the organization. If anyone is in doubt about a suspicious event, they should be encouraged to contact the critical incident response function-point or a senior manager. Through a bit of conversation, the matter can be screened with more action to follow, or the employee can be told there is nothing about which to be concerned.

Interviewing System Administrators

Many suspected critical incidents would either be escalated to a higher level of action or classified as anomalous after a discussion with system administrators. At no other time is this more evident than in the case of firewall or intrusion detection activity. Often the system administrator or firewall administrator can provide information that confirms the suspicious nature of the event or is in a position to indicate that nothing is faulty.

Here are some areas to be asked of administrators:

- What is the nature of any unusual activity?
- Who are the employees with root access to the system?
- What are the logging capabilities of the system in question?
- What do these logs show?
- What security safeguards are implemented on the target system?

Interviewing Managers

It is a good business procedure to contact managers that have responsibility for the compromised systems. The matter is twofold, they are responsible for critical assets and they are responsible to report to their stakeholders about the status of those assets. Frequently, they have information to which administrators and other employees are not entitled. For example, they have information regarding personnel matters such as those employees who have been investigated or disciplined previously.

Here are suggested areas that should be included when the manager is apprised of a suspicious event:

- What is the level of sensitivity surrounding the data and applications on the affected system?
- What, if any, are the personnel issues surrounding the affected systems? Are there personnel issues of which investigators should be aware?
- Is the systems manager aware of any authorized systems auditing or penetration scheduled at the time of the emergency? If so, who authorized this action and who is performing this audit?

Experience Note If the responders take any action or direct someone to take action, there must be a determination early in the response to determine if changes, precipitated by the responders, will change anything that could be used as evidence later. This is a critical move; if evidence is altered in any way, it could be rendered useless in future legal proceedings. Consequently, there must be a decision made pursuant to the response strategy recommendations very early in the response action.

If evidence is going to be collected, it must be preserved in such a fashion that it can be introduced at court; otherwise, it does not matter what changes are made. Obviously, there is a balance in getting the affected system back online and carefully collecting evidence.

Determining a Response Strategy

Assembling preliminary information, investigators should be able to formulate a viable response strategy and move to that end. Just because they have made their recommendations to senior managers does not necessarily mean they are locked into that course of action. After getting well into the problem, it is quite likely they will discover it to be different from their initial assessment requiring a change in their original plan. Creating their response strategy is in actuality devising their action plan. This plan answers the question, "Under the circumstances, as I currently know them, what is the best way to proceed considering the organization's goals and applicable legal requirements?"

The response strategy should take everything they know at this point into account as, the type of attack, sensitivity of compromised systems, policies of the organization, legal opinion, and recommendations of senior managers. Armed with an understanding of the initial facts and relevant opinions, they should be in a position to make a determination of whether the system merely needs to be cleanly restored or if a forensic investigation is warranted.

Restoring Service Operations

Restoring business operations has the goal of returning affected systems to normal service. In this action, there is not generally much care taken to collect and preserve evidence, attribute attack responsibility, or remove affected systems from operation. The primary goal is to contain damage, make changes precluding the damage from recurring, and restore the system to its operational state. Usually done at the some time is the examination of how and why the attack was successful. For example, if a virus attack were successful, owing to an outdated antivirus program, updating and change control documentation must take place before the system is restored.

This is probably the most common step dealing with attacks stemming from viruses and worms. Usually this action does not require much of an emergency response, rather it requires administrators to take appropriate action in locating the reason the virus was successful, patching the system, documenting and enabling approved changes, ensuring the system is ready for production, and placing the system back into service. Auditors are notified so they might include antivirus software patching in their next audit program.

An Attack Is Underway

There are many earmarks that identify a system under attack; here are a few:

- Sudden and dramatic increase in overall network traffic
- Traffic occurring at unusual times, usually during slack periods
- Unexplained root or user accounts
- Unexplained installed applications
- Sudden increase in the number of bad or malformed packets
- Large numbers of packets caught by routers or firewalls as egress items
- Unscheduled and unexplained server reboots
- Existence of known attack signatures in log files

Where Is the Attacker?

If investigators are tasked to identify the attacker, the investigation must proceed with great care and great length. Suppose the attacker is located within the organization, the matter may proceed with relative ease with senior managers, legal unit, human resources unit, and law enforcement cooperation. If the matter is deserving of civil or administrative action, immediate steps should be taken to preserve evidence for later proceedings.

In the case of an attacker being located outside the venue of law enforcement, do not despair if she is not identified. It is possible this person resides in a country that does not have a law enforcement assistance treaty with the country where the victim-system resides. In such cases, it is unlikely that criminal prosecution and extradition will be successful.

Do not take this statement as an axiom, as there have been cases where attackers have been lured to countries with extradition treaties and attackers have been extradited for criminal prosecution. There are cases where law officers traveled to the country where the offender resided and assisted law enforcement agencies in building a case against the offender there. Given a sufficient amount of gravity, it is possible for countries to agree to criminally prosecute an individual for analogous crimes in the country of origin. These cases usually happen where the violator cannot be extradited and the host country is interested in deterring this type of criminal behavior.

Prosecutions of a criminal nature are primarily intended to deprive a defendant of her liberty. Criminal prosecutions will not usually provide suitable financial restitution to damaged organizations. However, there is an increasing tendency of judges to order victim-restitution as part of the criminal's sentence.

Civil actions are intended to provide financial restitution for injured plaintiffs (and victims of crimes) for damages and possibly punish the defendant financially. It is a matter of how badly you want to punish the perpetrator and how much money you are willing to spend to be successful. If there have been many attacks launched by the same person and the victims can identify themselves as victims, then it is possible for them to bind together, forming a certified class, and sue the defendant collectively.

Law Enforcement Relations

Handling law enforcement relations is a delicate subject and most businesses are shy to handle it. Nevertheless, reporting allegations of a serious (felony) criminal nature, according to U.S. federal law and many state laws, is not optional. It is mandatory.

Title 18, U.S. Code Section 4, states:

> Whoever, having knowledge of the actual commission of a felony cognizable by a court of the United States, conceals and does not as soon as possible make known the same to some judge or other person in civil or military authority under the United States, shall be fined under this title or imprisoned not more than three years, or both.

Another matter worth consideration is the legal requirement of having an internal mechanism to detect criminal acts affecting financial statements in publicly traded companies. Under 15 U.S. Code 87 j–l, the requirements of financial and operational audits include this language:

> (a) In general, each audit required pursuant to this chapter of the financial statements of an issuer by an independent public accountant shall include, in accordance with generally accepted auditing standards, as may be modified or supplemented from time to time by the Commission
>
>> (1) procedures designed to provide reasonable assurance of detecting illegal acts that would have a direct and material effect on the determination of financial statement amounts;
>>
>> (2) procedures designed to identify related party transactions that are material to the financial statements or otherwise require disclosure therein; and
>>
>> (3) an evaluation of whether there is substantial doubt about the ability of the issuer to continue as a going concern during the ensuing fiscal year.
>
> (b) Required response to audit discoveries
>
>> (1) Investigation and report to management If, in the course of conducting an audit pursuant to this chapter to which subsection (a) of this section applies, the independent public accountant detects or otherwise becomes aware of information indicating that an illegal act (whether or not perceived to have a material effect on the financial statements of the issuer) has or

may have occurred, the accountant shall, in accordance with generally accepted auditing standards, as may be modified or supplemented from time to time by the Commission

(A)(i) determine whether it is likely that an illegal act has occurred; and (ii) if so, determine and consider the possible effect of the illegal act on the financial statements of the issuer, including any contingent monetary effects, such as fines, penalties, and damages; and

(B) as soon as practicable, inform the appropriate level of the management of the issuer and assure that the audit committee of the issuer, or the board of directors of the issuer in the absence of such a committee, is adequately informed with respect to illegal acts that have been detected or have otherwise come to the attention of such accountant in the course of the audit, unless the illegal act is clearly inconsequential.

(2) Response to failure to take remedial action. If, after determining that the audit committee of the board of directors of the issuer, or the board of directors of the issuer in the absence of an audit committee, is adequately informed with respect to illegal acts that have been detected or have otherwise come to the attention of the accountant in the course of the audit of such accountant, the independent public accountant concludes that

(A) The illegal act has a material effect on the financial statements of the issuer;

(B) The senior management has not taken, and the board of directors has not caused senior management to take, timely and appropriate remedial actions with respect to the illegal act; and

(C) the failure to take remedial action is reasonably expected to warrant departure from a standard report of the auditor, when made, or warrant resignation from the audit engagement; the independent public accountant shall, as soon as practicable, directly report its conclusions to the board of directors.

(3) Notice to Commission; response to failure to notify. An issuer whose board of directors receives a report under paragraph (2) shall inform the Commission by notice not later than 1 business day after the receipt of such report and shall furnish the independent public accountant making such report with a copy of the notice furnished to the Commission. If the independent public accountant fails to receive a copy of the notice before the expiration of the required 1-business-day period, the independent public accountant shall

(A) Resign from the engagement; or

(B) Furnish to the Commission a copy of its report (or the documentation of any oral report given) not later than 1 business day following such failure to receive notice.

(4) Report after resignation. If an independent public accountant resigns from an engagement under paragraph (3)(A), the accountant shall, not later than 1 business day following the failure by the issuer to notify the Commission under paragraph (3), furnish to the Commission a copy of the accountant's report (or the documentation of any oral report given).

(c) Auditor liability limitation. No independent public accountant shall be liable in a private action for any finding, conclusion, or statement expressed in a report made pursuant to paragraph (3) or (4) of subsection (b) of this section, including any rule promulgated pursuant thereto.

(d) Civil penalties in cease-and-desist proceedings. If the Commission finds, after notice and opportunity for hearing in a proceeding instituted pursuant to section 78u-3 of this title, that an independent public accountant has willfully violated paragraph (3) or (4) of subsection (b) of this section, the Commission may, in addition to entering an order under section 78u-3 of this title, impose a civil penalty against the independent public accountant and any other person that the Commission finds was a cause of such violation. The determination to impose a civil penalty and the amount of the penalty shall be governed by the standards set forth in section 78u-2 of this title.

(e) Preservation of existing authority. Except as provided in subsection (d) of this section, nothing in this section shall be held to limit or otherwise affect the authority of the Commission under this chapter.

(f) "Illegal act" defined. As used in this section, the term "illegal act" means an act or omission that violates any law, or any rule or regulation having the force of law.

Suspicious Activity Reports

Federally insured financial institutions are required to file Suspicious Activity Reports, SARs, in a timely fashion with copies being sent to at least the following federal authorities:

- Internal Revenue Service
- Federal Bureau of Investigation
- Secret Service

The legal requirement for SAR completion is detailed in 12 CFR Part 21, Subpart B–Reports of Suspicious Activities, Section 21.11 Suspicious Activity Report:

> (a) *Purpose and scope.* This section ensures that national banks file a Suspicious Activity Report when they detect a known or suspected violation of Federal law or a suspicious transaction related to a money-laundering activity or a violation of the Bank Secrecy Act. This section applies to all national banks as well as any Federal branches and agencies of foreign banks licensed or chartered by the OCC. (For clarification the "OCC" is the Office of the Comptroller of the Currency.)

SARs must provide basic details surrounding suspicious internal and external events. Suspicious activities include the violation of criminal statutes as well as those that constitute unethical behavior. SAR completion is not optional. It is a regulatory requirement.*

Law Enforcement Liaison

Dealing with law enforcement authorities means cooperating with them as soon as criminal behavior is suspected. In the most basic terms, it means anyone with knowledge must report crimes to authorities, both civil and military where it applies.

---

* More SAR-relevant information is available at www.occ.treas.gov/fr/cfrparts/12CFR21.htm#§%2021.11%20 Suspicious%20Activity%20Report and www.occ.treas.gov/sar.htm.

Most law enforcement entities have very strict procedures about evidence collection. Their goal is to collect, analyze, and preserve evidence so it can be used in legal proceedings. In cases where untrained and inexperienced crisis responders go about the process of collecting or analyzing it, they usually render it useless for legal purposes. Officers must be able to testify about the way the evidence was collected and trace its custody from origin, through examination and analysis to testimony.

Incident responders and their legal units should establish liaison with local and federal authorities assigned to computer and white collar crimes. In most regions, law enforcement officers have already formed computer crimes task forces to address technology crimes.

Senior managers and employees are responsible to contact these task force officers and create mutual policies and procedures regarding crime-reporting and evidence collection. In most instances, officers and agents welcome the opportunity to create goodwill with business organizations and are anxious to explain their evidence collection and case-processing requirements.

There are national organizations, with local chapters, having the purpose of facilitating communication between government and private industry sectors. These associations attempt to share knowledge about potential risks and provide an outlet for increased information flow between members.

Experience Note Such organizations are Infragard and the NIPC, sponsored by the federal government, with information available at www.infragard.net and www.nipc.gov. Privately sponsored organizations are ISACA (Information Systems Audit and Control Association), www.isaca.org; ISSA (Information Systems Security Association), www.issa.org; and HTCIA (High Technology Crime Investigators Association), htcia.org.

In the case of criminal investigation and subsequent prosecution, it is a lengthy process depending on the local agency's priorities, availability of prosecution resources, and congestion of court dockets. Responders will likely be requested to provide testimony in a wide variety of judicial hearings and trials. Usually law enforcement officers can perform much of the investigation, evidence collection and analysis and preliminary testimony themselves. However, when it comes to testimony before grand juries, evidence hearings, trials, and sentencing hearings, appropriate levels of business resources will be requested to appear.

Experience Note It is not unusual for criminal proceedings to take from several months to several years before they are finally adjudicated. Depending on appeals, this period might be extended to several more years.

Many law enforcement authorities are not allowed to provide copies of their investigative reports to interested parties who intend to use them for civil or administrative actions. However, anything said or presented as evidence in open-court is public information. Through public access such as the Freedom of Information and Public Access laws, private entities may obtain information about adjudicated criminal cases. The court reporter's office and the court clerk's office may provide transcripts of hearings and court proceedings that might be used in other legal actions.

Types of Attacks

In determining the correct response strategy, you must identify the type of attack affecting operations. Is the attack unauthorized e-mail access, denial of service, Web site vandalism, theft of sensitive information, or someone exploring the interior network? Knowing and classifying the attack for the response checklist decides response options.

- Computer intrusions. These are attacks against tax critical assets. Unauthorized intrusions can take a variety of forms while attackers attempt to disguise their identity. Attackers freely plant viruses, back doors, Trojans and worms; steal proprietary information; waste system resources; and delete or corrupt data.
- Denial-of service-attacks. DoS attacks can have origins with one source or in the case of a Distributed Denial of Service, DDoS, hundreds of attacking sources. Stopping them depends greatly on the updated configuration of firewall and gateway equipment. They can be nasty — stealing large amounts of bandwidth and crashing systems with outside connections. A devastating DDoS attack was experienced and chronicled by Steve Gibson at http://grc.com/dos/drdos.htm.
- Unauthorized use of resources is not really an attack, but it should be considered in this category. Usually it is an employee violating organization policy by using the workstation and network to do such things as shopping, download software, or distribute prohibited materials. In addressing internal violators, investigators usually focus on the employee's workstation and the media found in the work area.
- Web page vandalism is part of the intrusion category. Here the responder is faced with the circumstances of how the attacker gained access to the Web server and changed the content or the means by which the Web page interacted with the user. A major concern of senior managers is the extent attackers were able to penetrate the victim-network. Web page defacements often appear to be nothing more than acts of cyber-vandalism, but many times they are more insidious. Responders should review the compromised Web page and related systems to determine if intruders accessed sensitive data.

Administrator Facilitated Attacks

There are times when attacks are facilitated by negligent acts on the part of network and systems administrators. Systems administrators are often so busy handling fires; there is not enough time in their day to get done what they are asked to do. Consequently, they install a server platform or application with its default configuration settings.

Experience Note Default installations are a recipe for disaster. Attackers are counting default installations for their success. Attacks exploiting default system vulnerabilities must be addressed by policies and procedures, with compliance ensured by unannounced internal audits.

These are a few examples of potentially disastrous acts:

- Administrators perform default installations
- Administrators fail to remove or disable unnecessary services
- Administrators fail to close unnecessary ports
- Administrators fail to remove all unnecessary hardware from networked equipment such as firewalls, servers, and workstations
- Administrators fail to disable 'A' drives from their servers allowing floppy disks to be inserted containing software facilitating system penetration

- Administrators run services, at root, that should be run at account levels
- Administrators fail to review user activity logs for anomalous activities
- Administrators assign poor or no passwords to users
- Administrators fail to enforce user authentication before manually resetting passwords
- Administrators install network services with known security flaws such as telnet, FTP, rhost, etc.
- Administrators fail to adequately protect sensitive files and information
- Administrators install applications that fail to screen, and deny improper user input

Senior Manager's Approval

Completing their initial investigation, investigators should have enough information collected to decide the appropriate response level, methodology, and make recommendations to senior managers. The primary issue at this time is to present the action-plan in an understandable and concise way. As part of the presentation, legal unit representatives should be present during the action plan presentation so they might render an informed legal opinion.

Experience Note Actions taken during the response will likely impact the entire enterprise. Investigators and senior managers must proceed with caution and deliberation.

Present all relevant alternatives with their corresponding advantages and disadvantages. Narrow the best choices to one well-justified recommendation. If there is not a clear-cut alternative, investigators must be prepared to declare their best possible recommendations.

Other Relative Issues

In addition to the items mentioned above, there are other matters affecting how and when the responder will react to the critical incident. Often the location of the attacker will affect the response action and willingness to pursue criminal and civil prosecution. If an attacker is located in a country that protects its citizens from extradition or prosecution, then pursuing judicial recourse may not be the wisest course. In some cases, legal efforts might best be directed toward asset forfeiture or civil process focusing on the attacker's financial assets in the region where the attacker's victim resides.

However, if the attacker is located within the same national borders as her victim or in a country with treaties supporting prosecution or within the organization itself, then administrative, civil, and criminal actions should be pursued. Bear in mind, these investigations and prosecutions frequently span months. In some cases, it appears the benefit is relatively small by seeking criminal prosecution; however, if the public is made aware that attacking your business results in legal action with prison, asset forfeiture, and the collection of damages from attackers, it will likely deter other attackers. Basically, civil and criminal prosecutions are effective in the deterrence of unlawful acts only if the public is made aware of them.

Experience Note Unlawful acts are not deterred in a news-vacuum.

Business Considerations before Legal Actions

Before pursuing the track of lengthy legal actions, there are technical and business considerations that have to be made.

- Does the organization have the technical expertise, equipment, and time to pursue an investigation, analysis and resolution?
- Are there public or stockholder considerations to be made?
- Do these factors impact legally mandated reporting requirements?
- Does the organization possess sufficient financial resources to initiate and complete a full investigation?
- Will your organization be a repeat target in future attacks if legal action is not taken now?

Collecting Evidence

Before the information age, when investigators wanted to collect documentary evidence, by consent, search warrant, or some other legal means, they searched a suspect's wallet, pocketbook, office file cabinet, or trash containers. In today's business environment, many of these areas are still valid places for evidence; however, they pale when compared to the amount of evidence that can be found in the workstation, PDA, laptop, or other mobile device.

What Is Evidence?

The simplest way to define evidence is information, of probative value, confirming or dispelling an assertion. In more common language, evidence either supports allegations or it does not. This is a good reference for electronic evidence, found at the U.S. Department of Justice Web site available at www.usdoj.gov/criminal/cyber-crime/s&smanual2002.htm.

At this point, it may be a good idea to examine the role of computers, networks, and systems and their role as evidence:

- Computers may be used as instruments to commit unlawful acts. For example, if a person launched a denial-of-service attack directed to your E-commerce Web site, the computer used to launch this attack would be considered an instrument of the unlawful act.
- Computers may be used to store evidence of an unlawful act. For example, if an employee downloads pornography on his office workstation, storing it on the hard drive as well as removable media, the workstation and related media have the same role as a file cabinet holding the evidence.
- Organizations and their related systems can be victims of unlawful acts. For example, if an attacker gained access to a server and modified sensitive data, in this instance the organization is a victim of the unlawful act.
- Computers may be physically stolen and thereafter are considered fruits of an unlawful act. For example, a truck loaded with PDAs is hijacked. The handheld computers would be considered fruits of the crime.

In seizing, examining, and analyzing information technology, there are many relevant legal decisions impacting investigative acts. If law enforcement agents want to seize computer systems that form part of a network, unless done correctly, the resulting damaged evidence presents prosecutors with substantial barriers. So formidable are these issues, the prosecutor might decide judges and juries cannot be convinced of the case's merits. Consequently, the prosecution declines to take legal action.

For more information regarding computers and electronic evidence search and seizure, there is substantial information available at www.usdoj.gov/criminal/cyber-crime/searching.html.

Experience Note Seizing an entire network could irreparably damage business operations and possibly result in the business' closure. Search warrants and other judicial processes are intended to legally seize evidence or fruits of a crime under the Fourth Amendment. They cannot be used as *de facto* cease-and-desist orders to close a business. If their use exceeds legal mandates, allegations of outrageous conduct are often made against law enforcement agents. Protecting against outrageous government conduct is civil recourse available to plaintiffs (the damaged business). Legal actions are described under the Privacy Protection Act, 42 U.S. Code 2000aa and the Electronic Communications Privacy Act, 18 U.S. Code 2701–2712 and Steve Jackson Games, Inc. v. Secret Service, 816 F. Supp. 432, 440, 443.

Examining the contents of target hard drives and other related media must be driven by the needs of the investigation. In short, this is another one of those "bang for the buck" priority matters. With the average workstation having more than 60 Gb of storage capacity, it is virtually impossible to completely examine every file and byte of stored or deleted information from a practical standpoint.

Data stored centrally on a network server may contain incriminating e-mail, but it also stores irrelevant e-mail of innocent third parties that have a reasonable expectation of privacy. Investigators sifting through messages considered private or privileged might find themselves the object of civil suits and depending on the circumstances criminally prosecuted. Seizing electronic evidence where communications are considered privileged, as e-mail exchanges between clergy and their parishioners, medical doctors and their patients, attorneys and their clients, and husbands and wives, can also result in the materials being excluded from legal actions. At times, determining if media contain privileged communications is an issue decided by the presiding judge; consequently, it is a matter for judicial hearings listening to arguments and evidence from opposing sides.

Evidence Prioritization

In relative terms, 24 Gb of printed data would amount to a stack of paper roughly 500 feet high. Obviously, it would require a large team of investigators to catalog and understand such a large amount of information. Computer forensic examiners must follow standards of evidence collection and analysis in the pursuit of their cases.

Experience Note If evidence review and analysis standards are established, they will go a long way to projecting witness credibility.

Despite the fact examiners may have a legal right to examine and search every file in the system, time constraints or legal limitations may not permit it. Therefore, the examination of files is practically limited to those identified as being case-relevant having evidentiary value. However, there is a voice in opposition to merely looking at the case-relevant files ignoring other evidence in the examination process. For example, an investigator viewing files containing stolen intellectual property should not ignore the files where the subject stored financial information about laundering the financial proceeds of that stolen property. Investigators must prioritize their efforts looking for relevant case-related information and perform sufficient examinations so they are convinced that all files do not contain anything of further evidentiary value.

Examining Computer Evidence

In physical terms, computer evidence generally consists of central processing units, storage media, monitors, printers, routers, firewalls, switches, logs, and software. Evidence stored on physical items is considered latent and needs to be essentially "lifted" to another medium for collection, examination, and preservation. Collection, examination, and analysis are performed on this recovered media and must remain unchanged if going to be considered of evidentiary value.

Often senior managers ask why copied media must remain unaltered if it is going to be used in legal proceedings. The answer is not simple. In the most basic terms, opposing legal sides routinely challenge the media's authenticity and if it is discovered the content has been changed, it feeds arguments that the evidence was intentionally or accidentally altered rendering it useless. Judges and juries have been convinced that although the content was slightly altered by the collection or examination process, the argument was sufficiently enlarged by opposing lawyers that they chose to exclude the digital evidence from their deliberations. Consequently, if digital evidence is to have full evidentiary impact, it must remain unaltered.

Experience Note Computer evidence must be collected in such a fashion as to maintain the integrity of the original while examination is performed on forensically sound media copies. It is incumbent on professionals to safeguard the integrity of evidence while delivering valid and reliable analytical results.

To further support this concept, review the following quote from the Federal Rules of Evidence for year 2002:

> Rule 1001. Definitions
>
> The following definitions are applicable:
>
> > (1) Writings and recordings. — "Writings" and "recordings" consist of letters, words, or numbers, or their equivalent, set down by handwriting, typewriting, printing, photocopying, photographing, magnetic impulse, mechanical or electronic recording, or other form of data compilation.
> >
> > (2) Photographs. — "Photographs" include still photographs, x-ray films, video tapes, and motion pictures.
> >
> > (3) Original. — An "original" of a writing or recording is the writing or recording itself or any counterpart intended to have the same effect by a person executing or issuing it. An "original" of a photograph includes the negative or any print therefrom.
> >
> > If data are stored in a computer or similar device, any printout or other output readable by sight, shown to reflect the data accurately, is an "original".
> >
> > (4) Duplicate. — A "duplicate" is a counterpart produced by the same impression as the original, or from the same matrix, or by means of photography, including enlargements and miniatures, or by mechanical

or electronic re-recording, or by chemical reproduction, or by other equivalent techniques which accurately reproduces the original.

Rule 1002. Requirement of Original

To prove the content of a writing, recording, or photograph, the original writing, recording, or photograph is required, except as otherwise provided in these rules or by Act of Congress.

Rule 1003. Admissibility of Duplicates

A duplicate is admissible to the same extent as an original unless

(1) A genuine question is raised as to the authenticity of the original or

(2) In the circumstances it would be unfair to admit the duplicate in lieu of the original.

These rules permit investigators to use forensic software and other tools to reconstruct an accurate representation of the original data stored on the system. This means the data copied from the target computer may be introduced if it can be proven that this data is a fair and accurate representation of the original.

Of course, opposing sides are going to attack the integrity of the collected evidence; for this reason, it is imperative that when collecting evidence, no one exceeds her expertise, as it could render evidence useless.

Policies and Procedures

Policies and procedures provide instructions and structures and apply to the examination of computers and related media. Their adherence ensures quality and good practices by investigators making sure their efforts are planned, performed, monitored, and recorded. Formalized procedures ensure the integrity and quality of the work performed. Policies should require electronic examinations to be performed on forensically sound copies of the original evidence. This principle is based on the fact that bit-by-bit copies can be made of original digital evidence resulting in exact and true copies of the original.

Policies and procedures must dictate that investigative methods used recovering digital information from computers are valid and reliable. These methods must be technologically and legally acceptable ensuring all relevant information is recovered and preserved. Duplication methods must be legally defensible so nothing in the original was altered when it was forensically copied and that forensic copy is an exact duplicate of the original down to the last bit.

Common Mistakes when Handling Evidence

These are some common mistakes when collecting and preserving evidence:

- Altering the MAC (modify, access, and create) times
- Updating or patching affected systems before responders arrive at the scene
- Using tools that alter the content of the original media
- Writing over evidence by installing software on the target media
- Performing collection and analysis exceeding training and expertise
- Failing to initiate and maintain accurate documentation including chain of custody schedules, commands on the target system, tools to recover digital evidence, and history of actions taken by the responders

Chain of Custody Schedule

It is one of those critical elements often neglected by investigators — the chain of custody schedule. The reason it is called a schedule is that the document memorializes the history of evidence discovery, acquisition, processing and presentation.

A chain of custody schedule is a history documenting:

> Case number
>
> Date, time, and location the evidence was discovered
>
> Person who made the evidence discovery
>
> Date, time, and location of each person taking custody of the evidence
>
> Identifying number of the evidence
>
> Date each person accepted the evidence for storage
>
> Location of storage
>
> Each person who takes custody of the evidence for examination or presentation

Exhibit 3 is a typical chain of custody schedule example.

Experience Note In many cases where evidence is stored in a central location, there are logs documenting the name, time, and dates of every person who enters that facility, in addition to the chain of custody schedules.

A copy of the chain of custody should physically accompany the evidence item with the appropriate field being completed. A copy of the chain of custody schedule should be included with the investigative report as part of the attachments.

Exhibit 3   Chain of Custody Schedule

Case No.	*Evidence Item No.*		
From Location By whom	Date	Reason	To Location To whom
From Location By whom	Date	Reason	To Location To whom
From Location By whom	Date	Reason	To Location To whom
From Location By whom	Date	Reason	To Location To whom
From Location By whom	Date	Reason	To Location To whom

Evidence Tags

Investigators should prepare evidence tags for all collected items. All items are tagged whether retained or returned to the owner. These are generally small gummed or self-adhesive tags that can be secured to outside of the item. Evidence tags may be attached to heat-sealed, electostatically neutral plastic bags containing magnetic media or other types of digital evidence. Storing media in this fashion secures it from static electricity, the elements, and tampering. Sealing the bag with two witnesses present signing the chain of custody schedule avoids future legal arguments challenging changes and custody.

Evidence tags should have the case number, an item number, and date-time-place information as well as the name and initials of the collecting person. In some cases, investigators have a policy that two individuals must witness the collection of evidence. Many law enforcement officers use scribes or markers placing their initials, date, time, and place on the evidence, in addition to the evidence tag, so they can positively identify it in the future. Some investigators think evidence handling is a tedious process. It is. But conscientious attention to details, accompanied by intelligent redundancy, has successfully defused many legal challenges.

Activity Log

On receiving a critical incident notification, the person receiving the call should begin an activity log. It is a complete responder activity log and includes all activities such as:

- Initial notification (Who, What, When, Where, How, Why)
- Interviews
- Management contacts and interaction
- Law enforcement contacts
- Evidence searches, seizures, and inventory
- On-the-spot evidence analysis
- Tools and commands used by responders
- Any other relevant responder activities

This log is a flowing document kept by individuals and later compiled as a single document encompassing all activities by all relevant persons. Notes should be kept, as they will be necessary as part of future legal discovery processes.

Witness Reports

Everyone that is interviewed should have his or her comments noted by the investigator and documented in the form of a written report after the interview is completed. Notes should be made of every person who is interviewed whether they have anything of value or not. Interviewees should answer the questions: who, why, when, where, what, and how. Direct the interview addressing those facts that are known to the witness directly leaving conjecture, speculation, guessing, and "gut-feelings" to the end of the interview. Witness interview reports are not supposed to be verbatim transcripts of the interview, rather they are summaries of important details. Investigators should take careful notes, because from these notes the witness' statement will be formalized into a report. Witness interview reports should be reduced to a formal document reflecting the following information:

- Witness' full name
- Witness' address and identifying information such as the beginning date of employment, business unit, supervisor, duties, etc.
- Purpose of the interview should be briefly explained to the interviewee and documented in the interview
- Identity of the investigators
- Information provided by the witnesses
- Time-date-location of the interview (It is possible that the interview report should mention the specific location of the interview such as a conference room. Current court rulings have made interviews held in hostile locations excludable.)
- Case file number
- Any evidence or materials delivered to the investigators by the witness

If the interview is very important and it is possible the witnesses may later change or recant their statements, witnesses may be requested to reduce their statements to writing. This can be accomplished in several ways, but one of the most successful is to have the witnesses write their statements in their own words. It is a prudent step to have the witnesses review their statements, making any changes they wish as to reflect their recollection of pertinent events.

Signed witness statements should be signed by the interviewee, dated, noting the time and place, and witnessed by at least two other people that must have been present during the entire interview and written statement process.

Some interviews are noted in logs where details of the interview are documented:

- Time of first contact with interviewee
- Place of interview
- Identities of those present during the interview
- Times of any person leaving or entering the interview
- Any requests from the interviewee, for example, food, restroom, union representation, or attorney

Statements used in criminal court proceedings must pass the test of "voluntariness." For example, if an employee were threatened with dismissal if she did not describe how she stole proprietary information from the company and she made a statement admitting it. It is likely this statement will not be admissible in criminal proceedings due to the coercive circumstances under which the statement was obtained.

Recorded Statements

Other types of recordings may be acceptable to memorialize witness statements. Under some circumstances, audio and video recordings may be used documenting interviews. Record the entire interview from start to finish if investigators are going to use audio/video media. This step eliminates arguments that the witness was forced or intimidated while the recording device was not operating. The recording media of the witness' statement is evidentiary. It is handled exactly like all evidence. There should be a chain of custody, evidence identification tag, and storage. In some cases, there are laws regulating audio/video recordings; consult with legal counsel before proceeding.

Hostile Interview Environments

Environments can be considered hostile and intimidating to the witness:

- Was the interview site one where the witness was in a small room with two interviewers? Was the witness advised that they were free to leave the room/building?
- Was the witness under arrest?
- Was the witness threatened with dismissal if they did not cooperate?
- Were the interviewers acting as law enforcement agents?
- Was the witness physically searched before being interviewed?
- Was the interview tone conversational or was it an interrogation where the tone was accusatory?
- Was the witness physically touched in any way?
- Was the witness' liberty significantly impeded in any way?
- Was the room temperature comfortable?
- Were the room's furnishings or lighting unusual or intimidating?

Legal challenges have been successfully filed eliminating witness interviews as it was decided that the surroundings were inherently coercive and intimidating to the witness. For example, investigators should be mindful that unless a person is under arrest, the witness is free to depart the interview at any time. Failing to allow the witness to leave the interview or denying access to medications, food, or restrooms, will likely precipitate a lawsuit and possible criminal charges against the investigators and their employer.

Performing Forensic Duplication: When a Clone Really Is a Clone

In any critical incident response, the preferred methodology is to prepare for trial whether there is going to be one or not. Following the most stringent procedures will allow investigators to introduce their evidence regardless of future legal circumstances. Consequently, investigators should always follow the rules of evidence in performing their investigation.

Here are some areas that will likely trigger future legal action:

- Is the incident considered high-profile receiving significant internal and external attention?
- Does the incident involve unequal treatment?
- Does the incident involve criminal allegations?
- Does the incident involve individual privacy?
- Has there been a significant financial or business loss attributed to the incident?
- Is there a need to forensically examine slack space and unallocated free space in the examination to collect evidence in proving the case?

Here are some rules that have been formulated to make it difficult to limit successful legal challenges that the evidence has been altered in any fashion thereby reducing its value.

- The examination of evidence is performed on forensically sterile media. This means that it has been forensically proven that the media on which the original was copied was devoid of any electronic characters. Examining the media with a disk editor or creating a hash of it will generally suffice proving it to be sterile. An exact bit-by-bit copy is made of the original to the sterile media. Examinations and analyses are performed on copies, never on the originals.

- The target system and related data must be protected during the collection ensuring that the data is not altered in any fashion. This includes measures that preclude the target machine's operating system from accessing the media containing the evidence at any point.

- Examinations of media must be made in such a fashion, as the file attributes are not changed from the original. When this is not possible, examiners will perform analyses giving priority to examining the media rather than preserving attributes.

- All examinations are accompanied by an investigator's activity log. In this document, all examination/investigative activities are logged including but not limited to the following:
  - Time/date/place media was acquired for examination
  - Name and title of examiner
  - Hardware and software configuration of machine on which the examination took place
  - Software tools and their versions
  - Commands used in examination
  - Tools and respective commands used in examination
  - Logging should reflect case-relevant discoveries
  - Serial numbers, identification numbers, and other relevant identification of original and examined media
  - Screen prints of examined evidence should be made according to a formal procedure rather than on a random basis

Steps to Follow when Collecting Evidence

Collecting digital evidence consists of securing the target system, conducting an examination of the system and its surrounding environment, forensically duplicating the target media, and preserving the forensic copies. The following are suggested steps provided to assist investigators in collecting evidence:

- Secure the crime scene. Physically control people and possible evidence-items from entering and leaving the target area. In other words, when responders are notified about a possible critical incident, the physical and logical areas should be immediately secured so the critical incident cannot spread. Once this is performed, all persons not directly connected with the investigation should be asked leave the area. Of course, all employees should drop what they are doing and leave the area immediately. At no time is any employee allowed to remove anything from the area or access any device remotely. Designated first-response employees should immediately contain the spread of any damage. In these cases, first-responders are chosen to use finely tuned people-skills when securing an area in advance of the responders.

    Investigators must do their jobs while controlling the comings and goings of people and potential evidence inside the target-area. Regardless of who wants to enter the area, and position in the organization, unless that person is part of the investigation, he should be courteously asked to wait until evidence collection is completed.

- Shut down the victim-machine. Do not touch the keyboard; just unplug the machine from the power supply. There is a significant degree of discussion about this topic involving interacting with the system while an attack is live or concern about lost data when the power is extinguished on the target machines. This is an area where responders must use their experience and training.

Experience Note While responding to a systems attack, the responders interacted with the system for over an hour only to discover that there were several attackers. While the responders had been interacting with the system, other attackers carefully concealed their activities, disabled safeguards, and installed back-doors throughout the system. This was a tragedy as the investigators were out-foxed by the attackers.

Depending on the machine and its software, going through a normal shutdown may trigger logic bombs or other data-destroying software. It is also possible that going through the normal shut down routine could change file attributes. This is one of these judgment areas where it is possible that evidence may be lost versus the spread of any damage. Preference in this case must go to the prevention of more damage.

- Physically secure the system. If the machine is going to be seized and transported, it must be sealed before it is transported. Take photographs of the cabling and label all cables before disconnecting. Cables may be left attached to the machine for future reference and examination depending on circumstances. Machines and cables should be wrapped in electrostatically neutral plastic wrap and sealed before being entered as evidence. Wrapping the machine precludes contaminates from entering the machine during transportation and initial storage. The first person who removes the wrapping should be the examiner. It is recommended that a virgin blank floppy disk should be inserted into the corresponding drive to act as spacer.
- If the examination is going to take place on the target machine or if the target machine is going to be used to make forensic duplicates of the hard drive, then changing the boot sequence is going to be required. Investigators must determine the operating platform of the target machine before they begin their task. They should know how to change the boot settings before starting the machine. Change the boot sequence so that it recognizes the floppy drive first, then the CD drive, then hard drive. This process will allow investigators to use bootable floppy disks or bootable CDs to take control of the subject-machine away from its native operating system. Bootable floppy disks or bootable CDs have utilities that block writing to the original hard drives or other media as well as other utilities that allow a forensically viable copy to be made of the target media.

Different Approaches to Media Duplication

If there is going to be an examination that will possibly lead to legal action, there needs to be a defined procedure for creating a forensically sound duplicate. Forensically sound media duplicates must be bit-by-bit duplicates of the entire target media. In making forensic duplications there are essentially three approaches:

1. Image the storage medium by removing it from the target machine and connecting it to the forensic computer for duplication. The forensic computer will have software already installed:
   - Allowing an exact duplicate to be made
   - Block any writing to the target medium
   - Survive a critical third-party expert analysis as part of its use as a duplication tool

   This method removes the target media from the BIOS or any other hardware configuration of the original machine. In most cases, this is the preferred duplication procedure.
2. Image the storage media by attaching virgin-storage media to the target machine. This method usually involves using utilities that prevent writing to the target medium and delivers forensically sound duplicates of the target.
3. Image the storage medium by sending the disk image over a closed network to the forensics workstation remotely as it is forensically duplicated. For many, this is the preferred method. If this method is used, it must be thoroughly qualified so juries and judges will understand the process. It must also be shown that through the connected systems, none of the digital information was changed or missing.

Removing the Target Hard Drive

Trained and experienced forensic investigators have the ability to remove the target media, duplicate it on their specially prepared forensic machine and return it to the target. Many private and law enforcement investigators have already invested in purchasing or building forensic computers with the software required to complete a forensically sound duplicate, software that will not allow the target medium to be changed in any fashion, removable drive bays, and connections to complete most tasks. Carefully investigators document all physical details, cable attachments, model names, serial numbers, appropriate jumper settings, peripheral equipment, and cable connections.

Investigators must be trained to use specialized software proven to deliver forensically sound duplications. Hard drives and other electronic media may be duplicated with such software as Safeback, EnCase, Ghost, or the UNIX *dd* command. These are applications that have been popular with investigators for many years and have successfully withstood legal challenges when used correctly.

> Safeback is available from www.forensics-intl.com.
>
> EnCase is available from www.guidancesoftware.com.
>
> Ghost is available from www.symantec.com.

Information about using the UNIX or Linux *dd* command is available in the "*man dd*," the systems manuals that are accessible from the command line interface.

Experience Note Before any media is used to store a copy of the original, it should be "scrubbed" or "wiped" of any data that it may contain. This process ensures that the accepting-media is devoid of any data before being used. There are several applications that are considered adequate for cleansing media. After cleansing the media, perform a checksum (hash) of the media using a tool like MD-5 or similar tool. If it is devoid of any digital information, the checksum should read 00. This will show for future argument sake that the media was clean. Another method of verifying the cleanliness of the media is to manually examine it through a disk editor.

There are several advantages to using the investigator's machine in the duplication method:

- The investigators are in control of the situation by not allowing the target machine's operating system to be launched during any duplication or examining operation.
- The investigators can testify about the level professional due diligence they exercised in using their own tested machine.
- There should not be any surprises like configurations that unless discovered will result in files being changed during the startup process.
- This duplication method has been introduced many times previously in judicial proceedings and is understandable by individuals who do not have a great deal of background in technology matters.
- Using the investigator's forensic machine, rather than the target machine for duplication, eliminates problems of compatibility.

Attaching a Hard Drive

There is another duplicating approach — attaching another hard drive or other storage device to the target machine.

Experience Note Some responders install interfaces and drivers on the target machines to expedite duplication. Beware that installing software on target machines could be responsible for overwriting irretrievable evidence. Changing the original machine's logical and physical configuration may be the basis of future legal challenges.

The above two duplication methods are basically the same with the exception one is performed on the investigator's machine and the other is performed on the target machine. Attach a forensically cleansed hard drive to the target machine, while the power is off, then as the power comes on, enter the BIOS process and make certain it "sees" the new hard drive.

Safeback, Ghost, and EnCase duplication applications are sufficiently small — they can fit on a floppy disk or bootable CD, so the target machine boots to them and a forensically sound duplicate can be made. In this fashion, the target machine is not allowed to launch its own operating system thereby preserving file attributes.

Experience Note On launching, it is estimated that most operating systems routinely change the attributes of approximately 200 or more files.

A Word about BIOS

The Basic Input/Output System, BIOS, is the small firmware utility used during initial startup. When the workstation is started, the BIOS is activated, the system's basic configuration is consulted and each of the machine's devices is queried to see if it is present and functioning properly. Investigators should open the BIOS and consult its settings to determine the drive geometry for the media where suspected evidence is located and the boot sequence of the target machine. The BIOS of the target machine will show on the monitor how to access it when it starts up. At times it is accessed by the Delete key, the F2 key, or a combination of the Ctrl+Alt+Esc keys.

Investigators might go to a similar workstation having the same hardware and see the startup screen to determine the key, or combination of keys, to access the BIOS. Regardless, duplicating from the target machine where evidence is located is not for weak hearts. During the BIOS startup process, investigators will have one hand on the power switch and the other hand on the BIOS access key. They will be watching the monitor for the BIOS access notification. Be thoroughly prepared to stop the process if the system gets past the BIOS operation and start again.

Exhibit 4 is a sample of BIOS access information.

Power-On Self Test

Power-on self-test, also known as POST, is started the moment the computer is turned on. There are several initial steps involving the BIOS presented on the monitor in the order they occur:

- BIOS boot program initiates a series of system checks, known as Power-On Self-Tests (POST). The CPU first checks itself and the POST program by comparing code against identical permanent records.
- The CPU sends signals over the system bus to make sure it is functioning properly. The CPU checks the system's timer, which is responsible for making sure that all of the PC's operations function in a synchronized, orderly fashion.
- The POST then tests the video display adapter. This is usually the first information that appears on the monitor.
- POST checks for RAM. Usually it runs a test to ensure that the RAM chips are functioning properly by writing to and reading from each chip and comparing the result. An accounting of the amount of memory that's been checked is usually displayed on the monitor during this test.
- The CPU checks to make sure the keyboard is attached properly and looks to see if any keys have been pressed. Pressing a key at this point will often interrupt the POST process. This feature can often be disabled in the BIOS settings and not all brands of computers are configured to do this check from the factory.
- The POST sends signals over specific paths on the bus to any disk drives and listens for a response to determine what drives are available. The lights on the drives usually flash briefly during this process.
- The results of the POST are compared with a record of which components are installed and control is passed to the operating system.

BIOS Passwords

BIOS settings held in the CMOS, Complementary Metal Oxide Semiconductor, chip are refreshed by a small battery located on the computer's motherboard. Basic configuration settings regarding the computer's disk drives are stored here and launched every time the computer is started with power-on. Most BIOS systems may be configured to request a password when power is first applied to the computer and will not progress further until the correct password is entered. Because all essential configuration functions are suspended at this time, the computer will not proceed to the startup phase until the correct password is entered. The BIOS configuration cannot be either altered to remove the password requirement either until the password is entered. Of course, BIOS passwords are not intended to keep out determined intruders that have access to the workstation or server.

Exhibit 4   BIOS Access Information

Bios Manufacturer	Key Command(s)
ALR Advanced Logic Research, Inc.® PC/PCI	F2
ALR PC non-PCI	Ctrl+Alt+Esc
AMD® (Advanced Micro Devices, Inc.) BIOS	F1
AMI (American Megatrends, Inc.) BIOS	Del
Award™ BIOS	Ctrl+Alt+Esc
Award BIOS	Del
DTK® (Datatech Enterprises Co.) BIOS	Esc
Phoenix™ BIOS	Ctrl+Alt+Esc
Phoenix BIOS	Ctrl+Alt+S
Phoenix BIOS	Ctrl+Alt+Ins

Computer	Key Command(s)
Acer	F1, F2, Ctrl+Alt+Esc
AST	Ctrl+Alt+Esc, Ctrl+Alt+Del
Compaq	F10
CompUSA	Del
Cybermax	Esc
Dell	F3
Dell 400	F1
Dell Dimension	F2 or DEL
Dell Inspiron	F2
Dell Latitude	Fn+F1 (while booted)
Dell Latitude	F2 (on boot)
Dell Optiplex	Del
Dell Optiplex	F2
Dell Precision	F2
eMachine	Del
Gateway 2000 1440	F1
Gateway 2000 Solo	F2
HP	F1, F2
IBM	F1
IBM E-Pro Laptop	F2
IBM PS/2	Ctrl+Alt+Ins after Ctrl+Alt+Del
IBM Thinkpad (newer)	Windows Programs: Thinkpad CFG
Intel Tangent	Del
Micron	F1, F2, or Del
Packard Bell	F1, F2, Del
Sony VAIO	F2, F3
Tiger	Del
Toshiba 335 CDS	ESC
Toshiba Protege	ESC
Toshiba Satellite 205 CDS	F1
Toshiba Tecra	F1 or ESC

BIOS passwords sometimes represent a bit of a problem for investigators. To gain entry, the settings of the BIOS must be reset to the default settings removing the password protection. There are essentially three ways of doing this.

Experience Note Investigators must document changing the machine's BIOS configuration in their activity log.

One way of bypassing the BIOS password is to remove the target machine's hard drive and place it in the forensic machine for duplication. Because the BIOS is a process that is restricted to the target machine's motherboard, this effectively bypasses this barrier.

The next process involves opening the computer's case and accessing the motherboard. Located in a small case is a flat battery used to refresh the CMOS chip holding the configuration settings. Removing the battery for a period of several hours is usually sufficient to cause the BIOS to reset to its default settings. The default settings do not include a password. Replacing the battery after allowing the system to reset removes the password settings and permits accessing the system normally on applying power.

Investigators may try to enter a default password to the BIOS and, if successful, the configuration settings will be preserved. BIOS settings should be documented for the analysis report. BIOS default passwords are listed on the Internet and are usually specific to manufacturer. Again, the chip's manufacturer is usually marked on the chip and is usually located adjacent to the refresh-battery. With the manufacturer identified, it is a simple task to research the default password on the Internet. More BIOS password information is available at www.pwcrack.com/bios.shtml.

Hard Disk Construction

Hard disks are constructed of rigid platters composed of a supporting substrate material covered with a magnetic medium. The substrate is a non-magnetic base material, manufactured with a smooth finish and called a platter. Substrates are usually made of either aluminum alloy or a mixture of class and ceramic materials. To support magnetic data, both sides of each platter are coated with magnetic medium usually called a thin-film medium capable of storing roughly a billion bits per square inch of platter surface.

Platters may vary in size with common hard drive disk sizes in two basic forms, 5.25 inches and 3.5 inches.

Currently, manufacturers are tending toward glass technology, as this has better heat-resistance and permits thinner platters. The inside of the hard drive must be kept as dust-free as it was built at the factory. Basically, the platters are hermetically sealed in a metal case with the interior maintained in a partial vacuum. Often, this chamber is referenced as the head disk assembly and will often be written as HDA.

Hard disk construction places three or more platters in the HDA stacked on top of one another with a common spindle allowing the whole platter assembly to revolve at speeds of 5000 or 7500 rpm. Platter speeds have recently exceeded 12,000 rpm. High speeds are used to increase data transfer from the drive to other components of the machine. There is a gap between the platters that makes room for magnetic read/write heads that are mounted on the end of an actuator arm. These heads pass over the magnetic media covering the platters. Heads are mounted so close to the platter surface that they clear by only a fraction of a millimeter or about .07 mm. In the case of IDE or SCSI drives, the disk controller electronic circuits are usually incorporated into the drive-case design.

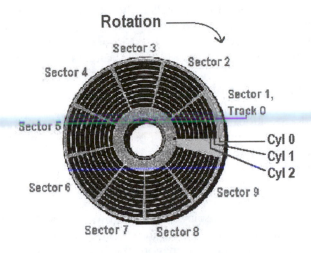

Exhibit 5   Typical Disk Geometry

When a hard drive disk undergoes a low-level format, it is divided into tracks and sectors. Tracks are concentric circles around the central spindle on both sides, top and bottom, of each platter. Tracks are located physically above each other and are grouped together into areas called cylinders. Cylinders are essentially the same areas spanning the vertical height of each platter. Cylinders are further divided into sectors containing 512 bytes each. The concept of cylinders is important because the same cylinder can be accessed without having to move the heads. In other words, cylinders are the areas of each platter that can be accessed by the heads without moving.

In physical addressing for disks, once the formatting is complete, each physical sector has a unique address based on the Cylinder, starting with cylinder 0; Head, starting with head 0; and Sector, starting with sector 1. The part of a cylinder that is the circular strip on a platter is called a track. If there are three platters in a hard drive, then there are six read/write heads. In reality, the outermost surface of most platters does not have heads above them so in these cases, there are only four heads.

Experience Note Sectors are the smallest parts of the disk that can be read or written at one time. The physical geometry of the disk is specified as the number of cylinders the disk contains, number of tracks the disk contains, number of heads, number of sectors per track, and the size of each sector measured in bytes.

In descending order, disk geometry is read CHS or Cylinder, Head, and Sector. Reading and calculating the physical layout of the hard drive would proceed like this example — the target hard drive has 1000 cylinders, 6 heads, 15 sectors per track, with each sector containing 512 bytes. Calculating the size of this drive results in about 46 megs (Exhibit 5).

Relative Addressing

There are two types of addressing, relative addressing and absolute addressing. An address found on a disk is specified indicating its distance from another address, called the base address. For example, a relative address might be B+15, with B being the base address and 15 the distance (called the offset). In absolute addressing, you specify the actual address (called the absolute address) of a memory location.

Relative and absolute addressing are used in a variety of circumstances. In programming, you can use either mode to identify locations in main memory or on mass storage devices.

Digital information is recorded on the magnetic surface of the disk in basically the same way as it is on floppy disks or tapes. Basically, the magnetic surface is an array of binary dot positions with each being set to either a "1" or "0." The position of each element is not identifiable as an absolute, so a scheme of guidance marks helps the read/write head find the positions on the disk. This is the reason why disks must be formatted before they can be used to record information.

When the computer reads data, the operating system works out where the data is located on the disk according to its filing system. In the Windows FAT (file allocation table), the operating system consults the FAT located at the beginning of the disk's partition. This alerts the operating system in which sector on which track the desired information is located. With this information, the head moves to the requested data (Exhibit 6).

Exhibit 7 is a table reflecting the typical floppy disk physical geometry.

Windows DOS-Based File Allocation Table

The FAT is really a table that resides at the top of the partition or volume.

Experience Note In explaining a FAT table to juries, investigators frequently compare it to index cards at a library. It is through their use that library patrons use the cards to locate books on their respective shelves.

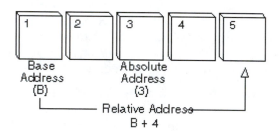

Exhibit 6   Relative Addressing

Exhibit 7   Typical Floppy Disk Geometry

3.5" Floppy Disk	Low Density	High Density
Bytes per sector	512	512
Sectors per track	9	18
Tracks per side	80	80
Sides	2	2
Capacity	720 kb	1.44 MB

Exhibit 8   Partitions and Cluster Sizes

Partition Size	FAT16 Cluster Size	FAT32 Cluster Size	NTFS Cluster Size
0 MB to 15 MB	4 kb	4 kb	512 bytes
16 MB to 127 MB	2 kb	4 kb	512 bytes
128 MB to 255 MB	4 kb	4 kb	512 bytes
256 MB to 511 MB	8 kb	4 kb	512 bytes
512 MB to 1023 MB	16 kb	4 kb	512 bytes
1 GB to 2 GB	32 kb	4 kb	1 kb
2 GB to 8 GB	N/A	4 kb	2 kb
8 GB to 16 GB	N/A	8 kb	4 kb
16 GB to 32 GB	N/A	16 kb	4 kb
More than 32 GB	N/A	32 kb	4 kb

FAT is a reference table present in the Windows DOS, 95, 98, and ME operating systems. As a safeguard, two copies of the FAT are preserved in the event one of them becomes damaged. The FAT tables and the root directory must be stored in fixed locations so the system's boot files can be correctly located.

A disk formatted with FAT is allocated in clusters. The size of these clusters is determined by the size of the volume. When a file is created by the operating system, an entry is created in the FAT directory and the first cluster number containing data is established at this time.

This entry in the FAT table either indicates that this entry is the last cluster of the file or it points to the next cluster. The table above compares the FAT with NTFS (Exhibit 8).

Updating the FAT table is imperative for the file system to function properly and it is resource consuming as well. If the FAT table is not regularly updated, it can result in lost data. The reason it is time consuming is because the read-heads must be repositioned to the drive's logical track zero each time the FAT table is updated. FAT supports only read-only, hidden, system, and archive file attributes.

FAT implements traditional 8.3 file naming convention, and all file names must be created within the ASCII character set. The names start with either a letter or number and can contain any characters except for the following: "/\ [ ] : ; | = . The following names are also reserved: CON, AUX, COM1, COM2, COM3, COM4, LPT1, LPT2, LPT3, PRN, and NUL.

Specialized software is required to perform an undelete function under Windows NT on any of the supported file systems. However, if the file was located on a FAT partition, and the system is restarted under MS-DOS, the deleted file can be undeleted and restored.

Experience Note   It is not possible to set file privileges on files within the FAT system.

Undeleting in Windows-Based Operating Systems

There are several tools that are useful when addressing Windows platforms, DOS-based (FAT), and NT. One such tool is called WinHex and is available at www.sf-soft.de/winhex/index-m.html. This hex editor is useful in granting access to floppy disks, CD-ROMs, DVD, ZIP, Smart Media, Compact Flash cards, and so on. It will read FAT12, FAT16, FAT32, and NTFS file systems. WinHex will recover data from deleted files manually or automatically in FAT and NTFS drives. This tool has many significant forensically valuable features such as drive cloning tolerating damaged sectors, erasing drive media and converting binary, hexadecimal, and ASCII.

R-Studio is a family of data recovery and undelete tools available at www.r-tt.com/RStudio.shtml. There is a comprehensive product for data recovery from FAT12, FAT16, FAT32, NTFS, NTFS5, and Ext2FS (Linux). It functions well on local and network disks that are damaged or contain deleted data.

Information Hiding in the Windows FAT

If a disk operating utility within the Windows DOS-based operating system marks the hard disk with a number of bad clusters or if clusters have been manually marked as bad, it is possible to unmark them using a disk editor. Regardless, investigators should verify that clusters are physically bad or are merely marked bad so they will not be recognized by the operating system. It is possible these bad clusters are being used to conceal information from prying eyes.

Experience Note   If investigators find a disk editor utility present on a target machine, it is possible that a user was engaged in hiding data in clusters marked "bad."

Clusters marked bad may be unmarked by the disk editor by locating the Find function of the disk editor and locating files with *F7 FF* for FAT16 and *F7 FF FF 0F* in the case of FAT32. It is possible for disk editors such as Winhex or Norton's Disk Editor (available at www.symantec.com) to recover data on a physical and on a logical level recovering data in clusters that have been marked as bad and reconstruct the clusters into the original file.

Windows NT File System

The main structure of the Windows NT file system, NTFS, consists of a logical partition on a disk. A disk may contain one or several partitions, also called volumes, with each volume containing files. There is no specially formatted space for the file system, rather all needed file system data such as bitmaps, directories, and system boot are stored as regular files. Files are divided as clusters on the disk with each cluster having a number of physical sectors. NTFS is not constrained to a certain sector size, such as 512 bytes. The cluster size varies with the size of the volume and is determined by the NTFS file format utility.

In NTFS, a file can be located on a disk through the master file table, MFT. This is a relational database, consisting of an array of file records contained in the volume. There is a record in the MFT for each file. Additionally, the MFT has its own record.

Each file in the volume is identified by a file reference consisting of a 64-bit value holding the file number and the sequence number. The file number records the position of the file's file record on the MFT and the sequence number is incremented each time an MFT file record position is reused. This enables the NTFS to perform consistency checks.

To reference a file's physical location on the disk, NTFS uses a logical cluster number, LCN, stored in the MFT. LCNs are simply the numbering of clusters in a volume from beginning to end. NTFS goes about the process of locating the physical disk address of a file by multiplying the LCN by the cluster factor.

A file directory in NTFS is simply an index of file names and their references. If the attributes of a directory are smaller than the record size, then all the information will be resident in the MFT.

NTFS has the ability to recover from a system failure and make the volume consistent again; it uses a system of logging transactions that occur within the volume. A log file created by the Format command and the log file service (LFS) is a series of kernel-mode routines, allow logging to be recorded.

Log files consist of a restart area and a logging area. The restart area stores information that allows NTFS to know where recovering should start, and there is a second copy of this information in case the first becomes inaccessible or corrupted. The logging area contains the records of transactions and I/O operations that alter files system data or change the volume's directory structure.

There are two types of records written to the log file, update records and checkpoint records. Included in an update record is "redo" information and "undo" information. The redo information tells how to redo one sub-operation of a transaction if system failure occurs before volume changes are flushed to disk. Undo information tells how to reverse one sub-operation of a transaction that has not been committed. A transaction is considered committed when a record indicating that the transaction is completed in the cache is sent to the log file. Committed transactions will be performed on disks even if a system failure subsequently occurs. NTFS records are updated for the following file actions: creating, deleting, extending, truncating, setting file information, renaming, and changing security.

Checkpoint records indicate where recovery should start after system failure. Every five seconds a transaction table, dirty page table, and the checkpoint record are written to the log file. These components of the log file are crucial to maintaining integrity for the volume (partition). The transaction table keeps track of transactions that have been started but were not committed at the point of system failure. The sub-operations of this transaction must be rolled back. The dirty page table keeps track of pages in the cache containing changes to the file system structure that have not been written to disk. Obviously, the data in these pages must be flushed to disk so the updating process is complete. The log file's restart area contains the LSN of the checkpoint record. Each checkpoint record stores LSNs for the nearest transaction table and dirty page table. This referencing allows NTFS to find these records quickly at the time of system recovery. At recovery, NTFS does three scans of the log file.

The first scan is the analysis pass. NTFS finds the most current transaction table and dirty page table indicated by the checkpoint record, and scans forward to the end of the log file. In doing so, any update records that are found are added to the two tables. Next the NTFS uses the tables to determine the LSN of the oldest update record containing an operation not written to disk.

Now the second scan can start, which is the redo pass. Starting at the LSN, the analysis pass found each update until the end of the log file is redone in the cache. These updates are then written to disk as a background action (lazy writing). Finally, NTFS does the undo pass using the transaction table to find transactions not committed at the time of the system failure. It then undoes each sub-operation of a transaction that is connected by backward pointers and continues undoing these transactions until all of them have been rolled back.

UNIX File System

Every item in a UNIX file system can be defined as belonging to one of our file types:

- Ordinary files. An ordinary file may contain text, data, or program information. It cannot contain another file or directory.

■ Directories. A directory is actually implemented as a file that has one line for each item contained in the directory. Each line in a directory file contains only the name of the item and a numerical reference to the location of the item. The reference is called an *I-number,* and is an index to a table called the *I-list*. The I-list is a complete list of all the storage space available to the UNIX file system.

■ Special files. Special files represent input/output (I/O) devices, like a tty (terminal), a disk drive or a printer. Because UNIX treats such devices as files, a degree of compatibility can be achieved between device I/O and ordinary file I/O, allowing for the more efficient use of software. Special files can be either *character special files,* that deal with streams of characters, or *block special files* that operate on larger blocks of data. Typical block sizes in UNIX are 512 bytes, 1024 bytes, and 2048 bytes.

■ Links. A link is a pointer to another file. Remember that a directory is nothing more than a list of the names and i-numbers of files. A directory entry can be a *hard link*, in which the i-number points directly to another file. A hard link to a file is indistinguishable from the file itself. When a hard link is made, the i-numbers of two different directory file entries point to the same inode. (Inodes are explained a bit later.) For that reason, hard links cannot span across file systems. A *soft link* (or *symbolic link*) provides an indirect pointer to a file. A soft link is implemented as a directory file entry containing a pathname. Soft links are distinguishable from files and can span across file systems. Not all versions of UNIX support soft links.

The I-list is actually referring to a physical memory location represented by a single I-list. Each UNIX machine has an I-list pointing to a special storage area, known as the root file system. The root file system contains the files for the operating system itself and is available at all times. Other file systems are removable. Removable file systems can be attached or mounted to the root file system. Typically, an empty directory is created on the root file system as a mount point and a removable file system is attached there. When a user issues a *cd* command to access the files and directories of a mounted removable file system, file operations will be controlled through the I-list of the removable file system.

The purpose of the I-list is to provide the operating system with a map into the memory of some physical storage device. This file map is constantly being revised, as files are created and removed and as they shrink and grow in size. In this fashion, the mechanism of mapping must be very flexible to accommodate changes in the number and size of files. The I-list is stored in a known location on the same memory storage device that it maps.

Each entry in an I-list is called an inode. An inode is a complex structure that provides the necessary flexibility to track the changing file system. Inodes contain the information necessary to get information from the storage device, which typically communicates in fixed-size disk blocks. An inode contains 10 direct pointers that point to disk blocks on the storage device. In addition, each inode also contains one indirect pointer, one double indirect pointer, and one triple indirect pointer. The indirect pointer points to a block of direct pointers. The double indirect pointer points to a block of indirect pointers and the triple indirect pointer points to a block of double indirect pointers.

In summary, the UNIX file directory is really a list of i-numbers; each i-number references a specific inode on a specific i-list. In operation, UNIX traces its way through a file path by following the inodes until it reaches the direct pointers that contain the actual location of file on the storage device.

Forensically Sound Duplication Tools

Here are requirements for a duplication tool to be considered trusted and sufficient to provide services that meet legal requirements:

- Applications must have the ability to create images of storage in a bit-by-bit fashion. Having a duplication of the files is not sufficient. The tool must have the ability to duplicate the entire medium including unallocated files space and free space known as slack space. Slack space includes file slack and RAM slack.
- Applications must not make any changes in the evidence-media being duplicated or in the copy it creates.
- Applications must have the ability to survive challenges and scrutiny by third-party experts.

Experience Note Investigators should use tools that have a positive history in judicial proceedings. This saves a significant amount of time and money and helps win cases. If the duplication tool does not have a favorable court history or is a tool used only by attackers, investigators are reminded they must justify the use of their procedures and tools. Under the law, procedures, standards, and results must be provided to the opposing attorneys and will likely be subjected to expert examination. However, if the tool has an extensive court presence, these cases may be cited when providing the tool and results to the opposing attorneys often resulting in fewer meritorious legal challenges.

- Applications must have the ability to generate a checksum or one-way hash of image creation and time. It is acceptable for the tool to generate this integrity safeguard during or after the image is completed.

Forensic Media Duplication Tools

The most commonly accepted forensic duplication tools are Safeback, EnCase, Ghost, and the UNIX *dd* utility. Safeback is probably the most common duplication tool, in that more digital evidence has been duplicated with this application than any other single application.

EnCase is an entire suite of tools directed to the purpose of duplicating evidence, organizing files and directories, viewing evidence, etc. It is an incredibly useful application and has an extensive legal history. Guidance Software, the manufacturer of EnCase, offers training sessions and certification in forensic examination.

The UNIX *dd* command is a duplication utility that gained popularity several years ago with investigators. Many investigators are unfamiliar with the flexibility and strength of UNIX commands, so they tend to shy away from them. Those who are comfortable with command line interface structures tend to use it.

There are many opinions about Symantec's Ghost as a forensic duplication tool. However, in the research done by many investigators, it appears to render forensically sound duplicates.

Producing Hash Values

A hash value, or simply stated as "hash," is a number generated from a string of text. Producing hash values ensures security and integrity of data. The hash is a number generated by an algorithm in such a way that it is extremely unlikely that other text can produce the same hash value. Hash is considered as encoding and is mathematically infeasible to reverse.

In essence, the hash program scans the text string and mathematically calculates the hash value. Hashes are generally substantially smaller than the text itself. Hashes play an important role in forensic examination where they ensure the duplicated material has not been altered in any way. Investigators commonly create hash values of collected digital evidence to ensure its integrity from the time it is duplicated, through the examination process, passing the evidence to the opposing counsel during the legal discovery process, and through judicial proceedings. Hashing can be applied to any size input and produce a fixed size output sometimes called the message digest.

Experience Note Remember that hashing is one-way, computationally infeasible to reverse, yet relatively easy to compute.

There are two hash algorithms that are in common usage: (1) the MD-5 hash function was designed by Ron Rivest, one of the trio of RSA public key encryption key engineers; and (2) the MD-5 algorithm produces a 128-bit output. More information is available at www.ietf.org/rfc/rfc1321.txt.

The SHA-1, Secure Hash Algorithm, is similar to the MD-5 algorithm. The SHA-1 algorithm produces a 160-bit output. More information is available at www.itl.nist.gov/fipspubs/fip180-1.htm.

Boot Disk

One of the most basic doctrines of forensic duplication is never permit the machine containing the evidence (target machine) to boot to its native operating system. Evidence files will be updated or their attributes changed by the native operating system. Altered files are subject to legal challenges disputing their integrity.

Experience Note One of the most common legal arguments in preserving digital evidence is the investigator changed the file's content during the collection, examination, or preservation process. Consequently, it is alleged the investigator tampered with the evidence and destroyed its evidentiary value in the process, relieving the defendant of the responsibility of the file and its content.

During the boot-phase, the workstations operating system updates file access times, registry configurations, log files, and system configuration files. Of course these file modifications are reflected in the file's attributes: Modified, Accessed, Created (MAC). When making media images, it is necessary to have an operating system outside the target machine. It may be located on a bootable floppy or CD, but the important point is to disable or remove control from the target machine's operating system.

One of the simpler ways to create a bootable floppy with an operating system on it is to create a DOS boot disk. Creating a Microsoft DOS boot floppy disk is a simple process. It is strongly recommended that a disk wiping utility be used here ensuring there are no stray commands or data on the boot disk. Just to be certain, it is a good idea to hash the disk with the resulting hash being 00. There are many hashing applications available. Dan Mares, a retired IRS Special Agent, has assembled many tools on his Web page plus links to other valuable tool sites.*

---

* www.dmares.com/maresware/forensic_tools.htm; Dan offers a hash tool at www.dmares.com/maresware/gk.htm#HASH.

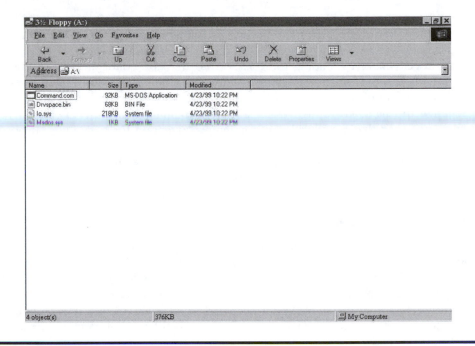

Exhibit 9   Boot Utilities

Boot Disk Creation

Using a copy of Microsoft DOS 6.22 or Windows 95, format a floppy disk using the following command:

```
C:\format a:/s
```

In creating this disk, you will notice there are four directories that are listed in Exhibit 9.

The first file listed and ready to be processed is IO.SYS. The code contained within this file loads the contents of MSDOS.SYS and begins to initialize the required device drivers, tests and resets the hardware, and loads the command line interpreter, COMMAND.COM. These files form the basic kernel of the DOS operating system.

If, during the process of loading the device drivers, a disk or partition is detected using compression software, IO.SYS loads the DRVSPACE.BIN driver. As DRVSPACE.BIN loads, it will mount the compressed file, uncompress it, and present the operating system with the uncompressed file. In this process, it changes the time and date stamps of the compressed file resulting in unacceptable changes to the file's attributes.

Experience Note DOS 6.22 and 7.0 are favorites for forensic investigations, as many investigators are convinced these operating systems do not change file attributes.

Disabling DRVSPACE.BIN

To make your boot disk useful, the DRVSPACE.BIN file must be disabled. It is not sufficient to remove the file, as IO.SYS is programmed to look at all root directories of all partitions for the file. Consequently, the most effective means of assuring the failure of DRVSPACE.BIN is to load IO.SYS into a hex editor and manually alter the strings. There are a variety of hex editors, also commonly called disk editors available.

One of the best editors is available as part of the Norton's Utilities available at www.symantec.com. There is another very useful hex editing tool available at the Hackman Web site (www.technologismiki.com/hackman/index.html).

The process involves loading the IO.SYS into the hex editor and executing the string search for the word *"SPACE."* You are searching for entries that refer to DriveSpace or DoubleSpace. Needing to have IO.SYS fail to execute this driver, you can change the name to *ZZZGONEZZZ.ZZZ*. The naming convention is immaterial, but it is suggested that you decide on a naming convention for continuity purposes. There are four instances in IO.SYS that need to be altered in the same fashion as the first. Use the hex editor in each case. Additionally, it is strongly recommended to remove the DRVSPACE.BIN file from the boot floppy disk.

Physical Write Blockers

As you can see, redundancy is one of the key features of forensic investigation because evidence is so fragile and volatile. Usually there is only one chance to obtain it. Such is the case with using a physical write blocker. Physical write blocker utilities use a technique termed interrupt masking to prevent writing requests. Interrupts are the method by which the operating system performs write functions. If a request is made to write to protected media, the write blocker discards the request, denying the ability to write to the media.

A very well written piece of physical write blocking software called PDBlock is available through the folks at Digital Intelligence (www.digitalintel.com/pdblock.htm). They offer useful software and hardware products with particular application to digital forensic investigations.

Using Safeback in Forensic Duplications

As mentioned earlier, Safeback has the ability to create bit-by-bit images of the evidence media and operates in four modes:

1. The copy function delivers backup and restores operations
2. The verify function verifies the checksum values generated by Safeback within the image file
3. The backup function creates the bit-by-bit duplication of the evidence media
4. The restore function restores the files created by the backup function

When Safeback is started from the bootable floppy disk, it will prompt for a location to create an audit file that serves to log the process by which the forensic duplication is made. This file is a convenient place for the storage of significant items related to the investigation of this particular medium, e.g., serial number of the medium, evidence tag number, case file number, time/date/place of the medium investigation, investigator's name and title, and other related information. Because this file constitutes an investigator's notes, it necessarily is an item to be retained as evidence. It is likely this file will be requested as part of the legal discovery process.

Safeback's options and features are fairly straightforward, having an easy-to-navigate interface. Safeback creates an image of the target media and writes that image to the media selected by the user. At some later time, the investigator restores the imaged drive and voila! her evidence is ready for review and analysis. There is one very interesting feature in that Safeback has the capability of filling the medium, where the copy is being written, with zeros. For example, this option is very useful if you are restoring a 10 Gb drive to a 20 Gb drive.

UNIX dd Commands

One of the best methods of ensuring originals and copies are exactly the same is to use an operating system that is not capable of writing to the target disk format. If investigators are going to use UNIX *dd* commands, it is prudent to remove all non-essential features from it. This may seem to be unnecessary, however, when the investigator is providing testimony. Removing all unnecessary features other than those necessary to create the forensic duplication will help establish the investigator's credibility and her professional due diligence.

Experience Note Investigators must be familiar with using UNIX *dd* before they use it to duplicate evidence. Showing up on a job and using UNIX *dd* for the first time is a recipe for disaster.

Information and instructions about using UNIX *dd* commands are available at www.cse.ogi.edu/cgi-bin/man-cgi?dd+1.

EnCase

EnCase is probably the most widely used forensic software suite in production today. EnCase has a significant following among law enforcement agencies and has faired well in legal challenges when used correctly. It is a suite of useful and tested tools for a Windows-based environment. EnCase permits investigators to duplicate original media and enables the duplication of multiple files using their own compression method. At the time of creation, each file is hashed and the hash is verified at the time of analysis. It supports file systems, FAT 16, FAT 32, NTFS, Linux, and Macintosh file systems. EnCase is supported by technical support, training, and a certification process. Information is available at www.guidancesoftware.com.

Forensic Investigation: Not Exactly a Needle in a Haystack

These are some logical areas that may interest an investigator in locating digital evidence:

- File space. This refers to blocks on the drive that either are assigned to an active file or assigned to the file system depending on the structure such as FAT (Windows) or inode (UNIX). Of course viewing interesting files from file space is merely a matter of using a disk editor, locating the file, and copying the file to another media for viewing by the investigator. In this fashion, the original media does not suffer from being changed.
- Slack space. This is the space made up of the file system blocks that are partially used by the operating system. Slack space is prevalent in file systems that have written to a sector, then overwritten that space with the newly written information not occupying the entire sector creating a slack space containing data from the previous data. Tools like EnCase or a disk editor will allow investigators to see the "junk" contained in the slack space. Slack space seldom contains enough information to see the entire file, however there is often

enough information to interest investigators. File names, file extensions, and pieces of text files are the usual finds.

- RAM space. RAM space is the term used to describe empty space between the data and the end of the sector. If there is an empty space, the operating system selects information from the data currently in RAM and writes it there. It can be similar to slack space in appearance.

Experience Note An investigator conducting an analysis on a target hard drive was able to effectively refute allegations made by a defendant that he had never installed pirated software on his workstation. The defendant had installed a number of expensive applications on his workstation and deleted them and attempted to write over the disk space. However, there were enough data left in the slack space to demonstrate he had indeed installed these applications. The most incriminating evidence was the extensions of the application's files.

- Unallocated file space. Any unclaimed sector falling within an active partition or not.
- Unclaimed sectors can often be restored by Undelete utilities depending on the operating system and if the unallocated file space is partially overwritten or not.

Physical Level Search

Investigators should consider begin looking at the raw data contained on the target media. Often these analyses are performed with tools like a disk editor or EnCase. With the forensically correct duplicated software, many experienced investigators will perform these principle processes:

- String search
- Slack space
- Free space examination

All analysis operations must be performed on the forensic image or the restored image of the evidence. Never perform examinations on the original evidence.

There is a frequently pursued avenue in running string searches to produce lists of data; for example:

- All e-mail addresses
- All Web site URLs
- All gif and jpeg file extensions
- String searches matching specific words
- String search

Experience Note There is a very handy DOS-based program called SearchString written by Dan Mares. It is available at www.maresware.com. This tool provides the context of the string search hit as well as the location being the byte offset from the beginning of the file. By inputting the specific string to be searched, this tool will scan the target media and produce the relative location of the item.

Also, most disk editors have well-developed string search capabilities. Many experienced investigators use disk editors to search for file extensions that are pertinent to the case, e.g., eml, png, gif, jpg, doc, txt, or exe.

File Slack and Free Space

Depending on the operating system's file system, there will be residue that can be located and examined when looking for evidence. File residue basically falls into two categories, file slack and free space.

Free space is that space located on a hard drive that is not allocated to a file. It can be space that has never been allocated to a file or space that is considered unallocated. This unallocated condition usually occurs after a file has been deleted. Unallocated file space occurring after a file has been deleted will often contain remnants of the deleted file. Fragmented data previously written could still reside in these areas and not be easily accessible to the everyday user. In order to gain visibility into these areas, it is necessary to work on the physical level.

In the case of slack space, this occurs when data is written to a storage medium in measures that fail to completely fill the block size as it is defined by the operating system. Investigators attempting to look into this area for evidence will also have to work beneath the operating system at the physical level of the medium.

Experience Note   An employee had been downloading obscene images to his workstation and subsequently deleting them. After a time, he performed word processing and other types of work thinking these had overwritten the images he had previously downloaded and would make viewing the images impossible. Fragments of these images and their file extensions were contained within the slack space and unallocated file space of his workstation hard drive. After forensically imaging the hard drive, investigators peered into slack areas using a disk editor. Investigators were aware that most photographic-quality image files have extensions such as .gif, .jpeg, and .png. They merely used the *find* function of the disk editor to perform a string search for these extensions. Experience and training taught them that deleted files in DOS-based operating systems are preceded by the σ character (lower-case sigma) and are listed with a hexadecimal value of E5h. They easily located the deleted files. After completing their search, they were able to identify the nature of the deleted files by their names and extensions and even recover some of the image fragments.

DOS-Based Operating Systems File Deletions

The file deletion process in DOS-based operating systems is a two-step process. In the first phase, the operating system marks the file entry with a lower-case sigma character σ. This character has a hexadecimal value of E5h. In phase two, it clears the FAT chain marking all data blocks as empty. In principle, many operating systems handle file deletions in similar fashion.

Using an undelete utility, like Norton's Utility suite, the file recovery software searches the file directory tree for file names beginning with σ and labeled with the value of hexadecimal E5h. Once found, the utility starts at the file cluster offset that is specified in the directory entry. If the file cluster is not claimed by another file in the block allocation table (FAT), then the utility will indicate the file has a good chance of recovery. Many commercial file recovery utilities will reconstruct the deleted file by replacing the sigma character with another recognizable character and rebuild the FAT table. In processing, the utility looks to the file size specified in the directory entry and determines if that block is free. If it is possible, the program will advise that the file has a good chance of being recovered.

Reading E-Mail Headers

As it appears in your e-mail client, it seems that e-mail is passed directly from the sender to the recipient without any intermediate steps. Typically, an e-mail passes through at least four computers in its route. In the case of an ISP whose users connect via dial-up, DSL, Cable Internet, or T1, the client is the user's machine and the actual mail server belongs to the client's ISP. To review the process, when a user sends e-mail, she normally composes the message on her workstation and sends it off to either the mail server located within the company of the ISP. At this point, her workstation usually keeps a copy of the e-mail in the *send* folder. Even if she deletes the contents of the *send* folder, the e-mail will reside in the *deleted* folder until she deletes them from this folder.

Experience Note It is possible that the e-mail client is configured to automatically empty the *deleted* folder, but as you have seen, there are ways to recover deleted files.

From her workstation, the e-mail server receives it and the server begins to look for the recipient's e-mail server, exchanging information packets with this server and eventually delivering the e-mail message. It does not really matter whether she is sending her e-mail through the Internet or merely within her own organization. For practical purposes, the process is basically the same. This e-mail will reside on this server until the recipient accesses his e-mail client and reads the e-mail. Of course, there are times depending on the type of e-mail configuration and the type of e-mail server, the e-mail server retains a copy of the e-mail or downloads the e-mail to the recipient's e-mail client located on the workstation. It is very possible that although the e-mail was downloaded to the recipient's workstation and the account emptied of the e-mail, there is a copy of the e-mail located on the e-mail server's backup storage. Tenacious investigators will pursue the chances of obtaining a copy of the e-mail from one of the many e-mail servers involved in the message transmission and receipt.

E-Mail Processing

For example, consider the users alice@largeU.edu and bob@biggycorp.com. Bob is a dial-up user at biggycorp.com while Alice is located on the university network, largeU.edu. If Alice wants to send an e-mail to Bob, she composes it at her workstation and the message is transmitted to the mail server at largeU.edu. In her mind, this is the last time she will see the e-mail. Alice's server contacts Bob's e-mail server at biggycorp.com and delivers Alice's message to Bob's e-mail server where it resides until Bob retrieves it through his e-mail client.

During this e-mail processing, there are headers added to the message: at the time of Alice's e-mail composition, when that program passes the e-mail to the largeU e-mail server, and when the e-mail is transmitted to Bob's e-mail server at biggycorp.com.

As generated by Alice's server and transmitted to e-mail.largeU.edu:

From: Alice@largeU.edu

To: Bob@biggycorp.com

Date: Tue, Mar 18 2003 18:20:15PST

X-Mailer: Sendmail v2.2

Subject: Up for lunch today?

This is the transmission from Alice's server to Bob's e-mail server:

Received: from theta.largeU.edu (theta.largeU.edu [106.104.3.33]) by e-mail.largeU.edu id 004A21; Tue, Mar 18 2003 14:36:17-0800 (PST)

From: Alice@largeU.edu

To: Bob@biggycorp.com

Date: Tue, Mar 18 2002 18:20:15PST

Message-Id: <rev011897133451-000145298@e-mail.largeU.edu>

X-Mailer: Sendmail v2.2

Subject: Up for lunch today?

Below is Alice's e-mail header when mailhost.biggycorp.com completes processing the message and stores it for Bob to retrieve:

Received: from e-mail.largeU.edu (e-mail.largeU.edu [127.234.3.78]) by mailhost.biggycorp.com with SMTP id CTX39794 for Tue, 18 Mar 2003 14:39:24-0800 (PST)

Received: from theta.largeU.edu (theta.largeU.edu [106.104.3.33]) by e-mail.largeU.edu id 004A21; Tue, Mar 18 2003 14:36:17-0800 (PST)

From: Alice@largeU.edu

To: Bob@biggycorp.com

Date: Tue, Mar 18 2003 18:20:15PST

Message-Id: <sdh011897133451-000145298@e-mail.largeU.edu>

X-Mailer: Sendmail v2.2

Subject: Up for lunch today?

Here's a line-by-line description of these headers and exactly what each one means:

Received: from email.largeU.edu	This e-mail was received from a machine calling itself email.largeU.edu.
(email.largeU.edu [127.234.3.78])	This header explains that it is really named email.largeU.edu and has the IP address 127.234.3.78.
with SMTP id CTX39794	The receiving server assigned the identification number CTX39794 to the message. This number is unique and can be used to look up the message in the server's log files.
for <Bob@biggycorp.com>;	This message was addressed to Bob@biggycorp.com
Tue, 18 Mar 2003 14:39:24-0800 (PST)	This e-mail was transmitted on Tuesday, March 18, 2003, at 14:39:24 (2:39:24 in the afternoon) Pacific Standard Time (which is 8 hours behind Greenwich Mean Time; hence the time written: "-0800").

Received: from theta.largeU.edu (theta.largeU.edu [106.104.3.33]) by email.largeU.edu id 004A21; Tue, Mar 18 2003 14:36:17-0800 (PST)	This line indicates the mail transmission from theta.largeU.edu (location of Alice's workstation) to email.largeU.edu (Alice's e-mail server) happened at 14:36:17 Pacific Standard Time. The sending machine called itself theta.largeU.edu. It is called theta.largeU.edu and has the IP address of 106.104.3.33. This line has assigned the ID number of 004A21 to this e-mail for internal logging and processing.
From: Alice@largeU.edu	The mail was sent by Alice@largeU.edu.
To: Bob@biggycorp.com	The letter is addressed to Bob@biggycorp.com.
Date: Tue, Mar 18 2003 18:20:15PST	The message was transmitted at 18:20:15 Pacific Standard Time on Tuesday, March 18, 2003.
Message-Id: alice031897143614–23446298@email.largeU.edu	The message has been given this number (by email.large.edu) to identify it. This ID is different from the SMTP ID numbers in the "Received" headers, because it is attached to this message for life; the other IDs are only associated with specific mail transactions at specific machines. In this fashion, one machine's ID number means nothing to another machine.
X-Mailer: Sendmail v2.2	The message was sent using a UNIX program called Sendmail, version 2.2.

E-Mail with Firewall Headers

From the vantage of another computer trying to deliver e-mail to a system behind a firewall, it has to exchange information with the firewall. Of course the firewall performs like another machine that is passing e-mail. Using our e-mail example from above, it would be modified somewhat to resemble this:

> Received: from firewall.biggycorp.com (firewall.biggycorp.com [121.214.13.129]) by mailhost.biggycorp.com with SMTP id CTX39794 for <Bob@biggycorp.com>; Tue, 18 Mar 2003 14:40:34-0800 (PST)
>
> Received: from email.largeU.edu (email.largeU.edu [127.234.3.78]) by firewall.biggycorp.com with SMTP id CTX39794 for; Tue, 18 Mar 2003 14:39:24-0800 (PST)
>
> Received: from theta.largeU.edu (theta.largeU.edu [106.104.3.33]) by email.largeU.edu id 004A21; Tue, Mar 18 2003 14:36:17-0800 (PST)
> From: Alice@largeU.edu
>
> To: Bob@biggycorp.com
>
> Date: Tue, Mar 18 2003 18:20:15PST
>
> Message-Id: <Alice :<alice031897143614-23446298@e-mail.largeU.edu>
> X-Mailer: Sendmail v2.2
>
> Subject: Up for lunch today?

If an outgoing e-mail message from largeU.edu were passed through a firewall, there would be an added Received line inserted by the outgoing firewall. In this same fashion, it is feasible that there are common routing points for this e-mail. For example, if biggycorp.com maintains machines in different physical locations and uses separate mail servers, it would not be outside the possibility of having many headers like this example:

Received: from mailgate.biggycorp.com (mailgate.biggycorp.com [121.214.34.102]) by mail5.biggycorp.com with SMTP id PDA30141 for <Bob@biggycorp.com>; Tue, 18 Mar 2003 14:41:08-0800 (PST)

Received: from firewall.biggycorp.com (firewall.biggycorp.com [121.214.13.129]) by mailgate.biggycorp.com with SMTP id CTX39794 for <Bob@biggycorp.com>; Tue, 18 Mar 2003 14:40:34-0800 (PST)

Received: from firewall.largeU.edu (firewall.largeU.edu [127.234.4.13]) by firewall.biggycorp.com with SMTP id PDA28874 for <Bob@biggycorp.com>; Tue, 18 Mar 2003 14:39:34-0800 (PST)

Received: from email.largeU.edu (email.largeU.edu [127.234.3.78]) by firewall.largeU.edu with SMTP id PDA61271; Tue, 18 Mar 2003 14:39:08-0800 (PST)

Received: from theta.largeU.edu (theta.largeU.edu [106.104.3.33]) by mail.largeU.edu id 004A21; Tue, Mar 18 2003 14:36:17-0800 (PST)

From: Alice@largeU.edu

To: Bob@biggycorp.com

Date: Tue, Mar 18 2003 18:20:15PST

Message-Id: <Alice031897143614-2344628@email.largeU.edu>

X-Mailer: Sendmail v2.2

Subject: Up for lunch today?

The history of the e-mail can be seen by reading the Received headers from bottom to top. It traveled from theta.largeU.edu to e-mail.largeU.edu, to firewall.largeU.edu to firewall.biggycorp.com to mailgate.biggycorp.com to mail5.biggycorp.com. Here the e-mail is stored, waiting for Bob to read it.

Relaying

The following examples provide some e-mail header possibilities:

Received: from emailserver.emailpassing.com (emailserver.emailpassing.com [98.134.34.32]) by email.largeU.edu id 004B32 for <Alice@largeU.edu>; Wed, Jul 20 2003 16:39:50-0800 (PST)

Received: from tipidwater.com ([104.128.23.205]) by emailserver.emailpassing.com with SMTP id PDA12741; Wed, Jul 20 2003 19:36:28-0500 (EST)

From: Shameless Spammer <junkmail@tipidwater.com>

To: (recipient list suppressed)

Message-Id: <w45ppz23-34ls5@emailserver.emailpassing.com>

X-Mailer: Massive Annoyance

Subject: FREE PRESCRIPTION DRUGS

From an investigator's point of view, there are some interesting features in this header example. The message originated at tipidwater.com and was transmitted to emailserver.emailpassing.com to its ultimate destination, email.largeU.edu. Basically, tipidwater.com merely connected to the SMTP port at e-mailserver.e-mailpassing.com and directed this server to transmit the e-mail message to Alice@largeU.edu. Spammers frequently use this type of e-mail forwarding in order to disguise their true e-mail location and avoid detection and identification. They simply look for an open SMTP machine that is poorly configured to relay e-mail from their location. Pointing their e-mail client to that e-mail relaying machine, spammers send their e-mail using the resources and bandwidth of the organization's SMTP server.

Experience Note E-mail servers should not be allowed to relay e-mail except from IP addresses originating within the organization's networks. Poorly configured e-mail servers mark the organization as having sloppy system configurations.

Common E-Mail Headers

- Message-Id: The Message-Id is a unique identifier assigned to the message usually by the first e-mail server. It is in the format of Alice@largeU.edu. "Alice" is the identification of the e-mail's origin and the second part is the name of the domain. Any e-mail where the message ID is malformed is not the real site of origin and is indicative of a forgery (spoofed).
- Content-Transfer-Encoding: This header information indicates MIME (Multipurpose Internet Mail Extensions). MIME is a method of enclosing non-text content in e-mail messages. It does not have any affect on delivery of e-mail, but it permits MIME-compliant mail programs to handle message content.
- Mime-Version: (also seen as MIME-Version) This is another MIME header. This header identifies the version of the MIME protocol used by the message-sender.
- Newsgroups: This header only appears in e-mail posted to a Usenet (Newsgroup).
- Reply-To: Identifies the reply e-mail address. Because this header has many purposes, it is often used by spammers to conceal their identities and origins.
- X-Confirm-Reading-To: This e-mail header requests an automated confirmation reply.
- X-Mailer: (also X-mailer) Information relating to the sender's e-mail software.

Network Resources

Here are two valuable resources when researching domain, ISP, and network contacts:

1. www.forensicsweb.com/downloads/cfid/isplist/isplist.htm
2. www.loc.gov/copyright/onlinesp/list/index.html

Networking Review

If a refresher is needed on IP addresses, a good resource is RFC 791, available at www.ietf.org/rfc/rfc0791.txt?number=791.

A review of the Open Systems Interconnect, OSI, model is available at www.inetdaemon.com/tutorials/theory/osi/.

A review of IP addresses is available at ftp://ftp.rfc-editor.org/in-notes/rfc1466.txt.

A review of domain name service is available at www.ietf.org/rfc/rfc1034.txt?number=1034.

A review of TCP/IP protocols is available at www.ietf.org/rfc/rfc1180.txt?number=1180.

There is a UNIX networking administration review available at www.uni-tuebingen.de/zdv/projekte/linux/books/nag/node1.html.

A review of TCP/IP networks is available at www.onlamp.com/lpt/a/345.

Responding to Windows NT Incidents

There is an old adage: "you've got to use the right tool for the right job." Responders must have the right tools in anticipation of the most common set of circumstances, so they are not looking around for their tools when precious time is wasting and profitability is declining.

Tools in the Tool Bag

In Windows operating system environment, there are two basic types of utility applications, those based on a Graphical User Interface (GUI) and those that are based on command line interface (CLI).

Following is a list of tools that are available at www.sysinternals.com:

- PsTools v1.56: The PsTools suite includes command-line utilities for listing the processes running on local or remote computers, running processes remotely, rebooting computers, dumping event logs, and more.
- Tokenmon v1.01: View security-related activity, including logon, logoff, privilege usage, and impersonation with this monitoring tool.
- Filemon v4.34: This monitoring tool lets you see all file system activity in real-time. It works on all versions of WinNT/2K, Windows 9x/Me, Windows XP 64-bit Edition, and Linux.
- PSLoggedon: An applet that displays both the locally logged on users and users logged on via resources for either the local computer or a remote one.
- TCPView v2.22: See all open TCP and UDP endpoints on Windows NT, 2000, and XP. TCPView displays the name of the process that owns each endpoint. Full source to the command-line version of this tool, netstat, is included.
- NTFSDOS Professional v4.0: Full read/write access to NTFS drives from DOS.

If investigators are going to use floppy disks or CDs, they must be rendered write-protected after writing.

There are several schools of thought concerning the use of tools in responding to critical incidents. Some responders have experienced vigorous cross examinations at the hands of knowledgeable attorneys where they did not keep copies of their programs and tools so these they could be examined by the opposing side's experts. Because this seems to be a current trend in qualifying witnesses, you must be sensitive to this tactic and ensure the versions of your tools are logged as part of your investigation. Investigators should maintain versions of all relevant tools so these tools can be produced when necessary.

Storing the Data

During the course of the response, there will be a lot of information gathered from the system. Consider the area where the incident has occurred as a crime scene because if investigators take the most restrictive posture when they respond, then should the matter proceed to court, their evidence should be introduced.

All media intended to be used to duplicate evidence must be cleansed using software intended for that exact purpose. This cleansing process includes all blank CDs, zip disks, jazz disks, tapes, floppies, hard drives, etc.

Experience Note Arriving on the scene is not the time to begin your preparations. Do you really want to take the stand and testify to your lack of professional diligence?

To Turn Off or not to Turn Off

If responders arrive at the scene before the system has been turned off, they might consider efforts to collect valuable evidence that could be lost otherwise. It is a matter of priorities. They should be included in the decision to be made by senior managers as part of the response posture. The balance is this one, if turning off the system will stop the progress of any further damage and whether turning off the system will likely result in the loss of evidence. Response postures should be certain to error on the side of caution and turn off relevant systems containing spreading damage. Following the firefighter model, it is a matter of business sense to contain the damage before worrying about evidence.

If the decision to keep the victim-system online, here is a list of items that should be considered as volatile and might disappear when the system is turned off:

- List of users logged onto the system
- List of currently running processes
- List of currently open ports
- List of currently listening services on their respective ports
- List of systems currently connected to the target system

When investigators approach the target system, they should have a plan outlining their general activities. Before anything actually takes place, an activity log should be initiated and maintained documenting all steps and their results. Log entries should include any and all tools deployed, system and application commands, who performed the action, the date/time/place, etc.

Essentially there are two reasons for maintaining an activity log, to gather information that will permit the reconstruction of the response-activities at a later date and protect the organization by demonstrating the responders exercised professional due diligence. More than once, logs have effectively answered legal and policy-compliance challenges.

System Users

If the response posture requires that an investigation proceed while the system is still active and the attacker is online, using the program, Psloggedon, written by Mark Russinovich, www.sysinternals.com, shows all users connected locally and remotely. If the system offers dial-up remote access, the investigators should determine the user accounts having remote-access privileges on the target system at the time of the incident. Depending on the number of logged on accounts, investigators may wish to remove the telephone lines, disconnecting online activity.

There is a command line tool, as part of the Remote Access Service, RAS, called *rasusers* that can be used to determine the users that have remote access to the target system. Rasusers is available at http://wettberg.home.texas.net/rasusers.htm.

```
MS-DOS Prompt                                                         _|□|×

Auto   ▼ □ ⓑ ⓑ ⊠ ⓐⓑ A

C:\WINDOWS>netstat -an

Active Connections

  Proto  Local Address         Foreign Address      State
  TCP    0.0.0.0:1118          0.0.0.0:0            LISTENING
  TCP    0.0.0.0:1173          0.0.0.0:0            LISTENING
  TCP    67.25.103.7:137       0.0.0.0:0            LISTENING
  TCP    67.25.103.7:138       0.0.0.0:0            LISTENING
  TCP    67.25.103.7:139       0.0.0.0:0            LISTENING
  TCP    67.25.103.7:1173      128.242.171.114:119  ESTABLISHED
  TCP    67.25.103.7:1234      207.46.181.55:110    TIME_WAIT
  TCP    67.25.103.7:1235      207.46.181.55:110    TIME_WAIT
  TCP    127.0.0.1:1025        0.0.0.0:0            LISTENING
  TCP    127.0.0.1:1029        0.0.0.0:0            LISTENING
  TCP    127.0.0.1:1058        0.0.0.0:0            LISTENING
  UDP    67.25.103.7:137       *:*
  UDP    67.25.103.7:138       *:*
  UDP    127.0.0.1:1025        *:*
  UDP    127.0.0.1:1029        *:*
  UDP    127.0.0.1:1058        *:*

C:\WINDOWS>_
```

Exhibit 10   Netstat Connections

Open Ports and Listening Services

The next step may provide one of the most significant steps in the real-time investigation. Determine what are the open ports and listening services. A handy tool, fport, is available from the Foundstone Web site at www.foundstone.com. This tool will show all listening processes.

The display format for fport is:

- Process identification
- Process name
- Port, Protocol
- Path

Of course, using the Netstat utility included as part of the Windows operating system will show some basic information. Complete netstat information can be obtained through Windows-based operating systems by the DOS prompt and typing *netstat* (Exhibit 10).

Processes Running on the Target Computer

Investigators usually want to know what processes were running on the target computer before powering off. Obviously, there is not a sure-fire way to record these processes with the power off. When a program is running on a Windows platform, a kernel object and an address space containing the executable program code are created. Using PSLIST will display all running processes and is available at www.sys-internals.com/ntw2k/freeware/pslist.shtml. This utility shows all legitimate and outlaw processes. Responders should recognize the critical processes from those that would disguise an attacker. For example, if an investigator ran PSLIST and discovered that a process was displayed by the name EXPLORER.EXE, this is a process responsible for the desktop start button. However, if there were a process observed by the name, *rwr*, this is not a legitimate function and may stand for a backdoor known as *rearviewer*.

Experience Note   Unless the investigators are very experienced and have an in-depth knowledge of the victim-system, they would be well advised to take the system offline and perform a forensic duplication of the target media. Live interaction with a system that is under attack is best left to investigators who have a significant amount of knowledge about networking. It may end up a battle of wits with the attackers. Engage in such exercises with the realization the person on the other end may be more talented than those attempting to interact with the online system.

Collecting Volatile Live-Time Evidence

Here are some steps to remember when collecting live-time evidence:

- Use utilities such as psloggedon to determine who is presently connected.
- Use netstat to see connections to listening ports.
- Use PSLIST to determine all the running system processes.
- Use fport, or similar tools, to determine which programs are running on particular ports.

Examining the Evidence: Taking a Look when You Have Time

If you choose to examine the evidence media itself, without creating a forensic duplication, it is very likely the evidence will be changed and it is possible that changes may subject your actions to vigorous challenges when introduced as evidence. Experienced investigators pursue the most constrained means of evidence collection. When the time arrives to introduce the evidence at a deposition, administrative, or criminal proceedings, it is a higher likelihood there will be few legal challenges to its acceptance.

Evidence on Windows Operating Systems

Investigators should have a plan before they begin to examine the forensically created duplicate. Depending on the details of the case, here are some areas where evidence is likely to be found when conducting an investigation on duplicated media:

- Slack space. This is the place where information will reside from previously deleted files and has been partially written over by the current file. This type of evidence will consist of file names, text information, and file extensions. Depending on the size of the slack space will depend on how much information will be retrievable.
- Unallocated or free space. This is space where a previous file has been deleted. Usually the file is identified by the lower-case sigma σ character. If the file has not been overwritten, a good file recovery utility should recover the file.
- Event logs maintained either on the affected application server or on the target workstation
- Windows Registry. Remember that this is the database containing configuration information and may be seen as a type of activity log file. Users usually do

not know that applications and activities are making entries and modifying the Registry where their activities may be documented at least in part.

- Application logs. These are event logs maintained by the applications running on the system and not managed by the operating system.
- History files. These are similar to the event logs mentioned above. These files log the user's activities with a particular Web browsing application. For example, in the case of Microsoft's Internet Explorer, there is a History file containing the URLs visited by the user. Depending on the configuration of this file will determine the length covered by the user's Internet browsing history. While it is possible for the user to delete file entries, they might be recoverable providing they have not been completely overwritten.
- Cookie files or caches. These files hold small text entries where the browser has stored accepted cookies from Web sites visited by the user. These text entries, when viewed by a text editor, will often reveal their Web site origin.
- Temporary and cache files. These files are created by many applications often at the time of installation. Temporary files may contain application installation files, previously viewed Internet Web pages, and previously viewed image files.
- Recycle Bin. This file is a place where logical file structures reside and deleted files may be found. Hidden within this file is the INFO or INFO2 file containing tree structure information of particular deleted files. Recovering the deleted files in the Recycle Bin or the INFO file can provide important information relevant to files that existed on that machine.
- E-mail in the Sent, Received, or Inbox, and Deleted files of the e-mail client.
- Newsgroup subscriptions. Read postings of newsgroups may reside in cached or temporary files.
- Internet Relay Chat rooms that are searched using the IRC client's utilities remain in the pull down menu and are viewable by starting the IRC client and looking at the search menu.

Logical File Review in Windows

When a Windows platform is started, a process is begun on recognizable drives where the metadata file system is updated. Running a Windows platform will typically access and update more than 200 files, depending on the version and whether it is 95, 98, ME, or NT. There are several options to ensure the host operating system does not alter the file system in any way.

In the case of NT, sysinternals.com offers a utility called NTFSDOS. This tool is a read-only driver for DOS on Windows and may be used with most Window 98 and ME platforms. By analyzing a forensically duplicated copy of the evidence, the investigator can navigate, view, and execute programs on NTFS systems without writing to the medium under investigation.

Using Linux is another option. Investigators can mount the media to be scrutinized as read-only, accessing the files on the media without being concerned about changing them. This command will mount an NTFS drive:

```
Mount -t ntfs/dev/hdb mnt/nameofdrive
```

Linux may be used as the host operating system where file analysis, contents inventory, and string searches is done. There is a successful methodology involving Linux and SAMBA. It is possible to set up sharing under SAMBA, as part of the read-only file system, and use a Windows system loaded with file-viewing utilities such as

Quickview Plus, Microsoft Word, Microsoft Excel, and Outlook to examine the contents without changing them. Installing Vmware, or another operating system emulator, will allow the Windows, Linux, and SAMBA to be installed on one forensic computer. Vmware is available at www.vmware.com.

Going Native

This is going to seem like a contradiction, but consider that steps taken one at a time usually lead to progress. It is likely at some time during the investigation that investigators will boot a duplicated disk into its native operating system to view configuration files, the desktop and its settings, and obtain a view of the system's state at the time of the original forensic duplication. For individual files, once they are located they may be copied to other media for viewing in the native operating system.

Experience Note It is a good idea to have multiple operating systems on the forensic machine. This can be accomplished by using an emulator like Vmware available at www.vmware.com.

As part of the analysis, it is going to be necessary to logon to the media that is going to be examined. This will likely be the last step and probably one of the most important steps you take in your investigation. To do this, you'll need the administrator user account name and the password. If the subject-user is cooperating, it is likely she will provide the pertinent information; however, it is quite likely that logging on will not be as easy as someone knowledgeable providing the information.

These are a few alternatives when folks are cooperative:

- Obtain the Windows NT SAM database (containing the password hashes) and run a password cracker, preferably a commercial one that has good customer service and a positive legal history.

Experience Note There are many opinions here, but using sound commercial tools has certain advantages over the tools commonly sponsored by attackers. Imagine testimony being vigorously challenged by knowledgeable attorneys where the witness is accused of using tools she obtained from a Web site that was sponsored by attackers. Using tools of this nature is not necessarily wrong, but it can provide a lot of fuel for cross-examination. Be prepared to justify and defend the tools used in the examination. There are some excellent password tools available at www.accessdata.com. Murphy's Law is usually going to apply to password cracking efforts regardless of the tools the investigator's use.

- Matching log entries with file attributes will show the diligence and professionalism of the examiner and avoid challenges to the integrity of the evidence.

Experience Note In the case of extremely critical investigations, having two examiners performing and logging their analyses will deflect future legal challenges.

Changing User Passwords

It is possible to use an offline tool that is feature-rich like CHNTPW, written by Petter Nordahl available at home.eunet.no/~pnordahl/ntpasswd. This is a Linux-based tool that permits viewing and changing the user passwords in the Windows NT SAM file. It also contains a Registry editor and disk editor. This is not a password cracker per se, rather it is a tool that permits the investigator to change the user's password to another one. Obviously, changing the password is an action that should be thoroughly documented in the investigator's log.

Cracking User Passwords

There are times when using a password cracker to brute force a password is the wisest path to follow. As was mentioned earlier, Access Data is a company that offers password cracking tools and other applications valuable to forensic investigators. NTI, www.forensics-intl.com, has an excellent reputation in providing password cracking tools as well as a host of other applications useful to investigators.

Looking at the Windows Registry

The Windows Registry is the database that contains information about the system's users, configuration preferences, and information about the network configuration. The Registry contains two types of files, system.dat and user.dat. If the system has been used by more than one user, the Registry will contain entries in these two categories for each user. The Registry is optimized for viewing with the native Windows operating system, so the best way to examine it is with the tools incorporated in Windows. This is accomplished with Windows 9x and ME with the command of Run | Regedit or in NT Run | Regedit32.

Although Windows has created a backup of the Registry, it is still a good idea to create one using the Export Registry File selection of the Registry menu. Save it somewhere away from the present location. An exported version to a floppy disk usually works well.

Windows Registry has a visible tree-structure, similar to Explorer. With the Registry window open, there are folder icons on the left side of the pane. These are called Keys and contain either other Keys or values. Next to the + sign, investigators may expand the key and see a list of subkeys.

As an example of the type of information stored in the Registry, if a user were using the Find Files function at the Start button, the investigator may pull down the menu and see the names that were input by the user. These values are stored in the Registry under the Windows, CurrentVersion, Explorer, then DocFindSpecMRU folder. These values should match each other and will provide the investigator with the specific search strings.

Autocomplete Entries in the Registry

Beginning with Microsoft Internet Explorer version 5, there is an option for users to save their passwords. With the AutoComplete option enabled, users may enter portions of their address, telephone numbers, e-mail addresses, etc. The blanks will be completed with data saved in the Registry. This information becomes critical should a user dispute they visited a Web site more than once. Autowhat is a utility that might help investigators view the values stored for each input field name. It supports Windows Internet Explorer browsers installed in Windows 95, 98, ME, and NT. It is available at www.pcmag.com/article2/0,4149,137603,00.asp.

In the Registry, the Explorer/RunMRU key may contain case-relevant information. This file contains the most recent commands launched from the Run window. If an investigator opens the Run window and pulls down the menu, she will see the entries made by the user to launch applications. These Registry entries are maintained in the RunMRU key.

If the user has installed Internet Explorer, its keys are located in the Registry Microsoft folder. These keys store the last downloaded file from the Internet and the user's Internet Start page. The keys may also contain a list of all the URLs typed into Internet Explorer's address field. There are other places that will store the URLs visited by the browser's users. There is a cache directory labeled Temporary Internet Files, where IE stores the URLs of visited Web pages. This file is configurable by the user. The settings for this file may be reviewed by accessing IE, going to Tools, then Internet Options, then General, then Settings.

Accessing the HKEY_LOCAL-MACHINE key will reveal information related to the workstation and its network connection. The Network/Logon key contains the last username used to log onto a network. This is useful knowledge if an investigator were attempting to tie a specific user's activity to a workstation.

Good Places for Evidence

One of the more logical places for investigators to look for files if they have an idea what they are looking for is the *My Documents* folder. This is a folder that is a default installation of Windows.

Experience Note There is nothing preventing a user from creating a folder at any location in the operating system, disguising it under some meaningless name, and storing data in it. However, many users stash data in the *My Documents* folder.

In the case of larger hard drives, it is common for users to partition them allowing for executables to be installed on one logical drive *C:* with data stored on *E:* for example.

Recycle Bin

Many users forget their Recycle Bin is used to store files before they are "permanently" emptied or they are overwritten at this location. Until this happens, these files are readily accessible. Although these files are marked for unlinking in the system, they will frequently remain in the Recycle Bin while user thinks they are gone.

There are some interesting features of the Recycle Bin in that it is a file that follows different rules than other Windows folders. In Windows 95 and 98, it is named *Recycle,* and in NT it is called *Recycler.* When a user deletes a file, it is moved to the Recycle Bin. There a few things that happen in this action:

- The file is deleted from the file's folder where it resided before deletion
- The deleted files' new folder entry is created in the Recycle Bin and the addition of pertinent information about the deleted file in a hidden file called INFO or INFO2 in the Recycle Bin

When a file is deleted, the file, its deletion date, and time are not recorded in the Recycle Bin. However, Windows records its date and time of deletion in the INFO file. There is more important information stored here: the deleted file's location prior to being sent to the Recycle Bin is recorded, its index number in the Recycle Bin (this is the order in the Recycle Bin), and its new file name by which it is labeled in the Recycle Bin. Files once entered in the Recycle Bin receive a new file name. For example, a file originally named "Testsample.doc" and stored at C:\My Test Documents is sent to the Recycle Bin. It would be renamed as DC0.DOC. The file's original name and path, along with its date and time of deletion, would be appended to the INFO file.

INFO maintains each file entry in 280 byte lengths. The part of the deleted file sent to the Recycle Bin is stored at offset 0 of the file's record in the Recycle Bin. The file's date and time of deletion are stored in eight bytes starting at offset 268 of the file's record in the Recycle Bin.

INFO files actually have very useful information about file histories and the intention and action of the computer's users. On Windows NT, when a user puts a file in the Recycle Bin, a subfolder is created in the C:\Recycler file. The subfolder is named with the user's SID and contains its INFO subfile. Knowing this system function allows investigators to determine which user account was used to delete the file.

Files that are deleted by the operating system do not have their information stored in the INFO file. Consequently, for a file to be recorded in the INFO subfile, it meant the user deliberately deleted the file. File deletion dates and times may lend credibility to statements made by the system's user.

Experience Note Noting the location of a downloaded file can provide the investigator with extremely valuable information. For example, if a computer user claimed she was not downloading pirated applications and an examination of her workstation revealed a directory named "Warez S.W." from which she had deleted the files, it would be very difficult for her to deny the existence of this directory and the existence of the deleted programs.

When the Recycle Bin is completely emptied, the Windows operating system deletes the files and the INFO subfile. If the INFO subfile is not overwritten completely, the deleted INFO subfile is available for investigators to undelete, recover, and review. If there are remaining portions of the INFO subfile in the slack space, it is possible there might be information fragments remaining, allowing the investigator to see the deleted file's name, extension indicating what type of file it was, and the former location of the file in the computer.

In attempting to locate INFO entries, on a FAT system, relating to a Recycle Bin file that has been emptied, examiners may locate the deleted folder by the first character E5h and possibly the rest of the entry intact. Of course, this depends on if it has been overwritten and how much was overwritten.

An investigator's challenge may be found when an INFO subfile is located in unallocated space that has been partially overwritten. In this case unique file characteristics may be difficult to find. In this situation, the investigator should attempt to find the individual INFO subfile records by looking in the unallocated area of the volume for their unique characteristics. For example, an investigator may wish to conduct an examination using the unique characteristics of the INFO subfile or other known file characteristics such as the original file path. Such an examination may be performed using a forensic suite such as EnCase or by using a hex editor and its Find function.

Experience Note If investigators review the INFO subfile and find it contains a reference to a volume (partition or attached drive) from which the file was deleted and the drive letter is not present in the seized system, they may deduce that the computer user had a drive that was not part of the seizure.

In today's world of multi-meg USB and Firewire drives the size of matchbooks, investigators must be creative in their search for all relevant media.

Partitions

Windows and UNIX-based systems use the word partition or "volume" to mean a divided portion of disk media. When the computer is turned on, the boot firmware stored in the CMOS chip launches the BIOS process where the machine's basic configuration information is stored. When the BIOS is finished checking the hardware, the boot-operation transfers startup execution to the boot sector (Master Boot Record) of the bootable disk partition. The Master Boot Record contains information relevant to the defined partitions and transfers control to the operation system address. The Master Boot Record occupies all 512 bytes of sector zero with 466 bytes comprising the bootstrap program and 66 bytes left. Of this amount, 64 bytes are dedicated to defining the fdisk partitions where the disk's partitioning information is contained.

There is a somewhat universal utility known by the name of "fdisk" used for creating, hiding, and "unhiding" partitions. There are many versions of fdisk with some allowing users to set values that others misread or ignore. Not all partition editors have the same feature-set, while some commercial programs (like Partition Magic, www.powerquest.com) can edit the MBR partition table itself.

Experience Note Examiners can look for hidden partitions using the DOS utility of fdisk and "unhide" them.

Partition Status

Partitions can be listed in three ways:

1. Status: Active or Inactive. In this case active means bootable. The status of any given partition is determined by whether "0" or "128" are written into the first variable "bootid" of the partition entry.
2. Primary, extended, or logical.
3. Visible or Hidden. This refers to the ability of the operating system to see the partition and assign a drive letter to it. It is important for investigators to note that fdisk programs can usually see "hidden" partitions.

Fdisk is a utility that should be made part of the investigator's initial boot disk. When a restore or rescue boot disk is made, Fdisk is usually one of those tools loaded to it. Fdisk may be launched from most DOS-based machines by launching the DOS Window and entering *fdisk*.

Partitions made by fdisk are destructive partitions in that data that is written in a disk is destroyed when fdisk creates partitions. However, when a program like Partition Magic creates partitions, disks retain data after being partitioned.

Experience Note If investigators discover their target machine has a partitioning program installed, it would be prudent to look for hidden partitions containing data.

Norton's Ghost 2002 and Symantec Ghost version 7.5 include a tool by the name Gdisk. These are very useful tools in displaying partition information in the cylinder/head/sector format. Gdisk is capable of "unhiding" partitions that are ignored by Windows NT systems. It is available at www.symantec.com.

In the investigation of the target media, it is a prudent step for investigators to use an fdisk type program to see if there are any hidden partitions where information is stored. It may only been seen by the user who knows of its existence.

Password-Protected and Encrypted Files

The purpose of encryption is to preserve the content of a file or traffic from being read by any one other than the intended party.

Many investigations will involve employees and other persons who have encrypted or placed a password on a document or application.

Experience Note If investigators are in the possession of significant computing power, time, money, and well-educated mathematicians, they are in a good position to tackle the task of breaking encrypted material. Absent an abundance of these elements, investigators are best advised to find a good program that will crack the guarding-application's password or obtain the password from the data's owner.

There are many free and commercial products targeting password cracking to decrypt documents and messages. Some applications are intended for specific operating systems and applications.

Here is a sample of a few commercial password cracking applications:

- Elcom: www.elcomsoft.com/
- AccessData: www.accessdata.com
- L0phtcrack: www.atstake.com/research/lc/index.html
- Lost Passwords: www.lostpassword.com

Here is a sample of a few shareware or freeware password cracking applications:

- John the Ripper: www.openwall.com/john/
- Lilo password cracker: www.cgsecurity.org/lilo.html
- FTP password cracker: members.ams.chello.nl/a.boros/fpr/index.htm

Here are Web pages dedicated to password cracking:

- www.password-crackers.com/pwdcrackfaq.html
- directory.google.com/Top/Computers/Security/Products_and_Tools/Password_Recovery/
- www.password-crackers.com/
- members.aol.com/jpeschel/crack.htm

Print Spooler Files

Printing files can deposit temporary files on a computer system that can provide the investigator with valuable information. Print spooling is accomplished by the operating system creating temporary files containing the data to be printed and information necessary to print the job.

For reference, there are two methods to spool print jobs, RAW and EMF. In both RAW and EMF formats, files with the extensions .SPL and .SHD are created for each print job. EMT and RAW are terms for spool file formats used in the Windows operating system. When a job is sent to the printer, if it is printing another file, the computer reads the new file and stores it usually on the hard drive for printing at a later time. Spooling permits multiple print jobs to be delivered to the printer one at a time. The EMF format is the 32-bit version of the Windows metafile format (WMF). The EMF format was created to solve deficiencies of the WMF format in printing graphics from some graphics programs. The EMF format is device-independent. This means the dimensions of the graphic are maintained on the printed copy regardless of the resolution in dots-per-inch of the printer.

A RAW spool file is sent to the Windows spooler unprocessed. The RAW file may also be used to send Postscript commands to a Postscript printer. Postscript commands are actually understood by the printer but are merely data to the Windows spooler. The RAW format is device-dependent and slower than the EMF.

In the RAW format, the file with the extension of .SPL contains names in the format EMFxxxxx.TMP. In the EMF format, the .SPL file has the name of the file printer, the method, and the data to be printed. The .SHD, .SPL, and .TMP files are deleted after the job is printed.

Experience Note With careful analysis, it is possible to restore and recover these deleted files.

Both .SPL and .SHD files may be found on both the target workstation and print server. Investigators are well advised to carefully examine the target media for allocated and deleted files with the extensions .SHD, .SPL, and ~EMFxxxxx.TMP. If investigators find the existence of files with these extensions, it indicates the user was deliberately engaged in printing a job. It is possible that if the original print job does not exist on the target machine, it exists in the enhanced metafile format.

Windows NT Logging

Logs in NT constitute event records for the target system and should show which users were accessing specific files, which users were attempting and successful at logging on to the system, which users were attempting to alter logging policy, and which changes were made to user privileges.

In all, there are three levels of log files in Windows NT systems:

- System log
- Application log
- Security log

System log entries record system processes and device driver activity. Included in system logs are devices that fail to start properly; hardware failures; and services that stop, start, and pause.

Application logs record activities related to user programs and commercial applications. Application events recorded by NT include errors or information that an application is specifically configured to report. Accordingly, application logs may contain events watched by the Performance Monitor including the number of failed logons and disk usage.

Security log entries record system auditing and security processes used by NT, including changes in user privileges, changes in audit policy, directory and file access, logins and logouts, and printer activities. Users can access and review the Application and System logs, but only users with administrator-level access can look at the Security logs.

Exhibit 11   Common Activity Codes

Identification Number	Information
516	Audit event records discarded
517	Audit log cleared
528	Successful logon
529	Failed logon
538	Successful logoff
576	Assignment and use of rights
578	Privileged service use
608	Rights policy change
610	New trusted domain
612	Audit policy change
624	New account added
626	User account enabled
630	User account deleted
636	Account group change
642	User account change
643	Domain policy change

Experience Note In the event of a critical incident, the Security logs are going to be the most useful logs to responders.

In the case of reviewing the logs while the system is connected to the network, NT has a utility called the Event Viewer that permits users to view the audit logs on a local machine. It is found going to Start | Programs | Administrative Tools | Event Viewer. In the Event Viewer, investigators see logged activities that are listed in a pane that are self-explanatory. However, there is a pane column labeled "Event" followed by a series of three digit numbers. The key to some of the more common activity codes is shown in Exhibit 11.

Windows NT is capable of logging the creation and termination of each process on the system; however, it is not a default configuration. To enable this feature, set the Audit policy to monitor the success and failure *detailed tracking*. Each process is assigned a unique identification called a PID or process identification. With detailed tracking enabled, each process executed on the system can be revealed by following the event identification.

Offline Log Reviews

By copying the logs from the evidence disk, investigators will see the secevent.evt, appevent.evt, and sysevent.evt files. Write them to a separate disk for examination. These files are generally located in the \WINNT\System32\Config file. Once recovered, these files are viewable by configuring the forensic workstation's NT in this fashion: *Event Viewer* | select log | *Open* and select the path to the copied .evt file to be viewed.

Experience Note It is prudent to disable the Security log on the forensic machine to avoid writing to the media holding the evidence. Windows NT restricts each log file to a maximum of 512 kb and a length of seven days. These are default settings. With the default installation, NT is set to log almost nothing at all. Consequently, if NT were installed at default, there would be very little for investigators to review in the way of logging.

When investigators are viewing NT logs offline, there are some considerations to be made. NT system logs are dependent on the DLL, dynamic link library, files and if the forensic machine does not have the same applications installed on it, it is possible that much of the information relevant to the description field of the Application log may be missing. This should not affect the Security log, however.

Experience Note By running Dumpel on the forensic system, and saving the output to a spreadsheet, the investigator can sort, search, and group data. Dumpel, Dump Event Log, is a command line tool outputting an event log for local or remote systems into a tab-separated text file. This tool can filter certain types of events aiding searches. More information and the dumpel utility are available at www.microsoft.com/windows2000/techinfo/reskit/tools/existing/dumpel-o.asp.

Looking for Specific Words

There are times when investigators will be provided with information relative to unlawful acts such as pornography, trafficking in pirated software, stolen proprietary information, narcotics dealing, and so on. In these cases, investigators will be looking for "key" word strings usually at the physical level of media. Many disk editors and searching tools are marketed as being able to conduct physical level string searches of the target drive. Using these tools, investigators input the key words to be searched and the tool locates them on the drive. Often these tools require the target system to be booted from a boot-floppy disk or other control media holding the search tool.

There are many search tools; for example, EnCase, NTI's DS2, and most hex editors also have string search capabilities.

Experience Note It is still wise to record all string search commands in a written investigative log, so they can be recalled in the future.

Searching for key words can literally be like "looking for a needle in a haystack." Investigators can reduce the time they spend looking at media if they spend a bit of time interviewing witnesses. Collecting enough information, narrowing allegations to specific terms about how the attacker was doing her "thing," can save many hours of fruitless disk searching.

Looking at Relevant Files

It's a lot like an old movie line when the police chief says, "round up the usual suspects." Investigators can save time by looking in the obvious storage locations on the target machine. Reviewing the forensically copied contents of the cookie cache, history file, temporary directories, recycle bin, and specific file extensions can provide significant amounts of relevant information. For example, if investigators responding to allegations that an employee has sent an obscene e-mail to another employee, investigators would likely start by reviewing the employee's e-mail client on his workstation.

Experience Note Go with the facts of the allegation before branching into other lesser-related areas.

The usual file "suspects" depend on the nature of the allegations but usually include files with the extensions of .png, .jpg, .gif, .vbs, .exe, log, .tmp, .wpd, .doc, and .txt. Obviously, it is not possible for the forensic machine to have all the necessary programs to open and see the files with all these extensions. However, there is a very useful program that will help in this effort; JASC's Quickview Plus supports more than 200 different file formats and allows users to view files including images, documents, spreadsheets, databases, presentations, and zip files. It is available from www.jasc.com/products/qvp/.

Here is a very valuable resource for researching file extensions: www.library. mcgill.ca/edrs/services/file_extensions.html.

Here's a handy Palm OS utility for listing and searching file extensions: www.free-warepalm.com/educational/file'snameextensionsdictionary.shtml.

Chronology of Events

There are many common elements between the investigation of a critical incident and a criminal act. A history of events must be established as one of the basic elements of any investigation. Establishing the timeline of created, modified, deleted, and accessed times will go a long way to determining the critical incident's sequence of events. Carefully scrutinize logs, listen to relevant witnesses, and by all means, consider the totality of the circumstances.

Critical incidents are rarely single-step happenings; rather they are like a good novel in that they have a beginning, middle, and end. The most effective and efficient means of establishing a timeline is the careful review of time-stamp information contained in the operating system logs as well as the application logs.

There is another aspect of event history that is worth detailing and that is the process of documenting the access privileges for affected directories and files. For example, investigators need to identify who placed unauthorized files on a server. There are two basic options, use a network based sniffer to monitor access to the file server. This depends on being able to know a significant amount of information before hand. Otherwise, a large data file is created with little chance of being productive.

The second alternative is to implement host logging on the affected machines where NT file access auditing is enabled through Local Security auditing. With the target directory or file selected, NT will log relevant events. Enable auditing for "success and failure" actions in the NT Audit policy.

Legal Cautions

Before installing network sniffers or any other type of traffic monitoring device/software, make certain that it is legally sound. This procedure can easily run afoul of an employee's reasonable expectation of privacy and can result in civil and possibly criminal charges.

UNIX-Based Investigations
UNIX File System Analysis

Briefly reviewing the UNIX file system, each disk drive is divided into one or more disk partitions with each containing a single file system. Within each file system is a list of inodes and a set of data blocks. Each inode holds almost all of the information that describes an individual file, including the size of the file, the location of disk blocks, etc. Inode numbers and their corresponding file names are stored in directory entries.

Data blocks are blocks of regularly sized data. The UNIX file system divides any data request to or from a file into logical blocks of data that correspond to the physical blocks on the disk. The downside of this methodology is that the data blocks are not necessarily contiguous to one another. Typically, the UNIX file system uses 8 KB as the size of its logical data blocks.

In UNIX when a file is deleted, the name remains in the directory, but the inode number, the name to which the name points, is removed. The inode itself is changed; consequently, the ctime is updated and the data block location is erased. As a file is deleted, UNIX decrements the inode's internal link to zero.

Removing all directory entry file name inode pairs performs this erase action. When the inode is deleted, the kernel marks its resources as available. The inode still contains all the data about the file and remains until it has been reallocated and overwritten. Having inodes containing some data but having a link count of zero reveals deleted inodes. Without having the file's content available, investigators can learn much about the file with only the metadata remaining in the directory entries and inodes.

To mount a file system, the UNIX kernel needs the sizes and locations of the file system metadata. The first piece of metadata is the super-block and it is stored at a known drive location. The super-block contains information such as the number of inodes and data blocks, size of a data block, etc. Predicated on the information contained in the super-block, the kernel is able to calculate the locations and sizes of the inode table and data portion of the disk. Inodes and data blocks are clustered together in groups scattered across the hard drive media. Usually UNIX maintains more than one super-block, one inode table, and one block array in the event of a disastrous data loss.

Undeleting UNIX

Undeleting UNIX files is different than handling Windows restoration issues. UNIX can be configured to make frequent backups, and it is not unusual for backups to be made hourly. Hopefully, there will be an easily accessed backup and it may be stored in */class/.snapshot*. Examining this file will reveal that it is a backup of the home directory from several points in the past. It is possible to copy from this directory the items lost or corrupted in the regular home directory.

There is a UNIX command that should find which directory the home account is stored in: *find/class/.snapshot/hourly.0 -name $USER -prune 2>/dev/null*

Backups may be in the following path examples:

/class/.snapshot/hourly.0/01

/class/.snapshot/hourly.1/01

/class/.snapshot/weekly.0/01

/class/.snapshot/weekly.1/01

Retrieving lost e-mail is a very similar process. UNIX makes copies of e-mail in a similar manner as it makes a copy of the home directory. Access to copies of e-mail can be accomplished through */var/mail/.snapshot*. By reviewing this directory, backups of deleted e-mail may be seen and captured. Be mindful that viewing e-mail contained in this folder will require it to be loaded into an e-mail client.

Data Hiding Techniques

Data "deleted" from UNIX files can be located by investigators with hex editors searching for specific files and file extensions. However, there is a technique where malicious individuals may attempt to "hide" data from forensic investigations. For the most part, it is effective in systems not using the Berkley Fast File System or FFS.

Experience Note FFS deprecated the bad data blocks inode, preventing individuals from hiding data in there.

By way of explanation, the bad blocks inode has been used to reference data blocks occupying bad sectors on the target disk thereby preventing these data blocks from being rewritten by live files. If investigators run the file system checker utility, fsck, it is possible that the file system can been seen as having been radically altered.

The first inode that is capable of allocating block resources on an ext2 file system is the bad blocks inode (inode 1) and not the root inode (inode 2). Because of this positioning, it is possible to store data on the blocks allocated to the bad blocks inode and have it hidden from many forensic tools. Malicious individuals have tools that will allow them to exploit flaws in the UNIX file system and store data outside the view of forensic tools. It is for this reason that investigators should look at the physical level of UNIX bad inode blocks before moving on to other areas.

Coroner's Toolkit

Responding to reports of critical incidents happening on UNIX-based systems, investigators establish a timeline of events beginning from the last time the system was stable and uncorrupted through the actual event and until it was discovered and brought to a halt. The Coroner's Toolkit is a collection of utilities that attempt to gather and analyze data in the target UNIX-based system where investigators can accomplish their goals.

The Coroner's Toolkit contains the following data-gathering tools:

- grave-robber, the main data-gathering program
- file, Ian Darwin's file command
- icat, copies a file by inode number
- ils, list file system inode information
- lastcomm, a portable lastcomm command
- mactime, the MAC time file system reporter
- md5, the RSA-based MD5 digital signature tool
- pcat, copies the address space of a running process
- unrm, uncovers unallocated blocks from a raw UNIX file system
- Lazarus, attempts to resurrect deleted files or data from raw data

Within the Coroner's Toolkit, available at www.porcupine.org/forensics/, there is a tool called *unrm* that can emit all the unallocated data blocks on a UNIX file system. It functions by reading the list of free data blocks, locating each logical block, and looking to see if they contain any blocks of unallocated data. The unrm should be used if investigators are looking for a specific file known to be deleted.

Another effective data recovery tool is *Lazarus*. Lazarus attempts to give unstructured data some structure that can be viewed and manipulated. Lazarus depends on UNIX never writing file data except in well-defined boundaries. UNIX generally writes files in contiguous data blocks, when possible, attempting to boost performance. For this reason, UNIX should never need a defragmenting utility, unlike some other popular operating systems. Lazarus maps the disk that is created and provides visibility into the disk seeing the data by content type. Lazarus is a very comprehensive program in that it takes a very broad view of deleted files.

Using unrm and Lazarus will fill significant amounts of disk space on the forensic machine. Because Lazarus takes a large view of its work, it does not run in just a few minutes, so investigators are advised to let it run for several hours, if not days, before being able to see the results.

Using unrm and Lazarus is not as easy as using a Windows file recovery tool, using them is a time consuming and laborious process. It would best be described as a "hit and miss" process.

Experience Note There is an interesting series of short articles about UNIX/Linux file system recoveries located at recover.sourceforge.net/linux.

Success rates restoring deleted UNIX files are spotty at best. The easiest way to restore deleted files from a UNIX system is to access an uncorrupted backup copy. UNIX administrators should back up all critical files on a regular basis observing the risk manager's axiom... the more important a file is, the more often it should be backed up.

Hiding Files

Users will go to many extremes to cover their tracks. Regrettably, employees and attackers employ a variety of ways to hide their nefarious acts by concealing files, including:

- Placing them in storage facilities located outside the workplace
- Secreting data in hidden hard disk partitions hoping no one will think to look there
- Encrypting data partitions of their hard drives with complex algorithms
- Encrypting data through the use of steganography

Web sites provide storage for users and may be accessed from any system with Internet access. For a small fee, files may be securely and privately stored on remote sites ready for access at some future date. In order for investigators to locate such services on target machines, it is recommended that a thorough review is made of pertinent files resident on subject's computer. Look for URLs in the history, temporary, and bookmark files indicating that files may have been stored there. If you have a very sophisticated user who could conceal his activities, check the user logs where access is made from the inside to the outside network for online storage sites.

In the case of having files, storage media, and hard drives encrypted by a password, investigators may try to obtain access by running a password cracking application. It is important to identify the application such as Word, Excel, or WordPerfect, as many cracking applications are specific to individual programs. With password protected files, it may be possible to run a tool like John the Ripper and brute force the password.

With encrypted hard drives; if investigators can identify the protection application, there are some manufacturers that provide a universal password that permits access in the event the hard drive owner forgot her password. By way of application, the encryption key is based on the password. If the drive's content is completely encrypted, consequently, working at a physical level is not going to provide any insight. Having the password is the only way to access an encrypted drive.

Steganography

Steganography is a concealment application where information is hidden in plain sight. By secreting data in an otherwise innocuous multimedia object (usually image or sound files) called carriers, steganography can hide information remaining essentially impervious to detection. Steganographic applications accomplish their task by first hiding the data's existence in the carrier and then encrypting it. Detecting these data-carrier files is a two-prong problem; first the multimedia file containing the data must be identified and then the data must be deciphered. With a workstation containing possibly hundreds or even thousands of such files, the task is formidable indeed.

Investigators can possibly determine if they have a steganography user by locating the program on the workstation's target hard drive or locating it at another location. Finding such an application might indicate the user has encrypted files with hidden data in them. Placing image or sound files in a steganographic application will result in a password prompt. This prompt does not necessarily mean the target file contains hidden data, so these tools cannot be used to screen potential files for hidden data. Most steganographic applications will prompt for passwords whether the file has data concealed in it or not.

There is one tool that claims to be able to detect steganographically hidden .jpg files and is available at www.outguess.org/download.php.

A wide variety of steganography tools are available at members.tripod.com/steganography/stego/software.html.

Creative investigators may well be served to obtain the passwords from the owner before attempting to brute force passwords in an effort to decipher encrypted files and drives. Failing this effort, using a technique such as the installation of a keyboard monitor to capture all the user's keystrokes may prove to be the answer. Outside of law enforcement, employers may implement keystroke monitors where employees do not have any reasonable expectation of privacy in their workstation or systems use.

Experience Note Within the statutory constraints applicable to law enforcement agencies, search warrants and court ordered wiretaps govern the use of keyboard monitors.

Software keyboard monitors and similar tools made by Spector Soft are available at www.spector.com.

Hardware keyboard monitors are available at www.keykatcher.com/index.htm.

Locating hardware keyboard monitors is a matter of tracing desktop cabling. These are small cylindrical or box-shaped devices that are placed in-series with cables connecting keyboards to desktop towers or between the desktop and the network. Investigators should be aware that keykatcher makes a keyboard that acts as a keyboard monitor eliminating the inline device.

Finding hardware keyboard monitor information is available at www.spycop.com/keyloggerremoval.htm.

Finding software keyboard monitor software information is available at www.spycop.com/spycop-free-product.htm.

Before using such a technique, it would be prudent to consult with prosecutors or corporate legal counsel. Also, consult with your legal counsel before attempting to provide the results of a keyboard monitor to law officers.

Strong Encrypted Protections

There seems to be a growing use of encryption with very strong protection features. While there are many talented investigators and analysts in the world today, the conversion of encrypted data to plain text data in most cases is virtually impossible. Unless data may be captured from the target keyboard through legal means, investigators have to accept the idea there will be information that cannot be accessed within the limits of current technology and resources.

File Recovery Alternatives for UNIX/Linux

There is an alternative file recovery utility for Ext2 files systems used in Linux and some flavors of UNIX. It uses proprietary technology and flexible settings providing control over the data recovery process. It is called R-Linux and is available at www.r-tt.com/RLinux.shtml. It is interesting to note that R-Linux is a Windows-based utility used to recover Linux data.

Understanding File Permissions

Here is a very brief refresher about file permissions. Included file permissions are Owner, Group, and the last set of permissions relevant to all other users on the system, except Superuser or root who have access to all files in the file system. In UNIX systems if *ls* is run, it tells you what the file is and what type of file access is granted. File access is simply defined as the ability to read, write, or execute.

- Read "r" access means that users can open a file and read the contents.
- Write "w" access means that users can overwrite the file with a new one or modify its contents.
- Execute "x" access means that users can execute programs if a file has execute bits set that users with this permission can launch the program.

File types are as follows:

File Contents	Meaning
—	Plain file
d	Directory
c	Character device, e.g., printer
b	Block device, e.g., CD-ROM

These are typical file permissions: *drwxr — r-r*. In this example, "d" means the file context is that of directory, "rwx" is the read, write, execute access granted to the file's owner, "r — " is the access of read-only granted to the group members, and all other non-owners and non-group members have read-only access.

File Stamps

File stamps are some of the investigator's most valued reconstruction resources. Most operating systems have at least three relevant timestamps for each file. They are termed mtime (modification time), atime (access time), and ctime (change of status time). In the case of Linux, EXT2, and filesystem, it also includes a delete time.

The knowledge investigators have of these MAC (modify, access, change) times will generally determine their effectiveness in reconstructing and interpreting events:

- Access time is exactly that, the last time a directory or file was accessed or opened for viewing.
- Modification time is time the contents of a file were last altered in any way.
- Changed status refers to changing information about the file, such as file ownership, permission, and group settings.

Experience Note In the Microsoft operating systems, the MAC is described as the Last Time Modified, Last Time Accessed, and Time Created.

Of course, there are tools that will perform timestamp reconstruction. The premier tool set for UNIX-based systems is The Coroner's Toolkit. This application is available at www.porcupine.org/forensics/tct.html. Within this set of tools is a utility called mactime, which compiles ASCII files making them suitable for viewing. After running "grave-robber," a program that captures data from a system including MAC timestamps, the mactime program is a utility used in viewing a focused portion of the timeline. Generally, mactime uses the database generated by the grave-robber program to deliver a chronological output. Mactime will deliver its output displaying all the programs executed for a given time period. This is very important to the investigator who is trying to reconstruct events, as this output reveals the relevant timestamps, the file permissions, group ID, and file name.

The typical output of mactimes is similar to the following:

Date	Size	MAC	Permissions	Owner	Group	File Name
Dec 09 02 18:15:01	2998	.a.	-rwxr-xr-x	root	finan	/usr/bin/login
	41556	.a.	-rwxr-xr-x	root	finan	/usr/etc/inetd
	21009	.a.	-rwxr-xr-x	root	finan	/etc/inetd
Dec 09 02 18:15:45	22756	m.c	-rw-rw-x	root	finan	/var/finadmin/lastlog
Dec 09 02 19:19:00	2147	m.c	-rw-r-r –	root	finan	/etc/passwd

Mactime can be used on networked UNIX machines as well as those that have been taken offline. It is not important for the target media times to be the same as the forensic machine. The mactime utility can also read and collect MAC times from an NTFS system.

Opening a file for reading will change the *atime*. Run the *lstat()* command before opening and note the information before opening the file for examination. Investigators should disable *atime* updates in the forensic machine so altering examined data does not occur.

In UNIX systems, when a file is removed, the *ctime* is set to the time when the last link to the file was removed noting the time when it was deleted. The inode is also deleted from the directory entry. This makes recovering UNIX file data very difficult to achieve. In most UNIX versions, if the target media can be forensically copied before the operating system synchronizes, it is possible that MAC times are preserved. In contrast, NTFS does not remove all the file information when a file is deleted, rather that information resides in the file record of the MFT, indicating to the system that the file is no longer in use and is available for overwriting.

MAC time of UNIX inodes that were once attached to files may be recovered using the "ILS" tool found in the Coroner's Toolkit. MAC times are a very important part of the puzzle that investigators need to reconstruct timetables surrounding critical events, but they are not the whole picture. If MAC times are going to be collected from a machine that is offline, collect them early, before the target machine is turned on.

Experience Note If an investigator were able to recover inodes information and corresponding MAC times of the unallocated file system, comparing them with the live file system; it might be possible to find the time when an intruder started changing and deleting files, and when the attacker entered and departed the system.

Baseline Comparison for SUID/SGID Files

If a system has an uncorrupted file system, for example found in the form of a backup recording, it might be possible to identify an attacker's backdoor.

Experience Note As a matter of course, it's a wise practice to make a comparison of SUID files between the target UNIX operating files and the "clean" backup. In discovering files outside this baseline comparison does not necessarily mean there is a backdoor; however, investigators and systems administrators must be able to account for any anomalous findings.

System Configuration

Investigators should check the/etc/syslog.conf file to determine where the system stores its logs and which events are logged. This configuration file establishes the storage facility, logging priorities, and the extent of logging.

User and Password Accounts

The file */etc/passwd* identifies user account names and may display password hashes, user and group identification, user home directories, and user general information. If the */etc/passwd* file contains password hashes, the system is vulnerable to password cracking. Investigators should consider this likelihood and after an initial review of a UNIX system, they should include checking for shared user ids. In reviewing the password file, note that user-id 0 is reserved for root access only. Any user-id 0 or shared user-ids should be questioned.

Log Files

These are a few of the system log files that could be encountered during an investigation:

By default, UNIX-based systems have the following log file names:

- *wtmp* and *wtmpx*. These logs keep track of login and logouts.
- *utmp* and *utmpx*. These logs keep track of users presently logged on the system.
- *lastlog*. This log tracks users' most recent login time and records their initiating IP address.
- *sulog*. This log records the usage of the switch *su* (substitute user).
- *syslogd*. This is a daemon referring to the configuration file.

- History file. This file records the history of recent commands used by the individual user.
- TCP Wrappers. Uses *syslogd* to facilitate connect logging.

Experience Note Root can arbitrarily name logs in the system log file, */etc/syslog.conf*. It is possible that some systems administrators have taken some latitude by renaming log files to apparently meaningless file names.

These UNIX programs are helpful to investigators and if installed, they can save investigators a lot of time in reconstructing events:

- Check Promiscuous Mode. It checks a system for any network interfaces in promiscuous mode. This may indicate that an attacker has broken in and started a packet snooping program.
- ifstatus. The ifstatus program was written by David Curry and checks a system for any network interface cards placed in promiscuous mode. This application is designed to be run as a scheduled event.
- Spar. Spar is a program intended to show process accounting records and is usually installed for computer-time billing purposes. However, in skilled hands, it is a valuable tool to establish when an attacker was using system resources.
- Tripwire. The Tripwire application is available from Purdue University. It scans designated files and computes hashes for them. At a future time, it can be used to check those files for changes indicating a possible attack.

All the above applications are available at ciac.llnl.gov/ciac/ToolsUNIXSysMon.html.

Types of Malicious Code Attacks: Even Kevlar Will not Stop all Attacks

As a matter of course, investigators are tasked to address rogue code attacks. Handling such an attack presents challenges in terms of priorities. For example, certain types of attacks spread very quickly affecting computers on networks in large numbers. The Morris Internet Worm was one such attack.

There are many demands placed on the responders once they are aware of a potential critical incident. The clear first priority is isolating the attack. Infected computers must be isolated from the surrounding system to prevent the infecting code from spreading to other systems. With this done, responders should ask themselves if it is important to determine the origins of the infection, or not. If the network and its connecting systems are cleansed of the rogue code, the evidence of its origin may be erased; however, if the systems containing the code are isolated, they remain inoperable until the investigation is completed, negatively affecting productivity.

Viruses

In a virus attack, it is very likely the virus has infected many systems. The responder's likely priority is isolating the infected machines, clean them, and return them to their users. In these cases, analyzing the virus and its origins is secondary. Tracing the virus is difficult, if not impossible in a large system, but there are some considerations that can be made:

- Make a forensically sound copy of one of the infected hard drives.
- Treat the hard drive as if it were evidence and a crime scene in its own right.
- Make a second forensic copy of the drive and use it as a work copy for future analysis.
- If the first infected computer in the system can be identified by timestamp analysis, it may be possible to identify the origin of the infestation.

Experience Note It is extremely difficult to identify the person who introduced a virus into a network. Anti-virus software must be constantly updated and users trained not to open e-mail attachments. Usually the best that can be done is to isolate the systems, cleanse them, return the systems to the production environment, and train users.

Trojan Horses and Logic Bombs

In many regards, these examples of malware code are easier to handle than viruses because they are usually confined to one machine. The problem is that they might remain dormant or unused on that machine until a triggering event takes place. Triggering events are items such as calendar dates, keystrokes made in a specific order, or the execution of program code. Once the triggering event takes place, the user discovers the malicious code and administrators take appropriate restoration steps. With the malicious code running, it's going to be fairly obvious where it is located. For example, if there is a logic bomb planted in a billing program, it is possible that users will know it when they try to execute the application and it does its damage.

With the execution of a logic bomb, the damage is done. Depending on the extent of possible legal action, the best solution is to cleanse the victim system and reinstall the software with clean backed-up data. It is possible that evidence could be collected, timestamps compared, and an attacker identified. Conducting such an investigation can be very time-consuming and resource intensive; consequently, it must be determined if it is worth the effort or not.

In the event of a suspected logic bomb hidden in an application, there are some specific steps that can be taken to prevent it from executing and doing its damage. It is important that a forensically sound copy of the suspected drive is made and preserved as evidence. Copy the evidence drive for performing all analyses and return a clean drive to the original system. The best way to locate the malicious code is to compare the victim system, where the malicious code is resident, with a clean backup copy. Investigators should review the date of the last change in the target media and compare it to the date of the last change for the same file in the backup copy. Continue to compare backups as far as is practical and compare dates. If there is a timestamp date change that cannot be explained or is not documented, the altered file is probably the guilty one.

If the investigators can gain visibility into the programmer's code (this may or may not be possible) there are editors that will automate the line by line comparison revealing any changes.

In the event of suspected malicious code, here are a few types of event logging that will help:

- Login and logoff
- File deletion
- Privilege changes

- Access by all root
- Failed login attempts
- Unused or dormant account access
- SU (Switch User) activity in UNIX-based systems
- System reboots
- Remote access of target system
- New user accounts

Things to Do after a Malicious Code Attack

If a system has been the victim of a malicious code attack or denial-of-service attack, either as a result of outside or inside activity, here are a few suggested measures:

- Contain the potential problem. The most efficient way to accomplish this is to simply remove the Ethernet cable from the NIC card, or isolate the affected systems from the rest of the network by some other means. If this cannot be accomplished, disable the power to the target machine. If you do not disconnect the target machine from the network, infections or attackers will cause havoc because they will continue to have access to the system.

Experience Note Managers should not be lulled into the idea that attackers having penetrated a system will not return. Once in, they will continuously attempt to intrude or deny service.

- Preserve the target media as evidence. This probably will mean making a forensic copy of the target drive and preserving it for evidence.
- Cleanse the original drive and return it to service. Make forensic copies of media containing the malicious code and preserve them as evidence. This will preserve the timestamp dates of infection. Cleansing media may consist of media degaussing, reformatting the drive, or launching a forensic erasing tool where the entire drive is overwritten several times destroying the offending code.
- A completely clean reinstallation will be more time consuming, but will ensure correct functionality rather than running the anti-virus software to delete or quarantine the offender.

Digital Bloodhounds

For matters that are going to be pursued to levels of litigation, it is important for investigators to discover the identities of those responsible for causing system damage. In many cases, civil and criminal legal processes can be, and should be, pursued on parallel tracks. It is not unusual for an individual to be criminally charged while the damaged parties file lawsuits to recover their losses. Considering all the different technologies that can be employed to conceal the attacker's identity such as anonymous e-mail re-mailers and compromised server accounts, it would seem attackers have a definite advantage over investigators.

Experience Note The Director of Risk Management for a credit card company noted that there were chat rooms dedicated to trading and verifying credit card information. After engaging several of the chat room operators in conversations over the course of many weeks, it was discovered many of them resided in countries that had few, if any, laws making credit card fraud a criminal act.

Further, it was discovered the subjects knew they were acting criminally and fully acknowledged they could not be extradited due to a lack of international treaties. Consequently, they knew they could steal credit card information, sell it, commit fraud with it, and not suffer any punishment.

IP Addresses

When investigators begin looking for evidence in an attacked a system, the most logical place to begin searching is the IP address. IP addresses create areas of difficulties when locating the offender.

It is possible, and indeed quite likely, that the source IP address is spoofed and not correctly resolved to the attacker.

It is possible, and indeed likely, that the source IP address used for an attack is many hops away from the actual origin of the attack. Experienced attackers will pass through multiple systems before actually launching an attack. It is very common for investigators to have to obtain information from the administrators of multiple systems in the attack-chain before arriving at the attacker's origin.

Experience Note Much of IP tracing depends on the investigator's skill and luck. This is not to say it is not successful, but realistically it can be difficult and discouraging.

The IP address is assigned to an individual machine. It may be difficult to determine who was using a particular machine at a particular time in a shared environment like a school or library.

Resolving IP Addresses

By way of review, IP addresses consist of four sets of numbers, such as 166.70.6.40. The resolution of this IP address is as follows:

OrgName: XMission

OrgID: XMIS

NetRange: 166.70.0.0 − 166.70.255.255

CIDR: 166.70.0.0/16

NetName: XMISSION-166-70-0-0

NetHandle: NET-166-70-0-0-1

Parent: NET-166-0-0-0-0

NetType: Direct Assignment

NameServer: NS.XMISSION.COM

NameServer: NS1.XMISSION.COM

NameServer: NS2.XMISSION.COM

Comment: Please use the abuse@xmission.com e-mail address for all complaints regarding UCE (spam), copyright violations, security intrusions, and other suspected network abuse sourcing from XMission networks. DO NOT COPY your complaint to any other ARIN XMission POCs or e-mail addresses on the XMission network. Failure to comply with this statement will result in your complaint being ignored.

RegDate: 1997-02-19

Updated: 2002-09-19

AbuseHandle: NETAB-ARIN

AbuseName: Netabuse Manager

AbusePhone: +1-801-539-0852

AbuseEmail: abuse@xmission.com

NOCHandle: NETWO22-ARIN

NOCName: Network Manager

NOCPhone: +1-801-539-0852

NOCEmail: net-manager@xmission.com

TechHandle: TECHN5-ARIN

TechName: Technical Support

TechPhone: +1-801-539-0852

TechEmail: support@xmission.com

OrgAbuseHandle: NETAB-ARIN

OrgAbuseName: Netabuse Manager

OrgAbusePhone: +1-801-539-0852

OrgAbuseEmail: abuse@xmission.com

OrgNOCHandle: NETWO22-ARIN

OrgNOCName: Network Manager

OrgNOCPhone: +1-801-539-0852

OrgNOCEmail: net-manager@xmission.com

OrgTechHandle: TECHN5-ARIN

OrgTechName: Technical Support

OrgTechPhone: +1-801-539-0852

OrgTechEmail: support@xmission.com

\# ARIN Whois database, last updated 2002-11-09 19:05

\# Enter ? for additional hints on searching ARIN's Whois database.

As can be seen, the IP address fell within the block of IP addresses assigned to xmission.com. The Domain Name Servers connect the IP address to the Fully Qualified Domain Name, FQDN, which is xmission.com in this case. Using the SamSpade tool to resolve the IP address revealed the screen shown in Exhibit 12.

Of course, using a tool like SamSpade or nslookup to resolve the IP address related to suspicious activities or attacks provides one of the first steps in the investigation. The resolution may lead to the address of a compromised system in a long chain of systems that are being used to launch more attacks. It is important to remember that the DNS system merely maps IP addresses to FQDNs.

Trace Route

There are two very useful tools that determine the route a packet follows getting from the origin to the destination. Trace route uses the IP's Time To Live (TTL) data field to obtain an Internet Control Message Protocol (ICMP) response from each

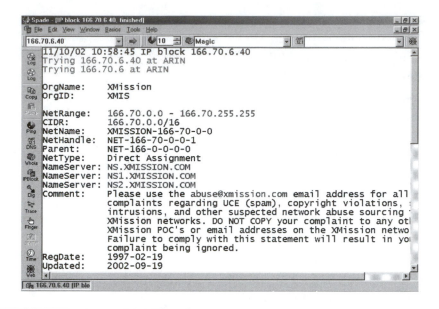

Exhibit 12   IP Resolution in SamSpade

router along the packet's path. Trace route is another of the tools available in the SamSpade application. Investigators can use trace route to determine the approximate geographical location of a system of interest. It is possible that the registered information for the domain owner may reveal her location to be in Maryland, yet the system of interest may be physically located in New York. Tracing the packet's routing may be helpful in revealing the real physical location of a system when considering legal jurisdiction.

Experience Note There are trace route tools that display their data in visual form available at www.visualware.com. This tool combines IP resolution, geographical information, and trace route information in one tool.

Of course, there is a built-in tool located in Windows operating systems called Tracert. It can be launched through the DOS prompt and by entering *tracert*, followed by the domain name at the prompt; for example, *C:\\windows> tracert www.fbi.gov*. This utility will count and display the hops, times, and connections.

Dynamic Host Control Protocol Tracing

DHCP provides dynamically assigned IP addresses to hosts accessing the network. This is the usual method that users are assigned IP addresses who are dialing up their ISP for Internet access. The process of assigning an IP address to a user is known as "leasing." In most cases, DHCP is normally a logged event regardless of whether the server platform is UNIX or Windows-based. By reviewing the DHCP server logs, investigators should be able to determine the leased IP addresses identifying connected machines.

In the case of UNIX platforms, the DHCP service is handled by the *dhcpd* program and uses the *syslogd* program to handle the IP address leases. In Windows platforms, the DHCP service is logged by the *DhcpSrvLog* file. With the DHCP address identified with a specific network card and matching it to the timestamp, it should be a simple

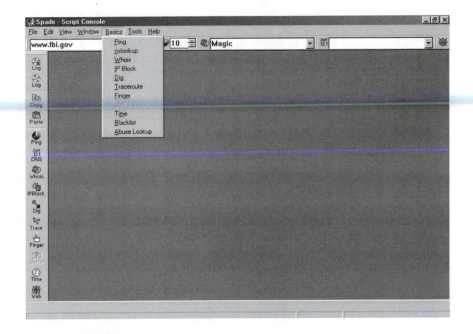

Exhibit 13   SamSpade Tools

matter of reviewing the organization's latest equipment inventory and matching the machine's identification with the assigned owner.

Investigating the Identity of the Attacker

It is sometimes worth the time, effort, and expense of discovering who is attacking the system and there are times that it is not. Investigators are advised to consult with their legal counsel before wasting resources in chasing a bandit down a blind alley. However, if investigators are inclined to discover their attacker's identity, here are some areas that may be fruitful. Use the SamSpade suite or similar tools to discover the domain registration of the attacker's IP address (Exhibit 13).

- Ping will discover if the target IP is online. Many administrators disable this service, so it should not be considered reliable.
- Nslookup will resolve the attacker's IP address and will provide relevant domain registration information. This information should provide a name, address, and telephone number of a responsible party with whom contact may be made to extend the investigation one more step backwards. It is often found the administrator of the previous system was unaware that her system was a launching pad for an attack on another system.
- Trace route will provide the route of information packets traveling from router to router.

Investigators may find situations where the attacker's trail passes through a system where activity logs do not exist or are insufficient to make the next hop toward the attacker. Talking to senior administrators, at these occasions, may reveal that they have relevant information identifying the next system back.

Experience Note Investigators are advised just because the administrator does not have complete logs, does not mean she does not have other helpful information.

In this same vein, just because an investigator finds an IP address going back many hops does not necessarily mean this is the attacker's address. It is very possible that the attacker was using a compromised account, and the administrator of that system will have to review logs and timestamps to determine the extent of the attacker's activity.

Convincing an administrator that this is an effort worthy of his time can be somewhat of a challenge in itself.

Experience Note Information collected by administrators and non-law enforcement investigators may be provided to law enforcement authorities. In some cases, law enforcement authorities are going to need international treaty enforcement or other processes to obtain this information depending on the location of the attacker.

This is a potential problem in that the administrator, along the attacker-trail, might be the attacker herself. So, it is important for non-law enforcement investigators to coordinate their efforts with law enforcement authorities and their respective legal counsel before proceeding. Failing to do so may have serious consequences. For example, if a corporate investigator alerted an attacker that she was under investigation by law enforcement authorities. As a result of this warning, the attacker destroyed evidence of her activities. In this case, the corporate investigator could possibly be charged with obstructing an investigation and evidence tempering.

Domain Registration Payments

There are times when investigators seem to hit a wall in their pursuit of their attacker's identity. Domain registration information is an extremely valuable resource. Registrations often provide some degree of information even if most of the registration information is false. Most domain registration entities require their clients to use credit cards or cashier's checks. Contacting the domain registration agency may provide the credit card number and other identifying information for the attacker's domain. It is possible the credit card was stolen, so law enforcement authorities may start a trail on the credit card number that might lead to the identity of the attacker and to charges of mail or interstate fraud.

Nicks and Monikers

Attackers frequently use monikers, also known as "Nicks," when boasting of their misdeeds in chat rooms. Sometimes these nicks are registered with chat room services similar to Dalnet or Undernet with valid e-mail addresses or other information. Do not forget that chat room servers may maintain user activity logs that will reveal the IP address of someone identified with an attack.

Experience Note Inexperienced attackers enjoy boasting of their destructive activities and often post their deeds in chat rooms or in Newsgroups. Monitoring relevant chat rooms immediately after an attack and logging the conversations will sometimes reveal the bragging-attacker and provide essentially a detailed confession. More than one investigator has maintained membership in such chat rooms specifically for this purpose.

Sometimes Nick-owners use anonymous Web-based mail thinking this will conceal their identities when they are logged on as chat room users. Such services as Yahoo and Hotmail provide Web-based e-mail services that may be used to thinly shield the user's identity. It is important to note that Web-based mail services carry the sender's IP address within the header content. If the sender were using a dynamically assigned IP address, this address would be contained in the header content. Web-based e-mail services usually maintain user logging.

If an attacker is using DHCP to connect to the network, this will not conceal her identity, as most ISPs maintain user-logging records that will reveal the leased IP address to a specific computer logged on to their system. If the attacker is located inside an organization's network, viewing the NAT (Network Address Translation) and firewall logs will generally reveal which user was using a particular IP address and was logged on the system at a particular time.

Searching the Newsgroups for an attacker's Nick or IP address or domain is another way of ascertaining an attacker's identity. Many attackers frequent Newsgroups looking for information or to engage in "flame-wars." They use their Nicks as identifiers and provide information about their interests and activities. Doing a bit of homework can reveal significant amounts of information about an attacker's interests and background. Newsgroups may be easily searched for information through search engines like www.google.com providing exact word or term searches.

Anonymous Re-Mailers

Frequently, questions about anonymous re-mailers arise and the degree of success investigators have in obtaining logs and other relevant information. The purpose of anonymous re-mailers is to conceal the user's true identity. Their philosophy is that privacy is assured by anonymity. People use re-mailers for the following reasons:

- Whistle blowing
- Discussion of personal or taboo issues
- Journalistic correspondence
- Spam protection
- Future anonymity
- Political speech
- Censorship avoidance
- Corporations and other organizations tend to use anonymous re-mailers for these reasons:
    - Research of competitors
    - Out-of-band communications
    - Avoidance of information leakage
    - Thwarting industrial espionage
    - Employee feedback

Anonymous re-mailers do not usually maintain user logs citing disk space and resource limitations. Often the truth is these entities are interested in user privacy concerns.

Experience Note Depending on the re-mailer owner's concerns for legal matters, they may be persuaded to be helpful in locating and identifying their users either through log analysis or active system monitoring.

It is possible for law enforcement officers to obtain relevant information from re-mailers. With legal authority such as search warrants, court orders, or subpoenas, re-mailers can be compelled to save specific incoming and outgoing messages. Second, it may be possible for officers to obtain a copy of a message from the sender, such as during the execution of a search warrant. It may be possible, with these message copies, that officers can obtain evidence from the ISP in the way of the time and date the sender logged on and sent the e-mail of interest.

To successfully obtain evidence from anonymous re-mailers, investigators must be prepared to obtain search warrants, court orders, and court ordered wiretaps. It is not impossible to obtain information from re-mailers; it depends on their degree of cooperation and the legal resources available to the investigators and prosecutors.

Forming a Critical Incident Response Team

In many descriptions you will see the words "Critical Incident Response Team" associated with critical incidents. Many incident response efforts are unsuccessful, not for lack of planning, but because many mistakes were made in creating a team that was not staffed with knowledgeable, dedicated employees. Many organizations use checklist methods of emergency response because of legal or policy mandates where senior managers think their systems' security is guaranteed because they mark a box. Feeling they have met all legal and policy requirements, they are lulled into a false sense of security.

Experience Note Locks only keep honest people, well, honest. They will not stop a knowledgeable, persistent thief. When visiting a small police department, a visiting dignitary was shown the department's new gymnasium and locker room. She noticed padlocks on the locker doors and asked the commander giving the tour, the reason why. Without missing a beat, the commander remarked the locks were present on the doors to, "keep honest people honest." Even in the police department, they were respectful of each other's belongings but they kept them secure by locking them up.

Security controls have the purpose of making unauthorized entry so unattractive and difficult, they compel attackers to go elsewhere. The only truly effective security systems are those that render important systems inoperable. Of course, that condition is ridiculous. Systems security before, during, and after a critical incident exists as part of the whole picture of good business practice. It ensures uptime, efficiency providing critical systems needed for daily business operations. The purpose of security is to preserve what belongs to the organization from being stolen, deleted, or modified. So, what happens when an attacker, inside or outside the organization, causes a critical incident?

Most organizations have long understood the importance of having fire suppression equipment installed in data-centers, emergency exits, and employee training for emergencies. These same organizations have extensive information security measures with firewalls, DMZs, VPNs, and physical security. Safeguards, like these, have the purpose of maintaining the organization's property and reputation in the community.

Regrettably, critical incident response and management are often neglected until a catastrophe actually strikes and the organization finds itself scrambling to recover.

Experience Note Critical incident management is determining which assets are needed to sustain profitability (profitability means the organization is accomplishing its goals), establishing policies and procedures addressing employee conduct, compliance audits and mechanisms to actually address crises when they occur.

CIRT

CIRTs should be composed of team members with specific roles supported by specialized training and experience. The CIRT must have a function-point or coordinator where all reports of critical incidents are made. The function-point is usually an individual senior employee or member of a business unit having significant managerial and business experience. She possesses a clear understanding of the organization's goals and objectives, and probably participates in the drafting of the business' operational plans sometime in her career.

It is not expected this person would have a complete knowledge of the organization's mission, goals, policies, and procedures, but it is important that she have sufficient knowledge. For the function-point person to deliver services, she must be available 24 hours, holidays, and weekends. Contact may be accomplished through telephone or other expedient means.

Under practical circumstances, it is immaterial whether the organization decides to use its own in-house talent or delegates the responsibility to outside consultants. The first contact is the employee who receives information relating to the critical incident and makes several important decisions relating to it:

- Does an actual critical incident exist?
- Where is the critical incident occurring?
- What is the extent of the damage?
- Has the damage been contained or is it continuing?
- Do I need to triage the damage at this moment?
- What resources do I need to deploy at this moment?
- Do I have the resources to address this crisis at this time?
- Do I have sufficient information to deliver a meaningful report to senior managers?
- When should I notify law enforcement authorities?

Using Outside Consultants

One of the greatest advantages in using outside consultants (commercial CIRTs) is that of overall reduced cost. This is particularly true in smaller organizations where their operational demands are less than larger organizations. In many cases, contract consultants specializing in critical incident response deal with a wide variety of matters resulting in a high degree of expertise. Additionally, many of their team members have specialties such as UNIX, Windows, or specific programming languages usually not available to employees of smaller businesses.

These are the advantages of commercial CIRTs:

- Most commercial firms have the ability to respond in a matter of hours depending on travel times.
- They provide 24-hour support and are in constant contact.
- They can offer full-service response-posture, as their services usually include forensic duplication and examination, litigation support, expert testimony, technical support, policy formulation, and legal expertise.

- Commercial CIRTs can provide mock-incident response training. Participants address imaginary, but logical, scenarios and interact with personnel, data, and facilities.
- Keeping abreast of current attack-trends. Commercial CIRTs are able to track attacker trends and tailor their response-posture to their clients. By assigning technically trained account executives to clients, they anticipate malicious behavior and are prepared to marshal resources accordingly.

Commercial CIRTs vary greatly in their abilities. Senior managers should do their homework before signing contracts for service.

- Be certain to ask for references from several recent customers and do not hesitate to ask for individual employee's qualifications and experience levels.
- Contact their references. Ask the most important question, "would you hire them again?"
- Determine their reputation in the business community by contact entities such as the Better Business Bureau to ascertain if complaints have been filed and are unresolved.
- Depending on circumstances, ask for financial references.
- Determine if they have bonding in the event of future legal action.

Using In-House Talent

The primary reason for initiating and developing an in-house CIRT is the ability to address emergencies observing the organization's policies and procedures. Staffed with employees, CIRT capability can be directed to address emergencies meeting cultural and internal needs. Because critical incidents often involve sensitive or political matters, in-house talents are more likely to address them in a fashion most advantageous to the organization.

In many cases, internal CIRTs are funded through the corporate offices or on a charge-back basis to the individual business units. Some CIRTs are funded through corporate headquarters paying salaries and other recurring expenses while the individual business units pay for the on-site expenses such as travel, lodging, or other expenses.

Here are a few advantages of the internal CIRTs:

- Direct support. Internal CIRTs will provide emergency response to affected business units with greater specific business-practice knowledge than commercial CIRTs. Generally, they have greater sensitivity to corporate culture than equivalent outside firms.
- Risk management, policy, and audit support. Although these functions are usually addressed by an organization's business units having an internal CIRT can provide invaluable input to heightened awareness and effectiveness. After all, the CIRT has a high vantage point from which to gauge their interaction and deliver this experience to risk managers, policy writers, and auditors on a continuing basis.
- Emergency drill participation. An internal CIRT can participate in emergency exercises testing the full range of recovery, resumption, and critical incident response capabilities. An emergency exercise consisting of an unannounced test can measure the effectiveness of personnel, equipment, and procedures.

Postmortem critiques, conducted among employees, are generally more productive and sensitive than sessions involving outsiders.

Ad Hoc CIRTs

This is a concept that has gained a lot of favor in the past few years for smaller businesses. Ad hoc CIRTs are developed utilizing existing talent, and where deficiencies are identified training is vigorously sought. For the most part, ad hoc CIRTs are composed of specially trained employees that have regularly assigned duties and when emergencies strike, they form their response team. For this concept to avoid being stillborn, it must have fanatical senior management sponsorship.

Here are a few suggestions for getting an ad hoc version of CIRT off the ground:

- Identify key technical employees that are qualified to address critical incidents. Such experts would include the IT manager, senior systems administrator, senior engineers, legal advisor, risk manager, human resources unit, etc.
- Draft response policies and procedures for the CIRT to screen initial reports, criteria for activation, response activities, and post-incident critique.
- Obtain senior management agreements with a minimum number of hours of participation on an annual basis for CIRT members. Provide financial incentives to employees for CIRT participation.
- Provide specialized training to CIRT members. This should be training that is complementary with their skills.
- Seek to train toward professional certifications. This is one of those incentive areas where CIRT participants can receive certifications qualifying them for advancement.

CIRT Requirements and Roles

As in any plan, the best place to start is with your deliverables and requirements. Experienced planners actually begin at the end by asking, "What is it we need the CIRT to do?" The most basic requirement for an incident response team is providing support and direction in successfully resolving critical incidents with a minimum degree of business disruption.

Basically, CIRTs are support units intended to provide critical incident response support to the organization as a whole and to the affected business unit specifically.

In this tasking, CIRTs usually serve in these potential roles:

- Direct hands-on emergency response where CIRT members are actively engaged in the containment and restoration of critical IT functions. The full-version of this activity is for the CIRT to assume complete response responsibility. Taking this posture potentially alienates employees already assigned to the affected business units. However, in the event of severe circumstances and if mandated by senior managers, this approach is efficient and effective.
- However, this role can suffer from a conflict of loyalties, as the CIRT is sometimes regarded as "big brother" when it appears on the scene and immediately takes control of the situation.
- Advisory/Shared role. In this role, the CIRT acts as a trusted advisor sharing response activities with the affected business unit. There is less conflict of loyalties in this role, meaning responsibilities are shared between entities.

Added CIRT Responsibilities

Because senior managers view full-time CIRTs as responding only when needed, sometimes they get the reputation of having little if anything to do unless they are responding to a crisis. Their perceived usefulness can be expanded by accepting added responsibilities:

- Acting as a problem screening unit. In this capacity, the CIRT acts as a unit where software patches, tools, and updated software versions are tried and tested before being applied. The practical side of this task rests in the CIRT being able to patch a corrupted system and know the patch they are applying has been tested. There is confidence this patch will not conflict with existing systems and is free from malicious code. Additionally, the CIRT acts like a clearinghouse for recurring or particularly troublesome system problems. They work closely with help desk coordinators and system administrators where any indications of critical incidents are reported and a determination is made if the CIRT should be activated either as an entire unit or in part.
- Coordinate inside emergency efforts and establish liaison with outside agencies. The CIRT coordinates the emergency response efforts of all organizational units in the event of a crisis and works to actively facilitate their drill and actual crises. The CIRT is tasked with the development of liaison with law enforcement and regulatory and legal entities. It actively seeks to participate in such entities as NIPC (National Infrastructure Protection Center), Infragard, HTCIA (High Tech Crime Investigators Association), ISACA (Information Security Audit and Control Association), ISSA (Information Systems Security Association), and the ACFE (Association of Certified Fraud Examiners).
- Provide training inside the organization and to outside entities. CIRT members should be in a very good position to deliver specialized training and increased awareness as one of their proactive jobs. Consider having the CIRT author technical articles in professional periodicals thereby benefiting them by having to do the research and delivering information to other professionals. Through this means, team members learn about developments and emerging trends while potentially providing a valuable service to their constituents and their organization.

CIRT Funding

Funding CIRTs, as are most business matters, is merely a matter of funding. Sometimes developing resources is more a matter of convincing bean counters of their value than anything else.

Here are a few basics to consider when developing your CIRT:

- CIRT as part of the IT function. Locating a CIRT as part of the organization's IT function can greatly facilitate productive interaction between the lessons learned as a result of responding to emergencies and improving development processes. Placing the CIRT as part of the IT function creates avenues of communication between responders and systems staff.
- Business units may benefit by having the CIRT as part of their operation. For example, the systems development unit could greatly benefit by having the knowledge and skills of the CIRT integrated as part of their operation. Having the CIRT as part of the IT audit unit could provide increased granularity and direction in audit programs.

- Corporate headquarters may wish to fund the cost of the CIRT's activities charged as an overhead cost to each of its business units. In this fashion, the cost of having the CIRT is spread to all affected business units, saving each unit from having to make preparations and fund critical response programs. In this fashion, there is an avoidance of duplicating response efforts between headquarters and the individual business units saving time and money. By adopting the "big picture" view, it allows the CIRT to respond to emergencies on the corporate level where trouble spots can be more readily recognized and addressed.

Who Does the CIRT Support?

The quick answer to this question is everybody. However, for a CIRT to adequately function, it must understand the people it serves mission and goals. For CIRT managers, it is suggested they track units calling for their services so they may gear their response accordingly. It is likely the same business units are requesting services time and again; consequently, it is important for CIRT to service their requests as if they were favored clients. For example, if the business units primarily supported by the CIRT consisted of systems users rather than findings produced by IT audit reports, CIRT's response would be less technical than the response delivered to the auditor's findings. Responding to the auditors would probably require more forensic skills than responding to worms and viruses encountered by users.

CIRT Communications

CIRT members should be mindful that their clients are the business units they service. Misplaced, flippant, or capricious remarks return poor dividends. Communications between the CIRT and the units it supports is not just something that is casually performed; it must be a matter of deliberation and coordinated efforts.

CIRTs should have specific communications goals when measuring their success:

- Timeliness. CIRTs must deliver information in a timely fashion. The means by which the information is transmitted may be e-mail, telephone calls, faxes, voice mail, company Web sites, memos, conferences and workshops, working groups, seminars, and bulletin boards. Basically, employees served by the CIRT should have information as soon as it is discovered. For example, the CIRT becomes aware that the BUGBEAR.exe virus is in the wild. The most efficient way to deliver a message warning about the proliferation and damage this virus can cause is by sending a voice mail message to each employee warning that e-mail attachments should not be opened. Sending an e-mail to each employee may result in the information arriving too late, as the employee may be checking e-mail by opening an attachment before getting to the CIRT warning. Timely and credible warnings will go a long way to developing the CIRT's position and credibility in the organization.
- Relevant communications are a must for a CIRT. If the units supported by them are primarily Windows platforms, it does little good to deliver information about UNIX and OS/2. Communications should be crafted so they are meaningful to their recipients.
- Digestibility. The intended audience must understand CIRT communications. For example, if the CIRT primarily serves workstation users, the CIRT should

not craft exhaustive communications dealing with the technical aspects of UNIX server configurations. Granted, there might be readers who enjoy the finer aspects of server configurations, but the broader appeal will be to the majority of the users. Reserve specialized information to specialized employees.

CIRTs should be mindful that there are many levels of employees that are going to read their material, including managers. Including a brief executive summary at the beginning of the communication is appreciated. Depending on the audience, it may serve to have two or even three versions of a communication to be disseminated. One version would be delivered to the general user population, one version to be sent to the managers, and another version intended for the technical staff.

- Accuracy of communications. Few actions will work to destroy the credibility of any business unit faster than to disseminate incorrect information. Get the facts, and get them straight before transmitting information to anyone. Every phrase and every term should be carefully scrutinized for accuracy before going out. CIRT managers must read the communication for technical accuracy and understanding. Of course, CIRT communications should be professional and courteous. This is not the place for colorless humor or sarcasm. Part of communication's accuracy is the assurance the intended audience receives them.

CIRTs should develop out-of-band communications. This means that CIRTs, their constituency, and management should know when and how to use OOBC. OOBC efforts require advance arrangements and coordination within a response team. CIRTs should analyze the organization's current communication structure and devise private alternate channels. OOBC may include private cellular telephones, text pagers, wireless equipment such as PDAs, out-of-business-area telephone communications, registered mail, encrypted e-mail, etc. CIRTs must ensure that each OOBC system is periodically tested and achieves acceptable levels of security.

Developing Critical Incident Cost Analyses

CIRTs should develop a means by which they can measure the cost of addressing critical incidents. The reason for this procedure is fairly simple, if their organization is going to pursue legal actions to recover damages, or criminal sentencing is directly tied to the amount of damage done, a monetary amount is necessary.

In recent years, almost everyone with an e-mail address has heard of or experienced the damage caused by the Melissa, SirCam, CodeRed, Nimda, Slammer, and Klez viruses.

Ask users and administrators how much "damage" they suffered as a result of these and other pieces of malicious software and you will hear, "Well, not much, I guess." From their perspective, how much does it cost to reformat hard drives and reinstall operating systems, applications, and data?

Adding up the time lost to handling critical incidents across a large organization and you are talking sizeable money amounts. If corporate executives, government administrators, or university regents were asked how much money is being lost to such incidents, they would likely answer they do not have any idea and they do not have any mechanism to collect such data.

The matter is simple if you know a few facts about responding CIRTs and affected systems. Such information can be obtained by answering a few questions:

- Who responded to the incident?
- What equipment and programs were used?

Exhibit 14

Item	Cost
Forensic computer	$5000 total cost, long-term asset; cost for this response is $0
Linux	Freeware $0
Coroner's ToolKit	Freeware $0
CIRT members (7)	7 × $42 = $294/hour labor
Total CIRT time expended (4 hours)	4 × $294 = $1176 total labor cost
Systems Administrators 2 @ $34/hour for 7 hours	2 × $34 × 7 = $476
Total overhead for labor @ 28 percent	$462.56
Total labor costs	$2114.56

- What post-incident analysis was performed pursuant to the incident?
- How many hours did each of them spend in that response? What are their salary levels?
- How many employees were prevented from working because of the emergency?
- How many hours of employee downtime were attributable to the emergency?
- Calculating an estimated amount of Internet business, what were the anticipated business losses attributable to not being able to conduct e-Business?
- What are the calculated overhead costs (insurance, sick leave, etc.) for each employee not able to work due to the critical incident?

The largest obstacle in obtaining such cost estimates is motivating employees to keep track of their billable time. CIRTs and systems administrators are usually anxious to return the system to productivity and usually do not keep careful notes of what they did and when they did it. However, if a civil action is filed or criminal charges leveled, the best means of ensuring accurate testimony is the employees' recollection supported by their notes.

Exhibit 14 is a table reflecting the costs related to a small incident.

CIRT Composition: What Kind of Skills and Talent Do I Need for a CIRT?

CIRT core membership should include the senior manager sponsor, IT security program manager, representatives from the legal counsel unit, public relations unit, human resources unit, and the CIRT manager. The CIRT manager should be someone who is a senior employee who has significant knowledge of the organization's operations as well as an employee capable of making sound business decisions.

The IT program manager is the head of the organization's IT security program and might double as the CIRT manager. In the case of a critical incident spanning regions or countries, one IT critical incident manager should be named for each office with all strategic efforts coordinated at the headquarters level. This representative will be responsible for tactical decisions, triage functions, and local resource deployment. It is the IT security program manager, with senior manager's approval, that is responsible for authorizing any release of information about the incident to the press. However, the program manager should not be the individual disclosing information to the press. A public relations unit employee should make contacts with the press. Delegating press responsibility relieves the program manager from having to evade sensitive questions or even having to lie to the press corps. Regardless, the public relations unit is going to be the place where the institutional knowledge and experience in this area is going to be found.

Legal Unit

Activating the CIRT requires an opinion from senior managers and specifically from the legal unit representative that is knowledgeable about the relevant laws dealing with the organization and its functions, intellectual property, information security, and privacy. In the case of CIRT deployment, it is the legal unit's responsibility to ensure that the CIRT does not violate laws and regulations while responding to a critical incident. Knowledgeable and experienced legal advise become particularly important when CIRTs are directed to follow attackers with the objectives of locating, identifying, assisting, apprehension, and prosecution. Legal representatives must be more than attorneys with general knowledge; they must possess a thorough understanding of information technology, business functions and civil, administrative and criminal matters. Through their participation on the CIRT core, they must initiate and develop relationships with law enforcement and regulatory authorities, professional support groups such as NIPC and Infragard. Often, this employee will serve as the primary contact for law enforcement.

Public Relations

Depending on the organization's size and funding, having a public relations unit representative is a decided advantage. This employee addresses all media requests for information and similarly handles authorized press releases. It is expected this employee will have developed relationships with media organizations as well as specific news agency representatives.

Human Resources Unit

A senior representative from the human resources unit must be part of the CIRT core. This person ensures that the CIRT team's response efforts do not violate employees' rights. Also, this person will make certain that appropriate disciplinary standards are applied should an employee be found to be the source of a critical incident. In the event an employee is an unwitting part of an attack, or if the employee is a victim, certain rights might be granted within the scope of their employment. The human resources unit representative is responsible for seeing that an employee's reasonable expectation of privacy is respected or knowing whether an employee is entitled to union representation in the event of an interview.

IT Investigative, Analysis, and Forensic Experts

These CIRT members ensure that the response is performed in a methodical and deliberate fashion, making certain all relevant evidence is properly collected, pre-served, and introduced at legal proceedings. CIRTs require their members to participate in addressing crises on an as-needed basis. Key participants should consist of IT security officers, systems administrators, telecommunications equipment specialists, database managers, engineers/software developers, and of course, systems owners.

IT Security Officers

Most organizations have individuals assigned full- or part-time to ensuring the security of systems. Often this employee performs duties in support of auditors, making certain the IT units are in compliance with the organization's policies, procedures, and standards. This employee helps in addressing attacks by knowing how the system was installed and configured before the attack. She will also be the person who provides CIRT with access and interpretation of logs.

Systems Administrators

These employees are the "bread-and-butter" individuals responsible for the day-to-day operation of the system, including hardware, software, and employee interaction with the system. Systems administrators should have in-depth knowledge of the function of the system's hardware, operations, and configurations. Depending on the organization, its culture and function, the systems administrators can provide immeasurable assistance to the CIRT.

Telecommunications Specialists

These employees are the ones who are most knowledgeable about the integration of the various components of the telephone and network border systems, including installation, security, configuration, and operation. Systems administrators sometimes perform this function in smaller organizations. These employees have intimate knowledge of the interaction between the various hardware/software components, cabling, telephone lines, PBXs, terminal equipment, routers, firewalls, gateways, and protocols like X.25 or Frame Relay. They are usually responsible for developing relationships with communications carriers including the interaction between the organization and the carrier's equipment.

Database Managers

Most organizations dealing with substantial amounts of data will employ database managers and administrators. These are the employees who have the responsibility of maintaining the integrity of the database; assessing the impact of proposed changes; and in the event of an attack, determining the effects of deletions, modifications, or additions.

Engineers/Software Developers

These employees have knowledge of the system's platforms and applications and how they interact with the hardware. They are the employees that know if the system is running according to design specifications.

System Owners

It is imperative that the systems owners be part of the CIRT, as it is their responsibility to see that the system personnel, data, and facilities are functioning effectively and efficiently. Owners should know the emergency response/recovery plans and their execution. They will be fully aware of backup and restoration procedures as well as equipment redundancies. Ultimately, the owners are responsible to the other stake-holders and will have to answer questions regarding the attack, including its effect on critical assets.

CIRT Management Skills

Possessing well-developed management skills is the single-most desirable attribute the CIRT team leader can have. When a critical incident arrives, it is incumbent on the CIRT manager to ensure the team has the requisite skills, resources, training, experi-ence, motivation, and attitude. Managing a CIRT is not really very different than managing any business unit that is populated by field-specific experts. CIRT managers do not need to have great technical proficiency, but on the other hand, they should have sufficient knowledge to make qualified decisions concerning team priorities and tactical deployments.

Technical Skills

Technical skills are absolutely essential in determining CIRT's efficiency and effective-ness. There is also a matter of the team's credibility. If the team does not earn a reputation for being able to handle emergencies, they will not be contacted for help and no one will listen to their warnings or advice. CIRT's technical skills should span relevant operating systems (UNIX, Linux, Windows, etc.); networking skills; program-ming languages such as C++, PERL, Java, XML, and HTML; and hardware equipment such as firewall appliances, routers, etc. Electrical engineering experience is a plus.

Staffing CIRTs with professionals that have skills in all relevant areas is extremely difficult and expensive. Such employees are going to command high salaries and are probably out of reach of most organizations. If this is not within the organization's budget, find individuals who have expertise in one or more areas and task them to work as a team. Teams, permanent and ad hoc, are composed of employees having key skills that mentor others in developing new skills. Foster a team culture of mutual dependence and spirit, it will pay dividends in the future.

Team Skills

These skills are vital in the CIRT's successful operation. Team skills are focused on:

- Having a common vision of the job to be done
- Division of responsibilities
- Ability of seeing the next item to be done without prompting
- Knowing when to tell and when to ask
- Knowing when the task exceeds an individual's skills resulting in getting help from another team member

Developing team skills is a direct result of management skills, so good managers tend to engender good team skills.

Communication Skills

Team members must be able to cooperate and communicate with coworkers as well as write and deliver effective formal presentations. If there are not employees that have technical writing skills, consider hiring technical writers to supplement team skills. Communications skills are so vital to CIRT's success, that if they are absent it is very possible that no amount of technical ability will compensate.

People Skills

In the event of a critical incident response, people skills are some of the most vital skills in the tool bag. There must be a dedicated team spirit in a CIRT when responding to critical incidents. Tempers, egos, and poor judgment cannot coexist in this type of teamwork environment. Being able to get along with team members as well as serving constituents are key elements in successfully addressing emergencies. At times, technical experts gain reputations as being difficult to work with; consequently, gathering team members with people skills can be challenging. In the arena of responding to critical incidents, team members must be adept at soothing a manager's bruised ego or an embarrassed administrator as they go about their work. Casting disparaging remarks about the employees that are responsible for day-to-day system operation certainly does not gain respect.

Incident Reporting

Along with the policy that potential or suspected critical incidents must be reported to the function-point, organizations must develop a standard for reporting emergencies that must be formalized as part of their response procedure. This procedure should include a standard checklist where critical information is elicited from the person reporting the incident.

Experience Note Do not get excited when fielding a complaint call. Do not request information that really does not have any bearing on the matter at hand; get to the point and collect enough information allowing a requirements assessment to take place and nothing more.

Here is an example of a proposed incident questionnaire:

- Date of the report. Obtain from the person reporting the incident, the time, date, and place the incident was first noticed.
- Duration of the incident. How long did the incident last and what were the indications that something had happened?
- What was the name of the system being attacked?
- Where is the system located?
- What is the operating system and affected applications?
- What was the data stored on the system?
- What was the sensitivity level of the data?
- Provide a detailed description of the incident.
- How widespread is the knowledge of the attack and its details?
- What are the implications of the incident, including adverse effects on the organization?
- Incident reporter's identity, contact information, and emergency contact information for supervisor, senior manager, and system owner.

Incident reporting should be made directly to the organization's function-point that acts as the incident screener and information collector. This employee, or business unit, collects the basic information making a determination whether it should receive a formal CIRT response or be treated as a system anomaly. The information collection form might serve as the front-end of an incident database by tracking their frequency, systems affected, response posture, and improvements.

What Should I Do if I Have Been Hit?

What organizations do in the face of crisis is determined by:

- Type of critical incident
- Its impact
- Anticipated legal actions
- Best way to return to normal operations

In essence, there are two tracks to follow when responding to incidents, one requires careful and detailed coordination where evidence is collected and preserved. The other track is one guided by the overarching philosophy of "let's restore operations as soon as possible and do not worry about evidence."

Response Steps for Legal Actions

In following the "locate and prosecute to the Nth degree" track, these are the basic measures to follow:

- Determine if the emergency is a real incident. This is the most important step for the employee acting as the function-point to take. If there truly is an attack under way, immediate and decisive action is warranted, but if there is merely something developed as a result of a user-error, then administrators should be told to take appropriate action.
- If there is a qualified opinion made by the function-point, terminate attack immediately. The CIRT or a CIRT-directed effort must halt any further damage from occurring to the system's elements. There can be a lot of discussion regarding this step, but the CIRT's actions must be guided by three priorities: personnel, data, and physical facilities. Any attack affecting the confidentiality, integrity, or availability of critical assets must receive immediate attention. Given that terminating an attacker while engaged in a "live" attack will probably result in the loss of amounts of potential evidence, senior managers must decide to create policies that terminate attacks first preserving operations and worry about evidence collection as a secondary matter.
- If there has been a decision to pursue the attacker, with advice of legal counsel, law enforcement authorities must be advised as soon as possible.
- In most cases, law enforcement agencies will not assume responsibility for taking over the emergency. That obligation rests fully with the organization. Rather, officers will work with CIRT members in the investigation and collection of evidence necessary for criminal prosecutions. Depending on the agency and its policies, copies of evidence collected by officers may or may not be provided to the organization's CIRT. Make certain that there are no misunderstandings when officers arrive at the scene.

- For many departments, copies of evidence collected by law officers cannot be provided to the CIRT as a matter of policy. There are many reasons for this policy:
  - Officers collecting evidence can be compelled to testify at civil and administrative hearings where the department does not have an interest.
  - Officers may provide testimony in these proceedings that could later be used to impeach their testimony at criminal proceedings.
  - Departments do not have the resources to provide copies to the organization.
- The collection of evidence for the organization is their responsibility.
- Any legal actions taken or anticipated on the part of the organization should be coordinated with law officers. Failure to do so may have a quelling effect on their criminal prosecution and result in damage to the law officer-organization relationship.
- CIRTs must document each action taken, including the date, time, place, system name, application, operating system, and who participated. Experienced CIRT members often follow the two-employee rule.
- Any action is observed and documented by at least two persons. The reason for the two-person rule is to lessen legal challenges. All notes are considered evidentiary and must be preserved as such.
- Isolate compromised systems from the network. This is one of those initial steps limiting the proliferation of any damage. Taking systems offline is a judgment call on the part of senior managers. Depending on circumstances such as systems redundancy, equipment availability, program availability, and personnel resources, determine if this is a step where affected systems are forensically duplicated and returned to service or not. This is another one of those items to discuss with law enforcement officers as they may wish to collect the forensic copies themselves, and if the organization has qualified employees, they might be directed to create forensic copies and deliver them later to the officers.
- Discover how the attacker gained access to the affected systems. Secure the attacker's access points on all unaffected systems first, then secure the affected systems as a matter of response priorities. It is imperative that the point of attack is discovered and closed. Many times the easiest way to detect the points of entry is to compare the affected systems with "clean" systems.
- There are experts that insist on directing the attacker to a secure system where her attack process can be captured and studied. These processes are frequently known as "honeypots." While honeypots provide a lot of material for study and vulnerability analysis, their value must be weighed very carefully.
- CIRTs must document the state of the compromised systems. Maintaining a system state log is important, memorializing whether the system is in production, offline, ready to be restored to production, or replaced by a redundant system.
- Restore the victim-systems to productivity. After locating the point of entry, compare the attacked systems with the last known system-state unaffected by attacks.

Experience Note Several years ago, attackers successfully invaded systems by exploiting documented vulnerabilities that were unpatched. On gaining unauthorized access, they installed backdoors, then downloaded and updated the systems.

By doing this, they precluded others from invading the same systems. The organization was oblivious to the updates and the attack.

- CIRTs should document their time, resource costs, and expenditures. The cost of responding, restoring, and business resumption can form the damage-basis for civil actions in the way of estimated damages along with the cost of the equipment, revenue losses, and employee-time losses. These accumulated costs can have a significant impact during criminal trials and sentencing. Many jurisdictions establish the degree of culpability, length of sentence, and victim restitution based on costs resulting from the defendant's actions.
- CIRT members must secure all affected systems logs, audits, notes, documentation, and any other relevant evidence created or collected at the time of the incident. The evidence collection process actually has its beginning the moment the attack begins and does not cease until litigation is completed. All evidence must be documented as part of a chain of custody schedule with a copy of this document accompanying evidence-items at all times. Error on the side of caution, evidence should be catalogued on a chain of custody and even the chain of custody schedule is regarded as part of the evidence package.
- After-action briefings. This is the presentation made to senior managers where they are briefed about the incident, effects, CIRT actions, legal actions, restoration, and current systems status. In this briefing, senior managers deliver their views about CIRT's efforts, expectations, and results. At this time, it is common for CIRT's constituents to have their say. This is not the place for injured egos and hurt feelings; CIRTs should consider any and all criticisms or praise in the spirit of accomplishment or improvement.
- Postmortem. The CIRT members including full-timers, part-timers, and ad hoc members attend this meeting. Depending on the sensitivity of the discussions, outsiders who participated in the critical incident response should be in attendance. The purpose of this meeting is for CIRT members to critically analyze their performance and deliverables.

CIRT Success Metrics

The likelihood of totally eliminating attacks from outside or inside the organization is zero. CIRTs are similar to fire departments; they have significant support costs but, when activated, they are literally worth their weight in gold. Consequently, crafting a series of success metrics is usually one that is left to the very last minute. Here are a few suggestions that should be considered during the CIRT creation process:

- How many incidents did the CIRT address in a given time period? (Time periods could be measured in months, quarters, or years.)
- What were the estimated amounts of financial damage averted by CIRT intervention?
- What has been the impression of CIRT's technical expertise with their constituency?
- What is the average time and employee resources needed to address each specific incident type?
- What is the documentation completed by individual CIRT members relative to the actions taken with each incident?
- What recognition or awards were presented to the CIRT?

- Postincident feedback from constituency. Basically, this mechanism is one where a questionnaire form is provided to the victim-business unit and the results compiled by the CIRT as part of their success metrics. Particular emphasis in these questionnaires should be placed on the anonymity of the person completing them, if so desired.
- Were significant changes brought to the organization's policies and procedures suggested by the CIRT as a result of their intercession with a critical incident?

CIRT Development Life Cycle

In various forms, CIRTs have been in existence for more than 20 years. In some cases, they have performed magnificently and made substantial contributions to their organizations; while in other cases, they have foundered and sometimes failed. The levels of CIRT competence and success in the organization are tied to their development life cycle. Consequently, these are the stages of the CIRT life cycle:

- Initiation and proposal. Here is the stage where it all begins. Usually, someone makes a proposal to senior managers testing the idea and follows with a written proposal containing:
  - Necessity studies
  - Plan
  - Resource requirements
  - Structure
  - Lines of reporting and authority
  - Staffing
  - Funding
  - Training needs
  - Deliverables
  - Success metrics

    Often the employee who will serve as the unit manager begins a small ad hoc CIRT team as a pilot program. This allows the organization time to get accustomed to the concept and its execution before submitting a formal proposal. Additionally, if immediate success is realized, it makes selling the proposal much easier if a good reputation is already earned. Most employees have not heard of CIRT in this phase and do not have any expectations, yet.
- Developmental. This phase is marked by the formation of the CIRT. Much of their direction will be guided by what is done at this time. In this phase, staffing is selected or recruited, an infrastructure is created, an office site is established, equipment and tools are procured, funding is allocated, duty rosters are developed ensuring that the function-point is available to screen trouble calls at all hours, policies and procedures applicable to the CIRT are instituted, and the team is advertised as operational.

    At this stage, precedence and reputation are going to be earned. When the fledgling CIRT responds, literally every critical eye will be focused on how it performs, how it interacts with managers, and how it interacts with its constituents. Of all times, this is not the one for judgment errors or other failings. The future of the team hinges on its ability to respond quickly and bring the emergency under control with a satisfactory solution. Failing to define and obtain senior management's approval of operational requirements, drafting deficient policies and procedures, forming meaningless outside liaison contacts, and training is staff poorly can quickly spell doom for the team and its effectiveness. On the other hand, if successful the team can move on to the next stage of development.

■ Establishment. In this phase startup and development problems are resolved. Constituents know when they should notify the CIRT and know what its course of action is when it arrives. In some instances, CIRTs are loaned or contracted to other organizations to assist in critical incidents. Through contracts and mutual assistance agreements, CIRTs may be deployed at business sites belonging to other organizations on a value-added basis. In this fashion, the cost of their existence is somewhat defrayed.

In this phase, senior managers have accepted the CIRT and formally recognized its efforts. At some time in this phase, the organization and team members realize the CIRT's existence is indefinite.

Plans are made for team progress by developing an institutional knowledge base. Team members might be considered promotions, relocation, rotation, or other work assignments. Working with the human resources unit, well-qualified prospective candidates are located and incentives provided, motivating them to consider team membership. The CIRT manager is also anxiously engaged in providing mentors for employees to upgrade training and professional certifications for her employees.

■ Postestablishment. This phase includes the expansion of the team to include operations and requirements not part of any previous phases. Usually these activities include the CIRT providing constituency training, delivering presentations as guest-lecturers, authoring articles for peer-review publications, and substantial research and analysis.

Chapter 5

Legal Matters

Legal Functions: More than Speeding Tickets

It is a well-worn cliché in the Information Age: criminals are on the cutting edge of technology while law enforcement officers are trailing far behind. The truth of the matter is this is not the case. Many venues are connected using state-of-the-art communications networks between individual law officers, their cars, and their precinct offices. At any moment, the officer can observe a license plate, touch the keys on her laptop, connect to the NCIC (National Crime Information Center), determine if the car has been reported stolen, and obtain a criminal history of its registered owner. Private and corporate investigators have advanced skills that allow them to access compromised workstations and servers, create forensic copies of relevant media, and quickly search for incriminating files.

Most law enforcement agencies and many investigators from the private sector are members of or have access to computer crimes task forces composed of officers and analysts from local, state, and federal agencies. Computer crimes task forces allow resource and jurisdiction pooling, so that qualified investigators and analysts are available to collect electronic evidence, analyze it, and provide credible testimony in legal proceedings. These same task forces have developed liaisons with private businesses that permit them to coordinate prevention and investigative efforts. Consequently, task force members are fully aware that evidence is more likely to be found on magnetic media than on multi-column ledger paper.

White-collar criminals have been known to use computer systems to steal an organization's trade secrets and transmit them to waiting competitors using the victim's own e-mail network. Drug dealers use spreadsheet software to track their purchases, assets, earnings, and persons owing them money. Even terrorists use computers to track their targets, financing, training manuals, contacts, and to communicate via the Internet.

Experience Note When the news broke about the "Beltway Snipers," John Allen Muhammad and Lee Malvo, there was a significant amount of press interest focused on the laptop computer stolen from a patron at a pizza parlor. It was reported that Muhammad and Malvo had kept a rolling journal, documenting their shootings, locations, and other crimes on the laptop.

In fact, one common definition of computer crime is criminal acts facilitated in any way by computers and computer-related equipment. Using computer networks can provide criminals and others with low-cost, easy access to victims and the means by which they can conceal their acts. Regardless of the degree of computer involvement in unlawful behavior, investigators must not forget their basic evidence collection training and guard against becoming overwhelmed by the magnitude of technical aspects relating to electronic evidence. Investigations of unlawful or abusive acts must be conducted with deliberation and good judgment.

The difference between investigating an ordinary unlawful act and one facilitated by technical equipment is very little when reduced to its basic doctrine: the investigator's skill in collecting and managing evidence and delivering credible testimony. It does not matter whether the investigation supports criminal, civil, or administrative actions; handling evidence must follow the same careful and deliberate process.

If electronic evidence is properly collected, analyzed, preserved, and followed by credible testimony, most legal challenges of alteration and mishandling can be avoided. In short, investigators must exercise a sound understanding of procedures and laws while preserving individual rights.

Experience Note Investigators wishing to avoid legal challenges to their testimony will collect evidence in accordance with established policies and procedures. Further, as a matter of procedure, they avoid engaging in evidence collection practices that exceed their training and experience.

Investigators are aware of the extreme volatility of digital evidence and the importance of not changing its content by even one bit if they intend to deliver credible testimony. Evidence collection is not the time for experimentation or guesswork.

Opposing attorneys will pounce on an investigator's lack of training and experience, using seemingly brutal examination tactics to discredit or detect weakness in testimony. For example, under vigorous examination at a deposition, an investigator can usually count on being questioned relative to experience delivering a forensically sound copy of the target media. If the investigator cannot recount her training, practices, and correct procedures, every question will focus attention on her inadequacies to the detriment of her credibility.

Investigators' Goals

In conducting an investigation, the goals of investigators, whether corporate or private, or law enforcement agents, are basically the same. They focus on professionally and legally collecting evidence. If the evidence is not collected within legal constraints, it is not admissible in legal proceedings, and any information derived from tainted evidence is going to be excluded. Books, movies, and television stories often do not accurately depict the process. If an officer or corporate investigator violates the law, regulations, or even the organization's policies, the investigator may be prosecuted and sued into oblivion, and any evidence collected or viewed is worthless.

Experience Note Law enforcement officers and those acting under the direction of law enforcement have a special burden because they may be sued for violating someone's rights in their evidence-searching efforts. Consequently, they might be held civilly liable for their acts under the legal decision *Bivens v. Six*

Unknown Federal Narcotics Agents, 403 U.S. 388, (1971). Briefly, this is a civil case where the civil petitioner, Bivens (plaintiff) alleged that agents of the Federal Bureau of Narcotics (unnamed defendants) acted under color of federal authority when they searched his apartment without a warrant and arrested him. Bivens was allegedly subjected to humiliation, embarrassment, and mental suffering and further alleged the agents had exercised unreasonable force. He sought $15,000 in the way of damages from each one of the agents. After hearing the matter, the U.S. Supreme Court decided the agents were not immune from civil action and that the petitioner was entitled to recover money damages for any injuries he suffered resulting from the agents violation of his Fourth Amendment rights.

Common Types of Unlawful Acts

In many cases, computer crimes do not involve attacks in the popular sense. Most administrators tend to think of system attacks originating with someone gaining access to a system by breaching outside fortifications. The truth of the matter is that most successful attacks are "inside jobs." The exact numbers depend on the survey or data, but they all state that the most successful and devastating attacks originate within the target organization. Employees, contractors, and former employees use their knowledge of the employer's systems to gain unauthorized access and wreak havoc. Often these acts include theft or denial-of-service attacks, destruction or modification of sensitive data, trafficking in software piracy, and theft of trade secrets and intellectual property. Following is a list of terms with which you should be familiar:

> **Espionage:** Collection and analysis of illicitly obtained information.
>
> **Trade secret:** Plan, concept, prototype, information, or property that has value by providing a business advantage over competitors who do not have the secret.
>
> **Corporate espionage:** Theft of trade secrets for economic gain.
>
> **Intellectual property:** Any product of the human intellect that is unique or novel, having some value in the marketplace. Patent, copyright, trademark, service mark, or trade secret protects intellectual property.
>
> **Cyber terrorism:** Unlawful use of force against persons or property to intimidate a government or a civilian population in furtherance of political or social objectives. Acts of terrorism usually have the goal of disrupting the public's faith in their institutions.
>
> **Economic espionage:** Illicit collection of information, sponsored by a foreign government for economic advantage.

Copyrights, Trademarks, Service Marks, Patents, and Trade Secrets Comprising Intellectual Property

Copyright protection is the means by which authors establish their rights of ownership in a fixed tangible medium of expression.* Authors may transfer their ownership rights

---

* More information is available at http://www.loc.gov/copyright/title17/92chap1.html and www4.law.cornell.edu/uscode/17.

to third-party owners, or it is possible that authors do not establish ownership because of contractual arrangements where the work is created by an author but owned by someone else. By copyright, an owner has basically five exclusive rights of the copyrighted work including:

1. *Right of reproduction.* The work's owner has the exclusive right to determine duplication, transcription, and imitations of the work.
2. *Right of modification.* The work's owner has the exclusive right to modify the work, thereby creating a new work. Legally, a work that is a modification of an original work is known as a derivative work.
3. *Right of distribution.* This is the right to determine the distribution of copies, including derivative works, to the public by sale, leasing, lending, or rental.
4. *Right of public performance.* This is the right to play, dance, recite, act, or display the work at public places, and to transmit the work to the public. In the case of audiovisual works such as movies, showing a movie is considered a public display.
5. There is a connected right called the *Right of public display* where the copyright owner has the right to control the showing of a copy of the work directly or by means of film or electronic transmission.

The copyright owner's rights are subject to a number of legal exceptions and limitations giving others the right to make limited use of a copyrighted item. Here are a few of the major exceptions:

- *Ideas and concepts.* Copyright laws only protect against the taking of a protected work's "expression" in an unauthorized fashion. Copyright does not include the copyrighted work's processes, procedures, ideas, concepts, discoveries, and methods of operation.
- *Originality.* A work's facts are not considered protected under copyright. Regardless of the measure of effort expended by the author or owner, copyright protects the work's originality only.
- *Separate and independent creation.* Copyright does not protect a work where someone else working independently creates an exact duplicate of a copyrighted work. Independent creation of an analogous, exact duplicate, or similar work does not violate the owner's rights.
- *Fair use of copyrighted works.* Using works under fair use is limited to criticism, news reporting, teaching, comment, scholarship, and research. Such use is not considered an infringement of the work's copyright. By virtue of the copyright, a work's owner is deemed to have consented to the use of their works by others within fair-use constraints.

Works that Can Be Copyrighted

Copyright laws protect the rights of ownership, grouping works into the following general categories:

- Literary works, which may consist of novels, nonfiction works, poetry, newspaper articles, magazines and magazine articles, computer software, software documentation, applicable software manuals, catalogs, training manuals, manuals, advertisements, and brochures
- Dramatic pieces such as plays, theater productions, and operas

- Musical works such as songs and instrumentals
- Movies and other audiovisual pieces, including movies, training films, documentaries, television programs, news programs, movie and television advertisements, video games, and interactive productions
- Choreographic works such as ballet, dances, and mime
- Graphic, pictorial, and sculptural works such as paintings, drawings, photographs, posters, works of fine art, display advertisements, graphic art productions, cartoon characters, statues, and toys
- Architectural works including building designs, plans, drawings, and the building itself

Copyright Protection

Interestingly, copyright protection arises automatically when an original work is marked with a tangible medium of expression. Registering the work with the Copyright Office is optional but must be completed before an infringement suit is filed. Copyright marking may take any of these forms:

- The symbol © followed by a date and name
- The word "Copyright" followed by a date and name
- The abbreviation "Copr" followed by a date and name

Duration of Copyright Protection

Currently, the effective term for copyrighted works created by individuals is the life of the author plus an additional 70 years. The period of copyright protection applying to works for hire is 95 years from the date of publication or 120 years from the date of first publication, whichever date is sooner.

Copyright Infringement

Copyright infringement is basically defined as violating any of the exclusive rights granted to the copyrighted work's owner. Copyright owners can recover actual and punitive damages resulting from infringement as well as reporting violations considered criminal. Federal district courts have the power to restrain infringers and order the seizure (impoundment) and destruction of illicit copies. Disputes over copyright ownership are civil matters and are settled through legal proceedings.

Criminal Actions in Copyright Cases

Federal criminal laws address copyright infringers, who may be prosecuted under 17 U.S. Code 506 and 18 U.S. Code 2319. Elements of these laws include any person infringing a copyright for the purpose of commercial or private gain by the reproduction or distribution of copyrighted works having a total retail value of more than $1,000.

Title 17, Section 506 specifies that evidence of a person involved in the reproduction or distribution of a copyrighted work is not sufficient to establish willful infringement.

Experience Note Judging from the criminal matters that have been prosecuted and adjudicated, there appears to be a need for financial gain motive before prosecution will move forward.

Criminal Copyright Forfeiture

Individuals who are criminally convicted for copyright violations may suffer additional punishment under legal provisions, including the forfeiture and destruction or other disposition of all infringing copies (more statute information is available at case-law.lp.findlaw.com/scripts/ts_search.pl?title=17&sec=506 and caselaw.lp.findlaw.com/scripts/ts_search.pl?title=18&sec=2319).

Resolving copyright matters is accomplished by civilly suing the defendants with the objective of financial settlement and criminal prosecution.

Works that Cannot Be Copyrighted

Works created by federal government employees as part of their official duties cannot be protected by copyright. For this reason, policies, procedures, laws, discussions, presentations, and related items originating with government agencies are not protected as copyrighted works. Consequently, these works are usually considered part of the public domain. Federal government employees may copyright works they produce on their own time but not those done as part of their official duties. Further, employees of state and local governments may copyright works they produce as part of their official duties.

Trademarks and Service Marks Protection

Trademarks and service marks are words, symbols, or other unique devices used by manufacturers to identify their goods and services, distinguishing them from similar goods and services sold by others. Trademarks are customarily used for goods, while service marks are used for services. When registered, they may not be used or displayed without consent of the mark's owner.

Trademarks and service marks are protected under the federal trademark statute, known as the Lanham Act.*

Criminal Prosecution for Trafficking in Counterfeit Goods or Services

Under the provisions of 18 U.S. Code 2320, it is prohibited for a person or persons to traffic in goods or services that are identified by identical or substantially indistinguishable marks registered with the U.S. Patent and Trademark Office. This law protects the mark's owners from those that would produce like or similar marks for their goods and services.**

Anyone criminally convicted for this crime, depending on the facts and circumstances, could receive a maximum prison sentence of not more than 10 years and a fine of not more than $2 million; if there are defendants acting together other than an individual (such as a business), then the fine could go as high as $5 million.

Protected Works

There are many types of trademarks that can be protected; for example, "Dell" is a registered trademark of Dell Computer Corporation, "IBM" is the registered trademark for International Business Machines Corporation, etc. Sounds, jingles, and shapes can

---

* Available at http://www.law.cornell.edu/topics/trademark.html.
** More information is available at caselaw.lp.findlaw.com/scripts/ts_search.pl?title=18&sec=2319.

also be registered as trademarks; for example, the music introducing the "Today Show," the shape of the Coca Cola bottle, or the Bar and Shield logo for Harley-Davidson Motorcycles.

Trademark protection is extendable to words, names, symbols, or unique devices distinguishing the goods and services offered by an owner from those offered by others. Basically, a trademark identifying a class of goods or services distinguishing the class of goods or services is not going to qualify for protection. Trademarks and service marks must apply to specific goods or services and not general classes. For example, the word "fishing rods" describes a class of instrument used for catching fish, where "Browning fly-rod" distinguishes the manufacturer and type of fishing rod.

Trademark and Service Mark Protection

Trademark and service mark protection is obtained by filing a registration application with the U.S. Patent Office.*

Protection under federal law is applicable to marks actually used, or intended to be used, in interstate commerce. In the case of federally registered trademarks or service marks, the use of public mark registration notice is optional. Registered trademark owners may provide symbolic or other type of notice indicating their trademark is registered by displaying the words, "Registered in the U.S. Patent and Trademark Office" or by merely displaying the ® symbol.

Trademark and service mark rights in the case of a federal registration can last indefinitely, provided the owner continues to use the mark on or in connection with goods or services and files the necessary documentation with the U.S. Patent and Trademark Office. Registration forms and filing times for marks are available at the U.S. Patent Office Web site.**

Federal trademark and service mark registrations actually remain in effect for 10 years, on the condition that an affidavit of continued commercial use is filed with the U.S. Patent and Trademark Office in the sixth year of the registration. Mark registrations may be renewed for an indefinite amount of 10-year terms, provided the mark continues to be in commercial use.

Trademark and Service Mark Ownership

Owning a registered mark provides several protections to owners:

- Exclusive commercial and private use of marks identifying specific goods and services as belonging to a particular organization or person
- Notice to the public of the mark's ownership
- Ability to enforce the mark's ownership through civil action in federal district court
- Use of the federal registration as a basis to obtain registration in foreign countries
- Use to file the U.S. registration with the U.S. Customs Service to prevent importation of infringing marks

---

* Available at http://www.uspto.gov.
** Available at http://www.uspto.gov/web/offices/tac/doc/basic.

Public Notification

Any time claims are made to a mark, the symbols ™ or ˢᴹ may be used to alert the public to the mark's claim, registered or not. However, the ® symbol may only be used after the mark is officially registered and only with goods and services listed in the federal trademark registration.

Internet Domain Names and Registered Marks

Domain names are the mechanism by which many private and open-ended computer systems function. Forming a computer network requires two basic elements: two or more computers connected together, and a common language or protocol allowing them to exchange information. Domain names are important to information providers because they deliver a user-easy name instead of the only-numbers method of connecting information seekers to information providers.

In short, regardless of the nature of the system, information cannot be exchanged easily through e-mail, newsgroups, instant messaging services, chat rooms, or the Web without domain names. Procuring a domain name for the Internet is as basic as contacting a registration authority (commonly known as a domain name registrar), determining that the desired domain name is not already registered, filing a domain name registration application, and paying the registration fee. Registration ensures that only one party can "own" the domain name at a time. And as long as the registrant pays the registration fees, he will continue to own that domain name indefinitely.

In the world of the Internet, if the information provider is a commercial entity, then its domain name will be significantly more effective if it is the same or similar to its registered marks. However, often it is discovered that someone has registered a domain name that corresponds to a business' trademark, preventing the business from owning it. What recourse does a business have when discovering that its domain name is unavailable for ownership or use? Should there be a regulation or law allowing the trademark owner to own a domain name corresponding to its trademark when it has been registered to someone else?

Acquiring exclusive trademark rights is as simple as using the trademark in commerce. Using trademarks or service marks, without registration, entitles users to common law trademark ownership. This type of trademark right extends only to the market boundaries where the mark's owner has actually used the mark.

Owners can obtain broader ownership rights by registering marks with the U.S. Patent and Trademark Office where the mark's exclusive use in a broad marketplace is guaranteed by federal registration.

Primarily, trademark rights are granted to protect the public from confusion about goods and services sold in the marketplace. Consequently, if it is discovered that someone other than the trademark's owner is using a trademark, causing confusion in the marketplace, the owner is able to file suit for infringement. An interesting case develops when similar trademarks are used for different goods or similar trademarks are used in separate geographical areas. Here, it is supposed there exists a small chance the public will be confused; consequently, both trademarks may be used simultaneously.

With the Internet, registered and unregistered marks change in a way that could not have existed a few years ago. Because the Internet allows virtually anyone to access goods, products, and services spanning all types of trade channels, it is possible there exists a significant degree of confusion between Porsche automobiles and Porsche umbrellas.

Cybersquatters

Enter the cybersquatters as factors in domain registration. These are people who register trademarks as a domain name for the purpose of selling it to the owner of the trademark. They have little, if any, intention of using the domain name in commerce. Many organizations and businesses have paid significant amounts of money to buy domain names containing their trademarks from cybersquatters who registered the domain name before the rightful owners were able to do so. Domain name registrars simply do not require registrants to show that there is any connection to the specific domain name. For example, in 1998, Compaq paid about $3 million for the domain name "Altavista.com" that was registered to someone other than Compaq, according to the *Wall Street Journal,* July 29, 1998.

Cybersquatting is generally identified by two basic elements:

1. Presence of a unique and famous trademark
2. Registration of a related domain name

In the event these cybersquatting elements are not present, a traditional trademark infringement assessment is pursued, looking at the uniqueness of the trademark to:

- Determine if the domain name is being used as a trademark or service mark
- Determine if the mark is legally protected
- Determine if the registered domain name results in a likelihood of consumer confusion between the domain name and the mark

There are organizations and famous individuals that choose to fight rather than pay for their namesake. For example, Panavision International was one of the first companies to sue and successfully prevail against a cybersquatter for diluting their trademark (*Panavision International, L.P. v. Toepen,* 141 F.3d 1316, 9th Circuit, 1998).

Cybersquatter-Victim Protection

With potential confusion looming about domain names and mark owners, there are two avenues to address cybersquatters: the *Anticybersquatting Consumer Protection Act,* 15 U.S. Code 1125.*

Administratively, domain name conflict resolutions can be affected through the ICANN (Internet Corporation for Assigned Names and Numbers) and their Uniform Domain Dispute Resolution Policy, available at icann.org/udrp/udrp.htm.

In the Anticybersquatting Act signed into law in November 1999, there is a means to predicate civil actions charging defendants with trademark infringement when domain names are in dispute. A mark's owner, the plaintiff, must prove that the cybersquatter registering the domain name infringed on the mark's owner and exhibited bad faith, intending to profit from the domain registration's sale. Elements that support bad faith on the part of the cybersquatter are:

- Determine any intellectual property rights the domain name registrant has with regard to the domain name

---

* The full text of this law is available at caselaw.lp.findlaw.com/casecode/uscodes/15/chapters/22/sub-chapters/iii/sections/section_1125.html.

- Determine the use of the domain name in the sale of goods or services on the part of the registrant
- Determine the domain name owner's intention to divert consumers from the plaintiff's Web site
- Determine the domain name owner's intention to dilute or tarnish the value of the trademark by confusing consumers
- Determine domain name registrant's efforts to sell or assign the domain name for financial gain without having used it for bona fide purposes

In 1999, ICANN approved the Uniform Domain Name Dispute Resolution Policy providing a procedure for resolving domain name disputes. This is an administrative procedure and not a judicial one. To be successful, complainants must:

- Identify how the domain name is identical or sufficiently confusing with respect to the mark in question
- Identify that the domain name owner has no legitimate interest in the name
- Identify why the domain name should be considered as having been registered in bad faith

All domain name registration agencies are bound by this policy, and all registrants agree when applying to register a domain name or renewing a domain name registration. The domain name registrant warrants or agrees to the following:

- Information made in the Registration Agreement is complete and accurate
- Domain name registration will not infringe upon or otherwise violate the rights of any third party
- Domain name is not being registered for any unlawful purpose
- Domain name registration is not in violation of applicable laws or regulations
- It is the responsibility of the registrant to determine if the domain name registration infringes or violates another's rights

The Uniform Domain Name Dispute Resolution Policy considers bad faith registration as the registration of the domain name primarily for the purpose of selling, renting, or transferring the domain name to the trademark's owner. Administration of this dispute policy is usually completed in roughly six weeks with fees approximating $1000. If the complainant is successful, the domain name registrar (domain name registration agency) will either disconnect the domain name or transfer it to the complainant.

Complainants must allege facts and circumstances focused in the following areas:

- The domain name in question is identical or confusingly similar to a trademark or service mark in which the complainant has legitimate rights
- The domain name registrant has no rights with respect to the domain name
- The domain name has been registered and is being used in bad faith

Victims of cybersquatting can select between remedies based in federal civil law and those administered by ICANN. Actions filed under the Anticybersquatting Act permit victims to sue defendants for infringement, unfair competition, and mark dilution. Remedies available under this law include but are not limited to:

- Actual damages
- Punitive damages

- Attorney's fees
- Injunction against defendants pending the resolution of claims

ICANN's Domain Name Dispute Policy provides a measure of conflict resolution by canceling the registrant's domain name or transferring the domain name to the successful claimant. Of course, the resolution must be supported by evidence before the arbitration board. ICANN's policy process is significantly more economical and expedient than civil actions filed under the federal statute and yet does not preclude future legal action against the domain name registrant.*

Patent Protections

Patents are issued only by the U.S. Patent and Trademark Office, as individual states are prohibited from granting them. Patents are basically property rights delivered to an invention's owner. In the language of the Patent Act is the grant of ownership providing for the ability to exclude others from making, using, offering for sale, or selling the invention in the United States or importing similar inventions to the United States.**

Patent laws protecting inventions are known as utility patents, while ornamental designs for articles of manufacture are known as design patents. Utility patents include any new and useful processes, machine, manufacture, or composition of an item or any new useful improvement.

Inventions may be electrical, mechanical, biological, or chemical. Internet-related inventions such as interfaces, networking protocols, information retrieval methods, and encryption might be protected by utility patents.

Qualifications for Design Patents

In order to be granted a design patent, the invention must be new, original, and ornamental. Design patents are limited to the ornamental appearance of an item and little more.

Qualifications for Utility Patents

Utility patents are granted for inventions that are new, useful, and not obvious. To qualify for registration, the invention must be unknown or used by others in the United States before a patent may be granted. Utility patents are granted for unique devices that add to the public's knowledge and are useful to society. Inventions must be sufficiently distinct from currently existing technology and must not be obvious to a person of ordinary skill in the invention's field.

"Firstest with the Mostest"

The inventor who actually invents the claimed item, not the inventor who files first for the patent, becomes the patent owner. This is a significant departure from many

---

* A current listing of domain name registrars is available at http://www.icann.org/registrars/accredited-list.html.

** Information and details about patents are contained in the Patent Act (http://www.law.cornell.edu/patent/patent.overview.html).

other countries that have the first-to-patent rule granting the patent to the first inventor to file for an invention's patent.

Utility patents are difficult to obtain in the United States. If an invention meets the levels of uniqueness, usefulness, and lack of obviousness, a patent may not be granted if the invention was described more than a year before the actual patent application date. This also applies to inventions in public use or sale in the United States for more than one year before the patent application date.

Filing for Patent Protection

Before filing a patent, there are several considerations that should be made. Although individuals without specialized training and experience can file a patent application, the process is expensive and time consuming, generally taking upwards of two years or more. In applying for patents, it is highly recommended that patent attorneys and patent agents (persons who have passed Patent Office examinations) are used in the process to avoid pitfalls and unnecessary delays.

Patent Ownership

Patent owners have the right to exclude others from manufacturing, selling or offering for sale, using, or importing a similar item to the United States. This exclusive ownership has a term of the patent. Anyone who violates these ownership rights is deemed an infringer.

Patent Terms

Current laws allow utility patents to be granted for a period of 20 years from the date the patent's application was filed.

Patent Validity

Patents might be subject to legal challenges based on infringement allegations. Infringement suits question the patent's validity by alleging the patented invention was not sufficiently novel or not obvious or belongs to someone else.

Trade Secrets

Trade secrets are basically defined as information that is valuable and maintained as secret. To qualify as trade secrets, information must be preserved as secret by the owner having taken reasonable steps to keep it from general knowledge.

Protected Trade Secrets

These are some types of business and technical information that are protected by trade secret laws:

> ... the term *trade secret* means all forms and types of financial, business, scientific, technical, economic, or engineering information, including patterns, plans, compilations, program devices, formulas, designs, prototypes, methods, techniques, processes, procedures, programs, or codes, whether tangible or

intangible, and whether (or how) stored, compiled, or memorialized physically, electronically, graphically, photographically, or in writing.

— 18 U.S. Code 1839

There is also a necessity of being the trade secret's owner and taking reasonable steps in keeping the information a secret:

> the owner thereof has taken reasonable measures to keep such information secret; and (B) the information derives independent economic value, actual or potential, from not being generally known to, and not being readily ascertainable through proper means by, the public; and (4) the term "owner," with respect to a trade secret, means the person or entity in whom or in which rightful legal or equitable title to, or license in, the trade secret is reposed.

— 18 U.S. Code 1839*

There are generally some factors that are considered to determine whether or not information qualifies as a trade secret:

- Extent to which the secret is known outside the owner's business
- Extent to which the secret is known by the owner's employees
- Specific measures taken by the owner guarding the information's secrecy
- Value of the secret to the secret's owner and the owner's competitors
- Ease at which the secret could be acquired from the secret's owner

There are two federal criminal statutes that apply to the theft of trade secrets; one applies to the theft of trade secrets by a foreign government or its agents (18 U.S. Code 1831),** and the other applies to the theft of trade secrets by individuals and their co-conspirators (18 U.S. Code 1832).*** In both statutes, the theft of trade secrets is contingent upon the following elements:

- Whether the entity stealing the trade secret is a foreign government or an individual
- Whether the trade secret is stolen by means of theft, copied, destroyed, etc.
- Whether the trade secret is received by an individual or foreign government
- In the case of trade secret theft (18 U.S. Code 1832), whether the trade secret is produced or included in a product placed in interstate or foreign commerce

Criminal Forfeiture

Individuals convicted of violating either of these trade secret criminal statutes can suffer the forfeiture of property connected with both of these laws (18 U.S. Code 1834):

> The court, in imposing sentence on a person for a violation of this chapter, shall order, in addition to any other sentence imposed, that the person forfeit to the United States

---

* The exact language of this statute defining trade secrets may be found at caselaw.lp.findlaw.com/scripts/ts_search.pl?title=18&sec=1839.

** Available at caselaw.lp.findlaw.com/scripts/ts_search.pl?title=18&sec=1831.

*** Available at caselaw.lp.findlaw.com/scripts/ts_search.pl?title=18&sec=1832.

(1) any property constituting, or derived from, any proceeds the person obtained, directly or indirectly, as the result of such violation; and

(2) any of the person's property used, or intended to be used, in any manner or part, to commit or facilitate the commission of such violation, if the court in its discretion so determines, taking into consideration the nature, scope, and proportionality of the use of the property in the offense.

(b) Property subject to forfeiture under this section, any seizure and disposition thereof, and any administrative or judicial proceeding in relation thereto, shall be governed by section 413 of the Comprehensive Drug Abuse Prevention and Control Act of 1970 (21 U.S. Code 853), except for subsections (d) and (j) of such section, which shall not apply to forfeitures under this section.*

Obtaining Trade Secrets Protection

Trade secrets protection automatically attaches when the information belonging to the owner is kept secret. Secret owners are not required to register or notify anyone with regard to their information. Trade secrets' owners have the right to see that civil and criminal actions are leveled at misappropriating or unauthorized use of their trade secret. Trade secrets protection, under the law, lasts as long as the owner engages in security measures protecting it from general knowledge. However, the owner loses protection if she fails to take reasonable steps to keep the trade secret concealed.

Interestingly, discovery of trade secret information by means of independent research or by means of reverse engineering is not legally considered theft or misappropriation. On another note, if an employee leaves her employment with knowledge of trade secrets, and does not have any binding agreements barring her disclosure of the protected information, then she may disclose it to her new employer.

Fraud in the Workplace

There are many surveys where American workers have been polled with results showing that they estimate their employers lose from 8 to 20 percent of every revenue-dollar to fraud in the workplace. Specific fraudulent acts were:

- Theft of office items
- Excessive expense accounts
- Theft of inventory
- Claiming extra hours that were not actually worked
- Accepting kickbacks from suppliers
- Embezzlement
- Employers skimming untaxed and unaccounted money
- Falsely representing financial information to stakeholders

Employees are likely to have an intimate knowledge of the organization's assets, disposition, procedures regarding accountability, and means by which such checks can be circumvented. They are members of the system and have the ability to plan

---

* Full information can be found at caselaw.lp.findlaw.com/scripts/ts_search.pl?title=18&sec=1834.

and execute dishonest acts that can effectively remain undetected. Insidiously, workplace fraud uses the resources of the organization to steal from it.

Experience Note Often, fraudsters maintain meticulous records of their misdeeds on the very workstations and servers owned by the victim of their crimes.

Fraud committed within the business is easily done through indirect means, and for that reason, it is extremely difficult to detect. Employees are trusted to make discretionary decisions in ways that auditing and management are unable to detect. For example, an accounts payable manager authorizes the purchase of supplies from a company owned by herself and her brother. Of course, she is not stealing directly from her employer, but the company is not likely receiving the best price for their money. The company loses money, the employee gains, and the misdeed is probably never going to be detected.

Experience Note The spectrum of unlawful and unethical employee actions (committed by all levels of employees) is only limited by the employee's imagination.

Employee Fraud Controls

As in all matters concerning critical assets, prevention is much better than cure. Detecting fraud and punishing those responsible tends to be expensive and time consuming. Lying in wait for employees to commit some unlawful deed, then punishing them, is a procedure that destroys morale and disrupts legitimate business activities. Developing mechanisms and cultures to ensure that employees act ethically from the outset will go a long way in preventing fraud.

Management Functions in Fraud Control

Management sets the example of workplace behavior and fraud prevention. If managers do nothing to prevent, detect, and control fraud, no one else will either. The traditional methods of fraud control such as auditing and internal controls are capable of detecting only a portion of unlawful employee acts. Consequently, fraud prevention is an outgrowth of management conduct and perception. Managers are responsible for creating an organizational culture of integrity. If the rules are enforced equally with clear responsibilities, accountabilities, and adequate records, then the basic platform exists where employees are able to do the right thing, provided they want to do the right thing.

Experience Note Locks exist to keep honest people honest.

There must be clear avenues for fraudulent acts to be reported. Whistleblowers must be supported to provide accurate and truthful information. Managers should draft policies and procedures where exposing fraud receives tangible bonuses, sending a clear message that fraud will be not be tolerated.

Accountability

In business procedures, it is essential to identify the employee responsible for specific tasks and to whom the employee reports. Accordingly, the manager must be held accountable for her staff's performance. In this fashion, whether something goes right or goes wrong, the responsible employees are known.

Records

Records are an important part of accountability. Organizations must have the requirement of maintaining adequate records of all significant acts permitting the reconstruction of decision processes. Unless such records are generated and maintained, it may not be clear who has performed certain actions, the criteria on which the action is based, and who is responsible. The existence of adequate records provides avenues for review and auditing as well as deterring employees who might otherwise regard themselves free from accountability.

Evidence, Its Collection, Preservation, Analysis, and Introduction at Trial

For the record, what is evidence, anyway? All types of legal matters are pursued based on the amount of available evidence. Evidence is defined as something physical and testimonial, material to an act. In order to pursue any legal action, administrative, civil or criminal, there needs to be a sufficiency of evidence supporting an allegation or complaint.

Evidence is something that must be collected in order to prove an event actually happened. The process by which evidence is collected usually follows one or more of these methods:

- Obtained by means of witness examination or deposition
- Obtained by means of interview or interrogation
- Obtained by means of conducting an inspection
- Obtained by means of legal discovery
- Surrendered to an investigator
- Through a search where authorized consent was obtained
- Obtained through the execution of search warrants
- Obtained by means of legal search without a search warrant
- Through court order or summons
- Obtained through a grand jury subpoena
- Obtained by means of a judicial subpoena

Evidence collection is a science governed by laws and regulations and refined by the courts. Unlike some movies and television shows, investigators, law enforcement authorities, and private investigators cannot legally enter into a room or an office uninvited, without a search warrant, and begin rifling through desks and cabinets, and downloading computers. Acts such as these hold our attention, but have dire consequences for the investigators and their evidence. The reason is simple. The evidence that is seen, seized, or derived from an unlawful search and seizure is considered "fruits of a poisonous tree" and will be excluded from any legal proceedings. In addition to having the evidence excluded from the case, investigators and possibly their managers or departments will be fired and sued into oblivion.

As a matter of course, investigators and attorneys have to answer this question with electronic evidence collection: Do the investigators have the right and authority to search and seize the computer, its contents and media, and search the surrounding area? An organization's policies and procedures likely grant this right. If employees understand and acknowledge that they do not have a reasonable expectation of privacy in the workplace, then the investigator's job is relatively simple. However, even with regard to employees that have waived their reasonable expectation of privacy, it is possible that they might have reserved their right to privacy by exchanging private e-mail, using instant messaging, or installing personal software. If their employer failed to take sufficient steps to discover and preclude these prohibited practices, it may be possible that a reasonable expectation of privacy exists. In such cases, investigators might find they cannot routinely search an employee's workstation, office, or e-mail stored on the company's servers. Regardless, investigators still must be very careful and consult with legal counsel before entering an office or equipment room and begin to search or seize evidence.

The Cost of Computer Crime

What does a computer crime cost? This is not an easy question to answer. If a Web page of a brick-and-mortar business such as a lumber store is attacked and taken offline, the damage will be significantly different than the damage suffered by a bookseller that does business exclusively online. There are many reasons that organizations should consider estimating the cost of damages inflicted as a result of unlawful or abusive behavior impacting their IT resources:

- Recovery of damages from the criminals and other types of unlawful behavior
- Recovery of damages from malicious employees, contractors, and former employees
- Criminal prosecution
- Administrative actions such as employee suspensions, censures, and dismissals

One generally accepted loss concept is that of calculating the actual financial impact of repairing the damage and restoring the system. These are relatively simple numbers to capture; however, when considering the damage resulting from lost reputation in the marketplace, things become more difficult. What about costs resulting from marketing to recover that reputation? And, what about missed sales opportunities? Can lost employee productivity be captured and calculated as damages? These are issues that are not clearly defined in the law and, for the most part, there is not much in the way of case law.

Challenging these questionable losses is addressed under the legal concept of "proximate causation." In effect, this means that if the loss of a sales opportunity was directly attributable to an attack, it would be more material to the organization's losses than if the organization's market reputation were damaged as a result of the attack. It is a matter of evidence showing that financial losses were a direct result of unlawful acts.

Estimating the damages resulting from the theft of trade secrets and intellectual property is also a point of legal contention. Arriving at the value of combinations of tangibles and intangibles is challenging. Including the costs of research and development, and calculating the cost of the trade secret is fairly simple; but what of the potential profits realized as a result of the product being released? How are those revenues estimated?

One of the most successful methods is that of licensing fees. If a competitor received stolen intellectual property or trade secret information that she otherwise would have needed to license before using, then the loss is the amount of the licensing fee and profits realized by the competitor directly attributable to the stolen information.

Effectively, corporations have four basic options that might be pursued when they have been victimized by attacks:

1. Conduct an internal investigation with the goal of pursuing civil action against the attacker.
2. Conduct an internal investigation with the goal of pursuing administrative action by dismissing, censuring, or suspending the offending employee.
3. Report unlawful acts to law enforcement authorities, thereby complying with applicable laws and regulations.
4. Do nothing hoping that legal and regulatory authorities and stakeholders do not discover the attack.

There are many reasons not to report an attack:

■ Loss of share price
■ Embarrassment
■ Senior managers may fear dismissal

Many companies choose not to report unlawful acts because the business may find itself incurring substantial legal expenses with little to show for it. Some senior managers have the attitude that if an attacker gains unauthorized entry, even many times, he will likely receive a minimum sentence without monetary fines. While this might be the case, they ignore the opportunities of publishing the attacker's apprehension and punishment. Further, they can present civil actions against the attacker and obtain sizable penalties, publicizing the fact that attackers are going to receive vigorous prosecution. The objective of such legal actions is to convince other potential attackers that the named organization is not going to stand still for being attacked.

Challenges mount and attitudes are forced to change when a company discovers regulations and laws requiring the reporting of suspicious or material events:

■ Publicly traded corporations are required to report material events affecting their business operations.
■ Publicly traded corporations are required to safeguard assets at the risk of being sued by government agencies and stakeholders.
■ Financial institutions, insured by federal insurance agencies, are required to report suspicious activities within 30 days of their discovery.

Title 18 U.S. Code Section 4 requires reporting of crimes over which the United States government has jurisdiction, by individuals who have knowledge. Failing to do so can result in felony prosecutions.

Criminal Law

Criminal acts are those acts offending society as a whole. Should an individual be the victim of a criminal act, it is deemed to be a criminal act against society. Interestingly, it is possible that criminal acts may also form the basis for civil suits. So the offender may suffer a criminal sentence for violating criminal statutes and may be sued, resulting in financial awards for victims. Criminal laws are found on federal, state, and local levels with many overlapping one another, resulting in jurisdiction controversies.

The primary distinction between criminal law and civil law is the degree and type of punishment. Criminal laws vary widely in their penalties, including fines, restitution, asset forfeiture, incarceration, and supervised probation. Because the nature of criminal punishment is so potentially devastating, there are many safeguards protecting the defendant's rights. Defendants have the right to be faced by their accusers, they have the right to competent legal counsel, they have the right against self-incrimination, they have the right to their possessions from unwarranted search and seizure, they have a right to have a jury of their peers decide their case, and they have the right to legal appeal.

Distinguishing criminal proceedings from civil actions is the assumption that defendants are not guilty, with the burden of proof resting on the prosecution. As criminal laws are found on multiple levels, so it is with prosecution. It is important to note that although there are different levels of prosecution, the steps taken by prosecutors are basically the same. Cases are characterized, regardless of venue, on the establishment of probable cause, with convictions proved beyond a reasonable doubt.

Allegations

In their most basic form, these are the steps of a criminal investigation and conviction.

Most cases start with an allegation. This allegation may be a factual statement made by a witness, a logical conclusion based on a credible witness' experience, a series of news reports, the findings of an audit, or something similar.

Two prongs must generally be present before starting an investigation: (1) are the allegations reasonable? and (2) are the allegations corroborable?

Investigations cannot be motivated by personal or political reasons; they must be based on articulated facts and circumstances. Law enforcement officers, agents, prosecutors, and the courts have many levels of supervisory, appellate, citizen, legislative, and legal safeguards. Administrative and legal penalties face law enforcement investigators if they engage in prohibited conduct, ranging from censure, dismissal, civil suit, and incarceration.

The Investigation

Investigators are tasked with evidence collection. The most valuable evidence comes from those who have direct knowledge of the criminal act supported by physical evidence. Of course, what a witness has observed or heard determines direct knowledge. If a witness sees someone committing a criminal act, that is direct knowledge. However, if the systems administrator tells her supervisor about an alleged criminal act committed by the help desk manager, that is considered hearsay and, depending on a number of circumstances, may or may not be admissible. Just because overheard statements may be hearsay does not necessarily diminish their value. For example, in most jurisdictions, statements made by defendants that are overheard by third parties are admissible as hearsay statements in legal proceedings. Hearsay should be documented as part of the investigator's interview report but only after documenting their direct knowledge. Investigators must separate what is direct knowledge from hearsay when interviewing witnesses.

Witnesses

For the most part, witnesses are divided into several categories. They may be witnesses of fact; they may possess specialized experience, training, and expertise and be called as expert witnesses; or they may be witnesses that may testify about a defendant's history, character, or credibility.

If witnesses or other people having material facts or evidence are reluctant to provide these facts, or it is deemed important to generate a transcript of testimony, these individuals may receive a summons or subpoena to appear before a grand jury or a judge. During such appearances, the witnesses are examined while a recording of their testimony is made. Such proceedings may be open to the public or in the case of a grand jury, they are held in secret.

Grand Juries

Grand juries are bodies of common persons empaneled for a period of a year or more who have the job of reviewing evidence and deciding the existence of probable cause. Prosecutors with supervision and oversight conduct grand jury proceedings by a presiding judge. Defense lawyers may not enter the chambers representing their client's interests. However, if a witness so desires, she may stop the proceeding and consult with her attorney outside the grand jury chambers. Grand juries listen to witness examinations conducted by prosecutors, review physical evidence, and listen to arguments from prosecutors. Defense attorneys are rarely allowed to address grand juries. This may seem unfair, but the task of the grand jury is merely that of deciding the existence of probable cause; they are not charged with deliberating the defendant's guilt or innocence. Grand juries decide whether sufficient probable cause exists that a crime has been committed and whether there is sufficient probable cause to believe that the defendant committed that crime. Grand juries are generally chosen from voter rolls or similar lists. Selection is random and the term of service may vary from one year to more than 18 months. Depending on the nature of the case under investigation, it is possible that a grand jury might be named to hear only one case. Depending on the matters before them, they may meet monthly or more often.

In most cases, grand jury proceedings are secret. Grand jurors, prosecutors, and reporters suffer criminal prosecution if they reveal the content of the proceedings; however; witnesses generally are free to discuss their testimony and the proceedings without sanction.

Experience Note Probable cause is a term that has vexed many people and is defined by legal terms that can become overly entwined. For argument's sake, consider that probable cause is defined by a set of facts and circumstances that lead reasonable people to believe that it is probable that an alleged event actually happened.

Grand juries have the task of deciding probable cause. Based on testimony and evidence:

- Is there probable cause to believe a crime has taken place?
- Is there probable cause to believe that a person, named or unnamed, committed that crime?

Grand juries may not be persuaded by conversations heard outside their deliberations or by news reports; they may only consider the case by the evidence and arguments presented in their chambers.

Transcripts of their proceedings include the examination of witnesses, introduction and examination of evidence, and statements made by the prosecutors. Grand jury deliberations are not recorded and are not subject to discovery. After hearing testimony, reviewing evidence, and hearing argument, grand juries deliberate. At this time, the prosecutor is not permitted to participate in their deliberations and is excused along with the recorder. Prosecutors present them with an indictment. Basically, an indictment is a formal document where a defendant is charged with violating the law. If grand jurors arrive at a decision, there are two paths: true bill and no bill. True bills result in indictments. Indictments mean the grand jury has decided there is sufficient probable cause to charge the defendant with a crime. Traditionally, indictments are divided by the number of times the defendant allegedly violated the law. In many jurisdictions, defendants are not invited to the grand jury and they do not have the opportunity to deliver evidence or testimony that would show that the evidence is not sufficient to accuse them. There are jurisdictions that send "target letters" to potential defendants who are subjects of grand jury investigations. They are invited to deliver any exculpatory evidence to the grand jury before they deliberate.

In the true bill, the grand jury decided there was probable cause and the prosecutor takes the indictment to the presiding judge, requesting either a warrant to arrest the defendant or a summons for the defendant to appear. In the case of a no bill, the prosecutor has the grand jury's decision and she must decide whether all the evidence has been presented and the matter is closed, or seek more evidence and present the matter again for further consideration.

In jurisdictions not having grand juries, the accusatory process is similar, except the matter is presented to a single judge listening to the witness testimony and reviewing physical evidence. In this case, the proceedings are recorded as they are before the grand jury. The judge is responsible for making the probable cause decision. This decision also results in either an arrest warrant or a summons to appear.

Arrest warrants are documents commanding law enforcement officers to arrest individuals, assuring their appearance before the court of jurisdiction, meaning the court where they are accused. If defendants are arrested outside the originating venue, then it becomes a matter of whether prosecutors will seek extradition of the defendant, wherever he may be found. Extradition may be waived or pursued at the pleasure of the defendant, as there are certain rights that attach. The defendant has the right to dispute whether he is the person named in the arrest warrant and to be represented during those proceedings. Summons are similar to invitations in that they command an individual to appear before the court; however, if they fail to do so, the judge will dismiss the summons to appear and issue an arrest warrant.

Arrest warrants can be executed by law officers and, depending on the circumstances, by ordinary citizens. They are enforceable at any hour on any day.

Subpoenas and Summons

Subpoenas may be issued by the grand jury and are basically predicated on investigative need. They are demands for a witness to appear or evidence to be brought before the grand jury. A summons is a document issued by judges demanding a witness appearance or evidence. Subpoenas may be quashed (dismissed) if the person named provides sufficient cause contesting the subpoena, validity of the subpoena, or the demands made by it.

Experience Note   A person receiving a grand jury subpoena is commanded to appear at the grand jury for testimony. She is not the same person as named in the subpoena and advises the court of the matter. The prosecutor is convinced she is the correct person and refuses to withdraw the subpoena, so her attorney files a motion to quash the subpoena triggering a hearing. At the hearing, the presiding judge hears testimony and argument, deciding if the subpoena should be enforced.

If there is sufficient cause to quash, then the court of jurisdiction withdraws the subpoena or summons. Failing to file a motion to quash, or sufficient other reason, the person must comply with the subpoena or summons, or the court issues an arrest warrant to have the named person arrested and brought before the court.

If a person is taken before the examining body, either a grand jury or judge, he retains his rights. In these proceedings, he has a right to legal counsel (although his lawyers may not appear before the grand jury, the proceedings may be stopped and they may consult with their client outside the grand jury room for advice), and he has the right against self-incrimination in his testimony. There have been many cases where an individual who received a subpoena and was commanded to appear before a grand jury invoked his Fifth Amendment rights when questioned. But he appeared because if he failed to do so, he would have been arrested.

There are generally two types of subpoenas: one resulting from a grand jury investigation and the other being issued by a judge. Both are documents based on need carrying the weight of the court. Judge-issued subpoenas are issued for witnesses and evidence to be presented before them at judicial proceedings, usually trials.

Search Warrants

Only law enforcement officers may obtain search warrants, as these documents carry the force of law in their execution. These are instruments that allow the search and seizure of evidence, persons in the case of third-party residences, assets to be seized, and instrumentalities or fruits of a crime. Because they carry force of law, force may be used in their execution should there be any impediment. However, if the executing officers fail to follow the law as well as their department's policies and procedures then they may be successfully sued.

Search warrants are not valid for civil and administrative actions and may not be executed to obtain evidence for these actions. Under the Fourth Amendment to the U.S. Constitution and subsequent case law, a law officer must provide a judge or magistrate with a sworn affidavit detailing the facts and circumstances surrounding the alleged crime. The information delivered by the affidavit must be complete, and the search warrant can only be weighed by its content. Search warrants usually contain the case's allegations, citations of criminal statute violations, a description of the area to be searched, and the reason there is probable cause to search the area. The presiding judge may ask questions by way of clarification, but the affidavit must be a document that stands on its own.

Basically, the judge is going to apply the following test to the affidavit:

- Is there probable cause to believe that a crime has been committed?
- Is there probable cause to believe that a person (named or not) committed that crime?
- Does this court have jurisdiction over the specified crime?
- Is there probable cause to believe that these fruits or instrumentalities are at that specified location now?

Search warrants are composed of two separate documents: the actual warrant and the affidavit. The search warrant is composed of a formal document describing in detail the area to be searched, the items to be seized, and the court of jurisdiction. Affidavits are statements of facts and circumstances supporting the search warrant.

Search warrants must specify what it is that is going to be seized. The actual area to be searched must be specified on the warrant and may not be expanded by the officers without obtaining another search warrant. Officers may use their observations in the currently valid search warrant to obtain probable cause for another search warrant to expand the area not covered in the first warrant. However, if an item of evidence or contraband is located "in plain sight" while legitimately executing the current search warrant, it may be seized even though the item was not specified on the warrant. This "plain sight seizure" may be used as predication for a second search warrant expanding the original one.

Experience Note While officers were executing a search warrant for electronic evidence, they ventured into a cabinet looking for storage media and relevant documentation. The cabinet was within the bounds of the warrant. One of the officers located a bag, weighing approximately one pound, of what appeared to be cocaine. The officer administered a commercially available field test for cocaine, returning a positive reaction. The bag was seized and, based on this discovery and other evidence, the cabinet's owner was charged with criminally distributing cocaine. The court ruled at a suppression hearing that the cocaine seizure was a "plain sight seizure" and was executed within the confines of the search warrant. The cocaine was admitted as evidence.

Any legal challenges to the search warrant such as the reliability of the affidavit's information, the freshness of the information, and the truthfulness of the information, must be addressed through formal hearings and may result in the exclusion of the seized evidence from proceedings or trial.

Experience Note It is unwise to impede the execution of a search warrant in any way. Such actions will generally result in the arrest of the person who is obstructing. In most jurisdictions, impeding or obstructing a search warrant is a felony and receives a commensurate sentence. However, persons legally present during a search warrant are well within their rights to ask for the identities of the executing officers, they may make notes or photographs of any officer conversations or actions that they witness, they may also leave the search area. Officers executing a search warrant secure the area, meaning they are going to look for persons or things that may be harmful or capable of evidence destruction.

Persons found at the location of a search warrant are to be told to move away from equipment, workstations, and media. It is also within the officer's purview to pat down the occupants, looking for weapons or devices that might destroy evidence. Once occupants have departed the search area, it is unlikely the officers will allow them to return, and this is a legal act on their part until the search warrant is completed. In some cases, officers may answer telephones and ask details of the callers.

Search warrants are valid only during daylight hours, meaning from 6 a.m. until 10 p.m., unless the officers have established that there are special circumstances that must be stated and justified to the court. Additionally, all search warrants must be executed by knocking and announcing the officers' identities and intentions at the door. Officers may provide special circumstances to the court relieving them of these knock-and-announce obligations. These are the infamous "no-knock" search warrants that have been widely publicized. If the executing officers can provide sufficient cause to the court that knocking and announcing will result in the destruction of evidence or place lives in peril, then the court may be moved to grant this type of warrant. Similarly, justification must be made to the court when officers want to execute the search warrant outside the daylight-hours provision.

Experience Note The fact that search warrants must be executed during daylight hours does not mean they must be completed in that time frame. It means the warrant must be started during that time frame.

When officers are executing search warrants, they are in control of the area, meaning they control people's comings and goings, telephone calls, computer activities, etc. If there are any objections to the fashion in which the search warrant was executed, the time and place for contesting a search warrant is in the courts, not during the search warrant execution.

Experience Note Search warrant execution has the goal of obtaining evidence or fruits of a crime. There cannot be another purpose such as using a search warrant to seize a business' computer network, resulting in the closure of the business.

The law enforcement agency is required to take every reasonable step to return the business to normal operation as soon as is reasonably possible. Officers must copy data and documentation and return the equipment necessary for the business to continue operation. Search warrants are not analogous to injunctions or cease-and-desist orders. Allegations of outrageous government conduct are often made regarding the fashion in which search warrants are executed or the reason for the warrant.

Experience Note Subpoenas and summons are based on "investigative need" and not probable cause. Obtaining a search warrant in place of a subpoena is basically at the discretion of the officer and prosecutor commensurate with the amount of probable cause.

If allegations of outrageous conduct have sufficient merit, they may trigger sanctions by the presiding court, evidence exclusion, civil suits against the officers and their agency as well as administrative actions against the offending officers.

Experience Note Search warrants are required in the case of third-party residence and if an officer wants to search for a person she wants to arrest. Also, search warrants must be obtained if an officer wants to search a location for assets to be seized pursuant to forfeiture actions.

When the search warrant is executed, whether anything was seized or not, a copy of the search warrant must be deposited at the location where it was executed along with an inventory of seized items. This search warrant is the document describing the area to be searched and the items to be taken. It does not include the supporting affidavit.

The second part of the search warrant is the affidavit constituting a sworn statement by the officer swearing to the truthfulness of the matter. The officer swearing to the warrant is known in legal terms as the affiant. The law does not require the affiant to have first-hand knowledge of the details of the statement, merely that he has reliable knowledge.

Court Orders

Court orders are issued by a court of jurisdiction and may be requested by law enforcement officers and non-law enforcement officers, depending on the nature of the case. Federal court orders may be filed for a wide variety of actions. For example, an officer installing a video camera on a public building to monitor the area below might require a court order. Court orders are also two-part documents with an application stating the facts and circumstances to the judge justifying the order and the second document being the actual court order.

Testimony

Witness testimony is obtained through interviews, depositions, and examinations. Remember that interviewing is a conversation directed toward specific events. Interrogations are different from interviews; they are deemed coercive, are conducted in a much more hostile atmosphere with the administration of advice of rights, and usually contemporaneous to an arrest. Interviews may be recorded in audio and video form or the investigator may take notes that serve as the basis for a written report of interview.

Experience Note Recording media and all forms of notes are considered evidence and must be retained along with a chain of custody schedule.

In the case of the report of interview, this document is not considered a verbatim transcript of the interview; rather, it is a synopsis of the witness statement and serves to deliver information to the prosecutor and defense, and may serve to refresh the witness' memory at trial.

Depositions are formal examinations attended by attorneys, parties to the action, and persons responsible for generating a formal record of the proceedings. Attorneys ask questions of the witnesses, attempting to ask questions that will cause the witness to provide testimony or evidence favorable to their side.

When a judge or magistrate judge examines a person, witnesses are sworn to tell the truth and the judge asks questions with the proceedings recorded. Attorneys representing their clients are present during these hearings along with the prosecution.

Expert Testimony

Typically, expert witnesses are people who are known for their expert knowledge in specific matters. Such knowledge may be technical, scientific, or by virtue of their experience. Federal Rules of Evidence, Rule 702, indicates that if scientific, technical, or other specialized knowledge will assist the trier of fact, then a witness qualified as an expert may testify in the form of an opinion. The U.S. Supreme Court expanded this rule (*Daubert v. Merrell Dow Pharmaceuticals, Inc.*) in that FRE Rule 702 requires an obligation from trial judges ensuring that expert testimony is reliable and relevant. In this decision, the Court ruled that there is a "gate keeping" obligation placed on judges applicable to all other types of expert testimony.

While it is common to label expert witnesses as people with advanced college degrees, many experts are people who are experienced systems administrators, help desk operators, or risk managers. It is possible to qualify someone as an expert witness just because the individual possesses great knowledge about a particular information technology system or a specific application. The advantage in using such expertise is that it brings a sense of honesty and sincerity to the courtroom.

The basic definition of an expert witness is someone who knows more about a particular topic than the jury and someone who can materially contribute to the jury's task. Nothing is specifically required in terms of background, training, knowledge, or education, other than a sufficient understanding of the relevant subject, contributing to the jury's ability to understand the truth of the matter at hand.

Expert witnesses might participate in grand jury proceedings, judicial hearings, trials, and sentencing.

Defense Arguments Relative to Expert Witnesses

While the expert witness may be someone who advertises or is well known among legal firms as available to testify, too often she is a person that regards herself as able to testify about almost everything.

It is important to note that these so-called experts base their abilities on an engineering background and education. Such experts are vulnerable to vigorous cross-examination by using their previous testimony or depositions. Usually a cross-examination enumerates the various cases that the expert witness has testified, showing that this person claims to be an expert on almost any subject. This activity has the effect of canceling her credibility.

There is an art to delivering expert testimony and not giving away the case. Many inexperienced witnesses tend to believe that the purpose of cross-examination is to discover the truth. The actual purpose of cross-examination might be to make the witnesses appear to be saying something different than what they are trying to say or have said previously. By contradicting themselves, they appear to be less credible to the jury. Experienced expert witnesses think carefully before they answer questions and tend to deliver answers that are exactly responsive to the question.

The Supreme Court further ruled that FRE Rule 702 does not distinguish between scientific, technical, and other specialized knowledge that might be the subject of expert testimony. The Court also highlighted that the essential function of gate keeping is to ensure the reliability of expert and experience-based testimony, and the trial court should consider tests where there are reasonable measures of reliability.

The simplest way of providing valuable testimony is to listen to the question; answer the question sincerely, truthfully, and completely; avoid incomplete responses; do not talk to the jury; and do not address matters outside your knowledge or expertise.

Computer Evidence

For more information, there is an article authored by Orin S. Kerr, Trial Attorney, Computer Crime and Intellectual Property Section, U.S. Department of Justice, written in March 2001.* His article is well documented, citing case law and addressing electronic evidence, its authenticity and reliability. There are many urban legends about electronic evidence and Mr. Kerr's article dispels many popular misconceptions.

In executing a search warrant, these are the usual steps by law officers ensuring credible testimony. Law enforcement officers should be trained in the legal and correct methods to collect evidence, ensuring its admissibility at the time of their testimony. If evidence is not gathered in accordance with the greatest attention of detail, it is likely that the evidence will be excluded from further use and may render the case impotent.

Law officers will gather evidence using a process similar to the following:

- Secure the area where potential evidence is stored, and remove anyone from equipment that could cause the alteration or destruction of the evidence.
- Ensure there are no devices or weapons that could be used to harm the officers or destroy evidence.
- Determine if the environment is networked to the outside in an effort to determine if all information is being obtained within the boundaries described by the search warrant. Search warrants are valid for very specific areas and

---

* Available at: http://www.cybercrime.gov/usamarch2001_4.htm.

may not be extended. If other potential evidence is discovered outside the scope of the search warrant, officers will secure the area and another search warrant sought to expand the search area. If officers expand the area to be searched without a superceding search warrant, any seized item will likely be rendered inadmissible when attempting to introduce it in court.

- An officer or examiner with technical forensic training will begin to conduct interviews in order to determine the types of equipment, software, network topology, location of network equipment, network connectivity, and location of backup media.
- Investigators will photograph and document the search site. This allows them to have a reference for evidence seizures as well as an inventory of seized items.
- Investigators will generally conduct interviews at this time.
- Depending on the search warrant, the investigators will seize the target machines or forensically copy the hard drives. Also depending on the search warrant, investigators will either forensically copy the removable media or seize it and copy it later.
- Investigators will likely seize documentation and media associated with the target machines. Documentation will likely include notes, scraps of paper, user documentation, calendars, diaries, "Post-Its," and items located in the trash.
- The investigators will initial, date, and tag all the seized items. Seized items will be entered on the seizure inventory. A chain-of-custody schedule will be made, documenting the discovery, location, and anyone who has custody of the evidence.
- Upon completing the search, the officers will deposit a copy of the search warrant, not including the affidavit, and a copy of the seized-item inventory.
- Within five days of the executed search warrant, the search warrant return must be made to the court that issued the search warrant. This return is the information that the search warrant was executed, when and where it was executed, and is accompanied by the seized-item inventory. Depending on the case, the search warrant, affidavit, and the inventory may be sealed and may not available until a motion for unsealing is filed.

Experience Note The Privacy Protection Act of 1980, 42 U.S. Code 2000aa, requires law enforcement officers to obtain a subpoena, rather than a search warrant, when acquiring materials that are reasonably believed to relate to publication, broadcast, or similar communication to the public.

Means of Collecting Electronic Evidence under Federal Statutes

The laws governing electronic collection are very specific. These statutes also apply to court-ordered wiretaps and microphone recordings (see Exhibit 1).

Federal Legal Requirements for Electronic Surveillance

Exhibit 2 details the legal requirements for law enforcement agencies to engage in electronic surveillance and monitoring.

Experience Note The term Title III refers to the section of the original 1968 law known as the Omnibus Crime and Safe Streets Act. Title III was the section that detailed the legal requirements of intercepting live wire and oral communications. Federal laws governing live interceptions of communications are found in 18 U.S. Code 2500.

Exhibit 1

Type of Communication	Court Order	Search Warrant	Subpoena
Wire, electronic, or oral communications (e.g., telephone calls, pager messages, facsimile, e-mail, computer transmissions, and face-to-face communications)	Pursuant to 18 USC 2510 (Title III); must be signed by a federal district court judge and based on affidavit and technique necessity. Interceptions are 30 or less unless extended by another affidavit		
Stored electronic communications (e.g., e-mail, pager messages, voice mails) in storage 180 days or less; see 18 USC 2703(a)	Unopened electronic communications require Title III warrant. Opened electronic communications require search warrant	18 USC 2703(a) and Rule 41, Federal Rules of Criminal Procedure; no prior notice to customer or subscriber required	
Stored electronic communications in electronic storage more than 180 days; see 18 USC 2703(a)	18 USC 2703(d); prior notice to customer or subscriber unless notice is delayed pursuant to § 2705; magistrate judge may sign	18 USC 2703(a), (b); no prior notice required	18 USC 2703(a), (b); prior notice to customer or subscriber unless notice is delayed under § 2705
Material held or maintained on a remote computing service (e.g., e-mail, business records, credit records, payroll records); see 18 USC 2703(b)	18 USC 2703(d); prior notice to customer or subscriber unless notice is delayed under § 2705; magistrate judge may sign	As provided for in 18 USC 2703(b); no prior notice required	As provided for in 18 USC 2703(b); prior notice to customer or subscriber unless notice is delayed under § 2705
A record of other information about a subscriber or customer of a communications service provider or remote computing service (not including the contents of a communication); see 18 USC 2703(B) (1)(B)	18 USC 2703(d); magistrate may sign; no prior notice to customer or subscriber is required	18 USC 2703(c) (1)(B); no prior notice to customer or subscriber is required	
Installation or use of a pen register or a trap-and-trace device	18 USC 3121, *et seq.*; magistrate judge may sign; order sealed until otherwise ordered by court		

Exhibit 2

Technique	Device	Authority	Statute	Official Authorizing	Duration of Authority	Weight of Evidence
Phone number dialed real-time (outgoing)	Pen register	Court order	18 USC 3121	U.S. Magistrate Judge	60 days	Relevance to investigation
Phone number dialed real-time (incoming)	Trap-and-trace	Court order	18 USC 3121	U.S. Magistrate Judge	60 days	Relevance to investigation
Face to face, oral communications w/o consenting party	Electronic device to capture and transmit	Title III court order	18 USC 2518	U.S. District Court Judge with DOJ approval	30 days	Probable cause and technique necessity
Computer messages sent via e-mail, Internet, computer network system (real-time interception)	Electronic devices including network equipment allowing real-time message interceptions, all nonpertinent transmissions must be minimized	Title III court order	18 USC 2518	U.S. District Court Judge with DOJ approval	30 days	Probable cause and technique necessity
Names and numbers from electronic address book	Electronic data notebook	Search warrant	Search warrant Rule 41 FRCP (Federal Rules of Criminal Procedure)	U.S. Magistrate Judge		Probable cause
Tracking device: transponder bumper, beeper, GPS	Search warrant (to install or monitor signal in Fourth Amendment protected area)	Search warrant	Rule 41 FRCP	U.S. Magistrate Judge		Probable cause
Wire communications (real-time): cellular phone, hard-wired telephone (business or residence), and cordless phone	Electronic devices including network equipment allowing real-time message interceptions, all nonpertinent transmissions must be minimized	Title III court order	18 USC 2518	U.S. District Court Judge with DOJ approval	30 days	Probable cause and technique necessity
Computer files stored or downloaded; computer, stand-alone		Search warrant (if information in storage 180 days or less)	18 USC 2703(a) and Rule 41 FRCP	U.S. Magistrate Judge		Probable cause

Evidence

Evidence has a lifecycle that is begun at the time it is generated and collected, and progresses until it is eventually returned to the original owner or destroyed. It is important to note that many law enforcement agencies have evidence destruction and retention policies. These are the general phases of the evidence lifecycle:

- *Evidence creation or generation.* This is the time or event when the evidence is created. For example, at this time an employee installs a pirated version of a graphics program on her office workstation and allows her coworkers to use it.
- *Collection or seizure.* At this time, the investigators (law enforcement or corporate) make forensic duplicates of the hard drive where the software is located on the employee's workstation.
- *Examination and analysis.* During this phase, the investigators or analysts will search the duplicated hard drive, discovering the location of the pirated software. Depending on the case circumstances, they will search the portions of the hard drive, looking for other pieces of evidence.
- *Storage and preservation.* After appropriate levels of examination and analysis have taken place, the hard drive will be stored in conditions preserving its integrity. Access to the evidence and related materials such as the chain-of-custody schedule will be extremely limited. For example, the only persons allowed to access the evidence will be the investigators in charge of the case.
- *Presentation in legal proceedings.* The evidence will be retrieved from storage and presented in legal proceedings. When they are completed, it will be returned to storage along with relevant materials.
- *Destruction or return to original owner.* At some future time, a determination will be made relative to the policy of whether or not the evidence should be returned to the owner. In the example of the pirated software, because the duplicated hard drive was not the property of the owner, it will be destroyed. The guiding principle of whether or not the evidence is retained depends greatly on whether it will be needed in the future. For example, if a person's hard drive containing pornography were seized, it may be cleansed of the contraband before being returned.

Criminal Procedure

After the officers have completed their job of collecting electronic evidence, they submit it for forensic analysis. Officers taking custody of evidence rarely perform analysis on it. The burden of proof rests with the prosecution, so examination and analysis are critical to proving or disproving the allegations. Crimes must be proved "beyond a reasonable doubt" that the accused defendant intended to violate specific criminal statutes and actually violated them. In the case of digital evidence, it might pass through a single analyst or it may pass through several in an effort to extract all relevant information from it.

After the evidence has been reviewed, officers draft an investigative report that will be transmitted first to their supervisor for review and approval and then to the corresponding prosecutor. This investigative summary contains reports of relevant interviews, list of evidence and its analysis, and relevant statutes. It is important to note that all evidence, whether incriminating or exculpatory, must be provided as discovery to the defense or the matter may be dismissed.

Prosecutors will carefully review the investigative report and determine if the case is attractive to prosecution. Depending on the nature of the investigation, the investigators may be asked to complete other interviews, collect more evidence, or conduct more analyses before the prosecutors determine the matter is sufficiently complete to present to a grand jury or a judge for a determination of probable cause.

Experience Note Because of laws such as the "Speedy Trial Act" (18 USC §§ 3161–3174), where defendants are guaranteed judicial proceedings within specific periods of time, prosecutors generally want the investigation sufficiently complete to bring to trial at the time of charging or shortly thereafter.

In some jurisdictions, prosecutors must prepare a document outlining arguments about why this matter should be prosecuted as well as anticipating any possible defense contentions. The prosecutor's report, including the officer's report, is then passed to the prosecutor's managers for a final determination as to the case's merit.

If there is some degree of urgency, the prosecutor will draft a complaint supported by an affidavit from the officers, and the matter will be presented before a judge, along with a request for an arrest warrant. As with the search warrant, the matter must be based on an affidavit (sworn statement) propounding the facts and circumstances of the matter within the test of probable cause.

Assuming the defendant is in custody, there are a series of hearings where the court ensures the defendant is aware of his rights and has the opportunity to retain counsel, or the court will appoint counsel preserving his Sixth Amendment rights.

Shortly after appearing at court, the defendant is entitled to an arraignment. At arraignment, the defendant will hear the charges against him, declare himself guilty or not guilty, and the court will ensure he has an attorney, appointing one if needed. If the defendant declares he is not guilty, the matter proceeds to trial; if he pleads guilty, he is scheduled for sentencing.

Once the defendant is charged and in custody, the prosecutor has essentially 70 days to bring the matter to trial under the provisions of the Speedy Trial Act, 18 U.S. Code 3161, unless the defendant waives this right. Cases have been dismissed if prosecutors failed to bring the matter to trial within the specific time limits.

Criminal Discovery

At this point, the process of discovery begins. The defense has the right to review the evidence — not only the incriminating evidence supporting the indictment, but also the exculpatory evidence must be delivered to the defendant's lawyer.

Rule 16 of the Federal Rules of Criminal Procedure provides for the defense to have access for the purpose of inspection, copying, or photographing the prosecution's relevant materials. Relevant materials include but are not necessarily limited to the following:

- Substance of any oral statement intended to be offered as evidence made by the defendant
- Defendant's statements made before the grand jury
- Defendant's prior criminal record
- Evidence material to the defendant's defense or intended to be introduced by the prosecution
- Items seized from the defendant and material to the defense
- Reports of examinations and tests material for the defense or intended to be used by the prosecution

Looking at this list would lead you to think that everything is discoverable; that is not the case. Internal documents consisting of memoranda or other nonevidentiary administrative documents are not subject to criminal discovery processes. For example, the prosecutor's office may require the prosecutor to prepare a memorandum summarizing the case, complete with possible defense arguments before being authorized to present the matter to the grand jury. This case summary would not be subject to discovery because it would be considered an administrative document and exempt as evidence.

Under the provisions of *Maryland v. Brady,* 373 U.S. 83 and 397 U.S. 742, the prosecution must deliver all relevant items, withholding nothing, including reports, analyses, affidavits, notes, criminal records of potential witnesses, list of potential witnesses, and a list of potential evidence to be introduced. This concept has been expanded to include relevant information about the pertinent law officers' backgrounds, including whether they have been disciplined for administrative infractions impacting their witness credibility. An example would be if a law officer were disciplined for violating an agency's policy regarding official use of an automobile, and during the internal investigation the officer lied to the investigators and was subsequently disciplined. This action would be an item impacting the officer's credibility and would have to be revealed to the defense as possibly affecting the officer's ability to deliver credible testimony.*

The discovery phase is one of the most critical phases in judicial proceedings, both criminal and civil. It is important to note that evidence may not be colored or tainted or it will likely be excluded from the case. For example, if it is discovered that seized digital files were encrypted and subsequently decrypted, then the decrypted materials must be provided to the defense. Failure to deliver the readable materials to the defendants will result in the case being dismissed or the evidence excluded from the proceedings.

Electronic Discovery

Computer-based discovery offers substantive advantages over the conventional documentary evidence that would have been difficult to manage in today's world. Documents that were previously lost or destroyed as routine are now retrievable. Most computer-mediated communications methods, from e-mail to videoconferences, are recorded and archived as digital records. Judges are becoming more sophisticated in their rulings about computer-related evidence. Attorneys are now quick to realize they cannot bamboozle the bench or stonewall their way through computer-based discovery. As a matter of course, attorneys seeking discovery of digital information should immediately notify the opposing counsel of that fact, identifying as clearly as possible the types and categories of information that is going to be sought, avoiding possible accusations of negligent spoliation.

E-Mail as Evidence

There is no correlation between e-mail and paper-based communications. E-mail usually is not filed in a rational filing system and is a problem for discovery purposes due to its sheer volume. The most important factor in e-mail as an object for discovery is its characteristic informal, casual, and often playful tone, even in the most formal

---

* More information is available at http://www.fbi.gov/publications/leb/1996/july966.txt.

business environments. These are characteristics that make e-mail very attractive for collection as evidence.

Prosecutors should have a clear understanding of the defendant's e-mail system with special attention paid to the nature of retention policies and procedures, and the extent of backed-up files. Backup tapes and other media are often maintained for months or possibly years. Backup tapes are not organized for retrieval of individual files, but their purpose is for emergencies, requiring large amounts of data are restored to the active system.

Criminal Plea Bargains

After the defendant and her lawyer have time to review the evidence disclosed in the discovery phase of the proceedings, it is common for a "plea bargain" to be sought. This action is one where the defendant agrees to enter a plea of guilty to specified charges, usually less than the original charges, and the prosecution agrees to accept the pleading in consideration of those lesser charges. In today's world, there are many factors impacting pleadings:

- The strength of the witnesses, defense, and prosecution
- The strength of the evidence
- Length of sentence relative to the charges
- Asset forfeiture action
- Civil remedies sought by the state or government
- Cooperation of the defendant impacting other defendants and crimes
- Return of goods
- Restitution paid to injured parties
- Fines paid to court

When the defendant enters a guilty plea, the matter is scheduled for sentencing. If the defendant enters a plea of not guilty, then the matter is scheduled for trial.

Trials

Basically, there are two types of trials: one heard by a judge and the other heard by a jury, called a petit jury, distinguishing it from a grand jury. Most jury panels are composed of ordinary citizens from the court's surrounding geographic area. Pursuant to questioning by both sides, jurors are qualified and candidates empanelled for the proceedings.

Experience Note   One of the most interesting facts about a petit jury trial is the jury is usually instructed as to what constitutes evidence and what is argument. This fact is significant in that they are instructed to rule on the evidence while excluding argument during their deliberations.

Jurors are instructed in great detail about their obligations and duties. After all the proceedings are completed, the jury adjourns to pursue its deliberations. The jury may only consider and weigh the evidence presented in court and from nowhere else. Argument, which is the attorneys' statements, is supposed to be separated from testimony. If they are convinced beyond a reasonable doubt of the defendant's guilt, then the defendant is found guilty and scheduled for sentencing. If they are not convinced of the defendant's guilt beyond a reasonable doubt, and they all agree that the defendant is not guilty, then the defendant is acquitted. If they cannot agree, then the matter is deadlocked. In this instance, if they cannot deliberate to a guilty verdict or acquittal, then the judge declares a mistrial and dismisses the charges. In this case, the prosecution must decide whether or not to charge the defendant again.

Sentencing

Sentencing the defendant is usually done after a court officer has prepared a report that synopsizes the case, victims and their losses, facts about the defendant's background and criminal history, extent of the crime, defendant's ability to make restitution and pay fines, and makes sentencing recommendations.

Experience Note Judges may accept or reject any plea bargain between the prosecutors and defense lawyers before the trial, but once the trial has begun, it is generally allowed to follow its own course.

Sentencing is the process by which the court levies monetary fines, demands victim restitution, declares that the defendant receives supervision in the form of probation, forfeits assets, or is remanded to a period of incarceration.

Appeals

Of course, under the system of justice in the United States, the defendant has the right of appeal. An appeal essentially states that there was an error committed in any part of the proceedings, including the constitutionality of the law under which the defendant was charged. Only matters of law and procedures are heard by appellate courts; they do not hear testimony and they do not review evidence. Decisions made by appellate courts consist of dismissing the matter, remanding the matter for another trial, or modifying the sentence.*

Civil Suits

Civil law, also commonly known as tort law, is a matter identifying a wrong against an individual, corporation, or business, resulting in damage or financial losses. Civil cases deal with matters of responsibility or liability, while criminal cases deal with matters of guilt. One principal difference between criminal and civil law is the level of proof that must be achieved in proving the case and the type of sentencing. Because civil matters deal with damage and losses, the remedies are in the form of financial penalties.

In civil matters, the amount of damages might be awarded by statute, or in the form of punitive or compensatory damages. Financial compensation is given to the plaintiff. It is important to remember that civil cases deal with financial remedies awarded to the victim or plaintiff and not decisions of guilt. Civil cases won by the defendant do not usually result in any monetary compensation unless further civil action is sought to recover expenses or punish the plaintiff for filing suit.

The burden of proof required of the plaintiff is significantly less than in a criminal case being beyond a reasonable doubt. In civil matters, the plaintiff need only prove 51 percent of the case or a preponderance of the evidence. It is important to note

---

* The latest version of the Federal Rules of Criminal Procedure is available at http://www2.law.cornell.edu/cgi-bin/foliocgiexe/frcrm. The latest version of the Federal Rules of Evidence is available at http://www.law.cornell.edu/rules/fre/overview.html.

that criminal charges may only be filed when a defendant has violated specific criminal statutes and had an intention to violate them.

In settling a civil matter, the parties agree on a monetary amount; however, if settlement cannot be reached, the matter proceeds to trial. In the civil trial, the jury decides if the defendant is liable and any amounts of financial settlement. Of course, as in the criminal matter, the losing side has the right of appeal.

Plaintiff's Burden of Proof

The burden of proof rests with the plaintiff. The plaintiff must show through a preponderance of evidence that the defendant caused her to suffer damages. The extent of these damages is measured in monetary values. Of course, the plaintiff must show actual damages and may ask the judge or jury to aware punitive damages, deterring similar acts from recurring in the future. In some cases, the amount of damages is a matter of language contained in legal statutes. The plaintiff is responsible for showing that:

- The defendant caused financial damages; if the plaintiff cannot then there is no reason for settlement and the case lacks merit.
- If applicable, there exists a standard of care or due diligence on the part of the defendant.
- If applicable, the defendant breached that due diligence.
- There exists causation between the defendant's conduct and lack of reasonable conduct caused the damages incurred by the plaintiff.

Cases where parties are in civil dispute involving a level of responsibility are measured by the "reasonable man" test. Basically, this test describes the behavior of a reasonable man and how he would act in the given set of circumstances. For example, it is not the acceptable conduct of a reasonable man to allow the public to have unfettered access to his offices.

In matters involving professional conduct, there is a still-higher test of responsibility called "due diligence." Due diligence is due professional care. Due diligence applies to the conduct of professionals in their particular area of expertise. Professional due diligence requires that the responsible person conducts sufficient investigation and responds appropriately. Plaintiffs must show to a level of preponderance (51 percent of the evidence) that the defendant, a professional, failed to take necessary precautions to inhibit or prohibit damages from occurring. It is the burden of the defendant to show that he acted prudently and within the scope of his professional due diligence.

Civil Processes

Civil suits often begin by filing complaints or petitions with the court, alleging the facts and circumstances of the plaintiff's case. In this document, the plaintiff attempts to demonstrate how she was damaged by the defendant, demanding a response from the defendant.

Experience Note Civil proceedings are allowed to draw certain inferences by the responses. For example, in criminal matters the defendant has the right against self-incrimination. However, in civil proceedings, if the defendant refuses to answer a particular question, then the opposing attorney is allowed to pronounce that the defendant was attempting to conceal her negligence by refusing to respond.

There is a series of filings that follow, depending on the particular civil procedure for the court. Various states have specific civil procedures that differ significantly from other states and the federal government.

Civil Discovery

The basic purpose of civil suits is the proof that the defendant wronged the plaintiff, causing damage, and plaintiff seeks financial settlement for those acts. One of the key activities of civil procedure is discovery. In most cases, discovery is where cases are made. Civil discovery is very different from criminal discovery. It is usually much more interactive between opposing sides. Discovery may include interrogatories where the opposing sides demand explanations for allegations and counter-allegations. It might include inspections; for example, the plaintiff physically inspects the workplace of the defendant. Discovery might include depositions where the opposing sides meet, examining each other and relevant witnesses, with the proceedings recorded. And, discovery might include the production of evidence, including electronic evidence. One of the favorite areas for discovery demands is the defendant's e-mail system.

Experience Note An important aspect of e-mail and other electronic evidence once a notice of civil action has been served is that destruction of any and all items should be suspended until the matter is settled, regardless of the destruction policy. Failure to suspend destruction policies can and likely will result in legal disasters.

E-Mail Discovery

In discovery actions, attorneys should meet and discuss the scope of anticipated e-mail discovery. Of course, the demanding side is going to request a very broad scope of e-mail discovery, with the opposition desiring a more narrow scope. Regardless, both sides need to agree on the protocol for relevant e-mail, including key words, dates, names, and sources to be searched.

The discovery of backup data tapes is usually within the scope of the discovery rules. They have the potential to deliver information that would be beyond conventional means to accurately search it and would likely result in prohibitive expenses. Before any discovery pretrial conferences, the opposing attorneys should agree on whether discovery of backed-up data is required, the extent to which it is going to be required, and who is going to pay for searching it.

Rule 34(b) of the Federal Rules of Civil Procedure allow an on-site inspection to take place. As part of this discovery process, an inspection may be necessary to observe the computer system in operation to ensure the discovery steps are being performed properly and to determine the adequacy of security and chain of custody, or to determine the source of relevant computer records. The nature of computer record storage and filing systems make it impossible to protect privileged or sensitive intellectual property.

Recently, federal courts have established a set of accepted computer inspection procedures:

- The parties agree on a neutral third-party expert who will execute the inspection as an officer of the court.
- The sides agree on the scope of the inspection, including target systems, search terms, ranges, and other defining criteria.
- The expert creates a "mirror image" (forensically sound, byte-by-byte copy of the computer data using accepted forensic procedures preserving the integrity of the original media).
- The expert searches the "mirror image" media and identifies relevant data according to previous agreements.
- The expert delivers the responsive data to the respondent's attorney.
- The respondent's attorney reviews the data for relevance and privilege.
- The respondent's attorney delivers the relevant, nonprivileged data to the requestor.

These steps will help the parties set obtainable objectives limiting discovery costs and scope while protecting privilege and privacy.

Experience Note The following federal cases formed the basis for the inspection protocols: *Playboy Enterprises, Inc. v. Welles, Northwest Airlines, Inc. v. Local 2000 International Brotherhood of Teamsters, AFL-CIO, et al.,* and *Simon Property Group, L.P. v. MySimon, Inc.*

The Federal Rules of Civil Procedure, Rule 26, states that the trial court has the power to limit discovery "if the burden or expense of the proposed discovery outweighs its likely benefit." This language was added to discourage excessively costly and time-consuming activities that are disproportionate to the nature of the case. The purpose of the discovery process is the collection and examination of evidence, not financial punishment.

If discovery efforts such as on-site inspections or recovery of deleted data are not justified by showing that the efforts are likely to result in relevant and material information, it is within the trial judge's discretion to limit discovery efforts.

More on Civil Discovery

The true purpose of civil discovery is to find evidence, narrow the issues, produce testimony, and avoid surprises causing case delays and mistrials. Attorneys must be mindful that goals are set relative to the direction of discovery so they know how much is necessary. Discovery forces the opposing sides to prepare for trial or dispositive motions, and causes opponents to better understand any weaknesses in the case, thereby facilitating settlements.

Experience Note Evidence can disappear, witnesses perish, memories fade, documents are destroyed, and physical evidence is misplaced or altered to a point that renders it useless. Witness testimony can be preserved by taking depositions either orally or by answering written questions. Should something happen to this witness, in a civil action, the recorded testimony can be entered as an exception to the hearsay rule. Early inspection of evidence will allow the recording of its condition and performance before it has diminished or been destroyed.*

---

* The latest version of the Federal Rules of Civil Procedure is available at http://www.law.cornell.edu/rules/frcp/overview.htm.

Federal Laws Applicable to Computer-Related Crimes

Following is a listing of federal statutes that have application to computer-related crimes:

- *18 USC 371:* Prohibits conspiracy to violate federal criminal statutes
- *18 USC 1028:* Identity theft, fraud, and related activity in connection with identification documents, including biometric data, electronic identification number, address or routing code, or telecommunications identifying number or access device
- *18 USC 1029:* Fraud and related activity in connection with access devices
- *18 USC 1030:* Fraud and related activity in connection with unauthorized access to computers
- *18 USC 1084:* Prohibits using a wire communication facility to transmit wagering information
- *18 USC 1831:* Prohibits stealing trade secrets to benefit foreign powers
- *18 USC 1832:* Prohibits stealing trade secrets by an individual
- *18 USC 2232:* Destruction or removal of property to prevent seizure
- *18 USC 2251, 2252:* Prohibits receipt or distribution by computer of material that contributes to the sexual exploitation of minors, including that which constitutes or contains child pornography
- *18 USC 2253:* Provides for forfeiture of property, profits, etc., of those convicted of sections 2251 and 2252
- *18 USC 2314:* Prohibits the interstate transportation of goods and travel in support of fraud in excess of $5000.
- *18 USC 2315:* Prohibits the sale or receipt of stolen goods transported between states
- *18 USC 2319:* Criminal infringement of a copyright
- *18 USC 2425, 2427:* Prohibits the use of interstate facilities to transmit information about a minor with the intent of enticing a person to engage in sexual activity
- *18 USC 2510, et seq.:* Prohibits interception and disclosure of wire, oral, or electronic communications without a warrant authorized by a federal district court judge
- *18 USC 2512:* Prohibits the manufacture, distribution, possession, and advertising of wire, oral, or electronic communication-intercepting devices
- *18 USC 2518:* Describes procedures for interception of wire, oral, or electronic communications
- *18 USC 2701:* Prohibits unlawful access to stored communications (Electronic Communications Privacy Law)
- *18 USC 2702:* Prohibits unauthorized disclosure of stored electronic communications
- *18 USC 2703:* Requires a federal or state warrant for governmental access to stored electronic communications
- *18 USC 2707:* Provides civil remedies for unlawful access to stored information by electronic communication service providers and subscribers
- *18 USC 2710:* Provides civil remedies for the unauthorized disclosure of video sales and rental records
- *47 USC 605:* Unauthorized publication or use of unlawfully intercepted communications

- *47 USC 1004:* Requires telecommunications carriers to ensure systems security and integrity
- *47 USC 1007:* Provides for enforcement orders when a telecommunications carrier fails to meet the government's demand for lawful interception of communications
- *50 USC 1809:* Prohibits unlawful electronic surveillance and provides criminal sanctions for violations against defendants
- *50 USC 1810:* Prohibits unlawful electronic surveillance and provides civil remedies for violations

Chapter 6

Privacy

Privacy Expectations

Privacy is a buzzword tossed around in the news currently, leaving the public and organizations confused and unable to decide whether they are entitled to privacy. Challenges currently face businesses and governments to decide privacy entitlements when weighed on balance with national security concerns.

Free and democratic societies are characterized by full legal privacy protection extended to choices, possessions, and persons. When social expectations rise, personal rights include the right to be "let alone." This right to be let alone is an essential definition of personal privacy and has early expression in an article found in the *Harvard Law Review*.*

The Bill of Rights guarantees, among other things, the rights of expression and association without having to answer to anyone. People have the right to privacy; that is, the right to be left alone in their lawful thoughts, activities, and expressions. Integral to collective freedom is the right to privacy and ownership regarding personal information. People are the owners of their information and only they can determine who has a legal right to see and use their property. For example, a person applying for a library card at a private institution completes a form with his name, date of birth, address, social security number, and e-mail address. Accompanying the application is a statement that states the reasons for collecting this information. This statement does not warn that the collected information is going to be sold. Applicants might expect the institution to treat their information confidentially. However, when the new library cardholder begins to receive unsolicited advertising, he soon realizes his information was sold by the library.

Governments must temper their voracious personal information needs with laws respecting individual privacy. Through individual interaction with government agencies involved with mail, taxes, property ownership, driver licensing, and pet and vehicle registration, governments at all levels are collecting vast amounts of information about their citizens. If not carefully and lawfully used, this information cannot be protected from the bias, scrutiny, and judgment of unqualified officials.

---

* Volume IV, No. 5, December 15, 1890 (www.lawrence.edu/fac/boardmaw/Privacy_brand_warr2.html).

Businesses have been collecting information about their customers, using it for every imaginable purpose. At times, providers of personal information are completely oblivious to its use and dissemination. For example, in the case of customer loyalty cards offered by merchants, persons making purchases are given discounts by showing their membership cards initially obtained by providing personal information. Each time a customer wants a discount, the membership card is shown. All purchases made by that customer are attributed to the name and identification number on the discount card. The merchant sells the collected purchase and customer information to vendors who then target the individual with selected advertising, and the merchant uses the revenue to offset the customer's discount.

With this process in mind, imagine this scenario: a customer is suspected of unethical acts by her employer. Pursuant to legal action by her employer, her membership card purchases, relevant or not, are obtained and made public through legal processes, causing significant embarrassment to her and her family.

Information Ownership

Information privacy is tied to information ownership. In many cases, it is easy to identify information ownership; however, in many cases, information does not belong exclusively to the individual as ownership passes to organizations and government entities.

Information Vulnerability in the Organization

All organizations are vulnerable to threats resulting from the compromise of personal information in their custody, even institutions that think they do not have sensitive information.

Experience Note While engaged in a practical exercise, student auditors were tasked with performing an audit on a local library in order to gain experience. One of the students, a young woman, could not see the reason for auditing public libraries because she believed they "did not have anything of value that could be exploited." Nevertheless, the instructor urged her to complete the assignment. During the audit, she discovered a spreadsheet on one of the library employee's workstations. She checked with the audit manager and the library's lawyer and determined that employees did not have a reasonable expectation to privacy on their workstations. Workstations were to be used for official use only and the spreadsheet software was not authorized. The student auditor accessed the spreadsheet program and saw an impressive list of books that had been checked out by local dignitaries. Each of the book titles dealt with subjects that, if made public, could possibly embarrass the readers and their families due to local community values. An employee was assigned to this workstation that required login before use. Checking the audit logs determined that only this particular employee had been using the workstation. The audit manager presented the results to the library director who questioned the employee. Subsequently, the employee was dismissed.

Certainly, one of the greatest vulnerabilities within an organization is the lack of understanding of the types of information the organization has collected:

- Under which circumstances and representations was the information collected?
- How is that information being used?

- To whom is that information being transmitted?
- How is that information being stored?
- Who has access, authorized or not, to that information?

Many businesses do not have an idea of how much data they collect, nor do they realize the damage that can be done when this information is lost or compromised.

Threats to Information Privacy

In essence, there are three fronts assaulting information privacy:

1. Willful or negligent misuse or theft of information
2. Unauthorized information disclosure or dissemination
3. Interaction of professionals and access to the organization's information assets

In the first case, malicious employees and outsiders target the theft of client lists, intellectual property, trade secrets, etc. In the second case, individuals who have legitimate access to information do not exercise due care and inadvertently share this information with unauthorized individuals that have malicious intentions. In the last case, professionals interested in sharing with others in solving problems can often be compromised into delivering sensitive information.

Experience Note The question most often asked of privacy professionals is "Isn't it the job of law enforcement authorities to provide information privacy protection?" Law enforcement authorities can do very little, generally, in protecting information privacy. It is outside their legal mandate. They are actually responsible for investigating allegations and collecting evidence of unlawful acts. It is not the responsibility of law enforcement agencies to provide protection for private information, rather these obligations rest at the individual and the organization levels.

Privacy Protection

Like so many other management challenges, planning for privacy is begun by determining needs and strategies. Organizations should consider information privacy something that will be threatened by corruption and theft. Start by using this simple model:

- What are my information privacy needs?
- What types of information exist in the organization?
- What information assets are available to employees connecting from outside the organization?
- What are the organization's legal and regulatory requirements?
- What is going to be the composition of the information privacy team?
- What business units must be represented on this team?
- Who is going to lead this team?
- Who is going to be the senior manager sponsoring the information privacy team?
- What is going to be the team's line of authority and reporting?
- What are the organization's information privacy assets?
- What are the threats to those privacy assets?
- What is the frequency of those threats?

- What are the organization's privacy vulnerabilities?
- What are the most feasible cost/benefit safeguards?
- What policies need to be drafted and approved to address these assets?
- Who is going to conduct employee training about information privacy?
- What is going to be the frequency of privacy training?
- Who is going to conduct internal compliance audits?
- What is the frequency of those audits?
- What is the level of intrusion of privacy audits?
- What penalties are going to be assessed against policy/law violators?

Information Assets Inventory

Organizations must develop an inventory to identify, locate, classify, and prioritize information requiring privacy safeguards. Like other organizational efforts, it is a wise idea to form a privacy team with representatives from pertinent business units. Team composition and functions are discussed in previous chapters.

The privacy team should be tasked with collecting as much information as possible about information collected and stored in the organization and record it as part of their inventory. Inventories of this nature are going to be inventories of origins of data and the types of data, not the data itself. For example, the privacy team will survey the organization's business units to determine the types and nature of information they collect as well as the information they access outside the organization. The survey should be simple yet sufficiently comprehensive to include the origin of the data, degree of sensitivity, classification, use, storage, and disposal.

A data inventory should include the following components at a minimum:

- Data description
- Origin of data
- Data ownership
- Responsible business unit
- Data classification or sensitivity
- How data is used in business unit
- To whom data is disseminated
- Individuals having access to data
- Authorization for access
- Existing relevant polices
- Current laws/regulations governing data
- Current and past material events affecting this data

Technology Relevant to Privacy Protection

It is the responsibility of the privacy team to assess the organization's technology requirements to protect and preserve the privacy of its data. This assessment requires a serious understanding of the organization's mission, implemented technologies, risk program, policies and procedures, audit program, and critical incident response. The privacy team will not likely decide the specific technology to deploy, but it will decide the functional parameters of such technology as well as relevant policies and procedures.

All information systems have their strengths and weaknesses depending on their implementation and deployment. Regardless of the system, the weakest link in all systems is the people interacting with it. The fundamental aspect of safeguarding information privacy is controlling access to the system. (Remember that systems are composed of people, data, and physical facilities.)

Access controls exist on a variety of levels including privileges assigned to employees and groups, password protections, tokens and smart cards, and biometrics and one-time passwords. An alternate method of controlling data access is to set user privileges meaning who can delete, add, modify, or manipulate data. Significant information privacy challenges exist in ensuring that products are installed and configured correctly so that only intended employees have access and corresponding privileges.

Policies and Procedures

Regrettably, in most organizations, there is a serious lack of strong policies and procedures regarding the use of the Internet, e-mail, chat rooms, and messaging services such as Instant Messenger. Employees generally do not understand the depth or variety of vulnerabilities that these communications technologies and their unrestrained use pose to information privacy.

Team members can expect to have challenges in understanding types of data, how that data are being used and by whom, to whom data are being transmitted, the means by which data are being transmitted, and which the data recipients is retransmitting data. With sufficient survey data collected, the team should have a good idea relative to the data transmission habits of the employees. Depending on the results, the team may recommend a widespread training program directed to deficiencies found in employee conduct. It is also quite possible that due to the sensitivity of the data and the employee's poor data-transmission habits, the team may recommend monitoring and filtering all transmissions for offending elements.

Experience Note Installing monitoring and filtering software for transmissions must not be considered the action of first resort. Like all privacy and security measures, it must be a total approach in achieving the best results. Enterprises may depend on monitoring and filtering software to solve their data-transmission behavior problems, but if they are dependent on this approach exclusively, malicious employees will find vulnerabilities circumventing filtering and monitoring software to the detriment of their information privacy program.

Educating employees is the best method to address data-transmission habits. They must understand the approved methods of communication and why these are approved. Included in these education sessions, must be the consequences for not complying with policies and procedures such as lost profits, lost market share, individual censure, dismissal, etc. Although many employees have excellent computer knowledge, they should glean from their training that their e-mail can be read, stolen, sent to unintended addressees, and retransmitted without their permission.

They should also understand their Internet browsing, e-mail, chat rooms, and instant messenger services may be monitored by their employer, government agencies, advertisers, and malicious individuals.

Auditing Privacy Practices

Tasking the organization's privacy team and audit unit, programs should be devised to test the viability of the privacy program. Audits should be unannounced, comprehensive, and conducted as if the future of the business depended upon their findings.

In today's world, it might! Auditors should be included as valued members of the privacy team and must participate as policies and procedures are developed and approved. Audits of the developing privacy plan will identify flaws and weaknesses that can be addressed before they become policy. If the chapter in this book about auditing has not been read, now is a good time.

Web Site Privacy

Handling data collected through the company's Web site essentially falls into the following categories:

1. Ensuring proper use of data collected through the Web site
2. Ensuring the privacy of individuals using the Web site
3. Ensuring the privacy of stored data

Privacy statements that can be read as part of the organization's Web site are complex legal and business processes. Most privacy statements displayed as part of the customer's Internet experience are fairly direct; however, there are Web sites that use circuitous or meaningless language leaving potential customers confused and bewildered (Exhibit 1).

Safeguarding, Processing, and Storing Privacy Data

Controls must be rigidly applied to the enterprise's data center, affecting employees with legitimate data access and those who would attempt unauthorized access. Information privacy procedures should include access to those individuals about whom the data is relevant. These are a few best practices relevant to data privacy:

- Data collection must be lawful and fair. Information collected from individuals and business entities must be lawful in purpose and relevant to the function for which it is being collected.
- There should be an established mechanism for individuals and organizations to discover what information is in the record, how it is being used, to whom it is being disclosed, and the ability to limit that disclosure and use. This process does not mean how it is intended to be used, rather it means how it is actually being used and distributed. There should be a mechanism for an individual to prevent information that was obtained for one purpose from being used or made available for other purposes without her informed consent. Also, there must be an avenue allowing individuals and organizations to correct, amend, or modify all relevant records. Any organization collecting, maintaining, storing, using, or disclosing records of personal data should ensure the reliability of data for their intended use and ensure adequate due diligence preventing misuse.
- Consent. At the time data is being collected from persons and organizations, they should be advised about the purposes for which the data is being collected, the conditions under which the data is collected, and which other parties will have access to the data.
- Quality. Organizations must take reasonable steps to ensure that collected data are accurate, relevant, and do not intrude into areas outside their stated purposes. In essence, it is a restatement of the "least privilege" concept. Organizations must not collect more information than is absolutely necessary

Exhibit 1   Sample Web Site Privacy Statement

The ABC Corporation is dedicated to your privacy and will not collect more information than is necessary to process your orders and provide a personalized shopping experience. For your privacy and peace of mind, we will not rent, sell, or trade your information with others.

How We Use Your Information.

When you place an order, we will ask for your name, e-mail address, mailing address, credit card number, billing address, CVV2 number, and credit card expiration date. This information permits us to expedite the order process and notify you of your orders status.

When you sign up for your Personalized Services we will send you information you have requested and we need only your e-mail address. When you selected the subjects listed under the Personalized Services, we will periodically provide updated information you requested. Through your Personalized Services, we will notify you of changes in our Web pages, www.ABCCorp.com we think you will find of value. These changes will include new products, services and sale items. You can modify or cancel this service at any time.

Information protection

When an order is placed through the www.ABCCorp.com Web site, a link with our secure server is made via Secure Sockets Layer, SSL, technology. All information exchanged between you and our Web site is encrypted for your security and protection. At all times, we safeguard your information against unauthorized access or use.

Cookies

Cookies are small pieces of text we place in your browser's storage so we may customize our Web site for you. Our cookies do not contain any personally identifying information about you but they enable us to provide Web site features such as personalized Web pages for you. It is not necessary to have our cookie on your computer to use our Web site services including browsing, shopping cart, purchases and shipping.

Summary

We are committed to your privacy and security while using the *www.ABCCorp.com* Web site. We use the information you provide to deliver your orders and provide a friendly and useful shopping experience. If for any reason you have any questions or you wish to review your information or its processing, please feel free to contact us at: *customerservice@abccorp.com* or

Joe Blow
Vice President
123 Elm Street
Anywhere, Anystate 11111
Tel: 111.555.2222

to deliver their goods or services and this should be clearly stated in their privacy policy. Persons and entities providing data should be advised under which provisions they might access their data for the purposes of limiting access, uses, or making corrections.

- Data disclosure. Organizations must not use personal or other proprietary data for purposes other than those stated in their policy. Organizations must not divulge protected information without the consent of the person/organization or authorized by law.
- Privacy enforcement. Data being collected and transmitted to relevant entities must be constrained by stated policies and procedures. There must be vigorous steps to ensure that data are used in the fashion it is stated, and nothing more. Auditing steps should be taken ensuring compliance with these policies.

Nonconsent Information Use

Using or disclosing information about someone without their consent or knowledge is not necessarily a violation of their privacy. For example, if Alice buys a new car, a brand name 4×4 Zoomie, she registers the car at the Department of Motor Vehicles knowing those records are publicly available. Publicly, she is seen driving this 4×4 Zoomie on a daily basis. Does she have a reasonable expectation of privacy when the Zoomie dealership sells her name to advertisers targeting consumers of this genre of vehicles? No, she does not. However, if the dealership disclosed the financial data Alice provided in her credit application, then that would be a potentially unlawful act because she does have an expectation of privacy in her financial dealings. They are not public information. She does not display her financial status for public review; it is her business and she is entitled to keep her information private.

Using information that is public does not grant its use to others to inflict or threaten harm. Information use and disclosure can proceed to civil liability regarding its use. If Alice discovers facts about Bob, these facts do not grant her the right to know all facts. When individuals or organizations provide information to third parties in confidence, they have a right to expect that it be protected as private information.

In this vein, it is the responsibility of data receivers to determine which information is private and which is not. There may be facts that are available to the public or a significantly large portion of the public that preclude the need of privacy. Organizations can use and transmit information of this nature without the individual's consent or knowledge. In most settings, individuals have the right to know why their information is collected, how it is going to be used, make corrections, and limit to whom it is going to be disseminated. However, the property rights extended to this data may limit the owner's right to confidentiality depending on how much of the information is already in the public domain.

Employee Privacy Training

Training employees in the nature and risks surrounding privacy is critical to all organizations. Training programs targeting end users about existing policies and procedures will go a long way to providing a sound basis of understanding before granting them access to sensitive information. Refresher training serves to update employees, who already have access, with changes in policies, procedures, and the law. Such training provides the opportunity for situational role playing where they learn to deal with real-life problems in a controlled setting. Employees transferring to a new business unit should receive proper training before data access is granted ensuring continuity in privacy. Challenges facing trainers rest in the fashion they deliver their message. Using tired handouts and boring formal presentations and lectures to teach privacy policies can be tedious and unproductive. Educators should be innovative in their approaches by reaching and involving their audiences. Using case studies, group participation, and practical exercises can go a long way to holding trainees' attention while delivering the message.

Training can also take the form of informal or spontaneous chats between employees. Many organizations have initiated and developed training programs based on mentors and other knowledgeable persons who, through a process of socialization, share their experiences. There are a few pitfalls in this approach, although it is a gentler and kinder way to impart knowledge. Problems exist in documenting the fact that training has actually taken place, attendance at training sessions and the effectiveness of such training.

Another area of concern in the informal training arena is that of bad habits being passed from senior employees to others. Because there is not a test for the correctness of information being disseminated, it is possible that misinformation and poor policy understanding are made part of a new employee's orientation.

Privacy Training Best Practices

Here are some suggestions for privacy training best practices:

- Deliver a basic summary of the organization's vision and mission. Include relevant but not overly detailed explanations of how privacy forms part of the organization's critical asset protection.
- Provide succinct summaries of applicable laws, regulations, and the organization's policies and procedures. It is suggested that much of this material can be made available on the business' internal network (Intranet) that may be browsed by employees at their leisure. Acknowledgements are a good idea to collect from participating employees for future audits.
- Provide training about the data's life cycle: why specific data is collected, its processing, its storage, and its disposal.
- Provide a relevant contact list so attendees know who to contact if they have a question.

Handling Privacy in Supply Chains

E-commerce companies frequently offer what appears to be one-stop shopping with ordering, shipping, and billing services. From the outside, the world sees that the Web site provides all these features, when in fact, many of these services may be actually performed by other companies under contract. For the purpose of understanding, networks of business that participate in such relationships are termed supply chains. In order to do business, companies are often required to pass along a customer's information to suppliers of goods or services so that orders can be placed and filled. Providers of those contracted goods and services are in turn responsible for the protection and security of information they receive during the course of business.

Good privacy procedures require organizations to ensure they collect only the minimum amount of information necessary to process transactions. Receivers of a customer's information are responsible to see how that information is transmitted to third parties and to ensure those third parties handle that data consistent with the original business' policies and procedures. Businesses that transmit client data to their partners must take appropriate steps ensuring that third parties take reasonable precautions to safeguard that data from misuse, unauthorized access, disclosure, modification, and destruction.

Sound business privacy practices will disclose to customers the types of information that are going to be disclosed to third parties and how that it is going to be used by them. In most cases, disclosing how the information will flow from one business to another in the supply chain would be considered prudent. As part of the working relationship between partners, an agreement is made ensuring that the data receivers will provide the same levels of privacy that the original receiver had. Of course, these agreements must be in the form of a contract and must be executed by the appropriate levels of senior management.

There are several areas of concern when making such agreements:

- Within the participating business entities, what is the actual level of data privacy protection?
- How are levels of privacy protection going to be audited? Who is going to conduct the audits? Are the results of these audits going to be made available to the other partners? What is the frequency of such audits?
- Which of the business partners is going to bear the expense of legal action?
- When a new supply chain participant enters, which of the partners is required to approve their admission to the supply chain?

Individual business partners should have the same levels of scrutiny that are applied to large supply chain systems regardless of the size and sponsorship. Agreements and contracts must detail a set of mutually agreed policies and procedures where the collection, processing, storage, and distribution of data are established. Each supply chain affiliate should provide a comprehensive report on data usage and data flow to all additional parties. Reports of data collection and distribution should be collected from all parties in the supply, even those that do not have a direct relationship with one another. This report becomes particularly important should a supply chain member use contractors. Tracking and documenting how all parties treat data might provide the basis for strong defense should legal action be pursued.

Ownership of business partners change often with mergers, acquisitions, closures, and bankruptcies. Supply chain members changing ownership or going out of business can have serious consequences on your ability to deliver goods and services and should be addressed by contingency plans. However, there are potential disasters when a company's structure changes and due diligence in handling data privacy is jeopardized. At this moment, financial risks, affecting all members of the supply chain, escalated. It should be the combined responsibility of the supply chain members to monitor ownership and the status of lawsuits, as these events may affect data privacy. For these reasons, data privacy agreements must be in the form of enforceable contracts applicable to all relevant third parties.

Auditing privacy management procedures might be accomplished by creating ghost personalities and accounts and placing orders that are going to be handled by the supply chain. Experienced auditors will direct their efforts to test goods and services that are delivered by all members of the supply chain and their subcontractors. Steps such as these will test and assess the internal processes and business practices. If an audit account is established and there is an increase of spam or unsolicited junk mail at the address designated as the receiver, it is likely that the account's data has been compromised. Using a bit of detective work and depending on the length of the supply chain, it is possible to locate a "leak."

Another audit technique employs social engineering; the audit contacts members of the supply chain and attempts to buy the customer list or other information. In order to ensure the integrity of data privacy, auditors should regularly test each member of the supply chain to determine if it will sell, rent, or trade data that should be kept private.

If problems are identified with supply chain members disclosing information, they should be immediately addressed in the manner detailed in the agreement or contract. Not surprisingly, it will likely be a matter for the legal unit to handle in consultation with other senior managers. Removing someone from the supply chain can have far reaching ramifications with risk management programs addressing such contingencies.

However, if a customer files a legal action as a result of a violation of privacy, the potential results can devastate all members of the business chain.

Employee Privacy: Is Monitoring the Same as Spying?

Most computer security statistics clearly demonstrate the most devastating information events happen as a result of employees (including full-time, part-time, interns, contractors, and volunteers). There are numbers amounting to more than 80 percent of unlawful computer acts committed by insiders with the remaining 20 percent resulting from individuals outside the organization's walls. The principal tool in the typical office is the workstation comprising the communication portal between employees and the outside world. Before organizations can safeguard their communications resources, they must understand why and what must be protected.

Experience Note   The organization's assets must be defined, identified, and prioritized before efforts can be mounted to keep them safe. Do not protect junk.

Governing the conduct of employees should be a set of well-established policies and procedures. Of course, employees are expected to conduct themselves in conformity with laws and regulations, but an organization's policies provide governance in situations tailored to the particular business structure and its needs. The employee's authority to act is derived from the lines of responsibility and reporting; consequently, there are some basic tenets when considering employee conduct:

- *Least privilege.* This is the practice of constraining a user's information access to the minimum level necessary for her to do her job and nothing more.
- *Separation of duties.* This is the practice of dividing critical function steps among employees so that no one employee has the ability to complete a transaction. For example, if an accounts payable clerk reviews incoming invoices and prepares checks, it is the vice president who must sign them before they may be sent.
- *Accountability.* This is the overarching goal of conscientious auditing to review business practices and determine if they are in conformity with laws, regulations, policies and procedures. Accountability looks for potential unlawful acts, abuse, single points of failure, business efficiency and effectiveness, separation of duties, and least privilege.

An employee's job-related conduct must not jeopardize the organization's critical assets, meaning the organization's legitimate ability to achieve its profitable goals.

Legalities in Employee Monitoring

There is much made of lawfully monitoring employees' conduct on the job. And, there seems to be a fair degree of misunderstanding on the part of senior managers and legal units. The fact of employee monitoring or auditing is this: the most active attacks on the organization's assets originate from outside the organization, but the most successful and financially devastating attacks come from employees, former employees, contractors, and others who had or have legitimate access to sensitive information.

Experience Note   Organizations can and will be held legally liable for the acts of their employees even if those employees are not longer employed. Unless organizations monitor and audit the activities of their employees, they are remiss in their legal responsibilities.

There are federal and state criminal statutes governing "listening" to employees' conversations and intercepting third-party electronic communications. These laws include actions such as eavesdropping on oral conversations, intercepting electronic communications, and the rights of those monitored by these techniques. Federal and many state laws define wire communications as electronically exchanged information through cable, wires, or transmitted through the air. Examples would include wireless local area networks, WLANs, conventional cable-connected networks, wire-connected telephones, cellular telephones, and cordless telephones.

Oral communications are exchanged in face-to-face situations, where one or more persons are vocalizing one to another without interceding technology. Intercepting communications is the process by which the contents of a communication, either oral, wireless or wire, is acquired by a third party. There is another type of employee monitoring where employers install video camera equipment to capture the activities of their employees and others on property under their control.

Oral Communications

There is federal law protection of oral communications not transmitted by means of electronic transmission such as telephone or voice over IP means. Federal laws protect the interception of oral communications or the disclosure of the contents of those communications that were unlawfully intercepted. Interestingly, legal privacy protection is only extended to oral communications that have a reasonable expectation of privacy. If there is a reasonable expectation of privacy, the only means by which an oral communication may be intercepted (absent a consenting third party) is by a law officer using a court ordered wiretap.

Experience Note If employers want to lawfully monitor the conversations of employees having a reasonable expectation of privacy, they must not use mechanical, electronic, or any other device to intercept the conversation. Intercepting an oral conversation may only take place where the people talking do not have a reasonable expectation of privacy. Employers may obtain consent from one or more of the persons present at the conversation and those persons may use electronic means to record the conversation. In the latter case, it is not a requirement that the consenting person speak during the conversation, it is only required that they have a legitimate right to be present during the conversation. It is important to note that several states have statutes outlawing the use of recording equipment. Ensure legal counsel is consulted before using this monitoring technique.

Wire Communications

Federal laws protect the sanctity of telephone communications and other electronically transmitted communications (Title 18, United States Code Section 2511). Under this statute if an employer intercepts or discloses the content of an unlawfully intercepted communication, it could result in a criminal prosecution. It is important to note that this statute has application to cellular telephones, cordless telephones, hard-wire telephones, and possibly wireless networks. However, there are some exceptions to this law:

- Consent of at least one of the participating parties to the electronic communication. As in the oral communication privacy law, it is required that only one person, having a legitimate presence, provide consent to monitoring. Currently, many organizations obtain continuing consent or waivers from their employees as a condition of their employment. Employers are wise to obtain signed employee acknowledgement and consent before monitoring.
- There is not a reasonable expectation of privacy to the electronic communication. Many employers announce that communications with their employees are possibly being monitored; this relieves the reasonable expectation of privacy. Employers might advise their employees and others that use of the organization's electronic equipment for any purpose other than business is not permitted.

Trap and Trace and Pen Register Installations

There are pieces of hardware known by their purpose of "trap and trace" that are installed to identify telephone numbers that are calling other telephones. Trapping and tracing telephone numbers refers to tracing a caller's telephone number to a telephone located at a specific location at a specific time. Equipment used to trap and trace a telephone call generally must be used in conjunction with the local telephone carrier and is restricted to law enforcement actions supported by court ordered installations. Pen registers are electronic devices that, when installed on a telephone line, identify the numbers dialed out from a targeted telephone. This equipment is installed only to identify telephone numbers either received or called. Trap and trace equipment will not and must not be used to monitor communication's content, merely the involved telephone numbers.

Under the provisions of Title 18 United States Code, Section 3121 there are general prohibitions regarding the installation of pen register and trap and trace equipment with the requirement of first obtaining a court order described under Section 3123. Court orders are generally obtained by law enforcement agents with an effective life of 60 days, and may be extended for additional periods of time. It is important to note that the application and court order for pen register and trap and trace equipment is applicable only to telephone lines. Using software applications and tools to locate IP addresses is not addressed in this statute and does not require any special type of court order or warrant.

Video and Still Camera Monitoring

Monitoring activities on property under the control of employers is allowed using video and still camera technology. It is a requirement, however, that only images are viewed and recorded, not communications either oral or electronic. For example, a bank uses hidden video camera or still camera technology to record the activities within the confines of the vault. As part of their employment, all employees are advised that only the bank's business may be conducted on the property during business hours and that employees are not entitled to a reasonable expectation of privacy with respect to their actions. During business hours, the camera captures an employee taking cash from her drawer and passing it to a customer in exchange for a small paper package that she immediately places in her pocketbook. No conversational exchange was recorded or intercepted. Is this a lawfully monitored incident? In all likelihood, the answer is "yes."

However, there are conditions under which employers may not record images as employees have expectations of privacy. For example, restroom stalls are areas where employees have a reasonable expectation of privacy. Monitoring their activities with video or still-camera equipment there would be prohibited. However, video camera surveillance of the work area where an employee can observe the equipment negates any reasonable expectation of privacy, *Vega-Rodriguez v. Puerto Rican Telephone Co.,* 110 F. 3d 174 (1997).

Monitoring E-Mail and the Employee Workstation Conduct

Employers' monitoring of e-mail used to be the $64,000 question. The matter is best addressed in the context that employers are liable for the conduct of their employees, even when employees are using the organization's equipment after business hours. Employees sending and receiving racist, sexist, and sexually explicit e-mail leave a trail that exposes an employer to liabilities based on claims of hostile work environment and negligence.

The courts have decided that it is the responsibility of employers to monitor the activities of their employees, and failing to do so can result in substantial settlements in the defendant's favor. In the matter of *Blakey v. Continental Airlines, Inc.,* June 1, 2000, the New Jersey Supreme Court unanimously decided that certain postings made to a work-related electronic bulletin board constituted a hostile work environment for which the employer could be held liable. The court decided that if the employer had noticed that its employees were posting messages to the bulletin board that were defamatory and harassing, the employer had a duty and responsibility to remedy that harassment.

Productivity and liability are issues that drive employers to monitor employee use of e-mail systems in the workplace. Failing to take appropriate levels of discipline often result in defendant's prevailing in civil suits. Presently, the courts have been inclined to side with the employer's position in the debate over employee's electronic privacy.

In *Smyth v. The Pillsbury Co.,* 914 F. Supp. 97 (Eastern District of Pa., 1996), the District Court decided that the employee did not have a reasonable expectation of privacy by his use of the internal e-mail system to communicate with his supervisor. The company had previously stated that e-mail communications would remain confidential. The court found that it was lawful for the company to intercept the employee's e-mail and terminate him for transmitting inappropriate communications using the company's e-mail. In this case, the court ruled that no employee had a reasonable expectation of privacy using e-mail sent over the company's e-mail network.

In the matter of *McLaren v. Microsoft Corp.,* No.05–97–00824-CV, 1999 Texas App. Texas Ct. App., May 28, 1999, the employee filed e-mail messages in "personal folders" on his office computer with password protection. The court ruled the employee did not have a reasonable expectation of privacy preventing the company from viewing these files. In their decision, the court determined the employee's e-mail messages were not his personal property, rather they were part of the employer's office environment. Accordingly, the employer's need to prevent inappropriate use of its e-mail system outweighed the employee's privacy, and the company had a legitimate right to access data stored in the employee's "personal folders."

Decisions made in the California State court system ruled that employees do not have cause of action for wrongful termination when they were fired because of their objections to their employers' e-mail monitoring activities. The relevant cases are *Bourke v. Nissan Motor Corp.,* No. B068705 (Cal. Ct. App. July 26, 1993); and *Shoars v. Epson America, Inc.,* No. B 073243 (Cal. Ct. App., rev. dec., No. S040065, 1994 Cal. LEXIS 3670, June 29, 1994, no published decision).

In 1986, the Electronic Communications Privacy Act (ECPA), 18 U.S. Code 2700 *et seq.* became federal law prohibiting the interception and unlawful use of intercepted electronic communications. Although the specific term of e-mail is not mentioned in the statute, the legislative history and current case law indicate that e-mail falls within its coverage. For the purposes of employers monitoring e-mail activities of their employees, there are three major exceptions:

1. *Provider exception to monitoring electronic communications.* The employer is the provider of the e-mail system and has the right to monitor its use preventing prohibited or unlawful behavior.
2. *Prior consent exception.* This exception is drawn on the conclusion that the employee has given her prior consent to having her electronic communications monitored.
3. *Business use exception.* This exception is based on the organization's policy that only proper official business may be conducted using the e-mail system.

Employee Legal Defense

With recent and past legal decisions regarding employees' privacy rights in the electronic workplace, there are some things that should be considered:

- Do not look to the Fourth Amendment to the Constitution for privacy protection as it only applies to the citizen's relationship with government and law enforcement agencies. Depending on an organization's policies and procedures, if an employer searches an employee's workstation where there is a reasonable expectation of privacy, then the employer may be held liable. If an employer searches an employee's workstation at the direction of law enforcement agents and it is determined there is a reasonable expectation of privacy, it is likely any evidence will be excluded from criminal proceedings under the doctrine of "fruits of a poisonous tree."
- For an invasion of an employee's privacy, an employee must have an expectation of privacy that society considers reasonable (*Medical Laboratory Management Consultants v. ABC, Inc.,* 30 F. Supp. 2d 1182, 1998). For an intrusion to be actionable in civil proceedings, it must violate the solitude or seclusion of another or her private affairs or concerns is subject to liability to the other for invasion of her privacy if the intrusion is highly offensive to a reasonable person. In determining whether the employees' privacy expectation is reasonable, the workplace should include areas and artifacts related to work that are under control of the employer even if employees bring personal items to work. Not everything brought into the workplace can be considered part of the workplace, e.g., pocketbooks, handbags, briefcases, etc. In the case, *O'Connor v. Ortega,* 480 U.S. 709 (1987), the court upheld the expectation of privacy as reasonable given that the employer had not discouraged employees from bringing personal items to their workplace neither had they established any privacy policies.
- Lack of formal official use policy. Even in today's world, some employers fail to institute policies governing official use only of business resources. Employees might be able to use the lack of enforced official use policy as grounds

for wrongful termination in the event of objectionable behavior. (*United States v. Slanina,* No. 00–20926 5th Cir. Feb. 21, 2002)

- Hard drive cleansing. There are super cleansing programs available for download offering differing levels of assurance that discarded data have been erased. Regrettably, as many have experienced, there are often records of e-mail and Internet browsing stored in other locations of the organization's network.
- Employees often deny they were viewing objectionable material and that the material in question was received from unsolicited sources. The viability of this argument will depend on the amount, type, and characteristics of the material. If material is discovered in the form of sexually explicit banner advertisements with a few thumbnail images, there might be some merit to the employee's argument. However, if there is a sizeable cache of full-size material that has been stored on the employee's workstation covering a lengthy period of time, then this argument is not persuasive.

Employee Monitoring Best Practices

The best philosophy for employee monitoring is to "get it out in the open." Do not hide the fact that employees are going to be monitored. If employers attempt to conceal employee-monitoring activities, it could result in employees having a reasonable expectation of privacy in their behavior at work. Employers choosing to engage in some type of employee monitoring should consider the following:

- Senior managers should formally identify the business purpose of employee monitoring and confine their monitoring to that purpose alone. It is a matter of legal business practices and continuing profitability. If employee monitoring is based in any other purpose, then prepare for endless litigation.
- Employers should have plainly written policies and procedures describing the nature, extent, and uses of monitoring. Wise employers will clarify that monitoring employee conduct is a matter of protecting the bottom line. Do not be afraid to reward good employee behavior that is discovered as a result of monitoring.
- Employers should selectively monitor electronic and oral communications unless there is a very strong reason to do otherwise.
- Advise employees, on all levels, that the organization has formal policies and procedures for monitoring. Identify what types of monitoring is going to be conducted such as e-mail, Internet browsing, telephone calls, voice mail, workstation files, server logs, router logs, video surveillance, etc.
- Advise employees and have them formally acknowledge that all equipment and resources belonging to the organization are for official use only and there is not any reasonable expectation of privacy for any employee, including senior managers. Employees should know that placing a password to protect a file does not ensure privacy. Organizations should determine if they are going to allow employees to use encryption and thereby evade monitoring. Rest assured if encryption is permitted, its use may be corrupted and the organization's intellectual property can be transmitted outside the company with little chance of detection.
- Should telephone calls between employees and outsiders be recorded, organizations should consider using a intercessory recording announcing that telephone conversations are being recorded for quality assurance or other purposes.

- Organizations must have designated procedures addressing the manner in which captured communications and recorded behavior will be reviewed for compliance. It is imperative that vigorous controls are in place relating to the dissemination of information obtained through employee monitoring.

Employee Polygraphs

This is a touchy topic and generally only employed by government agencies screening prospective and active employees who will have access to sensitive or classified information. The following are the conditions under which polygraphs are usually administered:

- Generally, employers cannot use polygraph testing to screen employees, except in cases of national defense or security concerns.
- Generally, employers can use polygraphs to screen employees who have direct access to controlled substances in the course of their employment.
- Generally, employers may screen employees who are security guards with access to sensitive areas.

Under the provisions of the federal Employee Polygraph Protection Act, Title 29 United States Code Section 2001–2007, testing employees must fall within the following investigation scope:

- There must be an ongoing investigation involving an actual economic loss.
- The employee that is going to be tested must have had access to items that resulted in the loss.
- There must be a reasonable suspicion that the employee was involved.
- Employees must be provided with a statement concerning the reasons why the test is to be performed. Employers must provide a statement containing the above listed information at least 48 hours before testing, it must be written so the employee can understand it, and an agency representative must sign it.

During polygraph testing the employee has the following rights:

- Polygraphs may not be used for random testing or for investigations of unspecified events.
- Employees may terminate the examination at any time.
- Employees cannot be asked intrusive or degrading questions.
- Employees cannot be asked questions concerning religious beliefs, racial opinions, political beliefs, sexual preferences, or beliefs about labor organizations.
- Employees cannot be tested if a qualified physician has advised, in writing, against testing on mental, physical, or medical grounds.

Industry-Specific Privacy Issues

Access to Financial Records Is Denied to Government Agencies

Title 12 United States Code Section 3402, access to financial records by U.S. government authorities is prohibited except in the following circumstances:

- The customer of financial records has authorized the disclosure.
- The relevant financial records are disclosed in response to an administrative subpoena or summons.
- The relevant financial records are disclosed in response to a judicial subpoena.
- The relevant financial records are disclosed in response to formal written request in conformity with the provisions of Section 3408 of Title 12.

Gramm–Leach–Bliley Act

This is a law intended to provide information privacy protection obligating each financial institution to respect the privacy of its customers and protect the security and confidentiality of the customers' nonpublic personal information, Title 15 United States Code Sections 6801–6810.

- Financial institutions may not disclose a customer's account number for the purpose of marketing by a third party.
- Financial institutions must develop procedures to protect information from unauthorized access that could result in harm to customers.
- Financial institutions must advise customers in a clear and timely manner of their policies regarding the disclosure of information with third parties.
- Financial institutions must provide a vehicle for customers to opt out of arrangements refusing permission to disclose their nonpublic information to third parties.

Health Insurance Portability and Accountability Act

HIPAA governs health care communications and practices knowing they play an essential role in ensuring individuals receive effective health care (45 CFR 160–164). HIPAA has the goal of improving the effectiveness and efficiency of the health care system including comprehensive measures not the least of which are provisions for protecting the privacy of individual health information. To this end, HIPAA mandates the adoption of privacy protections for individually identifiable health information.

Most health plans and health care providers are covered by the new rule (HIPAA) and must have complied with the new requirements by April 14, 2003. For the first time, HIPAA creates national standards safeguarding the privacy of individuals' health information:

- It provides patients with more control over the use and disclosure of their health records.
- It establishes safeguards that health care providers must achieve protecting the privacy of individuals' health information.
- It makes covered entities accountable, with civil and criminal laws when a patient's privacy rights are violated.
- It empowers patients to discover how their information might be used and about disclosures of their information that have been made.
- HIPAA limits the release of information reasonably needed for the specific purpose of the disclosure.
- HIPAA grants individuals the right to examine and obtain copies of their own health records, request corrections, and limit how they might be released.

- HIPAA grants individuals control over uses and disclosures of their health information.

Due to the nature of these types of communications and the environment in which individuals receive care, the potential for a person's health-related information to be disclosed is great. For example, a patient's conversation with their physician may be overheard in the confines of a two-patient hospital room.

HIPAA privacy rules are not intended to preclude customary or essential communications in the administration of patient care, nor does it require that all risk of disclosure be eliminated to satisfy its requirements. HIPAA privacy rules permit certain types of incidental uses or disclosures of protected health information when the covered health care entity has installed reasonable safeguards with required policies and procedures safeguarding privacy.

Generally HIPAA privacy rules require the following of the average health care provider or covered health plan:

- Notify individuals of their privacy rights and how their health care information can be used.
- Implement privacy procedures for covered entities, e.g., clinics, hospitals, health care plans, etc.
- Train employees of covered entities to understand and implement privacy procedures.
- Designate at least one individual to be responsible for the adoption and compliance with privacy procedures under HIPAA.
- Secure health records containing individually identifiable health information so they are not accessible to those not needing to know.

There are many important aspects of HIPAA, including the patient's right to file complaints regarding privacy to the covered health care entity or the Office of Inspector General, Department of Health and Human Services.

Compliance with the new HIPAA privacy standards is required of the covered entities:

- Health care plans
- Health care clearinghouses
- Health care providers who conduct certain financial and administrative transactions such as billing and fund transfers. These entities are bound by HIPAA privacy standards even if they contract with third parties to perform some functions.
- HIPAA Privacy rules compliance became effective April 14, 2003, with small health plans compliant by April 14, 2004.

Fair Credit Reporting Act

The federal Fair Credit Reporting Act (FCRA) was created to promote fairness, accuracy, and privacy of information relating to consumer credit histories held by Credit Reporting Agencies (15 United States Code Sections 1681–1681). As a matter of background, most credit reporting agencies are credit bureaus that collect and sell credit histories. Under provisions of the FCRA, consumers have very specific rights and in some cases, these rights have been expanded under state laws.

These are a few of the rights granted under the FCRA to consumers:

- Individuals and organizations have the right to review the information held in their file including a list of anyone who has requested to see the information. Credit reporting agencies are required to provide report copies for a nominal charge after proper request.
- Consumers must be advised if information from their credit file has been used to deny credit, insurance, or employment. This notification must include the name, address, and telephone number of the credit-reporting agency providing the credit history report.
- Consumers have the right to dispute inaccurate information with the credit-reporting agency. If notified of inaccuracies, it is the credit-reporting agency's responsibility to investigate the disputed items by presenting to its credit source all relevant evidence provided by the consumer unless it is determined the dispute is frivolous. The information source must review the consumer's evidence and report its findings to the credit-reporting agency that must deliver a written report of the investigation to the consumer. If the dispute cannot be resolved, then the consumer may add a statement to his file, and credit reports must normally include a summary of this statement in future reports.
- If a consumer disputes an item with the source of the information, they may not report the credit information to the credit-reporting agency without including notice of the dispute. Once the source of credit information is notified of an inaccuracy, it may not continue to report the identified inaccurate information.
- Access to credit history information is limited. The credit reporting agency may only provide information to individuals recognized by the FCRA: creditors, insurers, employers, landlords, and other relevant businesses.
- Consumers must provide consent for their credit history reports to be provided to employers or for reports that contain medical information. Credit reporting agencies may not provide information to employers, prospective employers, or reports containing medical information without the consumer's consent.

Penalties for failing to comply with FCRA tenets include:

- Civil liabilities for willful and negligent noncompliance including actual damages, attorneys' fees, punitive and statutory damages.
- Class actions can be brought under standards of civil liability.
- Criminal penalties for obtaining information under false pretenses and unauthorized disclosures. Of course, penalties include incarceration, fines, and restitution.
- Administrative actions may be sought by the Federal Trade Commission resulting in financial penalties against any person knowingly violating the FCRA.

Family Education Privacy Rights

Family educational and privacy rights are guaranteed by this federal law found at Title 20, United States Code, Section 1232g. Contingent upon the continued receipt of federal funding, it sets conditions for the availability of student records to parents who have children in school or for adults attending school. It grants the right to inspect and review education records of children and mandates that each institution establish appropriate procedures for granting requests by parents to inspect records. Under the tenets of this law, parents have the right to have a hearing challenging the content of such student's education records ensuring that the records are accurate or otherwise not in violation of the student's privacy rights. Such challenges may serve to correct, delete inaccuracies, or delete misleading or inappropriate data contained in the student's education records. Parents also have a right to insert into such records a written explanation respecting the content of these records. When a student has attained the age of eighteen or is attending post-secondary educational institutions, the permission or rights of the parents are accorded to the student.

Educational institutions have the right to disclose educational records to teachers and school officials including teachers and school officials in other schools having legitimate educational interest in the behavior and performance of the student.

By way of enforcement, the Secretary of Education must take appropriate actions enforcing this law and address violation. Failing to voluntarily comply can result in the Secretary terminating federal assistance to the educational institution.

Cable TV Privacy Act

Under the provisions of this law, 47 U.S. Code 551, at least yearly a cable TV operator must provide written notice to subscribers clearly and conspicuously advising of the nature of personally identifiable information collected with respect to the subscriber and the use of such information.

Cable operators are required to notify subscribers of the nature, frequency, and purpose of any disclosures, including the identification of persons to whom disclosure is made, the period during which this information is maintained by the operator, and the times and places at which the subscriber may have access to this information.

Cable operators cannot use the cable system to collect personally identifiable information about subscribers without the prior written consent of the subscriber.

Operators are prohibited from disclosing personally identifiable information concerning subscribers without their written consent. However, cable operators may use collected information or go about the process of collecting sufficient information in order to render services and conduct legitimate business. Operators may disclose personally identifiable information pursuant to a court order and must notify the subscriber of such orders. Disclosure of personally identifiable information to governmental entities will require a court order if there is clear and convincing evidence that the subscriber is reasonably suspected of engaging in criminal activity and the information sought is material to the case. In such cases, the law allows the subscriber to appear and contest the entity's claim.

A cable subscriber must be provided access to all personally identifiable information in the possession of the operator at reasonable times and places. Subscribers are provided reasonable opportunities to correct any errors. Cable operators may destroy personally identifiable information if the information is no longer necessary to conduct business.

Civil actions are directed to the United States district courts with damages, costs, and attorney's fees possibly awarded as part of any remedy.

Wrongful Disclosure of Videotape Rental or Sale Records (18 U.S. Code 2710)

Vendors engaged in the rental and sales of videotapes or similar products are prohibited from knowingly disclosing personally identifiable information concerning any consumer unless the following is met:

- There is informed written consent from the consumer given at the time the disclosure is sought.

- There is a warrant issued under the Federal Rules of Criminal Procedure, equivalent state warrant, grand jury subpoena, or court order.
- Pursuant to a court order in a civil proceeding, that is based on a showing of compelling need for the information that cannot be accommodated by any other means.
- Court orders authorizing personally identifying information disclosure shall only be issued with prior notice to the consumer and if the law enforcement agency shows there is probably cause to believe that the records or other information are relevant to a legitimate law enforcement inquiry.

If videotape service providers knowingly disclose to any person, personally identifiable information concerning any consumer of video tape sales or rentals, they can be held liable to the aggrieved person (consumer). Any person (plaintiff) alleging violations of this law by filing civil actions in U.S. District Court may seek financial remedies. The court may award actual damages to the plaintiff amounting to not less than $2,500, punitive damages in any appropriate amount, and other equitable relief the court determines to be appropriate and other reasonable fees including attorney's fees.

Children's Online Privacy Protection Act (COPPA)

Effective April 21, 2000, COPPA became law, addressing the online collection of personal information about children under the age of 13 must be safeguarded and limited (15 U.S. Code 6501). This law applies to the commercial operation of a Web site, online services, or general audience Web sites where vendors have knowledge these children are going to be providing personal information. There are actually several tests, applied by the Federal Trade Commission, responsible for this law's enforcement, to determine if the Web site is directed to children:

- Visual or audio content of the Web site
- Age of the models on the site
- Language of the site
- Advertising on the site appealing to children
- Information regarding the age of the actual or intended audience
- Use of animated characters
- Child-oriented features

Web site operators are defined as the persons responsible for ownership and control of the online services, individuals paying for the collection and maintenance of the information, individuals whose roles are defined by contract with respect to the collected information, and the role the target Web site has in collecting or maintaining the information.

Personal information, for the purposes of COPPA, is basically defined as a child's individually identifiable information collected through online services. Items such as name, home address, e-mail address, telephone numbers, age, or any other information permitting identification or making contact possible, are covered under the law. There are other items that frequently escape notice considered part of this pool of identifiable information:

- Hobbies
- Interests

- Tracking mechanisms such as cookies
- School attendance

On Web sites, operators must have links to privacy policies on their home page advising of information privacy practices and on each Web page where personally identifiable information is collected from children. Links to privacy notices must be clear and easy to see. They must be clearly written and plainly understandable and include:

- Name and contact information, address, telephone number, and e-mail address of Web site operator(s) collecting or maintaining children's information.
- If more than one Web site operator is collecting information at the Web site, the site may provide contact information for only one operator who is designated to respond to all inquiries from parents about the Web site's privacy, policies, and procedures.
- Kinds of personal information collected from children, e.g., name, address, etc.
- Means by which the information is collected, e.g., directly from children or indirectly using a mechanism such as cookies.
- Uses of the information by the operator. For example, is the information used for marketing purposes, contest participation, etc.?
- Operators must disclose whether the child's information is transmitted to third parties. If this is the case, the operator must disclose the kinds of business in which the information recipients are engaged, the general purposes they intend to use the information, and if the recipients have agreed to maintain the confidentiality and security of the personal information.
- Parents must have the option to agree to the collection and use of children's information without consenting to the disclosure of the information to third parties.
- Parents can review the child's personal information, requesting to have it deleted and refusing to permit any further collection or use of the child's information. The Web page's notice must also declare the procedures for parents to follow if they wish to take any action or make any inquiry.

The notice to parents must have the same information included on the notice on the Web site. Operators must notify parents that they wish to collect personal information from children, that the parent's consent is necessary for the collection, use and disclosure of the information, and of the means by which the parent can provide consent. The notice to parents must be written clearly and understandably.

It may not contain any unrelated or confusing information. Operators are allowed to use different methods of parental notification including sending an e-mail message to the parent, telephone call or by sending a notice by conventional mail. Operators must obtain verifiable parental consent, from the child's parent, before collecting or disclosing a child's personal information. In short, operators must take reasonable steps ensuring that a child's parent receives notice of the operator's information practices and consents to those practices before collecting, using, or disclosing a child's personal information.

Parental consent is not necessary in the following conditions:

- Operator collects an e-mail address belonging to a child or parent to provide notice to obtain consent.
- Operator collects an e-mail address to respond to a one-time request from a child, and then deletes it.

- Operator collects an e-mail address to respond more than once to specific requests. In this case, the operator must notify parents that it is communicating with the child and provide the parent with the opportunity to halt the communication before transmitting a second communication to the child.
- Operator collects a child's name or other contact information to protect the safety of the child who is participating on the site. In this fashion, the operator must notify parents and provide them the opportunity to prevent further use of the information.
- Operator collects a child's name or contact information to protect the security or liability of the Web site or to respond to law enforcement. The operator may not use the information for any other purpose.

Operators are required to send notices and seek consent from parents if there are material changes in their collection, use or change disclosure practices to which parents had consented previously. Operators must send parental notices and seek new consent, if the third parties materially change or if they change their information handling practices.

Operators must disclose the types of personal information they collect from children to parents when requested by the parents. Operators are legally required to employ reasonable procedures ensuring they are, in fact, communicating with the child's parents before they provide access to the child's personal information.

Experience Note Web site operators, appealing to young children, should have extensive documentation of their privacy policies and procedures. They must document their communications with parents and their children thoroughly if they wish to avoid legal actions. Vendors are wise to include the scope and existence of this documentation as part of their audit procedures.

Operators may deploy a variety of means in verifying parents' identities:

- Obtaining a personally signed form from the parent received by the operator via conventional mail or facsimile
- Operators may accept and verify a credit card number
- Operators may accept telephone calls from parents
- Operators may accept e-mail accompanied by the parent's digital signature Operators may accept an e-mail with a PIN or password obtained through a verification method

Web site operators following prudent and reasonable procedures, acting in good faith to a request for parental access to a child's personal information, may be protected from liability under federal law for inadvertent disclosures of a child's information to someone purporting to be a parent.

Parents may revoke their consent refusing to permit operators to further collect or use their child's information. They may advise operators they wish to have the information deleted and request operators to cease communicating further with their child.

COPPA enforcement is the responsibility of the Federal Trade Commission who examines operator's practices for deception and a lack of fairness. Their enforcement actions are pursued through civil processes and usually target representations, omissions, fraud, or deceptions where operators mislead consumers affecting behavior or decisions about the product or services.

Federal Privacy Act

In 1974, the federal government became bound by the Privacy Act, 5 U.S. Code 552. With the passage of this law, Congress established controls over the collection and disclosure of personal information. The federal government has a voracious personal information appetite collecting an incredibly wide range of individual information through military records, social security records, welfare programs, health care programs, federal employment, food stamps, farm subsidies, emergency assistance, government financial instruments, tax records, court records, grants, student loans, etc.

There are certain rights and controls within this law:

- Right to see one's records (there are certain exemptions)
- Right to amend that record if it contains inaccurate, irrelevant, untimely, or incomplete information
- Right to sue the government for violations of the statute, including unauthorized access, etc.

The Right to Privacy law mandates certain constraints on informational practices of federal agencies by requiring them to ensure their records are relevant, accurate, and complete. Federal agencies are prohibited in collecting or maintaining information about the way individuals exercise their First Amendment rights. Of course, agencies may collect this type of information if the individual consents to the practice or is within the scope of a legitimate law enforcement investigation.

Individuals may request to review their information but there are some conditions to this request. Requests only apply to information within the statutory definition of a "system of records." The system of records refers to records that can be retrieved by the individual's name, Social Security number, date of birth, or some other unique personal identifier. The Privacy Act does not apply to information about individuals contained in records that are filed under other subjects. For example, if a person purchased federal government bonds but they were purchased in the name of a business, it is likely the person actually making the purchase would not be indexed and her information would not likely be recoverable.

Any federal, state, or local government agency requesting an individual's Social Security number is required to advise that individual whether that information is mandatory or voluntary. If mandatory, they are required to cite the statutory or other authority by which the number is requested and their intended uses of it.

There are exemptions described in the Act under which an agency can withhold certain types of individual information. Such examples of exempted information are classified information or information contained in certain criminal investigations. Information relating to a confidential informant is exempted for obvious reasons as are individuals requesting confidentiality when they provide background information about someone seeking federal employment.

Information relating to an individual's name and address may not be sold, traded, or rented by an agency unless specifically authorized by law.

Safe Harbor Issues in the United States

In 2000, the European Union (EU) adopted the European Commissions Directive on Data Protection (Safe Harbor) prohibiting the transfer of personal data to non-EU nations that do not meet the EU standard for privacy protection. The United States has taken a different route to secure privacy protection adopting a combination of legislation, regulation, and self-regulation where the EU has adopted a stance of data protection agencies; registration of databases, and in some cases approval before personal data processing can be begun.

The Department of Commerce, acting with the European Commission, has developed a framework for "safe harbor" where U.S. businesses can avoid experiencing interruptions in their business operations with the EU or possibly face prosecution under EU privacy laws. The Department of Commerce has established a means certifying to the EU that U.S. registered companies provide adequate privacy safeguards as defined by the directive.*

Data controllers in Europe know which U.S. companies can receive data by the fact that the U.S. Department of Commerce, on this Web site, publicly posts those organizations that have joined Safe Harbor. By self-certification, U.S. companies can become placed on the Safe Harbor Web list. Through the self-certification process, U.S. organizations declare they will comply with Safe Harbor privacy requirements. European Union Data Protection Directive (95/46/EC) mandates that organizations provide adequate protection of data relevant to EU residents. If a U.S. organization publicly declares its compliance to Safe Harbor principles, it is presumed to provide adequate information protection. In their most basic form, Safe Harbor principles basically consist of the following:

- Notice of the purpose the information is being collected, its uses, and disclosures.
- Individual personal information may be reviewed making corrections, deletions, amendments, and modifications. The individual also has right to determine to whom the information might be revealed and which parts will be disclosed. The collector of the information is bound to safeguard the information for the time it is stored, whether it is being used or not.
- Entities receiving personal information from the original collector are bound to comply with the privacy principles of Safe Harbor.
- The collector of personal information is bound to adequately protect the information from unauthorized access, disclosure, or use.

After they certify, businesses are subject to oversight and enforcement by the Federal Trade Commission or the Department of Transportation dealing with unfair and deceptive practices. Subscribing organizations are required to identify an independent body whose purpose it is to resolve disputes so anyone with a complaint knows where to file.

One of the guiding principles of Safe Harbor is that the transfer of data to U.S. participants cannot be transmitted to others outside the Safe Harbor confines. The only exception to this rule is if the disclosure is made to a third party acting as an agent under the direction of a member of Safe Harbor. It is a requirement that receiving third parties have to observe similar information privacy protections as the member-business.

Experience Note Becoming a member of Safe Harbor is voluntary with the rules applying only to those who enlist.

Enforcement of Safe Harbor privacy requirements in the United States is essentially driven by filed complaints. Resolution forums established for that purpose address initial disputes. It is expected these entities will investigate and attempt to resolve complaints as an initial step. However, if members fail to adhere to rulings, then cases

---

* Complete information is available at www.export.gov/safeharbor/index.html.

will be transmitted to the Federal Trade Commission or Department of Transportation who have the ability to legally obligate them into compliance. If there are more serious cases of noncompliance, then they will be removed from the membership list, meaning they can no longer receive personal information data transfers from the EU under Safe Harbor.

Compliance with Safe Harbor membership has Federal Trade Commission enforcement through the Federal Trade Commission Act, making it unlawful to make misrepresentations or engage in deceptive practices misleading consumers. If businesses declare they are providing a specific set of information privacy protections and fail to do so, this is going to be interpreted as a deceptive practice resulting in civil or administrative enforcement actions from the Federal Trade Commission.

Organizations undergo the self-certify process by providing a letter, signed by an officer on behalf of the organization that it is joining Safe Harbor, containing the following information:

- Name of organization, mailing address, e-mail address, telephone and facsimile numbers
- Description of the organization's activities relating to personal information received from the EU
- Description of the organization's privacy policies for personal information protection including:
  - Where is the organization's privacy policy available for public viewing?
  - What is the privacy policy's effective date of implementation?
  - What is the organization's official contact for addressing complaints, information access requests, and other issues under Safe Harbor?
  - What is the statutory body having jurisdiction to hear complaints against the organization regarding allegations of unfair, deceptive practices, violations of laws and regulations?
  - What is the name of any privacy program in which the petitioning organization is a member?
  - What is the method of compliance verification?
  - What is the mechanism available to investigate unresolved complaints?

Adherence to the Safe Harbor rules is not limited to the time the organization is exchanging data with the EU. It means that the member-organization continues to observe and apply Safe Harbor rules to the EU data as long as the organization stores, uses, or discloses the information even if it leaves Safe Harbor membership.

Appendix A

The following is a list of assigned port numbers for Well-Known Ports TCP and UDP. A complete listing of assigned port numbers can be found at http://iana.org/assignments/port-numbers.

Port Numbers (Updated 2/9/2003)

Port numbers are divided into three ranges:

1. Well-Known Ports are those numbered from 0 through 1023.
2. Registered Ports are those numbered from 1024 through 49,151.
3. Dynamic or Private Ports are those numbered from 49,152 through 65,535.

Well-Known Port Numbers

The Well-Known Ports are assigned by the IANA (Internet Assigned Numbers Authority) and on most systems can only be used by system (or root) processes or by programs executed by privileged users. Ports are used in the TCP [RFC793] to name the ends of logical connections that carry long-term conversations. For the purpose of providing services to unknown callers, a service contact port is defined. This list specifies the port used by the server process as its contact port. The contact port is sometimes called the "well-known port." To the extent possible, these same port assignments are used with the UDP [RFC768].

Port Assignments

Keyword	Decimal	Description
	0/tcp	Reserved
	0/udp	Reserved
#		Jon Postel < postel@isi.edu >
tcpmux	1/tcp	TCP Port Service Multiplexer
tcpmux	1/udp	TCP Port Service Multiplexer
#		Mark Lottor < MKL@nisc.sri.com >

Keyword	Decimal	Description
compressnet	2/tcp	Management Utility
compressnet	2/udp	Management Utility
compressnet	3/tcp	Compression Process
compressnet	3/udp	Compression Process
#		Bernie Volz < VOLZ@PROCESS.COM >
#	4/tcp	Unassigned
#	4/udp	Unassigned
rje	5/tcp	Remote Job Entry
rje	5/udp	Remote Job Entry
#		Jon Postel < postel@isi.edu >
#	6/tcp	Unassigned
#	6/udp	Unassigned
echo	7/tcp	Echo
echo	7/udp	Echo
#		Jon Postel < postel@isi.edu >
#	8/tcp	Unassigned
#	8/udp	Unassigned
discard	9/tcp	Discard
discard	9/udp	Discard
#		Jon Postel < postel@isi.edu >
#	10/tcp	Unassigned
#	10/udp	Unassigned
systat	11/tcp	Active Users
systat	11/udp	Active Users
#		Jon Postel < postel@isi.edu >
#	12/tcp	Unassigned
#	12/udp	Unassigned
daytime	13/tcp	Daytime (RFC 867)
daytime	13/udp	Daytime (RFC 867)
#		Jon Postel < postel@isi.edu >
#	14/tcp	Unassigned
#	14/udp	Unassigned
#	15/tcp	Unassigned [was netstat]
#	15/udp	Unassigned
#	16/tcp	Unassigned
#	16/udp	Unassigned
qotd	17/tcp	Quote of the Day
qotd	17/udp	Quote of the Day
#		Jon Postel < postel@isi.edu >
msp	18/tcp	Message Send Protocol
msp	18/udp	Message Send Protocol
#		Rina Nethaniel < none >
chargen	19/tcp	Character Generator
chargen	19/udp	Character Generator
ftp-data	20/tcp	File Transfer [Default Data]
ftp-data	20/udp	File Transfer [Default Data]
ftp	21/tcp	File Transfer [Control]
ftp	21/udp	File Transfer [Control]
#		Jon Postel <postel@isi.edu>
ssh	22/tcp	SSH Remote Login Protocol
ssh	22/udp	SSH Remote Login Protocol

Keyword	Decimal	Description
#		Tatu Ylonen <ylo@cs.hut.fi>
telnet	23/tcp	Telnet
telnet	23/udp	Telnet
#		Jon Postel <postel@isi.edu>
	24/tcp	any private mail system
	24/udp	any private mail system
#		Rick Adams <rick@UUNET.UU.NET>
smtp	25/tcp	Simple Mail Transfer
smtp	25/udp	Simple Mail Transfer
#		Jon Postel <postel@isi.edu>
#	26/tcp	Unassigned
#	26/udp	Unassigned
nsw-fe	27/tcp	NSW User System FE
nsw-fe	27/udp	NSW User System FE
#		Robert Thomas <BThomas@F.BBN.COM>
#	28/tcp	Unassigned
#	28/udp	Unassigned
msg-icp	29/tcp	MSG ICP
msg-icp	29/udp	MSG ICP
#		Robert Thomas <BThomas@F.BBN.COM>
#	30/tcp	Unassigned
#	30/udp	Unassigned
msg-auth	31/tcp	MSG Authentication
msg-auth	31/udp	MSG Authentication
#		Robert Thomas <BThomas@F.BBN.COM>
#	32/tcp	Unassigned
#	32/udp	Unassigned
dsp	33/tcp	Display Support Protocol
dsp	33/udp	Display Support Protocol
#		Ed Cain <cain@edn-unix.dca.mil>
#	34/tcp	Unassigned
#	34/udp	Unassigned
	35/tcp	any private printer server
	35/udp	any private printer server
#		Jon Postel <postel@isi.edu>
#	36/tcp	Unassigned
#	36/udp	Unassigned
time	37/tcp	Time
time	37/udp	Time
#		Jon Postel <postel@isi.edu>
rap	38/tcp	Route Access Protocol
rap	38/udp	Route Access Protocol
#		Robert Ullmann <ariel@world.std.com>
rlp	39/tcp	Resource Location Protocol
rlp	39/udp	Resource Location Protocol
#		Mike Accetta <MIKE.ACCETTA@CMU-CS-A.EDU>
#	40/tcp	Unassigned
#	40/udp	Unassigned
graphics	41/tcp	Graphics
graphics	41/udp	Graphics
name	42/tcp	Host Name Server

Keyword	Decimal	Description
name	42/udp	Host Name Server
nameserver	42/tcp	Host Name Server
nameserver	42/udp	Host Name Server
nicname	43/tcp	Who Is
nicname	43/udp	Who Is
mpm-flags	44/tcp	MPM FLAGS Protocol
mpm-flags	44/udp	MPM FLAGS Protocol
mpm	45/tcp	Message Processing Module [recv]
mpm	45/udp	Message Processing Module [recv]
mpm-snd	46/tcp	MPM [default send]
mpm-snd	46/udp	MPM [default send]
#		Jon Postel <postel@isi.edu>
ni-ftp	47/tcp	NI FTP
ni-ftp	47/udp	NI FTP
#		Steve Kille <S.Kille@isode.com>
auditd	48/tcp	Digital Audit Daemon
auditd	48/udp	Digital Audit Daemon
#		Larry Scott <scott@zk3.dec.com>
tacacs	49/tcp	Login Host Protocol (TACACS)
tacacs	49/udp	Login Host Protocol (TACACS)
#		Pieter Ditmars <pditmars@BBN.COM>
re-mail-ck	50/tcp	Remote Mail Checking Protocol
re-mail-ck	50/udp	Remote Mail Checking Protocol
#		Steve Dorner <s-dorner@UIUC.EDU>
la-maint	51/tcp	IMP Logical Address Maintenance
la-maint	51/udp	IMP Logical Address Maintenance
#		Andy Malis <malis_a@timeplex.com>
xns-time	52/tcp	XNS Time Protocol
xns-time	52/udp	XNS Time Protocol
#		Susie Armstrong <Armstrong.wbst128@XEROX>
domain	53/tcp	Domain Name Server
domain	53/udp	Domain Name Server
#		Paul Mockapetris <PVM@Isi.edu>
xns-ch	54/tcp	XNS Clearinghouse
xns-ch	54/udp	XNS Clearinghouse
#		Susie Armstrong <Armstrong.wbst128@XEROX>
isi-gl	55/tcp	ISI Graphics Language
isi-gl	55/udp	ISI Graphics Language
xns-auth	56/tcp	XNS Authentication
xns-auth	56/udp	XNS Authentication
#		Susie Armstrong <Armstrong.wbst128@XEROX>
	57/tcp	any private terminal access
	57/udp	any private terminal access
#		Jon Postel <postel@isi.edu>
xns-mail	58/tcp	XNS Mail
xns-mail	58/udp	XNS Mail
#		Susie Armstrong <Armstrong.wbst128@XEROX>
	59/tcp	any private file service
	59/udp	any private file service
#		Jon Postel <postel@isi.edu>
	60/tcp	Unassigned

Keyword	Decimal	Description
	60/udp	Unassigned
ni-mail	61/tcp	NI MAIL
ni-mail	61/udp	NI MAIL
#		Steve Kille <S.Kille@isode.com>
acas	62/tcp	ACA Services
acas	62/udp	ACA Services
#		E. Wald <ewald@via.enet.dec.com>
whois++	63/tcp	whois++
whois++	63/udp	whois++
#		Rickard Schoultz <schoultz@sunet.se>
covia	64/tcp	Communications Integrator (CI)
covia	64/udp	Communications Integrator (CI)
#		Dan Smith <dan.smith@den.galileo.com>
tacacs-ds	65/tcp	TACACS-Database Service
tacacs-ds	65/udp	TACACS-Database Service
#		Kathy Huber <khuber@bbn.com>
sql*net	66/tcp	Oracle SQL*NET
sql*net	66/udp	Oracle SQL*NET
#		Jack Haverty <jhaverty@ORACLE.COM>
bootps	67/tcp	Bootstrap Protocol Server
bootps	67/udp	Bootstrap Protocol Server
bootpc	68/tcp	Bootstrap Protocol Client
bootpc	68/udp	Bootstrap Protocol Client
#		Bill Croft <Croft@SUMEX-AIM.STANFORD.EDU>
tftp	69/tcp	Trivial File Transfer
tftp	69/udp	Trivial File Transfer
#		David Clark <ddc@LCS.MIT.EDU>
gopher	70/tcp	Gopher
gopher	70/udp	Gopher
#		Mark McCahill <mpm@boombox.micro.umn.edu>
netrjs-1	71/tcp	Remote Job Service
netrjs-1	71/udp	Remote Job Service
netrjs-2	72/tcp	Remote Job Service
netrjs-2	72/udp	Remote Job Service
netrjs-3	73/tcp	Remote Job Service
netrjs-3	73/udp	Remote Job Service
netrjs-4	74/tcp	Remote Job Service
netrjs-4	74/udp	Remote Job Service
#		Bob Braden <Braden@isi.edu>
	75/tcp	any private dial out service
	75/udp	any private dial out service
#		Jon Postel <postel@isi.edu>
deos	76/tcp	Distributed External Object Store
deos	76/udp	Distributed External Object Store
#		Robert Ullmann <ariel@world.std.com>
	77/tcp	any private RJE service
	77/udp	any private RJE service
#		Jon Postel <postel@isi.edu>
vettcp	78/tcp	vettcp
vettcp	78/udp	vettcp
#		Christopher Leong <leong@kolmod.mlo.dec.com>

Keyword	Decimal	Description
finger	79/tcp	Finger
finger	79/udp	Finger
#		David Zimmerman <dpz@RUTGERS.EDU>
http	80/tcp	World Wide Web HTTP
http	80/udp	World Wide Web HTTP
www	80/tcp	World Wide Web HTTP
www	80/udp	World Wide Web HTTP
www-http	80/tcp	World Wide Web HTTP
www-http	80/udp	World Wide Web HTTP
#		Tim Berners-Lee <timbl@W3.org>
hosts2-ns	81/tcp	HOSTS2 Name Server
hosts2-ns	81/udp	HOSTS2 Name Server
#		Earl Killian <EAK@MORDOR.S1.GOV>
xfer	82/tcp	XFER Utility
xfer	82/udp	XFER Utility
#		Thomas M. Smith <Thomas.M.Smith@lmco.com>
mit-ml-dev	83/tcp	MIT ML Device
mit-ml-dev	83/udp	MIT ML Device
#		David Reed < — none — ->
ctf	84/tcp	Common Trace Facility
ctf	84/udp	Common Trace Facility
#		Hugh Thomas <thomas@oils.enet.dec.com>
mit-ml-dev	85/tcp	MIT ML Device
mit-ml-dev	85/udp	MIT ML Device
#		David Reed < — none — ->
mfcobol	86/tcp	Micro Focus Cobol
mfcobol	86/udp	Micro Focus Cobol
#		Simon Edwards < — none — ->
	87/tcp	any private terminal link
	87/udp	any private terminal link
#		Jon Postel <postel@isi.edu>
kerberos	88/tcp	Kerberos
kerberos	88/udp	Kerberos
#		B. Clifford Neuman <bcn@isi.edu>
su-mit-tg	89/tcp	SU/MIT Telnet Gateway
su-mit-tg	89/udp	SU/MIT Telnet Gateway
#		Mark Crispin <MRC@PANDA.COM>
########### PORT 90 also being used unofficially by Pointcast #########		
dnsix	90/tcp	DNSIX Security Attribute Token Map
dnsix	90/udp	DNSIX Security Attribute Token Map
#		Charles Watt <watt@sware.com>
mit-dov	91/tcp	MIT Dover Spooler
mit-dov	91/udp	MIT Dover Spooler
#		Eliot Moss <EBM@XX.LCS.MIT.EDU>
npp	92/tcp	Network Printing Protocol
npp	92/udp	Network Printing Protocol
#		Louis Mamakos <louie@sayshell.umd.edu>
dcp	93/tcp	Device Control Protocol
dcp	93/udp	Device Control Protocol
#		Daniel Tappan <Tappan@BBN.COM>
objcall	94/tcp	Tivoli Object Dispatcher

Keyword	Decimal	Description
objcall	94/udp	Tivoli Object Dispatcher
#		Tom Bereiter < — none — ->
supdup	95/tcp	SUPDUP
supdup	95/udp	SUPDUP
#		Mark Crispin <MRC@PANDA.COM>
dixie	96/tcp	DIXIE Protocol Specification
dixie	96/udp	DIXIE Protocol Specification
#		Tim Howes <Tim.Howes@terminator.cc.umich.edu>
swift-rvf	97/tcp	Swift Remote Virtual File Protocol
swift-rvf	97/udp	Swift Remote Virtual File Protocol
#		Maurice R. Turcotte <mailrus!uflorida!rm1!dnmrt%rmatl@uunet.UU.NET>
tacnews	98/tcp	TAC News
tacnews	98/udp	TAC News
#		Jon Postel <postel@isi.edu>
metagram	99/tcp	Metagram Relay
metagram	99/udp	Metagram Relay
#		Geoff Goodfellow <Geoff@FERNWOOD.MPK.CA.US>
newacct	100/tcp	[unauthorized use]
hostname	101/tcp	NIC Host Name Server
hostname	101/udp	NIC Host Name Server
#		Jon Postel <postel@isi.edu>
iso-tsap	102/tcp	ISO-TSAP Class 0
iso-tsap	102/udp	ISO-TSAP Class 0
#		Marshall Rose <mrose@dbc.mtview.ca.us>
gppitnp	103/tcp	Genesis Point-to-Point Trans Net
gppitnp	103/udp	Genesis Point-to-Point Trans Net
acr-nema	104/tcp	ACR-NEMA Digital Imag. & Comm. 300
acr-nema	104/udp	ACR-NEMA Digital Imag. & Comm. 300
#		Patrick McNamee < — none — ->
cso	105/tcp	CCSO name server protocol
cso	105/udp	CCSO name server protocol
#		Martin Hamilton <martin@mrrl.lut.as.uk>
csnet-ns	105/tcp	Mailbox Name Nameserver
csnet-ns	105/udp	Mailbox Name Nameserver
#		Marvin Solomon <solomon@CS.WISC.EDU>
3com-tsmux	106/tcp	3COM-TSMUX
3com-tsmux	106/udp	3COM-TSMUX
#		Jeremy Siegel <jzs@NSD.3Com.COM>
##########	106	Unauthorized use by insecure poppassd protocol
rtelnet	107/tcp	Remote Telnet Service
rtelnet	107/udp	Remote Telnet Service
#		Jon Postel <postel@isi.edu>
snagas	108/tcp	SNA Gateway Access Server
snagas	108/udp	SNA Gateway Access Server
#		Kevin Murphy <murphy@sevens.lkg.dec.com>
pop2	109/tcp	Post Office Protocol Version 2
pop2	109/udp	Post Office Protocol Version 2
#		Joyce K. Reynolds <jkrey@isi.edu>
pop3	110/tcp	Post Office Protocol Version 3
pop3	110/udp	Post Office Protocol Version 3

Keyword	Decimal	Description
#		Marshall Rose <mrose@dbc.mtview.ca.us>
sunrpc	111/tcp	SUN Remote Procedure Call
sunrpc	111/udp	SUN Remote Procedure Call
#		Chuck McManis <cmcmanis@freegate.net>
mcidas	112/tcp	McIDAS Data Transmission Protocol
mcidas	112/udp	McIDAS Data Transmission Protocol
#		Glenn Davis <support@unidata.ucar.edu>
ident	113/tcp	
auth	113/tcp	Authentication Service
auth	113/udp	Authentication Service
#		Mike St. Johns <stjohns@arpa.mil>
audionews	114/tcp	Audio News Multicast
audionews	114/udp	Audio News Multicast
#		Martin Forssen <maf@dtek.chalmers.se>
sftp	115/tcp	Simple File Transfer Protocol
sftp	115/udp	Simple File Transfer Protocol
#		Mark Lottor <MKL@nisc.sri.com>
ansanotify	116/tcp	ANSA REX Notify
ansanotify	116/udp	ANSA REX Notify
#		Nicola J. Howarth <njh@ansa.co.uk>
uucp-path	117/tcp	UUCP Path Service
uucp-path	117/udp	UUCP Path Service
sqlserv	118/tcp	SQL Services
sqlserv	118/udp	SQL Services
#		Larry Barnes <barnes@broke.enet.dec.com>
nntp	119/tcp	Network News Transfer Protocol
nntp	119/udp	Network News Transfer Protocol
#		Phil Lapsley <phil@UCBARPA.BERKELEY.EDU>
cfdptkt	120/tcp	CFDPTKT
cfdptkt	120/udp	CFDPTKT
#		John Ioannidis <ji@close.cs.columbia.ed>
erpc	121/tcp	Encore Expedited Remote Pro.Call
erpc	121/udp	Encore Expedited Remote Pro.Call
#		Jack O'Neil < — -none — ->
smakynet	122/tcp	SMAKYNET
smakynet	122/udp	SMAKYNET
#		Pierre Arnaud <pierre.arnaud@iname.com>
ntp	123/tcp	Network Time Protocol
ntp	123/udp	Network Time Protocol
#		Dave Mills <Mills@HUEY.UDEL.EDU>
ansatrader	124/tcp	ANSA REX Trader
ansatrader	124/udp	ANSA REX Trader
#		Nicola J. Howarth <njh@ansa.co.uk>
locus-map	125/tcp	Locus PC-Interface Net Map Ser
locus-map	125/udp	Locus PC-Interface Net Map Ser
#		Eric Peterson <lcc.eric@SEAS.UCLA.EDU>
nxedit	126/tcp	NXEdit
nxedit	126/udp	NXEdit
#		Don Payette <Don.Payette@unisys.com>
###########Port	126	Previously assigned to application below#######
#unitary	126/tcp	Unisys Unitary Login

Keyword	Decimal	Description
#unitary	126/udp	Unisys Unitary Login
#		<feil@kronos.nisd.cam.unisys.com>
###########Port	126	Previously assigned to application above#######
locus-con	127/tcp	Locus PC-Interface Conn Server
locus-con	127/udp	Locus PC-Interface Conn Server
#		Eric Peterson <lcc.eric@SEAS.UCLA.EDU>
gss-xlicen	128/tcp	GSS X License Verification
gss-xlicen	128/udp	GSS X License Verification
#		John Light <johnl@gssc.gss.com>
pwdgen	129/tcp	Password Generator Protocol
pwdgen	129/udp	Password Generator Protocol
#		Frank J. Wacho <WANCHO@WSMR-SIMTEL20.ARMY.MIL>
cisco-fna	130/tcp	cisco FNATIVE
cisco-fna	130/udp	cisco FNATIVE
cisco-tna	131/tcp	cisco TNATIVE
cisco-tna	131/udp	cisco TNATIVE
cisco-sys	132/tcp	cisco SYSMAINT
cisco-sys	132/udp	cisco SYSMAINT
statsrv	133/tcp	Statistics Service
statsrv	133/udp	Statistics Service
#		Dave Mills <Mills@HUEY.UDEL.EDU>
ingres-net	134/tcp	INGRES-NET Service
ingres-net	134/udp	INGRES-NET Service
#		Mike Berrow < — -none — ->
epmap	135/tcp	DCE endpoint resolution
epmap	135/udp	DCE endpoint resolution
#		Joe Pato <pato@apollo.hp.com>
profile	136/tcp	PROFILE Naming System
profile	136/udp	PROFILE Naming System
#		Larry Peterson <llp@ARIZONA.EDU>
netbios-ns	137/tcp	NETBIOS Name Service
netbios-ns	137/udp	NETBIOS Name Service
netbios-dgm	138/tcp	NETBIOS Datagram Service
netbios-dgm	138/udp	NETBIOS Datagram Service
netbios-ssn	139/tcp	NETBIOS Session Service
netbios-ssn	139/udp	NETBIOS Session Service
#		Jon Postel <postel@isi.edu>
emfis-data	140/tcp	EMFIS Data Service
emfis-data	140/udp	EMFIS Data Service
emfis-cntl	141/tcp	EMFIS Control Service
emfis-cntl	141/udp	EMFIS Control Service
#		Gerd Beling <GBELING@isi.edu>
bl-idm	142/tcp	Britton-Lee IDM
bl-idm	142/udp	Britton-Lee IDM
#		Susie Snitzer < — -none — ->
imap	143/tcp	Internet Message Access Protocol
imap	143/udp	Internet Message Access Protocol
#		Mark Crispin <MRC@CAC.Washington.EDU>
uma	144/tcp	Universal Management Architecture
uma	144/udp	Universal Management Architecture
#		Jay Whitney <jw@powercenter.com>

Keyword	Decimal	Description
uaac	145/tcp	UAAC Protocol
uaac	145/udp	UAAC Protocol
#		David A. Gomberg <gomberg@GATEWAY.MITRE.ORG>
iso-tp0	146/tcp	ISO-IP0
iso-tp0	146/udp	ISO-IP0
iso-ip	147/tcp	ISO-IP
iso-ip	147/udp	ISO-IP
#		Marshall Rose <mrose@dbc.mtview.ca.us>
jargon	148/tcp	Jargon
jargon	148/udp	Jargon
#		Bill Weinman <wew@bearnet.com>
aed-512	149/tcp	AED 512 Emulation Service
aed-512	149/udp	AED 512 Emulation Service
#		Albert G. Broscius <broscius@DSL.CIS.UPENN.EDU>
sql-net	150/tcp	SQL-NET
sql-net	150/udp	SQL-NET
#		Martin Picard << — -none — ->
hems	151/tcp	HEMS
hems	151/udp	HEMS
bftp	152/tcp	Background File Transfer Program
bftp	152/udp	Background File Transfer Program
#		Annette DeSchon <DESCHON@Isi.edu>
sgmp	153/tcp	SGMP
sgmp	153/udp	SGMP
#		Marty Schoffstahl <schoff@NISC.NYSER.NET>
netsc-prod	154/tcp	NETSC
netsc-prod	154/udp	NETSC
netsc-dev	155/tcp	NETSC
netsc-dev	155/udp	NETSC
#		Sergio Heker <heker@JVNCC.CSC.ORG>
sqlsrv	156/tcp	SQL Service
sqlsrv	156/udp	SQL Service
#		Craig Rogers <Rogers@Isi.edu>
knet-cmp	157/tcp	KNET/VM Command/Message Protocol
knet-cmp	157/udp	KNET/VM Command/Message Protocol
#		Gary S. Malkin <GMALKIN@XYLOGICS.COM>
pcmail-srv	158/tcp	PCMail Server
pcmail-srv	158/udp	PCMail Server
#		Mark L. Lambert <markl@PTT.LCS.MIT.EDU>
nss-routing	159/tcp	NSS-Routing
nss-routing	159/udp	NSS-Routing
#		Yakov Rekhter <Yakov@IBM.COM>
sgmp-traps	160/tcp	SGMP-TRAPS
sgmp-traps	160/udp	SGMP-TRAPS
#		Marty Schoffstahl <schoff@NISC.NYSER.NET>
snmp	161/tcp	SNMP
snmp	161/udp	SNMP
snmptrap	162/tcp	SNMPTRAP
snmptrap	162/udp	SNMPTRAP
#		Marshall Rose <mrose@dbc.mtview.ca.us>
cmip-man	163/tcp	CMIP/tcp Manager

Keyword	Decimal	Description
cmip-man	163/udp	CMIP/tcp Manager
cmip-agent	164/tcp	CMIP/tcp Agent
cmip-agent	164/udp	CMIP/tcp Agent
#		Amatzia Ben-Artzi < — -none — ->
xns-courier	165/tcp	Xerox
xns-courier	165/udp	Xerox
#		Susie Armstrong <Armstrong.whst128@XEROX.COM>
s-net	166/tcp	Sirius Systems
s-net	166/udp	Sirius Systems
#		Brian Lloyd <brian@lloyd.com>
namp	167/tcp	NAMP
namp	167/udp	NAMP
#		Marty Schoffstahl <schoff@NISC.NYSER.NET>
rsvd	168/tcp	RSVD
rsvd	168/udp	RSVD
#		Neil Todd <mcvax!ist.co.uk!neil@UUNET.UU.NET>
send	169/tcp	SEND
send	169/udp	SEND
#		William D. Wisner <wisner@HAYES.FAI.ALASKA.EDU>
print-srv	170/tcp	Network PostScript
print-srv	170/udp	Network PostScript
#		Brian Reid <reid@DECWRL.DEC.COM>
multiplex	171/tcp	Network Innovations Multiplex
multiplex	171/udp	Network Innovations Multiplex
cl/1	172/tcp	Network Innovations CL/1
cl/1	172/udp	Network Innovations CL/1
#		Kevin DeVault << — -none — ->
xyplex-mux	173/tcp	Xyplex
xyplex-mux	173/udp	Xyplex
#		Bob Stewart <STEWART@XYPLEX.COM>
mailq	174/tcp	MAILQ
mailq	174/udp	MAILQ
#		Rayan Zachariassen <rayan@AI.TORONTO.EDU>
vmnet	175/tcp	VMNET
vmnet	175/udp	VMNET
#		Christopher Tengi <tengi@Princeton.EDU>
genrad-mux	176/tcp	GENRAD-MUX
genrad-mux	176/udp	GENRAD-MUX
#		Ron Thornton <thornton@qm7501.genrad.com>
xdmcp	177/tcp	X Display Manager Control Protocol
xdmcp	177/udp	X Display Manager Control Protocol
#		Robert W. Scheifler <RWS@XX.LCS.MIT.EDU>
nextstep	178/tcp	NextStep Window Server
nextstep	178/udp	NextStep Window Server
#		Leo Hourvitz <leo@NEXT.COM>
bgp	179/tcp	Border Gateway Protocol
bgp	179/udp	Border Gateway Protocol
#		Kirk Lougheed <LOUGHEED@MATHOM.CISCO.COM>
ris	180/tcp	Intergraph
ris	180/udp	Intergraph
#		Dave Buehmann <ingr!daveb@UUNET.UU.NET>

Keyword	Decimal	Description
unify	181/tcp	Unify
unify	181/udp	Unify
#		Mark Ainsley <ianaportmaster@unify.com>
audit	182/tcp	Unisys Audit SITP
audit	182/udp	Unisys Audit SITP
#		Gil Greenbaum <gcole@nisd.cam.unisys.com>
ocbinder	183/tcp	OCBinder
ocbinder	183/udp	OCBinder
ocserver	184/tcp	OCServer
ocserver	184/udp	OCServer
#		Jerrilynn Okamura < — none — ->
remote-kis	185/tcp	Remote-KIS
remote-kis	185/udp	Remote-KIS
kis	186/tcp	KIS Protocol
kis	186/udp	KIS Protocol
#		Ralph Droms <rdroms@NRI.RESTON.VA.US>
aci	187/tcp	Application Communication Interface
aci	187/udp	Application Communication Interface
#		Rick Carlos <rick.ticipa.csc.ti.com>
mumps	188/tcp	Plus Five's MUMPS
mumps	188/udp	Plus Five's MUMPS
#		Hokey Stenn <hokey@PLUS5.COM>
qft	189/tcp	Queued File Transport
qft	189/udp	Queued File Transport
#		Wayne Schroeder <schroeder@SDS.SDSC.EDU>
gacp	190/tcp	Gateway Access Control Protocol
gacp	190/udp	Gateway Access Control Protocol
#		C. Philip Wood <cpw@LANL.GOV>
prospero	191/tcp	Prospero Directory Service
prospero	191/udp	Prospero Directory Service
#		B. Clifford Neuman <bcn@isi.edu>
osu-nms	192/tcp	OSU Network Monitoring System
osu-nms	192/udp	OSU Network Monitoring System
#		Doug Karl <KARL-D@OSU-20.IRCC.OHIO-STATE.EDU>
srmp	193/tcp	Spider Remote Monitoring Protocol
srmp	193/udp	Spider Remote Monitoring Protocol
#		Ted J. Socolofsky <Teds@SPIDER.CO.UK>
irc	194/tcp	Internet Relay Chat Protocol
irc	194/udp	Internet Relay Chat Protocol
#		Jarkko Oikarinen <jto@TOLSUN.OULU.FI>
dn6-nlm-aud	195/tcp	DNSIX Network Level Module Audit
dn6-nlm-aud	195/udp	DNSIX Network Level Module Audit
dn6-smm-red	196/tcp	DNSIX Session Mgt Module Audit Redir
dn6-smm-red	196/udp	DNSIX Session Mgt Module Audit Redir
#		Lawrence Lebahn <DIA3@PAXRV-NES.NAVY.MIL>
dls	197/tcp	Directory Location Service
dls	197/udp	Directory Location Service
dls-mon	198/tcp	Directory Location Service Monitor
dls-mon	198/udp	Directory Location Service Monitor
#		Scott Bellew <smb@cs.purdue.edu>
smux	199/tcp	SMUX

Keyword	Decimal	Description
smux	199/udp	SMUX
#		Marshall Rose <mrose@dbc.mtview.ca.us>
src	200/tcp	IBM System Resource Controller
src	200/udp	IBM System Resource Controller
#		Gerald McBrearty < — -none — ->
at-rtmp	201/tcp	AppleTalk Routing Maintenance
at-rtmp	201/udp	AppleTalk Routing Maintenance
at-nbp	202/tcp	AppleTalk Name Binding
at-nbp	202/udp	AppleTalk Name Binding
at-3	203/tcp	AppleTalk Unused
at-3	203/udp	AppleTalk Unused
at-echo	204/tcp	AppleTalk Echo
at-echo	204/udp	AppleTalk Echo
at-5	205/tcp	AppleTalk Unused
at-5	205/udp	AppleTalk Unused
at-zis	206/tcp	AppleTalk Zone Information
at-zis	206/udp	AppleTalk Zone Information
at-7	207/tcp	AppleTalk Unused
at-7	207/udp	AppleTalk Unused
at-8	208/tcp	AppleTalk Unused
at-8	208/udp	AppleTalk Unused
#		Rob Chandhok <chandhok@gnome.cs.cmu.edu>
qmtp	209/tcp	The Quick Mail Transfer Protocol
qmtp	209/udp	The Quick Mail Transfer Protocol
#		Dan Bernstein <djb@silverton.berkeley.edu>
z39.50	210/tcp	ANSI Z39.50
z39.50	210/udp	ANSI Z39.50
#		Mark H. Needleman <markn@sirsi.com>
914c/g	211/tcp	Texas Instruments 914C/G Terminal
914c/g	211/udp	Texas Instruments 914C/G Terminal
#		Bill Harrell < — -none — ->
anet	212/tcp	ATEXSSTR
anet	212/udp	ATEXSSTR
#		Jim Taylor <taylor@heart.epps.kodak.com>
ipx	213/tcp	IPX
ipx	213/udp	IPX
#		Don Provan <donp@xlnvax.novell.com>
vmpwscs	214/tcp	VM PWSCS
vmpwscs	214/udp	VM PWSCS
#		Dan Shia <dset!shia@uunet.UU.NET>
softpc	215/tcp	Insignia Solutions
softpc	215/udp	Insignia Solutions
#		Martyn Thomas < — -none — ->
CAllic	216/tcp	Computer Associates Int'l License Server
CAllic	216/udp	Computer Associates Int'l License Server
#		Chuck Spitz <spich04@cai.com>
dbase	217/tcp	dBASE Unix
dbase	217/udp	dBASE Unix
#		Don Gibson
#		<sequent!aero!twinsun!ashtate.A-T.COM!dong@uunet.UU.NET>
mpp	218/tcp	Netix Message Posting Protocol

Keyword	Decimal	Description
mpp	218/udp	Netix Message Posting Protocol
#		Shannon Yeh <yeh@netix.com>
uarps	219/tcp	Unisys ARPs
uarps	219/udp	Unisys ARPs
#		Ashok Marwaha < — -none — ->
imap3	220/tcp	Interactive Mail Access Protocol v3
imap3	220/udp	Interactive Mail Access Protocol v3
#		James Rice <RICE@SUMEX-AIM.STANFORD.EDU>
fln-spx	221/tcp	Berkeley rlogind with SPX auth
fln-spx	221/udp	Berkeley rlogind with SPX auth
rsh-spx	222/tcp	Berkeley rshd with SPX auth
rsh-spx	222/udp	Berkeley rshd with SPX auth
cdc	223/tcp	Certificate Distribution Center
cdc	223/udp	Certificate Distribution Center
#		Kannan Alagappan <kannan@sejour.enet.dec.com>
########### Possible Conflict of Port 222 with "Masqdialer"##############		
### Contact for Masqdialer is Charles Wright <cpwright@villagenet.com>###		
masqdialer	224/tcp	masqdialer
masqdialer	224/udp	masqdialer
#		Charles Wright <cpwright@villagenet.com>
#	225–241	Reserved
#		Jon Postel <postel@isi.edu>
direct	242/tcp	Direct
direct	242/udp	Direct
#		Herb Sutter <HerbS@cntc.com>
sur-meas	243/tcp	Survey Measurement
sur-meas	243/udp	Survey Measurement
#		Dave Clark <ddc@LCS.MIT.EDU>
inbusiness	244/tcp	inbusiness
inbusiness	244/udp	inbusiness
#		Derrick Hisatake <derrick.i.hisatake@intel.com>
link	245/tcp	LINK
link	245/udp	LINK
dsp3270	246/tcp	Display Systems Protocol
dsp3270	246/udp	Display Systems Protocol
#		Weldon J. Showalter <Gamma@MINTAKA.DCA.MIL>
subntbcst_tftp	247/tcp	SUBNTBCST_TFTP
subntbcst_tftp	247/udp	SUBNTBCST_TFTP
#		John Fake <fake@us.ibm.com>
bhfhs	248/tcp	bhfhs
bhfhs	248/udp	bhfhs
#		John Kelly <johnk@bellhow.com>
#	249–255	Reserved
#		Jon Postel <postel@isi.edu>
rap	256/tcp	RAP
rap	256/udp	RAP
#		J.S. Greenfield <greeny@raleigh.ibm.com>
set	257/tcp	Secure Electronic Transaction
set	257/udp	Secure Electronic Transaction
#		Donald Eastlake <dee3@torque.pothole.com>
yak-chat	258/tcp	Yak Winsock Personal Chat

Keyword	Decimal	Description
yak-chat	258/udp	Yak Winsock Personal Chat
#		Brian Bandy <bbandy@swbell.net>
esro-gen	259/tcp	Efficient Short Remote Operations
esro-gen	259/udp	Efficient Short Remote Operations
#		Mohsen Banan <mohsen@rostam.neda.com>
openport	260/tcp	Openport
openport	260/udp	Openport
#		John Marland <jmarland@dean.openport.com>
nsiiops	261/tcp	IIOP Name Service over TLS/SSL
nsiiops	261/udp	IIOP Name Service over TLS/SSL
#		Jeff Stewart <jstewart@netscape.com>
arcisdms	262/tcp	Arcisdms
arcisdms	262/udp	Arcisdms
#		Russell Crook (rmc@sni.ca>
hdap	263/tcp	HDAP
hdap	263/udp	HDAP
#		Troy Gau <troy@zyxel.com>
bgmp	264/tcp	BGMP
bgmp	264/udp	BGMP
#		Dave Thaler <thalerd@eecs.umich.edu>
x-bone-ctl	265/tcp	X-Bone CTL
x-bone-ctl	265/udp	X-Bone CTL
#		Joe Touch <touch@isi.edu>
sst	266/tcp	SCSI on ST
sst	266/udp	SCSI on ST
#		Donald D. Woelz <don@genroco.com>
td-service	267/tcp	Tobit David Service Layer
td-service	267/udp	Tobit David Service Layer
td-replica	268/tcp	Tobit David Replica
td-replica	268/udp	Tobit David Replica
#		Franz-Josef Leuders <development@tobit.com>
#	269–279	Unassigned
http-mgmt	280/tcp	http-mgmt
http-mgmt	280/udp	http-mgmt
#		Adrian Pell <PELL_ADRIAN/HP-UnitedKingdom_om6@hplb.hpl.hp.com>
personal-link	281/tcp	Personal Link
personal-link	281/udp	Personal Link
#		Dan Cummings <doc@cnr.com>
cableport-ax	282/tcp	Cable Port A/X
cableport-ax	282/udp	Cable Port A/X
#		Craig Langfahl <Craig_J_Langfahl@ccm.ch.intel.com>
rescap	283/tcp	rescap
rescap	283/udp	rescap
#		Paul Hoffman <phoffman@imc.org>
corerjd	284/tcp	corerjd
corerjd	284/udp	corerjd
#		Chris Thornhill <cjt@corenetworks.com>
#	285	Unassigned
fxp-1	286/tcp	FXP-1
fxp-1	286/udp	FXP-1

Keyword	Decimal	Description
#		James Darnall <jim@cennoid.com>
k-block	287/tcp	K-BLOCK
k-block	287/udp	K-BLOCK
#		Simon P Jackson <jacko@kring.co.uk>
#	288–307	Unassigned
novastorbakcup	308/tcp	Novastor Backup
novastorbakcup	308/udp	Novastor Backup
#		Brian Dickman <brian@novastor.com>
entrusttime	309/tcp	EntrustTime
entrusttime	309/udp	EntrustTime
#		Peter Whittaker <pww@entrust.com>
bhmds	310/tcp	bhmds
bhmds	310/udp	bhmds
#		John Kelly <johnk@bellhow.com>
asip-webadmin	311/tcp	AppleShare IP WebAdmin
asip-webadmin	311/udp	AppleShare IP WebAdmin
#		Ann Huang <annhuang@apple.com>
vslmp	312/tcp	VSLMP
vslmp	312/udp	VSLMP
#		Gerben Wierda <Gerben_Wierda@RnA.nl>
magenta-logic	313/tcp	Magenta Logic
magenta-logic	313/udp	Magenta Logic
#		Karl Rousseau <kr@netfusion.co.uk>
opalis-robot	314/tcp	Opalis Robot
opalis-robot	314/udp	Opalis Robot
#		Laurent Domenech, Opalis <ldomenech@opalis.com>
dpsi	315/tcp	DPSI
dpsi	315/udp	DPSI
#		Tony Scamurra <Tony@DesktopPaging.com>
decauth	316/tcp	decAuth
decauth	316/udp	decAuth
#		Michael Agishtein <misha@unx.dec.com>
zannet	317/tcp	Zannet
zannet	317/udp	Zannet
#		Zan Oliphant <zan@accessone.com>
pkix-timestamp	318/tcp	PKIX TimeStamp
pkix-timestamp	318/udp	PKIX TimeStamp
#		Robert Zuccherato <robert.zuccherato@entrust.com>
ptp-event	319/tcp	PTP Event
ptp-event	319/udp	PTP Event
ptp-general	320/tcp	PTP General
ptp-general	320/udp	PTP General
#		John Eidson <eidson@hpl.hp.com>
pip	321/tcp	PIP
pip	321/udp	PIP
#		Gordon Mohr <gojomo@usa.net>
rtsps	322/tcp	RTSPS
rtsps	322/udp	RTSPS
#		Anders Klemets <anderskl@microsoft.com>
#	323–332	Unassigned
texar	333/tcp	Texar Security Port

Keyword	Decimal	Description
texar	333/udp	Texar Security Port
#		Eugen Bacic <ebacic@texar.com>
#	334–343	Unassigned
pdap	344/tcp	Prospero Data Access Protocol
pdap	344/udp	Prospero Data Access Protocol
#		B. Clifford Neuman <bcn@isi.edu>
pawserv	345/tcp	Perf Analysis Workbench
pawserv	345/udp	Perf Analysis Workbench
zserv	346/tcp	Zebra server
zserv	346/udp	Zebra server
fatserv	347/tcp	Fatmen Server
fatserv	347/udp	Fatmen Server
csi-sgwp	348/tcp	Cabletron Management Protocol
csi-sgwp	348/udp	Cabletron Management Protocol
mftp	349/tcp	mftp
mftp	349/udp	mftp
#		Dave Feinleib <davefe@microsoft.com>
matip-type-a	350/tcp	MATIP Type A
matip-type-a	350/udp	MATIP Type A
matip-type-b	351/tcp	MATIP Type B
matip-type-b	351/udp	MATIP Type B
#		Alain Robert <arobert@par.sita.int>
# The following entry records an unassigned but widespread use		
bhoetty	351/tcp	bhoetty (added 5/21/97)
bhoetty	351/udp	bhoetty
#		John Kelly <johnk@bellhow.com>
dtag-ste-sb	352/tcp	DTAG (assigned long ago)
dtag-ste-sb	352/udp	DTAG
#		Ruediger Wald <wald@ez-darmstadt.telekom.de>
# The following entry records an unassigned but widespread use		
bhoedap4	352/tcp	bhoedap4 (added 5/21/97)
bhoedap4	352/udp	bhoedap4
#		John Kelly <johnk@bellhow.com>
ndsauth	353/tcp	NDSAUTH
ndsauth	353/udp	NDSAUTH
#		Jayakumar Ramalingam <jayakumar@novell.com>
bh611	354/tcp	bh611
bh611	354/udp	bh611
#		John Kelly <johnk@bellhow.com>
datex-asn	355/tcp	DATEX-ASN
datex-asn	355/udp	DATEX-ASN
#		Kenneth Vaughn <kvaughn@mail.viggen.com>
cloanto-net-1	356/tcp	Cloanto Net 1
cloanto-net-1	356/udp	Cloanto Net 1
#		Michael Battilana <mcb-iana@cloanto.com>
bhevent	357/tcp	bhevent
bhevent	357/udp	bhevent
#		John Kelly <johnk@bellhow.com>
shrinkwrap	358/tcp	Shrinkwrap
shrinkwrap	358/udp	Shrinkwrap
#		Bill Simpson <wsimpson@greendragon.com>

Keyword	Decimal	Description
nsrmp	359/tcp	Network Security Risk Management Protocol
nsrmp	359/udp	Network Security Risk Management Protocol
#		Eric Jacksch <jacksch@tenebris.ca>
scoi2odialog	360/tcp	scoi2odialog
scoi2odialog	360/udp	scoi2odialog
#		Keith Petley <keithp@sco.COM>
semantix	361/tcp	Semantix
semantix	361/udp	Semantix
#		Semantix <xsSupport@semantix.com>
srssend	362/tcp	SRS Send
srssend	362/udp	SRS Send
#		Curt Mayer <curt@emergent.com>
rsvp_tunnel	363/tcp	RSVP Tunnel
rsvp_tunnel	363/udp	RSVP Tunnel
#		Andreas Terzis <terzis@cs.ucla.edu>
aurora-cmgr	364/tcp	Aurora CMGR
aurora-cmgr	364/udp	Aurora CMGR
#		Philip Budne <budne@auroratech.com>
dtk	365/tcp	DTK
dtk	365/udp	DTK
#		Fred Cohen <fc@all.net>
odmr	366/tcp	ODMR
odmr	366/udp	ODMR
#		Randall Gellens <randy@qualcomm.com>
mortgageware	367/tcp	MortgageWare
mortgageware	367/udp	MortgageWare
#		Ole Hellevik <oleh@interlinq.com>
qbikgdp	368/tcp	QbikGDP
qbikgdp	368/udp	QbikGDP
#		Adrien de Croy <adrien@qbik.com>
rpc2portmap	369/tcp	rpc2portmap
rpc2portmap	369/udp	rpc2portmap
codaauth2	370/tcp	codaauth2
codaauth2	370/udp	codaauth2
#		Robert Watson <robert@cyrus.watson.org>
clearcase	371/tcp	Clearcase
clearcase	371/udp	Clearcase
#		Dave LeBlang <leglang@atria.com>
ulistproc	372/tcp	ListProcessor
ulistproc	372/udp	ListProcessor
#		Anastasios Kotsikonas <tasos@cs.bu.edu>
legent-1	373/tcp	Legent Corporation
legent-1	373/udp	Legent Corporation
legent-2	374/tcp	Legent Corporation
legent-2	374/udp	Legent Corporation
#		Keith Boyce < — -none — ->
hassle	375/tcp	Hassle
hassle	375/udp	Hassle
#		Reinhard Doelz <doelz@comp.bioz.unibas.ch>
nip	376/tcp	Amiga Envoy Network Inquiry Proto
nip	376/udp	Amiga Envoy Network Inquiry Proto

Keyword	Decimal	Description
#		Heinz Wrobel <hwrobel@gmx.de>
tnETOS	377/tcp	NEC Corporation
tnETOS	377/udp	NEC Corporation
dsETOS	378/tcp	NEC Corporation
dsETOS	378/udp	NEC Corporation
#		Tomoo Fujita <tf@arc.bs1.fc.nec.co.jp>
is99c	379/tcp	TIA/EIA/IS-99 modem client
is99c	379/udp	TIA/EIA/IS-99 modem client
is99s	380/tcp	TIA/EIA/IS-99 modem server
is99s	380/udp	TIA/EIA/IS-99 modem server
#		Frank Quick <fquick@qualcomm.com>
hp-collector	381/tcp	hp performance data collector
hp-collector	381/udp	hp performance data collector
hp-managed-node	382/tcp	hp performance data managed node
hp-managed-node	382/udp	hp performance data managed node
hp-alarm-mgr	383/tcp	hp performance data alarm manager
hp-alarm-mgr	383/udp	hp performance data alarm manager
#		Frank Blakely <frankb@hpptc16.rose.hp.com>
arns	384/tcp	A Remote Network Server System
arns	384/udp	A Remote Network Server System
#		David Hornsby <djh@munnari.OZ.AU>
ibm-app	385/tcp	IBM Application
ibm-app	385/udp	IBM Application
#		Lisa Tomita < — -none — ->
asa	386/tcp	ASA Message Router Object Def.
asa	386/udp	ASA Message Router Object Def.
#		Steve Laitinen <laitinen@brutus.aa.ab.com>
aurp	387/tcp	Appletalk Update-Based Routing Pro.
aurp	387/udp	Appletalk Update-Based Routing Pro.
#		Chris Ranch <cranch@novell.com>
unidata-ldm	388/tcp	Unidata LDM
unidata-ldm	388/udp	Unidata LDM
#		Glenn Davis <support@unidata.ucar.edu>
ldap	389/tcp	Lightweight Directory Access Protocol
ldap	389/udp	Lightweight Directory Access Protocol
#		Tim Howes <Tim.Howes@terminator.cc.umich.edu>
uis	390/tcp	UIS
uis	390/udp	UIS
#		Ed Barron < — -none — ->
synotics-relay	391/tcp	SynOptics SNMP Relay Port
synotics-relay	391/udp	SynOptics SNMP Relay Port
synotics-broker	392/tcp	SynOptics Port Broker Port
synotics-broker	392/udp	SynOptics Port Broker Port
#		Illan Raab <iraab@synoptics.com>
meta5	393/tcp	Meta5
meta5	393/udp	Meta5
#		Jim Kanzler <jim.kanzler@meta5.com>
embl-ndt	394/tcp	EMBL Nucleic Data Transfer
embl-ndt	394/udp	EMBL Nucleic Data Transfer
#		Peter Gad <peter@bmc.uu.se>
netcp	395/tcp	NETscout Control Protocol

Keyword	Decimal	Description
netcp	395/udp	NETscout Control Protocol
#		Anil Singhal < — -none — ->
netware-ip	396/tcp	Novell Netware over IP
netware-ip	396/udp	Novell Netware over IP
mptn	397/tcp	Multi Protocol Trans. Net.
mptn	397/udp	Multi Protocol Trans. Net.
#		Soumitra Sarkar <sarkar@vnet.ibm.com>
kryptolan	398/tcp	Kryptolan
kryptolan	398/udp	Kryptolan
#		Peter de Laval <pdl@sectra.se>
iso-tsap-c2	399/tcp	ISO Transport Class 2 Noncontrol over TCP
iso-tsap-c2	399/udp	ISO Transport Class 2 Noncontrol over UDP
#		Yanick Pouffary <pouffary@taec.enet.dec.com>
work-sol	400/tcp	Workstation Solutions
work-sol	400/udp	Workstation Solutions
#		Jim Ward <jimw@worksta.com>
ups	401/tcp	Uninterruptible Power Supply
ups	401/udp	Uninterruptible Power Supply
#		Charles Bennett <chuck@benatong.com>
genie	402/tcp	Genie Protocol
genie	402/udp	Genie Protocol
#		Mark Hankin < — -none — ->
decap	403/tcp	decap
decap	403/udp	decap
nced	404/tcp	nced
nced	404/udp	nced
ncld	405/tcp	ncld
ncld	405/udp	ncld
#		Richard Jones < — -none — ->
imsp	406/tcp	Interactive Mail Support Protocol
imsp	406/udp	Interactive Mail Support Protocol
#		John Myers <jgm+@cmu.edu>
timbuktu	407/tcp	Timbuktu
timbuktu	407/udp	Timbuktu
#		Marc Epard <marc@netopia.com>
prm-sm	408/tcp	Prospero Resource Manager Sys. Man.
prm-sm	408/udp	Prospero Resource Manager Sys. Man.
prm-nm	409/tcp	Prospero Resource Manager Node Man.
prm-nm	409/udp	Prospero Resource Manager Node Man.
#		B. Clifford Neuman <bcn@isi.edu>
decladebug	410/tcp	DECLadebug Remote Debug Protocol
decladebug	410/udp	DECLadebug Remote Debug Protocol
#		Anthony Berent <anthony.berent@reo.mts.dec.com>
rmt	411/tcp	Remote MT Protocol
rmt	411/udp	Remote MT Protocol
#		Peter Eriksson <pen@lysator.liu.se>
synoptics-trap	412/tcp	Trap Convention Port
synoptics-trap	412/udp	Trap Convention Port
#		Illan Raab <iraab@synoptics.com>
smsp	413/tcp	Storage Management Services Protocol
smsp	413/udp	Storage Management Services Protocol

Keyword	Decimal	Description
#		Murthy Srinivas <murthy@novell.com>
infoseek	414/tcp	InfoSeek
infoseek	414/udp	InfoSeek
#		Steve Kirsch <stk@infoseek.com>
bnet	415/tcp	BNet
bnet	415/udp	BNet
#		Jim Mertz <JMertz+RV09@rvdc.unisys.com>
silverplatter	416/tcp	Silverplatter
silverplatter	416/udp	Silverplatter
#		Peter Ciuffetti <petec@silverplatter.com>
onmux	417/tcp	Onmux
onmux	417/udp	Onmux
#		Stephen Hanna <hanna@world.std.com>
hyper-g	418/tcp	Hyper-G
hyper-g	418/udp	Hyper-G
#		Frank Kappe <fkappe@iicm.tu-graz.ac.at>
ariel1	419/tcp	Ariel
ariel1	419/udp	Ariel
#		Lennie Stovel <bl.mds@rlg.org>
smpte	420/tcp	SMPTE
smpte	420/udp	SMPTE
#		Si Becker <71362.22@CompuServe.COM>
ariel2	421/tcp	Ariel
ariel2	421/udp	Ariel
ariel3	422/tcp	Ariel
ariel3	422/udp	Ariel
#		Lennie Stovel <bl.mds@rlg.org>
opc-job-start	423/tcp	IBM Operations Planning and Control Start
opc-job-start	423/udp	IBM Operations Planning and Control Start
opc-job-track	424/tcp	IBM Operations Planning and Control Track
opc-job-track	424/udp	IBM Operations Planning and Control Track
#		Conny Larsson <cocke@VNET.IBM.COM>
icad-el	425/tcp	ICAD
icad-el	425/udp	ICAD
#		Larry Stone <lcs@icad.com>
smartsdp	426/tcp	smartsdp
smartsdp	426/udp	smartsdp
#		Alexander Dupuy <dupuy@smarts.com>
svrloc	427/tcp	Server Location
svrloc	427/udp	Server Location
#		<veizades@ftp.com>
ocs_cmu	428/tcp	OCS_CMU
ocs_cmu	428/udp	OCS_CMU
ocs_amu	429/tcp	OCS_AMU
ocs_amu	429/udp	OCS_AMU
#		Florence Wyman <wyman@peabody.plk.af.mil>
utmpsd	430/tcp	UTMPSD
utmpsd	430/udp	UTMPSD
utmpcd	431/tcp	UTMPCD
utmpcd	431/udp	UTMPCD
iasd	432/tcp	IASD

Keyword	Decimal	Description
iasd	432/udp	IASD
#		Nir Baroz <nbaroz@encore.com>
nnsp	433/tcp	NNSP
nnsp	433/udp	NNSP
#		Rob Robertson <rob@gangrene.berkeley.edu>
mobileip-agent	434/tcp	MobileIP-Agent
mobileip-agent	434/udp	MobileIP-Agent
mobilip-mn	435/tcp	MobilIP-MN
mobilip-mn	435/udp	MobilIP-MN
#		Kannan Alagappan <kannan@sejour.lkg.dec.com>
dna-cml	436/tcp	DNA-CML
dna-cml	436/udp	DNA-CML
#		Dan Flowers <flowers@smaug.lkg.dec.com>
comscm	437/tcp	comscm
comscm	437/udp	comscm
#		Jim Teague <teague@zso.dec.com>
dsfgw	438/tcp	dsfgw
dsfgw	438/udp	dsfgw
#		Andy McKeen <mckeen@osf.org>
dasp	439/tcp	dasp Thomas Obermair
dasp	439/udp	dasp tommy@inlab.m.eunet.de
#		Thomas Obermair <tommy@inlab.m.eunet.de>
sgcp	440/tcp	sgcp
sgcp	440/udp	sgcp
#		Marshall Rose <mrose@dbc.mtview.ca.us>
decvms-sysmgt	441/tcp	decvms-sysmgt
decvms-sysmgt	441/udp	decvms-sysmgt
#		Lee Barton <barton@star.enet.dec.com>
cvc_hostd	442/tcp	cvc_hostd
cvc_hostd	442/udp	cvc_hostd
#		Bill Davidson <billd@equalizer.cray.com>
https	443/tcp	http protocol over TLS/SSL
https	443/udp	http protocol over TLS/SSL
#		Kipp E.B. Hickman <kipp@mcom.com>
snpp	444/tcp	Simple Network Paging Protocol
snpp	444/udp	Simple Network Paging Protocol
#	[RFC1568]	
microsoft-ds	445/tcp	Microsoft-DS
microsoft-ds	445/udp	Microsoft-DS
#		Pradeep Bahl <pradeepb@microsoft.com>
ddm-rdb	446/tcp	DDM-RDB
ddm-rdb	446/udp	DDM-RDB
ddm-dfm	447/tcp	DDM-RFM
ddm-dfm	447/udp	DDM-RFM
#		Jan David Fisher <jdfisher@VNET.IBM.COM>
ddm-ssl	448/tcp	DDM-SSL
ddm-ssl	448/udp	DDM-SSL
#		Steve Ritland <srr@vnet.ibm.com>
as-servermap	449/tcp	AS Server Mapper
as-servermap	449/udp	AS Server Mapper
#		Barbara Foss <BGFOSS@rchvmv.vnet.ibm.com>

Keyword	Decimal	Description
tserver	450/tcp	Computer Supported Telecomunication Applications
tserver	450/udp	Computer Supported Telecomunication Applications
#		Harvey S. Schultz <harvey@acm.org>
sfs-smp-net	451/tcp	Cray Network Semaphore server
sfs-smp-net	451/udp	Cray Network Semaphore server
sfs-config	452/tcp	Cray SFS config server
sfs-config	452/udp	Cray SFS config server
#		Walter Poxon <wdp@ironwood.cray.com>
creativeserver	453/tcp	CreativeServer
creativeserver	453/udp	CreativeServer
contentserver	454/tcp	ContentServer
contentserver	454/udp	ContentServer
creativepartnr	455/tcp	CreativePartnr
creativepartnr	455/udp	CreativePartnr
#		Jesus Ortiz <jesus_ortiz@emotion.com>
macon-tcp	456/tcp	macon-tcp
macon-udp	456/udp	macon-udp
#		Yoshinobu Inoue <shin@hodaka.mfd.cs.fujitsu.co.jp>
scohelp	457/tcp	scohelp
scohelp	457/udp	scohelp
#		Faith Zack <faithz@sco.com>
appleqtc	458/tcp	apple quick time
appleqtc	458/udp	apple quick time
#		Murali Ranganathan <murali_ranganathan@quickmail.apple.com>
ampr-rcmd	459/tcp	ampr-rcmd
ampr-rcmd	459/udp	ampr-rcmd
#		Rob Janssen <rob@sys3.pe1chl.ampr.org>
skronk	460/tcp	skronk
skronk	460/udp	skronk
#		Henry Strickland <strick@yak.net>
datasurfsrv	461/tcp	DataRampSrv
datasurfsrv	461/udp	DataRampSrv
datasurfsrvsec	462/tcp	DataRampSrvSec
datasurfsrvsec	462/udp	DataRampSrvSec
#		Diane Downie <downie@jibe.MV.COM>
alpes	463/tcp	alpes
alpes	463/udp	alpes
#		Alain Durand <Alain.Durand@imag.fr>
kpasswd	464/tcp	kpasswd
kpasswd	464/udp	kpasswd
#		Theodore Ts'o <tytso@MIT.EDU>
urd	465/tcp	URL Rendesvous Directory for SSM
igmpv3lite	465/udp	IGMP over UDP for SSM
#		Toerless Eckert <eckert@cisco.com>
digital-vrc	466/tcp	digital-vrc
digital-vrc	466/udp	digital-vrc
#		Peter Higginson <higginson@mail.dec.com>
mylex-mapd	467/tcp	mylex-mapd
mylex-mapd	467/udp	mylex-mapd
#		Gary Lewis <GaryL@hq.mylex.com>

Keyword	Decimal	Description
photuris	468/tcp	proturis
photuris	468/udp	proturis
#		Bill Simpson <Bill.Simpson@um.cc.umich.edu>
rcp	469/tcp	Radio Control Protocol
rcp	469/udp	Radio Control Protocol
#		Jim Jennings +1–708–538–7241
scx-proxy	470/tcp	scx-proxy
scx-proxy	470/udp	scx-proxy
#		Scott Narveson <sjn@cray.com>
mondex	471/tcp	Mondex
mondex	471/udp	Mondex
#		Bill Reding <redingb@nwdt.natwest.co.uk>
ljk-login	472/tcp	ljk-login
ljk-login	472/udp	ljk-login
#		LJK Software, Cambridge, Massachusetts <support@ljk.com>
hybrid-pop	473/tcp	hybrid-pop
hybrid-pop	473/udp	hybrid-pop
#		Rami Rubin <rami@hybrid.com>
tn-tl-w1	474/tcp	tn-tl-w1
tn-tl-w2	474/udp	tn-tl-w2
#		Ed Kress <eskress@thinknet.com>
tcpnethaspsrv	475/tcp	tcpnethaspsrv
tcpnethaspsrv	475/udp	tcpnethaspsrv
#		Charlie Hava <charlie@aladdin.co.il>
tn-tl-fd1	476/tcp	tn-tl-fd1
tn-tl-fd1	476/udp	tn-tl-fd1
#		Ed Kress <eskress@thinknet.com>
ss7ns	477/tcp	ss7ns
ss7ns	477/udp	ss7ns
#		Jean-Michel URSCH <ursch@taec.enet.dec.com>
spsc	478/tcp	spsc
spsc	478/udp	spsc
#		Mike Rieker <mikea@sp32.com>
iafserver	479/tcp	iafserver
iafserver	479/udp	iafserver
iafdbase	480/tcp	iafdbase
iafdbase	480/udp	iafdbase
#		ricky@solect.com <Rick Yazwinski>
ph	481/tcp	Ph service
ph	481/udp	Ph service
#		Roland Hedberg <Roland.Hedberg@umdac.umu.se>
bgs-nsi	482/tcp	bgs-nsi
bgs-nsi	482/udp	bgs-nsi
#		Jon Saperia <saperia@bgs.com>
ulpnet	483/tcp	ulpnet
ulpnet	483/udp	ulpnet
#		Kevin Mooney <kevinm@bfs.unibol.com>
integra-sme	484/tcp	Integra Software Management Environment
integra-sme	484/udp	Integra Software Management Environment
#		Randall Dow <rand@randix.m.isr.de>

Keyword	Decimal	Description
powerburst	485/tcp	Air Soft Power Burst
powerburst	485/udp	Air Soft Power Burst
#		<gary@airsoft.com>
avian	486/tcp	avian
avian	486/udp	avian
#		Robert Ullmann <Robert_Ullmann/CAM/Lotus.LOTUS@crd.lotus.com>
saft	487/tcp	saft Simple Asynchronous File Transfer
saft	487/udp	saft Simple Asynchronous File Transfer
#		Ulli Horlacher <framstag@rus.uni-stuttgart.de>
gss-http	488/tcp	gss-http
gss-http	488/udp	gss-http
#		Doug Rosenthal <rosenthl@krypton.einet.net>
nest-protocol	489/tcp	nest-protocol
nest-protocol	489/udp	nest-protocol
#		Gilles Gameiro <ggameiro@birdland.com>
micom-pfs	490/tcp	micom-pfs
micom-pfs	490/udp	micom-pfs
#		David Misunas <DMisunas@micom.com>
go-login	491/tcp	go-login
go-login	491/udp	go-login
#		Troy Morrison <troy@graphon.com>
ticf-1	492/tcp	Transport Independent Convergence for FNA
ticf-1	492/udp	Transport Independent Convergence for FNA
ticf-2	493/tcp	Transport Independent Convergence for FNA
ticf-2	493/udp	Transport Independent Convergence for FNA
#		Mamoru Ito <Ito@pcnet.ks.pfu.co.jp>
pov-ray	494/tcp	POV-Ray
pov-ray	494/udp	POV-Ray
#		POV-Team Coordinator <iana-port.remove-spamguard@povray.org>
intecourier	495/tcp	intecourier
intecourier	495/udp	intecourier
#		Steve Favor <sfavor@tigger.intecom.com>
pim-rp-disc	496/tcp	PIM-RP-DISC
pim-rp-disc	496/udp	PIM-RP-DISC
#		Dino Farinacci <dino@cisco.com>
dantz	497/tcp	dantz
dantz	497/udp	dantz
#		Richard Zulch <richard_zulch@dantz.com>
siam	498/tcp	siam
siam	498/udp	siam
#		Philippe Gilbert <pgilbert@cal.fr>
iso-ill	499/tcp	ISO ILL Protocol
iso-ill	499/udp	ISO ILL Protocol
#		Mark H. Needleman <markn@sirsi.com>
isakmp	500/tcp	isakmp
isakmp	500/udp	isakmp
#		Mark Schertler <mjs@tycho.ncsc.mil>
stmf	501/tcp	STMF
stmf	501/udp	STMF

Keyword	Decimal	Description
#		Alan Ungar <aungar@farradyne.com>
asa-appl-proto	502/tcp	asa-appl-proto
asa-appl-proto	502/udp	asa-appl-proto
#		Dennis Dube <ddube@modicon.com>
intrinsa	503/tcp	Intrinsa
intrinsa	503/udp	Intrinsa
#		Robert Ford <robert@intrinsa.com>
citadel	504/tcp	citadel
citadel	504/udp	citadel
#		Art Cancro <ajc@uncnsrd.mt-kisco.ny.us>
mailbox-lm	505/tcp	mailbox-lm
mailbox-lm	505/udp	mailbox-lm
#		Beverly Moody <Beverly_Moody@stercomm.com>
ohimsrv	506/tcp	ohimsrv
ohimsrv	506/udp	ohimsrv
#		Scott Powell <spowell@openhorizon.com>
crs	507/tcp	crs
crs	507/udp	crs
#		Brad Wright <bradwr@microsoft.com>
xvttp	508/tcp	xvttp
xvttp	508/udp	xvttp
#		Keith J. Alphonso <alphonso@ncs-ssc.com>
snare	509/tcp	snare
snare	509/udp	snare
#		Dennis Batchelder <dennis@capres.com>
fcp	510/tcp	FirstClass Protocol
fcp	510/udp	FirstClass Protocol
#		Mike Marshburn <paul@softarc.com>
passgo	511/tcp	PassGo
passgo	511/udp	PassGo
#		John Rainford <jrainford@passgo.com>
exec	512/tcp	remote process execution;
#		authentication performed using passwords and UNIX login names
comsat	512/udp	
biff	512/udp	used by mail system to notify users # of new mail received; currently receives messages only from processes on the same machine
login	513/tcp	remote login a la telnet; automatic authentication performed based on privileged port numbers and distributed data bases which identify "authentication domains"
who	513/udp	maintains data bases showing who is logged in to machines on a local net and the load average of the machine
shell	514/tcp	cmd
#		like exec, but automatic authentication is performed as login server
syslog	514/udp	
printer	515/tcp	spooler
printer	515/udp	spooler
videotex	516/tcp	videotex
videotex	516/udp	videotex

Keyword	Decimal	Description
#		Daniel Mavrakis <system@venus.mctel.fr>
talk	517/tcp	like tenex link, but across machine; unfortunately, does not use link protocol (this is actually just a rendezvous port from which a tcp connection is established)
talk	517/udp	like tenex link, but across machine; unfortunately, does not use link protocol (this is actually just a rendezvous port from which a tcp connection is established)
ntalk	518/tcp	
ntalk	518/udp	
utime	519/tcp	unixtime
utime	519/udp	unixtime
efs	520/tcp	extended file name server
router	520/udp	local routing process (on site); uses variant of Xerox NS routing information protocol - RIP
ripng	521/tcp	ripng
ripng	521/udp	ripng
#		Robert E. Minnear <minnear@ipsilon.com>
ulp	522/tcp	ULP
ulp	522/udp	ULP
#		Max Morris <maxm@MICROSOFT.com>
ibm-db2	523/tcp	IBM-DB2
ibm-db2	523/udp	IBM-DB2
#		Peter Pau <pau@VNET.IBM.COM>
ncp	524/tcp	NCP
ncp	524/udp	NCP
#		Don Provan <donp@sjf.novell.com>
timed	525/tcp	timeserver
timed	525/udp	timeserver
tempo	526/tcp	newdate
tempo	526/udp	newdate
#	Unknown	
stx	527/tcp	Stock IXChange
stx	527/udp	Stock IXChange
custix	528/tcp	Customer IXChange
custix	528/udp	Customer IXChange
#		Ferdi Ladeira <ferdi.ladeira@ixchange.com>
irc-serv	529/tcp	IRC-SERV
irc-serv	529/udp	IRC-SERV
#		Brian Tackett <cym@acrux.net>
courier	530/tcp	rpc
courier	530/udp	rpc
conference	531/tcp	chat
conference	531/udp	chat
netnews	532/tcp	readnews
netnews	532/udp	readnews
netwall	533/tcp	for emergency broadcasts
netwall	533/udp	for emergency broadcasts
mm-admin	534/tcp	MegaMedia Admin
mm-admin	534/udp	MegaMedia Admin
#		Andreas Heidemann <a.heidemann@ais-gmbh.de>
iiop	535/tcp	iiop
iiop	535/udp	iiop

Keyword	Decimal	Description
#		Jeff M.Michaud <michaud@zk3.dec.com>
opalis-rdv	536/tcp	opalis-rdv
opalis-rdv	536/udp	opalis-rdv
#		Laurent Domenech <ldomenech@opalis.com>
nmsp	537/tcp	Networked Media Streaming Protocol
nmsp	537/udp	Networked Media Streaming Protocol
#		Paul Santinelli Jr. <psantinelli@narrative.com>
gdomap	538/tcp	gdomap
gdomap	538/udp	gdomap
#		Richard Frith-Macdonald <richard@brainstorm.co.uk>
apertus-ldp	539/tcp	Apertus Technologies Load Determination
apertus-ldp	539/udp	Apertus Technologies Load Determination
uucp	540/tcp	uucpd
uucp	540/udp	uucpd
uucp-rlogin	541/tcp	uucp-rlogin
uucp-rlogin	541/udp	uucp-rlogin
#		Stuart Lynne <sl@wimsey.com>
commerce	542/tcp	commerce
commerce	542/udp	commerce
#		Randy Epstein <repstein@host.net>
klogin	543/tcp	
klogin	543/udp	
kshell	544/tcp	krcmd
kshell	544/udp	krcmd
appleqtcsrvr	545/tcp	appleqtcsrvr
appleqtcsrvr	545/udp	appleqtcsrvr
#		Murali Ranganatha <Murali_Ranganathan@quickmail.apple.com>
dhcpv6-client	546/tcp	DHCPv6 Client
dhcpv6-client	546/udp	DHCPv6 Client
dhcpv6-server	547/tcp	DHCPv6 Server
dhcpv6-server	547/udp	DHCPv6 Server
#		Jim Bound <bound@zk3.dec.com>
afpovertcp	548/tcp	AFP over TCP
afpovertcp	548/udp	AFP over TCP
#		Leland Wallace <randall@apple.com>
idfp	549/tcp	IDFP
idfp	549/udp	IDFP
#		Ramana Kovi <ramana@kovi.com>
new-rwho	550/tcp	new-who
new-rwho	550/udp	new-who
cybercash	551/tcp	cybercash
cybercash	551/udp	cybercash
#		Donald E. Eastlake <dee@cybercash.com>
devshr-nts	552/tcp	DeviceShare
devshr-nts	552/udp	DeviceShare
#		Benjamin Rosenberg <brosenberg@advsyscon.com>
pirp	553/tcp	pirp
pirp	553/udp	pirp
#		D.J. Bernstein <djb@silverton.berkeley.edu>
rtsp	554/tcp	Real Time Stream Control Protocol

Keyword	Decimal	Description
rtsp	554/udp	Real Time Stream Control Protocol
#		Mob Lanphier <robla@prognet.com>
dsf	555/tcp	
dsf	555/udp	
remotefs	556/tcp	rfs server
remotefs	556/udp	rfs server
openvms-sysipc	557/tcp	openvms-sysipc
openvms-sysipc	557/udp	openvms-sysipc
#		Alan Potter <potter@movies.enet.dec.com>
sdnskmp	558/tcp	SDNSKMP
sdnskmp	558/udp	SDNSKMP
teedtap	559/tcp	TEEDTAP
teedtap	559/udp	TEEDTAP
#		Mort Hoffman <hoffman@mail.ndhm.gtegsc.com>
rmonitor	560/tcp	rmonitord
rmonitor	560/udp	rmonitord
monitor	561/tcp	
monitor	561/udp	
chshell	562/tcp	chcmd
chshell	562/udp	chcmd
nntps	563/tcp	nntp protocol over TLS/SSL (was snntp)
nntps	563/udp	nntp protocol over TLS/SSL (was snntp)
#		Kipp E.B. Hickman <kipp@netscape.com>
9pfs	564/tcp	plan 9 file service
9pfs	564/udp	plan 9 file service
whoami	565/tcp	whoami
whoami	565/udp	whoami
streettalk	566/tcp	streettalk
streettalk	566/udp	streettalk
banyan-rpc	567/tcp	banyan-rpc
banyan-rpc	567/udp	banyan-rpc
#		Tom Lemaire <toml@banyan.com>
ms-shuttle	568/tcp	microsoft shuttle
ms-shuttle	568/udp	microsoft shuttle
#		Mudolph Balaz <rudolphb@microsoft.com>
ms-rome	569/tcp	microsoft rome
ms-rome	569/udp	microsoft rome
#		Mudolph Balaz <rudolphb@microsoft.com>
meter	570/tcp	demon
meter	570/udp	demon
meter	571/tcp	udemon
meter	571/udp	udemon
sonar	572/tcp	sonar
sonar	572/udp	sonar
#		Keith Moore <moore@cs.utk.edu>
banyan-vip	573/tcp	banyan-vip
banyan-vip	573/udp	banyan-vip
#		Denis Leclerc <DLeclerc@banyan.com>
ftp-agent	574/tcp	FTP Software Agent System
ftp-agent	574/udp	FTP Software Agent System
#		Michael S. Greenberg <arnoff@ftp.com>

Keyword	Decimal	Description
vemmi	575/tcp	VEMMI
vemmi	575/udp	VEMMI
#		Daniel Mavrakis <mavrakis@mctel.fr>
ipcd	576/tcp	ipcd
ipcd	576/udp	ipcd
vnas	577/tcp	vnas
vnas	577/udp	vnas
ipdd	578/tcp	ipdd
ipdd	578/udp	ipdd
#		Jay Farhat <jfarhat@ipass.com>
decbsrv	579/tcp	decbsrv
decbsrv	579/udp	decbsrv
#		Rudi Martin <movies::martin"@movies.enet.dec.com>
sntp-heartbeat	580/tcp	SNTP HEARTBEAT
sntp-heartbeat	580/udp	SNTP HEARTBEAT
#		Louis Mamakos <louie@uu.net>
bdp	581/tcp	Bundle Discovery Protocol
bdp	581/udp	Bundle Discovery Protocol
#		Gary Malkin <gmalkin@xylogics.com>
scc-security	582/tcp	SCC Security
scc-security	582/udp	SCC Security
#		Prashant Dholakia <prashant@semaphorecom.com>
philips-vc	583/tcp	Philips Video-Conferencing
philips-vc	583/udp	Philips Video-Conferencing
#		Janna Chang <janna@pmc.philips.com>
keyserver	584/tcp	Key Server
keyserver	584/udp	Key Server
#		Gary Howland <gary@systemics.com>
imap4-ssl	585/tcp	IMAP4+SSL (use 993 instead)
imap4-ssl	585/udp	IMAP4+SSL (use 993 instead)
#		Terry Gray <gray@cac.washington.edu>
#		Use of 585 is not recommended, use 993 instead
password-chg	586/tcp	Password Change
password-chg	586/udp	Password Change
submission	587/tcp	Submission
submission	587/udp	Submission
#		Randy Gellens <randy@qualcomm.com>
cal	588/tcp	CAL
cal	588/udp	CAL
#		Myron Hattig <Myron_Hattig@ccm.jf.intel.com>
eyelink	589/tcp	EyeLink
eyelink	589/udp	EyeLink
#		Dave Stampe <dstampe@psych.toronto.edu>
tns-cml	590/tcp	TNS CML
tns-cml	590/udp	TNS CML
#		Jerome Albin <albin@taec.enet.dec.com>
http-alt	591/tcp	FileMaker, Inc. - HTTP Alternate (see Port 80)
http-alt	591/udp	FileMaker, Inc. - HTTP Alternate (see Port 80)
#		Clay Maeckel <clay_maeckel@filemaker.com>
eudora-set	592/tcp	Eudora Set
eudora-set	592/udp	Eudora Set

Keyword	Decimal	Description
#		Randall Gellens <randy@qualcomm.com>
http-rpc-epmap	593/tcp	HTTP RPC Ep Map
http-rpc-epmap	593/udp	HTTP RPC Ep Map
#		Edward Reus <edwardr@microsoft.com>
tpip	594/tcp	TPIP
tpip	594/udp	TPIP
#		Brad Spear <spear@platinum.com>
cab-protocol	595/tcp	CAB Protocol
cab-protocol	595/udp	CAB Protocol
#		Winston Hetherington
smsd	596/tcp	SMSD
smsd	596/udp	SMSD
#		Wayne Barlow <web@unx.dec.com>
ptcnameservice	597/tcp	PTC Name Service
ptcnameservice	597/udp	PTC Name Service
#		Yuri Machkasov <yuri@ptc.com>
sco-websrvrmg3	598/tcp	SCO Web Server Manager 3
sco-websrvrmg3	598/udp	SCO Web Server Manager 3
#		Simon Baldwin <simonb@sco.com>
acp	599/tcp	Aeolon Core Protocol
acp	599/udp	Aeolon Core Protocol
#		Michael Alyn Miller <malyn@aeolon.com>
ipcserver	600/tcp	Sun IPC server
ipcserver	600/udp	Sun IPC server
#		Bill Schiefelbein <schief@aspen.cray.com>
syslog-conn	601/tcp	Reliable Syslog Service
syslog-conn	601/udp	Reliable Syslog Service
#	MFC 3195	
#	602–604	Unassigned
soap-beep	605/tcp	SOAP over BEEP
soap-beep	605/udp	SOAP over BEEP
#		RFC3288 <ftp://ftp.isi.edu/in-notes/rfc3288.txt> April 2002
urm	606/tcp	Cray Unified Resource Manager
urm	606/udp	Cray Unified Resource Manager
nqs	607/tcp	nqs
nqs	607/udp	nqs
#		Bill Schiefelbein <schief@aspen.cray.com>
sift-uft	608/tcp	Sender-Initiated/Unsolicited File Transfer
sift-uft	608/udp	Sender-Initiated/Unsolicited File Transfer
#		Mick Troth <troth@rice.edu>
npmp-trap	609/tcp	npmp-trap
npmp-trap	609/udp	npmp-trap
npmp-local	610/tcp	npmp-local
npmp-local	610/udp	npmp-local
npmp-gui	611/tcp	npmp-gui
npmp-gui	611/udp	npmp-gui
#		John Barnes <jbarnes@crl.com>
hmmp-ind	612/tcp	HMMP Indication
hmmp-ind	612/udp	HMMP Indication
hmmp-op	613/tcp	HMMP Operation
hmmp-op	613/udp	HMMP Operation

Keyword	Decimal	Description
#		Andrew Sinclair <andrsin@microsoft.com>
sshell	614/tcp	SSLshell
sshell	614/udp	SSLshell
#		Simon J. Gerraty <sjg@quick.com.au>
sco-inetmgr	615/tcp	Internet Configuration Manager
sco-inetmgr	615/udp	Internet Configuration Manager
sco-sysmgr	616/tcp	SCO System Administration Server
sco-sysmgr	616/udp	SCO System Administration Server
sco-dtmgr	617/tcp	SCO Desktop Administration Server
sco-dtmgr	617/udp	SCO Desktop Administration Server
#		Christopher Durham <chrisdu@sco.com>
dei-icda	618/tcp	DEI-ICDA
dei-icda	618/udp	DEI-ICDA
#		David Turner <digital@Quetico.tbaytel.net>
compaq-evm	619/tcp	Compaq EVM
compaq-evm	619/udp	Compaq EVM
#		Jem Treadwell <Jem.Treadwell@compaq.com>
sco-websrvrmgr	620/tcp	SCO WebServer Manager
sco-websrvrmgr	620/udp	SCO WebServer Manager
#		Christopher Durham <chrisdu@sco.com>
escp-ip	621/tcp	ESCP
escp-ip	621/udp	ESCP
#		Lai Zit Seng <lzs@pobox.com>
collaborator	622/tcp	Collaborator
collaborator	622/udp	Collaborator
#		Johnson Davis <johnsond@opteamasoft.com>
asf-rmcp	623/tcp	ASF Remote Management and Control Protocol
asf-rmcp	623/udp	ASF Remote Management and Control Protocol
#		Carl First <Carl.L.First@intel.com>
cryptoadmin	624/tcp	Crypto Admin
cryptoadmin	624/udp	Crypto Admin
#		Tony Walker <tony@cryptocard.com>
dec_dlm	625/tcp	DEC DLM
dec_dlm	625/udp	DEC DLM
#		Rudi Martin <Rudi.Martin@edo.mts.dec.com>
asia	626/tcp	ASIA
asia	626/udp	ASIA
#		Michael Dasenbrock <dasenbro@apple.com>
passgo-tivoli	627/tcp	PassGo Tivoli
passgo-tivoli	627/udp	PassGo Tivoli
#		Chris Hall <chall@passgo.com>
qmqp	628/tcp	QMQP
qmqp	628/udp	QMQP
#		Dan Bernstein <djb@cr.yp.to>
3com-amp3	629/tcp	3Com AMP3
3com-amp3	629/udp	3Com AMP3
#		Prakash Banthia <prakash_banthia@3com.com>
rda	630/tcp	RDA
rda	630/udp	RDA
#		John Hadjioannou <john@minster.co.uk>
ipp	631/tcp	IPP (Internet Printing Protocol)

Keyword	Decimal	Description
ipp	631/udp	IPP (Internet Printing Protocol)
#		Carl-Uno Manros <manros@cp10.es.xerox.com>
bmpp	632/tcp	bmpp
bmpp	632/udp	bmpp
#		Troy Rollo <troy@kroll.corvu.com.au>
servstat	633/tcp	Service Status update (Sterling Software)
servstat	633/udp	Service Status update (Sterling Software)
#		Greg Rose <Greg_Rose@sydney.sterling.com>
ginad	634/tcp	ginad
ginad	634/udp	ginad
#		Mark Crother <mark@eis.calstate.edu>
rlzdbase	635/tcp	RLZ DBase
rlzdbase	635/udp	RLZ DBase
#		Michael Ginn <ginn@tyxar.com>
ldaps	636/tcp	ldap protocol over TLS/SSL (was sldap)
ldaps	636/udp	ldap protocol over TLS/SSL (was sldap)
#		Pat Richard <patr@xcert.com>
lanserver	637/tcp	lanserver
lanserver	637/udp	lanserver
#		Chris Larsson <clarsson@VNET.IBM.COM>
mcns-sec	638/tcp	mcns-sec
mcns-sec	638/udp	mcns-sec
#		Kaz Ozawa <k.ozawa@cablelabs.com>
msdp	639/tcp	MSDP
msdp	639/udp	MSDP
#		Dino Farinacci <dino@cisco.com>
entrust-sps	640/tcp	entrust-sps
entrust-sps	640/udp	entrust-sps
#		Marek Buchler <Marek.Buchler@entrust.com>
repcmd	641/tcp	repcmd
repcmd	641/udp	repcmd
#		Scott Dale <scott@Replicase.com>
esro-emsdp	642/tcp	ESRO-EMSDP V1.3
esro-emsdp	642/udp	ESRO-EMSDP V1.3
#		Mohsen Banan <mohsen@neda.com>
sanity	643/tcp	SANity
sanity	643/udp	SANity
#		Peter Viscarola <PeterGV@osr.com>
dwr	644/tcp	dwr
dwr	644/udp	dwr
#		Bill Fenner <fenner@parc.xerox.com>
pssc	645/tcp	PSSC
pssc	645/udp	PSSC
#		Egon Meier-Engelen <egon.meier-engelen@dlr.de>
ldp	646/tcp	LDP
ldp	646/udp	LDP
#		Bob Thomas <rhthomas@cisco.com>
dhcp-failover	647/tcp	DHCP Failover
dhcp-failover	647/udp	DHCP Failover
#		Bernard Volz <volz@ipworks.com>
rrp	648/tcp	Registry Registrar Protocol (RRP)

Keyword	Decimal	Description
rrp	648/udp	Registry Registrar Protocol (RRP)
#		Scott Hollenbeck <shollenb@netsol.com>
cadview-3d	649/tcp	Cadview-3d - streaming three-dimensional models over the Internet
cadview-3d	649/udp	Cadview-3d - streaming three-dimensional models over the Internet
#		David Cooper <david.cooper@oracle.com>
obex	650/tcp	OBEX
obex	650/udp	OBEX
#		Jeff Garbers <FJG030@email.mot.com>
ieee-mms	651/tcp	IEEE MMS
ieee-mms	651/udp	IEEE MMS
#		Curtis Anderson <canderson@turbolinux.com>
hello-port	652/tcp	HELLO_PORT
hello-port	652/udp	HELLO_PORT
#		Patrick Cipiere <Patrick.Cipiere@UDcast.com>
repscmd	653/tcp	RepCmd
repscmd	653/udp	RepCmd
#		Scott Dale <scott@tioga.com>
aodv	654/tcp	AODV
aodv	654/udp	AODV
#		Charles Perkins <cperkins@eng.sun.com>
tinc	655/tcp	TINC
tinc	655/udp	TINC
#		Ivo Timmermans <itimmermans@bigfoot.com>
spmp	656/tcp	SPMP
spmp	656/udp	SPMP
#		Jakob Kaivo <jkaivo@nodomainname.net>
rmc	657/tcp	RMC
rmc	657/udp	RMC
#		Michael Schmidt <mmaass@us.ibm.com>
tenfold	658/tcp	TenFold
tenfold	658/udp	TenFold
#		Louis Olszyk <lolszyk@10fold.com>
#	659	Removed (6-6-2001)
mac-srvr-admin	660/tcp	MacOS Server Admin
mac-srvr-admin	660/udp	MacOS Server Admin
#		Forest Hill <forest@apple.com>
hap	661/tcp	HAP
hap	661/udp	HAP
#		Igor Plotnikov <igor@uroam.com>
pftp	662/tcp	PFTP
pftp	662/udp	PFTP
#		Ben Schluricke <support@pftp.de>
purenoise	663/tcp	PureNoise
purenoise	663/udp	PureNoise
#		Sam Osa <pristine@mailcity.com>
asf-secure-rmcp	664/tcp	ASF Secure Remote Management and Control Protocol
asf-secure-rmcp	664/udp	ASF Secure Remote Management and Control Protocol
#		Carl First <Carl.L.First@intel.com>
sun-dr	665/tcp	Sun DR

Keyword	Decimal	Description
sun-dr	665/udp	Sun DR
#		Harinder Bhasin <Harinder.Bhasin@Sun.COM>
mdqs	666/tcp	
mdqs	666/udp	
doom	666/tcp	doom Id Software
doom	666/udp	doom Id Software <ddt@idcube.idsoftware.com>
disclose	667/tcp	campaign contribution disclosures - SDR Technologies
disclose	667/udp	campaign contribution disclosures - SDR Technologies
#		Jim Dixon <jim@lambda.com>
mecomm	668/tcp	MeComm
mecomm	668/udp	MeComm
meregister	669/tcp	MeRegister
meregister	669/udp	MeRegister
#		Armin Sawusch <armin@esd1.esd.de>
vacdsm-sws	670/tcp	VACDSM-SWS
vacdsm-sws	670/udp	VACDSM-SWS
vacdsm-app	671/tcp	VACDSM-APP
vacdsm-app	671/udp	VACDSM-APP
vpps-qua	672/tcp	VPPS-QUA
vpps-qua	672/udp	VPPS-QUA
cimplex	673/tcp	CIMPLEX
cimplex	673/udp	CIMPLEX
#		Ulysses G. Smith Jr. <ugsmith@cesi.com>
acap	674/tcp	ACAP
acap	674/udp	ACAP
#		Chris Newman <chris.newman@sun.com>
dctp	675/tcp	DCTP
dctp	675/udp	DCTP
#		Andre Kramer <Andre.Kramer@ansa.co.uk>
vpps-via	676/tcp	VPPS Via
vpps-via	676/udp	VPPS Via
#		Ulysses G. Smith Jr. <ugsmith@cesi.com>
vpp	677/tcp	Virtual Presence Protocol
vpp	677/udp	Virtual Presence Protocol
#		Klaus Wolf <wolf@cobrow.com>
ggf-ncp	678/tcp	GNU Generation Foundation NCP
ggf-ncp	678/udp	GNU Generation Foundation NCP
#		Noah Paul <noahp@altavista.net>
mrm	679/tcp	MRM
mrm	679/udp	MRM
#		Liming Wei <lwei@cisco.com>
entrust-aaas	680/tcp	entrust-aaas
entrust-aaas	680/udp	entrust-aaas
entrust-aams	681/tcp	entrust-aams
entrust-aams	681/udp	entrust-aams
#		Adrian Mancini <adrian.mancini@entrust.com>
xfr	682/tcp	XFR
xfr	682/udp	XFR
#		Noah Paul <noahp@ultranet.com>
corba-iiop	683/tcp	CORBA IIOP
corba-iiop	683/udp	CORBA IIOP

Keyword	Decimal	Description
corba-iiop-ssl	684/tcp	CORBA IIOP SSL
corba-iiop-ssl	684/udp	CORBA IIOP SSL
#		Henry Lowe <lowe@omg.org>
mdc-portmapper	685/tcp	MDC Port Mapper
mdc-portmapper	685/udp	MDC Port Mapper
#		Noah Paul <noahp@altavista.net>
hcp-wismar	686/tcp	Hardware Control Protocol Wismar
hcp-wismar	686/udp	Hardware Control Protocol Wismar
#		David Merchant <d.f.merchant@livjm.ac.uk>
asipregistry	687/tcp	asipregistry
asipregistry	687/udp	asipregistry
#		Erik Sea <sea@apple.com>
realm-rusd	688/tcp	REALM-RUSD
realm-rusd	688/udp	REALM-RUSD
#		Jerry Knight <jknight@realminfo.com>
nmap	689/tcp	NMAP
nmap	689/udp	NMAP
#		Peter Dennis Bartok <peter@novonyx.com>
vatp	690/tcp	VATP
vatp	690/udp	VATP
#		Atica Software <comercial@aticasoft.es>
msexch-routing	691/tcp	MS Exchange Routing
msexch-routing	691/udp	MS Exchange Routing
#		David Lemson <dlemson@microsoft.com>
hyperwave-isp	692/tcp	Hyperwave-ISP
hyperwave-isp	692/udp	Hyperwave-ISP
#		Gerald Mesaric <gmesaric@hyperwave.com>
connendp	693/tcp	connendp
connendp	693/udp	connendp
#		Ronny Bremer <rbremer@future-gate.com>
ha-cluster	694/tcp	ha-cluster
ha-cluster	694/udp	ha-cluster
#		Alan Robertson <alanr@unix.sh>
ieee-mms-ssl	695/tcp	IEEE-MMS-SSL
ieee-mms-ssl	695/udp	IEEE-MMS-SSL
#		Curtis Anderson <ecanderson@turbolinux.com>
rushd	696/tcp	RUSHD
rushd	696/udp	RUSHD
#		Greg Ercolano <erco@netcom.com>
uuidgen	697/tcp	UUIDGEN
uuidgen	697/udp	UUIDGEN
#		James Falkner <james.falkner@sun.com>
olsr	698/tcp	OLSR
olsr	698/udp	OLSR
#		Thomas Clausen <thomas.clausen@inria.fr>
accessnetwork	699/tcp	Access Network
accessnetwork	699/udp	Access Network
#		Yingchun Xu <Yingchun_Xu@3com.com>
#	700–703	Unassigned
elcsd	704/tcp	errlog copy/server daemon
elcsd	704/udp	errlog copy/server daemon

Keyword	Decimal	Description
agentx	705/tcp	AgentX
agentx	705/udp	AgentX
#		Bob Natale <natale@acec.com>
silc	706/tcp	SILC
silc	706/udp	SILC
#		Pekka Riikonen <priikone@poseidon.pspt.fi>
borland-dsj	707/tcp	Borland DSJ
borland-dsj	707/udp	Borland DSJ
#		Gerg Cole <gcole@corp.borland.com>
#	708	Unassigned
entrust-kmsh	709/tcp	Entrust Key Management Service Handler
entrust-kmsh	709/udp	Entrust Key Management Service Handler
entrust-ash	710/tcp	Entrust Administration Service Handler
entrust-ash	710/udp	Entrust Administration Service Handler
#		Peter Whittaker <pww@entrust.com>
cisco-tdp	711/tcp	Cisco TDP
cisco-tdp	711/udp	Cisco TDP
#		Bruce Davie <bsd@cisco.com>
#	712–728	Unassigned
netviewdm1	729/tcp	IBM NetView DM/6000 Server/Client
netviewdm1	729/udp	IBM NetView DM/6000 Server/Client
netviewdm2	730/tcp	IBM NetView DM/6000 send/tcp
netviewdm2	730/udp	IBM NetView DM/6000 send/tcp
netviewdm3	731/tcp	IBM NetView DM/6000 receive/tcp
netviewdm3	731/udp	IBM NetView DM/6000 receive/tcp
#		Philippe Binet (phbinet@vnet.IBM.COM)
#	732–740	Unassigned
netgw	741/tcp	netGW
netgw	741/udp	netGW
#		Oliver Korfmacher (okorf@netcs.com)
netrcs	742/tcp	Network based Rev. Cont. Sys.
netrcs	742/udp	Network based Rev. Cont. Sys.
#		Gordon C. Galligher <gorpong@ping.chi.il.us>
#	743	Unassigned
flexlm	744/tcp	Flexible License Manager
flexlm	744/udp	Flexible License Manager
#		Matt Christiano <globes@matt@oliveb.atc.olivetti.com>
#	745–746	Unassigned
fujitsu-dev	747/tcp	Fujitsu Device Control
fujitsu-dev	747/udp	Fujitsu Device Control
ris-cm	748/tcp	Russell Info Sci Calendar Manager
ris-cm	748/udp	Russell Info Sci Calendar Manager
kerberos-adm	749/tcp	kerberos administration
kerberos-adm	749/udp	kerberos administration
rfile	750/tcp	
loadav	750/udp	
kerberos-iv	750/udp	kerberos version iv
#		Martin Hamilton <martin@mrrl.lut.as.uk>
pump	751/tcp	
pump	751/udp	
qrh	752/tcp	

Keyword	Decimal	Description
qrh	752/udp	
rrh	753/tcp	
rrh	753/udp	
tell	754/tcp	send
tell	754/udp	send
#		Josyula R. Rao <jrrao@watson.ibm.com>
#	755–756	Unassigned
nlogin	758/tcp	
nlogin	758/udp	
con	759/tcp	
con	759/udp	
ns	760/tcp	
ns	760/udp	
rxe	761/tcp	
rxe	761/udp	
quotad	762/tcp	
quotad	762/udp	
cycleserv	763/tcp	
cycleserv	763/udp	
omserv	764/tcp	
omserv	764/udp	
webster	765/tcp	
webster	765/udp	
#		Josyula R. Rao <jrrao@watson.ibm.com>
#	766	Unassigned
phonebook	767/tcp	phone
phonebook	767/udp	phone
#		Josyula R. Rao <jrrao@watson.ibm.com>
#	768	Unassigned
vid	769/tcp	
vid	769/udp	
cadlock	770/tcp	
cadlock	770/udp	
rtip	771/tcp	
rtip	771/udp	
cycleserv2	772/tcp	
cycleserv2	772/udp	
submit	773/tcp	
notify	773/udp	
rpasswd	774/tcp	
acmaint_dbd	774/udp	
entomb	775/tcp	
acmaint_transd	775/udp	
wpages	776/tcp	
wpages	776/udp	
#		Josyula R. Rao <jrrao@watson.ibm.com>
multiling-http	777/tcp	Multiling HTTP
multiling-http	777/udp	Multiling HTTP
#		Alejandro Bonet <babel@ctv.es>
#	778–779	Unassigned
wpgs	780/tcp	

Keyword	Decimal	Description
wpgs	780/udp	
#		Josyula R. Rao <jrrao@watson.ibm.com>
#	781–785	Unassigned
#	786	Unassigned (Removed 2002-05-08)
#	787	Unassigned (Removed 2002-10-08)
#	788–799	Unassigned
mdbs_daemon	800/tcp	
mdbs_daemon	800/udp	
device	801/tcp	
device	801/udp	
#	802–809	Unassigned
fcp-udp	810/tcp	FCP
fcp-udp	810/udp	FCP Datagram
#		Paul Whittemore <paul@softarc.com>
#	811–827	Unassigned
itm-mcell-s	828/tcp	itm-mcell-s
itm-mcell-s	828/udp	itm-mcell-s
#		Miles O'Neal <meo@us.itmasters.com>
pkix-3-ca-ra	829/tcp	PKIX-3 CA/RA
pkix-3-ca-ra	829/udp	PKIX-3 CA/RA
#		Carlisle Adams <Cadams@entrust.com>
#	830–846	Unassigned
dhcp-failover2	847/tcp	dhcp-failover 2
dhcp-failover2	847/udp	dhcp-failover 2
#		Bernard Volz <volz@ipworks.com>
#	848–872	Unassigned
rsync	873/tcp	rsync
rsync	873/udp	rsync
#		Andrew Tridgell <tridge@samba.anu.edu.au>
#	874–885	Unassigned
iclcnet-locate	886/tcp	ICL coNETion locate server
iclcnet-locate	886/udp	ICL coNETion locate server
#		Bob Lyon <bl@oasis.icl.co.uk>
iclcnet_svinfo	887/tcp	ICL coNETion server info
iclcnet_svinfo	887/udp	ICL coNETion server info
#		Bob Lyon <bl@oasis.icl.co.uk>
accessbuilder	888/tcp	AccessBuilder
accessbuilder	888/udp	AccessBuilder
#		Steve Sweeney <Steven_Sweeney@3mail.3com.com>
#The following entry records an unassigned but widespread use		
cddbp	888/tcp	CD Database Protocol
#		Steve Scherf <steve@moonsoft.com>
#	889–899	Unassigned
omginitialrefs	900/tcp	OMG Initial Refs
omginitialrefs	900/udp	OMG Initial Refs
#		Christian Callsen <Christian.Callsen@eng.sun.com>
smpnameres	901/tcp	SMPNAMERES
smpnameres	901/udp	SMPNAMERES
#		Leif Ekblad <leif@rdos.net>
ideafarm-chat	902/tcp	IDEAFARM-CHAT
ideafarm-chat	902/udp	IDEAFARM-CHAT

Keyword	Decimal	Description
ideafarm-catch	903/tcp	IDEAFARM-CATCH
ideafarm-catch	903/udp	IDEAFARM-CATCH
#		Wo'o Ideafarm <wo@ideafarm.com>
#	904–910	Unassigned
xact-backup	911/tcp	xact-backup
xact-backup	911/udp	xact-backup
#		Bill Carroll <billc@xactlabs.com>
apex-mesh	912/tcp	APEX relay-relay service
apex-mesh	912/udp	APEX relay-relay service
apex-edge	913/tcp	APEX endpoint-relay service
apex-edge	913/udp	APEX endpoint-relay service
# [RFC3340]		
#	914–988	Unassigned
ftps-data	989/tcp	ftp protocol, data, over TLS/SSL
ftps-data	989/udp	ftp protocol, data, over TLS/SSL
ftps	990/tcp	ftp protocol, control, over TLS/SSL
ftps	990/udp	ftp protocol, control, over TLS/SSL
#		Christopher Allen <ChristopherA@consensus.com>
nas	991/tcp	Netnews Administration System
nas	991/udp	Netnews Administration System
#		Vera Heinau <heinau@fu-berlin.de>
#		Heiko Schlichting <heiko@fu-berlin.de>
telnets	992/tcp	telnet protocol over TLS/SSL
telnets	992/udp	telnet protocol over TLS/SSL
imaps	993/tcp	imap4 protocol over TLS/SSL
imaps	993/udp	imap4 protocol over TLS/SSL
ircs	994/tcp	irc protocol over TLS/SSL
ircs	994/udp	irc protocol over TLS/SSL
#		Christopher Allen <ChristopherA@consensus.com>
pop3s	995/tcp	pop3 protocol over TLS/SSL (was spop3)
pop3s	995/udp	pop3 protocol over TLS/SSL (was spop3)
#		Gordon Mangione <gordm@microsoft.com>
vsinet	996/tcp	vsinet
vsinet	996/udp	vsinet
#		Mob Juergens <robj@vsi.com>
maitrd	997/tcp	
maitrd	997/udp	
busboy	998/tcp	
puparp	998/udp	
garcon	999/tcp	
applix	999/udp	Applix ac
puprouter	999/tcp	
puprouter	999/udp	
cadlock2	1000/tcp	
cadlock2	1000/udp	
#	1001–1009	Unassigned
#	1008/udp	Possibly used by Sun Solaris????
surf	1010/tcp	surf
surf	1010/udp	surf
#		Joseph Geer <jgeer@peapod.com>
#	1011–1022	Reserved

Keyword	Decimal	Description
1023/tcp	Reserved	
1023/udp	Reserved	
#		IANA <iana@iana.org>

References

[RFC768] Postel, J., "User Datagram Protocol," STD 6, RFC 768, USC/Information Sciences Institute, August 1980.

[RFC793] Postel, J., Ed., "Transmission Control Protocol — DARPA Internet Program Protocol Specification," STD 7, RFC 793, USC/Information Sciences Institute, September 1981.

[RFC3077] Duros, E., W. Dabbous, H. Izumiyama, N. Fujii, and Y. Zhang, "A Link-Layer Tunneling Mechanism for Unidirectional Links", RFC 3077, March 2001.

[RFC3340] Rose, M., G. Klyne, and D. Crocker, "The Application Exchange Core," RFC 3340, July 2002.

Appendix B

Site Security Handbook RFC 2196*

Status

This memo provides information for the Internet community. It does not specify an Internet standard of any kind. Distribution of this memo is unlimited.

Abstract

This handbook is a guide to developing computer security policies and procedures for sites that have systems on the Internet. The purpose of this Appendix is to provide practical guidance to administrators trying to secure their information and services. The subjects covered include policy content and formation, a broad range of technical system and network security topics, and security incident response.

Table of Contents

Status.. 451

Abstract.. 451

Table of Contents 451

1. Introduction 452

    1.1 Purpose of this Work.. 453

    1.2 Audience 453

    1.3 Definitions.. 453

    1.4 Related Work 454

    1.5 Basic Approach 454

    1.6 Risk Assessment 454

---

* Editor information: Barbara Y. Fraser, Software Engineering Institute, Carnegie Mellon University, 5000 Forbes Avenue, Pittsburgh, PA 15213.

2. Security Policies 456
    2.1 What Is a Security Policy, and Why Have One? 456
    2.2 What Makes a Good Security Policy? 457
    2.3 Keeping the Policy Flexible 459
3. Architecture 459
    3.1 Objectives 459
    3.2 Network and Service Configuration 461
    3.3 Firewalls 466
4. Security Services and Procedures 468
    4.1 Authentication 468
    4.2 Confidentiality 471
    4.3 Integrity 471
    4.4 Authorization 472
    4.5 Access 472
    4.6 Auditing 475
    4.7 Securing Backups 477
5. Security Incident Handling 478
    5.1 Preparing and Planning for Incident Handling 479
    5.2 Notification and Points of Contact 481
    5.3 Identifying an Incident 486
    5.4 Handling an Incident 488
    5.5 Aftermath of an Incident 492
    5.6 Responsibilities 493
6. Ongoing Activities 493
7. Tools and Locations 494
8. Mailing Lists and Other Resources 495
9. References 496

1. Introduction

This document provides guidance to system and network administrators on how to address security issues within the Internet community. It builds on the foundation provided in RFC 1244 and is the collective work of a number of contributing authors:

Jules P. Aronson (aronson@nlm.nih.gov)

Nevil Brownlee (n.brownlee@auckland.ac.nz)

Frank Byrum (byrum@norfolk.infi.net)

Joao Nuno Ferreira (ferreira@rccn.net)

Barbara Fraser (byf@cert.org)

Steve Glass (glass@ftp.com)

Erik Guttman (erik.guttman@eng.sun.com)

Tom Killalea (tomk@nwnet.net)

Klaus-Peter Kossakowski (kossakowski@cert.dfn.de)

Lorna Leone (lorna@staff.singnet.com.sg)

Edward P. Lewis (Edward.P.Lewis.1@gsfc.nasa.gov)

Gary Malkin (gmalkin@xylogics.com)

Russ Mundy (mundy@tis.com)

Philip J. Nesser (pjnesser@martigny.ai.mit.edu)

Michael S. Ramsey (msr@interpath.net)

In addition to the principal writers, a number of reviewers provided valuable comments:

Eric Luiijf (luiijf@fel.tno.nl)

Marijke Kaat (marijke.kaat@sec.nl)

Ray Plzak (plzak@nic.mil)

Han Pronk (h.m.pronk@vka.nl)

A special thank you goes to Joyce Reynolds, ISI, and Paul Holbrook, CICnet, for their vision, leadership, and effort in the creation of the first version of this handbook. It is the working group's sincere hope that this version will be as helpful to the community as the earlier one was.

1.1 Purpose of this Work

This handbook is a guide to setting computer security policies and procedures for sites that have systems on the Internet (however, the information provided should also be useful to sites not yet connected to the Internet). This guide lists issues and factors that a site must consider when setting its policies. It makes a number of recommendations and provides discussions of relevant areas.

This guide is only a framework for setting security policies and procedures. In order to have an effective set of policies and procedures, a site will have to make many decisions, gain agreement, and then communicate and implement these policies.

1.2 Audience

The audience for this document is system and network administrators, and decision makers (typically "middle management") at sites. For brevity, we will use the term "administrator" throughout this document to refer to system and network administrators.

This document is not directed at programmers or those trying to create secure programs or systems. The focus of this document is on the policies and procedures that need to be in place to support the technical security features that a site may be implementing.

The primary audience for this work is sites that are members of the Internet community. However, this document should be useful to any site that allows communication with other sites. As a general guide to security policies, this document may also be useful to sites with isolated systems.

1.3 Definitions

For the purposes of this guide, a "site" is any organization that owns computers or network-related resources. These resources may include host computers that users use, routers, terminal servers, PCs, or other devices that have access to the Internet. A site may be an end user of Internet services or a service provider such as a mid-level network. However, most of the focus of this guide is on those end users of Internet services. We assume that the site has the ability to set policies and procedures for itself with the concurrence and support from those who actually own the resources. It will be assumed that sites that are parts of larger organizations will know when they need to consult, collaborate, or take recommendations from the larger entity.

The "Internet" is a collection of thousands of networks linked by a common set of technical protocols that make it possible for users of any one of the networks to communicate with or use the services located on any of the other networks (FYI4, RFC 1594).

The term "administrator" is used to cover all those people who are responsible for the day-to-day operation of system and network resources. This may be a number of individuals or an organization.

The term "security administrator" is used to cover all those responsible for the security of information and information technology. At some sites, this function may be combined with administrator; at others, this will be a separate position.

The term "decision maker" refers to the people who set or approve policy. These are often (but not always) the people who own the resources.

1.4 Related Work

The Site Security Handbook Working Group is working on a User's Guide to Internet Security. It will provide practical guidance to end users to help them protect their information and the resources they use.

1.5 Basic Approach

This guide is written to provide basic guidance in developing a security plan for your site. One generally accepted approach to follow is suggested by Fites et al. [1989] and includes the following steps:

1.   Identify what you are trying to protect.
2.   Determine what you are trying to protect it from.
3.   Determine how likely the threats are.
4.   Implement measures that will protect your assets in a cost-effective manner.
5.   Review the process continuously and make improvements each time a weakness is found.

Most of this document is focused on item 4 but the other steps cannot be avoided if an effective plan is to be established at your site. One old truism in security is that the cost of protecting yourself against a threat should be less than the cost of recovering if the threat were to strike you. Cost in this context should be remembered to include losses expressed in real currency, reputation, trustworthiness, and other less-obvious measures. Without reasonable knowledge of what you are protecting and what the likely threats are, following this rule could be difficult.

1.6 Risk Assessment

1.6.1 General Discussion

One of the most important reasons for creating a computer security policy is to ensure that efforts spent on security yield cost-effective benefits. Although this may seem obvious, it is possible to be misled about where the effort is needed. As an example, there is a great deal of publicity about intruders on computers systems; yet most surveys of computer security show that, for most organizations, the actual loss from "insiders" is much greater.

Risk analysis involves determining what you need to protect, what you need to protect it from, and how to protect it. It is the process of examining all of your risks, then ranking those risks by level of severity. This process involves making cost-effective decisions on what you want to protect. As mentioned previously, you should probably not spend more to protect something than it is actually worth.

A full treatment of risk analysis is outside the scope of this document. Fites [1989] and Pfleeger [1989] provide introductions to this topic. However, there are two elements of a risk analysis that will be briefly covered in the next two sections:

1. Identifying the assets
2. Identifying the threats

For each asset, the basic goals of security are availability, confidentiality, and integrity. Each threat should be examined with an eye to how the threat could affect these areas.

1.6.2 Identifying the Assets

One step in a risk analysis is to identify all the things that need to be protected. Some things are obvious, such as valuable proprietary information, intellectual property, and all the various pieces of hardware; but some are overlooked, such as the people who actually use the systems. The essential point is to list all things that could be affected by a security problem.

One list of categories is suggested by Pfleeger [1989]; this list is adapted from that source:

1. *Hardware:* CPUs, boards, keyboards, terminals, workstations, personal computers, printers, disk drives, communications lines, terminal servers, routers
2. *Software:* Source programs, object programs, utilities, diagnostic programs, operating systems, communications programs
3. *Data:* During execution, stored online, archived offline, backups, audit logs, databases, in transit over communications media
4. *People:* Users, administrators, hardware maintainers
5. *Documentation:* Programs, hardware, systems, local administrative procedures
6. *Supplies:* Paper, forms, ribbons, magnetic media

1.6.3 Identifying the Threats

Once the assets requiring protection are identified, it is necessary to identify threats to those assets. The threats can then be examined to determine what potential for loss exists. It helps to consider what threats you are trying to protect your assets from. The following are classic threats that should be considered. Depending on your site, there will be more specific threats that should be identified and addressed.

1. Unauthorized access to resources and information
2. Unintended and unauthorized disclosure of information
3. Denial of service

2. Security Policies

Throughout this document there will be many references to policies. Often these references will include recommendations for specific policies. Rather than repeat guidance in how to create and communicate such a policy, the reader should apply the advice presented in this chapter when developing any policy recommended later in this book.

2.1 What Is a Security Policy, and Why Have One?

The security-related decisions you make, or fail to make, as administrator largely determine how secure or insecure your network is, how much functionality your network offers, and how easy your network is to use. However, you cannot make good decisions about security without first determining what your security goals are.

Until you determine what your security goals are, you cannot make effective use of any collection of security tools because you simply will not know what to check for and what restrictions to impose.

For example, your goals will probably be very different from the goals of a product vendor. Vendors are trying to make configuration and operation of their products as simple as possible, which implies that the default configurations will often be as open (i.e., insecure) as possible. While this does make it easier to install new products, it also leaves access to those systems, and other systems through them, open to any user who wanders by.

Your goals will be largely determined by the following key trade-offs:

1. Services offered vs. security provided. Each service offered to users carries its own security risks. For some services the risk outweighs the benefit of the service and the administrator may choose to eliminate the service rather than try to secure it.
2. Ease of use vs. security. The easiest system to use would allow access to any user and require no passwords; that is, there would be no security. Requiring passwords makes the system a little less convenient but more secure. Requiring device-generated one-time passwords makes the system even more difficult to use but much more secure.
3. Cost of security vs. risk of loss. There are many different costs to security: monetary (i.e., the cost of purchasing security hardware and software such as firewalls and one-time password generators), performance (i.e., encryption and decryption take time), and ease of use (as mentioned previously). There are also many levels of risk: loss of privacy (i.e., the reading of information by unauthorized individuals), loss of data (i.e., the corruption or erasure of information), and the loss of service (e.g., the filling of data storage space, usage of computational resources, and denial of network access). Each type of cost must be weighed against each type of loss.

Your goals should be communicated to all users, operations staff, and managers through a set of security rules, called a "security policy." We are using this term, rather than the narrower "computer security policy," because the scope includes all types of information technology and the information stored and manipulated by the technology.

2.1.1 Definition of a Security Policy

A security policy is a formal statement of the rules by which people who are given access to an organization's technology and information assets must abide.

2.1.2 Purposes of a Security Policy

The main purpose of a security policy is to inform users, staff, and managers of their obligatory requirements for protecting technology and information assets. The policy should specify the mechanisms through which these requirements can be met. Another purpose is to provide a baseline from which to acquire, configure, and audit computer systems and networks for compliance with the policy; therefore, an attempt to use a set of security tools in the absence of at least an implied security policy is meaningless.

An Appropriate Use Policy (AUP) may also be part of a security policy. It should spell out what users shall and shall not do on the various components of the system, including the type of traffic allowed on the networks. The AUP should be as explicit as possible to avoid ambiguity or misunderstanding. For example, an AUP might list any prohibited USENET newsgroups.*

2.1.3 Who Should Be Involved when Forming Policy?

In order for a security policy to be appropriate and effective, it needs to have the acceptance and support of all levels of employees within the organization. It is especially important that corporate management fully support the security policy process; otherwise, there is little chance that it will have the intended impact. The following is a list of individuals who should be involved in the creation and review of security policy documents:

1. Site Security Administrator
2. Information technology technical staff (e.g., staff from computing center)
3. Administrators of large user groups within the organization (e.g., business divisions, computer science department within a university, etc.)
4. Security Incident Response Team
5. Representatives of the user groups affected by the security policy
6. Responsible management
7. Legal counsel (if appropriate)

The list is representative of many organizations but is not necessarily comprehensive. The idea is to bring in representation from key stakeholders, management who have budget and policy authority, technical staff who know what can and cannot be supported, and legal counsel who know the legal ramifications of various policy choices. In some organizations, it may be appropriate to include EDP audit personnel. Involving this group is important if resulting policy statements are to reach the broadest possible acceptance. It is also relevant to mention that the role of legal counsel will vary from country to country.

2.2 What Makes a Good Security Policy?

The characteristics of a good security policy are:

1. It must be implementable through system administration procedures, publishing of acceptable use guidelines, or other appropriate methods.
2. It must be enforceable with security tools, where appropriate, and with sanctions, where actual prevention is not technically feasible.

---

* Appropriate Use Policy is referred to as Acceptable Use Policy by some sites.

3. It must clearly define the areas of responsibility for the users, administrators, and management.

The components of a good security policy include:

1. Computer technology purchasing guidelines that specify required or preferred security features. These should supplement existing purchasing policies and guidelines.
2. A Privacy Policy that defines reasonable expectations of privacy regarding issues such as monitoring of electronic mail, logging of keystrokes, and access to users' files.
3. An Access Policy that defines access rights and privileges to protect assets from loss or disclosure by specifying acceptable use guidelines for users, operations staff, and management. It should provide guidelines for external connections, data communications, connecting devices to a network, and adding new software to systems. It should also specify any required notification messages (e.g., connect messages should provide warnings about authorized usage and line monitoring, and not simply say "Welcome").
4. An Accountability Policy that defines the responsibilities of users, operations staff, and management. It should specify an audit capability, and provide incident handling guidelines (e.g., what to do and who to contact if a possible intrusion is detected).
5. An Authentication Policy that establishes trust through an effective password policy, and by setting guidelines for remote location authentication and the use of authentication devices (e.g., one-time passwords and the devices that generate them).
6. An Availability Statement that sets users' expectations for the availability of resources. It should address redundancy and recovery issues, as well as specify operating hours and maintenance down-time periods. It should also include contact information for reporting system and network failures.
7. An Information Technology System and Network Maintenance Policy that describes how internal and external maintenance people are allowed to handle and access technology. One important topic to be addressed here is whether remote maintenance is allowed and how such access is controlled. Another area for consideration is outsourcing and how it is managed.
8. A Violations Reporting Policy that indicates which types of violations (e.g., privacy and security, internal and external) must be reported and to whom the reports are made. A nonthreatening atmosphere and the possibility of anonymous reporting will result in a greater probability that a violation will be reported if it is detected.
9. Supporting information that provides users, staff, and management with contact information for each type of policy violation; guidelines on how to handle outside queries about a security incident, or information that may be considered confidential or proprietary; and cross-references to security procedures and related information, such as company policies and governmental laws and regulations.

There may be regulatory requirements that affect some aspects of your security policy (e.g., line monitoring). The creators of the security policy should consider seeking legal assistance in the creation of the policy. At a minimum, the policy should be reviewed by legal counsel.

Once your security policy has been established, it should be clearly communicated to users, staff, and management. Having all personnel sign a statement indicating that they have read, understood, and agreed to abide by the policy is an important part of the process. Finally, your policy should be reviewed on a regular basis to see if it is successfully supporting your security needs.

2.3 Keeping the Policy Flexible

In order for a security policy to be viable for the long term, it requires a lot of flexibility based on an architectural security concept. A security policy should be (largely) independent from specific hardware and software situations (as specific systems tend to be replaced or moved overnight). The mechanisms for updating the policy should be clearly spelled out. This includes the process, the people involved, and the people who must sign off on the changes.

It is also important to recognize that there are exceptions to every rule. Whenever possible, the policy should spell out exceptions to the general policy that exist. For example, under what conditions is a system administrator allowed to go through a user's files? Also, there may be some cases when multiple users will have access to the same user ID. For example, on systems with a "root" user, multiple system administrators may know the password and use the root account.

Another consideration is called the "Garbage Truck Syndrome." This refers to what happens to a site when a key person is suddenly unavailable for his job function (e.g., illness or left the company unexpectedly). Despite the fact that the greatest security resides in the minimum dissemination of information, the risk of losing critical information increases when that information is not shared. It is important to determine what the proper balance is for your site.

3. Architecture

3.1 Objectives

3.1.1 Completely Defined Security Plans

All sites should define a comprehensive security plan. This plan should be at a higher level than the specific policies discussed in Chapter 2, and it should be crafted as a framework of broad guidelines into which specific policies will fit.

It is important to have this framework in place so that individual policies can be consistent with the overall site security architecture. For example, having a strong policy with regard to Internet access and having weak restrictions on modem usage is inconsistent with an overall philosophy of strong security restrictions on external access.

A security plan should define the list of network services that will be provided; the areas of the organization that will provide the services; the people who will have access to those services; how access will be provided; who will administer those services; etc.

The plan should also address how an incident will be handled. Chapter 5 provides an in-depth discussion of this topic but it is important for each site to define classes of incidents and corresponding responses. For example, sites with firewalls should set a threshold on the number of attempts made to foil the firewall before triggering a response. Escalation levels should be defined for both attacks and responses. Sites without firewalls will have to determine if a single attempt to connect to a host constitutes an incident. What about a systematic scan of systems?

For sites connected to the Internet, the rampant media magnification of Internet-related security incidents can overshadow a (potentially) more-serious internal security problem. Likewise, companies who have never been connected to the Internet may have strong, well-defined internal policies but fail to adequately address an external connection policy.

3.1.2 Separation of Services

There are many services that a site may wish to provide for its users, some of which may be external. There are a variety of security reasons to attempt to isolate services on dedicated host computers. There are also performance reasons in most cases, but a detailed discussion is beyond the scope of this appendix.

The services that a site may provide will, in most cases, have different levels of access needs and models of trust. Services that are essential to the security or smooth operation of a site would be better off being placed on a dedicated machine with very limited access (discussed in the section "Deny All/Allow All"), rather than on a machine that provides a service (or services) that has traditionally been less secure or requires greater accessibility by users who may accidentally suborn security.

It is also important to distinguish between hosts that operate within different models of trust (e.g., all the hosts inside of a firewall and any host on an exposed network).

Some of the services that should be examined for potential separation are outlined in the section "Protecting the Services." It is important to remember that security is only as strong as the weakest link in the chain. Several of the most-publicized penetrations in recent years have been through the exploitation of vulnerabilities in electronic mail systems. The intruders were not trying to steal electronic mail, but they used the vulnerability in that service to gain access to other systems.

If possible, each service should be running on a different machine whose only duty is to provide a specific service. This helps to isolate intruders and limit potential harm.

3.1.3 Deny All/Allow All

There are two diametrically opposed, underlying philosophies that can be adopted when defining a security plan. Both alternatives are legitimate models to adopt, and the choice between them will depend on the site and its needs for security.

The first option is to turn off all services and then selectively enable services on a case-by-case basis as they are needed. This can be done at the host or network level as appropriate. This model, which will hereafter be referred to as the "deny all" model, is generally more secure than the other model described in the next paragraph. More work is required to successfully implement a "deny all" configuration as well as a better understanding of services. Allowing only known services provides for a better analysis of a particular service/protocol and the design of a security mechanism suited to the security level of the site.

The other model, which will hereafter be referred to as the "allow all" model, is much easier to implement but is generally less secure than the "deny all" model. Simply turn on all services, usually the default at the host level, and allow all protocols to travel across network boundaries, usually the default at the router level. As security holes become apparent, they are restricted or patched at either the host or network level.

Each of these models can be applied to different portions of the site, depending on functionality requirements, administrative control, site policy, etc. For example, the policy may be to use the "allow all" model when setting up workstations for general use but adopt a "deny all" model when setting up information servers, such as an e-mail hub. Likewise, an "allow all" policy may be adopted for traffic between LANs internal to the site, but a "deny all" policy can be adopted between the site and the Internet.

Be careful when mixing philosophies as in these examples. Many sites adopt the theory of a hard "crunchy" shell and a soft "squishy" middle. They are willing to pay the cost of security for their external traffic and require strong security measures but are unwilling or unable to provide similar protections internally. This works fine as long as the outer defenses are never breached and the internal users can be trusted. Once the outer shell (firewall) is breached, subverting the internal network is trivial.

3.1.4 Identify Real Needs for Services

There is a large variety of services that may be provided, both internally and on the Internet. Managing security is, in many ways, managing access to services internal to the site and managing how internal users access information at remote sites.

Services tend to rush like waves over the Internet. Over the years many sites have established anonymous FTP servers, gopher servers, WAIS servers, Web servers, etc., as they became popular but not particularly needed at all sites. Evaluate all new services that are established with a skeptical attitude to determine if they are actually needed or just the current fad sweeping the Internet.

Bear in mind that security complexity can grow exponentially with the number of services provided. Filtering routers need to be modified to support the new protocols. Some protocols are inherently difficult to filter safely (e.g., RPC and UDP services), thus providing more openings to the internal network. Services provided on the same machine can interact in catastrophic ways. For example, allowing an anonymous FTP on the same machine as the Web server may allow an intruder to place a file in the anonymous FTP area and cause the HTTP server to execute it.

3.2 Network and Service Configuration

3.2.1 Protecting the Infrastructure

Many network administrators go to great lengths to protect the hosts on their networks. Few administrators make any effort to protect the networks themselves. There is some rationale to this. For example, it is far easier to protect a host than a network. Also, intruders are likely to be after data on the hosts; damaging the network would not serve their purposes; having said that, there are still reasons to protect the networks. For example, an intruder might divert network traffic through an outside host in order to examine the data (i.e., to search for passwords). Also, infrastructure includes more than the networks and the routers that interconnect them. Infrastructure also includes network management (e.g., SNMP), services (e.g., DNS, NFS, NTP, WWW), and security (i.e., user authentication and access restrictions).

The infrastructure also needs protection against human error. When an administrator configures a host incorrectly, that host may offer degraded service. This only affects users who require that host; and unless that host is a primary server, the number of affected users will therefore be limited. However, if a router is configured incorrectly, all users who require the network will be affected. Obviously, this is a far larger number of users than those depending on any one host.

3.2.2 Protecting the Network

There are several problems to which networks are vulnerable. The classic problem is a denial-of-service attack. In this case, the network is brought to a state in which it can no longer carry legitimate users' data. There are two common ways this can be done: by attacking the routers and by flooding the network with extraneous traffic. Please note that the term "router" in this section is used as an example of a larger class of active network interconnection components that also includes components such as firewalls, proxy servers, etc.

An attack on the router is designed to cause it to stop forwarding packets or to forward them improperly. The former case may be due to poor configuration, the injection of a spurious routing update, or a "flood attack" (i.e., the router is bombarded with packets that cannot be routed, causing its performance to degrade). A flood attack on a network is similar to a flood attack on a router, except that the flood packets are usually broadcast. An ideal flood attack is the injection of a single packet that exploits some known flaw in the network nodes and causes them to retransmit the packet or to generate error packets, each of which is picked up and repeated by another host. A well-chosen attack packet can even generate an exponential explosion of transmissions.

Another classic problem is spoofing. In this case, spurious routing updates are sent to one or more routers, causing them to misroute packets. This differs from a denial-of-service attack only in the purpose behind the spurious route. In denial of service, the object is to make the router unusable, a state that will be quickly detected by network users. In spoofing, the spurious route will cause packets to be routed to a host from which an intruder may monitor the data in the packets. These packets are then rerouted to their correct destinations. However, the intruder may or may not have altered the contents of the packets.

The solution to most of these problems is to protect the routing update packets sent by the routing protocols in use (e.g., RIP-2, OSPF). There are three levels of protection: clear-text password, cryptographic checksum, and encryption. Passwords offer only minimal protection against intruders who do not have direct access to the physical networks. Passwords also offer some protection against misconfigured routers (i.e., routers that, out of the box, attempt to route packets). The advantage of passwords is that they have a very low overhead in both bandwidth and CPU consumption. Checksums protect against the injection of spurious packets, even if the intruder has direct access to the physical network. Combined with a sequence number or other unique identifier, a checksum can also protect again "replay" attacks, wherein an old (but valid at the time) routing update is retransmitted by either an intruder or a misbehaving router. The most security is provided by complete encryption of sequenced or uniquely identified routing updates. This prevents an intruder from determining the topology of the network. The disadvantage to encryption is the overhead involved in processing the updates.

RIP-2 (RFC 1723) and OSPF (RFC 1583) both support clear-text passwords in their base design specifications. In addition, there are extensions to each base protocol to support MD5 encryption.

Unfortunately, there is no adequate protection against a flooding attack or a misbehaving host or router that is flooding the network. Fortunately, this type of attack is obvious when it occurs and can usually be terminated relatively simply.

3.2.3 Protecting the Services

There are many types of services, and each has its own security requirements. These requirements will vary based on the intended use of the service. For example, a service that should only be usable within a site (e.g., NFS) may require different protection mechanisms than a service provided for external use. It may be sufficient to protect the internal server from external access. However, a Web server which provides a home page intended for viewing by users anywhere on the Internet, requires built-in protection. That is, the service/protocol/server must provide whatever security may be required to prevent unauthorized access and modification of the Web database.

Internal services (i.e., services meant to be used only by users within a site) and external services (i.e., services deliberately made available to users outside a site) will, in general, have protection requirements that differ, as previously described. It is therefore wise to isolate the internal services to one set of server host computers and the external services to another set of server host computers. That is, internal and external servers should not be co-located on the same host computer. In fact, many sites go so far as to have one set of subnets (or even different networks) that are accessible from the outside and another set that may be accessed only within the site. Of course, there is usually a firewall that connects these partitions. Great care must be taken to ensure that such a firewall is operating properly.

There is increasing interest in using intranets to connect different parts of an organization (e.g., divisions of a company). While this appendix generally differentiates between external and internal (public and private), sites using intranets should be aware that they will need to consider three separations and take appropriate actions when designing and offering services. A service offered to an intranet would be neither public nor as completely private as a service to a single organizational sub-unit. Therefore, the service would need its own supporting system, separated from both external and internal services and networks.

One form of external service deserves some special consideration, and that is anonymous or guest access. This may be either anonymous FTP or guest (unauthenticated) login. It is extremely important to ensure that anonymous FTP servers and guest login user IDs are carefully isolated from any hosts and file systems from which outside users should be kept. Another area to which special attention must be paid concerns anonymous, writable access. A site may be legally responsible for the content of publicly available information, so careful monitoring of the information deposited by anonymous users is advised.

Now we shall consider some of the most popular services: name service, password/key service, authentication/proxy service, electronic mail, Web services, file transfer, and NFS. Because these are the most frequently used services, they are the most obvious points of attack. Also, a successful attack on one of these services can produce disaster all out of proportion to the innocence of the basic service.

3.2.3.1 Name Servers (DNS and NIS(+))

The Internet uses the Domain Name System (DNS) to perform address resolution for host and network names. The Network Information Service (NIS) and NIS+ are not used on the global Internet but are subject to the same risks as a DNS server. Name-to-address resolution is critical to the secure operation of any network. An attacker who can successfully control or impersonate a DNS server can reroute traffic to subvert security protections. For example, routine traffic can be diverted to a compromised system to be monitored; or users can be tricked into providing authentication secrets. An organization should create well-known, protected sites to act as secondary name servers and protect their DNS masters from denial-of-service attacks using filtering routers.

Traditionally, DNS has had no security capabilities. In particular, the information returned from a query could not be checked for modification or verified that it had come from the name server in question. Work has been done to incorporate digital signatures into the protocol which, when deployed, will allow the integrity of the information to be cryptographically verified (see RFC 2065).

3.2.3.2 Password/Key Servers (NIS(+) and KDC)

Password and key servers generally protect their vital information (i.e., the passwords and keys) with encryption algorithms. However, even a one-way encrypted password can be determined by a dictionary attack (wherein common words are encrypted to see if they match the stored encryption). It is therefore necessary to ensure that these servers are not accessible by hosts that do not plan to use them for the service, and even those hosts should only be able to access the service (i.e., general services such as Telnet and FTP should not be allowed by anyone other than administrators).

3.2.3.3 Authentication/Proxy Servers (SOCKS, FWTK)

A proxy server provides a number of security enhancements. It allows sites to concentrate services through a specific host to allow monitoring, hiding of internal structure, etc. This funneling of services creates an attractive target for a potential intruder. The type of protection required for a proxy server depends greatly on the proxy protocol in use and the services being proxied. The general rule of limiting access only to those hosts that need the services and limiting access by those hosts to only those services is a good starting point.

3.2.3.4 Electronic Mail

Electronic mail (e-mail) systems have long been a source for intruder break-ins because e-mail protocols are among the oldest and most widely deployed services. Also, by its very nature, an e-mail server requires access to the outside world; most e-mail servers accept input from any source. An e-mail server generally consists of two parts: a receiving/sending agent and a processing agent. Because e-mail is delivered to all users and is usually private, the processing agent typically requires system (root) privileges to deliver the mail. Most e-mail implementations perform both portions of the service, which means the receiving agent also has system privileges. This opens several security holes that this appendix will not describe.

There are some implementations available that allow a separation of the two agents. Such implementations are generally considered more secure but still require careful installation to avoid creating a security problem.

3.2.3.5 World Wide Web

The Web is growing in popularity exponentially because of its ease of use and the powerful ability to concentrate information services. Most Web servers accept some type of direction and action from the persons accessing their services. The most common example is taking a request from a remote user and passing the provided information to a program running on the server to process the request. Some of these programs are not written with security in mind and can create security holes. If a Web server is available to the Internet community, it is especially important that confidential information not be co-located on the same host as that server. In fact, it is recommended that the server have a dedicated host that is not "trusted" by other internal hosts.

Many sites may want to co-locate FTP service with their Web service, but this should only occur for anonymous FTP (anonftp) servers that only provide information (ftp-get). Anonftp puts, in combination with Web, might be dangerous (e.g., they could result in modifications to the information your site is publishing to the Web) and in themselves make the security considerations for each service different.

3.2.3.6 File Transfer (FTP, TFTP)

FTP and TFTP allow users to receive and send electronic files in a point-to-point manner. However, FTP requires authentication while TFTP does not. For this reason, TFTP should be avoided as much as possible.

Improperly configured FTP servers can allow intruders to copy, replace, and delete files at will anywhere on a host, so it is very important to configure this service correctly. Access to encrypted passwords and proprietary data and the introduction of Trojan horses are just a few of the potential security holes that can occur when the service is configured incorrectly. FTP servers should reside on their own host. Some sites choose to co-locate FTP with a Web server, because the two protocols share common security considerations However, the practice is not recommended, especially when the FTP service allows the deposit of files (see the section "World Wide Web"). As mentioned in the opening paragraphs of the section "Protecting the Services," services offered internally to your site should not be co-located with services offered externally. Each service should have its own host.

TFTP does not support the same range of functions as FTP and has no security whatsoever. This service should only be considered for internal use, and then it should be configured in a restricted way so that the server only has access to a set of predetermined files (instead of every world-readable file on the system). Probably the most common usage of TFTP is for downloading router configuration files to a router. TFTP should reside on its own host and should not be installed on hosts supporting external FTP or Web access.

3.2.3.7 NFS

The Network File Service allows hosts to share common disks. NFS is frequently used by diskless hosts who depend on a disk server for all of their storage needs. Unfortunately, NFS has no built-in security. It is therefore necessary that the NFS server is accessible only by those hosts that are using it for service. This is achieved by specifying which hosts the file system is being exported to and in what manner (e.g., read-only, read-write, etc.). File systems should not be exported to any hosts outside the local network because this will require that the NFS service be accessible externally. Ideally, external access to NFS service should be stopped by a firewall.

3.2.4 Protecting the Protection

It is amazing how often a site will overlook the most obvious weakness in its security by leaving the security server itself open to attack. Based on considerations previously discussed, it should be clear that: the security server should not be accessible from offsite; should offer minimum access, except for the authentication function, to users on-site; and should not be co-located with any other servers. Further, all access to the node, including access to the service itself, should be logged to provide a paper trail in the event of a security breach.

3.3 Firewalls

One of the most widely deployed and publicized security measures in use on the Internet is a firewall. Firewalls have been given the reputation of a general panacea for many, if not all, of the Internet security issues. They are not. A firewall is just another tool in the quest for system security. Firewalls provide a certain level of protection and are, in general, a way of implementing security policy at the network level. The level of security that a firewall provides can vary as much as the level of security on a particular machine. There are the traditional trade-offs between security, ease of use, cost, complexity, etc.

A firewall is any one of several mechanisms used to control and watch access to and from a network for the purpose of protecting it. A firewall acts as a gateway through which all traffic to and from the protected network or systems passes. Firewalls help to place limitations on the amount and type of communication that takes place between the protected network and the other network (e.g., the Internet or another piece of the site's network).

A firewall is generally a way to build a wall between one part of a network (e.g., a company's internal network) and another part (e.g., the global Internet). The unique feature about this wall is that there needs to be ways for some traffic with particular characteristics to pass through carefully monitored doors (gateways). The difficult part is establishing the criteria by which the packets are allowed or denied access through the doors. Books written on the subject use different terminology to describe the various forms of firewalls. This can be confusing to system administrators who are not familiar with firewalls. The thing to note here is that there is no fixed terminology for the description of firewalls.

Firewalls are not always or even typically a single machine. Rather, firewalls are often a combination of routers, network segments, and host computers. Therefore, for the purposes of this discussion, the term "firewall" can consist of more than one physical device. Firewalls are typically built using two different components, filtering routers and proxy servers.

Filtering routers are the easiest component to conceptualize in a firewall. A router moves data back and forth between two (or more) different networks. A "normal" router takes a packet from network A and "routes" it to its destination on network B. A filtering router does the same thing but decides not only how to route the packet but whether it should route the packet at all. This is done by installing a series of filters by which the router decides what to do with any given packet of data.

A discussion concerning capabilities of a particular brand of router running a particular software version is outside the scope of this appendix. However, when evaluating a router to be used for filtering packets, the following criteria can be important when implementing a filtering policy: source and destination IP address, source and destination TCP port numbers, state of the TCP "ack" bit, UDP source and destination port numbers, and direction of packet flow (i.e., A→B or B→A). Other information necessary to construct a secure filtering scheme is whether the router reorders filter instructions designed to optimize filters, which can sometimes change the meaning and cause unintended access, and whether it is possible to apply filters for inbound and outbound packets on each interface (if the router filters only outbound packets, then the router is "outside" of its filters and may be more vulnerable to attack). In addition to the router being vulnerable, this distinction between applying filters on inbound or outbound packets is especially relevant for routers with more than two interfaces. Other important issues are the ability to create filters based on IP header options and the fragment state of a packet. Building a good filter can be very difficult and requires a good understanding of the type of services (protocols) that will be filtered.

For better security, the filters usually restrict access between the two connected nets to just one host, the bastion host. It is only possible to access the other network via this bastion host. As only this host, rather than a few hundred hosts, can get attacked, it is easier to maintain a certain level of security because only this host has to be protected very carefully. To make resources available to legitimate users across this firewall, services have to be forwarded by the bastion host. Some servers have built-in forwarding (e.g., DNS servers or SMTP servers); for other services (e.g., Telnet, FTP), proxy servers can be used to allow access to the resources across the firewall in a secure way.

A proxy server is a way to concentrate application services through a single machine. There is typically a single machine (the bastion host) that acts as a proxy server for a variety of protocols (Telnet, SMTP, FTP, HTTP, etc.), but there can be individual host computers for each service. Instead of connecting directly to an external server, the client connects to the proxy server, which in turn initiates a connection to the requested external server. Depending on the type of proxy server used, it is possible to configure internal clients to perform this redirection automatically, without knowledge to the user; others might require that the user connect directly to the proxy server and then initiate the connection through a specified format.

There are significant security benefits that can be derived from using proxy servers. It is possible to add access control lists to protocols, requiring users or systems to provide some level of authentication before access is granted. Smarter proxy servers, sometimes called Application Layer Gateways (ALGs), can be written that understand specific protocols and can be configured to block only subsections of the protocol. For example, an ALG for FTP can tell the difference between the "put" command and the "get" command; an organization may wish to allow users to "get" files from the Internet but not be able to "put" internal files on a remote server. By contrast, a filtering router could either block all FTP access or none but not a subset.

Proxy servers can also be configured to encrypt data streams based on a variety of parameters. An organization might use this feature to allow encrypted connections between two locations whose sole access points are on the Internet.

Firewalls are typically thought of as a way to keep intruders out, but they are also often used as a way to let legitimate users into a site. There are many examples where a valid user might need to regularly access the "home" site while on travel to trade shows and conferences, etc. Access to the Internet is often available but may be through an untrusted machine or network. A correctly configured proxy server can allow certain users into the site while still denying access to other users.

The current best effort in firewall techniques is found using a combination of a pair of screening routers with one or more proxy servers on a network between the two routers. This setup allows the external router to block off any attempts to use the underlying IP layer to break security (IP spoofing, source routing, packet fragments), while allowing the proxy server to handle potential security holes in the higher layer protocols. The internal router's purpose is to block all traffic except to the proxy server. If this setup is rigidly implemented, a high level of security can be achieved.

Most firewalls provide logging that can be tuned to make security administration of the network more convenient. Logging may be centralized and the system may be configured to send out alerts for abnormal conditions. It is important to regularly monitor these logs for any signs of intrusions or break-in attempts. Because some intruders will attempt to cover their tracks by editing logs, it is desirable to protect these logs. A variety of methods is available, including write once, read many (WORM) drives; papers logs; and centralized logging via the syslog utility. Another technique is to use a fake serial printer but have the serial port connected to an isolated machine or PC that keeps the logs.

Firewalls are available in a wide range of quality and strengths. Commercial packages start at approximately $10,000 and go up to over $250,000. Homegrown firewalls can be built for smaller amounts of capital. It should be remembered that the correct setup of a firewall (commercial or homegrown) requires a significant amount of skill and knowledge of TCP/IP. Both types require regular maintenance, installation of software patches and updates, and regular monitoring. When budgeting for a firewall, these additional costs should be considered in addition to the cost of the physical elements of the firewall.

As an aside, building a homegrown firewall requires a significant amount of skill and knowledge of TCP/IP. It should not be trivially attempted because a perceived sense of security is worse in the long run than knowing that there is no security. As with all security measures, it is important to decide on the threat, the value of the assets to be protected, and the costs to implement security.

A final note about firewalls: A firewall can be a great aid when implementing security for a site and can protect against a large variety of attacks. But it is important to keep in mind that a firewall is only one part of the solution. A firewall cannot protect your site against all types of attack.

4. Security Services and Procedures

This appendix guides you through a number of topics that should be addressed when securing a site. Each section touches on a security service or capability that may be required to protect the information and systems at a site. The topics are presented at a fairly high level to introduce you to the concepts.

Throughout the appendix, you will find significant mention of cryptography. It is outside the scope of this appendix to delve into details concerning cryptography, but the interested reader can obtain more information from books and articles listed in the reference section.

4.1 Authentication

For many years, the prescribed method for authenticating users has been through the use of standard, reusable passwords. Originally, these passwords were used by users at terminals to authenticate themselves to a central computer. At the time, there were no networks (internally or externally), so the risk of disclosure of the clear-text password was minimal. Today, systems are connected together through local networks, and these local networks are further connected together and to the Internet. Users are logging in from all over the globe; their reusable passwords are often transmitted across those same networks in clear text, ripe for anyone in-between to capture. And indeed, the CERT* Coordination Center and other response teams are seeing a tre-

---

* CERT is registered in the U.S. Patent and Trademark Office.

mendous number of incidents involving packet sniffers that are capturing the clear-text passwords.

With the advent of newer technologies such as one-time passwords (e.g., S/Key), Pretty Good Privacy (PGP), and token-based authentication devices, people are using password-like strings as secret tokens and pins. If these secret tokens and pins are not properly selected and protected, the authentication will be easily subverted.

4.1.1 One-Time Passwords

As mentioned earlier, given today's networked environments, it is recommended that sites concerned about the security and integrity of their systems and networks consider moving away from standard, reusable passwords. There have been many incidents involving Trojan network programs (e.g., telnet and rlogin) and network packet-sniffing programs. These programs capture clear-text host name/account name/password triplets. Intruders can use the captured information for subsequent access to those hosts and accounts. This is possible because (1) the password is used over and over (hence the term "reusable"), and (2) the password passes across the network in clear text.

Several authentication techniques have been developed that address this problem. Among these techniques are challenge–response technologies that provide passwords that are only used once (commonly called one-time passwords). There are a number of products available that sites should consider using. The decision to use a product is the responsibility of each organization, and each organization should perform its own evaluation and selection.

4.1.2 Kerberos

Kerberos is a distributed network security system that provides for authentication across unsecured networks. If requested by the application, integrity, and encryption can also be provided. Kerberos was originally developed at MIT in the mid-1980s. There are two major releases of Kerberos, version 4 and version 5, which for practical purposes are incompatible.

Kerberos relies on a symmetric key database using a key distribution center (KDC) known as the Kerberos server. A user or service (known as "principals") is granted electronic "tickets" after properly communicating with the KDC. These tickets are used for authentication between principals. All tickets include a time stamp that limits the time period for which the ticket is valid. Therefore, Kerberos clients and servers must have a secure time source and be able to keep time accurately.

The practical side of Kerberos is its integration with the application level. Typical applications such as FTP, telnet, POP, and NFS have been integrated with the Kerberos system. There are a variety of implementations that have varying levels of integration. Please see Kerberos FAQ available at http://www.ov.com/misc/krb-faq.html for the latest information.

4.1.3 Choosing and Protecting Secret Tokens and PINs

When selecting secret tokens, take care to choose them carefully. Like the selection of passwords, they should be robust against brute-force efforts to guess them. That is, they should not be single words in any language, any common industry or cultural acronyms, etc. Ideally, they will be longer rather than shorter and consist of pass phrases that combine upper- and lower-case character, digits, and other characters.

Once chosen, the protection of these secret tokens is very important. Some are used as pins to hardware devices (such as token cards) and these should not be written down or placed in the same location as the device with which they are associated. Others, such as a secret PGP key, should be protected from unauthorized access.

One final word on this subject. When using cryptography products such as PGP, take care to determine the proper key length and ensure that your users are trained to do likewise. As technology advances, the minimum safe key length continues to grow. Make sure your site keeps up with the latest knowledge on the technology so that you can ensure that any cryptography in use is providing the protection you believe it is.

4.1.4 Password Assurance

While the need to eliminate the use of standard, reusable passwords cannot be overstated, it is recognized that some organizations may still be using them. While it is recommended that these organizations transition to the use of better technology, in the meantime we have the following advice to help with the selection and maintenance of traditional passwords. But remember, none of these measures provides protection against disclosure due to sniffer programs.

1. *The importance of robust passwords.* In many (if not most) cases of system penetration, the intruder needs to gain access to an account on the system. One way that goal is typically accomplished is through guessing the password of a legitimate user. This is often accomplished by running an automated password cracking program, which utilizes a very large dictionary, against the system's password file. The only way to guard against passwords being disclosed in this manner is through the careful selection of passwords that cannot be easily guessed (i.e., combinations of numbers, letters, and punctuation characters). Passwords should also be as long as the system supports and users can tolerate.

2. *Changing default passwords.* Many operating systems and application programs are installed with default accounts and passwords. These must be changed immediately to something that cannot be guessed or cracked.

3. *Restricting access to the password file.* In particular, a site wants to protect the encrypted password portion of the file so that would-be intruders do not have them available for cracking. One effective technique is to use shadow passwords, where the password field of the standard file contains a dummy or false password. The file containing the legitimate passwords is protected elsewhere on the system.

4. *Password aging.* When and how to expire passwords is still a subject of controversy among the security community. It is generally accepted that a password should not be maintained once an account is no longer in use, but it is hotly debated whether a user should be forced to change a good password that is in active use. The arguments for changing passwords relate to the prevention of the continued use of penetrated accounts. However, the opposition claims that frequent password changes lead to users writing down their passwords in visible areas (such as pasting them to a terminal), or to users selecting very simple passwords that are easy to guess. It should also be stated that an intruder will probably use a captured or guessed password sooner rather than later, in which case password aging provides little if any protection.

While there is no definitive answer to this dilemma, a password policy should directly address the issue and provide guidelines for how often a user should change the password. Certainly, an annual change in password is usually not difficult for most users, and you should consider requiring it. It is recommended that passwords are changed at least whenever a privileged account is compromised, a critical change in personnel (especially if it is an administrator!) occurs, or when an account has been compromised. In addition, if a privileged account password is compromised, all passwords on the system should be changed.

5. *Password/account blocking.* Some sites find it useful to disable accounts after a predefined number of failed attempts to authenticate. If your site decides to employ this mechanism, it is recommended that the mechanism does not "advertise" itself. After disabling, even if the correct password is presented, the message displayed should remain that of a failed login attempt. Implementing this mechanism will require that legitimate users contact their system administrator to request that their account be reactivated.

6. *A word about the finger daemon.* By default, the finger daemon displays considerable system and user information. For example, it can display a list of all users currently using a system or all the contents of a specific user's plan file. This information can be used by would-be intruders to identify user names and guess their passwords. It is recommended that sites consider modifying finger to restrict the information displayed.

4.2 Confidentiality

There will be information assets that your site will want to protect from disclosure to unauthorized entities. Operating systems often have built-in file protection mechanisms that allow an administrator to control who on the system can access, or "see," the contents of a given file. A more secure way to provide confidentiality is through encryption. Encryption is accomplished by scrambling data so that it is very difficult and time consuming for anyone other than the authorized recipients or owners to obtain the plain text. Authorized recipients and the owner of the information will possess the corresponding decryption keys that allow them to easily unscramble the text to a readable (clear text) form. We recommend that sites use encryption to provide confidentiality and protect valuable information.

The use of encryption is sometimes controlled by governmental and site regulations, so we encourage administrators to become informed of laws or policies that regulate its use before employing it. It is outside the scope of this document to discuss the various algorithms and programs available for this purpose but we do caution against the casual use of the UNIX crypt program, as it has been found to be easily broken. We also encourage everyone to take time to understand the strength of the encryption in any given algorithm/product before using it. Most well-known products are documented in the literature, so this should be a fairly easy task.

4.3 Integrity

As an administrator, you will want to make sure that information (e.g., operating system files, company data, etc.) has not been altered in an unauthorized fashion. This means you will want to provide some assurance as to the integrity of the information on your systems. One way to provide this is to produce a checksum of the unaltered file, store that checksum offline, and periodically check to make sure the checksum of the online file has not changed (which would indicate the data has not been modified).

Some operating systems come with checksumming programs, such as the UNIX sum program. However, these may not provide the protection you actually need. Files can be modified to preserve the result of the UNIX sum program! Therefore, we suggest that you use a cryptographically strong program, such as the message digesting program MD5, to produce the checksums you will be using to assure integrity.

There are other applications where integrity will need to be assured, such as when transmitting an e-mail message between two parties. There are products available that can provide this capability. Once you identify that this is a capability you need, you can go about identifying technologies that will provide it.

4.4 Authorization

Authorization refers to the process of granting privileges to processes and ultimately to users. This differs from authentication in that authentication is the process used to identify a user. Once identified (reliably), the privileges, rights, property, and permissible actions of the user are determined by authorization.

Explicitly listing the authorized activities of each user (and user process) with respect to all resources (objects) is impossible in a reasonable system. In a real system certain techniques are used to simplify the process of granting and checking authorization(s).

One approach, popularized in UNIX systems, is to assign to each object three classes of user: owner, group, and world. The owner is either the creator of the object or the user assigned as owner by the super-user. The owner permissions (read, write, and execute) apply only to the owner. A group is a collection of users that share access rights to an object. The group permissions (read, write, and execute) apply to all users in the group (except the owner). The world refers to everybody else with access to the system. The world permissions (read, write, and execute) apply to all users (except the owner and members of the group).

Another approach is to attach to an object a list that explicitly contains the identity of all permitted users (or groups). This is an Access Control List (ACL). The advantage of ACLs is that they are easily maintained (one central list per object) and it is very easy to visually check who has access to what. The disadvantages are the extra resources required to store such lists, as well as the vast number of such lists required for large systems.

4.5 Access

4.5.1 Physical Access

Restrict physical access to hosts, allowing access only to those people who are supposed to use the hosts. Hosts include "trusted" terminals (i.e., terminals that allow unauthenticated use such as system consoles, operator terminals, and terminals dedicated to special tasks), and individual microcomputers and workstations, especially those connected to your network. Make sure people's work areas mesh well with access restrictions; otherwise they will find ways to circumvent your physical security (e.g., jamming doors open).

Keep original and backup copies of data and programs safe. Apart from keeping them in good condition for backup purposes, they must be protected from theft. It is important to keep backups in a separate location from the originals, not only for damage considerations but also to guard against theft.

Portable hosts are a particular risk. Make sure it will not cause problems if one of your staff's portable computers is stolen. Consider developing guidelines for the kinds of data that should be allowed to reside on the disks of portable computers, as well as how the data should be protected (e.g., encryption) when it is on a portable computer.

Other areas where physical access should be restricted are the wiring closets and important network elements such as file servers, name server hosts, and routers.

4.5.2 Walk-Up Network Connections

By "walk-up" connections, we mean network connection points located to provide a convenient way for users to connect a portable host to your network.

Consider whether you need to provide this service, bearing in mind that it allows any user to attach an unauthorized host to your network. This increases the risk of attacks via techniques such as IP address spoofing, packet sniffing, etc. Users and site management must appreciate the risks involved. If you decide to provide walk-up connections, plan the service carefully and define precisely where you will provide it so that you can ensure the necessary physical access security.

A walk-up host should be authenticated before its user is permitted to access resources on your network. As an alternative, it may be possible to control physical access. For example, if the service is to be used by students, you might only provide walk-up connection sockets in student laboratories.

If you are providing walk-up access for visitors to connect back to their home networks (e.g., to read e-mail, etc.) in your facility, consider using a separate subnet that has no connectivity to the internal network.

Keep an eye on any area that contains unmonitored access to the network, such as vacant offices. It may be sensible to disconnect such areas at the wiring closet. Consider using secure hubs and monitoring attempts to connect unauthorized hosts.

4.5.3 Other Network Technologies

Technologies considered here include X.25, ISDN, SMDS, DDS, and Frame Relay. All are provided via physical links that go through telephone exchanges, providing the potential for them to be diverted. Crackers are certainly interested in telephone switches as well as in data networks!

With switched technologies, use Permanent Virtual Circuits or Closed User Groups whenever this is possible. Technologies that provide authentication and encryption (such as IPv6) are evolving rapidly; consider using them on links where security is important.

4.5.4 Modems

4.5.4.1 Modem Lines Must Be Managed

Although they provide convenient access to a site for its users, they can also provide an effective detour around the site's firewalls. For this reason it is essential to maintain proper control of modems.

Do not allow users to install a modem line without proper authorization. This includes temporary installations (e.g., plugging a modem into a facsimile or telephone line overnight).

Maintain a register of all your modem lines and keep your register up-to-date. Conduct regular (ideally automated) site checks for unauthorized modems.

4.5.4.2 Dial-In Users Must Be Authenticated

A user name and password check should be completed before a user can access anything on your network. Normal password security considerations are particularly important (see the section "One-Time Passwords").

Remember that telephone lines can be tapped, and that it is quite easy to intercept messages to cellular phones. Modern high-speed modems use more-sophisticated modulation techniques, which makes them somewhat more difficult to monitor, but it is prudent to assume that hackers know how to eavesdrop on your lines. For this reason, you should use one-time passwords if at all possible.

It is helpful to have a single dial-in point (e.g., a single large modem pool) so that all users are authenticated in the same way.

Users will occasionally mistype a password. Set a short delay — two seconds, perhaps — after the first and second failed logins, and force a disconnect after the third. This will slow down automated password attacks. Do not tell the user whether the user name, the password, or both were incorrect.

4.5.4.3 Call-Back Capability

Some dial-in servers offer call-back facilities (i.e., the user dials in and is authenticated, then the system disconnects the call and calls back on a specified number). Call-back is useful because if someone guesses a user name and password, the system disconnects and then calls back the actual user whose password was cracked; random calls from a server are suspicious, at best. This does mean users may only log in from one location (where the server is configured to dial them back), and of course there may be phone charges associated with the call-back location.

This feature should be used with caution; it can easily be bypassed. At a minimum, make sure that the return call is never made from the same modem as the incoming one. Overall, although call-back can improve modem security, you should not depend on it alone.

4.5.4.4 All Logins Should Be Logged

All logins, whether successful or unsuccessful, should be logged. However, do not keep correct passwords in the log. Rather, log them simply as a successful login attempt. Because most bad passwords are mistyped by authorized users, they only vary by a single character from the actual password. Therefore, if you cannot keep such a log secure, do not log it at all.

If Calling Line Identification is available, take advantage of it by recording the calling number for each login attempt. Be sensitive to the privacy issues raised by Calling Line Identification. Also be aware that Calling Line Identification is not to be trusted (because intruders have been known to break into phone switches and forward phone numbers or make other changes); use the data for informational purposes only, not for authentication.

4.5.4.5 Choose Your Opening Banner Carefully

Many sites use a system default contained in a message-of-the-day file for their opening banner. Unfortunately, this often includes the type of host hardware or operating system present on the host. This can provide valuable information to a would-be intruder. Instead, each site should create its own specific login banner, taking care to only include necessary information.

Display a short banner but do not offer an "inviting" name (e.g., University of XYZ, Student Records System). Instead, give your site name, a short warning that sessions may be monitored, and a user name/password prompt. Verify possible legal issues related to the text you put into the banner.

For high-security applications, consider using a "blind" password (i.e., give no response to an incoming call until the user has typed in a password). This effectively simulates a dead modem.

4.5.4.6 Dial-Out Authentication

Dial-out users should also be authenticated, particularly because your site will have to pay the telephone charges.

Never allow dial-out from an unauthenticated dial-in call, and consider whether you will allow it from an authenticated one. The goal here is to prevent callers using your modem pool as part of a chain of logins. This can be hard to detect, particularly if a hacker sets up a path through several hosts on your site.

At a minimum, do not allow the same modems and phone lines to be used for both dial-in and dial-out. This can be implemented easily if you run separate dial-in and dial-out modem pools.

4.5.4.7 Make Your Modem Programming as "Bullet-Proof" as Possible

Be sure modems cannot be reprogrammed while they are in service. At a minimum, make sure that three plus signs will not put your dial-in modems into command mode!

Program your modems to reset to your standard configuration at the start of each new call. Failing this, make them reset at the end of each call. This precaution will protect you against accidental reprogramming of your modems. Resetting at both the end and the beginning of each call will assure an even higher level of confidence that a new caller will not inherit a previous caller's session.

Check that your modems terminate calls cleanly. When a user logs out from an access server, verify that the server hangs up the phone line properly. It is equally important that the server forces logouts from whatever sessions were active if the user hangs up unexpectedly.

4.6 Auditing

This section covers the procedures for collecting data generated by network activity, which may be useful in analyzing the security of a network and responding to security incidents.

4.6.1 What to Collect

Audit data should include any attempt to achieve a different security level by any person, process, or other entity in the network. This includes login and logout, super-user access (or the non-UNIX equivalent), ticket generation (for Kerberos, for example), and any other change of access or status. It is especially important to note "anonymous" or "guest" access to public servers.

The actual data to collect will differ for different sites and for different types of access changes within a site. In general, the information you want to collect includes user name and host name for login and logout; previous and new access rights for a change of access rights; and a timestamp. Of course, there is much more information that might be gathered, depending on what the system makes available and how much space is available to store that information.

One very important note: Do not gather passwords. This creates an enormous potential security breach if the audit records should be improperly accessed. Do not gather incorrect passwords either, as they often differ from valid passwords by only a single character or transposition.

4.6.2 Collection Process

The collection process should be enacted by the host or resource being accessed. Depending on the importance of the data and the need to have it local in instances in which services are being denied, data could be kept local to the resource until needed or be transmitted to storage after each event.

There are basically three ways to store audit records: in a read/write file on a host, on a write-once/read-many device (e.g., a CD-ROM or a specially configured tape drive), or on a write-only device (e.g., a line printer). Each method has advantages and disadvantages.

File system logging is the least resource-intensive of the three methods and the easiest to configure. It allows instant access to the records for analysis, which may be important if an attack is in progress. File system logging is also the least-reliable method. If the logging host has been compromised, the file system is usually the first thing to go; an intruder could easily cover up traces of the intrusion.

Collecting audit data on a write-once device takes slightly more effort to configure than a simple file, but it has the significant advantage of greatly increased security because an intruder could not alter the data showing that an intrusion has occurred. The disadvantage of this method is the need to maintain a supply of storage media and the cost of that media. Also, the data may not be instantly available.

Line printer logging is useful in systems where permanent and immediate logs are required. A real-time system is an example of this, where the exact point of failure or attack must be recorded. A laser printer or other device that buffers data (e.g., a print server) may suffer from lost data if buffers contain the needed data at a critical instant. The disadvantage of paper trails is the need to keep the printer fed and the need to scan records by hand. There is also the issue of where to store the potentially enormous volume of paper that may be generated.

For each of the logging methods described, there is also the issue of securing the path between the device generating the log and actual logging device (i.e., the file server, tape/CD-ROM drive, printer).

If that path is compromised, logging can be stopped or spoofed or both. In an ideal world, the logging device would be directly attached by a single, simple point-to-point cable. Because that is usually impractical, the path should pass through the minimum number of networks and routers. Even if logs can be blocked, spoofing can be prevented with cryptographic checksums (it probably is not necessary to encrypt the logs because they should not contain sensitive information in the first place).

4.6.3 Collection Load

Collecting audit data may result in a rapid accumulation of bytes, so storage availability for this information must be considered in advance. There are a few ways to reduce the required storage space. First, data can be compressed, using one of many methods, or the required space can be minimized by keeping data for a shorter period of time with only summaries of that data kept in long-term archives. One major drawback to the latter method involves incident response. Often, an incident has been ongoing for some period of time when a site notices it and begins to investigate. At that point in time, it is very helpful to have detailed audit logs available. If these are just summaries, there may not be sufficient detail to fully handle the incident.

4.6.4 Handling and Preserving Audit Data

Audit data should be some of the most carefully secured data at the site and in the backups. If an intruder were to gain access to audit logs, the systems themselves in addition to the data would be at risk.

Audit data may also be crucial to the investigation, apprehension, and prosecution of the perpetrator of an incident. For this reason, it is advisable to seek the advice of legal council when deciding how audit data should be treated. This should happen before an incident occurs.

If a data-handling plan is not adequately defined prior to an incident, it may mean that there is no recourse in the aftermath of an event, and it may create liability resulting from improper treatment of the data.

4.6.5 Legal Considerations

Due to the content of audit data, there are a number of legal questions that arise that might need to be addressed by your legal counsel. If you collect and save audit data, you need to be prepared for consequences resulting both from its existence and its content.

One area concerns the privacy of individuals. In certain instances, audit data may contain personal information. Searching through the data, even for a routine check of the system's security, could represent an invasion of privacy.

A second area of concern involves knowledge of intrusive behavior originating from your site. If an organization keeps audit data, is it responsible for examining it to search for incidents? If a host in one organization is used as a launching point for an attack against another organization, can the second organization use the audit data of the first organization to prove negligence on the part of that organization?

These examples are meant to be comprehensive but should motivate your organization to consider the legal issues involved with audit data.

4.7 Securing Backups

The procedure of creating backups is a classic part of operating a computer system. Within the context of this document, backups are addressed as part of the overall security plan of a site. There are several aspects to backups that are important within this context:

1. Make sure your site is creating backups.
2. Make sure your site is using offsite storage for backups. The storage site should be carefully selected for both its security and its availability.
3. Consider encrypting your backups to provide additional protection of the information once it is offsite. However, be aware that you will need a good

key management scheme so that you will be able to recover data at any point in the future. Also, make sure you will have access to the necessary decryption programs at such time in the future as you need to perform the decryption.

4. Do not always assume that your backups are good. There have been many instances of computer security incidents that have gone on for long periods of time before a site has noticed the incident. In such cases, backups of the affected systems are also tainted.

5. Periodically verify the correctness and completeness of your backups.

5. Security Incident Handling

This section will supply guidance to be used before, during, and after a computer security incident occurs on a host, network, site, or multi-site environment. The operative philosophy in the event of a breach of computer security is to react according to a plan. This is true whether the breach is the result of an external intruder attack, unintentional damage, a student testing some new program to exploit software vulnerability, or a disgruntled employee. Each of the possible types of events, such as those just listed, should be addressed in advance by adequate contingency plans.

Traditional computer security, while quite important in the overall site security plan, usually pays little attention to how to actually handle an attack once one occurs. The result is that when an attack is in progress, many decisions are made in haste and can be damaging to tracking down the source of the incident, collecting evidence to be used in prosecution efforts, preparing for the recovery of the system, and protecting the valuable data contained on the system.

One of the most important but often overlooked benefits for efficient incident handling is an economic one. Having both technical and managerial personnel respond to an incident requires considerable resources. If trained to handle incidents efficiently, less staff time is required when one occurs.

Due to the worldwide network, most incidents are not restricted to a single site. Operating system vulnerabilities apply (in some cases) to several millions of systems, and many vulnerabilities are exploited within the network itself. Therefore, it is vital that all sites with involved parties are informed as soon as possible.

Another benefit is related to public relations. News about computer security incidents tends to be damaging to an organization's stature among current or potential clients. Efficient incident handling minimizes the potential for negative exposure.

A final benefit of efficient incident handling is related to legal issues. It is possible that in the near future, organizations may be held responsible if one of their nodes is used to launch a network attack. In a similar vein, people who develop patches or work-arounds may be sued if the patches or work-arounds are ineffective, resulting in compromise of the systems, or if the patches or work-arounds themselves damage systems. Knowing about operating system vulnerabilities and patterns of attacks and then taking appropriate measures to counter these potential threats is critical to circumventing possible legal problems.

The sections in this appendix provide an outline and starting point for creating your site's policy for handling security incidents:

1. Preparing and planning (what are the goals and objectives in handling an incident?)
2. Notification (who should be contacted in the case of an incident?)
   - Local managers and personnel

       – Law enforcement and investigative agencies
       – Computer security incidents handling teams
       – Affected and involved sites
       – Internal communications
       – Public relations and press releases

3. Identifying an incident (is it an incident and how serious is it?)
4. Handling (what should be done when an incident occurs?)
       – Notification (who should be notified about the incident?)
       – Protecting evidence and activity logs (what records should be kept before, during, and after the incident?)
       – Containment (how can the damage be limited?)
       – Eradication (how to eliminate the reasons for the incident?)
       – Recovery (how to reestablish service and systems?)
       – Follow up (what actions should be taken after the incident?)
5. Aftermath (what are the implications of past incidents?)
6. Administrative response to incidents

The remainder of this appendix will detail the issues involved in each of the important topics listed and provide some guidance as to what should be included in a site policy for handling incidents.

5.1 Preparing and Planning for Incident Handling

Part of handling an incident is being prepared to respond before the incident occurs. This includes establishing a suitable level of protections, as explained in the preceding chapters. Doing this should help your site prevent incidents as well as limit potential damage resulting from them when they do occur. Protection also includes preparing incident handling guidelines as part of a contingency plan for your organization or site. Having written plans eliminates much of the ambiguity that occurs during an incident, and will lead to a more appropriate and thorough set of responses. It is vitally important to test the proposed plan before an incident occurs through "dry runs." A team might even consider hiring a tiger team to act in parallel with the dry run. Learning to respond efficiently to an incident is important for a number of reasons:

1. Protecting assets that could be compromised
2. Protecting resources that could be utilized more profitably if an incident did not require their services
3. Complying with government or other regulations
4. Preventing the use of your systems in attacks against other systems (which could cause you to incur legal liability)
5. Minimizing the potential for negative exposure

As in any set of preplanned procedures, attention must be paid to a set of goals for handling an incident. These goals will be prioritized differently, depending on the site. A specific set of objectives can be identified for dealing with incidents:

1. Figure out how it happened
2. Find out how to avoid further exploitation of the same vulnerability
3. Avoid escalation and further incidents
4. Assess the impact and damage of the incident
5. Recover from the incident

6. Update policies and procedures as needed
7. Find out who did it (if appropriate and possible)

Due to the nature of the incident, there might be a conflict between analyzing the original source of a problem and restoring systems and services. Overall goals (such as assuring the integrity of critical systems) might be the reason for not analyzing an incident. Of course, this is an important management decision; but all involved parties must be aware that without analysis the same incident may happen again.

It is also important to prioritize the actions to be taken during an incident well in advance of the time an incident occurs. Sometimes an incident may be so complex that it is impossible to do everything at once to respond to it; priorities are essential. Although priorities will vary from institution to institution, the following suggested priorities may serve as a starting point for defining your organization's response:

1. Protect human life and people's safety; human life always has precedence over all other considerations.
2. Protect classified and sensitive data. Prevent exploitation of classified and sensitive systems, networks, or sites. Inform affected classified and sensitive systems, networks, or sites about penetrations that have already occurred. Be aware of regulations by your site or by government.
3. Protect proprietary, scientific, managerial, and other data because loss of data is costly in terms of resources. Prevent exploitations of other systems, networks, or sites and inform already affected systems, networks, or sites about successful penetrations.
4. Prevent damage to systems (e.g., loss or alteration of system files, damage to disk drives, etc.). Damage to systems can result in costly downtime and recovery.
5. Minimize disruption of computing resources (including processes). It is better in many cases to shut a system down or disconnect from a network than to risk damage to data or systems. Sites will have to evaluate the trade-offs between shutting down and disconnecting, and staying up. There may be service agreements in place that may require keeping systems up even in light of further damage occurring. However, the damage and scope of an incident may be so extensive that service agreements may have to be overridden.

An important implication for defining priorities is that once human life and national security considerations have been addressed, it is generally more important to save data than system software and hardware. Although it is undesirable to have any damage or loss during an incident, systems can be replaced. However, the loss or compromise of data (especially classified or proprietary data) is usually not an acceptable outcome under any circumstances.

Another important concern is the effect on others beyond the systems and networks where the incident occurs. Within the limits imposed by government regulations, it is always important to inform affected parties as soon as possible. Due to the legal implications of this topic, it should be included in the planned procedures to avoid further delays and uncertainties for the administrators.

Any plan for responding to security incidents should be guided by local policies and regulations. Government and private sites that deal with classified material have specific rules that they must follow.

The policies chosen by your site that determine how it reacts to incidents will shape your response. For example, it may make little sense to create mechanisms to monitor and trace intruders if your site does not plan to take action against the intruders if they are caught. Other organizations may have policies that affect your plans. Telephone companies often release information about telephone traces to law enforcement agencies only.

Handling incidents can be tedious and requires any number of routine tasks that could be handled by support personnel. To free the technical staff, it may be helpful to identify support staff that will help with tasks such as photocopying, faxing, etc.

5.2 Notification and Points of Contact

It is important to establish contacts with various personnel before a real incident occurs. Many times, incidents are not real emergencies. Indeed, often you will be able to handle the activities internally. However, there will also be many times when others outside your immediate department will need to be included in the incident handling. These additional contacts include local managers and system administrators, administrative contacts for other sites on the Internet, and various investigative organizations. Getting to know these contacts before incidents occur will help to make your incident handling process more efficient.

For each type of communication contact, specific points of contact (POC) should be defined. These may be technical or administrative in nature and may include legal or investigative agencies as well as service providers and vendors. When establishing these contacts, it is important to decide how much information will be shared with each class of contact. It is especially important to define ahead of time what information will be shared with the users at a site, with the public (including the press), and with other sites.

Settling these issues is especially important for the local person responsible for handling the incident, because that is the person responsible for the actual notification of others. A list of contacts in each of these categories is an important time-saver for this person during an incident. It can be quite difficult to find an appropriate person during an incident when many urgent events are ongoing. It is strongly recommended that all relevant telephone numbers (also electronic mail addresses and fax numbers) are included in the site security policy. The names and contact information of all individuals who will be directly involved in the handling of an incident should be placed at the top of this list.

5.2.1 Local Managers and Personnel

When an incident is underway, a major issue is deciding who is in charge of coordinating the activity of the multitude of players. A major mistake that can be made is to have a number of people who are each working independently but are not working together. This will only add to the confusion of the event and will probably lead to wasted or ineffective effort.

The single POC may or may not be the person responsible for handling the incident. There are two distinct roles to fill when deciding who will be the POC and who will be the person in charge of the incident. The person in charge of the incident will make decisions as to the interpretation of policy applied to the event. In contrast, the POC must coordinate the effort of all the parties involved with handling the event.

The POC must be a person with the technical expertise to successfully coordinate the efforts of the system managers and users involved in monitoring and reacting to the attack. Care should be taken when identifying who this person will be. It should not necessarily be the same person who has administrative responsibility for the compromised systems because such administrators often have knowledge sufficient for the day-to-day use of the computers but lack in-depth technical expertise.

Another important function of the POC is to maintain contact with law enforcement and other external agencies to assure that multi-agency involvement occurs. The level of involvement will be determined by management decisions as well as legal constraints.

A single POC should also be the single person in charge of collecting evidence because, as a rule of thumb, the more people that touch a potential piece of evidence, the greater the possibility that it will be inadmissible in court. To ensure that evidence will be acceptable to the legal community, collecting evidence should be done following predefined procedures in accordance with local laws and legal regulations.

One of the most critical tasks for the POC is the coordination of all relevant processes. Responsibilities may be distributed over the whole site, involving multiple independent departments or groups. This will require a well-coordinated effort in order to achieve overall success. The situation becomes even more complex if multiple sites are involved. When this happens, rarely will a single POC at one site be able to adequately coordinate the handling of the entire incident. Instead, appropriate incident response teams should be involved.

The incident handling process should provide some escalation mechanisms. In order to define such a mechanism, sites will need to create an internal classification scheme for incidents. Associated with each level of incident will be the appropriate POC and procedures. As an incident is escalated, there may be a change in the POC that will need to be communicated to all others involved in handling the incident. When a change in the POC occurs, the old POC should brief the new POC in all background information.

Finally, users must know how to report suspected incidents. Sites should establish reporting procedures that will work both during and outside normal working hours. Help desks are often used to receive these reports during normal working hours, while beepers and telephones can be used for out-of-hours reporting.

5.2.2 Law Enforcement and Investigative Agencies

In the event of an incident that has legal consequences, it is important to establish contact with investigative agencies (e.g., the FBI and Secret Service in the U.S.) as soon as possible. Local law enforcement, local security offices, and campus police departments should also be informed as appropriate. This section describes many of the issues that will be confronted, but it is acknowledged that each organization will have its own local and governmental laws and regulations that will impact how they interact with law enforcement and investigative agencies. The most important point to make is that each site needs to work through these issues.

A primary reason for determining these points of contact well in advance of an incident is that once a major attack is in progress, there is little time to call these agencies to determine exactly who the correct point of contact is. Another reason is that it is important to cooperate with these agencies in a manner that will foster a good working relationship, and that will be in accordance with the working procedures of these agencies. Knowing the working procedures in advance, and the expectations of your point of contact is a big step in this direction. For example, it is important to gather evidence that will be admissible in any subsequent legal proceedings, and this will require prior knowledge of how to gather such evidence. A final reason for establishing contacts as soon as possible is that it is impossible to know the particular agency that will assume jurisdiction in any given incident. Making contacts and finding the proper channels early on will make responding to an incident go considerably more smoothly.

If your organization or site has a legal counsel, you need to notify this office soon after you learn that an incident is in progress. At a minimum, your legal counsel needs to be involved to protect the legal and financial interests of your site or organization. There are many legal and practical issues, a few of which are:

1. Whether your site or organization is willing to risk negative publicity or exposure to cooperate with legal prosecution efforts.
2. Downstream liability — if you leave a compromised system as is so it can be monitored and another computer is damaged because the attack originated from your system, your site or organization may be liable for damages incurred.
3. Distribution of information — if your site or organization distributes information about an attack in which another site or organization may be involved or the vulnerability in a product that may affect ability to market that product, your site or organization may again be liable for any damages (including damage of reputation).
4. Liabilities due to monitoring — your site or organization may be sued if users at your site or elsewhere discover that your site is monitoring account activity without informing users.

Unfortunately, there are no clear precedents yet on the liabilities or responsibilities of organizations involved in a security incident or who might be involved in supporting an investigative effort. Investigators will often encourage organizations to help trace and monitor intruders. Indeed, most investigators cannot pursue computer intrusions without extensive support from the organizations involved. However, investigators cannot provide protection from liability claims, and these kinds of efforts may drag out for months and may take a lot of effort.

On the other hand, an organization's legal council may advise extreme caution and suggest that tracing activities be halted and an intruder shut out of the system. This, in itself, may not provide protection from liability, and may prevent investigators from identifying the perpetrator.

The balance between supporting investigative activity and limiting liability is tricky. You will need to consider the advice of your legal counsel and the damage the intruder is causing (if any) when making your decision about what to do during any particular incident.

Your legal counsel should also be involved in any decision to contact investigative agencies when an incident occurs at your site. The decision to coordinate efforts with investigative agencies is most properly that of your site or organization. Involving your legal counsel will also foster the multi-level coordination between your site and the particular investigative agency involved, which in turn results in an efficient division of labor. Another result is that you are likely to obtain guidance that will help you avoid future legal mistakes.

Finally, your legal counsel should evaluate your site's written procedures for responding to incidents. It is essential to obtain a "clean bill of health" from a legal perspective before you actually carry out these procedures.

It is vital, when dealing with investigative agencies, to verify that the person who calls asking for information is a legitimate representative from the agency in question. Unfortunately, many well intentioned people have unknowingly leaked sensitive details about incidents, allowed unauthorized people into their systems, etc., because a caller has masqueraded as a representative of a government agency.*

A similar consideration is using a secure means of communication. Because many network attackers can easily reroute electronic mail, avoid using electronic mail to communicate with other agencies (as well as others dealing with the incident at hand). Nonsecured phone lines (the phones normally used in the business world) are also frequent targets for tapping by network intruders, so be careful!

There is no one established set of rules for responding to an incident when the local government becomes involved. Normally (in the U.S.), except by legal order, no agency can force you to monitor, to disconnect from the network, to avoid telephone contact with the suspected attackers, etc. Each organization will have a set of local and national laws and regulations that must be adhered to when handling incidents. It is recommended that each site be familiar with those laws and regulations, and identify and get to know the contacts for agencies with jurisdiction well in advance of handling an incident.

5.2.3 Computer Security Incident Handling Teams

There are currently a number of Computer Security Incident Response Teams (CSIRTs) such as the CERT Coordination Center, the German DFN-CERT, and other teams around the globe. Teams exist for many major government agencies and large corporations. If such a team is available, notifying it should be of primary consideration during the early stages of an incident. These teams are responsible for coordinating computer security incidents over a range of sites and larger entities. Even if the incident is believed to be contained within a single site, it is possible that the information available through a response team could help in fully resolving the incident.

If it is determined that the breach occurred due to a flaw in the system's hardware or software, the vendor (or supplier) and a Computer Security Incident Handling team should be notified as soon as possible. This is especially important because many other systems are vulnerable, and these vendor and response team organizations can help disseminate help to other affected sites.

In setting up a site policy for incident handling, it may be desirable to create a subgroup, much like those teams that already exist, that will be responsible for handling computer security incidents for the site (or organization). If such a team is created, it is essential that communication lines be opened between this team and other teams. Once an incident is underway, it is difficult to open a trusted dialogue between other teams if none had existed before.

5.2.4 Affected and Involved Sites

If an incident has an impact on other sites, it is good practice to inform them. It may be obvious from the beginning that the incident is not limited to the local site, or it may emerge only after further analysis.

Each site may choose to contact other sites directly or it can pass the information to an appropriate incident response team. It is often very difficult to find the responsible POC at remote sites and the incident response team will be able to facilitate contact by making use of already established channels.

---

* This word of caution actually applies to all external contacts.

The legal and liability issues arising from a security incident will differ from site to site. It is important to define a policy for the sharing and logging of information about other sites before an incident occurs.

Information about specific people is especially sensitive, and may be subject to privacy laws. To avoid problems in this area, irrelevant information should be deleted and a statement of how to handle the remaining information should be included. A clear statement of how this information is to be used is essential. No one who informs a site of a security incident wants to read about it in the public press. Incident response teams are valuable in this respect. When they pass information to responsible POCs, they are able to protect the anonymity of the original source. But, be aware that, in many cases, the analysis of logs and information at other sites will reveal addresses of your site.

All the problems discussed above should not be taken as reasons not to involve other sites. In fact, the experiences of existing teams reveal that most sites informed about security problems are not even aware that their site had been compromised. Without timely information, other sites are often unable to take action against intruders.

5.2.5 Internal Communications

It is crucial during a major incident to communicate why certain actions are being taken, and how the users (or departments) are expected to behave. In particular, it should be made very clear to users what they are allowed to say (and not say) to the outside world (including other departments). For example, it would not be good for an organization if users replied to customers with something like, "I'm sorry the systems are down, we've had an intruder and we are trying to clean things up." It would be much better if they were instructed to respond with a prepared statement like, "I'm sorry our systems are unavailable, they are being maintained for better service in the future."

Communications with customers and contract partners should be handled in a sensible but sensitive way. One can prepare for the main issues by preparing a checklist. When an incident occurs, the checklist can be used with the addition of a sentence or two for the specific circumstances of the incident.

Public relations departments can be very helpful during incidents. They should be involved in all planning and can provide well-constructed responses for use when contact is necessary with outside departments and organizations.

5.2.6 Public Relations: Press Releases

There has been a tremendous growth in the amount of media coverage dedicated to computer security incidents in the United States. Such press coverage is bound to extend to other countries as the Internet continues to grow and expand internationally. Readers from countries where such media attention has not yet occurred, can learn from the experiences in the United States and should be forewarned and prepared.

One of the most important issues to consider is when, who, and how much to release to the general public through the press. There are many issues to consider when deciding this particular issue. First and foremost, if a public relations office exists for the site, it is important to use this office as liaison to the press. The public relations office is trained in the type and wording of information released, and will help to assure that the image of the site is protected during and after the incident (if possible). A public relations office has the advantage that you can communicate candidly with them, and provide a buffer between the constant press attention and the need of the POC to maintain control over the incident.

If a public relations office is not available, the information released to the press must be carefully considered. If the information is sensitive, it may be advantageous to provide only minimal or overview information to the press. It is quite possible that any information provided to the press will be quickly reviewed by the perpetrator of the incident. Also note that misleading the press can often backfire and cause more damage than releasing sensitive information.

While it is difficult to determine in advance what level of detail to provide to the press, some guidelines to keep in mind are:

1. *Keep the technical level of detail low.* Detailed information about the incident may provide enough information for others to launch similar attacks on other sites, or even damage the site's ability to prosecute the guilty party once the event is over.

2. *Keep the speculation out of press statements.* Speculation of who is causing the incident or the motives is very likely to be in error and may cause an inflamed view of the incident.

3. *Work with law enforcement professionals to assure that evidence is protected.* If prosecution is involved, assure that the evidence collected is not divulged to the press.

4. *Try not to be forced into a press interview before you are prepared.* The popular press is famous for the "2 a.m." interview, where the hope is to catch the interviewee off guard and obtain information otherwise not available.

5. *Do not allow the press attention to detract from the handling of the event.* Always remember that the successful closure of an incident is of primary importance.

5.3 Identifying an Incident

5.3.1 Is It Real?

This stage involves determining if a problem really exists. Of course many if not most signs often associated with virus infection, system intrusions, malicious users, etc., are simply anomalies such as hardware failures or suspicious system/user behavior. To assist in identifying whether there really is an incident, it is usually helpful to obtain and use any detection software that may be available. Audit information is also extremely useful, especially in determining whether there is a network attack. It is extremely important to obtain a system snapshot as soon as one suspects that something is wrong. Many incidents cause a dynamic chain of events to occur, and an initial system snapshot may be the most valuable tool for identifying the problem and any source of attack. Finally, it is important to start a log book. Recording system events, telephone conversations, time stamps, etc., can lead to a more rapid and systematic identification of the problem, and is the basis for subsequent stages of incident handling.

There are certain indications or "symptoms" of an incident that deserve special attention:

1. System crashes
2. New user accounts (the account RUMPELSTILTSKIN has been unexpectedly created) or high activity on a previously low usage account
3. New files (usually with novel or strange file names, such as data.xx or k.xx)

4. Accounting discrepancies (in a UNIX system you might notice the shrinking of an accounting file called/usr/admin/lastlog, something that should make you very suspicious that there may be an intruder)
5. Changes in file lengths or dates (a user should be suspicious if .EXE files in an MS DOS computer have inexplicably grown by over 1800 bytes)
6. Attempts to write to system (a system manager notices that a privileged user in a VMS system is attempting to alter rightslist.dat)
7. Data modification or deletion (files start to disappear)
8. Denial of service (a system manager and all other users become locked out of a UNIX system, now in single user mode)
9. Unexplained, poor system performance
10. Anomalies ("GOTCHA" is displayed on the console or there are frequent unexplained "beeps")
11. Suspicious probes (there are numerous unsuccessful login attempts from another node)
12. Suspicious browsing (someone becomes a root user on a UNIX system and accesses file after file on many user accounts
13. Inability of a user to log in due to modifications of his account

By no means is this list comprehensive; we have just listed a number of common indicators. It is best to collaborate with other technical and computer security personnel to make a decision as a group about whether an incident is occurring.

5.3.2 Types and Scope of Incidents

Along with the identification of the incident is the evaluation of the scope and impact of the problem. It is important to correctly identify the boundaries of the incident in order to effectively deal with it and prioritize responses.

In order to identify the scope and impact, a set of criteria should be defined that is appropriate to the site and to the type of connections available. Some of the issues include:

1. Is this a multi-site incident?
2. Are many computers at your site affected by this incident?
3. Is sensitive information involved?
4. What is the entry point of the incident (network, phone line, local terminal, etc.)?
5. Is the press involved?
6. What is the potential damage of the incident?
7. What is the estimated time to close out the incident?
8. What resources could be required to handle the incident?
9. Is law enforcement involved?

5.3.3 Assessing the Damage and Extent

The analysis of the damage and extent of the incident can be quite time consuming but should lead to some insight into the nature of the incident, and aid investigation and prosecution. As soon as the breach has occurred, the entire system and all of its components should be considered suspect. System software is the most probable target. Preparation is crucial to be able to detect all changes for a possibly tainted system. This includes checksumming all media from the vendor using an algorithm that is resistant to tampering.

Assuming original vendor distribution media is available, an analysis of all system files should commence, and any irregularities should be noted and referred to all parties involved in handling the incident. It can be very difficult, in some cases, to decide which backup media are showing a correct system status. Consider, for example, that the incident may have continued for months or years before discovery, and the suspect may be an employee of the site, or otherwise have intimate knowledge or access to the systems. In all cases, the pre-incident preparation will determine what recovery is possible.

If the system supports centralized logging (most do), go back over the logs and look for abnormalities. If process accounting and connect time accounting are enabled, look for patterns of system usage. To a lesser extent, disk usage may shed light on the incident. Accounting can provide much helpful information in an analysis of an incident and subsequent prosecution. Your ability to address all aspects of a specific incident strongly depends on the success of this analysis.

5.4 Handling an Incident

Certain steps are necessary to take during the handling of an incident. In all security related activities, the most important point to be made is that all sites should have policies in place. Without defined policies and goals, activities undertaken will remain without focus. The goals should be defined by management and legal counsel in advance.

One of the most fundamental objectives is to restore control of the affected systems and to limit the impact and damage. In the worst-case scenario, shutting down the system, or disconnecting the system from the network, may be the only practical solution.

As the activities involved are complex, try to get as much help as necessary. While trying to solve the problem alone, real damage might occur due to delays or missing information. Most administrators take the discovery of an intruder as a personal challenge. By proceeding this way, other objectives as outlined in the local policies may not always be considered. Trying to catch intruders may be a very low priority, compared to system integrity, for example. Monitoring a hacker's activity is useful but it might not be considered worth the risk to allow the continued access.

5.4.1 Types of Notification and Exchange of Information

When you have confirmed that an incident is occurring, the appropriate personnel must be notified. How this notification is achieved is very important to keeping the event under control both from a technical and emotional standpoint. The circumstances should be described in as much detail as possible, in order to aid prompt acknowledgment and understanding of the problem. Great care should be taken when determining to which groups detailed technical information is given during the notification. For example, it is helpful to pass this kind of information to an incident handling team, as they can assist you by providing helpful hints for eradicating the vulnerabilities involved in an incident. On the other hand, putting the critical knowledge into the public domain (e.g., via USENET newsgroups or mailing lists) may potentially put a large number of systems at risk of intrusion. It is invalid to assume that all administrators reading a particular newsgroup have access to operating system source code, or can even understand an advisory well enough to take adequate steps.

First of all, any notification to either local or offsite personnel must be explicit. This requires that any statement (be it an electronic mail message, phone call, fax, beeper, or semaphore) providing information about the incident be clear, concise, and fully qualified. When you are notifying others that will help you handle an event, a "smoke screen" will only divide the effort and create confusion. If a division of labor is suggested, it is helpful to provide information to each participant about what is being accomplished in other efforts. This will not only reduce duplication of effort but allow people working on parts of the problem to know where to obtain information relevant to their part of the incident.

Another important consideration when communicating about the incident is to be factual. Attempting to hide aspects of the incident by providing false or incomplete information may not only prevent a successful resolution to the incident but may even worsen the situation.

The choice of language used when notifying people about the incident can have a profound effect on the way that information is received. When you use emotional or inflammatory terms, you raise the potential for damage and negative outcomes of the incident. It is important to remain calm both in written and spoken communications.

Another consideration is that not all people speak the same language. Due to this fact, misunderstandings and delay may arise, especially if it is a multi-national incident. Other international concerns include differing legal implications of a security incident and cultural differences. However, cultural differences do not only exist between countries. They even exist within countries, between different social or user groups. For example, an administrator of a university system might be very relaxed about attempts to connect to the system via telnet, but the administrator of a military system is likely to consider the same action as a possible attack.

Another issue associated with the choice of language is the notification of non-technical or offsite personnel. It is important to accurately describe the incident without generating undue alarm or confusion. While it is more difficult to describe the incident to a nontechnical audience, it is often more important. A nontechnical description may be required for upper-level management, the press, or law enforcement liaisons. The importance of these communications cannot be underestimated and may make the difference between resolving the incident properly and escalating to some higher level of damage.

If an incident response team becomes involved, it might be necessary to fill out a template for the information exchange. Although this may seem to be an additional burden and adds a certain delay, it helps the team to act on this minimum set of information. The response team may be able to respond to aspects of the incident of which the local administrator is unaware. If information is given out to someone else, the following minimum information should be provided:

1. Time zone of logs in GMT or local time
2. Information about the remote system, including host names, IP addresses, and (perhaps) user IDs
3. All log entries relevant for the remote site
4. Type of incident (what happened, why you should care)

If local information (i.e., local user IDs) is included in the log entries, it will be necessary to sanitize the entries beforehand to avoid privacy issues. In general, all information that might assist a remote site in resolving an incident should be given out, unless local policies prohibit this.

5.4.2 Protecting Evidence and Activity Logs

When you respond to an incident, document all details related to the incident. This will provide valuable information to yourself and others as you try to unravel the course of events. Documenting all details will ultimately save you time. If you do not document every relevant phone call, for example, you are likely to forget a significant portion of information you obtain, requiring you to contact the source of information again. At the same time, recording details will provide evidence for prosecution efforts, providing the case moves in that direction. Documenting an incident will also help you perform a final assessment of damage (something your management, as well as law enforcement officers, will want to know), and will provide the basis for later phases of the handling process: eradication, recovery, and follow-up "lessons learned."

During the initial stages of an incident, it is often infeasible to determine whether prosecution is viable, so you should document as if you are gathering evidence for a court case. At a minimum, you should record:

1. All system events (audit records)
2. All actions you take (time tagged)
3. All external conversations (including the person with whom you talked, the date and time, and the content of the conversation)

The most straightforward way to maintain documentation is keeping a log book. This allows you to go to a centralized, chronological source of information when you need it, instead of requiring you to page through individual sheets of paper. Much of this information is potential evidence in a court of law. Thus, when a legal follow-up is a possibility, one should follow the prepared procedures and avoid jeopardizing the legal follow-up by improper handling of possible evidence. If appropriate, the following steps may be taken.

1. Regularly (e.g., every day) turn in photocopied, signed copies of your logbook (as well as media you use to record system events) to a document custodian.
2. The custodian should store these copied pages in a secure place (e.g., a safe).
3. When you submit information for storage, you should receive a signed, dated receipt from the document custodian.

Failure to observe these procedures can result in invalidation of any evidence you obtain in a court of law.

5.4.3 Containment

The purpose of containment is to limit the extent of an attack. An essential part of containment is decision making (e.g., determining whether to shut a system down, disconnect from a network, monitor system or network activity, set traps, disable functions such as remote file transfer, etc.).

Sometimes this decision is trivial; shut the system down if the information is classified, sensitive, or proprietary. Bear in mind that removing all access while an incident is in progress obviously notifies all users, including the alleged problem users, that the administrators are aware of a problem; this may have a deleterious effect on an investigation. In some cases, it is prudent to remove all access or functionality as soon as possible, then restore normal operation in limited stages. In other cases, it is worthwhile to risk some damage to the system if keeping the system up might enable you to identify an intruder.

This stage should involve carrying out predetermined procedures. Your organization or site should, for example, define acceptable risks in dealing with an incident, and should prescribe specific actions and strategies accordingly. This is especially important when a quick decision is necessary and it is not possible to first contact all involved parties to discuss the decision. In the absence of predefined procedures, the person in charge of the incident will often not have the power to make difficult management decisions (like to lose the results of a costly experiment by shutting down a system). A final activity that should occur during this stage of incident handling is the notification of appropriate authorities.

5.4.4 Eradication

Once the incident has been contained, it is time to eradicate the cause. But before eradicating the cause, great care should be taken to collect all necessary information about the compromised system(s) and the cause of the incident, as they will likely be lost when cleaning up the system.

Software may be available to help you in the eradication process, such as anti-virus software. If any bogus files have been created, archive them before deleting them. In the case of virus infections, it is important to clean and reformat any media containing infected files. Finally, ensure that all backups are clean. Many systems infected with viruses become periodically re-infected simply because people do not systematically eradicate the virus from backups. After eradication, a new backup should be taken.

Removing all vulnerabilities once an incident has occurred is difficult. The key to removing vulnerabilities is knowledge and understanding of the breach.

It may be necessary to go back to the original distribution media and re-customize the system. To facilitate this worst-case scenario, a record of the original system setup and each customization change should be maintained. In the case of a network-based attack, it is important to install patches for all operating system vulnerabilities that were exploited.

A security log can be most valuable during this phase of removing vulnerabilities. The logs showing how the incident was discovered and contained can be used later to help determine how extensive the damage was from a given incident. The steps taken can be used in the future to make sure the problem does not resurface. Ideally, one should automate and regularly apply the same test as was used to detect the security incident.

If a particular vulnerability is isolated as having been exploited, the next step is to find a mechanism to protect your system. The security mailing lists and bulletins would be a good place to search for this information, and you can get advice from incident response teams.

5.4.5 Recovery

Once the cause of an incident has been eradicated, the recovery phase defines the next stage of action. The goal of recovery is to return the system to normal. In general, bringing up services in the order of demand to allow a minimum of user inconvenience is the best practice. Understand that the proper recovery procedures for the system are extremely important and should be specific to the site.

5.4.6 Follow-Up

Once you believe that a system has been restored to a "safe" state, it is still possible that holes, and even traps, could be lurking in the system. One of the most important stages of responding to incidents is also the most often omitted, the follow-up stage. In the follow-up stage, the system should be monitored for items that may have been missed during the cleanup stage. It would be prudent to utilize some of the tools mentioned in Chapter 7 as a start. Remember, these tools do not replace continual system monitoring and good systems administration practices.

The most important element of the follow-up stage is performing a postmortem analysis. Exactly what happened, and at what times? How well did the staff involved with the incident perform? What kind of information did the staff need quickly, and how could they have gotten that information as soon as possible? What would the staff do differently next time?

After an incident, it is prudent to write a report describing the exact sequence of events: the method of discovery, correction procedure, monitoring procedure, and a summary of lesson learned. This will aid in the clear understanding of the problem. Creating a formal chronology of events (including time stamps) is also important for legal reasons.

A follow-up report is valuable for many reasons. It provides a reference to be used in case of other similar incidents. It is also important to, as quickly as possible, obtain a monetary estimate of the amount of damage the incident caused. This estimate should include costs associated with any loss of software and files (especially the value of proprietary data that may have been disclosed), hardware damage, and manpower costs to restore altered files, reconfigure affected systems, and so forth. This estimate may become the basis for subsequent prosecution activity. The report can also help justify an organization's computer security effort to management.

5.5 Aftermath of an Incident

In the wake of an incident, several actions should take place. These actions can be summarized as follows:

1. An inventory should be taken of the systems' assets, (i.e., a careful examination should determine how the system was affected by the incident).
2. The lessons learned as a result of the incident should be included in revised security plan to prevent the incident from recurring.
3. A new risk analysis should be developed in light of the incident.
4. An investigation and prosecution of the individuals who caused the incident should commence, if it is deemed desirable.

If an incident is based on poor policy, and unless the policy is changed, then one is doomed to repeat the past. Once a site has recovered from an incident, site policy and procedures should be reviewed to encompass changes to prevent similar incidents. Even without an incident, it would be prudent to review policies and procedures on a regular basis. Reviews are imperative due to today's changing computing environments.

The whole purpose of this postmortem process is to improve all security measures to protect the site against future attacks. As a result of an incident, a site or organization should gain practical knowledge from the experience. A concrete goal of the postmortem is to develop new proactive methods. Another important facet of the aftermath may be end user and administrator education to prevent a reoccurrence of the security problem.

5.6 Responsibilities

5.6.1 Not Crossing the Line

It is one thing to protect one's own network but quite another to assume that one should protect other networks. During the handling of an incident, certain system vulnerabilities of one's own systems and the systems of others become apparent. It is quite easy and may even be tempting to pursue the intruders in order to track them. Keep in mind that at a certain point it is possible to "cross the line," and, with the best of intentions, become no better than the intruder.

The best rule when it comes to propriety is to not use any facility of remote sites that is not public. This clearly excludes any entry onto a system (such as a remote shell or login session) that is not expressly permitted. This may be very tempting; after a breach of security is detected, a system administrator may have the means to "follow it up," to ascertain what damage is being done to the remote site. Do not do it! Instead, attempt to reach the appropriate point of contact for the affected site.

5.6.2 Good Internet Citizenship

During a security incident, there are two choices one can make. First, a site can choose to watch the intruder in the hopes of catching him; or, the site can go about cleaning up after the incident and shut the intruder out of the systems. This is a decision that must be made very thoughtfully, as there may be legal liabilities if you choose to leave your site open, knowing that an intruder is using your site as a launching pad to reach out to other sites. Being a good Internet citizen means that you should try to alert other sites that may have been impacted by the intruder. These affected sites may be readily apparent after a thorough review of your log files.

5.6.3 Administrative Response to Incidents

When a security incident involves a user, the site's security policy should describe what action is to be taken. The transgression should be taken seriously, but it is very important to be sure of the role the user played. Was the user naive? Could there be a mistake in attributing the security breach to the user? Applying administrative action that assumes the user intentionally caused the incident may not be appropriate for a user who simply made a mistake. It may be appropriate to include sanctions more suitable for such a situation in your policies (e.g., education or reprimand of a user) in addition to more stern measures for intentional acts of intrusion and system misuse.

6. Ongoing Activities

At this point in time, your site has hopefully developed a complete security policy and has developed procedures to assist in the configuration and management of your technology in support of those policies. How nice it would be if you could sit back and relax at this point and know that you were finished with the job of security. Unfortunately, that is not possible. Your systems and networks are not a static environment, so you will need to review policies and procedures on a regular basis.

There are a number of steps you can take to help you keep up with the changes around you so that you can initiate corresponding actions to address those changes. The following is a starter set and you may add others as appropriate for your site:

1. Subscribe to advisories that are issued by various security incident response teams, like those of the CERT Coordination Center, and update your systems against those threats that apply to your site's technology.
2. Monitor security patches that are produced by the vendors of your equipment, and obtain and install all that apply.
3. Actively watch the configurations of your systems to identify any changes that may have occurred, and investigate all anomalies.
4. Review all security policies and procedures annually (at a minimum).
5. Read relevant mailing lists and USENET newsgroups to keep up to date with the latest information being shared by fellow administrators.
6. Regularly check for compliance with policies and procedures. This audit should be performed by someone other than the people who define or implement the policies and procedures.

7. Tools and Locations

This appendix provides a brief list of publicly available security technology that can be downloaded from the Internet. Many of the items described below will undoubtedly be surpassed or made obsolete before this document is published.

Some of the tools listed are applications such as end user programs (clients) and their supporting system infrastructure (servers). Others are tools that a general user will never see or need to use but may be used by applications, or by administrators to troubleshoot security problems or to guard against intruders.

A sad fact is that there are very few security-conscious applications currently available. Primarily, this is caused by the need for a security infrastructure that must first be put into place for most applications to operate securely. There is considerable effort currently taking place to build this infrastructure so that applications can take advantage of secure communications.

Most of the tools and applications described below can be found in one of the following archive sites:

1. CERT Coordination Center: ftp://info.cert.org:/pub/tools
2. DFN-CERT: ftp://ftp.cert.dfn.de/pub/tools/
3. Computer Operations, Audit, and Security Tools (COAST): coast.cs.pur-due.edu:/pub/tools

It is important to note that many sites, including CERT and COAST, are mirrored throughout the Internet. Be careful to use a well-known mirror site to retrieve software, and to use verification tools (MD5, checksums, etc.) to validate that software. A clever cracker might advertise security software that has intentionally been designed to provide access to data or systems.

Tools

COPS	rpcbind/portmapper replacement
DES	SATAN
Drawbridge	sfingerd

Tools	
identd (not really a security tool)	smrsh
ISS	S/KEY
Kerberos	ssh
logdaemon	swatch
lsof	TCP-Wrapper
MD5	tiger
PEM	Tripwire[a]
PGP	TROJAN.PL

[a] Tripwire is registered in the U.S. Patent and Trademark Office.

8. Mailing Lists and Other Resources

It would be impossible to list all of the mailing lists and other resources dealing with site security. However, these are some "jump-points" from which the reader can begin. All of these references are for the Internet constituency. More specific (vendor and geographical) resources can be found through these references.

8.1 Mailing Lists

8.1.1 CERT™ Advisory

Send mail to: cert-advisory-request@cert.org

Message Body: subscribe cert <FIRST NAME> <LAST NAME>

A CERT advisory provides information on how to obtain a patch or details of a workaround for a known computer security problem. The CERT Coordination Center works with vendors to produce a workaround or a patch for a problem, and does not publish vulnerability information until a workaround or a patch is available. A CERT advisory may also be a warning to our constituency about ongoing attacks (e.g., "CA-91:18.Active.Internet.tftp.Attacks").

CERT advisories are also published on the USENET newsgroup: comp.security.announce.

CERT advisory archives are available via anonymous FTP from info.cert.org in the/pub/cert_advisories directory.

8.1.2 VIRUS-L List

Send mail to: listserv%lehiibm1.bitnet@mitvma.mit.edu

Message Body: subscribe virus-L FIRSTNAME LASTNAME

VIRUS-L is a moderated mailing list with a focus on computer virus issues. For more information, including a copy of the posting guidelines, see the file "virus-l.README," available by anonymous FTP from cs.ucr.edu.

8.1.3 Internet Firewalls

Send mail to: majordomo@greatcircle.com

Message Body: subscribe firewalls user@host

The Firewalls mailing list is a discussion forum for firewall administrators and implementers.

8.1.4 USENET Newsgroups

1. comp.security.announce: The comp.security.announce newsgroup is moderated and is used solely for the distribution of CERT advisories.
2. comp.security.misc: The comp.security.misc is a forum for the discussion of computer security, especially as it relates to the UNIX® operating system.
3. alt.security: The alt.security newsgroup is also a forum for the discussion of computer security, as well as other issues such as car locks and alarm systems.
4. comp.virus: The comp.virus newsgroup is a moderated newsgroup with a focus on computer virus issues. For more information, including a copy of the posting guidelines, see the file "virus-l.README," available via anonymous FTP on info.cert.org in the/pub/virus-l directory.
5. comp.risks: The comp.risks newsgroup is a moderated forum on the risks to the public in computers and related systems.

8.1.5 World Wide Web Pages

1. http://www.first.org: Computer Security Resource Clearinghouse. The main focus is on crisis response information; information on computer security-related threats, vulnerabilities, and solutions. At the same time, the Clearinghouse strives to be a general index to computer security information on a broad variety of subjects, including general risks, privacy, legal issues, viruses, assurance, policy, and training.
2. http://www.telstra.com.au/info/security.html: This reference index contains a list of links to information sources on network and computer security. There is no implied fitness to the tools, techniques, and documents contained within this archive. Many, if not all, of these items work well but we do not guarantee that this will be so. This information is for the education and legitimate use of computer security techniques only.
3. http://www.alw.nih.gov/Security/security.html: This page features general information about computer security. Information is organized by source and each section is organized by topic. Recent modifications are noted in What's New page.
4. http://csrc.ncsl.nist.gov: This archive at the National Institute of Standards and Technology's Computer Security Resource Clearinghouse page contains a number of announcements, programs, and documents related to computer security.

9. References

The following references may not be available in all countries.

[ABA, 1989] American Bar Association, Section of Science and Technology, Guide to the Prosecution of Telecommunication Fraud by the Use of Computer Crime Statutes, American Bar Association, 1989.

[Appelman et al., 1995] Appelman, Heller, Ehrman, White, and McAuliffe, The Law and The Internet, USENIX 1995 Technical Conference on UNIX and Advanced Computing, New Orleans, January 16–20, 1995.

[Aucoin, 1989] R. Aucoin, Computer Viruses: Checklist for Recovery, *Computers in Libraries,* 9, 2, 4, February 1989.

[Barrett, 1996] D. Barrett, Bandits on the Information Superhighway, O'Reilly & Associates, Sebastopol, CA, 1996.

[Bates, 1992] R. Bates, *Disaster Recovery Planning: Networks, Telecommunications and Data Communications,* McGraw-Hill, New York, 1992.

[Bellovin, 1989] S. Bellovin, Security Problems in the TCP/IP Protocol Suite, *Computer Communication Review,* 19, 2, 32–48, April 1989.

[Bellovin, 1990] S. Bellovin, and M. Merritt, Limitations of the Kerberos Authentication System, *Computer Communications Review,* October 1990.

[Bellovin, 1992] S. Bellovin, There Be Dragon, USENIX: Proceedings of the Third Usenix Security Symposium, Baltimore, September, 1992.

[Bender, 1894] D. Bender, *Computer Law: Evidence and Procedure,* M. Bender, New York, 1978–present.

[Bloombecker, 1990] B. Bloombecker, *Spectacular Computer Crimes,* Dow Jones–Irwin, Homewood, IL, 1990.

[Brand, 1990] R. Brand, *Coping with the Threat of Computer Security Incidents: A Primer from Prevention through Recovery,* R. Brand, 8 June 1990.

[Brock, 1989] J. Brock, November 1988 Internet Computer Virus and the Vulnerability of National Telecommunications Networks to Computer Viruses, GAO/T-IMTEC-89–10, Washington, D.C., 20 July 1989.

[BS 7799] British Standard, BS Tech Committee BSFD/12, Info. Sec. Mgmt, BS 7799: 1995 Code of Practice for Information Security Management, British Standards Institution, London, 54, effective 15 February 1995.

[Caelli, 1988] W. Caelli, Ed., Computer Security in the Age of Information, Proceedings of the 5th IFIP International Conference on Computer Security, IFIP/Sec '88.

[Carroll, 1987] J. Carroll, *Computer Security,* 2nd ed., Butterworth Publishers, Stoneham, MA, 1987.

[Cavazos and Morin, 1995] E. Cavazos and G. Morin, *Cyber-Space and The Law,* MIT Press, Cambridge, MA, 1995.

[CCH, 1989] Commerce Clearing House, Guide to Computer Law (Topical Law Reports), Chicago, 1989.

[Chapman, 1992] B. Chapman, Network (In) Security Through IP Packet Filtering, USENIX: Proceedings of the 3rd UNIX Security Symposium, Baltimore, September 1992.

[Chapman and Zwicky, 1995] B. Chapman and E. Zwicky, *Building Internet Firewalls,* O'Reilly & Associates, Sebastopol, CA, 1995.

[Cheswick, 1990] W. Cheswick, The Design of a Secure Internet Gateway, Proceedings of the Summer Usenix Conference, Anaheim, CA, June 1990.

[Cheswick, 1994] W. Cheswick, An Evening with Berferd in which a Cracker is Lured, Endured, and Studied, AT&T Bell Laboratories.

[Cheswick and Bellovin, 1994] W. Cheswick and S. Bellovin, *Firewalls and Internet Security: Repelling the Wily Hacker,* Addison-Wesley, Reading, MA, 1994.

[Conly, 1989] C. Conly, Organizing for Computer Crime Investigation and Prosecution, U.S. Dept. of Justice, Office of Justice Programs, under Contract Number OJP-86-C-002, National Institute of Justice, Washington, D.C., July 1989.

[Cooper, 1989] J. Cooper, *Computer and Communications Security: Strategies for the 1990s,* McGraw-Hill, New York, 1989.

[CPSR, 1989] Computer Professionals for Social Responsibility, CPSR Statement on the Computer Virus, *Communications of the ACM,* 32, 6, 699, June 1989.

[CSC-STD-002-85, 1985] Department of Defense, Password Management Guideline, CSC-STD-002-85, 12 April 1985.

[Curry, 1990] D. Curry, Improving the Security of Your UNIX System, SRI International Report ITSTD-721-FR-90–21, April 1990.

[Curry, 1992] D. Curry, *UNIX System Security: A Guide for Users and Systems Administrators,* Addison-Wesley, Reading, MA, 1992.

[DDN88] Defense Data Network, BSD 4.2 and 4.3 Software Problem Resolution, DDN MGT Bulletin #43, DDN Network Information Center, 3 November 1988.

[DDN89] DCA DDN Defense Communications System, DDN Security Bulletin 03, DDN Security Coordination Center, 17 October 1989.

[Denning, 1990] P. Denning, Ed., *Computers Under Attack: Intruders, Worms, and Viruses,* ACM Press, New York, 1990.

[Eichin and Rochlis, 1989] M. Eichin and J. Rochlis, With Microscope and Tweezers: An Analysis of the Internet Virus of November 1988, Massachusetts Institute of Technology, February 1989.

[Eisenberg et al., 1989] T. Eisenberg, D. Gries, J. Hartmanis, D. Holcomb, M. Lynn, and T. Santoro, The Computer Worm, Cornell University, 6 February 1989.

[Ermann, Williams, and Gutierrez, 1990] D. Ermann, M. Williams, and C. Gutierrez, Eds., *Computers, Ethics, and Society,* Oxford University Press, New York, 1990.

[Farmer and Spafford, 1990] D. Farmer and E. Spafford, The COPS Security Checker System, Proceedings of the Summer 1990 USENIX Conference, Anaheim, CA, pp. 165–170, June 1990.

[Farrow, 1991] R. Farrow, *UNIX Systems Security,* Addison-Wesley, Reading, MA, 1991.

[Fenwick, 1985] W. Fenwick, Chair, Computer Litigation, 1985: Trial Tactics and Techniques, Litigation Course Handbook Series No. 280, prepared for distribution at the Computer Litigation, 1985: Trial Tactics and Techniques Program, February–March 1985.

[Fites et al., 1989] M. Fites, P. Kratz, and A. Brebner, *Control and Security of Computer Information Systems,* Computer Science Press, Rockville, MD, 1989.

[Fites, Johnson, and Kratz, 1992] Fites, Johnson, and Kratz, *The Computer Virus Crisis,* 2nd ed., Van Nostrand Reinhold, New York, 1992.

[Forester and Morrison, 1990] T. Forester and P. Morrison, *Computer Ethics: Tales and Ethical Dilemmas in Computing,* MIT Press, Cambridge, MA, 1990.

[GAO/IMTEX-89-57, 1989] General Accounting Office, Computer Security — Virus Highlights Need for Improved Internet Management, United States General Accounting Office, Washington, D.C., 1989.

[Garfinkel and Spafford, 1991] S. Garfinkel and E. Spafford, *Practical Unix Security,* O'Reilly & Associates, Sebastopol, CA, May 1991.

[Garfinkel, 1995] S. Garfinkel, *PGP: Pretty Good Privacy,* O'Reilly & Associates, Sebastopol, CA, 1996.

[Garfinkel and Spafford, 1996] S. Garfinkel and E. Spafford, *Practical UNIX and Internet Security,* O'Reilly & Associates, Sebastopol, CA, 1996.

[Gemignani, 1989] M. Gemignani, Viruses and Criminal Law, *Communications of the ACM,* Vol. 32, No. 6, Pgs. 669–671, June 1989.

[Goodell, 1996] J. Goodell, *The Cyberthief and the Samurai: The True Story of Kevin Mitnick — And The Man Who Hunted Him Down,* Dell Publishing, New York, 1996.

[Gould, 1989] C. Gould, Ed., *The Information Web: Ethical and Social Implications of Computer Networking,* Westview Press, Boulder, CO, 1989.

[Greenia, 1989] M. Greenia, *Computer Security Information Sourcebook,* Lexikon Services, Sacramento, CA, 1989.

[Hafner and Markoff, 1991] K. Hafner and J. Markoff, *Cyberpunk: Outlaws and Hackers on the Computer Frontier,* Touchstone, Simon & Schuster, New York, 1991.

[Hess, Safford, and Pooch] D. Hess, D. Safford, and U. Pooch, A Unix Network Protocol Security Study: Network Information Service, Texas A&M University.

[Hoffman, 1990] L. Hoffman, *Rogue Programs: Viruses, Worms, and Trojan Horses,* Van Nostrand Reinhold, NY, 1990.

[Howard, 1995] G. Howard, *Introduction to Internet Security: From Basics to Beyond,* Prima Publishing, Rocklin, CA, 1995.

[Huband and Shelton, 1986] F. Huband and R. Shelton, Eds., Protection of Computer Systems and Software: New Approaches for Combating Theft of Software and Unauthorized Intrusion, papers presented at a workshop sponsored by the National Science Foundation, 1986.

[Hughes, 1995] L. Hughes Jr., *Actually Useful Internet Security Techniques,* New Riders Publishing, Indianapolis, IN, 1995.

[IAB-RFC1087, 1989] Internet Activities Board, Ethics and the Internet, RFC1087, IAB, January 1989.

[Icove, Seger, and VonStorch, 1995] D. Icove, K. Seger, and W. VonStorch, *Computer Crime: A Crimefighter's Handbook,* O'Reilly & Associates, Sebastopol, CA, 1995.

[IVPC, 1996] International Virus Prevention Conference '96 Proceedings, NCSA, 1996.

[Johnson and Podesta] D. Johnson and J. Podesta, Formulating a Company Policy on Access to and Use and Disclosure of Electronic Mail on Company Computer Systems, International Virus Prevention Conference '96 Proceedings, NCSA, 1996.

[Kane, 1994] P. Kane, *PC Security and Virus Protection Handbook: The Ongoing War Against Information Sabotage,* M&T Books, New York, 1994.

[Kaufman, Perlman, and Speciner, 1995] C. Kaufman, R. Perlman, and M. Speciner, *Network Security: PRIVATE Communication in a PUBLIC World,* Prentice Hall, Englewood Cliffs, NJ, 1995.

[Kent, 1990] S. Kent, E-Mail Privacy for the Internet: New Software and Strict Registration Procedures will be Implemented this Year, *Business Communications Review,* 20, 1, 55, 1 January 1990.

[Levy, 1984] S. Levy, *Hacker: Heroes of the Computer Revolution,* Delta, 1984.

[Lewis, 1996] S. Lewis, Disaster Recovery Yellow Pages, The Systems Audit Group, 1996.

[Littleman, 1996] J. Littleman, *The Fugitive Game: Online with Kevin Mitnick,* Little, Brown, Boston, 1996.

[Lu and Sundareshan, 1989] W. Lu and M. Sundareshan, Secure Communication in Internet Environments: A Hierarchical Key Management Scheme for End-to-End Encryption, *IEEE Transactions on Communications,* 37, 10, 1014, 1 October 1989.

[Lu and Sundareshan, 1990] W. Lu and M. Sundareshan, A Model for Multilevel Security in Computer Networks, *IEEE Transactions on Software Engineering,* 16, 6, 647, 1 June 1990.

[Martin and Schinzinger, 1989] M. Martin and R. Schinzinger, *Ethics in Engineering,* 2nd ed., McGraw Hill, New York, 1989.

[Merkle] R. Merkle, A Fast Software One-Way Hash Function, *Journal of Cryptology,* 3, 1990.

[McEwen, 1989] J. McEwen, Dedicated Computer Crime Units, report contributors: D. Fester and H. Nugent, prepared for the National Institute of Justice, U.S. Department of Justice, by Institute for Law and Justice, Inc., under contract number OJP-85-C-006, Washington, D.C., 1989.

[MIT, 1989] Massachusetts Institute of Technology, Teaching Students About Responsible Use of Computers, MIT, 1985–1986.

[Mogel, 1989] Mogel, J., Simple and Flexible Datagram Access Controls for UNIX-based Gateways, Digital Western Research Laboratory Research Report 89/4, March 1989.

[Muffett, 1992] A. Muffett, Crack Version 4.1: A Sensible Password Checker for Unix, NCSAI, 1992.

[NCSA1, 1995] NCSA, NCSA Firewall Policy Guide, 1995.

[NCSA2, 1995] NCSA, NCSA's Corporate Computer Virus Prevention Policy Model, NCSA, 1995.

[NCSA, 1996] NCSA, Firewalls and Internet Security Conference '96 Proceedings, 1996.

[NCSC-89-660-P, 1990] National Computer Security Center, Guidelines for Formal Verification Systems, The Center, Fort George G. Meade, MD, 1 April 1990.

[NCSC-89-254-P, 1988] National Computer Security Center, Glossary of Computer Security Terms, The Center, Fort George G. Meade, MD, 21 October 1988.

[NCSC-C1-001-89, 1989] Tinto, M., Computer Viruses: Prevention, Detection, and Treatment, National Computer Security Center C1 Technical Report C1-001-89, June 1989.

[NCSC Conference, 1989] National Computer Security Conference, 12th National Computer Security Conference: Baltimore Convention Center, Baltimore, 10–13 October, 1989: Information Systems Security, Solutions for Today — Concepts for Tomorrow, National Institute of Standards and National Computer Security Center, 1989.

[NCSC-CSC-STD-003-85, 1985] National Computer Security Center, Guidance for Applying the Department of Defense Trusted Computer System Evaluation Criteria in Specific Environments, CSC-STD-003-85, NCSC, 25 June 1985.

[NCSC-STD-004-85, 1985] National Computer Security Center, Technical Rationale Behind CSC-STD-003-85: Computer Security Requirements, CSC-STD-004-85, NCSC, 25 June 1985.

[NCSC-STD-005-85, 1985] National Computer Security Center, Magnetic Remanence Security Guideline, CSC-STD-005-85, NCSC, 15 November 1985.

[NCSC-TCSEC, 1985] National Computer Security Center, Trusted Computer System Evaluation Criteria, DoD 5200.28-STD, CSC-STD-001-83, NCSC, December 1985.

[NCSC-TG-003, 1987] NCSC, A Guide to Understanding Discretionary Access Control in Trusted Systems, NCSC-TG-003, Version 1, 30 September 1987, 29 pages.

[NCSC-TG-001, 1988] NCSC, A Guide to Understanding AUDIT in Trusted Systems, NCSC-TG-001, Version 2, 1 June 1988, 25 pages.

[NCSC-TG-004, 1988] National Computer Security Center, Glossary of Computer Security Terms, NCSC-TG-004, NCSC, 21 October 1988.

[NCSC-TG-005, 1987] National Computer Security Center, Trusted Network Interpretation, NCSC-TG-005, NCSC, 31 July 1987.

[NCSC-TG-006, 1988] NCSC, A Guide to Understanding Configuration Management in Trusted Systems, NCSC-TG-006, Version 1, 28 March 1988, 31 pages.

[NCSC-TRUSIX, 1990] National Computer Security Center, Trusted UNIX Working Group (TRUSIX) rationale for selecting access control list features for the UNIX system, The Center, Fort George G. Meade, MD, 1990.

[NRC, 1991] National Research Council, *Computers at Risk: Safe Computing in the Information Age,* National Academy Press, 1991.

[Nemeth et al., 1995] E. Nemeth, G. Snyder, S. Seebass, and T. Hein, UNIX Systems Administration Handbook, Prentice Hall PTR, Englewood Cliffs, NJ, 1995.

[NIST, 1989] National Institute of Standards and Technology, Computer Viruses and Related Threats: A Management Guide, NIST Special Publication 500–166, August 1989.

[NSA] National Security Agency, Information Systems Security Products and Services Catalog, NSA, Quarterly Publication.

[NSF, 1988] National Science Foundation, NSF Poses Code of Networking Ethics, *Communications of the ACM,* 32, 6, 688, June 1989.

[NTISSAM, 1987] NTISS, Advisory Memorandum on Office Automation Security Guideline, NTISSAM COMPUSEC/1–87, 16 January 1987.

[OTA-CIT-310, 1987] United States Congress, Office of Technology Assessment, Defending Secrets, Sharing Data: New Locks and Keys for Electronic Information, OTA-CIT-310, October 1987.

[OTA-TCT-606] Congress of the United States, Office of Technology Assessment, Information Security and Privacy in Network Environments, OTA-TCT-606, September 1994.

[Palmer and Potter, 1989] I. Palmer and G. Potter, *Computer Security Risk Management,* Van Nostrand Reinhold, New York, 1989.

[Parker, 1989] D. Parker, Computer Crime: Criminal Justice Resource Manual, U.S. Dept. of Justice, National Institute of Justice, Office of Justice Programs, Under Contract Number OJP-86-C-002, Washington, D.C., August 1989.

[Parker, Swope, and Baker, 1990] D. Parker, S. Swope, and B. Baker, *Ethical Conflicts: Information and Computer Science, Technology and Business,* QED Information Sciences, Wellesley, MA.

[Pfleeger, 1989] C. Pfleeger, *Security in Computing,* Prentice-Hall, Englewood Cliffs, NJ, 1989.

[Quarterman, 1990] J. Quarterman, *The Matrix: Computer Networks and Conferencing Systems World-wide,* Digital Press, Bedford, MA, 1990.

[Ranum1, 1992] M. Ranum, An Internet Firewall, Proceedings of World Conference on Systems Management and Security, 1992.

[Ranum2, 1992] M. Ranum, A Network Firewall, Digital Equipment Corporation Washington Open Systems Resource Center, June 12, 1992.

[Ranum, 1993] M. Ranum, Thinking About Firewalls, 1993.

[Ranum and Avolio, 1994] M. Ranum and F. Avolio, A Toolkit and Methods for Internet Firewalls, Trusted Information Systems, 1994.

[Reinhardt, 1993] R. Reinhardt, An Architectural Overview of UNIX Network Security, ARINC Research Corporation, February 18, 1993.

[Reynolds-RFC1135, 1989] The Helminthiasis of the Internet, RFC 1135, USC/Information Sciences Institute, Marina del Rey, CA, December 1989.

[Russell and Gangemi, 1991] D. Russell and G. Gangemi, *Computer Security Basics,* O'Reilly & Associates, Sebastopol, CA, 1991.

[Schneier 1996] B. Schneier, *Applied Cryptography: Protocols, Algorithms, and Source Code in C,* 2nd ed., John Wiley & Sons, New York, 1996.

[Seeley, 1989] D. Seeley, A Tour of the Worm, Proceedings of 1989 Winter USENIX Conference, Usenix Association, San Diego, CA, February 1989.

[Shaw, 1986] E. Shaw Jr., Computer Fraud and Abuse Act of 1986, Congressional Record (3 June 1986), Washington, D.C., 3 June 1986.

[Shimomura, 1996] T. Shimomura with J. Markoff, *Takedown: The Pursuit and Capture of Kevin Mitnick, America's Most Wanted Computer Outlaw — by the Man Who Did It,* Hyperion, 1996.

[Shirey, 1990] R. Shirey, Defense Data Network Security Architecture, *Computer Communication Review,* 20, 2, 66, 1 April 1990.

[Slatalla and Quittner, 1995] M. Slatalla and J. Quittner, *Masters of Deception: The Gang that Ruled Cyberspace,* Harper Collins, New York, 1995.

[Smith, 1989] M. Smith, *Commonsense Computer Security: Your Practical Guide to Preventing Accidental and Deliberate Electronic Data Loss,* McGraw-Hill, New York, 1989.

[Smith, 1995] D. Smith, Forming an Incident Response Team, 6th Annual Computer Security Incident Handling Workshop, Boston, MA, July 25–29, 1995.

[Spafford, 1988] E. Spafford, The Internet Worm Program: An Analysis, *Computer Communication Review,* 19, 1, ACM SIGCOM, January 1989.

[Spafford, 1989] G. Spafford, An Analysis of the Internet Worm, Proceedings of the European Software Engineering Conference 1989, Warwick England, September 1989. Proceedings published by Springer-Verlag as: Lecture Notes in Computer Science #387. Also issued as Purdue Technical Report #CSD-TR-933.

[Spafford, Keaphy, and Ferbrache, 1989] E. Spafford, K. Heaphy, and D. Ferbrache, Computer Viruses: Dealing with Electronic Vandalism and Programmed Threats, ADAPSO, 1989.

[Stallings1, 1995] W. Stallings, *Internet Security Handbook,* IDG Books, Foster City CA, 1995.

[Stallings2, 1995] W. Stallings, *Network and InterNetwork Security,* Prentice Hall, Englewood Cliffs, NJ, 1995.

[Stallings3, 1995] W. Stallings, *Protect Your Privacy: A Guide for PGP Users,* PTR Prentice Hall, Englewood Cliffs, NJ, 1995.

[Stoll, 1988] C. Stoll, Stalking the Wily Hacker, *Communications of the ACM,* 31, 5, 484–497, May 1988.

[Stoll, 1989] C. Stoll, *The Cuckoo's Egg,* Doubleday, Garden City, NY, 1989.

[Treese and Wolman, 1993] G. Treese and A. Wolman, X Through the Firewall, and Other Applications Relays, Digital Equipment Corporation, Cambridge Research Laboratory, CRL 93/10, May 3, 1993.

[Trible, 1986] P. Trible, The Computer Fraud and Abuse Act of 1986, U.S. Senate Committee on the Judiciary, 1986.

[USENIX, 1988] USENIX, USENIX Proceedings: UNIX Security Workshop, Portland, OR, August 29–30, 1988.

[USENIX, 1990] USENIX, USENIX Proceedings: UNIX Security II Workshop, Portland, OR, August 27–28, 1990.

[USENIX, 1992] USENIX, USENIX Symposium Proceedings: UNIX Security III, Baltimore, MD, September 14–16, 1992.

[USENIX, 1993] USENIX, USENIX Symposium Proceedings: UNIX Security IV, Santa Clara, CA, October 4–6, 1993.

[USENIX, 1995] USENIX, The Fifth USENIX UNIX Security Symposium, Salt Lake City, UT, June 5–7, 1995.

[Wood et al., 1987] C. Wood, W. Banks, S. Guarro, A. Garcia, V. Hampel, and H. Sartorio, *Computer Security: A Comprehensive Controls Checklist,* John Wiley & Sons, New York, 1987.

[Wrobel, 1993] L. Wrobel, *Writing Disaster Recovery Plans for Telecommunications Networks and LANs,* Artech House, 1993.

[Vallabhaneni, 1989] S. Vallabhaneni, *Auditing Computer Security: A Manual with Case Studies,* Wiley, New York, 1989.

[Venema] W. Venema, TCP Wrapper: Network monitoring, access control, and booby traps, Mathematics and Computing Science, Eindhoven University of Technology, The Netherlands.

Appendix C

Below is a useful list for senior managers, auditors, and security administrators.

Tools

Application	Description Information	Availability URL
BlackWidow	Web site information tool	http://www.softbytelabs.com
Crack	Password cracker tool	ftp://ftp.cert.dfn.de/pub/tools/password/Crack
Dumpsec	Dumps NT logs	http://www.microsoft.com/ntworkstation/downloads/ Recommended/Featured/NTKit.asp
Ethereal	Sniffing and analysis tool	http://www.ethereal.com
Forensic Toolkit	Foundstone tool bundle	http://www.foundstone.com/knowledge/proddesc/ forensic-toolkit.html
Fport	TCP/UDP port discoverer	http://www.foundstone.com/knowledge/proddesc/ fport.html
Ghost	Disk imaging tool	http://www.symantec.com
John the Ripper	Password cracker (Unix/Windows)	http://www.openwall.com/john
Jphs	Unix/Windows steganographic tool	linux01.gwdg.de/~alatham/stego.html
Keylogger	Keystroke logging solution	http://www.amecisco.com
Legion	Windows-based scanner	http://www.zimmermantech.com/legion.html
Lopht Crack	Password cracker	http://www.atstake.com/research/lc/whatsnew.html
NTFSDOS	NT utilities	http://www.sysinternals.com
MN Desk Reference	Network reference guide	http://www.hackerhost.com/archives/computers/ DeskReference.txt
Nessus	Unix/Linux-based vulnerability tool	http://www.nessus.org
Nmap	Unix/Linux-based port scanner	http://www.insecure.org/nmap

Application	Description Information	Availability URL
PGP	Personal encryption tool	http://www.pgpi.org
SamSpade 1.14	Network toolkit	http://www.samspade.org/ssw
Snort	IDS and packet capture	http://www.snort.org
Strobe	Port Scanner	http://www.prosolve.com/software
SuperScan	Windows-based port scanner	http://www.webattack.com/get/superscan.shtml
THC (The Hacker's Choice)	War dialer	http://www.infowar.co.uk/thc/releases.htm
VMWare	Operating system emulator	http://www.vmware.com
Whisker	Web site vulnerability scanner	http://www.wiretrip.net/rfp/p/doc.asp/i2/d21.htm
Winscan	Windows-based scanner	http://www.prosolve.com/software

Vulnerability Lists

Site Information	URL
Open Source Vulnerability Database	http://www.osvdb.org
Internet Storm Center	http://isc.incidents.org
National Institute of Standards and Technology	http://icat.nist.gov
Mitre Corp	http://cve.mitre.org
CERT	http://www.cert.org/nav/index_red.html
Internet Security Systems	http://xforce.iss.net/index.php
Network and Applications	http://www.securityfocus.com

Bulletins and Listservs

Site Information	URL
HIPAA discussion groups	http://groups.yahoo.com/group/HIPAA-TCS
	http://groups.yahoo.com/group/HIPAA-CISSP
Privacy discussion groups	http://groups.yahoo.com/group/privacy-forum
CERT advisories	majordomo@cert.org
Bugtraq	bugtraq-subscribe@securityfocus.com
Spyware	alt.privacy.spyware
Vulnerability watch	http://www.vulnwatch.org
Windows NT	listserv@listserv.ntsecurity.net
Redhat Linux	linux-security-request@RedHat.com
Windows 2000	listserv@listserv.ntsecurity.net
Linux	comp.os.linux.advocacy
Unix	comp.unix.aix
Unix	comp.unix.admin

Index

A

Absolute addressing, 275, 276
Access
    Control List (ACL), 472
    controls, discretionary, 156
    point (AP), 207
Accounting discrepancies, 487
Accreditation Manual for Hospitals, 9
Achilles configuration, 199
ACL, *see* Access Control List
Activity
    codes, common, 305
    logs, protection of, 490
Addressing
    absolute, 275, 276
    relative, 275, 276
Address Resolution Protocol (ARP), 211
Administrative support and supplies sub-team,
    36
ALE, *see* Annualized loss expectancy
ALGs, *see* Application Layer Gateways
Annualized loss expectancy (ALE), 5, 21
Annualized rate of occurrence (ARO), 5, 22
Anticybersquatting Consumer Protection, 349
Antivirus software, 2, 103, 153, 190
AP, *see* Access point
Application
    firewalls, 93
    Layer Gateways (ALGs), 467
    logging, 241
Appropriate Use Policy (AUP), 457
ARO, *see* Annualized rate of occurrence
ARP, *see* Address Resolution Protocol
Arpwatch, 211
Asset(s)
    criticality, 20
    definition of, 5
    identification, 455
    protection schedule, 30
    ranking of, 20
    value, 5
Attack(s)
    administrator facilitated, 258
    automated, 212
    common, 136
    denial-of-service, 3, 23, 70
        origin of, 240, 258
        wireless, 211
    financial, 196
    malicious code, 315
    replay, 462
    resistance to, 70
    system, 253
        most frequent, 230
        recognition of, 70
    tools, 213
    types of, 257
    unicode input, 198
    virus, 23
Attacker
    definition of, 5
    identity, 321
Attorney–client communications, e-mail, 64
Audit
    findings, 202
    management planning, 129, 131, 132
    program development, 135
    report, 143, 144
    risk, 130
    trails, 92, 113, 158
Auditing, 111–227
    audit conferences, 145–150
        audit program for small IT department,
            147–150
        exit conferences, 146

opening conferences, 145
other conferences, 145–146
summary of audit steps, 146–147
auditing for masses, 111–113
    auditor responsibilities, 111–112
    authority and responsibility, 113
    documentation, 113
    general controls, 112
    internal controls, 112
    performance checks and accountability, 113
    separation of duties and least privilege, 112–113
    specific controls, 112
audit management planning, 129–144
    auditing common systems vulnerabilities, 137–143
    audit programs, 132–133
    audit report, 143–144
    audit risk, 130
    audit work papers, 143
    common attacks, 136
    development of audit program, 135
    flawed systems, 136–137
    planning of audit, 130–132
    standard audit programs, 133–134
    useful Internet sites, 136
auditors, 113–117
    attributes, 114–115
    code of ethics and conduct, 115
    external impairments, 116
    free and independent, 115–116
    organizational impairments, 116
    personal impairments, 116–117
    qualifications, 113–114
controls, 117–118
E-commerce Web sites, 214–227
    auditing Windows NT and XP, 227
    auditing workstations, 219–220
    audit program items, 216–217
    chargeback issues, 216
    cookies, 226–227
    credit card authentication, 215–216
    e-mail sent by employees, 224–225
    first steps, 220
    implementing fraud screening to identify high-risk transactions, 217–218
    keystroke monitors, 227
    looking in right places, 225–226
    organizing and searching file systems, 221–222
    settlement, 216
    signs of possible online credit card fraud, 218–219
    unformatting and undeleting, 222
    Windows Registry investigations, 222–224

evidence collection, 121–129
    flowcharts, 126
    homework, 122–123
    interview analysis, 124
    interviewing for evidence of controls, 123–124
    interview preparation, 122
    interviews, 121–122
    interview steps, 123
    questionnaires, 125–126
    taking care of stakeholders, 128–129
    types of flowcharts, 126–127
firewall auditing, 204–206
    barbarians at wall, 204–205
    firewall rulebase, 205–206
    logging, 206
network vulnerability assessments, 171–191
    assessment safety, 176–177
    automated vulnerability tools, 185–187
    discovering character of audit target, 177–180
    domain name server, DNS, and zone transfers, 184–185
    homework, 187–191
    identifying operating systems, 183–184
    IP address confirmation, 176
    rules of engagement, 173–174
    social engineering, 174–176
    system parts that are alive, 180–182
remote system administration, 202–204
security measures preventing automated attacks, 212–214
    root tools to gain access, 212–213
    users of attacking tools, 213–214
specialized auditing matters, 154–171
    access controls, 156
    auditing databases, 154
    auditing UNIX, 163–166
    auditing Windows NT, 168–171
    audit trail controls, 158
    database concurrency controls in distributed environment, 157–158
    database definitions, 154–156
    database existence controls, 158–159
    discretionary access controls, 156
    domain servers, 159–162
    format of /etc/passwd file, 167–168
    format of shadow file, 168
    mandatory access controls, 156–157
    object reuse, 158
    protecting against DNS cache corruption, 162–163
    software controls and update protocols, 157
    UNIX shadow password file, 166–167
subsystem interaction and reliability, 118–121
    audit procedures, 120–121

generally accepted government auditing
        standards, 120
    risks affecting auditors, 119–120
vulnerability self-assessments, 150–154
    disaster recovery and business
        resumption, 153
    emergency power management, 152
    employee security awareness training, 154
    environmental conditions, 152
    hardware, 151
    media, 153–154
    network protocols, 152
    physical security, 151
    software, 153
Web application vulnerability assessments,
        191–202
    accidental error messages, 194–195
    Achilles, 199
    audit findings, 202
    audit issues, 202
    automated Web tools, 199–201
    Cookie Pal, 198–199
    get vs. post commands in CGI forms,
        196–197
    hidden form elements, 195–196
    HTML examination, 192
    overflow vulnerabilities, 195
    quality control issues, 201
    reporting vulnerability assessment results,
        201–202
    testing for indexed directories, 192–193
    unexpected user input, 195
    unicode input attack, 198
    Web page referrer fields, 198
    Web server examination, 193–194
Windows NT, 227
wireless networks, 206–212
    auditor considerations for wireless
        networks, 211–212
    basic wi-fi architecture, 207–208
    cloaking SSIDs, 209
    802.11b headers, 208
    802.11b information packet types, 208
    WEP, 209
    wi-fi audit program features, 209–210
    wi-fi network detection, 208
    wireless denial-of-service attacks, 211
workstation, 219, 220
Auditor(s), 103
    attributes, 114
    data controls, 104
    disaster recovery, 104
    risk assessment reviews by, 38
    systems development and programming
        policies, 104
    workstation audit policies, 104
AUP, *see* Appropriate Use Policy
Authentication, 92, 475

B

Back doors, 24
Back Orifice, 251
Backup(s), 242
    definition of, 5
    e-mail, 53, 54
    procedures, 158
    security, 477
Bank examiners, risk assessment reviews by, 38
Banner(s), 68, 69
    definition of, 5
    opening, 474
Banyan VINES, 169
Basic input/output system (BIOS), 5, 101
    access information, 273
    activation, 271
    passwords, 101, 151, 274
Beltway Snipers, 341
Berkley Internet Domain (BIND), 138
BIND, *see* Berkley Internet Domain
BIOS, *see* Basic input/output system
Bivens v. Six Unknown Federal Narcotics Agents,
        342–343
Black-hat system attacking, 172
BlackWidow, 503
Blakey v. Continental Airlines, Inc., 394
Boot
    disk, 282, 283
    utilities, 283
Bourke v. Nissan Motor Corp., 394
Broadcast domains, 250
Browsing, suspicious, 487
Brutus, 200
Buffer overflows, 137
Business
    plan, 37
    recovery, 35, 37
Busting root, 212
BWINET, 211

C

C++, 172
Cable TV Privacy Act, 401
Cache corruption, 163
California Business and Professional Code, 64
Calling Line Identification, 474
Capability Maturity Model® (CMM), 44, 47
Cellular telephones, 145, 151
CERT, *see* Computer Emergency Response Team
CERT Coordination Center, 468, 484, 494
Certified Information Systems Auditor (CISA),
        115
CGI, *see* Common Gateway Interface
Chain of custody schedule, 264
Change control management, 192

Chart(s)
    Critical Path Method, 12, 13
    examples, 13
    Gantt, 12, 13
    organizational, 122
Children's Online Privacy Protection Act
    (COPPA), 402, 404
CIA, *see* Confidentiality, integrity, and availability
CIDR, *see* Classless Inter-Domain Routing
CIRT
    ad hoc, 327
    commercial, 325
    communications, 329
    development life cycle, 339
    funding, 328
    in-house, 326
    management skills, 334
    people skills, 335
    requirements, 327
    success metrics, 338
CISA, *see* Certified Information Systems Auditor
Civil suits, 374
    civil discovery, 376
    civil processes, 375
    e-mail discovery, 376
    federal laws applicable to computer-related
        crimes, 378
    plaintiff's burden of proof, 375
Classless Inter-Domain Routing (CIDR), 238, 239
Classroom training sessions, 51
CLI, *see* Command line interface
CMM, *see* Capability Maturity Model®
CMOS, *see* Complementary Metal Oxide
    Semiconductor
Coaching, 18
COBIT™, 133
Code of ethics and conduct, auditor, 115
CodeRed virus, 329
Cold sites, 30
Cold telephone calls, 67
Command line interface (CLI), 293
Command post (CP), 233
Common Gateway Interface (CGI), 23, 138
    Output, 201
    scanner, PERL language-based, 200
    vulnerabilities, 199
Common Vulnerability and Exposure (CVE), 136,
    137, 186, 202
Communications sub-team, 36
Company assets, laws affecting protection of, 8,
    9
Complementary Metal Oxide Semiconductor
    (CMOS), 272
Computer
    crime, cost of, 357
    Crime and Security Survey, 230
    Emergency Response Team (CERT), 1
    evidence, examination of, 262

    forensics examiners, 81
    intrusions, 258
    names, 1
    Security Incident Response Teams (CSIRTs),
        484
Computer Security Institute (CSI), 2, 229
Computer Security Resource Clearinghouse, 496
Confidentiality, 471
    attorney–client, 64
    auditor, 115
    integrity, and availability (CIA), 26, 154
Consultant procedures, 88
Contract language, 88
Controls
    audit trail, 158
    database
        concurrency, 157
        existence, 158
Cookie(s), 198
    caches, 297
    definition of, 226
    disabling of, 102
Cookie Pal, 198, 199
COPPA, *see* Children's Online Privacy Protection
    Act
Copyright(s), 344
    cases, criminal actions in, 345
    employee, 61
    infringement, 345
    laws, 61
    protection, 345
    sample, 62
    violation, 57
Corporate espionage, 343
Corrective controls, 117
Counterfeit goods, criminal prosecution for
    trafficking in, 346
CP, *see* Command post
CPM chart, *see* Critical Path Method chart
Crack, 503
Credit card
    authentication, 215
    fraud, 218
Credit-reporting agency, 400
Crime scene investigation, 250
Criminal law, 358
    allegations, 359
    appeals, 374
    computer evidence, 366
    court orders, 364
    criminal discovery, 371
    criminal plea bargains, 373
    criminal procedure, 370
    defense arguments relative to expert
        witnesses, 366
    electronic discovery, 372
    e-mail as evidence, 372
    expert testimony, 365

federal legal requirements for electronic
surveillance, 367
grand juries, 360
investigation, 359
means of collecting electronic evidence, 367
search warrants, 362
sentencing, 374
subpoenas and summons, 361
testimony, 365
trials, 373
witnesses, 359
Critical assets
damage to, 3
definition of, 5
management of, 112
priority-ranked, 32
safeguarding of, 119
Critical incident analysis, parts of, 11
Critical incident response and CIRT
development, 229–340
CIRT composition, 331–340
CIRT development life cycle, 339–340
CIRT management skills, 334
CIRT success metrics, 338–339
communication skills, 334–335
crisis, 336
database managers, 333
engineers/software developers, 333
human resources unit, 332
incident reporting, 335–336
IT investigative, analysis, and forensic
experts, 332
IT security officers, 333
legal unit, 332
people skills, 335
public relations, 332
response steps for legal actions, 336–338
system owners, 333–334
systems administrators, 333
team skills, 334
technical skills, 334
telecommunications specialists, 333
collecting evidence, 260–267
activity log, 265
chain of custody schedule, 264
common mistakes when handling
evidence, 263
definition of evidence, 260–261
evidence prioritization, 261–262
evidence tags, 265
examining computer evidence, 262–263
hostile interview environments, 267
policies and procedures, 263
recorded statements, 266
witness reports, 265–266
critical incident detection, 235–260
administrator facilitated attacks, 258–259
application logging, 241–242

attack underway, 253
business considerations before legal
actions, 260
business issues, 245
critical incident checklist, 249
critical incident response personnel, 247
critical incident response tools, 246–247
critical incident symptoms, 236
determining response strategy, 252
DNS, 239
frequent backups, 242–243
hardening servers, 242
interviewing managers, 252
interviewing system administrators, 251
interviewing users, 251
interviews, 250
IP addresses, 238–239
IP addressing, 237–238
law enforcement liaison, 256–257
law enforcement relations, 254–256
legal issues, 245
locating origin of denial-of-service attacks,
240
location of attacker, 253–254
mission statement, 247–248
other relative issues, 259
political issues, 245–246
resources, 240
response to scene, 248
response strategy, 236–237
restoring service operations, 253
senior manager's approval, 259
suspicious activity reports, 256
system map, 250
system monitoring structure, 244–245
system security architecture, 243–244
time stamps, 244
types of attacks, 257–258
UNIX logging, 240–241
user security training, 243
Windows logging, 241
critical incident management, 229–235
command post operations, 233–235
critical incident planning, 232–233
critical incident response, 230–231
critical incident response strategy,
231–232
firefighter response model, 231
evidence examination, 296–307
autocomplete entries in registry, 299–300
changing user passwords, 298–299
chronology of events, 307
cracking user passwords, 299
evidence on Windows operating systems,
296–297
going native, 298
good places for evidence, 300
legal cautions, 307

logical file review in Windows, 297–298
looking at relevant files, 306–307
looking for specific words, 306
looking at Windows registry, 299
offline log reviews, 305–306
partitions, 302
partition status, 302–303
password-protected and encrypted files,
    303
print spooler files, 303–304
recycle bin, 300–302
Windows NT logging, 304–305
forensic investigation, 285–293
    common e-mail headers, 292
    DOS-based operating systems file
        deletions, 287–288
    e-mail with firewall headers, 290–291
    e-mail processing, 288–290
    file slack and free space, 287
    networking review, 292–293
    network resources, 292
    physical level search, 286–287
    reading e-mail headers, 288
    relaying, 291–292
forming critical incident response team,
    324–331
    added CIRT responsibilities, 328
    ad hoc CIRTs, 327
    CIRT, 325
    CIRT communications, 329–330
    CIRT funding, 328–329
    CIRT requirements and roles, 327
    developing critical incident cost analyses,
        330–331
    people supported by CIRT, 329
    using in-house talent, 326–327
    using outside consultants, 325–326
malicious code attacks, 315–324
    anonymous remailers, 323–324
    digital bloodhounds, 317–318
    domain registration payments, 322
    dynamic host control protocol tracing,
        320–321
    investigating identity of attacker, 321–322
    IP addresses, 318
    nicks and monikers, 322–323
    resolving IP addresses, 318–319
    things to do after, 317
    trace route, 319–320
    Trojan horses and logic bombs, 316–317
    viruses, 315–316
performing forensic duplication, 267–285
    attaching hard drive, 271
    BIOS, 271–272
    BIOS passwords, 272–274
    boot disk, 282, 283
    different approaches to media
        duplication, 269–270

disabling DRVSPACE.BIN, 283–284
EnCase, 285
forensically sound duplication tools, 281
forensic media duplication tools, 281
hard disk construction, 274–275
information hiding in Windows FAT, 278
physical write blockers, 284
Power-On Self Test, 272
producing hash values, 281–282
relative addressing, 275–276
removing target hard drive, 270–271
steps to follow when collecting evidence,
    268–269
undeleting in Windows-based operating
    systems, 277–278
UNIX dd commands, 285
UNIX file system, 279–280
using Safeback in forensic duplications,
    284–285
Windows DOS-based file allocation table,
    276–277
Windows NT file system, 278–279
responding to Windows NT incidents,
    293–296
    collecting volatile live-time evidence, 296
    data storage, 293–294
    open ports and listening services, 295
    processes running on target computer,
        295–296
    responders turned off, 294
    system users, 294
    tolls in tool bag, 293
UNIX-based investigations, 307–315
    baseline comparison for SUID/SGID files,
        314
    coroner's toolkit, 309–310
    data hiding techniques, 309
    file recovery alternatives for UNIX/Linux,
        312
    file stamps, 312–314
    hiding files, 310–311
    log files, 314–315
    steganography, 311
    strong encrypted protections, 312
    system configuration, 314
    undeleting UNIX, 308
    understanding file permissions, 312
    UNIX file system analysis, 307–308
    user and password accounts, 314
Critical Incident Response Team, 153
Critical Path Method (CPM) chart, 12, 13
CRM, *see* Customer Resource Management
Crying wolf, 232
Cryptography, 468
CSI, *see* Computer Security Institute
CSIRTs, *see* Computer Security Incident
        Response Teams
Customer Resource Management (CRM), 52

CVE, *see* Common Vulnerability and Exposure
Cybersquatters, 349

D

DAC, *see* Discretionary Access Control
Data
    administration management, 118
    backup practices, 29
    blocks, 308
    classification, 28
    controls, 104
    disclosure, 387
    entry, 99
    flowchart, 127
    fragmented, 287
    -gathering tools, 309
    hiding techniques, 309
    integrity, 119
    libraries, 98
    manipulation, 155
    privacy, Best Practices, 386
    recovery sub-team, 36
    storage, Windows NT incidents, 293
    -transmission habits, 385
Database(s)
    administration, 99
    auditing of, 154
    chronology, 235
    concurrency controls, 157
    definitions, 154
    existence controls, 158
    management system (DBMS), 154
    managers, 333
    Securities Exchange Commission, 178
Daubert v. Merrell Dow Pharmaceuticals, Inc.,
    365
DBMS, *see* Database management system
Defamation
    claims of, 57–58
    definition of, 24
Demilitarized zone (DMZ), 5, 97, 152, 160, 185,
    324
Denial-of-service (DoS) attacks, 3, 23, 70
    origin of, 240, 258
    wireless, 211
Department Operating Procedure (DOP),42
Design patents, 351
Detective controls, 117
DHCP, *see* Dynamic Host Control Protocol
Dial-in users, 474
Digital certificates, 92
Directory privileges, unauthorized changes of,
    236
Disaster recovery, 104
    plans, 32
    training, 34

Discretionary Access Control (DAC), 155
Discrimination
    claims of, 57–58
    definition of, 24
Disk geometry, 275
Distributed denial-of-service attacks, 23
DMZ, *see* Demilitarized zone
DNS, *see* Domain Name System
Document flowcharts, 126, 127
Domain Name System (DNS), 23, 138, 159, 184,
    462
    cache corruption, 162
    names, 176, 239
    purpose of, 239
Domain registration
    payments, 322
    queries, 178
DOP, *see* Department Operating Procedure
DoS attacks, *see* Denial-of-service attacks
DOS-based operating systems file deletions, 287
Driver licensing, 381
Dumpsec, 503
Duplication tools, forensically sound, 281
Dynamic Host Control Protocol (DHCP), 85, 320

E

Earthquake threat, 22
E-commerce, 191
    merchants, 216
    one-stop shopping, 389
    sites, attacker invading, 219
    Web sites, auditing of, 214
Economic espionage, 343
Economic Espionage Act, 62
ECPA, *see* Electronic Communications Privacy
    Act
Electronic communications, privacy of, 55
Electronic Communications Privacy Act (ECPA),
    5, 58
Electronic evidence, means of collecting, 367
Electronic media, 50
Electronic privacy statement, 60
E-mail
    accounts, size of, 54
    attachments, 56
        employees opening, 41
        viruses executed through, 23
    attorney–client, 65
    backing up of, 53
    client communications using, 64
    confidentiality of, 55
    deletion of, 53
    delivery, 464
    discovery, 376
    employee, 15, 224
    encrypted, 57

forwarded, 56
good, 52
headers, 288, 292
interior network handling, 94
message
    employee filing of in personal folders, 394
    priority, 56
naming conventions, 177
PIN, 404
policy
    risks of, 51
    violation, 46
privacy policies, 57
processing, 288
retention policy, 55
services, Web-based, 323
signatures, 56
spelling and grammar, 56
unsolicited, 63
Web-based, 224
Embezzlement, 159, 354
Emergency
    assessment, information collected during, 237
    management team, 35
    operation(s)
        center (EOC), 34
        plans, 33
        sub-team, 35
    processes, 34
    recovery processes, 34
Employee(s)
    behavior
        policy information, most-valuable source
            of, 15
        reasons for monitor, 59
    copyright concerns, 61
    e-mail, 15, 224
    feedback, 323
    fraud controls, 355
    Internet activity logs, 225
    IT, 105
    labor organization, 63
    monitoring best practices, 396
    polygraphs, 397
    privacy, 57, 391
        policy, 91
        rights, 248
        training, 388
    responsibility for entry methods, 67
    security awareness training, 153
    software installation, 68, 69
    termination, 107
    trade secrets and, 62
    training, 108
        business recovery processes, 35
        disaster recovery, 34
        emergency processes, 34
        evacuation, 34

notification process, 34
orientation, 34
promotion, 34
relocation procedures, 35
salvage operations, 35
standardized, 33
working at home, 59
EnCase, 270, 271, 285
    law enforcement agency use of, 285
    string search capability of, 306
EOC, *see* Emergency operations center
Error messages, accidental, 194
Espionage, 343
Ethereal, 503
Eudora, 224, 246
European Commissions Directive on Data
    Protection, 405
European Union Data Protection Directive,
    406
Event logs, creation of, 70
Evidence, 356
    collection, 121, 260
        flowcharts, 126
        homework, 122
        interviews, 121, 122, 123, 124
        questionnaires, 125–126
        taking care of stakeholders, 127
    common mistakes when handling, 263
    computer, examination of, 262
    definition of, 260
    electronic, means of collecting, 367
    e-mail as, 372
    examination, 296
        autocomplete entries in Registry, 299
        changing user passwords, 298
        chronology of events, 307
        cracking user passwords, 299
        going native, 298
        good places for evidence, 300
        legal cautions, 307
        logical file review in, 297
        looking at relevant files, 306
        looking for specific words, 306
        offline log reviews, 305
        partitions, 302
        partition status, 302
        password-protected and encrypted files,
            303
        print spooler files, 303
        Recycle Bin, 300
        Windows NT logging, 304
        Windows operating systems, 296
        Windows Registry, 299
    good places for, 300
    live-time, 296
    prioritization, 261
    recovery, 81
    steps to follow when collecting, 268

tags, 265
writing over, 263
Exposure value, 5

F

Facilities
    outsourcing, 30
    sub-team, 36
Failure, definition of, 70
Fair Credit Reporting Act (FCRA), 399
Family education privacy rights, 400
FAT, *see* File allocation table
Fault tolerance, 5, 20, 69
FCRA, *see* Fair Credit Reporting Act
Fear, uncertainty, doubt (FUD), 5, 8, 41
Federal Bureau of Investigation, 229, 482
Federal law, suspected violation of, 256
Federal Privacy Act, 405
Federal Rules of Criminal Procedure, 371
Federal Rules of Evidence, 81
Federal Trade Commission, 400, 404
Federal Trade Commission Act, 407
File(s)
    allocation table (FAT), 276
        disk formatted with, 277
        information hiding in, 278
    permissions, 312
    stamps, 312
    system logging, 476
    Transfer Protocol (FTP), 169
Financial attack, 196
Finanzoffice, 211
Fire
    safety, 76
    threat of, 22
Firefighter response model, 231
Firewall(s), 2
    administration, 98
        policy, 94, 95
        remote, 95
        unit, audit management plan for, 132
    application, 93
    auditing, 204
    backup policy, 95
    breach, 243
    hardware, 93
    headers, e-mail with, 290
    logs, 206
    mailing list, 495
    packet-filtering, 92
    policy, 91
    reputation of, 466
    rulebase, 205
    types, 92
    ultimate, 10
Flame-wars, 323

Flowchart(s)
    data, 127
    document, 126, 127
    program, 129
Foreign Corrupt Practices Act, 9
Forensic duplication, 267, 284
Forensic investigation, 285
    common e-mail headers, 292
    DOS-based operating systems file deletions,
        287
    e-mail with firewall headers, 290
    e-mail processing, 288
    file slack and free space, 287
    networking review, 292
    network resources, 292
    physical level search, 286
    reading e-mail headers, 288
    relaying, 291
Forensic software, 247, 285
Forensic Toolkit, 503
For Official Use Only (FOUO), 52
Foundstone Web site, 295
FOUO, *see* For Official Use Only
Fourth Amendment, 362
Fport, 503
FQDN, *see* Fully Qualified Domain Name
Frame Relay, 250, 473
Fraud, 216
    credit card, 218
    -detection services, 215
    rate, 217
    screening, 217
    workplace, 354
        accountability, 355
        employee fraud controls, 355
        management functions in fraud control,
            355
        records, 356
FTP, *see* File Transfer Protocol
FTP servers
    anonymous, 461, 463
    improperly configured, 465
FUD, *see* Fear, uncertainty, doubt
Fully Qualified Domain Name (FQDN), 319

G

GAGAS, *see* Generally Accepted Government
        Auditing Standards
Gantt charts, 12, 13
Generally Accepted Government Auditing
        Standards (GAGAS), 120
Ghost, 270, 271, 281, 503
GISRA, *see* Government Information Security
        Reform Act
Glass technology, 274
Globally Unique Identifier (GUID), 220

Google, 178, 196
Gopher servers, 461
Government Information Security Reform Act
    (GISRA), 9
Gramm–Leach–Bliley Act, 9, 398
Grand jury subpoena, 356
Granularity, definition of, 5
Graphical user interface (GUI), 177, 293
Grave-robber, 313
Gray-hat system attacking, 172
GUI, *see* Graphical user interface
GUID, *see* Globally Unique Identifier

H

Hacker
    activity, monitoring of, 488
    definition of, 5
Harassment
    claims of, 57
    sexual, 61
Hard disk construction, 274
Hard drive
    formatting of, 275
    removal of target, 270
Hard link, 280
Hardware
    keyboard monitors, 311
    tools, critical incident response, 246
Hash
    definition of, 5
    value, 281
HDA, *see* Head disk assembly
Head disk assembly (HDA), 274
Health Insurance Portability and Accountability
    Act (HIPAA), 9, 398, 399
Help desk, server, 100
Hex editor, 277, 283, 306
High Technology Crime Investigators
    Association (HTCIA), 257
HIPAA, *see* Health Insurance Portability and
    Accountability Act
Honeypots, 337
Host, definition of, 5
Hot grounders, 145
Hotmail, 323
Hot sites, 31
HRMail, 211
HTCIA, *see* High Technology Crime Investigators
    Association
HTML, *see* HyperText Markup Language
HTTP
    referrer header field, 198
    server, 193
Human threats, 23
HyperText Markup Language (HTML), 192, 247
    delimiter characters, 195

examination, 192
hidden form elements, 195

I

ICANN, *see* Internet Corporation for Assigned
    Names and Numbers
ICMP, *see* Internet Control Management Protocol
IDE drives, 274
IDS, *see* Intrusion Detection System
IEEE, *see* Institute of Electrical and Electronics
    Engineers
Industrial Revolution, 25
Industries, laws affecting, 9
INFO files, 301
Information
    assets inventory, 384
    classification schedule, 28
    flow, charts documenting, 16
    hiding, 278
    ownership, 382
    privacy, threats to, 383
    systems
        attacks concentrating on, 2
        managers, 118
        support policies, 98
    technology (IT), 105
        audit, major steps of, 129
        auditors, goals of, 119
        department, audit program for small,
            147–150
        security officers, 333
    vulnerability, 382
Information Systems Audit and Control
    Association (ISACA), 115, 133, 257
Information Systems Security Association (ISSA),
    257
Instant Messenger, 385
Institute of Electrical and Electronics Engineers
    (IEEE), 83, 207
Insurance, definition of, 25
Intellectual property, 232, 343, 455
Internal controls, 112
International Standards Organization, 43, 134
Internet
    activity logs, employee, 225
    browsing, 102, 246
    connection, 69, 233
    Control Management Protocol (ICMP), 181
    default password on, 274
    domain names, 348
    firewall policy, 91
    Protocol (IP), 237
        address architecture, 240
        address blocks, 238
        address confirmation, 176
        spoofing, 467

Relay Chat (IRC), 85, 297
Service Providers, 217
Web sites, audit management planning, 136
Internet Corporation for Assigned Names and Numbers (ICANN), 349
Interview
environments, hostile, 267
method, most time-consuming, 14
Intrusion attack(s)
detection of, 70
patterns, 70
Intrusion Detection System (IDS), 2, 211
dream, 96
host-based, 96
product vendors, 96
Inventory
information assets, 384
theft, 354
Investigator goals, 342
IP, *see* Internet Protocol
IRC, *see* Internet Relay Chat
IRS Procedure 86-19, 9
ISACA, *see* Information Systems Audit and Control Association
ISO 9000, 43, 47
ISO 17799, 134
ISSA, *see* Information Systems Security Association
IT, *see* Information technology

J

Java, 172, 247
Job
interviews, 106
performance measurement, 107
John the Ripper, 503
Jphs, 503
Judges, risk assessment reviews by, 38

K

KDC, *see* Key distribution center
Kerberos, 469
Key distribution center (KDC), 469
Keylogger, 503
Keystroke monitors, 227
KISS idea, 28
Klez virus, 329

L

Labor organization, employee, 63
LANs, *see* Local area networks

Laser printer, 476
Law enforcement agents, risk assessment reviews by, 38
Lawyers, risk assessment reviews by, 38
Lazy writing, 279
Least privilege, 113, 391
Legal matters, 341–379
civil suits, 374–375
civil discovery, 376, 377
civil process, 375–376
e-mail discovery, 376–377
federal laws applicable to computer-related crimes, 378–379
plaintiff's burden of proof, 375
common types of unlawful acts, 343
cost of computer crime, 357–358
criminal law, 358–374
allegations, 359
appeals, 374
computer evidence, 366–367
court orders, 364–365
criminal discovery, 371–372
criminal plea bargains, 373
criminal procedure, 370–371
defense arguments relative to expert witnesses, 366
electronic discovery, 372
e-mail as evidence, 372–373
evidence, 370
expert testimony, 365
federal legal requirements for electronic surveillance, 367
grand juries, 360–361
investigation, 359
means of collecting electronic evidence under federal statutes, 367
search warrants, 362–364
sentencing, 374
subpoenas and summons, 361–362
testimony, 365
trials, 373–374
witnesses, 359–360
evidence collection, preservation, analysis, and introduction at trial, 356–357
fraud in workplace, 354–356
accountability, 355
employee fraud controls, 355
management functions in fraud control, 355
records, 356
intellectual property, 343–354
copyright infringement, 345
copyright protection, 345
criminal actions in copyright cases, 345
criminal copyright forfeiture, 346
criminal forfeiture, 353–354
criminal prosecution for trafficking in counterfeit goods or services, 346

cybersquatters, 349
cybersquatter-victim protection, 349–351
duration of copyright protection, 345
filing for patent protection, 352
Internet domain names and registered
    marks, 348
inventor, 351–352
obtaining trade secrets protection, 354
patent ownership, 352
patent protections, 351
patent terms, 352
patent validity, 352
protected trade secrets, 352–353
protected works, 346–347
public notification, 348
qualifications for design patents, 351
qualifications for utility patents, 351
trademark and service mark ownership,
    347
trademark and service mark protection,
    346, 347
trade secrets, 352
works that can be copyrighted, 344–345
works that cannot be copyrighted, 346
investigators' goals, 342–343
legal functions, 341–342
Legislatures, risk assessment reviews by, 38
LFS, *see* Log file service
Line-of-authority documentation, 122
Line printer logging, 476
Linux, 139
    evidence examination, 297
    password-protected user accounts, 102
Listservs, bulletins and, 504
Local area networks (LANs), 99
Log
    entries, gaps in, 236
    file service (LFS), 279
    reviews, 305
Logging
    application, 241
    file system, 476
    line printer, 476
    UNIX, 240
    Windows, 241, 304
Logic bombs, 316

M

MAC, *see* Mandatory Access Control
Mailing lists, 488, 495
    CERT™ advisory, 495
    Internet firewalls, 495
    USENET newsgroups, 496
    VIRUS-L list, 495
    World Wide Web pages, 496
Malicious code attacks, 315

anonymous remailers, 323
attacker identity, 321
digital bloodhounds, 317
domain registration payments, 322
Dynamic Host Control Protocol, 320
IP addresses, 318
nicks and monikers, 322
trace route, 319
Trojan horses and logic bombs, 316
viruses, 315
Malicious programming, 24
Malware, 5
Management metrics, 43
Mandatory Access Control (MAC), 155, 156
Maryland v. Brady, 372
McLaren v. Microsoft Corp., 394
Media
    contact log, 37
    duplication, 269
    mirror image, 377
Medical Laboratory Management Consultants v.
    ABC, Inc., 395
Melissa virus, 329
Mentor assignment, 108
Merchant accounts, 214
Microsoft, *see also* Windows
    Internet Information Server, 242
    Script Debugger, 169
Mirror image media, 377
MN Desk Reference, 503
Model(s)
    Capability Maturity, 44, 47
    firefighter response, 231
    quality, 43
Modem lines, management of, 473
Morris Worm, 229
Murphy's Law, 32, 139–140, 176

N

NAT, *see* Network Address Translation
National Crime Information Center (NCIC), 341
National Fire Protection Association, 22
National Infrastructure Protection Center (NIPC),
    22, 23
National Institute for Standards and Technology
    (NIST), 134
National Labor Relations Act (NLRA), 63
National Oceanic and Atmospheric
    Administration, 22
National Transportation Safety Board, 17
NCIC, *see* National Crime Information Center
Need-to-know concept, 28
Nessus, 187, 188, 189, 190, 191, 503
NetScan Tools, 177
Network(s)
    Address Translation (NAT), 93, 323

-based products, 96
-based scanners, 186
cable-connected, 392
classes, 238
connections, walk-up, 473
File Service (NFS), 465
IDS sensors, 96
information capture program, 162
Information Service (NIS), 462
interface card (NIC), 93, 209, 246
management policies, 77
open-ended, 159
protection, 462
protocols, 152
resources, forensic investigation, 292
topology map, 244
vulnerabilities, 82, 171
New York Stock Exchange (NYSE), 3
NFS, *see* Network File Service
NIC, *see* Network interface card
Nimda virus, 1, 329
NIPC, *see* National Infrastructure Protection
Center
NIS, *see* Network Information Service
NIST, *see* National Institute for Standards and
Technology
NLRA, *see* National Labor Relations Act
Nmap, 180, 182, 183, 503
No-knock search warrants, 363
Novell NetWare, 169
NTFS, *see* Windows NT file system
NTFSDOS, 503
NYSE, *see* New York Stock Exchange

O

Object reuse, 158
OCC, *see* Office of the Comptroller of the
Currency
Occam's razor, 14
O'Connor v. Ortega, 395
OFAC, *see* Office of Foreign Asset Control
Office of the Comptroller of the Currency (OCC),
256
Office of Foreign Asset Control (OFAC), 9
Office of Management and Budget (OMB), 8
OMB, *see* Office of Management and Budget
OOB communications, *see* Out-of-band
communications
Open-ended networks, 69, 70, 159
Operating systems
default installations of, 139
identification, 183
Operations management, 118
Oral communications, 392
Organization
impairments, auditor, 116

information vulnerability in, 392
threats occurring within, 25
Out-of-band (OOB) communications, 57
Outlook, 224
Outsourcing
facilities, 30
policies and procedures involving, 89
potentials, 88

P

Packet filtering
firewalls, 92
security table, 161
Panavision International, L.P. v. Toepen, 349
Partition status, 302
Password(s), 65, 66
accounts, 314
aging, 470
assurance, 470
BIOS, 101, 151, 274
brute force, 194, 311
changing, 298
cracking, 299
applications, 303
utilities, 236
Web pages, 303
default, 274
file, shadow, 166
hashes, 314
maintenance, 67
one-time, 66, 469
-protected
files, 303
screensaver, 101
removal, 139
screensaver, 151
weak, 139
Patent
protection, 351, 352
validity, 352
Payment gateway, 215
PBX, *see* Telephone Branch Exchange
PDA, *see* Personal digital assistant
PDD 63, *see* President's Decision Directive
Pen register installation, 393
Performance
checks, 113
metrics, 43
reviews, 107
standards, 43
testing, 69
PERL, 172
Personal digital assistant (PDA), 82
PGP, 504
Physical and environmental safety, 76
access controls, 76

building collapse, 76
fire safety factors, 76
plumbing leaks, 76
utilities failures, 76
workplace safety, 76
Physical facilities
    protection strategies concerning, 30
    redundant, 30
Physical write blocker utilities, 284
POC, *see* Points of contact
Points of contact (POC), 481, 482
Policies and procedures, 41–109
    auditors, 103–105
        data controls, 104
        disaster recovery and business continuity,
            104–105
        systems development and programming
            policies, 104
        workstation audit policies, 105
    connecting to Internet, 69–71
    e-mail policy, 51
    e-mail storage, 54
    employee privacy expectations and legal
        rights, 57–69
        attorney–client communications using e-
            mail, 64–65
        copyright violation, 68
        ECPA, 58
        employee copyright concerns, 61–62
        employee labor organization, 63
        employee software installation, 68
        employees and trade secrets, 62–63
        employees working at home, 59–60
        harassment, discrimination, and
            defamation, 60–61
        part-time and full-time employees, 60
        passwords, 65–66
        privacy acknowledgments, 59
        privacy arguments, 59
        reasons to monitor and audit employee
            behavior, 59
        security through obscurity, 67
        shoulder surfing, 67
        something person has, 66
        something person is, 66
        something person knows, 66
        spamming, spoofing, and organization,
            63–64
        use of banners, 68–69
    employee use of e-mail, 54–57
        attachments, 56
        bad news, 55
        confidentiality, 55
        e-mail for managers, 57
        encrypted communications, 57
        forwarded e-mail, 56
        message priority, 56
        negotiations, 55

out-of-band communications, 57
plain, professional language, 55–56
salutations and signatures, 56
spam, 56
spelling and grammar, 56–57
enhancements to written policies, 50–51
    audio/video productions, 50–51
    classroom training sessions, 51
forensics policy, 78–81
    secure sockets layer, 84
    service set identifier, 83–84
    virtual privacy network, 84
    wireless network security, 82–85
    wireless policies, 84–85
information systems support policies, 98–100
    data entry, 99
    technical support, 99–100
information technology human resources
        management policies, 105–108
    employee departures on good terms, 108
    employee termination, 107–108
    getting best candidates for position,
        105–106
    job interviews, 106–107
    performance reviews, 107
information tsunami, 51–52
Internet firewall policy, 91–95
    application firewalls, 93
    authentication, 92
    firewall administration, 94
    firewall types, 92–93
    hardware firewall architectures, 93–94
    remote firewall administration, 95
intrusion detection policies, 95–96
    host-based IDs, 96
    network and host IDs, 96
network management policies, 77–78
network vulnerability assessment policies,
        85–87
    identifying exposures, 86–87
    plan to conduct vulnerability assessments,
        86
    resolving exposures, 87
organization of documents, 53–54
physical and environmental safety, 76–77
policies and procedures involving
        outsourcing, 89–91
policies, procedures, standards, and politics,
        41–42
policy distributions, 50
policy of policy development, 44–48
    changes, 46
    common policy components, 45–46
    doing policy right first time, 48
    executive approvals, 46
    policy exemptions, 46
    policy team members, 45
    team leadership, 45

vetting policies, 48
violations, 46–48
policy writing techniques, 48–50
application, 49
eternal view, 49
gender words, 49
plain language, 48–49
responsibility for compliance, 50
spelling and grammar, 49
securing systems, 100–103
systems development life cycle, 71–75
benefits, 72
documentation, 73–74
integrated product team, 72–73
management controls, 73
system accreditation and certification, 74–75
trust models, 44
vendor policies and procedures, 87–89
consultant procedures, 88–89
evaluating proposals, 89
outsource potentials, 88
outsource vendor selection procedures, 89
Web server policies and procedures, 97–98
Web server security policies and procedures, 97
Policy(ies)
employee privacy, 91
exemptions, 46
firewall administration, 94, 95
firewall backup, 95
forensics, 78
information system support, 98
Internet firewall, 91
intrusion detection, 95
IT human resources management, 105
outsourcing, 89
reasons for documenting, 43
systems development, 75, 104
vendor, 87
Web server, 97
wireless, 84
workstation audit, 104
Polygraph testing, 397
Pornography, 6
Port numbers, well-known, 409–449
POST, *see* Power-On Self Test
Power-On Self Test (POST), 272
President's Decision Directive (PDD 63), 8
Press
relations, 36, 37
releases, 485
Preventive controls, 117
Printer
laser, 476
logging, 476
sharing, 142

Print spooler files, 303
Privacy, 381–407
acknowledgments, 59
arguments, 59
employee, 391–397
employee legal defense, 395–396
employee monitoring best practices, 396–397
employee polygraphs, 397
legalities in employee monitoring, 391–392
monitoring e-mail and employee workstation conduct, 394–395
oral communications, 392
trap and trace and pen register installations, 393
video and still camera monitoring, 393–394
wire communications, 392–393
expectations, 381–383
information ownership, 382
information vulnerability in organization, 382–383
threats to information privacy, 383
industry-specific issues, 397–402
access to financial records, 397–398
Cable TV Privacy Act, 401
Children's Online Privacy Protection Act, 402–404
Fair Credit Reporting Act, 399–400
Family Education Privacy Rights, 400–401
Federal Privacy Act, 405
Gramm–Leach–Bliley Act, 398
Health Insurance Portability and Accountability Act, 398–399
safe harbor issues in United States, 405–407
wrongful disclosure of videotape rental or sale records, 401–402
protection, 383–391
auditing of privacy practices, 385–386
employee privacy training, 388–389
handling privacy in supply chains, 389–391
information assets inventory, 384
nonconsent information use, 388
policies and procedures, 385
privacy training best practices, 389
safeguarding, processing, and storing privacy data, 386–387
technology relevant to, 384–385
Web site privacy, 386
violations, 24
Privilege escalation, 23
Professional conduct, 61
Program flowchart, 129
Project failure, 11
Property ownership, 381

Prosecutors, risk assessment reviews by, 38
Protected works, 346
Proximate causation, 357
Proxy server, 464, 466
Public key encryption, RSA, 282
Public relations, 331, 485
Public service announcements, 231

Q

QOS, *see* Quality Operating Procedure
Qualitative analysis, 21
Quality
    assurance testing, 192
    models, 43
    Operating Procedure (QOS), 42
Quantitative analysis, 21
Questionnaire, sample, 19

R

RAM space, 286
RAS, *see* Remote Access Service
Recovery procedures, 32, 158–159
Recycle Bin, 297, 300
Relative addressing, 275, 276
Remote Access Service (RAS), 294
Remote control programs, 24
Remote Procedure Calls (RPC), 139
Remote system administration, 202
Replay attacks, 462
Responsibility(ies)
    compliance, 50
    unwritten, 33
Risk
    analysis report, 6
    assessment(s), 14
        best practices in, 16
        report, 38, 39
        schedule, 27
    audit, 130
    definition of, 6
Risk management, 1–40
    advice, 38
    ancient history, 1–3
        game plan, 2–3
        Maginot Line, 3
        recent events, 1–2
        senior management responsibilities, 3
    asset criticality, 20–21
    best practices in risk assessments, 16–18
        executive sponsorship, 16
        information resources, 16–17
        scope, 16
        team management dynamics, 17–18
    CIA, 9

critical incidents, 3–4
    disaster recovery plans, 32–35
    emergency management team, 35–36
        administrative support and supplies sub-team, 36
        communications sub-team, 36
        data recovery sub-team, 36
        emergency operations sub-team, 35
        facilities sub-team, 36
        transportation sub-team, 35
    facts, 18–20
    fear, uncertainty, and doubt, 7–8
    goal, 10–11
    law, 8–9
    mathematics, 21–22
    organization, 14–16
    original documentation, 37
    PDD 63, 8
    planning, 11–14, 71
        acquire and implement, 13
        assessment and critical incident program requirements, 11
        charting, 12–13
        monitor and revise, 13–14
        plan, 12
    press relations, 36–37
    programs, 2, 10
    protection strategies, 26–31
        backups, 29–30
        data classification, 28
        facilities outsourcing, 30–31
        getting organized, 31
        need-to-know, 28–29
        personnel, 26
        physical facilities, 30
        redundant physical facilities, 30
    questions, 20
    risk assessment reports, 38–39
        organizational change, 39
        simple risk management advice, 38
    risk-business, 10
    risk definitions, 5–7
    suggestions, 39–40
    team, 104
    testing of plan, 37–38
    threats, 22–26
Roadway Express v. NLRB, 63
Roll-back operation, 159
Root, definition of, 6
Rooting, 212
RPC, *see* Remote Procedure Calls
RSA public key encryption, 282

S

Sabotage, 25
Safeback, 270, 271, 284

Safeguards
  cost/benefit analysis of, 25
  definition of, 6
Safe harbor issues, United States, 405
SAINT, 186
SAM, *see* Security Account Manager
SAMBA, 297
SamSpade, 179, 320, 321, 504
SARA, 186
SARs, *see* Suspicious Activity Reports
Satellite-linked Internet connections, 233
Schwartzkopf, Norman, 36
Screensaver passwords, 101, 151
SCSI drives, 274
SDLC, *see* Systems development lifecycle
SearchString, 286
Search warrants, 362, 363
SEC, *see* Securities Exchange Commission
Secret Service, 482
Secure Sockets Layer (SSL), 84, 193
Securities Exchange Commission (SEC), 178
  database, 178
  filings, 179
Security
  Account Manager (SAM), 171
  log entries, 304
  policies, 456
  through obscurity, 67
Separation of duties, 112, 391
September 11, 2001, 1
Server
  FTP, 461, 463, 465
  help desk, 100
  proxy, 464, 466
  reboots, unexplained, 253
Service mark protection, 346, 347
Service Set Identifier (SSID), 83, 207, 208, 209
Sexual harassment, 61
Shadow file, 166, 168
Shareware, 180
Shoars v. Epson America, Inc., 394–395
Shoulder surfing, 67
Single loss expectancy (SLE), 6, 21, 22
SirCam virus, 329
SiteScan, 200
Site Security Handbook RFC 2196, 451–501
  abstract, 451
  architecture, 459–468
    firewalls, 466–468
    network and service configuration, 461–466
    objectives, 459–461
  introduction, 452–455
    audience, 453
    basic approach, 454
    definitions, 453–454
    purpose, 453

  related work, 454
  risk assessment, 454–456
mailing lists and other resources, 495–496
  CERT™ advisory, 495
  Internet firewalls, 495–496
  USENET newsgroups, 496
  VIRUS-L list, 495
  World Wide Web pages, 496
ongoing activities, 493–494
security incident handling, 478–493
  incident aftermath, 492–493
  incident handling, 488–492
  incident identification, 486–488
  notification and points of contact, 481–486
  preparing and planning for, 479–481
  responsibilities, 493
security policies, 456–459
  characteristics of good, 457–459
  definition, 456–457
  keeping policy flexible, 459
security services and procedures, 468–478
  access, 472–475
  auditing, 475–477
  authentication, 468–471
  authorization, 472
  confidentiality, 471
  integrity, 471–472
  securing backups, 477–478
status, 451
tools and locations, 494–495
Slammer virus, 329
SLE, *see* Single loss expectancy
Smart cards, 66, 154
Smoke screen, 489
SMTP Service, 169
Smyth v. The Pillsbury Co., 394
SNA Server, 169
Snort, 504
Social engineering, 172, 174, 175, 390
Soft link, 280
Software
  access, 67
  antivirus, 103, 153, 190
  configurations, default, 242
  controls, 157
  copyright sample, 62
  destructive, 68
  forensic, 247, 285
  installation
    employee, 68, 69
    policies, 139
  license, 153
  manuals, 244
  piracy, 343
  support, 100
  tools, critical incident response, 246

unauthorized, 101
        vulnerability self-assessment, 153
Solaris, 139
SOP, *see* Standard Operating Procedure
Source code, 90
Spam, 6, 56, 63, 323
Speedy Trial Act, 371
Spoofing, 64
Spyware, 102
SQL Server, 169
SSID, *see* Service Set Identifier
SSL, *see* Secure Sockets Layer
Standard Operating Procedure (SOP), 42
Stockholders, risk assessment reviews by,
        38
Strobe, 504
SUID/SGID files, comparison of, 314
SuperScan, 181, 504
Supply chains, handling privacy in, 389
Surge suppressor power strips, 246
Survivability, definition of, 69
Suspicious Activity Reports (SARs), 256
Suspicious browsing, 487
Symantec Ghost, 281, 302
Symbolic link, 280
System(s)
    administration, remote, 202
    attack(s)
        most frequent, 230
        recognition of, 70
        threats, 22–23
        white-hat, 172
    controls, understanding of, 120
    crashes, 486
    definition of, 6
    effectiveness, 119
    efficiency, 119
    flawed, 136
    intrusions, 486
    map, 250
    monitoring structure, 244
    owners, 333
    risks, 171
    security consultants, 173
Systems development lifecycle (SDLC), 71,
        135, 151
    benefits, 72
    design phase, 72
    development, 72, 86
    disposition phase, 73
    documentation, 73
    implementation phase, 73
    integration and test phase, 73
    management controls, 73
    methodology, 71
    operations and maintenance phase, 73
    planning phase, 72
    requirements analysis phase, 72

system accreditation and certification,
        74
system concept development phase, 72
vendor services and, 88

T

TCP, *see* Transmission Control Protocol
TCPdump, 162, 205
TCP/IP, 468
    protocols, 94
    stack, 193
Team(s)
    emergency management, 35
    formulation process, 12
    leadership, 45
    management dynamics, 17
    members, questions formulated by, 20
    risk management, 104
    SDLC project, 72
    skills, CIRT, 334
    vulnerabilities of to problems, 17
Telecommunications specialists, 333
Telecommuter(s)
    media convenient for, 50
    understanding of policies by, 60
Telephone
    Branch Exchange (PBX), 151
    numbers, trapping and tracing of, 393
Testimony, legal challenges to, 342
THC, 504
Threat(s), 6
    frequency, 22
    human, 23
    identification, 19, 22, 455
    system-attacker, 22–23
ThumbsPlus, 222
Time stamps, 158, 244
Trademark
    infringement, 349
    protection, 346, 347
Trade secret(s), 343
    employees and, 15, 62
    protected, 352, 354
Training
    classroom, 51
    employee, 108
        privacy, 388
        security awareness, 153
    user security, 243
Transaction
    management, 156
    tests, 121
Transferring risk safeguard, 4
Transmission Control Protocol (TCP), 181
Transportation sub-team, 35
Trap door, 6

Trap and trace installation, 393
Trojan horse, 6, 68, 70, 316

U

UDP, *see* User Datagram Protocol
Unicode input attack, 198
Uniform Domain Name Dispute Resolution
    Policy, 349, 350
United States v. Slanina, 396
UNIX, 136
    auditing, 163
    boot disk for, 246
    crypt program, 471
    dd command, 270, 281, 285
    file system, 279, 280
    hardware inventory, 164
    logging, 240
    shadow password file, 166
    sum program, 472
UNIX-based investigations, 307
    baseline comparison for SUID/SGID files,
        314
    coroner's toolkit, 309
    data hiding techniques, 309
    file recovery alternatives, 312
    file stamps, 312
    file system analysis, 307
    hiding files, 310
    log files, 314
    steganography, 311
    strong encrypted protections, 312
    system configuration, 314
    undeleting UNIX, 208
    understanding file permissions, 312
    user and password accounts, 314
Unlawful acts, types of, 343
URL, 227
U.S. copyright laws, 61
U.S. Department of Justice, 366
USENET newsgroups, 488, 496
User(s)
    acceptance testing, 192
    Datagram Protocol (UDP), 181
    dial-in, 474
    identification, 139
    passwords
        changing, 298
        cracking, 299
    security training, 243
U.S. government
    employees, 29
    publications, 134
U.S. Patent and Trademark Office, 346, 348
Utility(ies)
    failures, 76
    patents, 351

V

Vega-Rodriguez v. Puerto Rican Telephone Co.,
    394
Vendor
    policies, 87
    selection procedures, 89
Vetting policies, 48
Video camera monitoring, 393
Videotape rentals, wrongful disclosure of, 401
Virtual Privacy Network (VPN), 82, 84, 203, 210,
    324
Virus(es), 68, 315
    attacks, 23
    CodeRed, 329
    Klez, 329
    Melissa, 329
    Nimda, 1, 329
    SirCam, 329
    Slammer, 329
VMWare, 504
Voluntariness, test of, 266
VPN, *see* Virtual Privacy Network
Vulnerability(ies)
    assessments, 85
        organizational policy and, 87
        plan to conduct, 86
        Web application, 191
    definition of, 6, 25
    lists, 504
    overflow, 195
    scanners, 187
    self-assessment, 151
        configuration management, 152
        disaster recovery and business
            resumption, 153
        emergency power management, 152
        employee security awareness training, 153
        environmental conditions, 152
        hardware, 151
        media, 153
        network protocols, 152
        physical security, 151
        software, 153
    tools, automated, 185

W

WAN, *see* Wide area network
War driving, 209
Warm sites, 30
Web
    application assessments, 191, 201
    -based e-mail, 224, 323
    pages, password cracking, 303
    proxy, 199
    server policies, 97

site(s)
    E-commerce, 214
    privacy statement, 387
    vandalism, 257, 258
    tools, automated, 199
Well-known ports, 409–449
WEP, *see* Wired Equivalent Privacy
What-if idea, 15
Whisker, 200, 504
White-hat system attacking, 172
Wide area network (WAN), 26, 99
Wilbur, 221
Windows
    Advanced Server for LAN Management, 168
    -based operating systems, undeleting in, 277
    Developers Conference, 168
    FAT, information hiding in, 278
    file allocation table, 276
    logging, 241
    logical file review in, 297
    NT, auditing, 168, 227
    NT audit policy, 307
    NT file system (NTFS), 278, 279
    NT incidents, responding to, 293
        collecting volatile live-time evidence, 296
        data storage, 293
        open ports and listening services, 295
        processes running on target computer, 295
        system turned off, 294
        system users, 294
        tools in tool bag, 293
    NT logging, 304
    NT Server multi-user core, 169
    operating systems, evidence on, 296

password-protected user accounts, 102
Registry, 222, 299
Server Message Block, 142
system documentation, 141
    Windump, 162, 205
Winscan, 504
Wire communications, 392
Wired Equivalent Privacy (WEP), 83,85, 208, 209, 210
Wireless local area network (WLAN), 82, 207
Wireless networks, auditing, 206
Wireless policies, 84
Witness reports, 265
WLAN, *see* Wireless local area network
Workplace
    fraud, 354
    safety, 76, 77
Workstation auditing, 68, 104, 219, 220
World Wide Web, search, 85, *see also* Web
WORM media, *see* Write Once, Read Many media
Worms, 23, 70, 229
WPRM media, 78
Write Once, Read Many (WORM) media, 70

Y

Yahoo, 323

Z

Zone transfers, 184